Get + tape

FAMILY
CLASSICS

Fantasia

CineBooks Home Library Series
No. 2

FAMILY CLASSICS

Films ideally suited for family viewing

CineBooks

CineBooks, Inc.
Evanston, Illinois, 1988

Editors: James J. Mulay, Daniel Curran, Jeffrey H. Wallenfeldt, Jenny Mueller.

Editorial Director: William Leahy; Research Director: William C. Clogston;
Production Assistant: Jeannette Hori; Research Assistant: Jennifer Howe.

President: Anita L. Werling; Business Manager: Jack Medor;
Advertising Manager: Craig Carter; Assistants: Bernie Gregoryk
Michaela Tuohy, Lena Hicks.

Editorial & Sales Offices
CINEBOOKS
990 Grove Street
Evanston, IL 60201

ISBN: 0-933997-19-1

CINEBOOKS, INC. is a McPherson's Publishing Company

Printed in the United States
First Edition

1   2   3   4   5   6   7   8   9   10

Table of Contents

Foreword

What a pleasure for me to be afforded the opportunity to write the introduction to this guide book for some of the most heartwarming films ever made, films that truly are Family Classics.

Family Classics are those films that each and every member of our family can watch, enjoy and understand. They make us better people, teach us lessons about virtues and tug at our heartstrings, with their very real understanding of the human condition. They are classics because their stories and lessons are timeless, they mean as much today and tomorrow as they did yesterday.

It is their timeless quality that transports us out of our living rooms, opening doors to exotic lands filled with mystery, intrigue, humor and people just like us. These are films that bring history and literature to life, that let kangaroos talk and lions turn cowardly.

I have worked in films all my life and these are the types of movies I like to make most. Imagine my thrill at being able to bring to life Mark Twain's HUCKLEBERRY FINN (1939). I learned a lot of valuable lessons from that story, lessons that have stuck with me all my life.

People always ask me what are my favorite films. That is difficult for me to say because I like all types of films, but I guess that if I must make a list it would have to include those films that I watched and enjoyed as a child, that I then watched with my children and will watch with my grandchildren. My list would be long, but would have to include THE ADVENTURES OF ROBIN HOOD (1938), with my good friend Errol Flynn; almost all Walt Disney films, but especially BAMBI (1942) and OLD YELLER (1957), and my other favorite dog film BENJI (1974). I want my children and grandchildren to be there fighting to the end with Davy Crockett (played by John Wayne) at THE ALAMO (1960) and to experience the great debates as Raymond Massey portrays our 16th President in ABE LINCOLN IN ILLINOIS. Somehow I know that it wouldn't be Christmas without seeing Frank Capra's IT'S A WONDERFUL LIFE, Natalie Wood in THE MIRACLE ON 34TH STREET and hearing Bing Crosby sing in WHITE CHRISTMAS (1954). What's Easter without Irving Berlin's EASTER PARADE?

I guess that my list wouldn't be complete if I left out a very special person in a very special film, perhaps the epitome of a Family Classic and that would have to be Judy Garland in THE WIZARD OF OZ (1939). Every time I see that film she comes to life again for me and I get a warm, teary-eyed good feeling and a glow that lasts for days. That is the special quality of all these films and I hope that this book helps you and your family discover all the joys that the films have brought to me and my family through the years.

Mickey Rooney

FILMS BY GENRE

All films contained in this volume are listed by the genre (category) best suited to the film. Those films which can be classified in more than one genre are listed under each of the genres in which they fit. For example the Horror/Comedy ABBOTT AND COSTELLO MEET FRANKENSTEIN is listed under both of those genres.

ADVENTURE
ADVENTURES OF BULLWHIP GRIFFIN, THE (1967)
ADVENTURES OF ROBIN HOOD, THE (1938)
ADVENTURES OF THE WILDERNESS FAMILY, THE (1975)
ADVENTURES OF HUCKLEBERRY FINN, THE (1960)
ADVENTURES OF TOM SAWYER, THE (1938)
ADVENTURES OF ROBINSON CRUSOE, THE (1954)
AFRICA—TEXAS STYLE! (1967)
AFRICAN QUEEN, THE (1951)
ALI BABA AND THE FORTY THIEVES (1944)
ALONE ON THE PACIFIC (1964)
AMAZING MRS. HOLLIDAY (1943)
ARABIAN NIGHTS (1942)
AROUND THE WORLD IN 80 DAYS (1956)
BLACK STALLION, THE (1979)
BOMBA THE JUNGLE BOY (1949)
BOY TEN FEET TALL, A (1965)
CALL OF THE WILD (1935)
CAPTAINS COURAGEOUS (1937)
CLARENCE, THE CROSS-EYED LION (1965)
CONNECTICUT YANKEE IN KING ARTHUR'S COURT, A (1949)
CONNECTICUT YANKEE, A (1931)
COUNT OF MONTE CRISTO, THE (1934)
COURT JESTER, THE (1956)
DAVY CROCKETT, KING OF THE WILD FRONTIER (1955)
DOVE, THE (1974)
DRUMS ALONG THE MOHAWK (1939)
EMIL AND THE DETECTIVES (1964)
FIGHTING PRINCE OF DONEGAL, THE (1966)
FLIGHT OF THE DOVES (1971)
FOR THE LOVE OF BENJI (1977)
GOLDEN VOYAGE OF SINBAD, THE (1974)
IN SEARCH OF THE CASTAWAYS (1962)

INCREDIBLE JOURNEY, THE (1963)
ISLAND AT THE TOP OF THE WORLD, THE (1974)
ISLAND OF THE BLUE DOLPHINS (1964)
JACK THE GIANT KILLER (1962)
JASON AND THE ARGONAUTS (1963)
JOHN AND JULIE (1957)
JOHNNY ON THE RUN (1953)
JOURNEY OF NATTY GANN, THE (1985)
JUNGLE BOOK, THE (1942)
KIDNAPPED (1938)
KIM (1950)
KING KONG (1933)
KING SOLOMON'S MINES (1950)
LASSIE'S GREAT ADVENTURE (1963)
LITTLE ARK, THE (1972)
MISTY (1961)
MOBY DICK (1956)
MY SIDE OF THE MOUNTAIN (1969)
NEVER CRY WOLF (1983)
NIKKI, WILD DOG OF THE NORTH (1961)
PAINTED HILLS, THE (1951)
PRINCE AND THE PAUPER, THE (1937)
PRINCESS BRIDE, THE (1987)
SEA GYPSIES, THE (1978)
SINBAD THE SAILOR (1947)
STANLEY AND LIVINGSTONE (1939)
STORY OF ROBIN HOOD, THE (1952)
SWALLOWS AND AMAZONS (1977)
SWISS FAMILY ROBINSON (1960)
TAIL OF THE TIGER (1984)
TARZAN, THE APE MAN (1932)
THREE MUSKETEERS, THE (1948)
TOM SAWYER (1930)
TOM SAWYER (1973)
TREASURE ISLAND (1950)
TREASURE ISLAND (1934)
WATER BABIES, THE (1979)
WINGS OF MYSTERY (1963)

ANIMATION
ADVENTURES OF ICHABOD AND MR. TOAD (1949)
ALICE IN WONDERLAND (1951)
AMERICAN TAIL, AN (1986)
ARISTOCATS, THE (1970)
BAMBI (1942)
BON VOYAGE, CHARLIE BROWN (AND DON'T COME BACK) (1980)
BUGS BUNNY, SUPERSTAR (1975)
CHARLOTTE'S WEB (1973)
CHIPMUNK ADVENTURE, THE (1987)
CINDERELLA (1950)
DOT AND THE KOALA (1985)
DUMBO (1941)
FANTASIA (1940)
FOX AND THE HOUND, THE (1981)
FUN AND FANCY FREE (1947)
GAY PURR-EE (1962)
GREAT AMERICAN BUGS BUNNY-ROAD RUNNER CHASE (1979)
GULLIVER'S TRAVELS (1939)
HUGO THE HIPPO (1976)
JUNGLE BOOK, THE (1967)
LADY AND THE TRAMP (1955)
MAKE MINE MUSIC (1946)
MAN CALLED FLINTSTONE, THE (1966)
MELODY TIME (1948)
MIGHTY MOUSE IN THE GREAT SPACE CHASE (1983)
MR. BUG GOES TO TOWN (1941)
OF STARS AND MEN (1961)
ONE HUNDRED AND ONE DALMATIANS (1961)
1001 ARABIAN NIGHTS (1959)
PETER PAN (1953)
PHANTOM TOLLBOOTH, THE (1970)
PINOCCHIO AND THE EMPEROR OF THE NIGHT (1987)
PINOCCHIO (1940)
RESCUERS, THE (1977)
ROBIN HOOD (1973)
SECRET OF NIMH, THE (1982)
SLEEPING BEAUTY (1959)
SNOOPY, COME HOME (1972)

SNOW WHITE AND THE SEVEN DWARFS (1937)
SONG OF THE SOUTH (1946)
THREE CABALLEROS, THE (1944)
TIKI TIKI (1971)
WACKY WORLD OF MOTHER GOOSE, THE, (1967)
WATER BABIES, THE (1979)
WHO FRAMED ROGER RABBIT? (1988)
WORLD OF HANS CHRISTIAN ANDERSEN, THE (1971)

BIOGRAPHY

ABE LINCOLN IN ILLINOIS (1940)
ADVENTURES OF MARK TWAIN, THE (1944)
ANNIE OAKLEY (1935)
ANNIE GET YOUR GUN (1950)
BABE RUTH STORY, THE (1948)
BEST THINGS IN LIFE ARE FREE, THE (1956)
BOYS TOWN (1938)
BUFFALO BILL (1944)
CHARIOTS OF FIRE (1981)
DEEP IN MY HEART (1954)
EDISON, THE MAN (1940)
HANS CHRISTIAN ANDERSEN (1952)
JOHN WESLEY (1954)
KNUTE ROCKNE—ALL AMERICAN (1940)
MADAME CURIE (1943)
MAGIC BOX, THE (1952)
MAGNIFICENT YANKEE, THE (1950)
MAN CALLED PETER, THE (1955)
ONE FOOT IN HEAVEN (1941)
PRIDE OF THE YANKEES, THE (1942)
PRIDE OF ST. LOUIS, THE (1952)
SERGEANT YORK (1941)
SEVEN LITTLE FOYS, THE (1955)
SONG OF BERNADETTE, THE (1943)
SOUND OF MUSIC, THE (1965)
SPIRIT OF ST. LOUIS, THE (1957)
STARS AND STRIPES FOREVER (1952)
STORY OF LOUIS PASTEUR, THE (1936)
STORY OF WILL ROGERS, THE (1952)
STORY OF G.I. JOE, THE (1945)
STORY OF ALEXANDER GRAHAM BELL, THE (1939)
STRATTON STORY, THE (1949)
WONDERFUL WORLD OF THE BROTHERS GRIMM, THE (1962)
YANKEE DOODLE DANDY (1942)
YOUNG TOM EDISON (1940)

COMEDY

ABBOTT AND COSTELLO MEET FRANKENSTEIN (1948)
ABSENT-MINDED PROFESSOR, THE (1961)
ADVENTURES OF BULLWHIP GRIFFIN, THE (1967)
AFRICA SCREAMS (1949)
AH, WILDERNESS! (1935)
ALIVE AND KICKING (1962)
ANIMAL CRACKERS (1930)
AT THE CIRCUS (1939)
BACHELOR AND THE BOBBY-SOXER, THE (1947)
BAD NEWS BEARS, THE (1976)
BANK DICK, THE (1940)
BAREFOOT EXECUTIVE, THE (1971)
BELLES OF ST. TRINIAN'S, THE (1954)
BENJI (1974)
BLACKBEARD'S GHOST (1968)
BLOCKHEADS (1938)
BLONDIE (1938)
BOY WHO STOLE A MILLION, THE (1960)
BRIGHT EYES (1934)
CALLAWAY WENT THATAWAY (1951)
CANTERVILLE GHOST, THE (1944)
CAT FROM OUTER SPACE, THE (1978)
CAUGHT IN THE DRAFT (1941)
CHAMPAGNE FOR CAESAR (1950)
CHARLEY'S AUNT (1941)
CHEAPER BY THE DOZEN (1950)
CHRISTMAS IN CONNECTICUT (1945)
CHRISTMAS STORY, A (1983)
COME TO THE STABLE (1949)
COMPUTER WORE TENNIS SHOES, THE (1970)
CONNECTICUT YANKEE, A (1931)
COURT JESTER, THE (1956)
COURTSHIP OF EDDIE'S FATHER, THE (1963)
CUCKOOS, THE (1930)
DATE WITH JUDY, A (1948)
DAY AT THE RACES, A (1937)
DEAR WIFE (1949)
DREAMBOAT (1952)
DUCK SOUP (1933)
EASTER PARADE (1948)
EMPEROR WALTZ, THE (1948)
EXCUSE MY DUST (1951)
FARMER'S DAUGHTER, THE (1947)
FATHER GOOSE (1964)

FATHER'S LITTLE DIVIDEND (1951)
FEARLESS FAGAN (1952)
FITZWILLY (1967)
FIVE LITTLE PEPPERS AND HOW THEY GREW (1939)
FLUFFY (1965)
FLYING DEUCES, THE (1939)
FRANCIS IN THE HAUNTED HOUSE (1956)
FRANCIS (1949)
FRASIER, THE SENSUOUS LION (1973)
FREAKY FRIDAY (1976)
FULLER BRUSH MAN (1948)
FULLER BRUSH GIRL, THE (1950)
GHOST BREAKERS, THE (1940)
GIDGET (1959)
GIRL CRAZY (1943)
GREAT RUPERT, THE (1950)
GREAT MUPPET CAPER, THE (1981)
HAPPY TIME, THE (1952)
HARVEY GIRLS, THE (1946)
HARVEY (1950)
HEAVENS ABOVE! (1963)
HELLO, DOLLY! (1969)
HENRY ALDRICH FOR PRESIDENT (1941)
HERBIE RIDES AGAIN (1974)
HERE COME THE CO-EDS (1945)
HOLD THAT GHOST (1941)
HOPE AND GLORY (1987)
HORN BLOWS AT MIDNIGHT, THE (1945)
HUCKLEBERRY FINN (1939)
IN THE GOOD OLD SUMMERTIME (1949)
INSPECTOR GENERAL, THE (1949)
IT HAPPENS EVERY SPRING (1949)
IT'S A GIFT (1934)
IT'S A MAD, MAD, MAD, MAD WORLD (1963)
IT'S A WONDERFUL LIFE (1946)
JALOPY (1953)
JOHN AND JULIE (1957)
KID FROM SPAIN, THE (1932)
KID FROM BROOKLYN, THE (1946)
LET'S GO NAVY (1951)
LI'L ABNER (1959)
LIFE WITH FATHER (1947)
LITTLE ROMANCE, A (1979)
LIVE WIRES (1946)
LOVE FINDS ANDY HARDY (1938)
LOVE BUG, THE (1968)
MA AND PA KETTLE ON VACATION (1953)
MA AND PA KETTLE (1949)

LITTLEST REBEL, THE (1935)
LOVE FINDS ANDY HARDY (1938)
MANHATTAN PROJECT, THE (1986)
MELODY (1971)
MIDSUMMER NIGHT'S DREAM, A (1961)
MIRACLE WORKER, THE (1962)
MISTER 880 (1950)
MR. SCOUTMASTER (1953)
MR. SMITH GOES TO WASHINGTON (1939)
MOBY DICK (1956)
MY FRIEND FLICKA (1943)
NATIONAL VELVET (1944)
NEXT VOICE YOU HEAR, THE (1950)
C. HENRY'S FULL HOUSE (1952)
OLD YELLER (1957)
OLIVER TWIST (1951)
RASCAL (1969)
SECRET GARDEN, THE (1949)
SKIPPY (1931)
SMALL CHANGE (1976)
SOUNDER (1972)
STORM BOY (1976)
SUN COMES UP, THE (1949)
SYLVESTER (1985)
TALE OF TWO CITIES, A (1935)
THOSE CALLOWAYS (1964)
THUNDERHEAD-SON OF FLICKA (1945)
TO KILL A MOCKINGBIRD (1962)
TOBY TYLER (1960)
TRUMAN CAPOTE'S TRILOGY (1969)
WEE GEORDIE (1956)
WEE WILLIE WINKIE (1937)
WHO SAYS I CAN'T RIDE A RAINBOW? (1971)
WILD CHILD, THE (1970)
WOLFPEN PRINCIPLE, THE (1974)
WORLD OF HENRY ORIENT, THE (1964)
YEARLING, THE (1946)
YOURS, MINE AND OURS (1968)

FANTASY
ALI BABA AND THE FORTY THIEVES (1944)
ALICE IN WONDERLAND (1933)
ARABIAN NIGHTS (1942)
BABES IN TOYLAND (1934)
BEAUTY AND THE BEAST (1947)
BEDKNOBS AND BROOMSTICKS (1971)
BLACKBEARD'S GHOST (1968)
BOY WHO COULD FLY, THE (1986)

CHITTY CHITTY BANG BANG (1968)
CHRISTMAS CAROL, A (1938)
DARBY O'GILL AND THE LITTLE PEOPLE (1959)
DAYDREAMER, THE (1966)
DOCTOR DOLITTLE (1967)
DR. COPPELIUS (1968)
FABULOUS WORLD OF JULES VERNE, THE (1961)
5,000 FINGERS OF DR. T, THE (1953)
FLIGHT OF THE NAVIGATOR (1986)
FUN AND FANCY FREE (1947)
GHOST AND MRS. MUIR, THE (1942)
GNOME-MOBILE, THE (1967)
GOLDEN VOYAGE OF SINBAD, THE (1974)
HERE COMES SANTA CLAUS (1984)
HILDUR AND THE MAGICIAN (1969)
IN SEARCH OF THE CASTAWAYS (1962)
IT'S A WONDERFUL LIFE (1946)
JACK FROST (1966)
JACK THE GIANT KILLER (1962)
JASON AND THE ARGONAUTS (1963)
LABYRINTH (1986)
MIRACLE ON 34TH STREET, THE (1947)
NUTCRACKER: THE MOTION PICTURE (1986)
PETER RABBIT AND TALES OF BEATRIX POTTER (1971)
PETE'S DRAGON (1977)
PHANTOM TOLLBOOTH, THE (1970)
SAND CASTLE, THE (1961)
SCROOGE (1970)
SEVEN FACES OF DR. LAO (1964)
SEVENTH VOYAGE OF SINBAD, THE (1958)
SHAGGY D.A., THE (1976)
SHAGGY DOG, THE (1959)
SINBAD AND THE EYE OF THE TIGER (1977)
SINBAD THE SAILOR (1947)
SONG OF THE SOUTH (1946)
THIEF OF BAGHDAD, THE (1940)
THREE LIVES OF THOMASINA, THE (1963)
THUMBELINA (1970)
TIME BANDITS (1981)
TOM THUMB (1958)
WILLIE MCBEAN AND HIS MAGIC MACHINE (1965)

WILLY WONKA AND THE CHOCOLATE FACTORY (1971)
WISHING MACHINE (1971)
WIZARD OF OZ, THE (1939)
WONDERFUL WORLD OF THE BROTHERS GRIMM, THE (1962)

HISTORICAL
JOHNNY TREMAIN (1957)

HORROR
ABBOTT AND COSTELLO MEET FRANKENSTEIN (1948)

MUSICAL
ANNIE (1982)
AT THE CIRCUS (1939)
BABES IN ARMS (1939)
BEST THINGS IN LIFE ARE FREE, THE (1956)
BUGSY MALONE (1976)
CONNECTICUT YANKEE IN KING ARTHUR'S COURT, A (1949)
DATE WITH JUDY, A (1948)
DAY AT THE RACES, A (1937)
DEEP IN MY HEART (1954)
EASTER PARADE (1948)
EMPEROR WALTZ, THE (1948)
EXCUSE MY DUST (1951)
GIRL CRAZY (1943)
GREAT MUPPET CAPER, THE (1981)
HARVEY GIRLS, THE (1946)
HELLO, DOLLY! (1969)
HIT THE DECK (1955)
IN THE GOOD OLD SUMMERTIME (1949)
INSPECTOR GENERAL, THE (1949)
KID FROM SPAIN, THE (1932)
KID FROM BROOKLYN, THE (1946)
KING AND I, THE (1956)
LI'L ABNER (1959)
LILI (1953)
LITTLE MISS MARKER (1934)
MARY POPPINS (1964)
MEET ME IN ST. LOUIS (1944)
MELODY TIME (1948)
MUPPET MOVIE, THE (1979)
MUSIC MAN, THE (1962)
MY FAIR LADY (1964)
MY SISTER EILEEN (1955)
OKLAHOMA! (1955)
OLIVER! (1968)
ONE NIGHT IN THE TROPICS (1940)
RIDE 'EM COWBOY (1942)
ROAD TO RIO (1947)
ROAD TO MOROCCO (1942)
ROAD TO UTOPIA (1945)
ROAD TO ZANZIBAR (1941)

SCROOGE (1935)
SEVEN BRIDES FOR SEVEN
BROTHERS (1954)
SEVEN LITTLE FOYS, THE (1955)
SING YOU SINNERS (1938)
SLIPPER AND THE ROSE, THE
(1976)
SO DEAR TO MY HEART (1949)
SOUND OF MUSIC, THE (1965)
STARS AND STRIPES FOREVER
(1952)
STOWAWAY (1936)
STRIKE UP THE BAND (1940)
SUMMER HOLIDAY (1948)
TAKE ME OUT TO THE BALL
GAME (1949)
THIS IS THE ARMY (1943)
THREE CABALLEROS, THE (1944)
TOM SAWYER (1973)
WHERE'S CHARLEY? (1952)
WHITE CHRISTMAS (1954)
WONDER MAN (1945)
WONDERFUL WORLD OF THE
BROTHERS GRIMM, THE (1962)
YANKEE DOODLE DANDY (1942)
YOUNG PEOPLE (1940)

MYSTERY
ADVENTURES OF SHERLOCK
HOLMES, THE (1939)
CHARLIE CHAN AT THE OPERA
(1936)
MOON-SPINNERS, THE (1964)
YOUNG SHERLOCK HOLMES
(1985)

RELIGIOUS
KING OF KINGS (1961)
TEN COMMANDMENTS, THE
(1956)

ROMANCE
AFRICAN QUEEN, THE (1951)
FARMER'S DAUGHTER, THE
(1947)
GHOST AND MRS. MUIR, THE
(1942)
KENTUCKY (1938)
PRIDE OF THE YANKEES, THE
(1942)
ROSEANNA McCOY (1949)

SCIENCE FICTION
CAT FROM OUTER SPACE, THE
(1978)
CLOSE ENCOUNTERS OF THE
THIRD KIND (1977)
E.T. THE EXTRA-TERRESTRIAL
(1982)
EMPIRE STRIKES BACK, THE
(1980)
ESCAPE TO WITCH MOUNTAIN
(1975)
FANTASTIC VOYAGE (1966)
FLASH GORDON (1936)
GLITTERBALL, THE (1977)
INVISIBLE BOY, THE (1957)
ISLAND AT THE TOP OF THE
WORLD, THE (1974)
JOURNEY TO THE CENTER OF
THE EARTH (1959)
MOON PILOT (1962)
MYSTERIOUS ISLAND (1961)
RETURN OF THE JEDI (1983)
STAR TREK: THE MOTION
PICTURE (1979)
STAR TREK II: THE WRATH OF
KHAN (1982)
STAR TREK III: THE SEARCH FOR
SPOCK (1984)
STAR TREK IV: THE VOYAGE
HOME (1986)
STAR WARS (1977)
SUPERMAN (1978)
SUPERMAN II (1980)
TIME MACHINE, THE (1960)
20,000 LEAGUES UNDER THE
SEA (1954)
VOYAGE TO THE BOTTOM OF
THE SEA (1961)

SPORTS
ANGELS IN THE OUTFIELD (1951)
KARATE KID, THE (1984)
PHAR LAP (1984)
BABE RUTH STORY, THE (1948)
BAD NEWS BEARS, THE (1976)
CHAMP, THE (1931)
CHARIOTS OF FIRE (1981)
IT HAPPENS EVERY SPRING
(1949)
KNUTE ROCKNE—ALL
AMERICAN (1940)
PALOOKA (1934)

PRIDE OF ST. LOUIS, THE (1952)
PRIDE OF THE YANKEES, THE
(1942)
STRATTON STORY, THE (1949)
TAKE ME OUT TO THE BALL
GAME (1949)
WORLD'S GREATEST ATHLETE,
THE (1973)

WAR
AIR FORCE (1943)
ALAMO, THE (1960)
BATAAN (1943)
BATTLE OF BRITAIN, THE (1969)
BATTLE OF THE BULGE (1965)
EMPIRE OF THE SUN (1987)
FATHER GOOSE (1964)
FIGHTING 69TH, THE (1940)
GREAT ESCAPE, THE (1963)
JOURNEY FOR MARGARET
(1942)
SANDS OF IWO JIMA (1949)
SERGEANT YORK (1941)
SON OF LASSIE (1945)
STORY OF G.I. JOE, THE (1945)
YANK IN THE R.A.F., A (1941)

WESTERN
ANNIE GET YOUR GUN (1950)
ANNIE OAKLEY (1935)
BELLS OF ROSARITA (1945)
BUFFALO BILL (1944)
CATTLE DRIVE (1951)
DAVY CROCKETT, INDIAN
SCOUT (1950)
HOW THE WEST WAS WON
(1962)
KING OF THE COWBOYS (1943)
KONGA, THE WILD STALLION
(1939)
LAST ROUND-UP, THE (1947)
MY PAL TRIGGER (1946)
SEVEN FACES OF DR. LAO (1964)
SHANE (1953)
SHUT MY BIG MOUTH (1942)
THREE GODFATHERS, THE
(1948)
TRUE GRIT (1969)
WAY OUT WEST (1937)

FILMS BY YEAR

All films included in this volume are listed below by their year of release.

1930
ANIMAL CRACKERS
CUCKOOS, THE
TOM SAWYER

1931
CHAMP, THE
CONNECTICUT YANKEE, A
SKIPPY

1932
KID FROM SPAIN, THE
TARZAN, THE APE MAN

1933
ALICE IN WONDERLAND
DUCK SOUP
KING KONG
LITTLE WOMEN

1934
BABES IN TOYLAND
BRIGHT EYES
COUNT OF MONTE CRISTO, THE
IT'S A GIFT
LITTLE MISS MARKER
PALOOKA
YOU'RE TELLING ME
TREASURE ISLAND

1935
AH, WILDERNESS!
ANNIE OAKLEY
CALL OF THE WILD
CAPTAIN JANUARY
DAVID COPPERFIELD
LADDIE
LITTLEST REBEL, THE
NIGHT AT THE OPERA, A
SCROOGE
TALE OF TWO CITIES, A

1936
CHARLIE CHAN AT THE OPERA
FLASH GORDON
LITTLE LORD FAUNTLEROY
MILKY WAY, THE
STORY OF LOUIS PASTEUR, THE
STOWAWAY

1937
CAPTAINS COURAGEOUS
DAY AT THE RACES, A
HEIDI
PRINCE AND THE PAUPER, THE

SNOW WHITE AND THE SEVEN
   DWARFS
THREE SMART GIRLS
TOPPER
WAY OUT WEST
WEE WILLIE WINKIE

1938
ADVENTURES OF ROBIN HOOD,
   THE
ADVENTURES OF TOM SAWYER,
   THE
ANGELS WITH DIRTY FACES
BLOCKHEADS
BLONDIE
BOYS TOWN
CHRISTMAS CAROL, A
JUDGE HARDY'S CHILDREN
KENTUCKY
KIDNAPPED
LOVE FINDS ANDY HARDY
SING YOU SINNERS
YANK AT OXFORD, A

1939
ADVENTURES OF SHERLOCK
   HOLMES, THE
AT THE CIRCUS
BABES IN ARMS
DRUMS ALONG THE MOHAWK
FIVE LITTLE PEPPERS AND HOW
   THEY GREW
FLYING DEUCES, THE
GOODBYE MR. CHIPS
GULLIVER'S TRAVELS
HUCKLEBERRY FINN
JUDGE HARDY AND SON
KONGA, THE WILD STALLION
LITTLE PRINCESS, THE
MR. SMITH GOES TO
   WASHINGTON
STANLEY AND LIVINGSTONE
STORY OF ALEXANDER
   GRAHAM BELL, THE
WIZARD OF OZ, THE

1940
ABE LINCOLN IN ILLINOIS
BANK DICK, THE
EDISON, THE MAN
FANTASIA
FIGHTING 69TH, THE
GHOST BREAKERS, THE
KNUTE ROCKNE—ALL
   AMERICAN

ONE NIGHT IN THE TROPICS
PINOCCHIO
SIDEWALKS OF LONDON
STRIKE UP THE BAND
THIEF OF BAGHDAD, THE
YOUNG PEOPLE
YOUNG TOM EDISON

1941
CAUGHT IN THE DRAFT
CHARLEY'S AUNT
DUMBO
HENRY ALDRICH FOR
   PRESIDENT
HOLD THAT GHOST
HOW GREEN WAS MY VALLEY
MR. BUG GOES TO TOWN
ONE FOOT IN HEAVEN
ROAD TO ZANZIBAR
SERGEANT YORK
YANK IN THE R.A.F., A

1942
ARABIAN NIGHTS
BAMBI
GHOST AND MRS. MUIR, THE
JOURNEY FOR MARGARET
JUNGLE BOOK, THE
MY SISTER EILEEN
PRIDE OF THE YANKEES, THE
RIDE 'EM COWBOY
ROAD TO MOROCCO
SHUT MY BIG MOUTH
TALES OF MANHATTAN
YANKEE DOODLE DANDY

1943
AIR FORCE
AMAZING MRS. HOLLIDAY
BATAAN
GIRL CRAZY
KING OF THE COWBOYS
LASSIE, COME HOME
MADAME CURIE
MY FRIEND FLICKA
SONG OF BERNADETTE, THE
THIS IS THE ARMY
YOUNGEST PROFESSION, THE

1944
ADVENTURES OF MARK TWAIN,
   THE
ALI BABA AND THE FORTY
   THIEVES
BUFFALO BILL
CANTERVILLE GHOST, THE

TEN COMMANDMENTS, THE
WEE GEORDIE

1957
INVISIBLE BOY, THE
JOHN AND JULIE
JOHNNY TREMAIN
OLD YELLER
SPIRIT OF ST. LOUIS, THE

1958
INN OF THE SIXTH HAPPINESS,
   THE
LIGHT IN THE FOREST, THE
MY UNCLE
SEVENTH VOYAGE OF SINBAD,
   THE
TOM THUMB

1959
CRY FROM THE STREET, A
DARBY O'GILL AND THE LITTLE
   PEOPLE
DOG OF FLANDERS, A
FOUR HUNDRED BLOWS, THE
GIDGET
JOURNEY TO THE CENTER OF
   THE EARTH
LI'L ABNER
MOUSE THAT ROARED, THE
1001 ARABIAN NIGHTS
SHAGGY DOG, THE
SLEEPING BEAUTY
TIGER BAY

1960
ADVENTURES OF
   HUCKLEBERRY FINN, THE
ALAMO, THE
BOY WHO STOLE A MILLION,
   THE
POLLYANNA
SCHOOL FOR SCOUNDRELS
SWISS FAMILY ROBINSON
TIME MACHINE, THE
TOBY TYLER

1961
ABSENT-MINDED PROFESSOR,
   THE
FABULOUS WORLD OF JULES
   VERNE, THE
GREYFRIARS BOBBY
KING OF KINGS
MIDSUMMER NIGHT'S DREAM, A
MR. HOBBS TAKES A VACATION
MISTY
MYSTERIOUS ISLAND
NIKKI, WILD DOG OF THE
   NORTH
OF STARS AND MEN
ONE HUNDRED AND ONE
   DALMATIANS

PARENT TRAP, THE
POCKETFUL OF MIRACLES
SAND CASTLE, THE
VOYAGE TO THE BOTTOM OF
   THE SEA

1962
ALIVE AND KICKING
DOG AND THE DIAMONDS, THE
GAY PURR-EE
HOW THE WEST WAS WON
IN SEARCH OF THE CASTAWAYS
JACK THE GIANT KILLER
MIRACLE WORKER, THE
MOON PILOT
MUSIC MAN, THE
TO KILL A MOCKINGBIRD
WONDERFUL WORLD OF THE
   BROTHERS GRIMM, THE

1963
COURTSHIP OF EDDIE'S
   FATHER, THE
FLIPPER
GREAT ESCAPE, THE
HEAVENS ABOVE!
INCREDIBLE JOURNEY, THE
IT'S A MAD, MAD, MAD, MAD
   WORLD
JASON AND THE ARGONAUTS
LASSIE'S GREAT ADVENTURE
SON OF FLUBBER
SUMMER MAGIC
THREE LIVES OF THOMASINA,
   THE
WINGS OF MYSTERY

1964
ALONE ON THE PACIFIC
EMIL AND THE DETECTIVES
FATHER GOOSE
FLIPPER'S NEW ADVENTURE
ISLAND OF THE BLUE DOLPHINS
MARY POPPINS
MOON-SPINNERS, THE
MY FAIR LADY
SEVEN FACES OF DR. LAO
THOSE CALLOWAYS
WORLD OF HENRY ORIENT, THE

1965
BATTLE OF THE BULGE
BOY TEN FEET TALL, A
CLARENCE, THE CROSS-EYED
   LION
FLUFFY
SOUND OF MUSIC, THE
THAT DARN CAT
THOSE MAGNIFICENT MEN IN
   THEIR FLYING MACHINES; OR
   HOW I FLEW FROM LONDON

TO PARIS IN 25 HOURS AND 11
   MINUTES
WILLIE MCBEAN AND HIS
   MAGIC MACHINE

1966
BORN FREE
DAYDREAMER, THE
FANTASTIC VOYAGE
FIGHTING PRINCE OF
   DONEGAL, THE
FOLLOW ME, BOYS!
JACK FROST
MAN CALLED FLINTSTONE, THE
STOLEN DIRIGIBLE, THE

1967
ADVENTURES OF BULLWHIP
   GRIFFIN, THE
AFRICA—TEXAS STYLE!
DOCTOR DOLITTLE
FITZWILLY
GENTLE GIANT
GNOME-MOBILE, THE
JUNGLE BOOK, THE
SWAN LAKE, THE
WACKY WORLD OF MOTHER
   GOOSE, THE

1968
BLACKBEARD'S GHOST
DR. COPPELIUS
CHITTY CHITTY BANG BANG
LOVE BUG, THE
OLIVER!
YOURS, MINE AND OURS

1969
BATTLE OF BRITAIN, THE
HELLO, DOLLY!
HILDUR AND THE MAGICIAN
MY SIDE OF THE MOUNTAIN
RASCAL
TRUE GRIT
TRUMAN CAPOTE'S TRILOGY

1970
ARISTOCATS, THE
COMPUTER WORE TENNIS
   SHOES, THE
PHANTOM TOLLBOOTH, THE
SCROOGE
THUMBELINA
WILD CHILD, THE

1971
BAREFOOT EXECUTIVE, THE
BEDKNOBS AND BROOMSTICKS
FLIGHT OF THE DOVES
MELODY
PETER RABBIT AND TALES OF
   BEATRIX POTTER

TIKI TIKI
WHO SAYS I CAN'T RIDE A
 RAINBOW?
WILLY WONKA AND THE
 CHOCOLATE FACTORY
WISHING MACHINE
WORLD OF HANS CHRISTIAN
 ANDERSEN, THE

1972
LITTLE ARK, THE
NOW YOU SEE HIM, NOW YOU
 DON'T
SNOOPY, COME HOME
SOUNDER
WHAT'S UP, DOC?

1973
CHARLOTTE'S WEB
FRASIER, THE SENSUOUS LION
PLAYTIME
ROBIN HOOD
TOM SAWYER
WORLD'S GREATEST ATHLETE,
 THE

1974
BENJI
DOVE, THE
GOLDEN VOYAGE OF SINBAD,
 THE
HERBIE RIDES AGAIN
ISLAND AT THE TOP OF THE
 WORLD, THE
WOLFPEN PRINCIPLE, THE

1975
ADVENTURES OF THE
 WILDERNESS FAMILY, THE
ALL CREATURES GREAT AND
 SMALL
BUGS BUNNY, SUPERSTAR
ESCAPE TO WITCH MOUNTAIN

1976
BAD NEWS BEARS, THE
BELSTONE FOX, THE
BUGSY MALONE
FOREVER YOUNG, FOREVER
 FREE
FREAKY FRIDAY

HUGO THE HIPPO
SHAGGY D.A., THE
SLIPPER AND THE ROSE, THE
SMALL CHANGE
STORM BOY

1977
CLOSE ENCOUNTERS OF THE
 THIRD KIND
FOR THE LOVE OF BENJI
GLITTERBALL, THE
LITTLEST HORSE THIEVES, THE
PETE'S DRAGON
RESCUERS, THE
SINBAD AND THE EYE OF THE
 TIGER
STAR WARS
SWALLOWS AND AMAZONS

1978
CAT FROM OUTER SPACE, THE
SEA GYPSIES, THE
SUPERMAN

1979
ALL THINGS BRIGHT AND
 BEAUTIFUL
BLACK STALLION, THE
GREAT AMERICAN BUGS
 BUNNY-ROAD RUNNER CHASE
LITTLE ROMANCE, A
MUPPET MOVIE, THE
STAR TREK: THE MOTION
 PICTURE
WATER BABIES, THE

1980
BON VOYAGE, CHARLIE BROWN
 (AND DON'T COME BACK)
EMPIRE STRIKES BACK, THE
SUPERMAN II

1981
CHARIOTS OF FIRE
FOX AND THE HOUND, THE
GREAT MUPPET CAPER, THE
TIME BANDITS

1982
ANNIE

E.T. THE EXTRA-TERRESTRIAL
SECRET OF NIMH, THE
STAR TREK II: THE WRATH OF
 KHAN

1983
CHRISTMAS STORY, A
MIGHTY MOUSE IN THE GREAT
 SPACE CHASE
NEVER CRY WOLF
RETURN OF THE JEDI

1984
HERE COMES SANTA CLAUS
KARATE KID, THE
MUPPETS TAKE MANHATTAN,
 THE
PHAR LAP
STAR TREK III: THE SEARCH FOR
 SPOCK
TAIL OF THE TIGER

1985
DOT AND THE KOALA
JOURNEY OF NATTY GANN, THE
SYLVESTER
YOUNG SHERLOCK HOLMES

1986
AMERICAN TAIL, AN
BOY WHO COULD FLY, THE
FLIGHT OF THE NAVIGATOR
LABYRINTH
MANHATTAN PROJECT, THE
NUTCRACKER: THE MOTION
 PICTURE
STAR TREK IV: THE VOYAGE
 HOME

1987
CHIPMUNK ADVENTURE, THE
EMPIRE OF THE SUN
HOPE AND GLORY
PINOCCHIO AND THE EMPEROR
 OF THE NIGHT
PRINCESS BRIDE, THE

1988
WHO FRAMED ROGER RABBIT?

FILMS BY SERIES

Films in this volume which are part of a series are listed below by the series title. In many cases there may be more films in a particlar series than are listed here since this volume deals only with those which are ideally suited for family viewing.

ABBOTT AND COSTELLO
AFRICA SCREAMS (1949)
ABBOTT AND COSTELLO MEET
  FRANKENSTEIN (1948)
HERE COME THE COEDS (1945)
HOLD THAT GHOST (1941)
NOOSE HANGS HIGH (1948)
ONE NIGHT IN THE TROPICS
  (1940)
RIDE 'EM COWBOY (1942)
TIME OF THEIR LIVES (1946)

ANDY HARDY
JUDGE HARDY AND SON (1939)
JUDGE HARDY'S CHILDREN
  (1938)
LOVE FINDS ANDY HARDY (1938)

BENJI
BENJI (1974)
FOR THE LOVE OF BENJI (1977)

BLONDIE
BLONDIE (1938)

BOWERY BOYS
JALOPY (1953)
LET'S GO NAVY (1951)
LIVE WIRES (1946)
NEWS HOUNDS (1947)

CHARLIE CHAN
CHARLIE CHAN AT THE OPERA
  (1936)

FRANCIS THE TALKING MULE
FRANCIS (1949)
FRANCIS IN THE HAUNTED
  HOUSE (1956)

GENE AUTRY
LAST ROUND-UP, THE (1947)

HENRY ALDRICH
HENRY ALDRICH FOR
  PRESIDENT (1941)

HERBIE, THE LOVE BUG
HERBIE RIDES AGAIN (1974)
LOVE BUG, THE (1968)

LASSIE
CHALLENGE TO LASSIE (1949)
COURAGE OF LASSIE (1946)
HILLS OF HOME (1948)
LASSIE, COME HOME (1943)
LASSIE'S GREAT ADVENTURE
  (1963)
SON OF LASSIE (1945)

LAUREL AND HARDY
BABES IN TOYLAND (1934)
BLOCKHEADS (1938)
FLYING DEUCES, THE (1939)
WAY OUT WEST (1937)

MA AND PA KETTLE
MA AND PA KETTLE ON
  VACATION (1953)
MA AND PA KETTLE (1949)

MARX BROTHERS
AT THE CIRCUS (1939)
ANIMAL CRACKERS (1930)
DAY AT THE RACES, A (1937)
DUCK SOUP (1933)
NIGHT AT THE OPERA, A (1935)

MUPPETS
GREAT MUPPET CAPER, THE
  (1981)
MUPPET MOVIE, THE (1979)
MUPPETS TAKE MANHATTAN,
  THE (1984)

PEANUTS
BON VOYAGE, CHARLIE BROWN
  (AND DON'T COME BACK)
  (1980)
SNOOPY, COME HOME (1972)

ROAD TO
ROAD TO MOROCCO (1942)

ROAD TO RIO (1947)
ROAD TO UTOPIA (1945)
ROAD TO ZANZIBAR (1941)

ROY ROGERS
KING OF THE COWBOYS (1943)
MY PAL TRIGGER (1946)

SHERLOCK HOLMES
ADVENTURES OF SHERLOCK
  HOLMES, THE (1939)
YOUNG SHERLOCK HOLMES
  (1985)

SINBAD
GOLDEN VOYAGE OF SINBAD,
  THE (1974)
SEVENTH VOYAGE OF SINBAD,
  THE (1958)
SINBAD AND THE EYE OF THE
  TIGER (1977)
SINBAD THE SAILOR (1947)

STAR TREK
STAR TREK: THE MOTION
  PICTURE (1979)
STAR TREK II: THE WRATH OF
  KHAN (1982)
STAR TREK III: THE SEARCH FOR
  SPOCK (1984)
STAR TREK IV: THE VOYAGE
  HOME (1986)

STAR WARS
EMPIRE STRIKES BACK, THE
  (1980)
RETURN OF THE JEDI (1983)
STAR WARS (1977)

SUPERMAN
SUPERMAN (1978)
SUPERMAN II (1980)

TARZAN
TARZAN, THE APE MAN (1932)

FAMILY CLASSICS

Film Reviews

A

ABBOTT AND COSTELLO MEET FRANKENSTEIN

(1948) 83m UNIV bw (GB: ABBOTT AND COSTELLO MEET THE GHOSTS)

Bud Abbott *(Chick Young)*, Lou Costello *(Wilbur Grey)*, Lon Chaney, Jr. *(Lawrence Talbot/The Wolf Man)*, Bela Lugosi *(Dracula)*, Glenn Strange *(The Monster)*, Lenore Aubert *(Sandra Mornay)*, Jane Randolph *(Joan Raymond)*, Frank Ferguson *(McDougal)*, Charles Bradstreet *(Dr. Stevens)*, Howard Negley *(Harris)*, Vincent Price *(Voice of the Invisible Man)*, Clarence Straight *(Man in Armor)*, Helen Spring *(Woman)*, Harry Brown *(Photographer)*, Joe Kirk, George Barton, Carl Sklover, Joe Walls *(Men)*, Paul Stader *(Sergeant)*, Bobby Barber *(Waiter)*.

In this hilarious spoof, Abbott and Costello play railway porters who unwittingly deliver the "undead" bodies of Frankenstein's Monster (Glenn Strange) and Dracula (Bela Lugosi) to a wax museum, where the bodies are revived. Thus awakened, Dracula becomes intent on replacing the Monster's brain with Costello's, because the Monster has become too intelligent and difficult to control. Lawrence Talbot (Lon Chaney, Jr.) attempts to help the boys, but he's got a problem himself: he turns into a wolf man whenever there's a full moon. Never were horror and comedy mixed more successfully than in this very funny film, which featured more than a few offscreen laughs as well. Reportedly, Lugosi, Chaney, and Strange joined Abbott and Costello in pie-throwing contests during filming breaks. In one such melee, Strange tripped over a cable and broke an ankle, so that Chaney had to fill in as the Monster for one scene. On the heels of this very successful outing, Abbott and Costello made several other pictures in which they "met" Hollywood monsters, but none was as lively and entertaining as this effort.

p, Robert Arthur; d, Charles T. Barton; w, Robert Lees, Frederic I. Rinaldo, John Grant (based on the novel *Frankenstein* by Mary Shelley); ph, Charles Van Enger; m, Frank Skinner.

Comedy/Horror   **Cas.**   **(MPAA:NR)**

ABE LINCOLN IN ILLINOIS

(1940) 110m RKO bw (GB: SPIRIT OF THE PEOPLE)

Raymond Massey *(Abraham Lincoln)*, Gene Lockhart *(Stephen Douglas)*, Ruth Gordon *(Mary Todd Lincoln)*, Mary Howard *(Ann Rutledge)*, Dorothy Tree *(Elizabeth Edwards)*, Harvey Stephens *(Ninian Edwards)*, Minor Watson *(Joshua Speed)*, Alan Baxter *(Billy Herndon)*, Howard Da Silva *(Jack Armstrong)*, Maurice Murphy *(John Mc-Neil)*, Clem Bevans *(Ben Mattling)*, Herbert Rudley *(Seth Gale)*, Roger Imhof *(Mr. Crimmin)*, Edmund Elton *(Mr. Rutledge)*, George Rosener *(Dr. Chandler)*, Trevor Bardette *(John Hanks)*, Elisabeth Risdon *(Sarah Lincoln)*, Napo-

leon Simpson *(Gobey)*, Aldrich Bowker *(Judge Bowling Green)*, Louis Jean Heydt *(Mentor Graham)*, Harlan Briggs *(Denton Offut)*, Andy Clyde *(Stage Driver)*, Leona Roberts *(Mrs. Rutledge)*, Florence Roberts *(Mrs. Bowling Green)*, Fay Helm *(Mrs. Seth Gale)*, Syd Saylor *(John Johnston)*, Charles Middleton *(Tom Lincoln)*, Alec Craig *(Trem Cogdall)*.

In adapting Robert E. Sherwood's popular play about the early years of Abraham Lincoln, the filmmakers wisely chose Raymond Massey, who played the title role on stage, to continue his portrayal in the film. Massey heads an impressive cast in a picture spanning 30 years of Lincoln's life, following his career from his beginnings as a woodsman and shopkeeper to his entry into law and politics and culminating with his election as the 16th president of the United States. The film includes some memorable scenes of Lincoln's debates with his longtime political rival, Stephen Douglas (Gene Lockhart), and offers a vivid account of 19th-century life in the Midwest, with particular attention paid to the political processes of the day.

p, Max Gordon; d, John Cromwell; w, Robert E. Sherwood (based on his play); ph, James Wong Howe; m, Roy Webb.

Biography   **Cas.**   **(MPAA:NR)**

ABSENT-MINDED PROFESSOR, THE

(1961) 97m Disney/BV bw

Fred MacMurray *(Prof. Ned Brainard)*, Nancy Olson *(Betsy Carlisle)*, Keenan Wynn *(Alonzo Hawk)*, Tommy Kirk *(Bill Hawk)*, Leon Ames *(Rufus Daggett)*, Elliott Reid *(Shelby Ashton)*, Edward Andrews *(Defense Secretary)*, Wally Brown *(Coach Elkins)*, Forrest Lewis *(Officer Kelly)*, James Westerfield *(Officer Hanson)*, Ed Wynn *(Fire Chief)*, David Lewis *(Gen. Singer)*, Belle Montrose *(Mrs. Chatsworth)*, Alan Carney *(Referee)*, Gage Clarke *(Rev. Bosworth)*, Alan Hewitt *(Gen. Hotchkiss)*, Jack Mullaney *(Captain)*, Raymond Bailey *(Adm. Olmstead)*, Wendell Holmes *(Gen. Poynter)*, Don Ross *(Lenny)*, Charlie Briggs *(Sig)*, Wally Boag *(TV Newsman)*.

In this screwy comedy, quirky college professor Ned Brainard (Fred MacMurray) invents flying rubber, which he dubs "flubber." The substance has gravity-defying properties that, when it's adhered to the soles of shoes, enable the wearer to leap incredible heights. Naturally, a variety of wacky situations ensue from this invention; meanwhile, the evil Alonzo Hawk (Keenan Wynn) plots to steal the formula for his own personal gain. The film's special effects will delight viewers of all ages. In 1964, a less successful sequel was released, titled THE SON OF FLUBBER.

p, Walt Disney; d, Robert Stevenson; w, Bill Walsh (based on a story by Samuel W. Taylor); ph, Edward Colman; m, George Bruns.

Comedy   **Cas.**   **(MPAA:NR)**

ADVENTURES OF BULLWHIP GRIFFIN, THE

(1967) 110m Disney/BV c

Roddy McDowall *(Bullwhip Griffin)*, Suzanne Pleshette *(Arabella Flagg)*, Karl Malden *(Judge Higgins)*, Harry Guardino *(Sam Trimble)*, Bryan Russell *(Jack Flagg)*, Richard Haydn *(Quentin Bartlett)*, Liam Redmond *(Capt. Swain)*, Hermione Baddeley *(Irene Chesney)*, Cecil Kellaway *(Mr. Pemberton)*, Joby Baker *(Bandido Leader)*, Mike Mazurki *(Mountain Ox)*, Alan Carney *(Joe Turner)*, Parley Baer *(Chief Executioner)*, Arthur Hunnicutt *(Referee)*, Dub Taylor *(Timekeeper)*, Pedro Gonzalez-Gonzalez *(Bandido)*, Burt Mustin, Gil Lamb, John Qualen, Dave Willock.

THE ADVENTURES OF BULLWHIP GRIFFIN is a happy Disney effort in which 14-year-old Jack Flagg (Bryan Russell) heads for California and the Gold Rush after the death of his grandfather in Boston in 1847. The grandfather's death has left orphan Jack and his sister Arabella (Suzanne Pleshette) penniless, and Jack plans to hit it big out west. He's followed by Griffin (Roddy McDowall), the prim and proper family butler. Along the way they get involved with an impoverished actor, a treasure map, and a villainous judge (Karl Malden), while a lucky punch from Griffin knocks out a huge bouncer, earning him the nickname "Bullwhip." The film features plenty of enjoyable action, a couple of catchy musical numbers from Pleshette, and a delightful portrait of California during the frenzied days of the Gold Rush.

p, Walt Disney, Bill Anderson; d, James Neilson; w, Lowell S. Hawley (based on "By the Great Horn Spoon" by Sid Fleischman); ph, Edward Colman; m, George Bruns.

Adventure/Comedy   **Cas.**   **(MPAA:NR)**

ADVENTURES OF HUCKLEBERRY FINN, THE

(1960) 107m MGM c

Tony Randall *(The King)*, Eddie Hodges *(Huckleberry Finn)*, Archie Moore *(Jim)*, Patty McCormack *(Joanna)*, Neville Brand *(Pap)*, Mickey Shaughnessy *(The Duke)*, Judy Canova *(Sheriff's Wife)*, Andy Devine *(Mr. Carmody)*, Sherry Jackson *(Mary Jane)*, Buster Keaton *(Lion Tamer)*, Finlay Currie *(Capt. Sellers)*, Josephine Hutchinson *(Widow Douglas)*, Parley Baer *(Grangerford Man)*, John Carradine *(Slave Catcher)*, Royal Dano *(Sheriff)*, Dolores Hawkins *(Riverboat Singer)*, Sterling Holloway *(Barber)*, Dean Stanton [Harry Dean Stanton] *(Slave Catcher)*.

This is a sprightly account of the adventures of Mark Twain's all-American boy, following Huck Finn (Eddie Hodges) and the slave Jim (Archie Moore) as they travel down the Mississippi on a raft in the mid-1800s. Along the way they are reluctantly drawn into the schemes of a pair of con men (Tony Randall and Mickey Shaughnessy), find work on a riverboat, and join the circus. Though it's not entirely faithful to the book (the riverboat and circus scenes have been added), this is nonetheless a well-crafted film featuring strong performances from Randall and former middleweight boxing champion Moore, with rich photography that beautifully captures authentic Mississippi River locations. This was Hollywood's second attempt to film the Huck Finn story, Mickey Rooney having played the title role in 1939's HUCKLEBERRY FINN.

p, Samuel Goldwyn, Jr.; d, Michael Curtiz; w, James Lee (based on the novel by Mark Twain); ph, Ted McCord (CinemaScope, Metrocolor); m, Jerome Moross.

Adventure   **Cas.**   **(MPAA:NR)**

ADVENTURES OF ICHABOD AND MR. TOAD

(1949) 68m Disney/RKO c

Voices of: Bing Crosby, Basil Rathbone, Eric Blore, Pat O'Malley, John Floyardt, Colin Campbell, Campbell Grant, Claude Allister, The Rhythmaires.

Split into two sequences, this feature-length cartoon is one of Disney's finest efforts, with attention paid to every animated detail. The first sequence deals with the wonderful, aristocratic Mr. Toad of Kenneth Grahame's British classic *The Wind in the Willows*, a haughty amphibian who thinks himself too good for such fellows as Mr. Pig and the stuffed shirt Mr. Rat. Toad, who is obsessed with planes and autos, lands through his own recklessness in trouble, debt, and jail, and it's up to his friends to get him out and to defeat the band of thieving weasels that framed him. The second segment, concerning the exceedingly thin Ichabod Crane of Washington Irving's "The Legend of Sleepy Hollow," is delightfully narrated by Bing Crosby, who also croons some eerie tunes with The Rhythmaires. Ichabod, the new schoolmaster in a small New England village, has a memorable Halloween night when he is chased by the legendary Headless Horseman. For pure imaginative animation, the pell-mell race through forests and glens has gone unequalled. Superb family entertainment, although very young children may find the climactic sequence of the "Sleepy Hollow" portion too frightening. The two segments have been released separately on videocassette.

p, Walt Disney; d, Jack Kinney, Clyde Geronimi, James Algar; w, Erdman Penner, Winston Hibler, Joe Rinaldi, Ted Sears, Homer Brightman, Harry Reeves (based on the stories "The Legend of Sleepy Hollow" by Washington Irving and "The Wind in the Willows" by Kenneth Grahame).

Animation   **Cas.**   **(MPAA:NR)**

ADVENTURES OF MARK TWAIN, THE

(1944) 130m WB bw

Fredric March *(Samuel Clemens)*, Alexis Smith *(Olivia Langdon)*, Donald Crisp *(J.B. Pond)*, Alan Hale *(Steve Gillis)*, C. Aubrey Smith *(Oxford Chancellor)*, John Carradine *(Bret Harte)*, William Henry *(Charles Langdon)*, Robert Barrat *(Horace E. Bixby)*, Walter Hampden *(Jervis Langdon)*, Joyce Reynolds *(Clara Clemens)*, Whitford Kane *(Joe Goodwin)*, Percy Kilbride *(Billings)*, Nana Bryant *(Mrs. Langdon)*, Dickie Jones *(Sam Clemens, Age 15)*, Kay Johnson *(Jane Clemens)*, Jackie Brown *(Sam Clem-*

ens, *Age 12)*, Eugene Holland *(Huck Finn)*, Michael Miller *(Tom Sawyer)*, Joseph Crehan *(Promoter)*, Cliff Saum *(Prospector)*, Harry Tyler *(Assistant Editor)*, Roland Drew *(Editor)*, Douglas Wood *(William Dean Howells)*, Willie Best *(George)*, Burr Caruth *(Oliver W. Holmes)*, Harry Hilliard *(John G. Whittier)*, Brandon Hurst *(Ralph W. Emerson)*, Davison Clark *(Henry W. Longfellow)*, Monte Blue *(Captain)*, Paul Newlan *(Boss Deckhand)*, Ernest Whitman *(Stoker)*, Emmett Smith *(Repeater)*, Pat O'Malley *(Captain's Mate)*, Chester Conklin *(Judge)*, George Lessey *(Henry H. Rogers)*, Dorothy Vaughan *(Kate Leary)*, Gloria Ann Crawford *(Susie as a child)*, Lynne Baggett *(Susie)*, Carol Joyce Coombs *(Clara as a child)*, Charlene Salerno *(Jean as a child)*, Joyce Tucker *(Jean)*, Charles Waldron *(Dr. Quintard)*, Paul Scardon *(Rudyard Kipling)*.

A rich biography of Mark Twain is rendered here, with a masterpiece of incisive acting by Fredric March as the young adventurer who left Hannibal, Missouri, to learn the Mississippi River's tricky ways as a navigator. In one scene, the young navigator is attempting to steer a riverboat through fogbound waters when he hears a deckhand, after throwing out a weight to determine the water's depth, shout: "Mark the twain [twine—the rope tied about the weight] 15 [feet]." Thus the *nom de plume* of one of America's finest writers and humorists. Sharp, witty dialog sparks the story line as Twain moves from the Mississippi to the West as a newspaper editor, then on to Gold Rush California, where he writes the short story "The Celebrated Jumping Frog of Calaveras County," the success of which starts him on his literary career. The episodic film chronicles Twain's meetings with the greats of his day (U.S. Grant, Bret Harte, Oliver Wendell Holmes, Ralph Waldo Emerson, etc.), as well as his courtship of and marriage to Olivia Langdon (Alexis Smith), as it follows Twain from young manhood to old age. March imbues his character with quiet nobility, projecting the forceful, courageous soul of the immortal Twain.

p, Jesse L. Lasky; d, Irving Rapper; w, Alan LeMay, Harry Chandlee (based on an adaptation by Alan LeMay and Harold M. Sherman of biographical material owned by the Mark Twain Co.); ph, Sol Polito, Laurence Butler, Edward Linden, Don Siegel, James Leicester; m, Max Steiner.

Biography (MPAA:NR)

ADVENTURES OF ROBIN HOOD, THE

(1938) 102m WB-FN c

Errol Flynn *(Sir Robin of Locksley/Robin Hood)*, Olivia de Havilland *(Maid Marian)*, Basil Rathbone *(Sir Guy of Gisbourne)*, Claude Rains *(Prince John)*, Patric Knowles *(Will Scarlet)*, Eugene Pallette *(Friar Tuck)*, Alan Hale *(Little John)*, Melville Cooper *(High Sheriff of Nottingham)*, Ian Hunter *(King Richard the Lion-Hearted)*, Una O'Connor *(Bess)*, Herbert Mundin *(Much, the Miller's Son)*, Montagu Love *(Bishop of Black Canons)*, Leonard Willey *(Sir Essex)*, Robert Noble *(Sir Ralf)*, Kenneth Hunter *(Sir Mortimer)*, Robert Warwick *(Sir Geoffrey)*, Colin Kenny *(Sir Baldwin)*, Lester Matthews *(Sir Ivor)*, Harry Cording *(Dickon Malbete)*, Howard Hill *(Captain of Archers)*, Ivan Simpson *(Tavern Proprietor)*, Charles McNaughton *(Crippen)*, Lionel Belmore *(Humilty Prin)*, Janet Shaw *(Humility's Daughter)*, Crawford Kent *(Sir Norbert)*, Austin Fairman *(Sir Nigel)*, Leonard Mudie *(Town Crier)*, Holmes Herbert *(Referee)*.

When Richard the Lion-Hearted (Ian Hunter), king of England, is captured by Austrians and held for ransom, the evil Prince John (Claude Rains) declares himself ruler of England and makes no attempt to secure Richard's safe return. Though John has all the nobles and their armies on his side, it doesn't sway a lone knight, Robin Hood (Errol Flynn), who swears his allegiance to Richard and sets out to raise the ransom money by stealing from the caravans of the rich that cross through Sherwood Forest. Robin is aided by his lady love, Maid Marian (Olivia de Havilland), and his band of merry men, including Little John (Alan Hale) and Friar Tuck (Eugene Pallette), as he battles the false monarch and the villainous Sheriff of Nottingham (Melville Cooper) in his effort to return the throne to its rightful owner. This is one of the truly great adventure films of all time, and features a terrific performance by the perfectly cast Flynn. Handsome, dashing, and athletic, Flynn is everything that Robin Hood should be—and more, as he imbues his character with a delightful sense of humor. His adversaries, of course, are all memorable villains, particularly Basil Rathbone as the conniving Sir Guy of Gisbourne. Rathbone spent many hours with a fencing instructor to prepare for his climactic duel with Flynn, one of the most exciting battles ever put on film. Only a spirited and extravagant production could do justice to the Robin Hood legend; this film is more than equal to the task.

p, Hal B. Wallis, Henry Blanke; d, Michael Curtiz, William Keighley; w, Norman Reilly Raine, Seton I. Miller (based on ancient Robin Hood legends); ph, Sol Polito, Tony Gaudio (Technicolor); m, Eric Wolfgang Korngold.

Adventure Cas. (MPAA:NR)

ADVENTURES OF ROBINSON CRUSOE, THE

(1954) 90m UA c

Dan O'Herlihy *(Robinson Crusoe)*, Jaime Fernandez *(Friday)*, Felipe De Alba *(Capt. Oberzo)*, Chel Lopez *(Bos'n)*, Jose Chavez, Emilio Garibay *(Leaders of the Mutiny)*.

Shipwrecked in a storm, sailor Robinson Crusoe (Dan O'Herlihy) finds himself washed up on the shore of a desert island. All other hands have been killed in the storm, but Crusoe is able to salvage a cat, a dog, and some weapons and provisions from the wreckage. He takes up residence in a cave and begins living as his prehistoric ancestors must have done, learning to hunt, build a fire, grow corn, and make bread, all the while striving to overcome his oppressive loneliness. After going 18 years without seeing another human being, he is shocked when a small band of natives visits the island one day. They are about to kill and eat one of their party when Crusoe intervenes, saves the intended victim, and chases off the others. Since he rescues the native on a Friday, Crusoe gives him that name and the two develop a strong relationship as they spend another 10 years on the island, after which Crusoe is finally returned to civilization by the crew of a ship that anchors off-shore. Written in 1719, Daniel Defoe's *The Life and Strange Surprising Adventures of Robinson Crusoe* is an enduring classic that has fascinated readers since its first publication. This is a fairly faithful adaptation of that classic by the great Spanish director Luis Bunuel, photographed in Mexico. The film is particularly effective in evoking the loneliness of the stranded survivor and in depicting the changes that gradually occur within him as his memories of civilization begin to fade.

p, Oscar Dancigers, Henry Ehrlich; d, Luis Bunuel; w, Philip Roll, Luis Bunuel (based on the novel *The Life and Strange Surprising Adventures of Robinson Crusoe* by Daniel Defoe); ph, Alex Philips (Pathecolor); m, Anthony Collins.

Adventure (MPAA:NR)

ADVENTURES OF SHERLOCK HOLMES, THE

(1939) 85m FOX bw (GB: SHERLOCK HOLMES)

Basil Rathbone *(Sherlock Holmes),* Nigel Bruce *(Dr. Watson),* Ida Lupino *(Ann Brandon),* Alan Marshal *(Jerrold Hunter),* Terry Kilburn *(Billy),* George Zucco *(Prof. Moriarty),* Henry Stephenson *(Sir Ronald Ramsgate),* E.E. Clive *(Inspector Bristol),* Arthur Hohl *(Bassick),* May Beatty *(Mrs. Jameson),* Peter Willes *(Lloyd Brandon),* Mary Gordon *(Mrs. Hudson),* Holmes Herbert *(Justice),* George Regas *(Mateo),* Mary Forbes *(Lady Conyngham),* Frank Dawson *(Dawes),* William Austin *(Stranger),* Anthony Kemble Cooper *(Tony).*

A taut script, sharp and witty dialog, and attention to production detail make this one of the finest crime adventures ever, a superb effort by the Basil Rathbone-Nigel Bruce team that was to prove so successful in the subsequent series concerning the great sleuth. Rathbone is the quintessential Sherlock Holmes, almost a double of the famous sketches by Sidney Paget that accompanied the original Doyle stories in *Strand Magazine,* while Bruce matches him in the public's imagination as *the* Dr. Watson—bumbling, dogged, ever-loyal. The film has just the right Victorian setting, with lots of foggy atmosphere, antique buildings, and hansom cabs. The evil Prof. Moriarty (George Zucco) is at the plot's center, trying to make good his threat to Holmes to "bring off right under [Holmes'] nose the most incredible crime of the century." Moriarty's plan is to steal the crown jewels while sidetracking Holmes with two foul murders. All of Holmes' fascinating quirks and preoccupations—his violin playing, his scientific experiments—are worked into the character, and the Baker Street rooms he shared with Watson are meticulously re-created, cluttered with books and criminal artifacts. This is the best of the Holmes movies and well worth watching.

p, Darryl F. Zanuck, Gene Markey; d, Alfred Werker; w, Edwin Blum, William Drake (based on a play by William Gillette and works of Arthur Conan Doyle); ph, Leon Shamroy.

Mystery Cas. (MPAA:NR)

ADVENTURES OF THE WILDERNESS FAMILY, THE

(1975) 94m Pacific c

Robert F. Logan *(Skip),* Susan Damante Shaw *(Pat),* Hollye Holmes *(Jenny),* Ham Larsen *(Toby).*

Made in Utah, this back-to-nature film stars Robert F. Logan as a construction worker fed up with city life. He takes his family to the high mountains, where his asthmatic daughter can breathe clean, fresh air. They build a log cabin and fend off attacks by ferocious bears while making friends with the tamer species—including raccoons, wild dogs, and coyotes. A well-done ode to the simpler life and a production that has universal family appeal.

p, Arthur R. Dubbs; d&w, Stewart Raffil; m, Gene Kauer, Douglas Lackey.

Adventure Cas. (MPAA:NR)

ADVENTURES OF TOM SAWYER, THE

(1938) 93m SELZ c

Tommy Kelly *(Tom Sawyer),* Jackie Moran *(Huckleberry Finn),* Ann Gillis *(Becky Thatcher),* May Robson *(Aunt Polly),* Walter Brennan *(Muff Potter),* Victor Jory *(Injun Joe),* David Holt *(Sid Sawyer),* Victor Kilian *(Sheriff),* Nana Bryant *(Mrs. Thatcher),* Olin Howland *(Schoolmaster),* Donald Meek *(Superintendent),* Charles Richman *(Judge Thatcher),* Margaret Hamilton *(Mrs. Harper),* Marcia Mae Jones *(Mary Sawyer),* Mickey Rentschler *(Joe Harper),* Cora Sue Collins *(Amy Lawrence),* Philip Hurlie *(Jim).*

Mark Twain's beloved Tom Sawyer comes to life in this excellent production, with Tommy Kelly portraying the brave, mischievous boy. He's caught between the manners of his very proper home, ruled by tough but loving Aunt Polly (May Robson), and the wild, roaming, trouble-seeking nature of his friend Huckleberry Finn, ably portrayed by Jackie Moran. The great Sawyer adventures are faithfully re-created—the conning of the two boys into whitewashing his aunt's fence, a wild ride down the Mississippi on a raft, the witnessing of Injun Joe's crimes, and his pursuit of Tom and the terrified Becky Thatcher (Ann Gillis) into the giant cave. The incorrigible boys even witness their own funeral ceremony before informing the grieving townsfolk that they are still among the living. A lively production featuring a quick pace, lots of action, and more than a little wit.

p, David O. Selznick, William H. Wright; d, Norman Taurog; w, John V.A. Weaver (based on the novel by Mark Twain); ph, James Wong Howe, Wilfrid Cline (Technicolor).

Adventure Cas. (MPAA:NR)

AFRICA SCREAMS

(1949) 79m UA bw

Bud Abbott *(Buzz Johnson)*, Lou Costello *(Stanley Livingston)*, Hillary Brooke *(Diana Emerson)*, Max Baer *(Boots)*, Buddy Baer *(Grappler)*, Shemp Howard *(Gunner)*, Joe Besser *(Harry)*, Clyde Beatty, Frank Buck *(Themselves)*.

This top-flight, though generally unheralded, Abbott and Costello comedy opens with the boys working in the book department of a large store. An attractive woman (Hillary Brooke) comes to their counter asking for an out-of-print tome titled *Dark Africa*. To impress the lady, Abbott tells her that his pal (Costello) was a personal friend of the author's and is very knowledgeable about Africa. As a result, the duo is later kidnaped and taken to the Dark Continent, where they are expected to help the woman and her evil henchmen find a fortune in diamonds. The production offers plenty of laughs, as the pair takes great advantage of the African setting.

p, Edward Nassour; d, Charles Barton; w, Earl Baldwin; ph, Charles Van Enger.

Comedy   **Cas.**   **(MPAA:NR)**

AFRICA—TEXAS STYLE!

(1967 US/Brit.) 110m Vantors/PAR c

Hugh O'Brian *(Jim Sinclair)*, John Mills *(Wing Comdr. Howard Hayes)*, Nigel Green *(Karl Bekker)*, Tom Nardini *(John Henry)*, Adrienne Corri *(Fay Carter)*, Ronald Howard *(Hugo Copp)*, Charles Malinda *(Sampson)*, Honey Wamala *(Mr. Oyondi)*, Charles Hayes *(Veterinary)*, Stephen Kikumu *(Peter)*, Ali Twaha *(Turk)*, Mohammed Abdullah *(Witch Doctor)*, Hayley Mills *(Girl)*.

Fast-paced direction and action-filled scenes make this production first-rate, as does the exceptional acting by John Mills as Howard Hayes, a Briton living in Africa. Hayes imports two Texas cowboys (Hugh O'Brian and Tom Nardini) to round up thousands of wild animals that are being systematically killed and that are on the verge of extinction. The good guys are opposed by a ruthless hunter who presents obstacles to their humane plan. Action and beautiful scenery abound in this film, which offers a worthwhile lesson on the need for conservation. It served as the pilot for the TV series "Cowboy in Africa."

p, Ivan Tors, Andrew Marton; d, Andrew Marton; w, Andy White; ph, Paul Beeson (Eastmancolor); m, Malcolm Arnold.

Adventure   **Cas.**   **(MPAA:NR)**

AFRICAN QUEEN, THE

(1951, US/Brit.) 105m Horizon-Romulus/UA c

Humphrey Bogart *(Charlie Allnut)*, Katharine Hepburn *(Rose Sayer)*, Robert Morley *(Rev. Samuel Sayer)*, Peter Bull *(Captain of "Louisa")*, Theodore Bikel *(1st Officer)*, Walter Gotell *(2nd Officer)*, Gerald Onn *(Petty Officer)*, Peter Swanick *(1st Officer at Shona)*, Richard Marner *(2nd Officer at Shona)*.

THE AFRICAN QUEEN ~~has everything~~—adventure, humor, spectacular photography, superb acting, and exciting motion. It tells the story of roustabout Charlie Allnut (Humphrey Bogart), who runs a little tramp steamer that brings supplies to small villages in East Africa at the onset of WW I. A series of events puts him in the position of having to transport Rose Sayer (Katharine Hepburn), the spinster sister of a recently deceased missionary, downriver in his barely seaworthy craft. The trials and travails they must overcome result in the development of a loving relationship between the unlikely pair, while their determination to play a part in the war effort grows. The marvelous script is packed with sprightly dialog, creating a punchy, tongue-in-cheek satire that filled the screen with hilarious humanity. Bogart deservedly won an Academy Award for his portrayal of a kind-hearted drifter risking all for the woman he loves.

p, S.P. Eagle [Sam Spiegel]; d, John Huston; w, James Agee, John Huston (based on the novel by C.S. Forester); ph, Jack Cardiff (Technicolor); m, Alan Gray.

Adventure/Romance   **Cas.**   **(MPAA:NR)**

AH, WILDERNESS!

(1935) 101m MGM bw

Wallace Beery *(Sid Davis)*, Lionel Barrymore *(Nat Miller)*, Aline MacMahon *(Lily Davis)*, Eric Linden *(Richard Miller)*, Cecilia Parker *(Muriel McComber)*, Spring Byington *(Essie Miller)*, Mickey Rooney *(Tommy Miller)*, Charles Grapewin *(Mr. McComber)*, Frank Albertson *(Arthur Miller)*, Edward Nugent *(Wint Selby)*, Bonita Granville *(Mildred Miller)*, Helen Flint *(Belle)*, Helen Freeman *(Miss Hawley)*.

Famed American playwright Eugene O'Neill's only comedy, written in five weeks, is a dream of the sweet, unaffected boyhood he never had, culminating in one long summer during which adolescence struggles into manhood. Eric Linden plays Richard Miller, a young man of sincerity and some charming stupidity. His mother busies herself with household problems, his mischievous brother and unruly sister vex him, his father nervously avoids instructing him in the ways of the world, and his often-inebriated uncle teaches him about life. It's a marvelous portrait of a family, filled with funny and tender scenes as young Richard strives to understand himself and those around him.

p, Hunt Stromberg; d, Clarence Brown; w, Albert Hackett, Frances Goodrich (based on the play by Eugene O'Neill); ph, Clyde De Vinna; m, Herbert Stothart.

Comedy   **(MPAA:NR)**

AIR FORCE

(1943) 124m WB bw

John Ridgely *(Capt. Mike Quincannon)*, Gig Young *(Lt. Bill Williams)*, Arthur Kennedy *(Lt. Tommy McMartin)*, Charles Drake *(Lt. Munchauser)*, Harry Carey *(Sgt. Robby White)*, George Tobias *(Cpl. Weinberg)*, Ward Wood *(Cpl.*

Peterson), Ray Montgomery (Pvt. Chester), John Garfield (Sgt. Joe Winocki), James Brown (Lt. Tex Rader), Stanley Ridges (Maj. Mallory), Willard Robertson (Colonel), Moroni Olsen (Col. Blake), Edward Brophy (Sgt. J.J. Callahan), Richard Lane (Maj. W.G. Roberts), Faye Emerson (Susan McMartin), Bill Crago (Lt. Moran), Addison Richards (Maj. Daniels), James Flavin (Maj. A.M. Bagley), Ann Doran (Mary Quincannon), Dorothy Peterson (Mrs. Chester), James Millican (Marine with Dog), William Forrest (Jack Harper), Murray Alper (Corporal of Demolition Squad), George Neise (Hickam Field Officer), Tom Neal (Marine), Henry Blair (Quincannon's Son), Warren Douglas (Control Officer), Ruth Ford (Nurse), William Hopper (Sergeant).

This is a thrilling salute to the Air Force told through the exploits of one B-17, the Mary Ann by name. The film opens before the US enters WW II, introducing the varied crew of the Mary Ann, whom we soon come to know better when they find themselves thrown into the war after the bombing of Pearl Harbor. It's an inspiring and gripping tale with excellent performances all around, particularly those of John Garfield, as the cynical airman who washed out of pilot school, and Harry Carey, as the tough old crew chief. The dialog is both meaningful and believable, and Hawks' direction is masterful, particularly when the plane is attacked by scores of Japanese Zeroes over Bataan in scenes that are harrowing and frighteningly realistic.

p, Hal B. Wallis; d, Howard Hawks; w, Dudley Nichols; ph, James Wong Howe, Elmer Dyer; m, Franz Waxman.

War   **Cas.**   **(MPAA:NR)**

ALAMO, THE

(1960) 192m Batjac/UA c

John Wayne (Col. David Crockett), Richard Widmark (Col. James Bowie), Laurence Harvey (Col. William Travis), Frankie Avalon (Smitty), Patrick Wayne (Capt. James Butler Bonham), Linda Cristal (Flaca), Joan O'Brien (Mrs. Dickinson), Chill Wills (Beekeeper), Joseph Calleia (Juan Sequin), Ken Curtis (Capt. Almeron Dickinson), Carlos Arruza (Lt. Reyes), Jester Hairston (Jethro), Veda Ann Borg (Blind Nell), John Dierkes (Jocko Robertson), Denver Pyle (Gambler), Aissa Wayne (Angelina Dickinson), Hank Worden (Parson), Bill Henry (Dr. Sutherland), Bill Daniel (Col. Neill), Wesley Lau (Emil), Chuck Roberson (A Tennessean), Guinn "Big Boy" Williams (Lt. Finn), Olive Carey (Mrs. Dennison), Ruben Padilla (Gen. Santa Anna), Richard Boone (Gen. Sam Houston).

This is an excellent re-creation of the defense of the Alamo in 1836 Texas, when 187 Americans and Texicans stood against Santa Anna's forces (more than 7,000 men) for 13 days. In addition to the battle, the movie shows how those men came to be inside the mission converted into a tiny fort in the dusty village of San Antonio, focusing on Col. William Travis, played archly by Laurence Harvey; Jim Bowie, enacted angrily by Richard Widmark; and Davy Crockett, expansively portrayed by John Wayne, coonskin cap and all. Much time is spent devel-

oping the rivalry between Travis and Bowie, who both attempt to take command of the fort. The screen rivalry is based upon fact, as is the moving scene in which Travis draws a line in the dirt and asks every man who is willing to defend the Alamo to cross it, knowing it means doom. As directed by Wayne, the film is an inspiring history lesson.

p&d, John Wayne; w, James Edward Grant; ph, William H. Clothier (Todd-AO, Technicolor); m, Dmitri Tiomkin.

War   **Cas.**   **(MPAA:NR)**

ALI BABA AND THE FORTY THIEVES

(1944) 87m UNIV c

Maria Montez (Amara), Jon Hall (Ali Baba), Turhan Bey (Jamiel), Andy Devine (Abdullah), Kurt Katch (Hulagu Khan), Frank Puglia (Cassim), Fortunio Bonanova (Baba), Moroni Olsen (Caliph), Ramsey Ames (Nalu), Chris-Pin Martin (Fat Thief), Scotty Beckett (Ali as a Child), Yvette Duguay (Amara as a Girl), Noel Cravat (Mongol Captain), Jimmy Conlin (Little Thief), Harry Cording (Mahmoud).

This lush and lavish Arabian Nights fantasy follows the exploits of the Caliph of Baghdad's son, who runs off into the desert after his father is killed by raiding Mongols. There he encounters the legendary 40 thieves and watches in amazement as their command, "Open Sesame," magically parts a solid rock wall, revealing a cavernous hiding place filled with treasures. He is adopted by the thieves, dubbed "Ali Baba," and grows up to be their leader. As an adult, Ali sets out to avenge his father's death and to free his land from the reigning Mongols. While the film is set in the ancient Middle East, there is much in the script that is reminiscent of THE ADVENTURES OF ROBIN HOOD, and some have likened it to a western. It holds its own, however, as a fast-action story of legendary Arabia, with plenty of wonders and miracles to excite any child and amuse any adult.

p, Paul Malvern; d, Arthur Lubin; w, Edmund L. Hartmann; ph, George Robinson, W. Howard Green; m, Edward Ward; ed, Russell Schoengarth.

Adventure/Fantasy   **(MPAA:NR)**

ALICE IN WONDERLAND

(1933) 90m PAR bw

Charlotte Henry (Alice), Richard Arlen (Cheshire Cat), Roscoe Ates (Fish), William Austin (Gryphon), Gary Cooper (White Knight), Jack Duffy (Leg of Mutton), Leon Errol (Uncle Gilbert), Louise Fazenda (White Queen), W.C. Fields (Humpty Dumpty), Alec B. Francis (King of Hearts), Skeets Gallagher (White Rabbit), Cary Grant (Mock Turtle), Lillian Harmer (Cook), Raymond Hatton (Mouse), Sterling Holloway (Frog), Edward Everett Horton (Mad Hatter), Roscoe Karns (Tweedledee), Baby LeRoy (Joker), Lucien Littlefield (Father William's Son), Mae Marsh (Sheep), Polly Moran (Dodo Bird), Jack Oakie (Tweedledum), Edna May Oliver (Red Queen), George Ovey (Plum Pudding), May Robson (Queen of Hearts),

Charlie Ruggles *(March Hare)*, Jackie Searle *(Dormouse)*, Alison Skipworth *(Duchess)*, Ned Sparks *(Caterpillar)*.

Hollywood's biggest stars of the day play the bizarre characters in this surrealistic version of Lewis Carroll's nonsensical, often frightening fantasy. Most of the superstars in this fascinating but offbeat production are thoroughly unrecognizable, buried under pounds of makeup or smothered in cumbersome costumes—Cary Grant, as the Mock Turtle, and Gary Cooper, as the White Knight, could be extras for all the costuming obscuring their identities. Jack Oakie, as Tweedledum, is identifiable, as are W.C. Fields, as Humpty-Dumpty; Edward Everett Horton, as the Mad Hatter; Sterling Holloway, as the Frog; and Edna May Oliver, as the Red Queen, though this recognizability is due to their distinctive voices. The film is a technical marvel for its year, with lavish sets, costuming, and makeup, and offers a fairly faithful adaptation of Carroll's work.

p, Louis D. Lighton; d, Norman McLeod; w, Joseph L. Mankiewicz, William Cameron Menzies (based on the novels *Alice's Adventures in Wonderland* and *Alice Through the Looking Glass* by Lewis Carroll); ph, Henry Sharp, Bert Glennon; m, Dmitri Tiomkin.

Fantasy   **(MPAA:NR)**

ALICE IN WONDERLAND

(1951) 74m Disney/RKO c

Voices of: Kathryn Beaumont *(Alice)*, Ed Wynn *(Mad Hatter)*, Richard Haydn *(Caterpillar)*, Sterling Holloway *(Cheshire Cat)*, Jerry Colonna *(March Hare)*, Verna Felton *(Queen of Hearts)*, Pat O'Malley *(Walrus/Carpenter/Dee/Dum)*, Bill Thompson *(White Rabbit/Dodo)*, Heather Angel *(Alice's Sister)*, Joseph Kearns *(Doorknob)*, Larry Grey *(Bill)*, Queenie Leonard *(Bird in the Tree)*, Dink Trout *(King of Hearts)*, Doris Lloyd *(The Rose)*, James Macdonald *(Dormouse)*, The Mellomen *(Card Players)*.

Disney's beautifully animated version of Alice's tale remains popular today, partly because it is aimed at a children's market for which Disney eschews intellectual interpretations of Carroll's story, playing it straight like a crazy dream/nightmare. All of Alice's adventures are in place, including her tea party with the Mad Hatter and friends, her meeting with the bewildering Cheshire Cat, and her strange game of croquet with the temperamental Queen of Hearts. The film is dazzling in its use of color and odd shapes, and is enhanced by the distinctive voices of Ed Wynn as the Mad Hatter, Sterling Holloway as the Cheshire Cat, Jerry Colonna as the March Hare, and Verna Felton as the Queen of Hearts. A delight for children and the young at heart.

p, Walt Disney; d, Clyde Geronimi, Hamilton Luske, Wilfred Jaxon; m, Oliver Wallace.

Animation   **Cas.**   **(MPAA:NR)**

ALIVE AND KICKING

(1962, Brit.) 95m Pathe/Seven Arts bw

Sybil Thorndike *(Dora)*, Kathleen Harrison *(Rosie)*, Estelle Winwood *(Mabel)*, Stanley Holloway *(MacDonagh)*, Liam Redmond *(Old Man)*, Marjorie Rhodes *(Old Woman)*, Richard Harris *(Lover)*, Olive McFarland *(Lover)*, John Salew *(Solicitor)*, Eric Pohlmann *(Captain)*, Colin Gordon *(Birdwatcher)*, Joyce Carey *(Matron)*, Anita Sharp Bolster *(Postmistress)*, Paul Farrell *(Postman)*, Patrick McAlinney *(Policeman)*, Raymond Manthorpe *(Little Boy)*.

Dora, Rosie, and Mabel (Sybil Thorndike, Kathleen Harrison, and Estelle Winwood) leave their tranquil old folks' home when they discover that they are to be separated. Cleverly eluding the police, army, navy, and air force, the three spunky old ladies make their escape and are off on a series of adventures that includes encounters with Russian fishermen and a millionaire, and a plot to bring prosperity to a poor island village. This delightfully zany British comedy gets added spark from the three main actresses and Stanley Holloway, who plays the millionaire.

p, Victor Skutezky; d, Cyril Frankel; w, Denis Cannan, ph, Gilbert Taylor; m, Philip Green.

Comedy   **(MPAA:NR)**

ALL CREATURES GREAT AND SMALL

(1975, Brit.) 92m EMI c

Simon Ward, Anthony Hopkins, Lisa Harrow, Brian Stirner, Freddie Jones, T.P. McKenna, Brenda Bruce, John Collin, Daphne Oxenford, Christine Buckley, Jane Collins.

This warmhearted story of a country vet and his practice in rural England depicts the day-to-day feeding and care of animals, as well as focusing on the children who love them. Based on actual incidents in the life of veterinarian James Herriot, the film provides excellent family entertainment. A sequel, ALL THINGS BRIGHT AND BEAUTIFUL (see below), was produced in 1979.

p, David Susskind, Duane Bogle; d, Claude Whatham; w, Hugh Whitemore (based on the book by James Herriot); ph, Peter Suschitzky; m, Wilfred Josephs.

Drama   **Cas.**   **(MPAA:NR)**

ALL THINGS BRIGHT AND BEAUTIFUL

(1979, Brit.) 94m Susskind/WORLD c

John Alderson *(James)*, Colin Blakely *(Siegfried)*, Lisa Harrow *(Helen)*, Bill Maynard *(Hinchcliffe)*, Paul Shelley *(Richard)*, Richard Pearson *(Granville)*, Rosemary Martin *(Mrs. Dalby)*, Raymond Francis *(Col. Bosworth)*, John Barrett *(Crump)*, Philip Stone *(Jack)*, Clifford Kershaw *(Kendall)*, Kevin Moreton *(William)*, Liz Smith *(Mrs. Dodds)*, Leslie Sarony *(Kirby)*, Gwen Nelson *(Mrs. Kirby)*, Juliet Cooke *(Jean)*, Stacy Davies *(Harry)*, Christine Hargreaves *(Mrs. Butterworth)*, May Warden *(Mrs. Tompkins)*, Richard Griffiths *(Sam)*, Ian Hastings *(Jackson)*.

The continuing exploits of a compassionate veterinarian as he takes care of animals and children alike in a small British community during the Depression. Like its predecessor, ALL CREATURES GREAT AND SMALL, this is a thoroughly uplifting, nonviolent family film with only one message: life is fascinating and full of joy for those who take the time to appreciate it.

p, Margaret Matheson; d, Eric Till; w, Alan Plater (based on books by James Herriot); ph, Arthur Ibbetson; m, Laurie Johnson.

Drama **(MPAA:NR)**

ALONE ON THE PACIFIC

(1964, Jap.) 104m Ishihara International c (AKA: MY ENEMY THE SEA)

Yuiro Ishihara *(The Youth)*, Kinuyo Tanaka *(His Mother)*, Masayuki Mori *(His Father)*, Ruriko Asoka *(His Sister)*, Hajime Hana *(His Friend)*.

ALONE ON THE PACIFIC is a testimony to the human spirit and a well-crafted film in which a youth (Yuiro Ishihara) fulfills his boyhood dream of crossing the ocean. He paddles his little craft past the Osaka Bay coast guard and is immediately hurled into deep waters by a raging blue-black typhoon that seems sure to send him to his ancestors. He survives the storm, however, and flashbacks of his life show his stern father, understanding mother, loving sister, and devoted friend, all of whom he informs of his desire to sail to America. Throughout the impossible voyage—through more storms, doldrums, and days upon days without food or water—the plucky, determined youth courageously sails onward to realize his dream. Excellent film fare, sharply directed and well acted.

p, Akira Nakai; d, Kon Ichikawa; w, Natto Wada (based on a logbook by Kenichi Horie); ph, Yoshihiro Yamazaki; m, Yasushi Akatagawa, Tohru Takemitsu.

Adventure **(MPAA:NR)**

AMAZING MRS. HOLLIDAY

(1943) 97m UNIV bw

Deanna Durbin *(Ruth)*, Edmond O'Brien *(Tom)*, Barry Fitzgerald *(Timothy)*, Arthur Treacher *(Henderson)*, Harry Davenport *(Commodore)*, Grant Mitchell *(Edgar)*, Frieda Inescort *(Karen)*, Elisabeth Risdon *(Louise)*, Jonathan Hale *(Ferguson)*, Esther Dale *(Lucy)*, Gus Schilling *(Jeff)*, J. Frank Hamilton *(Dr. Kirke)*, Christopher Severn, Yvonne Severn, Vido Rich, Mila Rich, Teddy Infuhr, Linda Bieber, Diane Dubois, Bill Ward.

This is a rather Cinderella-like adventure in which a young woman (Deanna Durbin) tries to get a group of orphan children out of South China and to safety in America. She poses as the wife of a steamship magnate lost at sea and manages to establish the kids in the wealthy man's huge mansion, but confesses her fraud to the magnate's grandson, who protects her and the chil-

dren. The pleasant outing is highlighted by two songs sung by Durbin in Chinese.

p&d, Bruce Manning; w, Frank Ryan, John Jacoby (based on a story by Boris Ingster and Leo Townsend); ph, Woody Bredell; m, Frank Skinner, H.J. Salter.

Adventure **(MPAA:NR)**

AMERICAN TAIL, AN

(1986) 80m Amblin Entertainment/UNIV c

Voices of: Erica Yohn *(Mama Mousekewitz)*, Nehemiah Persoff *(Papa Mousekewitz)*, Amy Green *(Tanya Mousekewitz)*, Phillip Glasser *(Fievel Mousekewitz)*, Christopher Plummer *(Henri)*, John Finnegan *(Warren T. Rat)*, Will Ryan *(Digit)*, Hal Smith *(Moe)*, Pat Musick *(Tony Toponi)*, Cathianne Blore *(Bridget)*, Neil Ross *(Honest John)*, Madeline Kahn *(Gussie Mausheimer)*, Dom DeLuise *(Tiger)*.

A beautifully animated feature, AN AMERICAN TAIL opens in turn-of-the-century Russia, where the Mousekewitz family, a clan of Jewish mice, is forced to emigrate after suffering under the rule of Czarist cats. Little Fievel Mousekewitz is separated from his family en route to New York and washes up on the shores of the New Land inside a bottle. Once in the big city, Fievel encounters a variety of mice, both friendly and vicious, and discovers that America has its share of cats—all the while attempting to be reunited with his family. The story is moving, and the animation includes some powerful images. Some of the early scenes depicting the suffering of the mice in Russia may be too frightening for younger viewers.

p, Don Bluth, John Pomeroy, Gary Goldman; d, Don Bluth; w, Judy Freudberg, Tony Geiss (based on a story by David Kirschner, Judy Freudberg and Tony Geiss); m, James Horner.

Animation **(MPAA:G)**

ANGELS IN THE OUTFIELD

(1951) 99m MGM bw (GB: ANGELS AND THE PIRATES)

Paul Douglas *(Guffy McGovern)*, Janet Leigh *(Jennifer Paige)*, Keenan Wynn *(Fred Bayles)*, Donna Corcoran *(Bridget White)*, Lewis Stone *(Arnold P. Hapgood)*, Spring Byington *(Sister Edwitha)*, Bruce Bennett *(Saul Hellman)*, Marvin Kaplan *(Timothy Durney)*, Ellen Corby *(Sister Veronica)*, Jeff Richards *(Dave Rothberg)*, John Gallaudet *(Reynolds)*, King Donovan *(McGee)*, Don Haggerty *(Rube Robinson)*, Paul Salata *(Tony Minelli)*, Fred Graham *("Chunk")*, John McKee *(Bill Baxter)*, Patrick J. Molyneaux *(Patrick J. Finley)*.

This is a silly but fun baseball film about gruff manager Guffy McGovern (Paul Douglas), who must sit by while his dismal team loses game after game. Suddenly the squad begins winning, and a newspaper reporter writes a story about a little orphan girl who swears she's seen angels standing among Guffy's players, trying to help them win. Not long after, Guffy is hit in the head by a line

drive and admits to the press that, indeed, angels *have* been helping the team. The baseball commissioner thinks he's gone nuts and starts an investigation into the manager's sanity as the team continues to win. Great performances by all make this a little gem of a film. Dwight Eisenhower, interviewed during his presidency, named this as his favorite movie.

p&d, Clarence Brown; w, Dorothy Kingsley, George Wells (based on a story by Richard Conlin); ph, Paul C. Vogel; m, Daniele Amfitheatrof.

Comedy/Sports (MPAA:NR)

ANGELS WITH DIRTY FACES

(1938) 97m WB bw

James Cagney *(Rocky Sullivan)*, Pat O'Brien *(Jerry Connelly)*, Humphrey Bogart *(James Frazier)*, Ann Sheridan *(Laury Ferguson)*, George Bancroft *(Mac Keefer)*, Billy Halop *(Soapy)*, Bobby Jordan *(Swing)*, Leo Gorcey *(Bim)*, Bernard Punsley *(Hunky)*, Gabriel Dell *(Patsy)*, Huntz Hall *(Crab)*, Frankie Burke *(Rocky as a Boy)*, William Tracy *(Jerry as a Boy)*, Marilyn Knowlden *(Laury as a Girl)*, Joe Downing *(Steve)*, Adrian Morris *(Blackie)*, Oscar O'Shea *(Guard Kennedy)*, Edward Pawley *(Guard Edwards)*, William Pawley *(Bugs the Gunman)*, Charles Sullivan, Theodore Rand *(Gunmen)*, John Hamilton *(Police Captain)*, Earl Dwire *(Priest)*, The St. Brendan's Church Choir *(Themselves)*.

As youths, Rocky Sullivan and his pal Jerry Connelly are caught in the act of breaking into a railroad car. Jerry escapes, but Rocky is caught and sent to reform school. The film then jumps ahead several years, with Rocky (now played by James Cagney) a hardened criminal and Jerry (Pat O'Brien) a priest in the neighborhood where the boys grew up. Rocky, recently released from jail, returns to the neighborhood and a battle begins between the criminal and the priest for the hearts and minds of some tough kids in the neighborhood, while Rocky also tries to get his double-crossing ex-partner (Humphrey Bogart) to come up with the $100,000 he owes him. With Cagney, O'Brien, and Bogart plus the young actors who would come to be known as the Dead End Kids, this film offers a host of terrific characters, crisp dialog, and not a little humor. Particularly comic is the scene in which Rocky gives the young toughs a lesson in how to play basketball. Stories of two boyhood friends who go down different paths in life were popular in movies of the 1930s, but the tale was never more effectively told than in this fast-paced drama.

p, Sam Bischoff; d, Michael Curtiz; w, John Wexley, Warren Duff (based on a story by Rowland Brown); ph, Sol Polito; m, Max Steiner.

Crime Cas. (MPAA:NR)

ANIMAL CRACKERS

(1930) 97m PAR bw

Groucho Marx *(Capt. Jeffrey Spaulding)*, Harpo Marx *(The Professor)*, Chico Marx *(Signor Emanuel Raveld)*, Zeppo Marx *(Horatio Jamison)*, Lillian Roth *(Arabella Rittenhouse)*, Margaret Dumont *(Mrs. Rittenhouse)*, Louis Sorin *(Roscoe Chandler)*, Hal Thompson *(John Parker)*, Margaret Irving *(Mrs. Whitehead)*, Kathryn Reece *(Grace Carpenter)*, Robert Greig *(Hives)*, Edward Metcalf *(Hennessey)*.

This zany comedy featuring the zaniest film comics ever opens with a party in a posh mansion during which a priceless oil painting is unveiled. The rest of the story—if you can call it that—concerns the painting's theft and recovery. Even though the script was tightly written, the movie appears to be one big ad-lib in the style of COCONUTS, the first smash film by the Marx Brothers. Groucho's wise-guy delivery is fast-paced as usual, but even he is repelled at times by his own puns, turning at one point to the camera to grimace and say, "Well, *all* the jokes can't be good!" He also sings the memorable "Hooray for Captain Spaulding," the tune that would become his theme song throughout his long career. Harpo is in his usual delightful and daffy character, as is Chico as Groucho's maddening antagonist.

d, Victor Heerman; w, Morris Ryskind (based on the musical play by Morris Ryskind and George S. Kaufman); ph, George Folsey.

Comedy Cas. (MPAA:NR)

ANNIE

(1982) 130m COL c

Albert Finney *(Daddy Warbucks)*, Carol Burnett *(Miss Hannigan)*, Bernadette Peters *(Lily)*, Ann Reinking *(Grace Farrell)*, Tim Curry *(Rooster)*, Aileen Quinn *(Annie)*, Geoffrey Holder *(Punjab)*, Roger Minami *(Asp)*, Toni Ann Gisondi *(Molly)*, Rosanne Sorrentino *(Pepper)*, Lara Berk *(Tessie)*, April Lerman *(Kate)*, Lucie Stewart *(Duffy)*, Robin Ignico *(July)*, Edward Herrmann *(FDR)*, Lois DeBanzie *(Eleanor Roosevelt)*, Peter Marshall *(Bert Healy)*, Loni Ackerman, Murphy Cross, Nancy Sinclair *(Boylan Sisters)*, I.M. Hobson *(Drake)*, Lu Leonard *(Mrs. Pugh)*, Mavis Ray *(Mrs. Greer)*, Pam Blair *(Annette)*, Colleen Zenk *(Celette)*, Victor Griffin *(Saunders)*, Jerome Collamore *(Frick)*, Jon Richards *(Frack)*, Wayne Cilento *(Photographer)*, Ken Swofford *(Weasel)*, Larry Hankin *(Pound Man)*, Irving Metzman *(Bundles)*, Angela Martin *(Mrs.McKracky)*, Kurtis Epper Sanders *(Spike)*.

This charming musical based on the comic strip character Little Orphan Annie features many a memorable song and pleasant dance numbers, to which the versatile Albert Finney, as Daddy Warbucks; the leggy Ann Reinking, as Grace Farrell; and Aileen Quinn, an adorable, near-perfect Annie, tap, shuffle, waltz, glide, and leap for all they're worth. A great supporting cast includes Carol Burnett spoofing the role of the heartless Miss Hannigan, overseer of a group of orphan girls, and Geoffrey Holder as Punjab, Warbucks' magician servant who finds no feat impossible. The slim story has the child Annie escaping from the orphanage, returned, then selected to spend a short time with billionaire Warbucks, who grows to love her. The music includes the unforgettable song "Tomorrow," which receives several renditions and is worth the whole film. The production itself is rich, and certain to appeal to all ages.

p, Ray Stark; d, John Huston; w, Carol Sobieski (based on the musical play by Thomas Meehan, Charles Strouse, and Martin Charnin and the comic strip "Little Orphan Annie"); ph, Richard Moore (Panavision, Metrocolor).

Musical   **Cas.**   **(MPAA:PG)**

ANNIE GET YOUR GUN

(1950) 107m MGM c

Betty Hutton (Annie Oakley), Howard Keel (Frank Butler), Louis Calhern (Buffalo Bill), J. Carrol Naish (Chief Sitting Bull), Edward Arnold (Pawnee Bill), Keenan Wynn (Charlie Davenport), Benay Venuta (Dolly Tate), Clinton Sundberg (Foster Wilson), James H. Harrison (Mac), Bradley Mora (Little Jake), Susan Odin (Jessie), Diane Dick (Nellie), Chief Yowlachie (Little Horse), Eleanor Brown (Minnie), Evelyn Beresford (Queen Victoria), Andre Charlot (President Loubet of France), John Mylong (Kaiser Wilhelm II), Nino Pipitone (King Victor Emmanuel of Italy).

This sprightly songfest captivated audiences with its tunes that became instant standards, large sets, armies of extras, and Wild West motif. In a glove-fitting role, Betty Hutton blasts her way on and off the screen as the sharp-shooting Annie Oakley Mozie (1860-1926), a girl from the Ozarks who becomes queen of Buffalo Bill's renowned Wild West Show, pitting her talents against marksman Frank Butler (Howard Keel), whom she loves. Keel is excellent as the smug star of the show, J. Carrol Naish, the versatile character actor, is top-notch as a shrewd Sitting Bull, and Louis Calhern is superb as a noble but slippery Buffalo Bill. Standout numbers include "Doin' What Comes Natur'lly," sung by Hutton, and the fantastic finale number, "There's No Business Like Show Business."

p, Arthur Freed; d, George Sidney; w, Sidney Sheldon (based on the musical play by Herbert Fields and Dorothy Fields); ph, Charles Rosher (Technicolor).

Biography/Musical/Western   Cas.   (MPAA:NR)

ANNIE OAKLEY

(1935) 79m RKO bw

Barbara Stanwyck (Annie Oakley), Preston Foster (Toby Walker), Melvyn Douglas (Jeff Hogarth), Moroni Olsen (Buffalo Bill), Pert Kelton (Vera Delmar), Andy Clyde (MacIvor), Chief Thundercloud (Sitting Bull), Margaret Armstrong (Mrs. Oakley), Delmar Watson (Wesley Oakley), Philo McCullough (Officer), Eddie Dunn, Ernie S. Adams (Wranglers), Harry Bowen (Father), Theodore Lorch (Announcer), Sammy McKim (Boy at Shooting Gallery).

Barbara Stanwyck stars in this lively historical fare as the rugged Ozark sharpshooter Annie Oakley. Stanwyck is particularly fine in the opening scenes, in which Annie

is discovered as an awkward, thoroughly uncultured and untutored backwoodsian. She joins Buffalo Bill's Wild West Show and becomes its star marksperson, vying for attention and falling in love with sharpshooter Toby Walker (Preston Foster). The show's manager, played by Melvyn Douglas, is himself hopelessly in love with Annie, but doesn't stand a chance as she goes tenaciously after Walker, getting help from Chief Thundercloud as Sitting Bull. Thundercloud provides many laughs in his encounters with the white man's world of folding beds and gas lights. The film is elaborately produced, with scores of Indians and cowboys making up Cody's legendary show, although the facts are bent a bit for dramatic effect.

p, Cliff Reid; d, George Stevens; w, Joel Sayre, John Twist (based on a story by Joseph A. Fields, Ewart Adamson); ph, J. Roy Hunt.

Western   **(MPAA:NR)**

ARABIAN NIGHTS

(1942) 86m UNIV c

Sabu (Ali Ben Ali), Jon Hall (Haroun al Raschid), Maria Montez (Sherazad), Leif Erikson (Kamar), Billy Gilbert (Ahmad), Edgar Barrier (Hadan), Richard Lane (Corporal), Turhan Bey (Captain), John Qualen (Aladdin), Shemp Howard (Sinbad), "Wee Willie" Davis (Valda), Thomas Gomez (Hakim, the Slave Trader), Jeni Le Gon (Dresser to Sherazad), Robert Greig (Eunuch, Story Teller), Charles Coleman (Eunuch), Adia Kuznetzoff (Slaver), Emory Parnell (Harem Sentry), Harry Cording (Blacksmith), Robin Raymond (Slave Girl), Carmen D'Antonio, Virginia Engels, Nedra Sanders, Mary Moore, Veronika Pataky, Jean Trent, Frances Gladwin, Rosemarie Dempsey, Patsy Mace, Pat Starling, June Ealey (Harem Girls), Andre Charlot, Frank Lackteen, Anthony Blair, Robert Barron, Art Miles, Murdock MacQuarrie (Bidders), Elyse Knox (Duenna), Burna Acquanetta (Ishya), Ernest Whitman (Nubian Slave), Eva Puig (Old Woman), Ken Christy (Provost Marshal), Johnnie Berkes (Blind Beggar), Cordell Hickman, Paul Clayton (Black Boys), Phyllis Forbes, Peggy Satterlee, Helen Pender, Eloise Hardt (Virgins), Alaine Brandes (Street Slave Girl).

The film plays fast and loose with the 1880s translations by British explorer Sir Richard Burton, but this version of the Arabian Nights is nevertheless filled with action and rich with color. The legal heir to the throne of the Caliph, played by Jon Hall, is attacked and almost murdered by his evil brother, played by Leif Erikson, who seizes the throne. A dancing girl (Maria Montez) finds the wounded heir and nurses him back to health. They fall in love, and he sets off on a series of adventures, accompanied by a trusted friend (Sabu), an aging Aladdin in search of his mislaid lamp (John Qualen), and a bragging, shiftless Sinbad in his declining years (Shemp Howard). It's all adolescent adventure, but great fun, and the production is lavish in all areas, particularly the costumes, sets, and wonderful lush color.

p, Walter Wanger; d, John Rawlins; w, Michael Hogan, True Boardman; ph, Milton Krasner; m, Frank Skinner.

Adventure/Fantasy (MPAA:NR)

ARISTOCATS, THE

(1970) 78m BV c

Voices of: Maurice Chevalier *(Title Song)*, Scatman Crothers *(Scat Cat)*, Paul Winchell *(Chinese Cat)*, Lord Tim Hudson *(English Cat)*, Vito Scotti *(Italian Cat)*, Thurl Ravenscroft *(Russian Cat)*, Dean Clark *(Berlioz)*, Liz English *(Marie)*, Gary Dubin *(Toulouse)*, Nancy Kulp *(Frou Frou)*, Pat Buttram *(Napoleon)*, George Lindsay *(Lafayette)*, Monica Evans *(Abigail)*, Carole Shelley *(Amelia)*, Charles Lane *(Lawyer)*, Hermione Baddeley *(Madame)*, Roddy Maude-Roxby *(Butler)*, Bill Thompson *(Uncle Waldo)*, Phil Harris *(O'Malley)*, Eva Gabor *(Duchess)*, Sterling Holloway *(Roquefort)*.

An enjoyable mix of fine animation, catchy songs, and outstanding voice characterizations, THE ARISTOCATS concerns an eccentric, wealthy Frenchwoman who leaves her fortune to her cat, Duchess (Eva Gabor), and her three kittens. The woman's butler is next in line for the fortune if anything should happen to the cats; finding this out, the butler is determined to get rid of the animals. He drugs them and dumps them in the countryside in the hope that they won't find their way home, but the felines meet up with a tough alley cat (Phil Harris) who helps them regain their fortune. On the way they meet a wide variety of animals, and even stop to listen to the Scat Cat (Scatman Crothers) and his jazz band. Maurice Chevalier came out of retirement to sing the film's theme song.

p, Wolfgang Reitherman, Winston Hibler; d, Wolfgang Reitherman; w, Larry Clemmons, Vance Gerry, Ken Anderson, Frank Thomas, Eric Cleworth, Julius Svendsen, Ralph Wright, Tom Rowe, Tom McGowan; ph, (Technicolor); m, George Bruns.

Animation (MPAA:G)

AROUND THE WORLD IN 80 DAYS

(1956) 175m UA c

David Niven *(Phileas Fogg)*, Cantinflas *(Passepartout)*, Shirley MacLaine *(Princess Aouda)*, Robert Newton *(Inspector Fix)*, Charles Boyer *(Mons. Casse)*, Joe E. Brown *(Stationmaster)*, Martine Carol *(Tourist)*, John Carradine *(Col. Proctor Stamp)*, Charles Coburn *(Clerk)*, Ronald Colman *(Railway Official)*, Melville Cooper *(Steward)*, Noel Coward *(Hesketh-Baggott)*, Finlay Currie *(Whist Partner)*, Reginald Denny *(Police Chief)*, Andy Devine *(1st Mate)*, Marlene Dietrich *(Hostess)*, Luis Miguel Dominguin *(Bullfighter)*, Fernandel *(Coachman)*, Hermione Gingold *(Sportin' Lady)*, Jose Greco *(Dancer)*, Sir John Gielgud *(Foster)*, Sir Cedric Hardwicke *(Sir Francis Gromarty)*, Trevor Howard *(Falletin)*, Glynis Johns *(Companion)*, Buster Keaton *(Conductor)*, Evelyn Keyes *(Flirt)*, Beatrice Lillie *(Revivalist)*, Peter Lorre *(Steward)*, Edmund Lowe

(Engineer), Victor McLaglen *(Helmsman)*, Colonel Tim McCoy *(Commander)*, Mike Mazurki *(Character)*, John Mills *(Cabby)*, Alan Mowbray *(Consul)*, Robert Morley *(Ralph)*, Edward R. Murrow *(Narrator)*, Jack Oakie *(Captain of "S.S. Henrietta")*, George Raft *(Bouncer at Barbary Coast Saloon)*, Gilbert Roland *(Achmed Abdullah)*, Cesar Romero *(Henchman)*, Frank Sinatra *(Saloon Pianist)*, Red Skelton *(Drunk)*, Ronald Squire, A.E. Matthews, Basil Sydney *(Club Members)*, Ava Gardner *(Spectator)*, Harcourt Williams *(Hinshaw)*.

David Niven is the punctual Phileas Fogg of the famous Jules Verne novel, who makes a bet with his fellow club members in London that he can encircle the globe within 80 days—this in 1872, when travel proceeded at a snail's pace. Fogg is accompanied by his bumbling valet (the great Mexican mimic Cantinflas) and along the way picks up a wandering princess (Shirley MacLaine), while being pursued by a London detective (Robert Newton) who believes the globetrotter has somehow robbed the Bank of England. Around these leads an army of 46 famous personalities of the day appear in bit parts. (This was the film that began the trend of stars appearing in cameo roles.) The star-spotting is fun, but so is the adventure, as Fogg journeys by train, ship, hot-air balloon, and elephant across Europe, India, Japan, the Pacific, the US, and the Atlantic in a race to win his bet. The film was shot in more than 100 natural settings and on 140 special sets. Everything about this big, beautiful movie smacks of authenticity, excitement, and massive showmanship.

p, Michael Todd; d, Michael Anderson; w, S.J. Perelman (John Farrow, James Poe, uncredited) (based on the novel by Jules Verne); ph, Lionel Lindon (Todd-AO, Eastmancolor); m, Victor Young.

Adventure **Cas.** (MPAA:NR)

AT THE CIRCUS

(1939) 86m MGM bw

Groucho Marx *(Attorney Loophole)*, Chico Marx *(Antonio)*, Harpo Marx *(Punchy)*, Kenny Baker *(Jeff Wilson)*, Florence Rice *(Julie Randall)*, Eve Arden *(Peerless Pauline)*, Margaret Dumont *(Mrs. Dukesbury)*, Nat Pendleton *(Goliath)*, Fritz Feld *(Jardinet)*, James Burke *(John Carter)*, Jerry Marenghi *(Little Professor Atom)*, Barnett Parker *(Whitcomb)*.

In this Marx Brothers romp, the nutty siblings team up to help a struggling circus owner save his business. Along the way, they battle a midget, a strong man, a trapeze artist, and other assorted villains intent on acquiring the circus. Since the brothers could turn any situation into a circus, they're right at home in the environment and make the most of it. A wild finish has the frantic trio doing impossible gyrations on the flying rings while attempting to avoid an escaped gorilla. The film features several songs, the most memorable of which, rendered by Groucho in his marvelous off-key voice, is "Lydia, the Tattooed Lady." The film marks the decline of the Marx Brothers style into Hollywood production numbers and a relinquishment of their distinctive set pieces as they slipped from original satire to studio burlesque; it is nevertheless a Marx must.

p, Mervyn Leroy; d, Edward Buzzell; w, Irving Brecher; ph, Leonard M. Smith; m, Franz Waxman.

Comedy/Musical   **Cas.**   **(MPAA:NR)**

BABE RUTH STORY, THE

(1948) 106m MON/AA bw

William Bendix *(Babe Ruth)*, Claire Trevor *(Claire Hodgson)*, Charles Bickford *(Brother Mathias)*, Sam Levene *(Phil Conrad)*, William Frawley *(Jack Dunn)*, Gertrude Niesen *(Nightclub Singer)*, Fred Lightner *(Miller Huggins)*, Stanley Clements *(Western Union Boy)*, Bobby Ellis *(Babe Ruth as a Boy)*, Lloyd Gough *(Baston)*, Matt Briggs *(Col. Ruppert)*, Paul Cavanagh *(Dr. Menzies)*, Pat Flaherty *(Bill Corrigan)*, Tony Taylor *(The Kid)*, Richard Lane *(Coach)*, Mark Koenig *(Himself)*, Harry Wismer, Mel Allen *(Sports Announcers)*, H.V. Kaltenborn *(News Announcer)*, Knox Manning *(Narrator)*.

This biography of Babe Ruth opens with the Babe as a boy in an orphanage. There the tough but kindly Brother Mathias (Charles Bickford) squeezes delinquency from his oversized frame and sends him out to the sandlot, where baseball becomes his first nature. As an adult, Ruth (William Bendix) starts his baseball career as a speed-demon hurler for the Boston Red Sox, then becomes the most powerful batsman in the world with the New York Yankees. Little attempt is made to portray the real-life Sultan of Swat, except for physical imitation— Bendix studied films of Ruth endlessly until he was able to imitate perfectly his stance, walk, unique mannerisms, and facial expressions. The resulting impression is of a larger-than-life Babe, a sports hero with tremendous heart and warmth. It's corny, but a fitting tribute to the man who is probably America's most legendary athlete.

p, Joe Kaufman; d, Roy Del Ruth; w, Bob Considine, George Callahan (based on the book by Bob Considine); ph, Phillip Tannura; m, Edward Ward.

Biography/Sports   **Cas.**   **(MPAA:NR)**

BABES IN ARMS

(1939) 93m MGM bw

Mickey Rooney *(Mickey Moran)*, Judy Garland *(Patsy Barton)*, Charles Winninger *(Joe Moran)*, Guy Kibbee *(Judge Black)*, June Preisser *(Rosalie Essex)*, Grace Hayes *(Florrie Moran)*, Betty Jaynes *(Molly Moran)*, Douglas McPhail *(Don Brice)*, Rand Brooks *(Jeff Steele)*, Leni Lynn *(Doby Martini)*, John Sheffield *(Bobs)*, Henry Hull

(Maddox), Barnett Parker *(William)*, Ann Shoemaker *(Mrs. Barton)*, Margaret Hamilton *(Martha Steele)*, Joseph Crehan *(Mr. Essex)*, George McKay *(Brice)*, Henry Roquemore *(Shaw)*, Lelah Taylor *(Mrs. Brice)*, Lon McCallister *(Boy)*.

Based on the Rodgers and Hart play of the same name, this is the first film teaming Judy Garland and Mickey Rooney. As it opens, Joe and Florrie Moran (Charles Winninger and Grace Hayes) are old vaudevillians who begin a touring show utilizing many of their senior pals. Their children want to go along, but the old folks refuse, so the kids start their own show. Son Mickey Moran (Rooney), pushed on by his friend Patsy Barton (Garland), writes the show, which he will star in as well as direct. The kids must also prove that they don't belong in a state-administered trade school, and a judge gives them 30 days to make the show a success or else. Against that backdrop, Garland, Rooney, and a host of talented singers and dancers serve up a fast-moving and tuneful romp, a great example of the popular MGM musicals of the 1930s and 1940s.

p, Arthur Freed; d, Busby Berkeley; w, Jack McGowan, Kay Van Riper (based on the musical play by Richard Rodgers and Lorenz Hart); ph, Ray June.

Musical   **Cas.**   **(MPAA:NR)**

BABES IN TOYLAND

(1934) 77m MGM bw (AKA: MARCH OF THE WOODEN SOLDIERS)

Stan Laurel *(Stanley Dum)*, Oliver Hardy *(Oliver Dee)*, Charlotte Henry *(Bo-Peep)*, Felix Knight *(Tom-Tom)*, Henry Kleinbach [Henry Brandon] *(Barnaby)*, Florence Roberts *(Widow Peep)*, Ferdinand Munier *(Santa Claus)*, William Burress *(Toymaker)*, Virginia Karns *(Mother Goose)*, Johnny Downs *(Little Boy Blue)*, Jean Darling *(Curly Locks)*, Frank Austin *(Justice of the Peace)*, Gus Leonard *(Candle Snuffer)*, Alice Dahl *(Little Miss Muffett)*, Peter Gordon *(Cat and the Fiddle)*, Sumner Getchell *(Tom Thumb)*, Kewpie Morgan *(Old King Cole)*, John George *(Barnaby's Minion)*, Billy Bletcher *(Chief of Police)*, Alice Cook *(Mother Hubbard)*, Alice Moore *(Queen of Hearts)*.

This is a terrific vehicle for the classic comedy of Laurel and Hardy. As Stanley Dum and Oliver Dee, they become the unsung heroes of Toyland when they save the Widow Peep's daughter, Bo, from marrying the evil Barnaby, save the widow's abode (a multilevel shoe), rescue Tom-Tom from his exile to Bogeyland, and ultimately rid Toyland of the evil Barnaby forever. It makes for a thoroughly enjoyable family film, with the "March of the Toys" number offering five minutes of raucous action that end the film on a high note.

p, Hal Roach; d, Gus Meins, Charles Rogers; w, Nick Grinde, Frank Butler (based on the musical comedy by Victor Herbert); ph, Art Lloyd, Francis Corby.

Fantasy/Musical   **(MPAA:NR)**

BACHELOR AND THE BOBBY-SOXER, THE

(1947) 95m RKO bw (GB: BACHELOR KNIGHT)

Cary Grant *(Dick)*, Myrna Loy *(Margaret)*, Shirley Temple *(Susan)*, Rudy Vallee *(Tommy)*, Ray Collins *(Beemish)*, Harry Davenport *(Thaddeus)*, Johnny Sands *(Jerry)*, Don Beddoe *(Tony)*, Lillian Randolph *(Bessie)*, Veda Ann Borg *(Agnes Prescott)*, Dan Tobin *(Walters)*, Ransom Sherman *(Judge Treadwell)*, William Bakewell *(Winters)*, Irving Bacon *(Melvin)*, Ian Bernard *(Perry)*, Carol Hughes *(Florence)*, William Hall *(Anthony Herman)*, Gregory Gaye *(Maitre d'hotel)*.

In this delightful farce, a guest lecturer at a high school becomes involved in a strange relationship with a student. Susan (Shirley Temple) sees Dick (Cary Grant), literally, as her knight in shining armor, but he brushes off her adolescent advances. She invites herself to Dick's room, shocking not only him, but also her sister (Myrna Loy), a judge who, accompanied by the assistant district attorney (Rudy Vallee), has come looking for Dick. The judge has already had a courtroom run-in with Dick over a nightclub fracas, and is in no mood for excuses. Before long, Grant again finds himself in court, where he is sentenced to an awful punishment—he must escort the love-struck teen everywhere until her infatuation disappears. Given this silly situation, Grant makes the most of it, donning teenage clothes, indulging in hip slang, pulling stunts at picnics and basketball games, and generally aping every teenager in the world in side-splittingly funny antics. The explosion of flamboyant, childlike behavior from one of the most sophisticated actors that ever graced the screen makes for a riotously funny film.

p, Dore Schary; d, Irving Reis; w, Sidney Sheldon; ph, Robert de Grasse, Nicholas Musuraca; m, Leigh Harline.

Comedy   **Cas.**   **(MPAA:NR)**

BAD NEWS BEARS, THE

(1976) 102m PAR c

Walter Matthau *(Coach Buttermaker)*, Tatum O'Neal *(Manda Whurlizer)*, Vic Morrow *(Roy Turner)*, Joyce Van Patten *(Cleveland)*, Ben Piazza *(Councilman Whitewood)*, Jackie Earle Haley *(Kelly Leak)*, Alfred W. Lutter *(Ogilvie)*, Brandon Cruz *(Joey Turner)*, Shari Summers *(Mrs. Turner)*, Joe Brooks *(Umpire)*, Maurice Marks *(Announcer)*, Quinn Smith *(Lupus)*, Gary Lee Cavagnaro *(Engelberg)*, Erin Blunt *(Ahmad)*, David Stambaugh *(Toby Whitewood)*, Jaime Escobedo, George Gonzales *(Agilar Boys)*, David Pollock, Chris Barnes, Scott Firestone, Brett Marx *(Other Boys)*.

THE BAD NEWS BEARS is a charming and funny film that bridges the gap between children and adults. Its PG rating (for language) should not deter most from seeing this gentle and warm ribbing of the Little League system. Coach Buttermaker (Walter Matthau) is a one-time minor leaguer who manages a Little League team, Manda Whurlizer (Tatum O'Neal) is his girl pitcher, and the rest of the team is a pretty ragtag group. Nevertheless, Buttermaker is able to overcome his own deficiencies and turn the team into a competitive squad. A lot of messages are conveyed, but with such deftness that the only memory you'll carry away is of having watched a terrifically emotional, hilarious movie. The great success it enjoyed prompted two sequels, THE BAD NEWS BEARS IN BREAKING TRAINING and THE BAD NEWS BEARS GO TO JAPAN; neither was as entertaining as this one, however.

p, Stanley R. Jaffe; d, Michael Ritchie; w, Bill Lancaster; ph, John A. Alonzo (Movielab Color); m, Jerry Fielding.

Comedy/Sports   **Cas.**   **(MPAA:PG)**

BAMBI

(1942) 70m Disney/RKO c

Voices of: Bobby Stewart *(Bambi)*, Peter Behn *(Thumper)*, Stan Alexander *(Flower)*, Cammie King *(Phylline)*, Donnie Dunagan, Hardie Albright, John Sutherland, Tim Davis, Sam Edwards, Sterling Holloway, Ann Gillis.

As this animated classic opens, the newborn fawn Bambi is adjusting to his unfamiliar surroundings. We watch Bambi mature from youth to a position as leader, with his father, of the herd—in what could be the story of any youngster facing trials and tribulations, even though the youngster this time is a deer. Bambi experiences numerous triumphs and setbacks, including the loss of his mother, and finds love with the doe Phylline. The climactic forest fire scene ranks among the animated highlights in the history of the technique, while comedy is provided by Thumper the rabbit as he teaches the young Bambi how to make it in the forest. To see Disney's animation of so many years ago, and to see what now passes for animation on television, is to realize that the art has gone backward since BAMBI. There is virtually no mention of humans in the movie and "man" is the only word Bambi fears, because it represents attack against his world's sylvan tranquility. This is definitely a film for the entire family.

p, Walt Disney, David D. Hand; w, Perce Pearce, Larry Morey (based on the book by Felix Salten); m, Frank Churchill, Edward Plumb.

Animation   **(MPAA:NR)**

BANK DICK, THE

(1940) 69m UNIV bw (GB: BANK DETECTIVE, THE)

W.C. Fields *(Egbert Souse)*, Cora Witherspoon *(Agatha Souse)*, Una Merkel *(Myrtle Souse)*, Evelyn Del Rio *(Elsie Mae Adele Brunch Souse)*, Jessie Ralph *(Mrs. Hermisillo Brunch)*, Franklin Pangborn *(J. Pinkerton Snoopington)*, Shemp Howard *(Joe Guelpe)*, Richard Purcell *(Mackley Q. Greene)*, Grady Sutton *(Og Oggilby)*, Russell Hicks *(J. Frothingham Waterbury)*, Pierre Watkin *(Mr. Skinner)*, Al Hill *(Repulsive Rogan)*, George Moran *(Loudmouth McNasty)*, Bill Wolfe *(Otis)*, Jack Norton *(A. Pismo Clam)*, Pat West *(Assistant Director)*, Reed Hadley *(Francois)*, Heather Wilde *(Miss Plupp)*, Harlan Briggs *(Doctor Stall)*, Bill Alston *(Mr. Cheek)*, Jan Duggan *(Woman in Bank)*,

Kay Sutton *(Young Woman on Bench)*, Fay Adler *(Bank President's Secretary)*, Bobby Larson *(Boy in Bank)*, Russell Cole *(Bank Clerk)*, Pat O'Malley *(Cop)*, Billy Mitchell *(Black Bank Customer)*, Eddie Dunn *(James, the Chauffeur)*, Emmett Vogan *(Hotel Desk Clerk)*, Margaret Seddon *(Old Lady in Car)*, Eddie Acuff *(Reporter)*, Mary Field *(Woman)*.

THE BANK DICK is classic W.C. Fields, providing manic mirth. The great comedian is an unemployed, much-henpecked family man not too eagerly seeking work who accidentally captures a bank robber and is rewarded with a guard job inside the bank. When not busy bothering customers (as when he apprehends a patron's son brandishing a toy gun inside the bank), he runs between his horrid family and The Black Pussy Cat Cafe, where the proprietor spends most of his time pouring the guard, his only customer, a series of stiff ones. The movie is filled with a marvelous series of Fields-patented comic bits. Fields, who wrote the script under one of his standard impossible pseudonyms, plays a character named Souse, which he pronounces Sou-say; the rest of the world calls him "souse," as in "drunk." Fields' personal drinking problem at this time was reaching debilitating proportions; he had developed a kidney ailment that made work often painful. THE BANK DICK would be his last major film before his death on Christmas Day, 1946, at age 67. Visiting the great clown a few days before he passed on, a close friend found a Bible at Fields' bedside. The self-avowed agnostic appeared flustered at the friend's discovery. "Bill, of all people," the friend asked, "what are *you* doing with a Bible?" Replied W.C. with squinting eyes and a corner-of-the-mouth delivery: "Looking for loopholes."

d, Edward Cline; w, Mahatma Kane Jeeves [W.C. Fields]; ph, Milton Krasner.

| Comedy | Cas. | (MPAA:NR) |

BAREFOOT EXECUTIVE, THE

(1971) 96m BV c

Kurt Russell *(Steven Post)*, Joe Flynn *(Francis X. Wilbanks)*, Harry Morgan *(E.J. Crampton)*, Wally Cox *(Mertons)*, Heather North *(Jennifer Scott)*, Alan Hewitt *(Farnsworth)*, Hayden Rorke *(Clifford)*, Raffles *(Himself)*, John Ritter *(Roger)*, Jack Bender *(Tom)*, Tom Anfinsen *(Dr. Schmidt)*, George N. Neise *(Network Executive)*, Ed Reimers *(Announcer)*, Morgan Farley *(Advertising Executive)*, Ed Prentiss *(Justice Department)*, Fabian Dean *(Jackhammer Man)*, Iris Adrian *(Woman Shopper)*, Jack Smith *(Clatworthy)*.

This very funny satire of the TV business may have more truth to it than one would believe. The action takes place at UBC, a TV network that's always last in the ratings. One of the pages has a girl friend who owns a pet chimp with an unerring eye and ear for picking hit TV shows. Network employee Steven Post (Kurt Russell) uses the simian to great advantage and soon his star is rising. But the secret to Post's success soon leaks out and everyone wants the brilliant chimp, leading to a variety of complications. Lots of serious laughter here from a basically

funny situation. Look for a very young John Ritter already showing his stuff as Roger.

p, Bill Anderson; d, Robert Butler; w, Joseph L. McEveety (based on a story by Lila Garrett, Bernie Kahn, Stewart C. Billett); ph, Charles F. Wheeler (Technicolor); m, Robert F. Brunner.

| Comedy | Cas. | (MPAA:G) |

BATAAN

(1943) 113m MGM bw

Robert Taylor *(Sgt. Bill Dane)*, George Murphy *(Lt. Steve Bentley)*, Thomas Mitchell *(Cpl. Jake Feingold)*, Lloyd Nolan *(Cpl. Barney Todd/Danny Burns)*, Lee Bowman *(Capt. Lassiter)*, Robert Walker *(Leonard Purckett)*, Desi Arnaz *(Felix Ramirez)*, Barry Nelson *(F.X. Matowski)*, Phillip Terry *(Gilbert Hardy)*, Roque Espiritu *(Cpl. Juan Katigbak)*, Kenneth Spencer *(Wesley Epps)*, J. Alex Havier *(Yankee Salazar)*, Tom Dugan *(Sam Malloy)*, Donald Curtis *(Lieutenant)*, Lynne Carver, Mary McLeod, Dorothy Morris *(Nurses)*, Bud Geary *(Infantry Officer)*, Ernie Alexander *(Wounded Soldier)*, Phil Schumacher *(Machine Gunner)*.

BATAAN is the tough, uncompromising war story of a group of determined American and Filipino soldiers fighting on Bataan, knowing they must delay the masses of advancing Japanese troops and that they will be doomed in the attempt. Based on the heroic defense of the Philippines in early 1942, this film portrays soldiers from all over America—as well as Filipinos fighting for their own soil—with a rugged lead performance from Robert Taylor as the grim but kind sergeant commanding the small group. Tay Garnett's direction is appropriately action-filled and the lulls are properly taken up with establishing each man's identity. Taylor, later described by Garnett as "one of the world's great gentlemen," gave an inspired performance. This was his last film for MGM before he became a fighter pilot for the US Navy.

p, Irving Starr; d, Tay Garnett; w, Robert D. Andrews (based partly on the 1934 film THE LOST PATROL); ph, Sidney Wagner; m, Bronislau Kaper.

| War | Cas. | (MPAA:NR) |

BATTLE OF BRITAIN, THE

(1969, Brit.) 133m Spitfire/UA c

Harry Andrews *(Senior Civil Servant)*, Michael Caine *(Squadron Leader Canfield)*, Trevor Howard *(Air Vice Marshal Keith Park)*, Curt Jurgens *(Baron von Richter)*, Ian McShane *(Sgt. Pilot Andy)*, Kenneth More *(Group Capt. Baker)*, Laurence Olivier *(Air Chief Marshal Sir Hugh Dowding)*, Nigel Patrick *(Group Capt. Hope)*, Christopher Plummer *(Squadron Leader Harvey)*, Michael Redgrave *(Air Vice Marshal Evill)*, Ralph Richardson *(British Minister in Switzerland)*, Robert Shaw *(Squadron Leader Skipper)*, Patrick Wymark *(Air Vice Marshal Trafford Leigh-Mallory)*, Susannah York *(Section Officer Maggie Harvey)*, Michael Bates *(W.O. Warrick)*, Isla Blair *(Andy's*

Wife), John Baskcomb *(Farmer)*, Tom Chatto *(Willoughby's Asst. Controller)*, James Cosmo *(Jamie)*, Robert Flemyng *(Wing Comdr. Willoughby)*, Barry Foster *(Squadron Leader Edwards)*, Edward Fox *(Pilot Officer Archie)*, W.G. Foxley *(Squadron Leader Evans)*, David Griffin *(Sgt. Pilot Chris)*, Jack Gwillim *(Senior Air Staff Officer)*, Myles Hoyle *(Peter)*, Duncan Lamont *(Flight Sgt. Arthur)*.

This great, stirring saga of England's defense of its homeland features a staggering, star-studded cast. Laurence Olivier is at his best as Sir Hugh Dowding, whose crafty tactics with his limited fighter command induced the Luftwaffe to make fatal errors that led to its destruction. Robert Shaw is superb as an exhausted but relentlessly tough fighter commander ordering his men again and again into the air. The film is a paean of praise for the RAF in its "finest hour," with recognition also given to the Czech and Polish flyers who fought alongside their British comrades. The aerial photography of the German bombing and the dogfights between the British and German fighters are spectacular and fascinating. Ironically, Adolf Galland, among the sharpest of the German aces that vexed the British during WW II, was used as a technical adviser on the film.

p, Harry Saltzman, S. Benjamin Fisz; d, Guy Hamilton; w, James Kennaway, Benjamin Fisz, Wilfred Greatorex; ph, Freddie Young, Bob Huke (Panavision, Technicolor); m, Sir William Walton, Ron Goodwin.

War   **Cas.**   **(MPAA:G)**

BATTLE OF THE BULGE

(1965) 167m Cinerama/WB c

Henry Fonda *(Lt. Col. Kiley)*, Robert Shaw *(Col. Hessler)*, Robert Ryan *(Gen. Grey)*, Dana Andrews *(Col. Pritchard)*, George Montgomery *(Sgt. Duquesne)*, Ty Hardin *(Schumacher)*, Pier Angeli *(Louise)*, Barbara Werle *(Elena)*, Charles Bronson *(Wolenski)*, Werner Peters *(Gen. Kohler)*, Hans Christian Blech *(Conrad)*, James MacArthur *(Lt. Weaver)*, Telly Savalas *(Guffy)*, Karl Otto Alberty *(Von Diepel)*, William Conrad *(Narrator)*, Steve Rowland, Donald Pickering.

Henry Fonda stars here as Lt. Col. Kiley, a US Army commander in Europe during WW II who keeps telling his superiors that he expects an attack from the German army. They won't hear of it. Fonda is vindicated and the rest of the film is an inch-by-inch view of the battle as the Germans make a last-ditch attempt to vanquish Allied troops in Europe. The battle scenes are well staged and the acting is solid, particularly that of Robert Shaw as a German colonel. This is a foot-slogging account of war with little of the heroics that normally dominate Hollywood war films. In that alone, it merits attention.

p, Milton Sperling, Philip Yordan; d, Ken Annakin; w, Philip Yordan, Milton Sperling, John Melson; ph, Jack Hildyard (Panavision, Technicolor); m, Benjamin Frankel.

War   **Cas.**   **(MPAA:NR)**

BEAUTY AND THE BEAST

(1947, Fr.) 90m Discina International/Lopert Films bw (LA BELLE ET LA BETE)

Jean Marais *(Avenant/The Beast/The Prince)*, Josette Day *(Beauty)*, Marcel Andre *(The Merchant)*, Mila Parely *(Adelaide)*, Nane Germon *(Felice)*, Michel Auclair *(Ludovic)*.

French poet and director Jean Cocteau took a classic fairy tale and created a film fantasy that is a visual masterpiece. The story concerns a merchant who accidentally trespasses upon land owned by a beast (Jean Marais). The beast decrees that the man be punished with death, but allows him to return to his home to say goodbye to his family. Upon hearing his story, his beautiful daughter (Josette Day) refuses to allow her father to die, and goes to the beast's castle in his place. Overwhelmed by her beauty, the beast falls in love with her, and the remainder of the film recounts how she comes to know, understand, and love her captor. The whole fantastic experience is a marvel, with camerawork that has seldom been equalled. The sets are awesome and fascinating, the decor of the castle patterned after illustrations by Gustave Dore. Many of the castle's exteriors were shot at the Chateau de Raray outside Senlis, with Cocteau taking visual advantage of the estate's strange animal statuary that dots the landscape. BEAUTY AND THE BEAST is a memorable and enduring film from the first frame to the last.

p, Andre Paulve; d&w, Jean Cocteau (based on the fairy tale by Mme. Leprince de Beaumont); ph, Henri Alekan; m, Georges Auric.

Fantasy   **Cas.**   **(MPAA:NR)**

BEDKNOBS AND BROOMSTICKS

(1971) 117m BV c

Angela Lansbury *(Eglantine Price)*, David Tomlinson *(Emelius Browne)*, Roddy McDowall *(Mr. Jelk)*, Sam Jaffe *(Bookman)*, John Ericson *(Col. Heller)*, Bruce Forsyth *(Swinburne)*, Reginald Owen *(Gen. Teagler)*, Tessie O'Shea *(Mrs. Hobday)*, Arthur E. Gould-Porter *(Capt. Greer)*, Ben Wrigley *(Street Sweeper)*, Rick Traeger, Manfred Lating *(German Sergeants)*, John Orchard *(Vendor)*, Roy Smart *(Paul)*, Cindy O'Callaghan *(Carrie)*, Ian Weighall *(Charlie)*, Robert Holt *(Voice of Codfish)*, Lennie Weinrib *(Voice of Secretary Bird and Lion)*.

Similar in many ways to MARY POPPINS, BEDKNOBS AND BROOMSTICKS is filled with unique special effects and delightful music. Angela Lansbury stars as Eglantine Price, the owner of a seaside house in England who has three children foisted on her during WW II. At first, the children aren't thrilled about being relocated. Then they learn that Eglantine is studying witchcraft by mail and has much mischief planned for the Nazis if they ever land in England. With a bedstead as their magic carpet, Eglantine takes the kids on a wonderful ride into several fantastic worlds. Animation is neatly mixed with live action and all performances are good.

BELLES OF ST. TRINIAN'S, THE—

p, Bill Walsh; d, Robert Stevenson; w, Bill Walsh, Don DaGradi (based on the book by Mary Norton); ph, Frank Phillips (Technicolor).

Fantasy/Musical   Cas.   (MPAA:G)

BELLES OF ST. TRINIAN'S, THE

(1954, Brit.) 91m London Films/BL bw

Alastair Sim *(Millicent Fritton/Clarence Fritton)*, Joyce Grenfell *(Sgt. Ruby Gates)*, George Cole *(Flash Harry)*, Vivienne Martin *(Arabella)*, Eric Pohlmann *(Sultan of Makyad)*, Lorna Henderson *(Princess Fatima)*, Hermione Baddeley *(Miss Drownder)*, Betty Ann Davies *(Miss Waters)*, Rene Houston *(Miss Brimmer)*, Beryl Reid *(Miss Dawn)*, Balbina *(Mlle. de St. Emilion)*, Jane Henderson *(Miss Holland)*, Diana Day *(Jackie)*, Lloyd Lamble *(Supt. Kemp-Bird)*, Jill Braidwood *(Florrie)*, Annabelle Covey *(Maudie)*, Pauline Drewitt *(Celia)*, Jean Langston *(Rosie)*, Guy Middleton *(Eric Rowbotham-Smith)*, Richard Wattis *(Manton Bassett)*.

This is a very funny comedy based on Ronald Searles' cartoons of a monstrous girls' school known as St. Trinian's. The plot has to do with the horsenaping of a famous steed that is foiled by some of the school's girls. Among the girls' antics: making gin in the school's science lab, which is then sold by the crooked Flash Harry (George Cole). Alastair Sim is wonderful in two roles, playing the headmistress as well as her ne'er-do-well brother. Joyce Grenfell is also quite amusing as a police spy. This one was a winner, spawning less successful sequels (BLUE MURDER AT ST. TRINIAN'S; THE PURE HELL OF ST. TRINIAN'S; and THE GREAT ST. TRINIAN'S TRAIN ROBBERY).

p, Frank Launder, Sidney Gilliat; d, Frank Launder; w, Frank Launder, Sidney Gilliat, Val Valentine (based on cartoons by Ronald Searle); ph, Stanley Pavey; m, Malcolm Arnold.

Comedy   Cas.   (MPAA:NR)

BELLS OF ROSARITA

(1945) 68m REP bw

Roy Rogers *(Himself)*, George "Gabby" Hayes *(Baggy Whittaker)*, Dale Evans *(Sue Farnum)*, Adele Mara *(Patty Phillips)*, Grant Withers *(William Ripley)*, Janet Martin *(Rosarita)*, Addison Richards *(Slim Phillips)*, Roy Barcroft *(Maxwell)*, Sons of the Pioneers *(Themselves)*, Wild Bill Elliott, Allan "Rocky" Lane, Don "Red" Barry, Robert Livingston, Sunset Carson.

One of the best of the Roy Rogers westerns, THE BELLS OF ROSARITA concerns the daughter of a former circus performer who is being cheated by her late father's ex-partner. Roy can never stand to see a lady in distress, and he rides to the rescue, along with Trigger, Dale, and his ever-present sidekick, Gabby Hayes. As if those forces weren't enough, Roy gets assistance from several other movie western heroes of the day, including Wild

Bill Elliott, Rocky Lane, Red Barry, and Sunset Carson. A classic, with great action and songs by Roy and Dale, and a melange of bad guys to match wits and fists with the good guys.

p, Edward J. White; d, Frank McDonald; w, Jack Townley; ph, Ernest Miller; md, Morton Scott.

Western   Cas.   (MPAA:NR)

BELLS OF ST. MARY'S, THE

(1945) 126m Rainbow/RKO bw

Bing Crosby *(Father Chuck O'Malley)*, Ingrid Bergman *(Sister Benedict)*, Henry Travers *(Mr. Bogardus)*, Ruth Donnelly *(Sister Michael)*, Joan Carroll *(Patsy)*, Martha Sleeper *(Patsy's Mother)*, William Gargan *(Joe Gallagher)*, Rhys Williams *(Dr. McKay)*, Dickie Tyler *(Eddie)*, Una O'Connor *(Mrs. Breen)*, Bobby Frasco *(Tommy)*, Matt McHugh *(Clerk)*, Edna Wonacott *(Delphine)*, Jimmy Crane *(Luther)*, Minerva Urecal *(Landlady)*, Cora Shannon *(Old Lady)*, Gwen Crawford, Aina Constant, Eva Novak *(The Sisters)*.

Touchingly sentimental, but strong in all the right places, this is the sequel to GOING MY WAY and nearly as excellent as that classic. Bing Crosby is trouble-shooting priest Father Chuck O'Malley, who is sent to the financially ailing St. Mary's. There he runs smack into charming, clever Sister Benedict (Ingrid Bergman), a mother superior who rules her students with a gentle but decisive hand. She is too rigid for Father O'Malley and he's too permissive for her, setting up a confrontation of styles that's a joy to behold. It's a gentle, uplifting story, and features some fine songs by Crosby, including "Adeste Fidelis," "In the Land of Beginning Again," and the sprightly "Aren't You Glad You're You."

p&d, Leo McCarey; w, Dudley Nichols (based on a story by Leo McCarey); ph, George Barnes; m, Robert Emmett Dolan.

Drama   Cas.   (MPAA:NR)

BELSTONE FOX, THE

(1976, Brit.) 103m RANK/FOX c

Eric Porter *(Asher)*, Rachel Roberts *(Cathie)*, Jeremy Kemp *(Kendrick)*, Bill Travers *(Tod)*, Dennis Waterman *(Stephen)*, Heather Wright *(Jenny)*.

A hunting hound and baby fox settle into a happy, friendly relationship that continues until humans pit them against each other in a hunt. Eric Porter is solid as the huntsman who brings the baby fox to be nurtured by the hound. Hats off to the trainers and technical experts who let the animals steal the show.

p, Julian Wintle; d, James Hill; ph, John Wilcox, James Allen (Todd-AO, Eastmancolor); m, Laurie Johnson.

Drama   Cas.   (MPAA:G)

BENJI

(1974) 85m Mulberry Square c

Higgins (Benji), Patsy Garrett (Mary), Allen Fiuzat (Paul), Cynthia Smith (Cindy), Peter Breck (Dr. Chapman), Frances Bavier (Lady with Cat), Terry Carter (Officer Tuttle), Edgar Buchanan (Bill), Tom Lester (Riley), Christopher Connelly (Henry), Deborah Walley (Linda), Mark Slade (Mitch), Herb Vigran (Lt. Samuels), Larry Swartz (Floyd), J.D. Young (2nd Policeman), Erwin Hearne (Mr. Harvey), Katie Hearne (Mrs. Harvey), Don Puckett (Plainclothesman), Ed DeLatte (Bob Fielding), Victor Raider-Wexler (Payton), Charles Starkey (Custodian), Ben Vaughn (Man).

BENJI is a captivating and irresistible film. A dog of questionable lineage, Benji lives in a vacant house until he is adopted by a family. When that family's children are kidnaped and taken to the very same house Benji once occupied, the pooch has his work cut out for him in rescuing them. Much of the film is shot from a dog's-eye view and it works perfectly. The human actors are good, but not as good as the animal star. Sequel: FOR THE LOVE OF BENJI.

p&d&w, Joe Camp; ph, Don Reddy; m, Euel Box.

Comedy   **Cas.**   **(MPAA:G)**

BEST THINGS IN LIFE ARE FREE, THE

(1956) 104m FOX c

Gordon MacRae (B.G. "Buddy" De Sylva), Dan Dailey (Ray Henderson), Ernest Borgnine (Lew Brown), Sheree North (Kitty), Tommy Noonan (Carl), Murvyn Vye (Manny), Phyllis Avery (Maggie Henderson), Larry Keating (Sheehan), Tony Galento (Fingers), Norman Brooks (Al Jolson), Jacques D'Amboise (Specialty Dancer), Roxanne Arlen (Perky Nicholas), Bryon Palmer (Hollywood Star), Linda Brace, Patty Lou Hudson, Larry Kerr, Julie Van Zandt, Charles Victor, Eugene Borden, Harold Miller, Paul Glass.

This is a thoroughly charming biography of songwriters Buddy De Sylva, Lew Brown, and Ray Henderson, who were responsible for a score of hits. There's not much of a story, just the usual saga of pals who get together and have some success until greed and ambition threaten to split them, but in the end they reconcile and go on writing the hummable tunes that highlight the film. Gordon MacRae, Ernest Borgnine, and Dan Dailey are excellent as the three songwriters. Among the many standards performed in the movie are "Birth of the Blues," "Black Bottom," "Button Up Your Overcoat," "Keep Your Sunnyside Up," and the title song.

p, Henry Ephron; d, Michael Curtiz; w, William Bowers, Phoebe Ephron (based on a story by John O'Hara); ph, Leon Shamroy (Deluxe Color); m, Lionel Newman.

Biography/Musical   **(MPAA:NR)**

BLACK STALLION, THE

(1979) 118m UA c

Kelly Reno (Alec Ramsey), Mickey Rooney (Henry Dailey), Teri Garr (Alec's Mother), Clarence Muse (Snoe), Hoyt Axton (Alec's Father), Michael Higgins (Neville), Ed McNamara (Jake), Doghmi Larbi (The Arab), John Burton, John Buchanan (Jockeys), Kristen Vigard (Becky), Fausto Tozzi (Rescue Captain).

THE BLACK STALLION is a "G" picture as in "Great" and "Gifted," as in "Gee, I didn't think they made films like this anymore." Based on the Walter Farley book, the screenplay (one of the writers cowrote E.T. and another did the 1984 COUNTRY) combines suspense, wit, fantasy, and joy, with none of the mawkish sentimentality often found in films about horses and kids. There's one stretch of about 30 minutes in which not a word is spoken and all we hear are the natural sounds of boy and horse, and it's riveting. The plot is simple: Alec Ramsey (Kelly Reno) and his father (Hoyt Axton) are on board a ship that also carries the stallion. The boat catches fire and the boy and horse end up on a deserted island. They are later rescued and brought back to Alec's small-town home. Once there, Alec meets Henry Dailey (Mickey Rooney), an ex-jockey who shows Alec how truly special the stallion is. The film tugs the heart, offering a series of affecting moments, and is a dazzling visual experience. The saga continued in 1983 with THE BLACK STALLION RETURNS, but that film didn't measure up in quality to its predecessor.

p, Tom Sternberg, Fred Roos; d, Carroll Ballard; w, Melissa Mathison, Jeanne Rosenberg, William Witliff (based on the novel by Walter Farley); ph, Caleb Deschanel; m, Carmine Coppola.

Adventure   **Cas.**   **(MPAA:G)**

BLACKBEARD'S GHOST

(1968) 106m BV c

Peter Ustinov (Captain Blackbeard), Dean Jones (Steve Walker), Suzanne Pleshette (Jo Anne Baker), Elsa Lanchester (Emily Stowcraft), Joby Baker (Silky Seymour), Elliott Reid (TV Commentator), Norman Grabowski (Virgil), Michael Conrad (Pinetop Purvis), Lou Nova (Leon).

BLACKBEARD'S GHOST is a charming fantasy-comedy in which the ghost of legendary pirate Captain Blackbeard (Peter Ustinov) comes to help some aging damsels in distress. Emily Stowcraft (Elsa Lanchester) and her friends are trying to protect a small resort island from being acquired by a criminal element and turned into a haven for gamblers. Track coach Steve Walker (Dean Jones) finds a witch's book that reveals the secret for summoning Blackbeard from the grave, and shares this information with Emily. Once Blackbeard shows up, special effects abound, but they never detract from the story. It's all good fun, and Ustinov is very amusing as Blackbeard.

p, Bill Walsh; d, Robert Stevenson; w, Bill Walsh, Don

DaGradi (based on the novel by Ben Stahl); ph, Edward Colman (Technicolor); m, Robert F. Brunner.

Comedy/Fantasy　　　**Cas.**　　　**(MPAA:NR)**

BLOCKHEADS

(1938) 58m MGM bw

Stan Laurel *(Himself)*, Oliver Hardy *(Himself)*, Patricia El-lis *(Mrs. Gilbert)*, Minna Gombell *(Mrs. Hardy)*, Billy Gilbert *(Himself)*, James Finlayson *(Mr. Finn)*.

Late in their brilliant careers, Stan and Ollie made this delightful comedy that begins with the absurd situation of Laurel having guarded his WW I trench for 20 years, simply because nobody ever came back to give him the order to halt. Hardy discovers his old comrade on a return visit to the battlefield and brings Laurel back home to his wife, with predictable but hilarious results. Two of the greatest comic performers ever, Laurel and Hardy easily made the transition from their silent classics to sound films, but their material in most of the sound pictures never equalled that of their great silents. BLOCK-HEADS is an exception, with a few sequences that are among the duo's best.

p, Hal Roach; d, John G. Blystone; w, Charles Rogers, Felix Adler, James Parrott, Harry Langdon, Arnold Belgard; ph, Art Lloyd.

Comedy　　　**Cas.**　　　**(MPAA:NR)**

BLONDIE

(1938) 68m COL bw

Penny Singleton *(Blondie)*, Arthur Lake *(Dagwood)*, Larry Simms *(Baby Dumpling)*, Gene Lockhart *(C.P. Hazlip)*, Ann Doran *(Elsie Hazlip)*, Jonathan Hale *(J.C. Dithers)*, Gordon Oliver *(Chester Franey)*, Stanley Andrews *(Mr. Hicks)*, Danny Mummert *(Alvin)*, Kathleen Lockhart *(Mrs. Miller)*, Dorothy Moore *(Dorothy)*, Fay Helm *(Mrs. Fuddle)*, Richard Fiske *(Nelson)*, Irving Bacon *(Mailman)*, Ian Wolfe *(Judge)*, Daisy the Dog.

In this first film of the very successful "Blondie" series based on the popular comic strip by Chic Young, harried Dagwood Bumstead (Arthur Lake) loses his job on the eve of his and Blondie's (Penny Singleton) fifth anniversary. Not as exaggerated as the comic strip, the series was very simple in its approach and managed to poke some fun at social customs. Singleton and Lake, perfectly cast as the famous husband-and-wife cartoon characters, bring charm and spontaneity to this film and to each entry in the series.

p, Robert Sparks; d, Frank R. Strayer; w, Richard Flournoy (based on the comic strip created by Chic Young); ph, Henry Freulich.

Comedy　　　**(MPAA:NR)**

BOMBA THE JUNGLE BOY

(1949) 70m MON bw

Johnny Sheffield *(Bomba)*, Peggy Ann Garner *(Pat Harland)*, Onslow Stevens *(George Harland)*, Charles Irwin *(Andy Barnes)*, Smoki Whitfield *(Eli)*, Martin Wilkins *(Mufti)*.

Johnny Sheffield, fresh from playing "Boy" in the "Tarzan" series, was immediately dropped into another serial as Bomba the Jungle Boy. In this, the first of the series, photographer George Harland (Onslow Stevens) journeys to the Dark Continent with his daughter (Peggy Ann Garner). They encounter Bomba and when the daughter becomes lost, it's Bomba who finds her and brings her back to her party, despite locust plagues, jungle fires, and dangerous animals. Though hardly a classic, the "Bomba" series did offer some entertaining adventure yarns, and this was the best of the lot.

p, Walter Mirisch; d, Ford Beebe; w, Jack DeWitt (based on characters created by Roy Rockwood); ph, William Sickner.

Adventure　　　**(MPAA:NR)**

BON VOYAGE, CHARLIE BROWN (AND DON'T COME BACK)

(1980) 75m PAR c

Voices of: Daniel Anderson, Scott Beach, Casey Carlson, Debbie Muller, Patricia Patts, Laura Planting, Arrin Skelley, Bill Melendez, Annalisa Bortolin, Roseline Rubens, Pascale De Bardlet.

This is the fourth and the best of the animated films devoted to the charming antics of the "Peanuts" gang, based on the comic strip created by Charles Schulz. This time Charlie Brown fans get a bagful of surprises that include jet flights, spooky chateaus, and a dose of danger rarely seen in Peanuts films, as the crew is transported to France for two weeks in a student exchange program. It is there that Charlie Brown and Linus are invited to stay at a chateau where grim things happen. Fans will love Snoopy's first-class flight to London and his stopover there, during which he plays tennis at Wimbledon. The film was in production for three years, and it was time well spent.

p, Lee Mendelson, Bill Melendez; d, Bill Melendez; w, Charles M. Schulz (based on "Peanuts" characters created by Charles M. Schulz); ph, Nick Vasu (Movielab Color); m, Ed Bogas, Judy Munsen.

Animation　　　**Cas.**　　　**(MPAA:G)**

BORN FREE

(1966) 95m COL c

Virginia McKenna *(Joy Adamson)*, Bill Travers *(George Adamson)*, Geoffrey Keen *(Kendall)*, Peter Lukoye *(Nuru)*, Omar Chambati *(Makkede)*, Bill Godden *(Sam)*, Bryan Epson *(Baker)*, Robert Cheetham *(Ken)*, Robert Young

(James), Geoffrey Best *(Watson)*, Surya Patel *(Indian Doctor)*.

A heartwarming true story with an African locale, BORN FREE has a pseudo-documentary style. It tells the story of Joy Adamson (Virginia McKenna) and her husband, George (Bill Travers), a Kenyan game warden, who adopt a slain lioness' cubs. One of the cubs, Elsa, is raised to adulthood and becomes a primary fixture in the couple's life. But soon they are faced with their inability to keep an enormous, potentially dangerous (if domesticated) lioness as a house pet. Rather than follow orders that Elsa be sent to a zoo, they set about teaching her techniques of hunting and surviving in the wilderness. A great success when released, the film won Academy Awards for score and the title song. The nature photography is excellent and real-life husband and wife McKenna and Travers are very good, their genuine affection transferring to the screen. The real Joy Adamson was later reported, ironically, to have been killed by a lion; investigation proved her death to be murder at the hands of a disgruntled ex-employee, however. In 1972, the story was continued in LIVING FREE—also an enjoyable film, but not as captivating as this one.

p, Sam Jaffe, Paul Radin; d, James Hill; w, Gerald L.C. Copley (based on books by Joy Adamson); ph, Kenneth Talbot (Technicolor); m, John Barry.

Drama   **Cas.**   **(MPAA:NR)**

BOY TEN FEET TALL, A

(1965, Brit.) 88m PAR c (AKA: SAMMY GOING SOUTH)

Edward G. Robinson *(Cocky Wainwright)*, Fergus McClelland *(Sammy Hartland)*, Constance Cummings *(Gloria Van Imhoff)*, Harry H. Corbett *(Lem)*, Paul Stassino *(Spyros Dracondopolous)*, Zia Mohyeddin *(The Syrian)*, Orlando Martins *(Abu Lubaba)*, John Turner *(Heneker)*, Zena Walker *(Aunt Jane)*, Jack Gwillim *(District Commissioner)*, Patricia Donahue *(Cathie)*, Jared Allen *(Bob)*, Guy Deghy *(Doctor)*, Marne Maitland *(Hassan)*, Steven Scott *(Egyptian Policeman)*, Frederick Schiller *(Head Porter)*.

When 10-year-old Sammy Hartland (Fergus McClelland) is orphaned after his parents are killed in an air raid in Egypt, the boy sets out to reach his aunt 5,000 miles away in Durban, South Africa. Along the way he meets Cocky Wainwright (Edward G. Robinson), a grizzled old diamond smuggler, who regales the boy with tales of his checkered past. Cocky proves to be an encouragement to Sammy as he strives to overcome the seemingly insurmountable odds against his completing his walk across Africa. A marvelous and inspiring adventure, the film also features a terrific performance by Robinson.

p, Hal Mason; d, Alexander Mackendrick; w, Denis Cannan (based on the novel *Sammy Going South* by W.H. Canaway); ph, Erwin Hillier (Eastmancolor); m, Tristram Cary.

Adventure   **(MPAA:NR)**

BOY WHO COULD FLY, THE

(1986) 114m FOX c

Lucy Deakins *(Milly)*, Jay Underwood *(Eric)*, Bonnie Bedelia *(Charlene)*, Fred Savage *(Louis)*, Colleen Dewhurst *(Mrs. Sherman)*, Fred Gwynne *(Uncle Hugo)*, Mindy Cohn *(Geneva)*, Janet MacLachlan *(Mrs. D'Gregario)*, Jennifer Michas *(Mona)*, Michelle Bardeaux *(Erin)*, Aura Pithart *(Colette)*, Cam Bancroft *(Joe)*, Jason Priestly *(Gary)*, Chris Arnold *(Sonny)*, Sean Kelso *(Bad Boy)*, Meredith B. Woodward *(Female Administrator)*, Raimund Stamm, Dan Zale *(Attendants)*, Dwight Koss *(Dad)*, James McLarty *(Tour Guide)*, Betty Phillips *(Institute Receptionist)*, Terry D. Mulligan *(Mr. Brandt)*, Tannis Rae *(Ms. O'Neil)*, Tom Heaton *(Dr. Nelson)*, Angela Gann *(Mrs. Betuel)*, Scott Irvine *(Officer)*, Karen Siegel *(Dr. Karen Siegel)*, John Carpenter, Nick Castle, Tommy Wallace *(The Coupe de Villes)*, Warren Carr *(Guest Coupe)*, Jake the Dog *(Max)*.

The idea of human flight is a fascinating one; providing a variation on that theme, this film is also a gentle, often touching evocation of adolescent pains and joys. As the film opens, the recently widowed Charlene (Bonnie Bedelia) has moved into a new home with her 15-year-old daughter, Milly (Lucy Deakins), and 8-year-old son, Louis (Fred Savage). As the family struggles to adjust to the new surroundings, Milly becomes friendly with her autistic neighbor (Jay Underwood), a boy who believes he can fly. Rich in many respects, THE BOY WHO COULD FLY delicately interweaves the story's dark and light elements, creating a work of striking originality.

p, Gary Adelson; d&w, Nick Castle; ph, Steven Poster, Adam Holender (Panavision, Deluxe Color); m, Bruce Broughton.

Drama/Fantasy   **Cas.**   **(MPAA:PG)**

BOY WHO STOLE A MILLION, THE

(1960, Brit.) 81m BL bw

Virgilio Texera *(Miguel)*, Maurice Reyna *(Paco)*, Marianne Benet *(Maria)*, Harold Kasket *(Luis)*, George Coulouris *(Bank Manager)*, Bill Nagy *(Police Chief)*, Warren Mitchell *(Pedro)*, Tutte Lemkow *(Mateo)*, Xan Das Bolas *(Knife Grinder)*, Francisco Bernal *(Blind Man)*, Edwin Richfield *(Commissionare)*, Barta Barri *(Gang Leader)*, Herbert Curiel *(Organ Grinder)*, Gaylord Cavallaro *(Reporter)*, Paul Whitsun Jones *(Desk Sergeant)*, Robert Rietty *(Detective)*, Mike Brendel *(Carlos I)*, Juan Olaguivel *(Carlos II)*, Victor Mojica *(Chico)*, Curt Christian *(Currito)*, Cyril Shaps *(Bank Clerk)*, Antonio Fuentes *(Assistant Organ Grinder)*, Andrea Malandrinos *(Shoemaker)*, Goyo Lebrero *(Street Vendor)*.

This charming tale, shot in Valencia, Spain, stars Maurice Reyna as a 12-year-old boy who "borrows" a million pesetas from the local bank to help his widowed father get his taxicab out of hock. This attracts the attention of the police as well as of the underworld, and the boy finds himself constantly on the run from all manner of characters who want the money. With his faithful dog at his side, the boy proves to be quite adept at evading his would-be captors in a number of funny and exciting chase sequences. The chase scenes have a bizarre style, making this a lively and entertaining film.

p, George H. Brown; d, Charles Crichton; w, Charles Crichton, John Eldridge (based on a story by Neils West Larsen and Antonio de Leon); ph, Douglas Slocombe; m, Tristram Cary.

Comedy (MPAA:NR)

BOYS TOWN

(1938) 96m MGM bw

Spencer Tracy *(Father Edward Flanagan),* Mickey Rooney *(Whitey Marsh),* Henry Hull *(Dave Morris),* Leslie Fenton *(Dan Farrow),* Addison Richards *(The Judge),* Edward Norris *(Joe Marsh),* Gene Reynolds *(Tony Ponessa),* Minor Watson *(The Bishop),* Jonathan Hale *(John Hargraves),* Bob Watson *(Pee Wee),* Martin Spellman *(Skinny),* Mickey Rentschler *(Tommy Anderson),* Frankie Thomas *(Freddie Fuller),* Jimmy Butler *(Paul Ferguson),* Sidney Miller *(Mo Kahn),* Robert Emmett Keane *(Burton),* Victor Kilian *(The Sheriff).*

When Father Edward J. Flanagan said there were no "bad boys," he meant it, and then went about saving homeless, underprivileged, and victimized youths by building a sanctuary called Boys Town in Omaha, Nebraska. This is the story of Father Flanagan and the creation of Boys Town, with Spencer Tracy playing the benevolent priest. The film depicts the early days of the sanctuary, then focuses on Flanagan's efforts to save a boy named Whitey Marsh (Mickey Rooney) from the life of crime upon which Marsh's older brother has embarked. Tracy won an Academy Award for his portrayal, after studying long and hard to play the priest who made a crusade of saving boys. The actor went to Boys Town before the production and spent hours talking with the real Father Flanagan, finding him a strong but gentle man without sanctimonious airs. Tracy emulated Flanagan's attitudes and mannerisms, and when he won the Oscar announced that it really belonged to the priest, sending it to Flanagan with an inscription that read: "To Father Edward J. Flanagan, whose great human qualities, kindly simplicity, and inspiring courage were strong enough to shine through my humble effort. Spencer Tracy." Sequel: MEN OF BOYS TOWN.

p, John W. Considine, Jr.; d, Norman Taurog; w, John Meehan, Dore Schary (based on a story by Dore Schary, Eleanore Griffin); ph, Sidney Wagner; m, Edward Ward.

Biography (MPAA:NR)

BRIGHT EYES

(1934) 84m FOX bw

Shirley Temple *(Shirley Blake),* James Dunn *(Loop Merritt),* Jane Darwell *(Mrs. Higgins),* Judith Allen *(Adele Martin),* Lois Wilson *(Mary Blake),* Charles Sellon *(Uncle Ned Smith),* Walter Johnson *(Thomas),* Jane Withers *(Joy Smythe),* Theodor von Eltz *(J. Wellington Smythe),* Dorothy Christy *(Anita Smythe),* Brandon Hurst *(Higgins),* George Irving *(Judge Thompson),* Dave O'Brien *(Tex).*

Little Shirley Blake (Shirley Temple) finds herself a center of attention after her mother dies, when three people vie to become her new parent. These would-be parents include the fabulously wealthy Ned Smith (Charles Sellon); his niece, Adele Martin (Judith Allen); and adventurous flyboy Loop Merritt (James Dunn), who was the little girl's father's friend. The always-cute Temple skips through a series of adventures with each until the parental question is happily resolved. An endearing film that features Temple's classic rendition of "On the Good Ship Lollipop."

p, Sol Wurtzel; d, David Butler; w, William Conselman, Edwin Burke, David Butler; ph, Arthur Miller.

Comedy (MPAA:NR)

BUFFALO BILL

(1944) 90m FOX c

Joel McCrea *(Buffalo Bill),* Maureen O'Hara *(Louisa Cody),* Linda Darnell *(Dawn Starlight),* Thomas Mitchell *(Ned Buntline),* Edgar Buchanan *(Sgt. Chips),* Anthony Quinn *(Yellow Hand),* Moroni Olsen *(Sen. Frederici),* Frank Fenton *(Murdo Carvell),* Matt Briggs *(Gen. Blazier),* George Lessey *(Mr. Vandevere),* Frank Orth *(Sherman),* George Chandler *(Trooper Clancy),* Chief Many Treaties *(Tall Bull),* Nick Thompson *(Medicine Man),* Chief Thundercloud *(Crazy Horse),* Sidney Blackmer *(President Theodore Roosevelt),* William Haade *(Barber),* Evelyn Beresford *(Queen Victoria),* Edwin Stanley *(Doctor),* John Dilson *(President Hayes),* Cecil Weston *(Maid),* Merrill Rodin *(Bellboy),* Vincent Graeff *(Crippled Boy),* Fred Graham *(Editor).*

This slam-bang western epic tells the story of "Buffalo Bill" Cody, the legendary frontier scout, fighter, buffalo hunter, and showman. Cody is played by Joel McCrea, and the story chronicles his days as an Indian fighter (for which he is awarded the Congressional Medal of Honor), his turbulent marriage, his criticism of the US government for its treatment of the Indians, and finally his creation of the Wild West show that thrilled crowds throughout the East. Though the film clearly embellishes the exploits of Buffalo Bill and is sometimes overly melodramatic, it remains a vivid, spacious, and exciting film, offering an entertaining portrait of one of the West's great heroes.

p, Harry A. Sherman; d, William A. Wellman; w, Aeneas MacKenzie, Clements Ripley, Cecile Kramer (based on a story by Frank Winch); ph, Leon Shamroy (Technicolor); m, David Buttolph.

Biography/Western (MPAA:NR)

BUGS BUNNY, SUPERSTAR

(1975) 90m WB c

Voices of: Bob Clampett, Tex Avery, Friz Freleng, Mel Blanc; narration by Orson Welles.

Fans of the immortal wisecracking rabbit will be entranced by the artistry of the "old-fashioned" realistic animation technique, as well as the humor, in this collection of 10 cartoons.

d, Larry Jackson.

Animation (MPAA:G)

BUGSY MALONE

(1976, Brit.) 93m PAR c

Scott Baio *(Bugsy Malone),* Jodie Foster *(Tallulah),* Florrie Dugger *(Blousey),* John Cassisi *(Fat Sam),* Paul Murphy *(Leroy),* Albin Jenkins *(Fizzy),* Martin Lev *(Dandy Dan),* Davidson Knight *(Knuckles),* Paul Chirelstein *(Smolsky),* Paul Besterman *(Yonkers),* Ron Melelu *(Doodle),* Jorge Valdez *(Bronx Charlie),* Michael Kirby *(Angelo),* Donald Waugh *(Snake Eyes),* Peter Holder *(Ritzy),* John Lee *(Benny),* Jon Zebrowski *(Shoulders),* Michael Jackson *(Razamataz),* Andrew Paul *(O'Dreary),* Helen Corran *(Bangles),* Dexter Fletcher *(Baby Face),* Vivienne McKonne *(Velma),* Jeffrey Stevens *(Louis),* Kevin Reul, Brian Hardy, Bonita Langford, Mark Curry, Katherine Apanowicz, Lynn Aulbaugh, Nick Amend, John Williams, Herbert Norville, Louise English, Kathy Spaulding.

Charming, delightful, and all the things a picture rated G should be, BUGSY MALONE is a spoof of 1920s gangster movies replete with all the cliched characters—except that this film is a musical and everyone in it is teenaged or less. You've seen every single one of these characters played by Edward G. Robinson or James Cagney or Humphrey Bogart, but they come to life again when such tried-and-true lines as "I thought I tol' ya ta stay outta da Sout' side, Blackie" come out of the mouths of babes. The film failed at the box office, but the lovely score by Paul Williams and fine, funny script by Alan Parker make it well worth a look.

p, Alan Marshall; d&w, Alan Parker; ph, Michael Seresin, Peter Biziou (Eastman Color); m, Paul Williams.

Musical Cas. (MPAA:PG)

CALL OF THE WILD

(1935) 89m FOX bw

Clark Gable *(Jack Thornton),* Loretta Young *(Claire*

Blake), Jack Oakie *(Shorty Hoolihan),* Frank Conroy *(John Blake),* Reginald Owen *(Smith),* Sidney Toler *(Groggin),* Katherine DeMille *(Marie),* Lalos Encinas *(Kali),* Charles Stevens *(Francois),* James Burke *(Ole),* Duke Green *(Frank),* Marie Wells *(Hilda),* Tommy Jackson, Russ Powell, Herman Bing, George McQuarrie.

This epic Alaskan adventure story features Clark Gable as prospector Jack Thornton. After losing his money gambling, Thornton acquires a huge dog, Buck, which is considered too vicious to be a sled dog. Thornton patiently trains the animal, then sets out with his friend Shorty Hoolihan (Jack Oakie) for the wilderness in search of gold. Thereafter they must battle the weather, the wilds, and crooks in their attempts to make their fortunes, and Thornton finds a love interest in the wife of a missing prospector. This hearty film was shot on the snowy slopes of Washington's Mount Baker, at 5,000 feet, where the harsh winter snows forced cast and crew to use snowplows to get to their daily locations. Through the hardships, they created a stirring adventure, loosely based on the writings of Jack London.

p, Darryl F Zanuck; d, William Wellman; w, Gene Fowler, Leonard Praskins (based on the novel by Jack London); ph, Charles Rosher; m, Alfred Newman.

Adventure (MPAA:NR)

CALLAWAY WENT THATAWAY

(1951) 81m MGM bw (GB: THE STAR SAID NO)

Fred MacMurray *(Mike Frye),* Dorothy McGuire *(Deborah Patterson),* Howard Keel *("Stretch" Barnes/"Smoky" Callaway),* Jesse White *(George Markham),* Fay Roope *(Tom Lorrison),* Natalie Schafer *(Martha Lorrison),* Douglas Kennedy *(Drunk),* Elisabeth Fraser *(Marie),* Johnny Indrisano *(Johnny Tarranto),* Stan Freberg *(Marvin),* Don Haggerty *(Director),* Clark Gable, Elizabeth Taylor, Esther Williams *(Guest Stars),* Dorothy Andre *(Girl),* James Harrison, Carl Sepulveda *(Heavies),* Hank Weaver *(Announcer),* Ned Glass *(Mailman).*

In this delightful spoof of early TV advertising and promotion executives, TV promoters Mike Frye (Fred MacMurray) and Deborah Patterson (Dorothy McGuire) are handed the assignment of finding "Smoky" Callaway, a yesteryear star of B westerns who has become an overnight smash, with millions of youngsters watching his old oaters on TV. They are unable to find Callaway, but do discover real-life cowboy Stretch Barnes (Howard Keel), a double for the missing actor, and induce him to impersonate Callaway. Trouble begins as success goes to Stretch's head and he becomes a thoroughly obnoxious "star." The situation worsens when the real Callaway (also played by Keel) shows up. It's a lot of fun, and offers an interesting portrait of the early days of television.

p,d&w, Norman Panama, Melvin Frank; ph, Ray June; m, Marlin Skiles.

Comedy (MPAA:NR)

CANTERVILLE GHOST, THE

(1944) 95m MGM bw

Charles Laughton (*Sir Simon de Canterville/The Ghost*), Robert Young (*Cuffy Williams*), Margaret O'Brien (*Lady Jessica de Canterville*), William Gargan (*Sgt. Benson*), Reginald Owen (*Lord Canterville*), Rags Ragland (*Big Harry*), Una O'Connor (*Mrs. Umney*), Donald Stuart (*Sir Valentine Williams*), Elisabeth Risdon (*Mrs. Polverdine*), Frank Faylen (*Lt. Kane*), Lumsden Hare (*Mr. Potts*), Mike Mazurki (*Metropolus*), William Moss (*Hector*), Bobby Readick (*Eddie*), Marc Cramer (*Bugsy McDougle*), William Tannen (*Jordan*), Peter Lawford (*Anthony de Canterville*).

This might instead have been called "The Cowardly Ghost," since the title spirit, played by Charles Laughton, is afraid of his own footfalls. Set in England during WW II, the story concerns an ancient English castle where a group of American soldiers are billeted. The lady of the manor is young Jessica de Canterville (Margaret O'Brien), who introduces the Americans to the ghost, a dead relative who has haunted the premises for more than 300 years since the day he was walled up in the dungeon by his father because of his cowardice. One of the soldiers, Cuffy Williams (Robert Young), is a distant relative of the Cantervilles, and he becomes concerned that he might also be a coward. The action centers on the efforts of Cuffy and the ghost to prove their mettle. Laughton is very funny as the frightened, rather than frightening, spirit in a film that was enormously popular when released in the 1940s and continues to provide wonderful entertainment today.

p, Arthur L. Field; d, Jules Dassin; w, Edwin Harvey Blum (based on the story by Oscar Wilde); ph, Robert Planck; m, George Bassman.

Comedy   **(MPAA:NR)**

CAPTAIN JANUARY

(1935) 78m FOX bw

Shirley Temple (*Star*), Guy Kibbee (*Capt. January*), Slim Summerville (*Capt. Nazro*), June Lang (*Mary Marshall*), Buddy Ebsen (*Paul Roberts*), Sara Haden (*Agatha Morgan*), Jane Darwell (*Eliza Croft*), Jerry Tucker (*Cyril Morgan*), Nella Walker (*Mrs. John Mason*), George Irving (*John Mason*), James Farley (*Deputy Sheriff*), Si Jenks (*Old Sailor*).

After Capt. January (Guy Kibbee) rescues young Star (Shirley Temple) during a storm that claims the lives of the little girl's parents, Star moves in with the kindly lighthouse keeper. Life is good for the pair, who are often joined by the captain's jovial friend Capt. Nazro (Slim Summerville). Then one day a truant officer decides that Star is not being brought up properly, and she is shipped off to boarding school. The remainder of the film deals with the Captain's desperate efforts to be reunited with Star. A particularly effective melodrama, which includes Temple and Buddy Ebsen providing a delightful song and dance routine to the tune "At the Codfish Ball."

p, Darryl F. Zanuck; d, David Butler; w, Sam Hellman, Gladys Lehman, Harry Tugend (based on a story by Laura E. Richards); ph, John Seitz.

Drama/Musical   **Cas.**   **(MPAA:NR)**

CAPTAINS COURAGEOUS

(1937) 115m MGM bw

Freddie Bartholomew (*Harvey*), Spencer Tracy (*Manuel*), Lionel Barrymore (*Disko*), Melvyn Douglas (*Mr. Cheyne*), Charley Grapewin (*Uncle Salters*), Mickey Rooney (*Dan*), John Carradine (*"Long Jack"*), Oscar O'Shea (*Cushman*), Jack La Rue (*Priest*), Walter Kingsford (*Dr. Finley*), Donald Briggs (*Tyler*), Sam McDaniel (*"Doc"*), Billy Burrud (*Charles*), Christian Rub (*Old Clement*), Dave Thursby (*Tom*), William Stack (*Elliott*), Leo G. Carroll (*Burns*), Charles Trowbridge (*Dr. Walsh*), Richard Powell (*Steward*), Jay Ward (*Pogey*), Kenneth Wilson (*Alvin*), Roger Gray (*Nate Rogers*), Gladden James (*Secretary Cobb*), Tommy Bupp, Wally Albright (*Boys*), Katherine Kenworthy (*Mrs. Disko*), Philo McCullough, James Kilgannon, Bill Fisher, Dick Howard, Larry Fisher, Gil Perkins, Jack Sterling, Stubby Kreuger (*Crew*), Dave Wengren (*Lars*).

Young Harvey (Freddie Bartholomew) the spoiled-rotten son of a business tycoon, believes he can lie, cheat, and whine his way through life. On a trip to Europe with his father, the young man falls off a posh ocean liner into the sea and is rescued by a boat filled with Portuguese fishermen. One of the sailors is Manuel (Spencer Tracy), a big-hearted veteran of the seas who has a lot to teach the selfish Harvey about life. CAPTAINS COURAGEOUS is a wonderful sea adventure with a heartwarming drama at its core. Tracy is excellent as the gentle fisherman, turning in a performance that won him a Best Actor Oscar. The following year, he won the statuette again for BOYS TOWN, and he remains the only actor to capture the award two years in a row.

p, Louis D. Lighton; d, Victor Fleming; w, John Lee Mahin, Marc Connelly, Dale Van Every (based on the novel by Rudyard Kipling); ph, Harold Rosson; m, Franz Waxman.

Adventure   **Cas.**   **(MPAA:NR)**

CAT FROM OUTER SPACE, THE

(1978) 103m BV c

Ken Berry (*Frank*), Sandy Duncan (*Liz*), Harry Morgan (*Gen. Stilton*), Roddy McDowall (*Stallwood*), McLean Stevenson (*Link*), Jesse White (*Emie*), Alan Young (*Wenger*), Hans Conried (*Heffel*), Ronnie Schell (*Sgt. Duffy*), James Hampton (*Capt. Anderson*), Howard T. Platt (*Col. Woodruff*), William Prince (*Olympus*), Ralph Manza (*Weasel*), Tom Pedi (*Honest Harry*), Hank Jones (*Officer*), Rick Hurst (*Dydee Guard*), John Alderson (*Mr. Smith*), Tiger Joe Marsh (*Omar*), Arnold Soboloff (*NASA Executive*).

THE CAT FROM OUTER SPACE is an entertaining Disney film that is a sort of E.T.-in-a-litter-box. Zunar J5/90 Doric 4-7, a cat more conveniently known as Jake, crash lands on earth and turns to a local physicist for aid. The feline alien needs $120,000 in gold for repairs to his malfunctioning spacecraft. It's soon discovered that this cat has special powers and can predict sports winners. The cat, however, is inadvertently put into a deep sleep by a bumbling vet and soon the military is snooping around, mistakenly looking for spacemen. A fine Disney product scripted by cartoonist Ted Key, who is also credited with GUS and THE $1,000,000 DUCK. Jake was played by two different Abyssinian cats—Rumpler and his sister, Amber.

p, Ron Miller, Norman Tokar; d, Norman Tokar; w, Ted Key; ph, Charles F. Wheeler (Technicolor); m, Lalo Schifrin.

Comedy/Science Fiction   Cas.   (MPAA:G)

CATTLE DRIVE

(1951) 77m UNIV c

Joel McCrea *(Dan Mathews)*, Dean Stockwell *(Chester Graham, Jr.)*, Chill Wills *(Dallas)*, Leon Ames *(Mr. Graham)*, Henry Brandon *(Jim Currie)*, Howard Petrie *(Cap)*, Bob Steele *(Careless)*, Griff Barnett *(Conductor O'Hara)*.

Photographed in Death Valley, this outstanding western features young Dean Stockwell as Chester Graham, Jr., the snobbish son of a railroad tycoon who is inadvertently left behind in the sun-blistered desert when his father's train pulls away without him. Dan Mathews (Joel McCrea, perfectly cast) is an old trail boss who looks after the lad as he drives his cattle toward civilization. Oddly, this western contains not one female character, except for a picture the cattleman carries with him of his wife (actor McCrea's real-life wife, Frances Dee), who represents the ideal that waits for him at the end of the trail. Strongly reminiscent of CAPTAINS COURAGEOUS.

p, Aaron Rosenberg; d, Kurt Neumann; w, Jack Natteford, Lillie Hayward; ph, Maury Gertsman (Technicolor).

Western   (MPAA:NR)

CAUGHT IN THE DRAFT

(1941) 82m PAR bw

Bob Hope *(Don Gilbert)*, Dorothy Lamour *(Tony Fairbanks)*, Lynne Overman *(Steve)*, Eddie Bracken *(Bert)*, Clarence Kolb *(Col. Peter Fairbanks)*, Paul Hurst *(Sgt. Bums)*, Ferike Boros *(Yetta)*, Phyllis Ruth *(Margie)*, Irving Bacon *(Cogswell)*, Arthur Loft *(Director)*, Edgar Dearing *(Recruiting Sergeant)*, Murray Alper *(Makeup Man)*, Dave Willock *(Colonel's Orderly)*, Rita Owen *(Cleaning Nurse)*, Frances Morris *(Stretcher Nurse)*, Ella Neal, Eleanor Stewart, Earlene Heath, Gloria Williams, Marie Blake *(Nurses)*, Terry Ray [Ellen Drew], Ed Peil, Jr. *(Patients)*, Jimmy Dodd *(Indignant Patient)*, Archie Twitchell *(Stretcher Patient)*, Jack Chapin, Victor Cutler *(Rookies)*, Jack Luden, Jerry Jerome, Frank Mitchell *(Captains)*, Ray Flynn *(Lieutenant Colonel)*, David Oliver *(Cameraman)*,

Frank O'Connor *(Major)*, Frank Marlowe *(Twitchell)*, Heinie Conklin *(Sign Hanger)*.

In one of Bob Hope's ~~best and funniest roles~~, he plays Don Gilbert, a Hollywood star trying to evade the draft during WW II. Tony Fairbanks (Dorothy Lamour) is the daughter of an Army colonel whom Don plans to marry in a scheme he thinks will keep him out of the service. The plot backfires and Don is dumped into a training camp. This situation evokes every laugh in the book as Hope's rapid-fire delivery makes a burlesque of every subject at hand—including the Army, love, and Hollywood—in 82 minutes of sustained zaniness.

p, B.G. DeSylva; d, David Butler; w, Harry Tugend (based on a story by Harry Tugend); ph, Karl Struss; m, Victor Young.

Comedy   (MPAA:NR)

CHALLENGE TO LASSIE

(1949) 76m MGM c

Edmund Gwenn *(John Traill)*, Donald Crisp *("Jock" Gray)*, Geraldine Brooks *(Susan Brown)*, Reginald Owen *(Sgt. Davie)*, Alan Webb *(James Brown)*, Ross Ford *(William Traill)*, Henry Stephenson *(Sir Charles Loring)*, Alan Napier *(Lord Provost)*, Sara Allgood *(Mrs. MacFarland)*, Edmond Breon *(Magistrate)*, Arthur Shields *(Dr. Lee)*, Lumsden Hare *(MacFarland)*, Charles Irwin *(Sergeant Major)*, Lassie.

Canine hero Lassie, in one of ~~her noblest roles~~, watches faithfully over her dead master's grave. Her antagonist, this time around, is a policeman who oversteps his authority and ignores his heart in ordering the collie out of the cemetery. Sensible townsfolk, however, come to the dog's aid. Featuring a strong cast, CHALLENGE TO LASSIE holds the interest of both of kids and adults.

p, Robert Sisk; d, Richard Thorpe; w, William Ludwig (based on the novel *Greyfriars Bobby* by Eleanor Atkinson); ph, Charles Schoenbaum (Technicolor); m, Andre Previn.

Drama   (MPAA:NR)

CHAMP, THE

(1931) 85m MGM bw

Wallace Beery *(Champ)*, Jackie Cooper *(Dink)*, Irene Rich *(Linda)*, Roscoe Ates *(Sponge)*, Edward Brophy *(Tim)*, Hale Hamilton *(Tony)*, Jesse Scott *(Jonah)*, Marcia Mae Jones *(Mary Lou)*.

Wallace Beery won an Oscar for his role as a down-at-the-heels ex-heavyweight boxing champion who trains for a comeback in Tijuana in between boozing and/or gambling. He has his son (Jackie Cooper) and the thought of getting back into the ring, a pipe dream rather than a reality. He wins some money and buys the boy a racehorse, which the boxer promptly loses in a crap game. The boy's mother (Irene Rich) and her new husband (Hale Hamilton) are very rich and they convince the boxer that the boy would be better off with them. The champ reluctantly agrees, but the boy later sneaks back to his father's side, as love proves stronger than logic. In the final reel, the old boxer finally engages in a brutal battle against a much younger opponent while his son, lower lip quivering, is ringside watching his dad. Audiences sobbed audibly at almost every showing of this tailored-to-make-you-cry picture. Writer Frances Marion won her second Oscar for the original story of THE CHAMP and Wallace Beery tied with Fredric March for his Oscar as Best Actor. Director King Vidor and the picture were also nominated. There are those cynics who pooh-pooh the emotions of THE CHAMP and call it mawkish, overly sentimental, etc.—but they probably didn't cry when Bambi's mother died, either. Avoid those people at all costs and see this film when you can. (Remade as THE CLOWN in 1953 and again in 1979.)

p, Harry Rapf; d, King Vidor; w, Leonard Praskins (based on an original story by Frances Marion); ph, Gordon Avil.

Drama/Sports (MPAA:NR)

CHAMPAGNE FOR CAESAR

(1950) 99m UA bw

Ronald Colman *(Beauregard Bottomley)*, Celeste Holm *(Flame O'Neil)*, Vincent Price *(Burnbridge Waters)*, Barbara Britton *(Gwenn Bottomley)*, Art Linkletter *(Happy Hogan)*, Gabriel Heatter, George Fisher *(Announcers)*, Byron Foulger *(Gerald)*, Ellye Marshall *(Frosty)*, Vici Raaf *(Waters' Secretary)*, Douglas Evans *(Radio Announcer)*, John Eldredge *(Executive No. 1)*, Lyle Talbot *(Executive No. 2)*, George Leigh *(Executive No. 3)*, John Hart *(Executive No. 4)*, Mel Blanc *(Caesar)*, Peter Brocco *(Fortune Teller)*, Brian O'Hara *(Buck)*, Jack Daly *(Scratch)*, Gordon Nelson *(Lecturer)*, Herbert Lytton *(Chuck Johnson)*, George Meader *(Mr. Brown)*.

Beauregard Bottomley (Ronald Colman) is an unemployed Ph.D. and genius who reads the encyclopedia for enjoyment and never forgets a thing he's read. He applies for work at a soap company owned by Burnbridge Waters (Vincent Price), but is rebuffed by the suds magnate. Beauregard is so annoyed by the treatment he receives at Waters' hands that he decides to bankrupt the company by becoming a contestant on the popular radio quiz show it sponsors. As the weeks pass, Beauregard keeps doubling his winnings and when the company attempts to cut him off, he appeals to the audience in the theater as well as to the listening millions, who all agree he should be allowed to continue. Desperate, the soap company tries another way to end Beauregard's winning streak—they dispatch a spy to find a weakness in his knowledge. CHAMPAGNE FOR CAESAR is one of the funniest movies ever made. It did not get the full benefit of a national run when it was released but went almost immediately to television, where it has been cut to fit that medium's time limits. If you're ever fortunate enough to see the complete 99-minute version, be prepared to howl.

p, Harry Popkin, George Moskov; d, Richard Whorf; w, Hans Jacoby, Fred Brady; ph, Paul Ivano, m, Dimitri Tiomkin.

Comedy **Cas.** (MPAA:NR)

CHARIOTS OF FIRE

(1981, Brit.) 123m Enigma/FOX c

Ben Cross *(Harold Abrahams)*, Ian Charleson *(Eric Liddell)*, Nigel Havers *(Lord Andrew Lindsay)*, Nicholas Farrell *(Aubrey Montague)*, Ian Holm *(Sam Mussabini)*, John Gielgud *(Master of Trinity)*, Lindsay Anderson *(Master of Caius)*, Nigel Davenport *(Lord Birkenhead)*, Cheryl Campbell *(Jennie Liddell)*, Alice Krige *(Sybil Gordon)*, Dennis Christopher *(Charles Paddock)*, Brad Davis *(Jackson Scholz)*, Patrick Magee *(Lord Cadogan)*, Peter Egan *(Duke of Sutherland)*, Struan Rodger *(Sandy McGrath)*, David Yelland *(Prince of Wales)*, Yves Beneyton *(George Andre)*, Daniel Gerroll *(Henry Stallard)*, Jeremy Sinden *(President, Gilbert and Sullivan Society)*, Gordon Hammersley *(President, Cambridge Athletic Club)*, Andrew Hawkins *(Secretary, Gilbert and Sullivan Society)*, Richard Griffiths *(Head Porter, Caius College)*, John Young *(Rev. J.D. Liddell)*, Benny Young *(Rob Liddell)*, Yvonne Gilan *(Mrs. Liddell)*, Jack Smethurst *(Sleeping Car Attendant)*, Gerry Slevin *(Col. Keddie)*, Peter Cellier *(Savoy Head Waiter)*, Stephen Mallatratt *(Watson)*, Colin Bruce *(Taylor)*, Alan Polonsky *(Paxton)*, Edward Wiley *(Fitch)*, Philip O'Brien *(American Coach)*, Ralph Lawton *(Harbormaster)*.

Winner of four Academy Awards, nominated for four others, and winner of British awards for best picture and costume design, CHARIOTS OF FIRE is almost, if not completely, worthy of all the accolades it received. This true story, which was directed by Hugh Hudson from an original script by Colin Welland, examines what it means to win and what one must do to achieve it. Eric Liddell (Ian Charleson) is a serious Scottish Christian who runs for the glory of Jesus and who believes that Christ is his trainer. Harold Abrahams (Ben Cross) is an English Jew who is extremely sensitive to prejudice and whose main motivation is to be accepted. The movie delineates and crosscuts between the lives of both men as they meet and run at the 1924 Olympics in Paris. The real-life Liddell later became a Christian missionary, went to China, and eventually died in a Japanese prisoner of war camp, true to his faith to the end. Harold Abrahams went on to become the spokesman for English amateur athletics, was knighted, and died in 1978, a venerated and respected elder statesman. CHARIOTS OF FIRE won Oscars for Best Picture, Best Screenplay, Best Costume Design, and Best Musical Score. The Oscar nominations went to Ian Holm, Hudson, and Terry Rawlings.

p, David Puttnam; d, Hugh Hudson; w, Colin Welland; ph, David Watkin; m, Vangelis Papathanassiou.

Biography/Sports **Cas.** (MPAA:PG)

CHARLEY'S AUNT

(1941) 80m FOX bw (GB: CHARLEY'S AMERICAN AUNT)

Jack Benny *(Babbs)*, Kay Francis *(Donna Lucia)*, James Ellison *(Jack Chesney)*, Anne Baxter *(Amy Spettigue)*, Edmund Gwenn *(Stephen Spettigue)*, Reginald Owen *(Redcliff)*, Laird Cregar *(Sir Francis Chesney)*, Arleen Whelan *(Kitty Verdun)*, Richard Haydn *(Charley Wyckham)*, Ernest Cossart *(Brasset)*, Morton Lowry *(Harley Stafford)*, Lionel Pape *(Babberly)*, Claude Allister, William Austin *(Spectators)*, Russell Burroughs, Gilchrist Stuart, John Meredith *(Teammates)*, Bob Conway, Bob Cornell, Basil Walker, Herbert Gunn *(Students)*, Will Stanton *(Messenger)*, C. Montague Shaw *(Elderly Man)*, Maurice Cass *(Octogenarian)*.

This was the third of many screen adaptations of "Charley's Aunt," the beloved 19th-century stage farce. The first starred Sydney Chaplin in 1925 and the second (released in 1930) featured Charlie Ruggles in the lead. Jack Benny stars here as Babbs, an Oxford student who masquerades as his friend Charley Wyckham's (Richard Haydn) aunt from Brazil, who will be the chaperon for Charley and Jack (James Ellison) as they court Amy (Anne Baxter) and Kitty (Arleen Whelan). Once Babbs is in drag, however, he must fend off romantic advances from gigolo Sir Francis Chesney (Laird Cregar) and from Stephen Spettigue (Edmund Gwenn), the girl's guardian. Jack Benny was never better (with the possible exception of his classic TO BE OR NOT TO BE) and carries the film with a top-flight performance. This was his first role of any consequence other than his previous tailor-made parts with radio jokes flying thick and fast around his well-known persona. In CHARLEY'S AUNT, Benny had to play a part totally alien to what he'd done before and he proved more than worthy of the task. This was Cregar's fifth role in a career that only lasted five years. He died in 1944 at age 28 from a heart attack that resulted from his constant crash dieting, having got it into his head that he would become a handsome leading man, instead of the fine, whalelike character actor he was, if only he could shed his hulking body by 100 pounds. Remade as the musical WHERE'S CHARLEY? in 1952.

p, William Perlberg; d, Archie Mayo; w, George Seaton (based on the play by Brandon Thomas); ph, Peverell Marley; m, Alfred Newman.

Comedy   **Cas.**   **(MPAA:NR)**

CHARLIE CHAN AT THE OPERA

(1936) 66m FOX bw

Warner Oland *(Charlie Chan)*, Boris Karloff *(Gravelle)*, Keye Luke *(Lee Chan)*, Charlotte Henry *(Mlle. Kitty)*, Thomas Beck *(Phil Childers)*, Margaret Irving *(Mme. Lilli Rouchelle)*, Gregory Gaye *(Enrico Barelli)*, Nedda Harrigan *(Mme. Lucretia Barelli)*, Frank Conroy *(Mr. Whitely)*, Guy Usher *(Inspector Regan)*, William Demarest *(Sgt. Kelly)*, Maurice Cass *(Mr. Arnold)*, Tom McGuire *(Morris)*, Fred Kelsey *(Cop)*, Selmer Jackson, Emmett Vogan

(Newspaper Wire-Photo Technicians), Benson Fong *(Opera Extra)*.

One of the best of the "Charlie Chan" series, this entry has the added attraction of Boris Karloff as Gravelle, an opera star who is caught in a fire at the theater and presumed dead. The baritone survives, however, and is admitted, suffering from amnesia and unidentified, into a mental hospital. When a picture of his opera singer wife appears in the newspaper, Gravelle's memory is spurred and he recalls that it was his unfaithful wife and her lover who set the fire in an attempt to kill him. Seething with a desire for vengeance, Gravelle escapes the mental hospital and heads for the opera house, and when several opera employees turn up dead, Charlie Chan (Warner Oland) is called in to investigate. Karloff plays his role to the hilt; in one scene a fellow performer comments, "Who do you think you are, Frankenstein?" Included in the film is the opera "Carnival," composed especially for the picture by Oscar Levant. So well made was the movie—and so much fun does it seem today—that its interest ranges far beyond the usual circle of Chan buffs.

p, John Stone; d, H. Bruce Humberstone; w, Scott Darling, Charles S. Belden (based on a story by Bess Meredyth and the character created by Earl Derr Biggers); ph, Lucien Andriot.

Mystery   **(MPAA:NR)**

CHARLOTTE'S WEB

(1973) 94m PAR c

Voices of: Debbie Reynolds *(Charlotte)*, Paul Lynde *(Templeton)*, Henry Gibson *(Wilbur)*, Rex Allen *(Narrator)*, Martha Scott *(Mrs. Arable)*, Dave Madden *(Old Sheep)*, Danny Bonaduce *(Avery)*, Don Messick *(Geoffrey)*, Herb Vigran *(Lurvy)*, Agnes Moorehead *(The Goose)*, Pam Ferdin *(Fern Arable)*, Joan Gerber *(Mrs. Zuckerman/Mrs. Fussy)*, Robert Holt *(Homer Zuckerman)*, John Stephenson *(Arable)*, William B. White *(Henry Fussy)*.

This is a charming cartoon adaptation of E.B. White's fantasy. Wilbur is a runt pig who has been raised as the pet of a New England farmer. He is sold to a neighboring farm, where a sheep informs him that he's fated to become what goes with cheese on rye. Wilbur is understandably frightened, until he meets a spider named Charlotte, who devotes her arachnoidal life to saving Wilbur from the fate of most porkers, and who weaves words into her web that convince the superstitious farmer that Wilbur is some sort of miraculous hog. The voices of Debbie Reynolds, Henry Gibson, and all the rest are perfectly cast, and the songs by the Sherman Brothers are solid, although none of them stepped out to become hits like those the Shermans wrote for such Disney movies as MARY POPPINS. A treat for everyone.

p, Joe Barbera, William Hannah; d, Charles A. Nichols, Iwao Takamoto; w, Earl Hamner, Jr. (based on the book by E.B. White); ph, Roy Wade, Dick Blundell, Dennis Weaver,

Ralph Migliori, George Epperson (Movielab color); m, Richard M. Sherman, Robert B. Sherman.

Animation   **Cas.**   **(MPAA:G)**

CHEAPER BY THE DOZEN

(1950) 85m FOX c

Clifton Webb *(Frank Bunker Gilbreth)*, Jeanne Crain *(Ann Gilbreth)*, Myrna Loy *(Mrs. Lillian Gilbreth)*, Betty Lynn *(Libby Lancaster)*, Edgar Buchanan *(Dr. Burton)*, Barbara Bates *(Ernestine)*, Mildred Natwick *(Mrs. Mebane)*, Sara Allgood *(Mrs. Monahan)*, Anthony Sydes *(Fred Gilbreth)*, Roddy McCaskill *(Jack Gilbreth)*, Norman Ollestad *(Frank Gilbreth, Jr.)*, Carole Nugent *(Lillie Gilbreth)*, Jimmy Hunt *(William Gilbreth)*, Teddy Driver *(Dan Gilbreth)*, Betty Barker *(Mary Gilbreth)*, Evelyn Varden *(School Principal)*, Frank Orth *(Higgins)*, Craig Hill *(Tom Black)*, Virginia Brissac *(Mrs. Benson)*, Walter Baldwin *(Jim Bracken)*, Benny Bartlett *(Joe Scales)*, Syd Saylor *(Plumber)*, Ken Christy *(Mailman)*, Mary Field *(Music Teacher)*.

Frank Bunker Gilbreth (Clifton Webb) is the strict but adoring father of 12 children in this charming family film set at the turn of the century. He is married to Lillian (Myrna Loy), and the way she's kept her sense of humor and her figure after a dozen births is enough to signify the film as fantasy. Frank is an efficiency expert, a stern taskmaster who wants everything his own way; Lillian is a psychologist who uses much of her knowledge in dealing with her spouse. The film has no particular driving story, presenting instead a host of engaging family incidents that show the closeness of the 14 people. Among these events: Frank escorts the eldest daughter, Ann (Jeanne Crain), to the high school prom and winds up the hit of the dance; a mass tonsillectomy; 12 cases of whooping cough; etc. In short, the movie is whatever can happen to an only child—times 12. An altogether lovely film, rich with humanity and fine work on all levels. A sequel, BELLES ON THEIR TOES, followed in 1952.

p, Lamar Trotti; d, Walter Lang; w, Lamar Trotti (based on the novel by Frank B. Gilbreth, Jr., and Ernestine Gilbreth Carey); ph, Leon Shamroy (Technicolor); m, Cyril Mockridge.

Comedy   **(MPAA:NR)**

CHIPMUNK ADVENTURE, THE

(1987) 76m Bagdasarian/Samuel Goldwyn c

Voices of: Ross Bagdasarian [Jr.], Janice Karman, Dody Goodman, Susan Tyrrell, Anthony DeLongis, Frank Welker, Nancy Cartwright, Ken Samsom, Charles Adler, Philip Clark, George Poulos, Pat Pinney.

Some 30 years ago Ross Bagdasarian, Sr., came up with a multimillion-dollar idea when he speeded up voices on a record and called the resulting creatures "The Chipmunks." Since then, many records have been pressed and there has been a TV series, movies, etc., featuring the cheeky squirrels. Ross, Sr., has passed away and his son, Ross, Jr., has taken over, carrying on the family tradition with this animated feature, and the results are good. Dave Seville is being sent abroad on a business venture and the Chipmunks are rankled because he hasn't asked them along, so that they have to stay in the care of an old lady instead. The boys are rock musicians (as in their TV show), always short of acorns and barely escaping trouble. When a female smuggler of precious stones happens across the Chipmunks and their friends the Chipettes, she uses the critters as unknowing couriers by placing the illegal gems in toy dolls and challenging the trios to a round-the-globe race. Thus begins a world tour, as the animals visit climes far and wide, including Greece, Africa, Mexico, the Alps, the South Seas, Egypt, Brazil, Bermuda, and Europe. Though the animation here isn't spectacular, the music is definitely a cut above that of most children's films, and the voice work is simply excellent. The slick score includes: "Witch Doctor," "Come On-a My House," "Diamond Dolls," "The Girls of Rock and Roll," and "Wooly Bully."

p, Ross Bagdasarian [Jr.]; d, Janice Karman; w, Janice Karman, Ross Bagdasarian [Jr.]; m, Randy Edelman.

Animation   **(MPAA:G)**

CHITTY CHITTY BANG BANG

(1968, Brit.) 156m Warfield/UA c

Dick Van Dyke *(Caractacus Potts)*, Sally Ann Howes *(Truly Scrumptious)*, Lionel Jeffries *(Grandpa Potts)*, Gert Frobe *(Baron Bomburst)*, Anna Quayle *(Baroness Bomburst)*, Benny Hill *(Toymaker)*, James Robertson Justice *(Lord Scrumptious)*, Robert Helpmann *(Child Catcher)*, Heather Ripley *(Jemima)*, Adrian Hall *(Jeremy)*, Barbara Windsor *(Blonde)*, Davy Kaye *(Admiral)*, Alexander Dore, Bernard Spear *(Spies)*, Stanley Unwin *(Chancellor)*, Peter Arne *(Captain of Guard)*, Desmond Llewelyn *(Coggins)*, Victor Maddern *(Junkman)*, Arthur Mullard *(Big Man)*, Ross Parker *(Chef)*, Gerald Campion, Felix Felton, Monti de Lyle *(Ministers)*, Totti Truman Taylor *(Duchess)*, Larry Taylor *(Lieutenant)*, Max Bacon *(Orchestra Leader)*, Max Wall, John Heawood, Michael Darbyshire, Kenneth Waller, Gerald Taylor, Eddie Davis *(Inventors)*, Richard Wattis *(Secretary at Sweet Factory)*, John Baskcomb *(Chef)*.

Many of the MARY POPPINS staff joined Dick Van Dyke in this big-budget attempt to re-create the magic of that earlier Disney film. Caractacus Potts (Van Dyke) is a widower with a penchant for things mechanical. He and his children (Heather Ripley and Adrian Hall) rescue an old car from the scrap heap and create a new motor car with the ability to fly and float. Trouble looms, however, in the form of Baron Bomburst (Gert Frobe), the monarch of a small but wealthy principality who hates children. The baron is after the magical car and wants the vehicle, and its inventor, kidnaped. Based on an Ian Fleming collection of stories, CHITTY CHITTY BANG BANG was made in Britain for American consumption, but its magic works on kids and adults of any nationality.

p, Albert R. Broccoli; d, Ken Hughes; w, Roald Dahl,

Hughes, Richard Maibaum (based on the book by Ian Fleming); ph, Christopher Challis (Super-Panavision, Technicolor).

Fantasy/Musical   **Cas.**   **(MPAA:G)**

CHRISTMAS CAROL, A

(1938) 68m MGM bw

Reginald Owen (*Ebenezer Scrooge*), Gene Lockhart (*Bob Cratchit*), Kathleen Lockhart (*Mrs. Cratchit*), Terry Kilburn (*Tiny Tim*), Barry Mackay (*Fred*), Lynne Carver (*Bess*), Leo G. Carroll (*Marley's Ghost*), Lionel Braham (*Spirit of Christmas Present*), Ann Rutherford (*Spirit of Christmas Past*), D'Arcy Corrigan (*Spirit of Christmas Future*), Ronald Sinclair (*Young Scrooge*), Charles Coleman (*Charity Canvasser*), Halliwell Hobbes (*Vicar*), Billy Bevan (*Watch Officer*).

This superb adaptation of the Dickens classic stars Reginald Owen as hard-hearted Ebenezer Scrooge, in probably the best role of his long and distinguished career. Gene Lockhart is terrific as the much-harassed Bob Cratchit and the rest of the cast do honor to their historic parts. Although this wonderful story has been made many times, Owen's rendition of the miser-turned-Maecenas is the best and most believable, even bettering the TV skinflint so wonderfully enacted by George C. Scott. Owen represents the essential Scrooge, never an introspective man, whose discovery of his own past, present, and future is a singular revelation, bringing about not a startling transformation of character but the emergence of a kind soul that was only waiting all along to struggle out of ledgerbooks and tally sheets. A great and eternally heartwarming film that can stand an appreciative viewing every year in every decade.

p, Joseph L. Mankiewicz; d, Edwin L. Marin; w, Hugo Butler (based on the story by Charles Dickens); ph, Sidney Wagner; m, Franz Waxman.

Drama/Fantasy   **Cas.**   **(MPAA:NR)**

CHRISTMAS IN CONNECTICUT

(1945) 102m WB-FN bw (GB: INDISCRETION)

Barbara Stanwyck (*Elizabeth Lane*), Dennis Morgan (*Jefferson Jones*), Sydney Greenstreet (*Alexander Yardley*), Reginald Gardiner (*John Sloan*), S.Z. Sakall (*Felix Bassenak*), Robert Shayne (*Dudley Beecham*), Una O'Connor (*Norah*), Frank Jenks (*Sinkewicz*), Joyce Compton (*Mary Lee*), Dick Elliott (*Judge Crothers*), Betty Alexander (*Nurse Smith*), Allen Fox (*Postman*), Lillian Bronson (*Prim Secretary*), Charles Sherlock (*Bartender*), Emmett Smith (*Sam*), Arthur Aylesworth (*Sleigh Driver*), Jody Gilbert (*Mrs. Gerseg*), Charles Arnt (*Mr. Higgenbottom*), Fred Kelsey (*Harper*), Walter Baldwin (*Potter*), Jack Mower, John Dehner (*State Troopers*), Marie Blake (*Mrs. Wright*), Olaf Hytten (*Elkins*).

A hilarious farce is made even funnier by the scheming of Elizabeth Lane (Barbara Stanwyck), a successful columnist for a housekeeping magazine who pretends to be a happy housewife expert in all wifely duties. She is compelled to take in a Navy hero, Jefferson Jones (Dennis Morgan), for the holidays, a promotion gimmick concocted by her publisher, Alexander Yardley (Sydney Greenstreet). There's one thing wrong with the plan: Elizabeth does not have the country home she writes about, she can't cook, and she's not married. In desperation, Elizabeth fakes her literary persona by persuading a friend to act as her husband, renting a rustic house, and hiring a world-famous chef (S.Z. Sakall) to teach her to cook. Embarrassing complications, of course, ensue. The action is lively from director Peter Godfrey and Stanwyck proves her considerable flair for comedy. A wonderful holiday romp.

p, William Jacobs; d, Peter Godfrey; w, Lionel Houser, Adele Commandini (based on a story by Aileen Hamilton); ph, Carl Guthrie; m, Frederick Hollander.

Comedy   **(MPAA:NR)**

CHRISTMAS STORY, A

(1983) 98m MGM/UA c

Melinda Dillon (*Mother*), Darren McGavin (*Old Man*), Peter Billingsley (*Ralphie*), Ian Petrella (*Randy*), Scott Schwartz (*Flick*), R.D. Robb (*Schuartz*), Tedde Moore (*Miss Shields*), Yano Anaya (*Grover*), Zack Ward (*Scot*), Jeff Gillen (*Santa Claus*), Colin Fox (*Ming*), Paul Hubbard (*Flash Gordon*), Les Carlson (*Tree Man*), Jim Hunter (*Freight Man*), Patty Johnson (*Head Elf*), Dew Hocevar (*Male Elf*), David Svoboda (*Goggles*), Dwayne McLean (*Black Bart*), Helen E. Kaider (*Wicked Witch*), John Wong (*Chinese Father*), Rocco Bellusci (*Street Kid*), Tommy Wallace (*Boy in School*), Johan Sebastian Wong, Fred Lee, Dan Ma (*Waiters*).

Based on the anecdotes of midwestern humorist Jean Shepherd (who is also the first-person narrator), A CHRISTMAS STORY is an episodic comedy, set in the 1940s, about the family life of young Ralphie (Peter Billingsley) as Christmas approaches. The plot loosely revolves around Ralphie's desire for a Red Ryder BB gun for Christmas, despite the fact that his mother (Melinda Dillon) has forbidden it, warning, "You'll shoot your eye out, Ralph." Among Shepherd's childhood recollections are his narrow escapes from the neighborhood bullies, the old man's (Darren McGavin) battles with the smoke-belching furnace, Mom's attempts to get little brother Randy (Ian Petrella) to eat, and a nightmarish visit with Santa at the local department store. The cast is wonderful—especially McGavin—the laughs nonstop, and the whole thing deserves to become a Christmastime classic. A must see.

p, Rene Dupont, Bob Clark; d, Bob Clark; w, Jean Shepherd, Leigh Brown, Bob Clark (based on the novel *In God We Trust, All Others Pay Cash* by Jean Shepherd); ph, Reginald H. Morris; m, Carl Ziffrer, Paul Zaza.

Comedy   **Cas.**   **(MPAA:PG)**

CINDERELLA

(1950) 74m Disney/RKO c

Voices of: Ilene Woods *(Cinderella)*, William Phipps *(Prince Charming)*, Eleanor Audley *(Stepmother)*, Verna Felton *(Fairy Godmother)*, James MacDonald *(Jacques and Gus-Gus)*, Rhoda Williams *(Anastasia)*, Lucille Bliss *(Drusilla)*, Luis Van Rooten *(King and Grand Duke)*, Don Barclay, Claire DuBrey.

Although not originally met with the kind of praise that Disney's SNOW WHITE or PINOCCHIO had received, CINDERELLA stands up just as well after all these years. In the familiar plot, poor Cinderella meets a handsome young prince at the ball, with the help of her fairy godmother. The prince falls in love, but Cinderella must leave before the godmother's magic spell wears off. On her way out, Cinderella loses one of her glass slippers. With the slipper as his only clue, the prince searches the countryside for the foot that fits it. To help pad out the simple and well-known storyline, the Disney people created a variety of animal characters, including Jacques and Gus-Gus, two adorable mice who draft a flock of bluebirds to help make Cinderella a dress so she can go to the ball. Excellent animation, marvelous color, good voices, and lovely music make for a delight all the way around. Oliver Wallace and Paul Smith received Oscar nominations for the music, as did Mack David, Jerry Livingston, and Al Hoffman for the hit "Bibbidi Bobbidi Boo."

p, Walt Disney; d, Wilfred Jackson, Hamilton Luske, Clyde Geronimi; w, William Peet, Ted Sears, Homer Brightman, Kenneth Anderson, Erdman Penner, Winston Hibler, Harry Reeves, Joe Rinaldi (based on the story by Charles Perrault); ph, (Technicolor); m, Oliver Wallace, Paul Smith.

Animation   **(MPAA:NR)**

CLARENCE, THE CROSS-EYED LION ✓

(1965) 92m Ivan Tors/MGM c

Marshall Thompson *(Dr. Marsh Tracy)*, Betsy Drake *(Julie Harper)*, Richard Haydn *(Rupert Rowbotham)*, Cheryl Miller *(Paula)*, Alan Caillou *(Carter)*, Rockne Tarkington *(Juma)*, Maurice Marsac *(Gregory)*, Bob DoQui *(Sergeant)*, Albert Amos *(Husseini)*, Dinny Powell *(Dinny)*, Mark Allen *(Larson)*, Laurence Conroy *(Tourist)*, Allyson Daniel *(Tourist's Wife)*, Janee Michele *(Girl in Pit)*, Naaman Brown, Napoleon Whiting *(Villagers)*, Chester Jones *(Old Man)*, Clarence the Lion, Doris the Chimpanzee, Mary the Python.

Executive producer Ivan Tors was expert at bringing this kind of moppet movie to the screen, and CLARENCE, THE CROSS-EYED LION presents no exception to his excellent record, which includes RHINO; FLIPPER; NAMU THE KILLER WHALE; and many more. Dr. Marsh Tracy (Marshall Thompson) is the boss of an African animal behavior center with a daughter, Paula (Cheryl Miller). The doctor falls in love with Julie Harper (Betsy Drake), who studies gorilla life. Dr. Marsh captures a lion

that suffers from a cross-eyed condition which prevents him from hunting. Paula names the friendly beast Clarence and treats him like a pet. Conflict arises when rebel troops arrive, determined to poach the wild gorillas for money to buy weapons. ~~Good fun.~~

p, Leonard B. Kaufman; d, Andrew Marton; w, Alan Caillou (based on a story by Art Arthur and Marshall Thompson); ph, Lamar Boren (Metrocolor); m, Al Mack.

Adventure   **(MPAA:NR)**

CLOSE ENCOUNTERS OF THE THIRD KIND

(1977) 135m COL c

Richard Dreyfuss *(Roy Neary)*, Francois Truffaut *(Claude Lacombe)*, Teri Garr *(Ronnie Neary)*, Melinda Dillon *(Jillian Guiler)*, Cary Guffey *(Barry Guiler)*, Bob Balaban *(Interpreter Laughlin)*, J. Patrick McNamara *(Project Leader)*, Warren Kemmerling *(Wild Bill)*, Roberts Blossom *(Farmer)*, Philip Dodds *(Jean Claude)*, Shawn Bishop, Adrienne Campbell, Justin Dreyfuss *(Neary Children)*, Lance Hendricksen *(Robert)*, Merrill Connally *(Team Leader)*, George Dicenzo *(Maj. Benchley)*, Carl Weathers *(M.P.)*, Roger Ernest *(Highway Patrolman)*, Josef Sommer *(Larry Butler)*, Gene Dynarski *(Ike)*, Gene Rader *(Hawker)*, Phil Dodds *(ARP Musician)*, F.J. O'Neil *(ARP Project Member)*.

Humans make contact with beings from another planet, and the results are unexpected and awe-inspiring. Of all the UFO films ever made, this is the most edifying, a wonder of ~~superb special~~ effects—from the cleverly designed spaceships to the manipulation of elements, weird cloud formations, winds, and lightning that all herald the UFOs' approach. What sets this film apart is its depiction of aliens that are loving and beneficent, rather than the raging creatures lusting for human lives found in THE THING or WAR OF THE WORLDS. CLOSE ENCOUNTERS OF THE THIRD KIND is space turned good and godlike, ending on a wonderfully optimistic note instead of fatalistic gloom and doom. Writer-director Steven Spielberg had long envisioned this film, even before making JAWS, and originally thought to have the lead played by a middle-aged man. He wanted Jack Nicholson for the part, but Richard Dreyfuss, who had appeared in JAWS, pleaded for the role and got it, proving himself to be a major talent. French director Francois Truffaut (THE 400 BLOWS, SMALL CHANGE, WILD CHILD) plays a role based on French UFO expert Jacques Vallee, who worked with American UFO scholar J. Allen Hynek (who makes a cameo appearance himself). Spielberg would later expand upon his obsession with the skies in E.T. (1982).

p, Julia and Michael Phillips; d&w, Steven Spielberg; ph, Vilmos Zsigmond, John A. Alonzo, William A. Fraker, Laszlo Kovacs, Douglas Slocombe, Dave Stewart, Robert Hall, Don Jarel, Dennis Muren, Richard Yuricich (Metrocolor); m, John Williams.

Science Fiction   **Cas.**   **(MPAA:PG)**

COME TO THE STABLE

(1949) 94m FOX bw

Loretta Young *(Sister Margaret)*, Celeste Holm *(Sister Scolastica)*, Hugh Marlowe *(Robert Mason)*, Elsa Lanchester *(Miss Potts)*, Thomas Gomez *(Luigi Rossi)*, Dorothy Patrick *(Kitty)*, Basil Ruysdael *(Bishop)*, Dooley Wilson *(Anthony James)*, Regis Toomey *(Monsignor)*, Mike Mazurki *(Heavy Man)*, Henri Letondal *(Father Barraud)*, Walter Baldwin *(Jarman)*, Tim Huntley *(Mr. Thompson)*, Virginia Kelley *(Mrs. Thompson)*, Louis Jean Heydt *(Mr. Newman)*, Pati Behrs, Nan Boardman, Louise Colombet, Georgette Duane, Yvette Reynard, Loulette Sablon *(Nuns)*, Ian MacDonald *(Mr. Matthews)*, Jean Prescott *(Mrs. Matthews)*, Gordon Gebert *(Willie)*, Gary Pagett *(Johnnie)*, Edwin Max *(Whitey)*, Russ Clark, Robert Falk *(Policemen)*, Marion Martin *(Manicurist)*.

This is a delightful and gentle story about two French nuns, Sister Margaret (Loretta Young) and Sister Scolastica (Celeste Holm), who leave their abbey in Europe and arrive in a New England town called Bethlehem, where they intend to establish a children's hospital. The nuns are determined to build the hospital and cannot be talked out of it. No one can resist their charm as they cajole their way into getting what they want. A painter who specializes in religious works, Miss Potts (Elsa Lanchester), allows them to use her studio—a stable she's converted and furnished—as a home base, and from there the nuns go forth and discreetly hustle everyone in the area in order to achieve their goal. Clare Booth Luce, a serious Catholic convert, wrote this story of faith and her beliefs show through every frame. Although very Catholic in intent, the movie celebrates tenacity in general and demonstrates that faith can move molehills, if not mountains.

p, Samuel G. Engel; d, Henry Koster; w, Oscar Millard, Sally Benson (based on a story by Clare Boothe Luce); ph, Joseph La Shelle; m, Cyril Mockridge.

Comedy/Drama **(MPAA:NR)**

COMPUTER WORE TENNIS SHOES, THE

(1970) 90m BV c

Cesar Romero *(A.J. Arno)*, Kurt Russell *(Dexter)*, Joe Flynn *(Dean Higgins)*, William Schallert *(Prof. Quigley)*, Alan Hewitt *(Dean Collingsgood)*, Richard Bakalyan *(Chillie Walsh)*, Debbie Paine *(Annie)*, Frank Webb *(Pete)*, Michael McGreevey *(Schuyler)*, Jon Provost *(Bradley)*, Frank Welker *(Henry)*, Alexander Clarke *(Myles)*, Bing Russell *(Angelo)*, Pat Harrington *(Moderator)*, Fabian Dean *(Little Mac)*, Fritz Feld *(Sigmund Van Dyke)*, Pete Renoudet *(Lt. Hannah)*, Hillyard Anderson *(J. Reedy)*.

Disney does it again in this delightful comedy. Dexter (Kurt Russell), a college student, acquires the entire contents of a computer's memory bank when an electrical accident causes its transfer into his brain. Unfortunately, along with other data, he now possesses information on the nefarious activities of the computer's original owner, gangster A.J. Arno (Cesar Romero). When Dexter be-

comes a contestant on a quiz show to raise money for the college, the word "applejack" triggers an enumeration of Arno's illegal activities. The chase is on, and an exciting one it is. The success of this film led to two follow-ups that also starred Russell: NOW YOU SEE HIM, NOW YOU DON'T, in which he discovers a formula that makes him invisible, and THE STRONGEST MAN IN THE WORLD, in which he discovers a formula that gives him great strength.

p, Bill Anderson; d, Robert Butler; w, Joseph L. McEveety; ph, Frank Phillips (Technicolor); m, Robert F. Brunner.

Comedy **Cas.** **(MPAA:G)**

CONNECTICUT YANKEE, A

(1931) 95m FOX bw

Will Rogers *(Hank)*, William Farnum *(King Arthur)*, Myrna Loy *(Queen Morgan Le Fay)*, Maureen O'Sullivan *(Alisande)*, Frank Albertson *(Clarence)*, Mitchell Harris *(Merlin)*, Brandon Hurst *(Sagramor)*.

This was the second version of Mark Twain's classic. Harry Myers starred in the first (1920) version after Doug Fairbanks turned it down. Bing Crosby did the musical version, A CONNECTICUT YANKEE IN KING ARTHUR'S COURT, a pleasant, colorful romp, while Disney did an updated remake in 1979 with UNIDENTIFIED FLYING ODDBALL. This picture combined Will Rogers' charm with an excellent adaptation of the book. Hank (Rogers) runs a small-town radio shop and is requested to visit a mysterious old house to install a battery. The owner of the house turns out to be a nut who thinks he can contact King Arthur if he has a powerful enough radio. When Hank is felled by an accidental blow on the head, he dreams his way back to days when knights were bold. The Camelot locals think he's a warlock and he manages to save his skin by predicting a solar eclipse. The picture was made during the depths of the Depression and Rogers does a lot of timely jokes that may be lost on today's audiences, but the visual gags (as when Rogers lassoes a Knight of the Round Table in the midst of one of their jousts) are just as funny as ever.

d, David Butler; w, William Conselman, Owen Davis (based on the novel *A Connecticut Yankee in King Arthur's Court* by Mark Twain); ph, Ernest Palmer.

Adventure/Comedy **(MPAA:NR)**

CONNECTICUT YANKEE IN KING ARTHUR'S COURT, A

(1949) 106m PAR c (GB: A YANKEE IN KING ARTHUR'S COURT)

Bing Crosby *(Hank Martin)*, William Bendix *(Sir Sagramore)*, Sir Cedric Hardwicke *(King Arthur)*, Rhonda Fleming *(Alisande La Carteloise)*, Murvyn Vye *(Merlin)*, Virginia Field *(Morgan Le Fay)*, Henry Wilcoxon *(Sir Lancelot)*, Richard Webb *(Sir Galahad)*, Joseph Vitale *(Sir Logris)*, Alan Napier *(High Executioner)*, Julia Faye *(Lady*

Penelope), Mary Field *(Peasant Woman)*, Ann Carter *(Peasant Girl)*.

Mark Twain's fantasy is pleasing from every angle in this lavishly mounted production, rich in color and songs. Bing Crosby, at the height of his immense popularity, stars as Hank Martin, the Connecticut blacksmith knocked unconscious in a wild rainstorm and sent into another world, waking up in King Arthur's Camelot. This film is a pure delight, certainly the most enjoyable of the many versions of the Twain story brought to the screen. The quality of the Crosby version far outstrips its predecessors, with wonderful sets, softly focused color lensing by Ray Rennahan, and memorable music. The famed art director Hans Dreier created a spectacular and authentic medieval castle for the film, with an enormous dining hall for King Arthur's knights, a huge ballroom, verdant gardens, courtyards, and jousting grounds. Rhonda Fleming's titian-haired beauty is stunning in the rich Technicolor process and Tay Garnett's direction is smooth and well paced. Most pleasing are the tunes: "Once and for Always," "If You Stub Your Toe on the Moon," "When Is Sometime?" "Twixt Myself and Me," and the memorable "Busy Doing Nothing." Remade and updated in 1979 as UNIDENTIFIED FLYING ODDBALL.

p, Robert Fellows; d, Tay Garnett; w, Edmund Beloin (based on the novel by Mark Twain); ph, Ray Rennahan (Technicolor); m, Victor Young.

Adventure/Musical   **Cas.**   **(MPAA:NR)**

COUNT OF MONTE CRISTO, THE

(1934) 113m Reliance/UA bw

Robert Donat *(Edmond Dantes)*, Elissa Landi *(Mercedes)*, Louis Calhern *(De Villefort, Jr.)*, Sidney Blackmer *(Mondego)*, Raymond Walburn *(Danglars)*, O.P. Heggie *(Abbe Faria)*, William Farnum *(Capt. Leclere)*, Georgia Caine *(Mme. De Rosas)*, Walter Walker *(Morrel)*, Lawrence Grant *(De Villefort, Sr.)*, Luis Alberni *(Jacopo)*, Irene Hervey *(Valentine)*, Douglas Walton *(Albert)*, Juliette Compton *(Clothilde)*, Clarence Wilson *(Fouquet)*, Eleanor Phelps *(HayDee)*, Ferdinand Munier *(Louis XVIII)*, Holmes Herbert *(Judge)*, Paul Irving *(Napoleon)*, Mitchell Lewis *(Vampa)*, Clarence Muse *(Ali)*, Lionel Belmore *(Prison Governor)*.

The oft-told tale by Alexandre Dumas *pere* was never better served than in this Edward Small production, with Robert Donat giving one of his finest performances. He is the wronged man, sailor Edmond Dantes, who has just received a promotion and is about to marry the beautiful Mercedes (Elissa Landi) when he is framed and imprisoned in the terrible sea-locked Chateau d'If, where he languishes for years. While wasting away in captivity, he meets an imprisoned clergyman (O.P. Heggie) who tells him of a fabulous pirate treasure hidden on the island of Monte Cristo. From that moment on Edmond works to escape from the prison and travel to Monte Cristo, where he will establish a new identity and seek vengeance on those who imprisoned him. Donat is captivating as the good-hearted victim and the cool seeker of justice,

measuring his vengeance with subtle moves and slow deliberation. Producer Small spared no expense in this lavish, technically top-notch production and director Rowland V. Lee, who aided in the adaptation, lends his usual flair for high drama and action.

p, Edward Small; d, Rowland V. Lee; w, Philip Dunne, Dan Totheroh, Rowland V. Lee (based on the novel by Alexandre Dumas); ph, Peverell J. Marley; m, Alfred Newman.

Adventure/Drama   **Cas.**   **(MPAA:NR)**

COURAGE OF LASSIE

(1946) 93m MGM c (AKA: BLUE SIERRA)

Elizabeth Taylor *(Kathie Merrick)*, Frank Morgan *(Harry McBain)*, Tom Drake *(Sgt. Smith)*, Selena Royle *(Mrs. Merrick)*, Harry Davenport *(Judge Payson)*, George Cleveland *(Old Man)*, Catherine McLeod *(Alice Merrick)*, Morris Ankrum *(Farmer Crews)*, Arthur Walsh *(Freddie Crews)*, Mitchell Lewis *(Farmer Elson)*, Jane Green *(Mrs. Ellison)*, David Holt *(Peter Merrick)*, William Lewin *(Sergeant)*, Minor Watson *(Sheriff Grayson)*, Windy Cook *(Youth)*, Donald Curtis *(Charlie)*, Clancy Cooper *(Casey)*, Byron Foulger *(Dr. Coleman)*, James Flavin *(Lt. Arnold)*, Charles Sullivan *(Officer Instructor)*, Addison Richards, Arthur Space *(Officers)*, Robert Emmett O'Connor *(Deputy)*, William "Bill" Phillips *(Sgt. Tyler)*, Douglas Cowan *(Sgt. Lewis)*, Lyle Mulhall *(Corporal)*.

A Lassie picture wherein the loyal collie plays a pooch named *Bill*, indicating a last-minute title change, obviously for box-office purposes. As a pup, Lassie/Bill is found by teenager Kathie Merrick (Elizabeth Taylor) who nurses the dog back to health after it has been accidentally shot by two boys out bird hunting. Soon Lassie/Bill becomes a healthy and useful dog and even helps out by rounding up stray sheep on kindly rancher Harry McBain's (Frank Morgan) land. Tragedy strikes one day when the pooch is hit by a car and, through a complicated series of events, ends up in the Army chewing up the Japanese in WW II. After the war the dog comes back shell-shocked and vicious. It takes all the kindness Kathie can muster to rehabilitate the canine veteran. Taylor received her first top billing in COURAGE OF LASSIE on the heels of her great success in NATIONAL VELVET (1944). The film is an oddity in the Lassie series as it really has no relation to either LASSIE COME HOME (1943) or SON OF LASSIE (1945).

p, Robert Sisk; d, Fred M. Wilcox; w, Lionel Houser; ph, Leonard Smith (Technicolor); m, Scott Bradley.

Drama   **(MPAA:NR)**

COURT JESTER, THE

(1956) 101m PAR c

Danny Kaye *(Hawkins)*, Glynis Johns *(Maid Jean)*, Basil Rathbone *(Sir Ravenhurst)*, Angela Lansbury *(Princess Gwendolyn)*, Cecil Parker *(King Roderick)*, Mildred Natwick *(Griselda)*, Robert Middleton *(Sir Griswold)*, Michael Pate *(Sir Locksley)*, Herbert Rudley *(Captain of the*

Guard), Noel Drayton (Fergus), Edward Ashley (Black Fox), John Carradine (Giacomo), Alan Napier (Sir Brockhurst), Lewis Martin (Sir Finsdale), Patrick Aherne (Sir Pertwee), Richard Kean (Archbishop), Larry Pennell (Novice Knight), Hermine's Midgets, The American Legion Zouaves, Tudor Owen, Charles Irwin, Leo Britt, Russell Gaige, Ray Kellogg, Eric Alden, William Pullen, Joel Smith, Robin Hughes, Robert E. Smith, Nels Nelson, Edward Gibbons, Thomas J. Cotton, Billy Curtis, A.J. Buster Resmondo, Irving Fulton, Frank Delfino, Little Billy Rhodes, Henry Lewis Stone.

THE COURT JESTER is outstanding entertainment starring Danny Kaye (in quite possibly his best film) as a lowly valet who rises to become the leader of a peasant rebellion aimed at restoring the rightful heir to the throne of England. He disguises himself as a court jester to gain access to an evil baron (played by Basil Rathbone), the real power behind the throne, and overthrow his oppressive rule. A great cast handles the laughs with dash and aplomb, but the real standout is Rathbone, whose charmingly villainous manner and comedic timing provide the perfect foil for Kaye's antics. In one of Kaye's classic routines he confuses a secret message beginning with the tongue-twisting line, "I've put a pellet of poison in the vessel with the pestle." A stylish, well-done genre parody.

p,d&w, Norman Panama, Melvin Frank; ph, Ray June, Tom McAdoo (VistaVision, Technicolor); m, Victor Schoen.

Adventure/Comedy   **Cas.**   **(MPAA:NR)**

COURTSHIP OF EDDIE'S FATHER, THE

(1963) 118m MGM c

Glenn Ford (Tom Corbett), Shirley Jones (Elizabeth Marten), Stella Stevens (Dollye Daly), Dina Merrill (Rita Behrens), Roberta Sherwood (Mrs. Livingston), Ronny Howard (Eddie), Jerry Van Dyke (Norman Jones), John LaSalle Jazz Combo.

This is the charming, if somewhat slow, story of widower Tom Corbett (Glenn Ford), who is raising his 6-year-old son Eddie (Ronny Howard, future director of SPLASH and WILLOW). Women are attracted to the handsome widower and all must pass muster with little Eddie, who has some very definite ideas on what kind of woman he might want his dad to marry. Mrs. Livingston (Roberta Sherwood) is the housekeeper and quite funny as she studies her Spanish, unaware that her trip to Brazil will be to a country where Portuguese is spoken. Eddie judges women by their eyes and busts and doesn't much like his pop's beloved, Rita Behrens (Dina Merrill), who, he thinks, has "skinny eyes"; he would much prefer that dad get together with the next door neighbor (Shirley Jones). Do you want three guesses as to who dad winds up with?

p, Joe Pasternak; d, Vincente Minnelli; w, John Gay

(based on the novel by Mark Toby); ph, Milton Krasner (Metrocolor); m, George Stoll.

Comedy/Drama   **(MPAA:NR)**

CRY FROM THE STREET, A

(1959, Brit.) 100m Eros bw

Max Bygraves (Bill Lowther), Barbara Murray (Ann Fairlie), Colin Petersen (Georgie), Dana Wilson (Barbie), Kathleen Harrison (Mrs. Farrer), Sean Barrett (Don Farrer), Eleanor Summerfield (Gloria), Mona Washbourne (Mrs. Daniels), Toke Townley (Mr. Daniels), Charles McShane (Derek), David Bushell (Alex), Tony Baker (Tony), Glyn Houston (Police Sergeant), Dandy Nicholls (Mrs. Jenks), Basil Dignam (Police Inspector), Avice Landone (Rachael Seymour), Vi Stevens (Mr. Robbins), Fred Griffiths (Mr. Hodges).

Any film featuring wide-eyed orphans simply cannot miss and, sure enough, this one doesn't. Welfare worker Ann Fairlie (Barbara Murray) grows fond of a group of homeless tots and with the help of the equally enraptured Bill Lowther (Max Bygraves) tries to bring them some happiness. Delightfully sensitive performances and fresh direction make this a thoroughly pleasurable film likely to bring tearful smiles. Bygraves sings "Gotta Have Rain" with the kids, a tune he also composed.

p, Ian Dalrymple; d, Lewis Gilbert; w, Vernon Harris (based on the novel The Friend In Need by Elizabeth Coxhead); ph, Harry Gilliam; m, Larry Adler.

Drama   **(MPAA:NR)**

CUCKOOS, THE

(1930) 90m RAD bw/c

Bert Wheeler (Sparrow), Robert Woolsey (Prof. Bird), June Clyde (Ruth), Hugh Trevor (Billy), Dorothy Lee (Anita), Ivan Lebedeff (The Baron), Marguerita Padula (Gypsy Queen), Mitchell Lewis (Julius), Jobyna Howland (Fanny Furst).

Sparrow (Bert Wheeler) and Prof. Bird (Robert Woolsey) are a pair of bogus fortune tellers hot on the trail of a kidnaped heiress. Based on a Broadway play, THE CUCKOOS is musical anarchy of a slightly different sort than what Laurel and Hardy were doing at the same time. Wheeler and Woolsey were both comedians, but they could also sing, dance, and act in high or low style. The pair went on to make many wonderfully wacky films until Woolsey died in 1938 at the early age of 49. It's too bad their years together were so short, but there are many films one can watch to see their versatility and charm.

d, Paul Sloane, Louis Sarecky; w, Cy Woods (based on the play "The Ramblers" by Guy Bolton, Harry Ruby, and Bert Kalmar).

Comedy   **(MPAA:NR)**

D

DARBY O'GILL AND THE LITTLE PEOPLE

(1959) 93m Disney/BV c

Albert Sharpe (Darby O'Gill), Janet Munro (Katie), Sean Connery (Michael McBride), Jimmy O'Dea (King Brian), Kieron Moore (Pony Sugrue), Estelle Winwood (Sheelah), Walter Fitzgerald (Lord Fitzpatrick), Dennis O'Dea (Fr. Murphy), J.G. Devlin (Tom Kerrigan), Jack MacGowran (Phadrig Oge), Farrell Pelly (Paddy Scanlon), Nora O'Mahony (Molly Malloy).

This excellent fantasy romps through the folklore world of Ireland, with Albert Sharpe starring as Darby O'Gill, the aging caretaker of a large estate. He falls into a well and lands in the cavernous realm of the Little People, ruled by King Brian (Jimmy O'Dea). Following a wild leprechaun celebration, the rock walls open and the king leads his men out on miniature horses to frolic in the Irish countryside. Later, Darby tricks King Brian into granting him three wishes, but quickly learns that one should be careful of what one wishes for. This wonderful tale is told with a brisk, imaginative pace and the special effects—whereby Darby interacts with the tiny leprechauns—are marvelously executed. The sharp camerawork is enhanced with brilliant colors and the music (by Oliver Wallace) is delightfully and capriciously Irish. As usual, the overall production reflects Walt Disney's perfectionist detail, as well it should, for Disney dreamed of making the film for 20 years and took a trip to Ireland in 1948 to do research. Any child who hasn't seen DARBY O'GILL AND THE LITTLE PEOPLE has missed an important bit of fancy, and that goes for adults too.

p, Walt Disney; d, Robert Stevenson; w, Lawrence E. Watkin (based on the Darby O'Gill stories by H.T. Kavanagh); ph, Winton C. Hoch (Technicolor); m, Oliver Wallace.

Fantasy   **Cas.**   **(MPAA:NR)**

DATE WITH JUDY, A

(1948) 113m MGM c

Wallace Beery (Melvin R. Foster), Jane Powell (Judy Foster), Elizabeth Taylor (Carol Pringle), Carmen Miranda (Rosita Conchelias), Xavier Cugat (Himself), Robert Stack (Stephen Andrews), Selena Royle (Mrs. Foster), Scotty Beckett (Ogden "Oogie" Pringle), Leon Ames (Lucien T. Pringle), George Cleveland (Gramps), Lloyd Corrigan (Pop Scully), Clinton Sundberg (Jameson), Jean McLaren (Mitzie), Jerry Hunter (Randolph Foster), Buddy Howard (Jo-Jo Hoffenpepper), Lillian Yarbo (Nightingale), Eula Guy (Miss Clarke), Francis Pierlot (Prof. Green), Rena Lenart (Olga), Sheila Stein (Little Girl in Drug Store), Paul Bradley (Headwaiter), Polly Bailey (Elderly Woman), Alice Kelley (Girl), Fern Eggen (Miss Sampson).

This cheerful musical began as a radio series, became a movie, and wound up a TV series. A Santa Barbara teenager, Judy Foster (Jane Powell), is seeing fellow teen Oogie Pringle (Scotty Beckett), but she soon falls for an older man (Robert Stack). Carol Pringle (Elizabeth Taylor) is Judy's best friend and they both misconstrue Judy's father's (Wallace Beery) relationship with the exotic Rosita Cochelias (Carmen Miranda) as an affair—when, in reality, the Brazilian Bombshell has been teaching him how to dance so he can surprise his wife. Romantic complications, both teen and adult, ensue until all is straightened out for a happy ending. Taylor is breathtakingly beautiful and most of the reviewers made mention of that, but the film's best performance is by Miranda, who purloins every scene. The music, dancing, and lighthearted comedy more than compensate for any lack of story involvement. Stanley Donen handled the choreography chores and the songs, by a raft of composers, which include Miranda's specialty, "Cuanto La Gusta."

p, Joe Pasternak; d, Richard Thorpe; w, Dorothy Cooper, Dorothy Kingsley (based on the radio series by Aleen Leslie); ph, Robert Surtees (Technicolor).

Comedy/Musical   **(MPAA:NR)**

DAVID COPPERFIELD

(1935) 133m MGM bw

W.C. Fields (Micawber), Lionel Barrymore (Dan Peggotty), Maureen O'Sullivan (Dora), Madge Evans (Agnes), Edna May Oliver (Aunt Betsey), Lewis Stone (Mr. Wickfield), Frank Lawton (David as a Man), Freddie Bartholomew (David as a Child), Elizabeth Allan (Mrs. Copperfield), Roland Young (Uriah Heep), Basil Rathbone (Mr. Murdstone), Elsa Lanchester (Clickett), Jean Cadell (Mrs. Micawber), Jessie Ralph (Nurse Peggotty), Lennox Pawle (Mr. Dick), Violet Kemble-Cooper (Jane Murdstone), Una O'Connor (Mrs. Gummidge), John Buckler (Ham), Hugh Williams (Steerforth), Ivan Simpson (Limmiter), Herbert Mundin (Barkis), Fay Chaldecott (Little Emily as a Child), Marilyn Knowlden (Agnes as a Child), Florine McKinney (Little Emily as a Woman), Harry Beresford (Dr. Chillip), Mabel Colcord (Mary Ann), Hugh Walpole (Vicar), Renee Gad (Janet), Arthur Treacher (Dishonest Coachman), Margaret Seddon.

To condense Charles Dickens' David Copperfield to a manageable 133 minutes of film and not lose one whit of the author's charm or sheer story-telling ability was a marvel of the screenwriter's art. Born six months after his father's death, young David Copperfield (Freddie Bartholomew) grows up in a household dominated by his mean stepfather, Mr. Murdstone (Basil Rathbone), whom his widowed mother married in desperation. David is terribly mistreated by Murdstone and is eventually sent to boarding school. When David's mother dies, his stepfather pulls the plucky youth out of school and puts him to work in Murdstone's dank export warehouse. There David meets Micawber (W.C. Fields), a complete pauper whose regal bearing belies his low financial station. The unlikely duo lodge together until Micawber is hauled off to debtors' prison. David escapes to Dover, where he grows into a man (now played by Frank Lawton) and overcomes his humble beginnings. Producer David O. Selznick was lavish with the budget, which enraged studio mogul Louis B. Mayer, who was against the project from the start and thought the novel unfilmable and uncommercial. He was wrong; the film was a hit at the box office and is now recognized as a classic. A cast of superior actors stocks the film, but the performer who got the most attention was W.C. Fields, cast against type. "He was born to play the part," director George Cukor later said, "... he realized he was working with something that was a classic and he behaved that way." In addition to the discovery of another side to Fields' talent, the film also contains the debut of Freddie Bartholomew, forever to be remembered as Spencer Tracy's "leetle feesh" in CAPTAINS COURAGEOUS.

p, David O. Selznick; d, George Cukor; w, Howard Estabrook, Hugh Walpole (based on the novel by Charles Dickens); ph, Oliver T. Marsh; m, Herbert Stothart

Drama   **Cas.**   **(MPAA:NR)**

DAVY CROCKETT, INDIAN SCOUT

(1950) 71m UA bw

George Montgomery *(Davy Crockett)*, Ellen Drew *(Frances)*, Philip Reed *(Red Hawk)*, Noah Beery, Jr. *(Tex)*, Paul Guilfoyle *(Ben)*, Addison Richards *(Capt. Weightman)*, Robert Barrat *(Lone Eagle)*, Erik Rolf *(Mr. Simms)*, William Wilkerson *(High Tree)*, John Hamilton *(Col. Pollard)*, Vera Marshe *(Mrs. Simms)*, Jimmy Moss *(Jimmy Simms)*, Chief Thundercloud *(Sleeping Fox)*, Kenneth Duncan *(Sgt. Gordon)*, Ray Teal *(Capt. McHale)*.

George Montgomery is a US military scout named after his famous uncle—Davy Crockett—who is assigned to stop Indian attacks on a defenseless group of wagon trains making their way west. Soon he realizes that someone in his outfit has been tipping the Indians off, because they seem to know what his next move will be before he makes it. Suspicion falls on Crockett's loyal Indian sidekick Red Hawk (Philip Reed), but the latter is vindicated when the real villain is revealed. Although this western adventure doesn't have anything to do with the renowned frontiersman from Tennessee, it is very enjoyable nonetheless. Five years later Walt Disney would make a film about the real Davy Crockett (see below) and start a national craze over the coonskin-capped hero.

p, Edward Small; d, Lew Landers; w, Richard Schayer (based on the story by Ford Beebe); ph, George Diskant, John Mescall; m, Paul Sawtell.

Western   **(MPAA:NR)**

DAVY CROCKETT, KING OF THE WILD FRONTIER

(1955) 90m Disney/BV c

Fess Parker *(Davy Crockett)*, Buddy Ebsen *(George Russel)*, Basil Ruysdael *(Andrew Jackson)*, Hans Conried *(Thimblerig)*, William Bakewell *(Tobias Norton)*, Kenneth

Tobey *(Col. Jim Bowie)*, Pat Hogan *(Chief Red Stick)*, Helene Stanley *(Polly Crockett)*, Nick Cravat *(Bustedluck)*, Don Megowan *(Col. Billy Travis)*, Mike Mazurki *(Bigfoot Mason)*, Jeff Thompson *(Charlie Two Shirts)*, Henry Joyner *(Swaney)*, Benjamin Hornbuckle *(Henderson)*, Hal Youngblood *(Opponent Political Speaker)*, Jim Maddux *(1st Congressman)*, Robert Booth *(2nd Congressman)*, Eugene Brindel *(Billy)*, Ray Whitetree *(Johnny)*, Campbell Brown *(Bruno)*.

Walt Disney spliced together three episodes from his "Wonderful World of Disney" television show to create this unbelievably lucrative box-office hit that also ushered in the coonskin cap craze of the 1950s. A basic plot shows the rise of Crockett (pleasantly played by Fess Parker) from his days as an Indian fighter to his time in Congress, concluding with his heroic death at the Alamo. At least audiences weren't gypped by the visuals, because the film was presented in widescreen Technicolor that was all but lost when originally shown on television. The theme song, "The Ballad of Davy Crockett," became a minor hit. Evidence that the Disney people did not expect Davy Crockett to become a national hero all over again abounds in the film; for example, Davy is seen bayoneting Indians and also venting his ego by announcing at one point, "We'll give 'em the old Crockett charge." After Davy became the idol of millions, writers Tom Blackburn and Norman Foster were more careful to make him a fault-free character.

p, Bill Walsh; d, Norman Foster; w, Tom Blackburn; ph, Charles Boyle (Technicolor); m, George Bruns.

Adventure/Biography   **Cas.**   **(MPAA:NR)**

DAY AT THE RACES, A

(1937) 109m MGM bw-c

Groucho Marx *(Dr. Hugo Z. Hackenbush)*, Chico Marx *(Tony)*, Harpo Marx *(Stuffy)*, Allan Jones *(Gil)*, Maureen O'Sullivan *(Judy)*, Margaret Dumont *(Mrs. Upjohn)*, Leonard Ceeley *(Whitmore)*, Douglas Dumbrille *(Morgan)*, Esther Muir *("Flo")*, Sig Rumann *(Dr. Steinberg)*, Robert Middlemass *(Sheriff)*, Vivien Fay *(Solo Dancer)*, Charles Trowbridge *(Dr. Wilmerding)*, Frank Dawson, Max Lucke *(Doctors)*, Frankie Darro *(Morgan's Jockey)*, Pat Flaherty *(Detective)*, Si Jenks *(Messenger)*, Hooper Atchley *(Race Judge)*, John Hyams, Wilbur Mack *(Judges)*, Mary MacLaren *(Nurse)*, Edward LeSaint *(Doctor)*, Jack Norton *(Drunk)*, Ivie Anderson, Crinoline Choir.

Hugo Z. Hackenbush (Groucho Marx) is a horse doctor who takes over a large sanitarium at the behest of hypochondriac socialite Mrs. Upjohn (Margaret Dumont). The sanitarium is owned by Judy (Maureen O'Sullivan), but she's having trouble paying off the mortgage. Luckily, with the help of Stuffy (Harpo Marx), Tony (Chico Marx), and a racehorse named Hi-Hat, she is able to save the hospital. Of course, the plot isn't important here; what really counts is the steady stream of wild comedy routines provided by the Marx Brothers, who poke fun at everything from the medical profession to high society. Striving for a worthy follow-up to the magnificent A

NIGHT AT THE OPERA, the comedians took their act on the road and performed these routines before live audiences throughout the country. The opulent-but-somewhat-dull musical production numbers prevent this from being as mesmerizing as its predecessor (indeed, a musical routine in which Harpo is mistaken for the angel Gabriel by blacks in a ghetto shantytown is racially offensive), but though it is a little dated, A DAY AT THE RACES is, nonetheless, a very entertaining comedy. Producer Irving Thalberg, to whom the Marxes were devoted, died during production.

p, Lawrence Weingarten; d, Sam Wood; w, Robert Pirosh, George Seaton, George Oppenheimer (based on a story by Robert Pirosh and George Seaton); ph, Joseph Ruttenberg; m, Bronislau Kaper, Walter Jurmann, Gus Kahn.

Comedy/Musical   **Cas.**   **(MPAA:NR)**

DAYDREAMER, THE

(1966) 101m Embassy c

Paul O'Keefe (Hans Christian Andersen), Jack Gilford (Papa Andersen), Ray Bolger (The Pieman), Margaret Hamilton (Mrs. Klopplebobbler), Robert Harter (Big Claus); voices of: Cyril Ritchard (The Sandman), Hayley Mills (The Little Mermaid), Burl Ives (Father Neptune), Tallulah Bankhead (The Sea Witch), Terry-Thomas (1st Tailor, Brigadier), Victor Borge (2nd Tailor, Zebro), Ed Wynn (The Emperor), Patty Duke (Thumbelina), Boris Karloff (The Rat), Sessue Hayakawa (The Mole), Robert Goulet (The Singer).

Live action combined with the Animagic process (stop-motion puppets) created this fantasy in which a young Hans Christian Andersen (Paul O'Keefe) daydreams some of his best fables. Nice songs and good voice talents for the animated characters, all presented with style and imagination, make this a memorable outing for children.

p, Arthur Rankin, Jr.; d, Jules Bass; w, Arthur Rankin, Jr. (based on the stories "The Little Mermaid," "The Emperor's New Clothes," "Thumbelina," and "The Garden of Paradise" by Hans Christian Andersen); ph, Daniel Cavelli, Tad Mochinaga (Animagic, Eastmancolor); m, Maury Laws.

Fantasy   **Cas.**   **(MPAA:NR)**

DEAR WIFE

(1949) 87m PAR bw

William Holden (Bill Seacroft), Joan Caulfield (Ruth Seacroft), Billy De Wolfe (Albert Kummer), Mona Freeman (Miriam Wilkins), Edward Arnold (Judge Wilkins), Arleen Whelan (Tommy Murphy), Mary Philips (Mrs. Wilkins), Harry Von Zell (Jeff Cooper), Raymond Roe (Ziggy), Elisabeth Fraser (Kate Collins), Bill Murphy (Dan Collins), Mary Field (Mrs. Bixby), Irving Bacon (Mike Man), Gordon Jones (Taxicab Driver), Marietta Canty (Dora), Don Beddoe (Metcalfe), Stanley Stayle (An Early

Riser), William Cartledge (Western Union Boy), Ralph Montgomery (Control Man), Franklyn Farnum, Edward Biby, Charles Dayton (Campaign Men), Claire DuBrey (Woman), Tim Ryan (Simmons the Cop), Ida Moore (Blowsy Woman), Leon Tyler (Gawky Boy), Harry Harvey (Mr. Channock), Tom Dugan (Painter), Len Hendry (Bank Teller), Bess Flowers (Mrs. Grindle), Paul E. Burns (Mr. Grindle), Harland Tucker (Mr. Burroughs), Patty Lou Arden (Clara).

In this sequel to 1947's DEAR RUTH, Bill (William Holden) and Ruth (Joan Caulfield) Seacroft are young marrieds with in-law problems. Bill's father-in-law (Edward Arnold) is a blustering judge whose word is law around the court and the house, and when Bill tells the judge that he doesn't know what a good breakfast is (the judge loves grapefruit in the morning and Bill hates it), the feathers fly. Kid sister-in-law Miriam Wilkins (Mona Freeman), who is socially conscious and very political, uses her wiles to get Bill into a race for the state senate. That wouldn't be a huge problem except that his opponent is the judge! A lighthearted family farce, the second in a series that would end with the next entry, DEAR BRAT (1951), featuring Freeman.

p, Richard Maibaum; d, Richard Haydn; w, Arthur Sheekman, N. Richard Nash (based on characters created by Norman Krasna for his play "Dear Ruth"); ph, Stuart Thompson.

Comedy   **Cas.**   **(MPAA:NR)**

DEEP IN MY HEART

(1954) 130m MGM c

Jose Ferrer (Sigmund Romberg), Merle Oberon (Dorothy Donnelly), Helen Traubel (Anna Mueller), Doe Avedon (Lillian Romberg), Walter Pidgeon (J.J. Shubert), Paul Henreid (Florenz Ziegfeid), Tamara Toumanova (Gaby Deslys), Paul Stewart (Bert Towsend), Isobel Elsom (Mrs. Harris), David Burns (Lazar Berrison, Sr.), Jim Backus (Ben Judson), Douglas Fowley (Harold Butterfield), Russ Tamblyn (Berrison, Jr.), Rosemary Clooney, Gene and Fred Kelly, Jane Powell, Vic Damone, Ann Miller, William Olvis, Cyd Charisse, James Mitchell, Howard Keel, Tony Martin, Joan Weldon (Guest Stars), Robert Easton (Cumberly), Suzanne Luckey (Arabella Bell), Ludwig Stossel (Mr. Novak), Else Neft (Mrs. Novak), Gordon Wynne (Treasurer), Mitchell Kowall (Oscar Hammerstein), Joe Roach (Groom), Dee Turnell (Bride).

An excellent screen biography of composer Sigmund Romberg, who was a power in the American musical genre for almost four decades. Romberg wrote more than 2,000 songs, did the scores for more than 80 plays, revues, and operettas, and still had time to lead a happy life. Born in Hungary, Romberg came to the US early, and his rise was steady and steep. Ferrer does well in the role of the young man who got his start in a little cafe on New York's Second Avenue. Its proprietress (Helen Traubel) encourages his work, as does Lazar Berrison (David Burns), a Brill Building song pusher. Romberg has a commercial smash when he changes the tempo of one of his tunes to ragtime, and a series of small-time shows follows until Romberg has such a hit with "Maytime" that one house won't hold it and, for the first time, *two* companies play the show on Broadway simultaneously. The picture mixes all the elements necessary to make a successful musical: songs like "One Alone," "The Desert Song," "Lover Come Back To Me," "Will You Remember," "Stouthearted Men," "Your Land and My Land"; dances by Ann Miller, Cyd Charisse, and James Mitchell; singing by Vic Damone, Jane Powell, Tony Martin, and Rosemary Clooney; and, of course, superior acting by all. The film takes some liberties with history and ascribes some songs to the wrong shows, but it's poetic license that even Romberg wouldn't have minded.

p, Roger Edens; d, Stanley Donen; w, Leonard Spigelgass (based on the book by Elliott Arnold); ph, George Folsey (Eastmancolor); m, Sigmund Romberg.

Biography/Musical   **Cas.**   **(MPAA:NR)**

DR. COPPELIUS

(1968, US/Span.) 97m Gala c (EL FANTASTICO MUNDO DEL DR. COPPELIUS)

Walter Slezak *(Dr. Coppelius),* Claudia Corday *(Swanilda/Coppelia),* Caj Selling *(Franz),* Eileen Elliott *(Brigitta),* Luis Prendes *(The Mayor),* Milord Moskovitch *(Hungarian Dance Champion),* Carmen Rojas *(Spanish Doll),* Veronica Rusmin *(Roman Doll),* Marcia Bellak, Kathy Jo Brown, Clara Cravey, Kathleen Garrison, Christine Holter. Sharon Kapner *(Swanhilda's Friends),* Helena Villarroya, Gran Teatro del Liceo Ballet, International Cine Ballet, Aurelio Bogado, Xenia Petrowsky.

In this film based on an 1870 ballet by Delibes and Nuitter, lonely Dr. Coppelius (Walter Slezak) creates a companion for himself—a beautiful dancing mechanical doll (Claudia Corday). Unfortunately, an amorous village lad, Franz (Caj Selling), spies the doll dancing on the balcony and falls in love with the doctor's creation. Coppelius kidnaps Franz and attempts to implant his soul into the doll, but Franz's jealous girl friend (Corday, playing a dual role) comes to his rescue. "Coppelia," the ballet that inspired this enthralling film, was itself derived from one of the tales of Hoffmann.

p, Frank J. Hale; d&w, Ted Kneeland (based on the ballet "Coppelia" by Clement Delibes and Charles Nuitter); ph, Cecilio Paniagua (Superpanorama, Technicolor); m, Clement Delibes, Raymond Guy Wilson.

Fantasy   **(MPAA:NR)**

DOCTOR DOLITTLE

(1967) 152m FOX c

Rex Harrison *(Dr. John Dolittle),* Anthony Newley *(Matthew Mugg),* Peter Bull *(Gen. Bellowes),* William Dix *(Tommy Stubbins),* Portia Nelson *(Sarah Dolittle),* Samantha Eggar *(Emma Fairfax),* Richard Attenborough *(Albert Blossom),* Muriel Landers *(Mrs. Blossom),* Geoffrey Holder *(Willie Shakespeare),* Norma Varden *(Lady Petherington).*

Doctor Dolittle (Rex Harrison) is considered a nut by his neighbors. After this "nuttiness" leads to his arrest, Dolittle decides to avoid people and to devote his life to animals since, as one who can speak all the animal tongues (he was taught 498 different languages by his parrot, Polynesia), he serves as a unique link between human and beast. With Matthew Mugg (Anthony Newley) and Emma Fairfax (Samantha Eggar) at his side, the doctor sails off to find the elusive Great Pink Sea Snail and the Giant Lunar Moth in the South Seas. The studio had high hopes for this movie and sank a lot of time and money into its production; unfortunately, it was a disaster at the box office. Problems on the set were many, especially with the use of so many live animals. More than 1,500 beasts took part and the average care and feeding cost for the featured animals was $750 a week. Alan Jay Lerner, originally set to write the book and lyrics, attempted to write for over a year but finally gave up and bailed out, whereupon Harrison wanted to leave as well. Actually, Harrison really hadn't wanted to star in a "children's film" in the first place, and it was only the presence of prestigious author-lyricist Lerner that attracted him to the project. Luckily, the songs by Lerner's replacement, Leslie Bricusse, pleased Harrison and he stayed with the production. Bricusse took an Oscar for best song with "Talk to the Animals."

p, Arthur P. Jacobs; d, Richard Fleischer; w, Leslie Bricusse (based on stories by Hugh Lofting); ph, Robert Surtees (Todd-AO, Deluxe Color); md, Lionel Newman, Alexander Courage.

Fantasy/Musical   **Cas.**   **(MPAA:NR)**

DOG AND THE DIAMONDS, THE

(1962, Brit.) 55m London Independent

Kathleen Harrison *(Mrs. Fossett),* George Coulouris *(Forbes),* Geoffrey Sumner *(Mr. Gayford),* Brian Oulton *(Mr. Plumpton),* Michael MacGuire *(Jimmy),* Robert Sandford *(Peter),* Robert Scroggins *(Ginger),* Barbara Brown *(Helen),* Molly Osborne *(Linda),* Hal Osmund, Arthur Lane, Dennis Wyndham *(Crooks).*

An enjoyable children's film about a group of kids who build a makeshift zoo because animals are *not* allowed in their apartment building. The zoo is set up in the garden of an abandoned manor that, the children discover, is the hideout for three jewel thieves. Kids and animals then join forces to battle the crooks.

p, Peter Rogers; d, Ralph Thomas; w, Patricia Latham.

Crime   **(MPAA:NR)**

DOG OF FLANDERS, A

(1959) 96m FOX c

David Ladd *(Nello),* Donald Crisp *(Daas),* Theodore Bikel *(Piet),* Max Croiset *(Mr. Cogez),* Monique Ahrens *(Corrie),* Siohban Taylor *(Alois),* Gijsbert Tersteeg, John Soer, Lo van Hernsbergen, Katherine Holland, Patrasche the Wonder Dog.

The third and finest film version of Ouida's classic children's novel of 1872 features David Ladd as Dutch boy Nello, a child who aspires to become a painter but seems to have no chance of ever attaining his dream. He lives with his grandfather (Donald Crisp) in Flanders, where they eke out a living by delivering milk from neighboring farms to Antwerp. They find a sickly dog and nurse it back to health, after which it becomes their cartdog. When the grandfather dies, the boy and dog struggle to make it on their own, with the help of a kindly artist (Theodore Bikel). Filmed on location in The Netherlands and Belgium, this film was awarded the Golden Lion at the Venice Film Festival and an award of merit from the Belgian government, and won acclaim from *Parents* magazine. The original movie version was a silent filmed in 1924 starring Jackie Coogan, which was followed by a 1935 talkie remake featuring Frankie Thomas.

p, Robert D. Radnitz; d, James B. Clark; w, Ted Sherdeman (based on the novel by Ouida); ph, Otto Heller (CinemaScope, Deluxe Color); m, Paul Sawtell, Bert Shefter.

Drama   **Cas.**   **(MPAA:NR)**

DOT AND THE KOALA

(1985, Aus.) 70m Gross c

Voices of: Robyn Moore, Keith Scott.

This animated children's feature from Australia—the fourth in a series—follows the adventures of the denizens of an animal town as they do battle with city hall. The mayor, Percy Pig, wants to build a new hydroelectric plant. To do so, a dam must be built on a nearby river, although the new structure will destroy much of the natural surroundings. Bruce, the Koala, along with his human friend Dot, joins forces with other animals to stop Percy and his henchman, a rat detective named Sherlock Bones. The film differs from other live-action/animation features in that the backgrounds used are real footage of the rugged Tasmanian countryside, where a similar real-life controversy actually took place.

p, Yoram Gross, Sandra Gross; d, Yoram Gross; w, Yoram Gross, Greg Flynn; ph, Graham Sharpe; m, Bob Young, John Sangster.

Animation   **(MPAA:NR)**

DOVE, THE

(1974, Brit.) 105m PAR c

Joseph Bottoms *(Robin Lee Graham)*, Deborah Raffin *(Patti Ratterree)*, John McLiam *(Lyle Graham)*, Dabney Coleman *(Charles Huntley)*, John Anderson *(Mike Turk)*, Colby Chester *(Tom Barkley)*, Ivor Barry *(Kenniston)*, Setoki Ceinaturoga *(Young Fijian)*, Rev. Nikula *(Minister)*, Apenisa Naigulevu *(Cruise Ship Captain)*, John Meillon *(Tim)*, Gordon Glenwright *(Darwin Harbor Master)*, Garth Meade *(South African Customs Official)*, Peter Gwynne

(Fred C. Pearson), Cecily Polsohn *(Mrs. Castaldi)*, Anthony Fridjohn *(License Bureau Clerk)*, Dale Cutts *(Reporter)*, Jose Augusto de Lima, Sampaio e Silva.

Based on the true adventures of 16-year-old Robin Lee Graham (played by Joseph Bottoms), this film follows the youngster as he sails solo around the world in a 23-foot sloop. The trip takes five years and brings the character to maturity and manhood. On the way he falls in love with Patti Ratterree (Deborah Raffin), who is his constant inspiration and follows him to Fiji, Australia, South Africa, Panama, and the Galapagos Islands. Upon the trip's triumphant conclusion, Robin becomes the youngest person every to sail around the world alone. Sven Nykvist's cinematography of the gorgeous locations is nothing less than stunning.

p, Gregory Peck; d, Charles Jarrott; w, Peter Beagle, Adam Kennedy (based on the book *Dove* by Robin Lee Graham with Derek Gill); ph, Sven Nykvist (Panavision, Technicolor); m, John Barry.

Adventure   **(MPAA:PG)**

DREAMBOAT

(1952) 83m FOX bw

Clifton Webb *(Thornton Sayre)*, Ginger Rogers *(Gloria)*, Anne Francis *(Carol Sayre)*, Jeffrey Hunter *(Bill Ainslee)*, Elsa Lanchester *(Dr. Coffey)*, Fred Clark *(Sam Levitt)*, Paul Harvey *(Harrington)*, Ray Collins *(Timothy Stone)*, Helene Stanley *(Mimi)*, Richard Garrick *(Judge Bowles)*, George Barrows *(Commandant)*, Jay Adler *(Desk Clerk)*, Marietta Canty *(Lavinia)*, Laura Brooks *(Mrs. Gunther)*, Emory Parnell *(Used Car Salesman)*, Helen Hatch *(Mrs. Faust)*, Harry Cheshire *(MacIntosh)*, Everett Glass *(George Bradley)*, Paul Maxey *(Clarence Bornay)*, Sandor Szabo *(Giant Arab)*, Leo Cleary *(Court Clerk)*, Lee Turnbull *(Denham)*, Helen Brown *(Dorothy)*, Al Herman *(Drunk)*, Howard Banks *(Hotel Clerk)*, Jack Mather *(Hotel Detective)*, Matt Mattox, Frank Radcliffe *(Men in Commercial)*, Gwen Verdon *(Girl in Commercial)*, Bob Easton, Marjorie Halliday *(TV Commercial)*, Donna Lee Hickey *(Cigarette Girl)*.

Charming spoof of television featuring Clifton Webb as Thornton Sayre, a highly regarded professor with a personal history no one knows about until a series of old films are shown on TV. It seems that this conservative educator had been a screen star back in the silent days, and the showing of his old features is destroying his credibility as a college instructor. His erstwhile costar, Gloria (Ginger Rogers), hosts the TV screenings and hawks perfume these days, making scads of money in the process. Thornton and his daughter (Anne Francis) seek to stop the showings and sue. However, the court case rekindles his love for acting and he soon finds that colleagues who once thought him bland and colorless now see him as the passionate swashbuckler he once played. Very few actors could essay righteous indignation as well as Webb, who plays it to the hilt in this role. While television is the film's main target, director Claude

Binyon has some fun with silent movie conventions as well.

p, Sol C. Siegel; d&w, Claude Binyon (based on a story by John D. Weaver); ph, Milton Krasner; m, Cyril J. Mockridge.

Comedy (MPAA:NR)

DRUMS ALONG THE MOHAWK

(1939) 103m FOX c

Claudette Colbert *(Lana "Magdelana" Martin)*, Henry Fonda *(Gil Martin)*, Edna May Oliver *(Mrs. Sarah McKlennar)*, Eddie Collins *(Christian Reall)*, John Carradine *(Caldwell)*, Doris Bowdon *(Mary Reall)*, Jessie Ralph *(Mrs. Weaver)*, Arthur Shields *(Rev. Rosenkrantz)*, Robert Lowery *(John Weaver)*, Roger Imhof *(Gen. Nicholas Herkimer)*, Francis Ford *(Joe Boleo)*, Ward Bond *(Adam Hartman)*, Kay Linaker *(Mrs. DeMooth)*, Russell Simpson *(Dr. Petry)*, Spencer Charters *(Innkeeper)*, Si Jenks *(Jacob Small)*, J. Ronald Pennick *(Amos Hartman)*, Arthur Aylesworth *(George Weaver)*, Chief Big Tree *(Blue Back)*, Charles Tannen *(Dr. Robert Johnson)*, Paul McVey *(Capt. Mark DeMooth)*, Elizabeth "Tiny" Jones *(Mrs. Reall)*, Beulah Hall Jones *(Daisy)*, Edwin Maxwell *(Rev. Daniel Gros)*, Robert Greig *(Mr. Borst)*, Clara Blandick *(Mrs. Borst)*.

A richly directed and acted colonial epic concerning Gil (Henry Fonda) and Lana (Claudette Colbert) Martin, young newlyweds starting out on the frontier of the Mohawk Valley just before the outbreak of the Revolutionary War. The transition from the life of privilege to that of the rugged frontier is difficult, especially for Lana. To help fend off Indian attacks engineered by the British, Gilbert joins the militia and goes off to fight; finally, after many battles and hardships, the future of the new Americans begins to look bright. This historical chronicle, directed by John Ford, is made believable through its attention to small details, presenting a mosaic of frontier life. One of Ford's biggest problems in making the spectacular film was the unavailability of necessary props and costumes. The movie studio had not specialized in costume or historical films, particularly those with 18th-century settings, and almost everything had to be made from scratch at great cost. The ancient flintlock muskets brandished by scores of extras were the real weapons of the era, however, not reproductions. A Fox prop man chased the flintlocks down in Ethiopia—where they had actually seen combat in the mid-1930s when they were used by Ethiopian soldiers trying to repel Mussolini's armies. This was Ford's first color film and he made the most of it, his cameras recording the lush forests and valleys of northern Utah. So rich and verdant is the color in this film that it later provided stock footage for several Fox productions, chiefly BUFFALO BILL (1944) and MOHAWK (1956).

p, Raymond Griffith; d, John Ford; w, Lamar Trotti, Sonya Levien (based on the novel by Walter D. Edmonds); ph, Bert Glennon, Ray Rennahan (Technicolor); m, Alfred Newman.

Adventure Cas. (MPAA:NR)

DUCK SOUP

(1933) 70m PAR bw

Groucho Marx *(Rufus T. Firefly)*, Chico Marx *(Chicolini)*, Harpo Marx *(Brownie)*, Zeppo Marx *(Bob Rolland)*, Raquel Torres *(Vera Marcal)*, Louis Calhern *(Ambassador Trentino)*, Margaret Dumont *(Mrs. Teasdale)*, Verna Hillie *(Secretary)*, Leonid Kinskey *(Agitator)*, Edmund Breese *(Zander)*, Edwin Maxwell *(Secretary of War)*, Edgar Kennedy *(Peddler)*.

Fast-moving, irreverent, almost anarchistic in style, DUCK SOUP is considered by many to be the Marx Brothers' greatest achievement. The story, if one can call it that, concerns Mrs. Teasdale (Margaret Dumont), a dowager millionairess who will donate $20 million to the destitute duchy of Freedonia if it will agree to make Rufus T. Firefly (Groucho) its dictator. Firefly woos Mrs. Teasdale and spends his spare time insulting Trentino (Louis Calhern), the ambassador from neighboring Sylvania. Trentino hires the sultry Vera Marcal (Raquel Torres) to vamp Firefly so that Trentino can move in on Mrs. Teasdale, marry her, and get control of Freedonia. To aid his chicanery, Trentino hires Chicolini (Chico), a peanut salesman, and his friend Brownie (Harpo) as spies. Eventually war breaks out and, after much manic double-crossing and side-switching, Freedonia emerges victorious. Perhaps the best, and funniest, depiction of the absurdities of war ever committed to celluloid, DUCK SOUP today remains a masterpiece of film comedy. The Marxes' depiction of two-bit dictators destroying their own countries was a direct slap at the rising fascists, so much so that Mussolini banned the film in Italy, thinking it a direct insult to Il Duce. Naturally, the Marx Brothers were thrilled to hear that.

p, Herman Mankiewicz; d, Leo McCarey; w, Bert Kalmar, Harry Ruby, Arthur Sheekman, Nat Perrin; ph, Henry Sharpe.

Comedy Cas. (MPAA:NR)

DUMBO

(1941) 64m Disney/RKO c

Voices of: Edward Brophy *(Timothy Mouse)*, Herman Bing *(Ringmaster)*, Verna Felton *(Elephant)*, Sterling Holloway *(Stork)*, Cliff Edwards *(Jim Crow)*.

One of Disney's finest films, this simple, short tale is set in a circus and centers around a baby elephant, Dumbo, who is mocked and ridiculed because his ears are too big. With the help of his friend Timothy the mouse, Dumbo discovers that he can use his gigantic ears to fly and becomes the hit of the circus. DUMBO is a flawless film, one of the shortest Disney ever made and inexpensive to boot, costing less than $1 million (whereas films like BAMBI shot well beyond the $2 million mark). A masterpiece of visual story-telling, the film contains very little dialog and Dumbo never speaks; his mother only speaks to him in the song "Baby Mine." Humans are shown in shadows and silhouettes, the animals taking center stage. As with all his major feature-length animation films, Disney made sure that none of the scenes were flat, that blades of grass rippled in the wind and leaves fluttered in the trees. It took the Disney geniuses a year and a half to design and execute this film of heart, taste, and overall beauty that will appeal to every child in the world and every adult who can still recall the happy world of childhood fantasies and fables.

p, Walt Disney; d, Ben Sharpsteen; w, Joe Grant, Dick Huemer (based on a book by Helen Aberson and Harold Pearl); ph, (Technicolor).

Animation   **Cas.**   **(MPAA:NR)**

E

E.T. THE EXTRA-TERRESTRIAL

(1982) 115m UNIV c

Dee Wallace *(Mary)*, Henry Thomas *(Elliott)*, Peter Coyote *(Keys)*, Robert MacNaughton *(Michael)*, Drew Barrymore *(Gertie)*, K.C. Martel *(Greg)*, Sean Frye *(Steve)*, Tom Howell *(Tyler)*, Erika Eleniak *(Pretty Girl)*, David O'Dell *(Schoolboy)*, Richard Swingler *(Science Teacher)*, Frank Toth *(Policeman)*, Robert Barton *(Ultra Sound Man)*, Michael Darrell *(Van Man)*, Milt Kogan *(Doctor)*, David Berkson, David Carlberg, Alexander Lampone, Rhoda Makoff, Robert Murphy, Richard Pesavento, Tom Sherry, Susan Cameron, Will Fowler, Jr., Barbara Hartnett, Di Ann Lampone, Mary Stein, Mitchell Suskin.

Elliott (Henry Thomas) finds E.T., a visitor from another planet left stranded on Earth, hiding in his backyard and, like any kid who finds a stray, decides to keep him. Hiding the alien from his mother, Elliott and the neighborhood kids befriend the creature. Although he becomes attached to Elliott and his friends, E.T. wants to get back to his own planet, and the children must save him from the government types who have been trying to capture and study him—against his will. A phenomenal hit at the box office, E.T. was embraced by audiences worldwide and instantly became absorbed into popular culture, becoming the most successful film of all time. Although the story is little more than a standard boy-and-his-dog tale, the fun comes with the rich detail that director Steven Spielberg and associate producer-writer Melissa Mathison have brought to the material. From E.T.'s amusing encounters with suburban living to the exhilaration felt when Elliott's bicycle magically soars into the air, viewers are under the spell of one of modern cinema's most skillful craftsmen.

p, Steven Spielberg, Kathleen Kennedy; d, Steven Spielberg; w, Melissa Mathison; ph, Allen Daviau (Technicolor); m, John Williams.

Science Fiction   **(MPAA:PG)**

EASTER PARADE

(1948) 107m MGM c

Judy Garland *(Hannah Brown)*, Fred Astaire *(Don Hewes)*, PeterLawford *(Jonathan Harrow III)*, Ann Miller *(Nadine Hale)*, Jules Munshin *(Francois)*, Clinton Sundberg *(Mike, the Bartender)*, Jeni LeGon *(Essie)*, Richard Beavers *(Singer)*, Dick Simmons *(Al, Stage Manager for Ziegfeld)*, Jimmy Bates *(Boy with Astaire in "Drum Crazy" Musical Number)*, Dee Turnell, Bobbie Priest, Patricia Jackson *(Specialty Girls)*, Lola Albright, Joi Lansing *(Hat Model Showgirls)*, Lynn and Jean Romer *("Delineator" Twins)*, Helene Heigh *(Modiste)*, Wilson Wood *(Marty)*, Peter Chong *(Sam, the Valet)*, Nolan Leary *(Drug Store Clerk)*, Doris Kemper *(Mary)*, Frank Mayo *(Headwaiter)*, Benay Venuta *(Bar Patron)*, Hector and His Pals—Carmi Tryon *(Dog Act)*, Jimmy Dodd *(Cabby)*, Robert Emmett O'Connor *(Cop Who Gives Johnny a Ticket)*.

The year is 1911 and Nadine Hale (Ann Miller) and Don Hewes (Fred Astaire) are dance partners. When Nadine is offered the lead in a new Ziegfeld extravaganza, she dumps Don and leaves. The jilted Don is angry and wants to prove he can make a star out of anyone he chooses, so he opts for the least likely future star he can find—a chorus girl named Hannah Brown (Judy Garland). Gene Kelly was supposed to have the lead, but injured his ankle playing volleyball, so he suggested to producer Arthur Freed that they prevail on Astaire to come out of his "retirement" for the role. Astaire had announced he was done after BLUE SKIES, but was obviously only waiting for someone to ask him, because he jumped at the opportunity and gave yet another classic performance. Irving Berlin wrote 17 tunes heard in the film and Johnny Green and Roger Edens won an Oscar for their musical adaptation. Making an appearance at the age of two-and-a-half is Liza Minnelli in the final sequence. The songs include "It Only Happens When I Dance with You," "Everybody's Doin' It Now," "A Fella with an Umbrella," "When the Midnight Choo-Choo Leaves for Alabam'," "Steppin' Out with My Baby," "A Couple of Swells," and, of course, "Easter Parade."

p, Arthur Freed; d, Charles Walters; w, Frances Goodrich, Albert Hackett, Sidney Sheldon, Guy Bolton (based on a story by Frances Goodrich and Albert Hackett); ph, Harry Stradling, Sr. (Technicolor).

Comedy/Musical   **Cas.**   **(MPAA:NR)**

EDISON, THE MAN

(1940) 104m MGM bw

Spencer Tracy *(Thomas Alva Edison)*, Rita Johnson *(Mary Stilwell)*, Lynne Overman *(Bunt Cavatt)*, Charles Coburn *(Gen. Powell)*, Gene Lockhart *(Mr. Taggart)*, Henry Travers *(Ben Els)*, Felix Bressart *(Michael Somon)*, Peter Godfrey *(Ashton)*, Frank Faylen *(Galbreath)*, Byron Foulger *(Edwin Hall)*, Guy D'Ennery *(Lundstrom)*, Addison Richards *(Dr. Johnson)*, Milton Parsons *(Acid Graham)*, Arthur Aylsworth *(Bigelow)*, Gene Reynolds *(Jimmy Price)*, Grant Mitchell *(Shade)*, Donald Douglas

(Jordan), Harlan Briggs *(Bisbee),* Charles Trowbridge *(Clark),* Harold Minjir *(Blair),* George Meader *(Minister),* Charles Waldron *(Commissioner),* Charles Lane *(Lecturer),* Irving Bacon *(Sheriff),* Edward Earle *(Broker),* Joe Whitehead *(Man),* Emmett Vogan *(Secretary),* Tom Mahoney *(Policeman),* Bruce Mitchell *(Coachman),* Milton Kibbee *(Workman),* Nell Craig *(Woman),* Ann Gillis, Jay Ward, George Lessey, Paul Hurst.

MGM suddenly decided to go all out for Thomas Alva Edison in 1940, producing two films on his life. One of them, YOUNG TOM EDISON, was a box-office flop, despite Mickey Rooney's energetic portrayal; EDISON, THE MAN was a much more lavish production, with Spencer Tracy giving a dynamic performance as the great inventor-humanitarian. The film opens as Edison, at age 82, is about to be honored on the 50th anniversary of his invention of the incandescent light. He is being interviewed by two youths, and begins to relate the story of his early manhood. The film then goes into flashback and chronicles Edison's most productive years, from ages 25 to 35, when he produced the phonograph, the dictaphone, and the electric light. Tracy studied every known detail about Edison, trying to capture his personality from rare films and books and staying in Edison's old laboratory in Menlo Park, studying the inventor's notebooks. After weeks of saturating himself thus, Tracy felt he understood the man, as well as admired him. This is a fine film biography.

p, John W. Considine, Jr., Orville O. Dull; d, Clarence Brown; w, Talbot Jennings, Bradbury Foote (based on a story by Dore Schary and Hugo Butler); ph, Harold Rosson; m, Herbert Stothart.

Biography   **(MPAA:NR)**

EMIL AND THE DETECTIVES

(1964) 99m BV c

Walter Slezak *(Baron),* Bryan Russell *(Emil),* Roger Mobley *(Gustav),* Heinz Schubert *(Grundeis),* Peter Ehrlich *(Muller),* Cindy Cassel *(Pony),* Elsa Wagner *(Nana),* Wolfgang Volz *(Stucke),* Eva-Ingeborg Scholz *(Frau Tischbein),* Franz Nicklisch *(Desk Sergeant),* Brian Richardson *(Professor),* David Petrychka *(Dienstag),* Robert Swann *(Hermann),* Ann Noland *(Frieda),* Ron Johnson *(Rudolf),* Rick Johnson *(Hans),* Paul Glawton *(Traffic Policeman),* Gerhard Retschy *(Officer Kiessling),* Viktor Hospach *(Newsstand Proprietor),* Konrad Thoms *(Waiter),* Egon Vogel *(Dispatcher),* Gert Wiedenhofen *(Policeman),* Georg Rebentisch *(Bus Driver),* Rolf Rolphs *(Butler),* Roswitha Habedank *(Parlor Maid).*

The sixth movie version of Erich Kastner's classic children's novel (of the other five, two versions were German, one each British, Japanese, and Brazilian) gets the full Disney treatment here. Bryan Russell plays the hapless Emil, a young boy who is robbed while on a bus ride to visit his aunt. Instead of going to the police, Emil enlists a group of kids who fancy themselves detectives to help him catch the pickpocket (Heinz Schubert). Director Pe-

ter Tewksbury uses the bombed-out buildings of Berlin to excellent advantage.

p, Walt Disney; d, Peter Tewksbury; w, A.J. Carothers (based on the novel by Erich Kastner); ph, Gunther Senftleben (Technicolor); m, Heinz Schreiter.

Adventure   **Cas.**   **(MPAA:NR)**

EMPEROR WALTZ, THE

(1948) 105m PAR c

Bing Crosby *(Virgil Smith),* Joan Fontaine *(Johanna Franziska Von Stultzenberg),* Roland Culver *(Baron Holenia),* Richard Haydn *(Emperor Franz Josef),* Lucile Watson *(Princess),* Sig Rumann *(Dr. Zwieback),* Julia Dean *(Archduchess Stephanie),* Harold Vermilyea *(Chamberlain),* Roberta Jonay *(Chambermaid),* John Goldsworthy *(Obersthofmeister),* Doris Dowling *(Tyrolean Girl),* James Vincent *(Abbe),* Harry Allen *(Gamekeeper),* Frank Elliot *(Von Usedon),* Paul de Corday *(Officer),* Jack Gargan *(Master of Ceremonies),* Cyril Delevanti *(Diplomat),* Frank Corsaro *(Marquess),* Bert Prival *(Chauffeur),* Alma Macrorie *(Proprietor of Tyrolean Inn),* Gerald Mohr *(Marques Alonso).*

A charming musical from the brains of Billy Wilder and Charles Brackett, two of the best screenwriters ever. Set in Franz Josef's Austria (but actually shot in Canada's Jasper National Park), the film features Bing Crosby as Virgil Smith, a phonograph salesman who tries to sell the emperor (Richard Haydn) one of his machines in the hope that the rest of Austria will begin clamoring for record players. At the palace he meets the emperor's haughty niece (Joan Fontaine) and takes an immediate dislike to her. But, as often happens in movies, these two who begin by despising each other eventually fall in love. It's hokey, but the dialog is so witty and the tunes so tuneful that the basic inanity of the story can be forgiven. And it is certainly funny. The songs include "The Emperor's Waltz," "Friendly Mountains," "Get Yourself a Phonograph," "The Kiss in Your Eyes," "I Kiss Your Hand, Madame," and "The Whistler and His Dog."

p, Charles Brackett; d, Billy Wilder; w, Charles Brackett, Billy Wilder; ph, George Barnes (Technicolor); m, Victor Young.

Comedy/Musical   **(MPAA:NR)**

EMPIRE OF THE SUN

(1987) 152m Amblin Ent./WB c

Christian Bale *(Jim Graham),* John Malkovich *(Basie),* Miranda Richardson *(Mrs. Victor),* Nigel Havers *(Dr. Rawlins),* Joe Pantoliano *(Frank Demerest),* Leslie Phillips *(Maxton),* Masato Ibu *(Sgt. Nagata),* Emily Richard *(Jim's Mother),* Rupert Frazer *(Jim's Father),* Peter Gale *(Mr. Victor),* Takatoro Kataoka *(Kamikaze Boy Pilot),* Ben Stiller *(Dainty),* David Neidorf *(Tiptree),* Ralph Seymour *(Cohen),* Robert Stephens *(Mr. Lockwood),* Zhai Nai She *(Yang),* Guts Ishimatsu *(Sgt. Uchida),* Emma Piper *(Amy Matthews),* James Walker *(Mr. Radik),* Jack Dearlove *(Singing*

Prisoner), Anna Turner *(Mrs. Gilmour),* Ann Castle *(Mrs. Phillips),* Yvonne Gilan *(Mrs. Lockwood),* Ralph Michael *(Mr. Partridge),* Sybil Maas *(Mrs. Hug),* Eric Flynn, James Greene, Simon Harrison, Barrie Houghton, Paula Hamilton, Thea Ranft, Tony Boncza, Nigel Leach, Sheridan Forbes, Peter Copley, Barbara Bolton, Francesca Longrigg, Samantha Warden *(British Prisoners),* Kieron Jecchinis, Michael Crossman, Gary Parker, Ray Charleson *(American Prisoners),* Burt Kwouk *(Mr. Chen),* Tom Danaher *(Col. Marshall),* Kong-Guo-Jun *(Chinese Youth),* Takao Yamada *(Japanese Truck Driver),* Hiro Arai *(Japanese Sergeant, Airfield).*

Based on the 1984 autobiographical novel by J.G. Ballard, EMPIRE OF THE SUN explores WW II through the eyes of an adolescent boy. Jim Graham (Christian Bale) is a nine-year-old spoiled English brat who has lived his entire life in Shanghai with his aristocratic parents. His perfectly sheltered life is shattered, however, after the Japanese conquer Shanghai. Jim and his parents are separated and, along with thousands of others, are hauled off to prison camps. Now alone for the first time in his life, Jim must learn to survive on his own. Rather than the celebration of innocent wonderment found in most of his work, director Steven Spielberg here made a film about the end of innocence—a young boy thrown into adulthood and an entire generation thrown into an atomic age. EMPIRE OF THE SUN, while based on a beautifully written novel, is a story told almost exclusively through images; although famed playwright Tom Stoppard wrote the screenplay, his words are not in the movie, nor are Ballard's. Spielberg relies on the purely visual and as a result EMPIRE OF THE SUN remains true to the spirit of the novel. EMPIRE OF THE SUN is a celebration of the spirit and an affirmation of Spielberg's passion for filmmaking—a passion all too rare in cinema today.

p, Steven Spielberg, Kathleen Kennedy, Frank Marshall; d, Steven Spielberg; w, Tom Stoppard, Menno Meyjes (uncredited) (based on the novel by J.G. Ballard); ph, Allen Daviau (Technicolor); m, John Williams.

Drama/War   **Cas.**   **(MPAA:PG)**

EMPIRE STRIKES BACK, THE

(1980) 124m FOX c

Mark Hamill *(Luke Skywalker),* Harrison Ford *(Han Solo),* Carrie Fisher *(Princess Leia),* Billy Dee Williams *(Lando Calrissian),* Anthony Daniels *(C-3PO),* David Prowse *(Darth Vader),* Peter Mayhew *(Chewbacca),* Kenny Baker *(R2-D2),* Frank Oz *(Yoda),* Alec Guinness *(Ben Kenobi),* Jeremy Bulloch *(Boba Fett),* John Hollis *(Lando's Aide),* Jack Purvis *(Chief Ugnaught),* Des Webb *(Snow Creature),* Kathryn Mullen *(Performing Assistant for Yoda),* Clive Revill *(Voice of Emperor),* Kenneth Colley *(Adm. Piett),* Julian Glover *(Gen. Veers),* Michael Sheard *(Adm. Ozzel),* Michael Culver *(Capt. Needa),* John Dicks, Milton Johns, Mark Jones, Oliver Maguire, Robin Scoby *(Officers),* Bruce Boa *(Gen. Rieekan),* Christopher Malcolm *(Zev),* Dennis Lawson *(Wedge),* Richard Oldfield *(Hobbie),*

John Morton *(Dak),* Ian Liston *(Janson),* John Ratzenberger *(Maj. Derlin),* Jack McKenzie *(Deck Lieutenant),* Jerry Harte *(Head Controller),* Norman Chancer, Norwich Duff, Ray Hassett, Brigitte Kahn, Burnell Tucker *(Officers).*

In this, the second chapter of the STAR WARS trilogy, the evil Darth Vader (David Prowse) is, once again, attempting to take over the universe. The rebel forces are on the ice planet Hoth and the evil empire sends troops to wipe them out. Forced to flee, Han Solo (Harrison Ford) and Princess Leia (Carrie Fisher) regroup in Cloud City, which is run by the roguish Lando Calrissian (Billy Dee Williams). Meanwhile, Luke Skywalker (Mark Hamill) searches for and finds Yoda, a wise little creature who teaches him the finer points of the Force. The whole thing climaxes with a showdown between Luke and Darth Vader whereby some incredible plot twists are revealed. It may prove upsetting to youngsters, since the dark side of the Force has the upper hand, but this is dramatically correct, setting the stage for the triumphant return of Good in part three. Audiences at the time were a bit dismayed at being left hanging for two years, but now, through the miracle of home video, you will only have to wait a matter of minutes to see how it comes out. Nominated for three Oscars, the film won one, plus a special achievement award. Sequel: RETURN OF THE JEDI.

p, Gary Kurtz; d, Irvin Kershner; w, Leigh Brackett, Lawrence Kasdan (based on a story by George Lucas); ph, Peter Suschitzky (Panavision, Deluxe Color); m, John Williams.

Science Fiction   **Cas.**   **(MPAA:PG)**

ESCAPE TO WITCH MOUNTAIN

(1975) 97m BV c

Eddie Albert *(Jason),* Ray Milland *(Aristotle Bolt),* Donald Pleasence *(Deranian),* Kim Richards *(Tia),* Ike Eisenmann *(Tony),* Walter Barnes *(Sheriff Purdy),* Reta Shaw *(Mrs. Grindley),* Denver Pyle *(Uncle Bene),* Alfred Ryder *(Astrologer),* Lawrence Montaigne *(Ubermann),* Terry Wilson *(Biff Jenkins),* George Chandler *(Grocer),* Dermott Downs *(Truck),* Shepherd Sanders *(Guru),* Don Brodie *(Gasoline Attendant),* Paul Sorenson *(Sgt. Foss),* Alfred Rossi *(Policeman No. 3),* Tiger Joe Marsh *(Lorko),* Harry Holcombe *(Capt. Malone),* Sam Edwards *(Mate),* Dan Seymour *(Psychic),* Eugene Daniels *(Cort),* Al Dunlap *(Deputy),* Rex Holman, Tony Giorgio *(Hunters).*

Tia (Kim Richards) and Tony (Ike Eisenmann) are a pair of orphaned children with psychic powers who suffer from amnesia and cannot remember where they came from. Evil tycoon Aristotle Bolt (Ray Milland) wants to use them toward his own nefarious ends, but kindly camper Jason (Eddie Albert) comes to their rescue, learning something quite surprising about the tots in the process. Sequel: RETURN FROM WITCH MOUNTAIN.

p, Jerome Courtland; d, John Hough; w, Robert Malcolm

Young (based on a book by Alexander Key); ph, Frank Phillips (Technicolor); m, Johnny Mandel.

Science Fiction   Cas.   (MPAA:G)

EXCUSE MY DUST

(1951) 82m MGM c

Red Skelton *(Joe Belden)*, Sally Forrest *(Liz Bullitt)*, Macdonald Carey *(Cyrus Random, Jr.)*, William Demarest *(Harvey Bullitt)*, Monica Lewis *(Daisy Lou Shultzer)*, Raymond Walburn *(Mayor Fred Haskell)*, Jane Darwell *(Mrs. Belden)*, Lillian Bronson *(Mrs. Matilda Bullitt)*, Guy Anderson *(Ben Parrot)*, Paul Harvey *(Cyrus Random, Sr.)*, Marjorie Wood *(Mrs. Random)*, Lee Scott *(Horace Antler)*, Alex Gerry *(Mr. Antler)*, Jim Hayward *(Nick Tosca)*, Will Wright *(Race Judge)*, Sheree North *(Club Member)*, Ed Peil, Sr. *(2nd Man)*.

Set at the turn of the century, this comedy features Red Skelton as Joe Belden, an eccentric inventor forever tinkering with gadgets and gizmos, much to his neighbors' and relatives' chagrin. Pretty, petite Liz Bullitt (Sally Forrest) loves his strange ways, but her father (William Demarest) just thinks he's a loony (as, for the most part, he is). Moreover, he owns a livery stable and the mere thought of Joe's proposed horseless carriage drives Dad into a rage. Woven expertly into this very funny film are some delightful numbers, including a period dance piece that cleverly segues into the modern era when the participants imagine what it will be like 50 years hence. This is a delightful comedy loaded with entertaining tunes, including "Spring Is Sprung," "Lorelei Brown," "That's for the Children," "Get a Horse," "Going Steady," and "I'd Like to Take You out Dreaming." Forrest's singing voice is dubbed by Gloria Grey.

p, Jack Cummings; d, Roy Rowland; w, George Wells; ph, Alfred Gilks (Technicolor).

Comedy/Musical   (MPAA:NR)

FABULOUS WORLD OF JULES VERNE, THE

(1961, Czech.) 83m Ceskoslovensky/WB bw (VYNALEZ ZKAZY)

Louis Tock *(Simon Hart)*, Ernest Navara *(Prof. Roche)*, Milo Holl *(Artigas)*, Francis Sherr *(Pirate Captain)*, Van Kissling *(Serke)*, Jane Zalata *(Jana)*.

A poetic re-creation of the atmosphere of Jules Verne's mystical novels—particularly *The Deadly Invention*—this Czech feature draws its remarkable visual style from the early works of film magician Georges Melies. Mixing live action with the 19th-century engravings that accompanied Verne's novels, the animators have come up with a technique they called "Mystimation." The story concerns the kidnaping of a scientist by pirates who want to exploit his knowledge of explosives. Originally released in 1958 in Czechoslovakia, the film was brought to the States by producer Joseph E. Levine, who tagged on an introduction by Hugh Downs.

p, Joseph E. Levine; d, Karel Zeman; w, Karel Zeman, Francis Gross, Milan Vacca (based on the novels of Jules Verne); ph, George Taran, B.S. Piccard, Anthony Hora; m, Sydney Fox.

Fantasy   Cas.   (MPAA:NR)

FANTASIA

(1940) 120m Disney/RKO c

Deems Taylor *(Himself)*, Leopold Stokowski and the Philadelphia Symphony Orchestra *(Themselves)*.

The most impressive animated feature ever to come out of the Disney studios, FANTASIA integrates great works of classical music with extraordinarily imaginative visuals that run the gamut from dancing hippos to the purely abstract. Among the wonderful combinations of sight and sound are J.S. Bach's "Toccata and Fugue in D Minor," Tchaikovsky's "Nutcracker Suite" (danced to by fairies, mushrooms, flower petals, fish, thistles, and orchids), Stravinsky's "Rite of Spring" (illustrated as the genesis of the planet), Mussorgsky's "Night on Bald Mountain" (whose Black God, Tchernobog, was pantomimed by Bela Lugosi for the Disney artists), and Schubert's "Ave Maria." Beethoven's "Pastoral Symphony" proved to be the most controversial segment, raising the hackles of music critics who didn't approve of the cartoon Bacchus, nymphs, and centaurs who accompanied it. The film's most famous segment, Paul Dukas' "Sorcerer's Apprentice," stars Mickey Mouse as the ambitious assistant who gets in way over his head when he uses his boss' magic hat to put a broom to work doing his chores. Originally intended as a short, "The Sorcerer's Apprentice" brought together Walt Disney and famed conductor Leopold Stokowski, but when the production ran over budget, Disney decided that the only way to recoup his investment would be to incorporate the segment into a feature. The film began to appear in limited roadshow engagements in 1940, but due to wartime difficulties in getting the materials for the sound system that had to be installed in each theater, it was not until 1942 that it received general release. In the late 1960s FANTASIA reemerged as a cult favorite and it continues to delight both children and adults today.

p, Walt Disney; d, Samuel Armstrong, James Algar, Paul Dukas, Bill Roberts, Paul Satterfield, Hamilton Luske, Jim Handley, Ford Beebe, T. Hee [Walt Disney], Norman Ferguson, Wilfred Jackson; m, Johann Sebastian Bach, Peter Ilich Tchaikovsky, Igor Stravinsky, Ludwig van Beethoven, Amilcare Ponchielli, Modest Mussorgsky, Franz Schubert.

Animation   (MPAA:NR)

FANTASTIC VOYAGE

(1966) 100m FOX c (AKA: MICROSCOPIA; STRANGE JOURNEY)

Stephen Boyd *(Grant)*, Raquel Welch *(Cora Peterson)*, Edmond O'Brien *(Gen. Carter)*, Donald Pleasence *(Dr. Michaels)*, Arthur O'Connell *(Col. Donald Reid)*, William Redfield *(Capt. Bill Owens)*, Arthur Kennedy *(Dr. Duval)*, Jean Del Val *(Jan Benes)*, Barry Coe *(Communications Aide)*, Ken Scott *(Secret Serviceman)*, Shelby Grant *(Nurse)*, James Brolin *(Technician)*, Brendan Fitzgerald *(Wireless Operator)*.

A medical crew (Stephen Boyd, Raquel Welch, William Redfield, Arthur Kennedy, and Donald Pleasence) and a submarine are miniaturized to remove a blood clot from the brain of a Czech scientist who was shot while defecting. Once shrunk and inside the body, the crew battle white corpuscles, while the heart and lungs also make their journey rougher. Early on, it becomes apparent that one of the crew members is a double agent, and matters become even more complex as they race against the clock to complete their mission before returning to normal size. Their voyage through the body's bloodstream, past different organs, is created by inventive special effects that make this one of the more visually interesting science-fiction films.

p, Saul David; d, Richard Fleischer; w, Harry Kleiner, David Duncan (based on the novel by Otto Klement and Jay Lewis Bixby); ph, Ernest Laszlo (CinemaScope, Deluxe Color); m, Leonard Rosenman.

Science Fiction   **Cas.**   **(MPAA:NR)**

FARMER'S DAUGHTER, THE

(1947) 96m RKO bw

Loretta Young *(Katrin Holstrom)*, Joseph Cotten *(Glenn Morley)*, Ethel Barrymore *(Mrs. Morley)*, Charles Bickford *(Clancy)*, Rose Hobart *(Virginia)*, Rhys Williams *(Adolph)*, Harry Davenport *(Dr. Mathew Sutven)*, Tom Powers *(Nordick)*, William Harrigan *(Ward Hughes)*, Lex Barker *(Olaf Holstrom)*, Harry Shannon *(Mr. Holstrom)*, Keith Andes *(Sven Holstrom)*, Thurston Hall *(Wilbur Johnson)*, Art Baker *(A.J. Finley)*, Don Beddoe *(Einar)*, James [James Arness] Aurness *(Peter Holstrom)*, Anna Q. Nilsson *(Mrs. Holstrom)*, Sven Hugo Borg *(Dr. Mattsen)*, John Gallaudet *(Van)*, William B. Davidson *(Eckers)*, Charles McGraw *(Fisher)*, Jason Robards *(Night Editor)*, Cy Kendall *(Sweeney)*, Frank Ferguson *(Mattemack)*, William Bakewell *(Windor)*, Charles Lane *(Jackson, Reporter)*, Douglas Evans *(Silbey, Politician)*, Robert Clarke *(Assistant Announcer)*, Bess Flowers *(Woman)*.

This winning Capraesque romantic comedy features Loretta Young as Katrin Holstrom, a Swedish farmer's daughter who comes to the capital in search of a nursing job but eventually becomes the maid for Congressman Glenn Morley (Joseph Cotten) and his powerful politico mother (Ethel Barrymore). Katrin is the perfect housekeeper in almost every way, but when the Morleys try to promote the Congressional candidacy of a man Katrin can't abide, she speaks out publicly and ends up as the rival party's candidate for the office. Young won an Academy Award for her delightful performance and Charles Bickford received a Best Supporting Actor Oscar nomination for his role as the butler who shows Katrin the ropes.

p, Dore Schary; d, H.C. Potter; w, Allen Rivkin, Laura Kerr (based on the play "Hulda, Daughter of Parliament" by Juhni Tervataa); ph, Milton Krasner; m, Leigh Harline.

Comedy/Romance   **Cas.**   **(MPAA:NR)**

FATHER GOOSE

(1964) 115m UNIV c

Cary Grant *(Walter Eckland)*, Leslie Caron *(Catherine Freneau)*, Trevor Howard *(Commodore Frank Houghton)*, Jack Good *(Lt. Stebbins)*, Verina Greenlaw *(Christine)*, Pip Sparke *(Anne)*, Jennifer Berrington *(Harriet)*, Stephanie Berrington *(Elizabeth)*, Laurelle Felsette *(Angelique)*, Nicole Felsette *(Dominique)*, Sharyl Locke *(Jenny)*, Simon Scott *(Submarine Captain)*, John Napier *(Submarine Executive)*, Richard Lupino *(Radioman)*, Alex Finlayson *(Doctor)*, Peter Forster *(Chaplain)*, Don Spruance *(Navigator)*, Ken Swofford *(Helmsman)*.

Playing against his sophisticated image, Cary Grant essays the role of Walter Eckland, a drunken beach bum who has been sitting out WW II on a South Seas island but is coerced by an Australian naval officer (Trevor Howard) into monitoring Japanese air activity. When Eckland travels to a nearby island to rescue another plane watcher, he finds the observer dead, but schoolteacher Catherine Freneau (Leslie Caron) and her seven young female charges very much alive after being marooned when their plane went down. They return with Eckland and clean up his act while he and Caron fall in love. Danger looms, however, as the Japanese forces close in. Grant's penultimate film, this romantic comedy won Best Screenplay Oscars for Frank Tarloff and Peter Stone, who worked on the script separately but were awarded a shared credit by a Writers Guild arbitration.

p, Robert Arthur; d, Ralph Nelson; w, Frank Tarloff, Peter Stone (based on the story "A Place of Dragons" by S.H. Barnett); ph, Charles Lang, Jr. (Technicolor); m, Cy Coleman.

Comedy/War   **Cas.**   **(MPAA:NR)**

FATHER'S LITTLE DIVIDEND

(1951) 82m MGM bw

Spencer Tracy *(Stanley Banks)*, Joan Bennett *(Ellie Banks)*, Elizabeth Taylor *(Kay Dunstan)*, Don Taylor *(Buckley Dunstan)*, Billie Burke *(Doris Dunstan)*, Moroni Olsen *(Herbert Dunstan)*, Richard Rober *(Police Sergeant)*, Marietta Canty *(Delilah)*, Rusty Tamblyn *(Tommy Banks)*, Tom Irish *(Ben Banks)*, Hayden Rorke *(Dr. Andrew Nordell)*, Paul Harvey *(Rev. Galsworthy)*, Frank Faylen *(Policeman)*, Beverly Thompson *(Nurse)*, Dabbs Greer *(Taxi Driver)*, Robert B. Williams *(Officer)*, Frank

Sully *(Diaper Man)*, James Menzies *(Mike)*, Thomas Menzies *(Red)*, Harry Hines *(Old Man)*, Nancy Valentine, Wendy Waldron *(Bridesmaids)*, Lon Poff *(Elderly Man on Porch)*, George Bruggeman *(Gym Instructor)*, Donald Clark *(The Dividend)*.

Spencer Tracy could hold his own acting opposite anyone, and in this excellent sequel to FATHER OF THE BRIDE (1950) he proves that not even a baby can upstage him. Tracy reprises his role as Stanley Banks, who, with his sons away at school and his daughter, Kay (Elizabeth Taylor), recently married, is finally ready for the good life with his wife (Joan Bennett). However, in no time Kay is expecting, and Stanley finds himself a most reluctant grandfather. The going gets a little rough when Tracy and Bennett and their in-laws don't see eye to eye on grandparenting, but everything turns out for the best in this comedy penned by the husband-and-wife screenwriting team of Frances Goodrich and Albert Hackett (THE DIARY OF ANNE FRANK, A CERTAIN SMILE, SEVEN BRIDES FOR SEVEN BROTHERS). Taylor was divorcing her first husband (hotel chain heir Nicky Hilton) at the time of the film's release and the resultant publicity helped at the box office.

p, Pandro S. Berman; d, Vincente Minnelli; w, Frances Goodrich, Albert Hackett (based on characters created by Edward Streeter); ph, John Alton; m, Albert Sendrey.

Comedy   Cas.   **(MPAA:NR)**

FEARLESS FAGAN

(1952) 79m MGM bw

Janet Leigh *(Abby Ames)*, Carleton Carpenter *(Pvt. Floyd Hilston)*, Keenan Wynn *(Sgt. Kellwin)*, Richard Anderson *(Capt. Daniels)*, Ellen Corby *(Mrs. Ardley)*, Barbara Ruick *(Nurse)*, John Call *(Mr. Ardley)*, Robert Burton *(Owen Gillman)*, Wilton Graff *(Col. Horne)*, Parley Baer *(Emil Tauchnitz)*, Jonathan Cott *(Cpl. Geft)*.

This enjoyable, well-written comedy focuses on a young draftee with a special problem: Pvt. Floyd Hilston (Carleton Carpenter) has grown up with a lion, named Fagan, as his pet, and the strong bond between them is not easily broken. Not wanting to sell his pet to a cruel circus trainer, Hilston asks his sergeant (Keenan Wynn) to help him find Fagan a home. The sergeant thinks it's a joke until the lion gets out of his cage and the Army is forced to send out search parties to recover him. With the help of Army publicity, the soldier is able to find a good home for his pet, but the big cat escapes again and causes havoc during troop maneuvers.

p, Edwin H. Knopf; d, Stanley Donen; w, Charles Lederer, Frederick Hazlitt Brennan (based on a story by Sidney Franklin, Jr., and Eldon W. Griffiths); ph, Harold Lipstein.

Comedy   **(MPAA:NR)**

FIGHTING PRINCE OF DONEGAL, THE

(1966, Brit.) 110m BV c

Peter McEnery *(Hugh O'Donnell)*, Susan Hampshire *(Kathleen MacSweeney)*, Tom Adams *(Henry O'Neill)*, Gordon Jackson *(Capt. Leeds)*, Andrew Keir *(Lord MacSweeney, Clan Leader)*, Maurice Roeves *(Martin, Prison Boy)*, Donal McCann *(Sean O'Toole, Prisoner)*, Richard Leech *(Phelim O'Toole, O'Neill Clan Leader)*, Peter Jeffrey *(Troop Sergeant)*, Marie Kean *(Mother)*, Bill Owen *(1st Officer Powell)*, Peggy Marshall *(Princess Ineen)*, Fidelma Murphy *(Moire)*, Maire O'Neill, Maire Ni Ghrainne *(Moire's Sisters)*, Norman Wooland *(Sir John Perrott)*, John Forbes-Robertson, Patrick Holt, Robert Cawdron, Roger Croucher, Keith McConnell, Inigo Jackson, Peter Cranwell.

Set in 16th-century Ireland, this lavish Disney swashbuckler hinges on the heroic attempts by Hugh O'Donnell (Peter McEnery), the newly crowned Prince of Donegal, to make good on the prophecy that "When Hugh succeeds Hugh, Ireland shall be free." In the process of uniting the Irish clans, Red Hugh falls in love with the daughter of one of his compatriots (Susan Hampshire) and is captured by the British, who imprison him in Dublin Castle. After a daring escape, Hugh and two of his comrades endeavor to liberate Donegal Castle, where his roguish English nemesis (Gordon Jackson) holds Hugh's true love.

p, Walt Disney, Bill Anderson; d, Michael O'Herlihy; w, Robert Westerby (based on the novel *Red Hugh, Prince of Donegal* by Robert T. Reilly); ph, Arthur Ibbetson (Technicolor); m, George Bruns.

Adventure   Cas.   **(MPAA:NR)**

FIGHTING 69TH, THE

(1940) 90m WB bw

James Cagney *(Jerry Plunkett)*, Pat O'Brien *(Father Duffy)*, George Brent *(Wild Bill Donovan)*, Jeffrey Lynn *(Joyce Kilmer)*, Alan Hale *(Sgt. Big Mike Wynn)*, Frank McHugh *("Crepe Hanger" Burke)*, Dennis Morgan *(Lt. Ames)*, William Lundigan *(Timmy Wynn)*, Dick Foran *(John Wynn)*, Guinn "Big Boy" Williams *(Paddy Dolan)*, Henry O'Neill *(The Colonel)*, John Litel *(Capt. Mangan)*, Sammy Cohen *(Mike Murphy)*, Harvey Stephens *(Maj. Anderson)*, William Hopper *(Pvt. Turner)*, Tom Dugan *(Pvt. McManus)*, George Reeves *(Jack O'Keefe)*, Charles Trowbridge *(Chaplain Holmes)*, Frank Wilcox *(Lt. Norman)*, Herbert Anderson *(Casey)*, J. Anthony Hughes *(Healey)*, Frank Mayo *(Capt. Bootz)*, John Harron *(Carroll)*, George Kilgen *(Ryan)*, Richard Clayton *(Tierney)*, Edward Dew *(Regan)*, Wilfred Lucas, Joseph Crehan, Emmett Vogan *(Doctors)*, Frank Sully *(Sergeant)*, James Flavin *(Supply Sergeant)*, George O'Hanlon *(Eddie)*, Jack Perrin *(Major)*.

One of the great patriotic films, THE FIGHTING 69TH offers James Cagney in a tour de force performance as Jerry Plunkett, a wisecracking would-be hero from Brooklyn who joins the all-Irish 69th New York regiment during WW I. After boasting his way through training camp, Plunkett panics when he actually comes under fire in France, and his cowardice brings about the deaths of scores of doughboys. Sentenced to death by a court martial, Plunkett is freed from confinement by an exploding enemy shell and rushes to the front, where he proves his mettle, heroically staving off a German attack with a mortar. Pat O'Brien gives one of his finest performances as Father Duffy, the famous battlefield priest whose statue stands in Times Square and whose "Holy Joe" message is rejected and then embraced by Plunkett. Featuring a terrific supporting cast, a touching, funny script, inspired direction by William Keighley, and virtuoso camerawork by Tony Gaudio, THE FIGHTING 69TH was an enormous hit for Warner Bros., who rightly assumed that the U.S. public, close to entering WW II, would respond well to a solid patriotic film. Warners spent a fortune on this marvelous production, which beat rival Fox to the punch. When Warners launched its Cagney film, Fox abandoned its own version of the story, tentatively titled "Father Duffy of the Fighting 69th."

p, Jack L. Warner; d, William Keighley; w, Norman Reilly Raine, Fred Niblo, Jr., Dean Franklin; ph, Tony Gaudio; m, Adolph Deutsch.

War **(MPAA:NR)**

FITZWILLY

(1967) 102m UA c (GB: FITZWILLY STRIKES BACK)

Dick Van Dyke (Fitzwilliam), Barbara Feldon (Juliet Nowell), Edith Evans (Victoria Woodworth), John McGiver (Albert), Harry Townes (Mr. Nowell), John Fiedler (Mr. Dunne), Norman Fell (Oderblatz), Cecil Kellaway (Buckmaster), Stephen Strimpell (Byron Casey), Anne Seymour (Grimsby), Helen Kleeb (Mrs. Mortimer), Sam Waterston (Oliver), Paul Reed (Prettikin), Albert Carrier (Pierre), Nelson Olmsted (Simmons), Dennis Cooney (Adams), Noam Pitlik (Charles), Antony Eustrel (Garland), Laurence Naismith (Cotty), Karen Norris (Kitty), Patience Cleveland (Dolly), Lew Brown (Frank), Monroe Arnold (Goldfarb), Bob Williams (Ryan), Billy Halop (Restaurant Owner).

Dick Van Dyke plays the title role in this entertaining Delbert Mann-helmed comedy. Fitzwilly is the devoted butler of the elderly Victoria Woodworth (Edith Evans) who, regrettably, isn't as rich as she thinks she is. To maintain her illusion of wealth, Fitzwilly and the rest of the servants pull off a score of robberies.

p, Walter Mirisch; d, Delbert Mann; w, Isobel Lennart (based on the novel A Garden of Cucumbers by Poyntz Tyler); ph, Joseph Biroc (Panavision, Deluxe Color); m, Johnny Williams.

Comedy **(MPAA:NR)**

FIVE LITTLE PEPPERS AND HOW THEY GREW

(1939) 58m COL bw

Edith Fellows (Polly Pepper), Clarence Kolb (Mr. King), Dorothy Peterson (Mrs. Pepper), Ronald Sinclair (Jasper), Charles Peck (Ben Pepper), Tommy Bond (Joey Pepper), Jimmy Leake (Davie Pepper), Dorothy Ann Seese (Phronsie Pepper), Leonard Carey (Martin), Bruce Bennett (Chauffeur), Paul Everton (Townsend), George Lloyd

(Truck Driver), Edward Le Saint (Dr. Emery), Linda Winters [Dorothy Comingore] (Nurse), Harry Hayden (Dr. Spence), Betty Roadman (Cook), Bessie Wade (Asst. Cook), Harry Bernard (Caretaker), Maurice Costello (Hart), Flo Campbell (Woman).

This fine entry from the "Five Little Peppers" series finds Polly (Edith Fellows), the oldest of the Pepper kids, taking care of the rest of the clan while Mrs. Pepper (Dorothy Peterson) works at a factory. Polly is befriended by Jasper (Ronald Sinclair), a rich boy who sneaks over to play with the Peppers. When the youngest Pepper gets the measles, Jasper and his grandfather, Mr. King (Clarence Kolb), are stuck in the quarantined house. Polly collapses from too much work, and King moves the whole family to his mansion. Things turn even brighter when it's discovered that Polly has inherited controlling shares in a mine that King wants to buy. Wouldn't you like to be a Pepper, too?

p, Jack Fier; d, Charles Barton; w, Nathalie Bucknall, Jefferson Parker (based on the novel by Margaret Sidney); ph, Henry Freulich.

Comedy/Drama **(MPAA:NR)**

5,000 FINGERS OF DR. T, THE

(1953) 89m COL c

Peter Lind Hayes (Zabladowski), Mary Healy (Mrs. Collins), Hans Conried (Dr. Terwilliker), Tommy Rettig (Bart), John Heasley (Uncle Whitney), Robert Heasley (Uncle Judson), Noel Cravat (Sgt. Lunk), Henry Kulky (Stroogo).

In this excellent surrealistic children's film (cowritten by Ted Geisel, better known as Dr. Seuss), Bart (Tommy Rettig) is a young boy who would rather play baseball than take piano lessons with his teacher, Dr. Terwilliker (Hans Conried). The boy dreams he's being chased by weird creatures with butterfly nets through a land of fog, cylinders, and odd-shaped mounds. He stumbles upon the castle of Dr. T, who runs a piano school for 500 captive boys. In the dungeon Dr. T keeps creatures who have grown green and moldy, put there for playing instruments other than the piano. The prisoners have built musical instruments out of odd materials and, in the best sequence of the film, perform a strange ballet. Bart, with the help of Zabladowski (Peter Lind Hayes), fights off two men on roller skates who are connected by their beards. The two also build a bomb that absorbs sound waves, and help Bart's mother escape from Dr. T's bizarre world.

p, Stanley Kramer; d, Roy Rowland; w, Ted Geisel [Dr. Seuss], Allan Scott; ph, Franz Planer (Technicolor); m, Frederick Hollander.

Fantasy/Musical **(MPAA:NR)**

FLASH GORDON

(1936) 97m UNIV bw (AKA: ROCKET SHIP, SPACESHIP TO THE UNKNOWN, SPACE SOLDIERS, ATOMIC ROCKETSHIP)

Larry "Buster" Crabbe (Flash Gordon), Jean Rogers

(Dale Arden), Charles Middleton *(Ming the Merciless),* Priscilla Lawson *(Princess Aura),* John Lipson *(King Vultan),* Richard Alexander *(Prince Barin),* Frank Shannon *(Dr. Zarkov),* Duke York, Jr. *(King Kala),* Earl Askam *(Officer Torch),* George Cleveland *(Prof. Hensley),* Theodore Lorch *(High Priest),* House Peters, Jr. *(Shark Man),* James Pierce *(King Thun),* Muriel Goodspeed *(Zona),* Richard Tucker *(Flash Gordon, Sr.),* Fred Kohler, Jr., Lane Chandler, Al Ferguson, Glenn Strange *(Soldiers).*

The one, the only, the original, and the best, this started as a 13-part serial shown weekly in movie houses during the 1930s. King Features' comic strip hero Flash Gordon (Olympic swimmer Buster Crabbe) and his companion, Dr. Zarkov (Frank Shannon), along with Flash's sweetheart Dale Arden (Jean Rogers), blast off to planet Mongo, trying to stop it from colliding with Earth. There Flash encounters evil Ming the Merciless (Charles Middleton, of bald head and cruel mustache) along with assorted hawk men, shark men, dinosaurs, horned gorillas, giant lobsters, space ships on none-too-subtle wires, and some nifty costumes. There's a great love triangle with Ming the Merciless lusting wantonly after Dale, while Princess Aura (Priscilla Lawson), Ming's outerspace daughter, has a heavy crush on Flash. The music and some sets were borrowed from THE BRIDE OF FRANKENSTEIN, released a year earlier. Great fun and not to be missed.

p, Henry MacRae; d, Frederick Stephani; w, Frederick Stephani, George Plympton, Basil Dickey, Ella O'Neill (based on the comic strip by Alex Raymond); ph, Jerry Ash, Richard Fryer; m, Franz Waxman.

Science Fiction **(MPAA:NR)**

FLIGHT OF THE DOVES

(1971) 101m COL c

Ron Moody *(Hawk Dove),* Jack Wild *(Finn Dove),* Dorothy McGuire *(Granny O'Flaherty),* Stanley Holloway *(Judge Liffy),* Helen Raye *(Derval Dove),* William Rushton *(Tobias Cromwell),* Dana *(Sheila),* John Molloy *(Mickser),* Barry Keegan *(Powder),* Brendan O'Reilly *(Michael),* Emmett Bergin *(Paddy),* Noel Purcell *(Rabbi),* Nial O'Brian *(Joe),* Ronnie Walsh *(Inspector Town),* Brenda Cauldwell *(Club Manager),* Thomas Hickey *(Garda Pat Flynn),* Tom Irwin, Joe Cahill, Clara Mullen, Des Keogh.

The engaging FLIGHT OF THE DOVES follows the adventures of a pair of adorable youngsters who are running away from their cruel British stepfather to the security of their Irish grandmother. Hawk Dove (Ron Moody)—the heir to a fortune if the kids fail to survive—tries to track the tots, who are beneficiaries to the grandfather's will. FLIGHT OF THE DOVES is especially entertaining for the younger set, though some of the production numbers may be less interesting for adults. Shot on location in Ireland, with an international cast, two of whom may be familiar to American audiences: Moody and Jack Wild were, respectively, Fagin and The Artful Dodger in the film version of the musical OLIVER! (1968).

p&d, Ralph Nelson; w, Frank Gabrielson, Ralph Nelson (based on a book by Walter Macken); ph, Harry Waxman; m, Roy Budd.

Adventure **(MPAA:G)**

FLIGHT OF THE NAVIGATOR

(1986) 90m PSO/Disney-BV c

Joey Cramer *(David Freeman),* Veronica Cartwright *(Helen Freeman),* Cliff De Young *(Bill Freeman),* Sarah Jessica Parker *(Carolyn McAdams),* Matt Adler *(Jeff, Age 16),* Howard Hesseman *(Dr. Faraday),* Paul Mall *(Max),* Robert Small *(Troy),* Albie Whitaker *(Jeff, Age 8),* Jonathan Sanger *(Dr. Carr),* Iris Acker *(Mrs. Howard),* Richard Liberty *(Mr. Howard),* Raymond Forchion *(Detective Banks),* Cynthia Caquelin *(Woman Officer),* Ted Bartsch *(Night Guard Brayton),* Gizelle Elliot *(Female Technician),* Brigid Cleary, Michael Strano *(Technicians),* Parris Buckner, Robyn Peterson *(Scientists),* Tony Tracy *(Observation Guard),* Philip Hoelcher *(NASA Officer),* Julio Mechoso, Butch Raymond *(Hangar Guards),* Bob Strickland, Michael Brockman *(Control Room Guards),* Louis Cutolo, Debbie Casperson *(Radar Technicians),* Chase Randolph *(Lt. King),* John Archie, Tony Calvino *(Agents),* Rusty Pouch *(Gas Station Attendant),* Robert Goodman *(Tourist Man),* Ryan Murray *(Tourist Child),* Keri Rogers *(Jennifer Bradley),* Peter Lundquist, Jill Beach *(Newscasters),* Kenny Davis *(Kid in Mustang),* Bruce Laks *(Bixby),* Arnie Ross, Fritz Braumer *(NASA Technicians).*

This charming Disney fantasy revolves around the extraordinary experiences of 12-year-old David Freeman (Joey Cramer), who, in 1978, falls into a ravine and is knocked unconscious. When he comes to, it's 1986, and while he is still 12 years old, his little brother is now his big brother. The folks at NASA are convinced that there is a connection between David's disappearance and the recent discovery of an alien spacecraft, and, using space-age technology, they discover heretofore unseen star charts imprinted on David's brain. Escaping from NASA, David is called to the spaceship that carried him away eight years previously and that was trying to take him home when its computer malfunctioned. With David aboard, the spacecraft takes off, and MAX, the HAL-like computer that operates the ship (given its voice and sense of humor by the uncredited Paul Reubens, aka Pee Wee Herman), uses the star charts in David's brain to plot its return voyage. Randal Kleiser (THE BLUE LAGOON; GREASE) provides a steady directorial hand for this film, which was being shot in Florida when the space shuttle disaster took place.

p, Robby Wald, Dimitri Villard; d, Randal Kleiser; w, Michael Burton, Matt MacManus (based on a story by Mark H. Baker); ph, James Glennon (Technicolor); m, Alan Silvestri.

Fantasy **Cas.** **(MPAA:PG)**

FLIPPER

(1963) 87m MGM c

Chuck Connors *(Porter Ricks)*, Luke Halpin *(Sandy Ricks)*, Connie Scott *(Kim Parker)*, Jane Rose *(Hettie White)*, Joe Higgins *(Mr. L.C. Porett)*, Robertson White *(Mr. Abrams)*, George Applewhite *(Sheriff Rogers)*, Kathleen Maguire *(Martha Ricks)*, Mitzi the Dolphin *(Flipper)*.

Youngster Sandy Ricks (Luke Halpin) nurses Flipper back to health after a spear is removed from the dolphin; however, Sandy's father (Chuck Connors) insists that Flipper be released from his tank and returned to his natural home. Sandy is understandably upset by the news, but Flipper proves his loyalty when he comes back and saves Sandy from sharks, providing some exciting underwater action. Highly recommended for kids, FLIPPER brings new life to the boy-and-his-trustworthy-pet formula.

p, Ivan Tors; d, James B. Clark; w, Arthur Weiss (based on a story by Ricou Browning and Jack Cowden); ph, Lamar Boren, Joseph Brun (Metrocolor); m, Henry Vars.

Drama **Cas.** **(MPAA:NR)**

FLIPPER'S NEW ADVENTURE

(1964) 92m MGM c (AKA: FLIPPER AND THE PIRATES)

Luke Halpin *(Sandy)*, Pamela Franklin *(Penny)*, Helen Cherry *(Julia)*, Tom Helmore *(Sir Halsey Hopewell)*, Francesca Annis *(Gwen)*, Brian Kelly *(Porter Ricks)*, Joe Higgins *(L.C. Porett)*, Lloyd Battista *(Gill)*, Gordon Dilworth *(Sea Captain)*, Courtney Brown, William Cooley *(Convicts)*, Dan Chandler *(Coast Guard Commander)*, Ricou Browning *(Dr. Clark Burton)*, Robert Baldwin, Ric O'Feldman *(Veterinarians)*, Susie the Dolphin *(Flipper)*.

This entertaining boy-and-his-dolphin sequel to FLIPPER takes Sandy Ricks (Luke Halpin) and his finned friend to a remote island in the Bahamas. There the two get mixed up with a gang that is holding a wealthy British family captive, and Flipper performs his usual ocean acrobatics in the service of Sandy and his new girl friend (Pamela Franklin). Not long after the release of this film, Flipper began delighting young fans on the TV series that starred Brian Kelly, who plays Sandy's dad here.

p, Ivan Tors; d, Leon Benson; w, Art Arthur (based on a story by Ivan Tors, from characters created by Ricou Browning, Jack Cowden); ph, Lamar Boren (Metrocolor); m, Henry Vars.

Drama **(MPAA:NR)**

FLUFFY

(1965) 92m UNIV c

Tony Randall *(Daniel Potter)*, Shirley Jones *(Janice)*, Edward Andrews *(Griswald)*, Howard Morris *(Sweeney)*, Ernest Truex *(Claridge)*, Jim Backus *(Sergeant)*, Frank Faylen *(Catfish)*, Celia Kaye *(Sally Brighton)*, Dick Sargent *(Tommy)*, Adam Roarke *(Bob Brighton)*, Whit Bissell *(Dr. Braden)*, Harriet MacGibbon *(Mrs. Claridge)*, Jim

Boles *(Pete)*, Parley Baer *(Police Captain)*, Connie Gilchrist *(Maid)*, Stuart Randall *(State Trooper)*, Sammee Tong *(Cook)*, Barry O'Hara *(Fireman No. 2)*, Sam Gilman *(Policeman)*, Milton Frome *(Tweedy Physicist)*, Doodles Weaver *(Yokel)*.

Scientist Daniel Potter (Tony Randall) domesticates Fluffy, a lion, to prove that even the wildest of animals can be kept as pets if they are trained properly. Needless to say, the mere sight of a lion sends Potter's fellow citizens, including the police, into a panic. Potter hides out in a hotel, where the owner's daughter (Shirley Jones) falls in love with both lion and master. Other notables who appear in this light hearted Disneyesque romp include Jim Backus as the police sergeant and Dick Sargent of TV's "Bewitched."

p, Gordon Kay; d, Earl Bellamy; w, Samuel Roeca; ph, Clifford Stine (Eastmancolor); m, Irving Gertz.

Comedy **(MPAA:NR)**

FLYING DEUCES, THE

(1939) 67m RKO bw

Stan Laurel *(Stan)*, Oliver Hardy *(Ollie)*, Jean Parker *(Georgette)*, Reginald Gardiner *(Francois)*, Charles Middleton *(Commandant)*, Jean Del Val *(Sergeant)*, Clem Wilenchick, Crane Whitley *(Corporals)*, James Finlayson *(Jailer)*, Richard Cramer *(Truck Driver)*, Michael Visaroff *(Innkeeper)*, Monica Bannister, Bonnie Bannon, Mary Jane Carey, Christine Cabanne *(Georgette's Girl Friends)*, Frank Clarke *(Pilot)*, Eddie Borden, Sam Lufkin *(Legionnaires Knocked Out by Corks)*, Kit Guard, Billy Engle, Jack Chefe *(Other Legionnaires)*.

Based loosely on the French film THE TWO ACES, this amusing Laurel and Hardy comedy casts the boys as Iowa fishmongers who travel to Paris and join the French Foreign Legion after Ollie is jilted by a waitress. Once in the famous fighting force, the boys become the victims of a series of comic mishaps, and when they attempt to desert, they are captured and condemned to death. They escape in an airplane and go on a mad ride through the skies until the plane crashes, and Hardy is reincarnated as a horse, while Laurel emerges totally unscathed. One of the film's cowriters was baby-faced Harry Langdon, who was in between pictures as an actor. Another silent film veteran, James Finlayson—who could get more laughs with a squint than most actors could get with a full page of dialog—has a small role as a prison jailer.

p, Boris Morros; d, A. Edward Sutherland; w, Ralph Spence, Alfred Schiller, Charles Rogers, Harry Langdon; ph, Art Lloyd; m, John Leopold, Leo Shuken.

Comedy **Cas.** **(MPAA:NR)**

FOLLOW ME, BOYS!

(1966) 131m Disney/BV c

Fred MacMurray *(Lemuel Siddons)*, Vera Miles *(Vida Downey)*, Lillian Gish *(Hetty Seibert)*, Charlie Ruggles *(John Everett Hughes)*, Elliott Reid *(Ralph Hastings)*, Kurt

Russell *(Whitey),* Luana Patten *(Nora White),* Ken Murray *(Melody Murphy),* Donald May *(Edward White, Jr.),* Sean McClory *(Edward White, Sr.),* Steve Franken *(POW Lieutenant),* Parley Baer *(Mayor Hi Plommer),* William Reynolds *(Hoodoo Henderson as a Man),* Craig Hill *(Leo as a Man),* Tol Avery *(Dr. Ferris),* Willis Bouchey *(Judge),* John Zaremba *(Ralph's Lawyer),* Madge Blake *(Cora Anderson),* Carl Reindel *(Tank Captain),* Hank Brandt *(Frankie Martin as a Man),* Richard Bakalyan *(Umpire),* Tim McIntire *(Corporal),* Willie Soo Hoo *(Quong Lee as a Man),* Tony Regan *(Hetty's Lawyer),* Robert B. Williams *(Artie),* Jimmy Murphy *(1st POW Soldier),* Adam Williams *(POW Sergeant),* Dean Moray *(Hoodoo Henderson).*

In a charming role, Fred MacMurray plays an ordinary fellow who packs up his saxophone and relocates in the country, where he plays melodies for the local Boy Scout troop. He soon wins over one of the town beauties (Vera Miles), who becomes his wife and understands his devotion to the kids. The highlight of the film, however, is the appearance of Lillian Gish as an eccentric and dainty rich lady. Disney sweetness abounds.

p, Walt Disney; d, Norman Tokar; w, Louis Pelletier (based on the book *God and My Country* by MacKinlay Kantor); ph, Clifford Stine (Technicolor); m, George Bruns.

Drama   **Cas.**   **(MPAA:NR)**

FOR THE LOVE OF BENJI

(1977) 85m Mulberry Square c

Higgins the Dog *(Benji),* Patsy Garrett *(Mary),* Cynthia Smith *(Cindy),* Allen Fiuzat *(Paul),* Ed Nelson *(Chandler Dietrich),* Art Vasil *(Stelios),* Peter Bowles *(Ronald),* Bridget Armstrong *(Elizabeth),* Mihalis Lambrinos *(Man in Baggage Room).*

As far as children's entertainment goes, you can't beat a good dog story for providing the necessary assortment of thrills. FOR THE LOVE OF BENJI fits the bill with one of the most expressive dogs (and actors, for that matter) to come out of Hollywood. The adorable canine in this film is a 2-year-old look-alike replacement for the original Benji. While in Greece, Benji is drugged and kidnaped by Chandler Dietrich (Ed Nelson), who imprints a coded message on the pooch's paw. Benji then proceeds to wander through Greece, getting in and out of trouble while eluding crooks. A great one for the kids.

p, Ven Vaughn; d&w, Joe Camp (based on a story by Ven Vaughn and Joe Camp); ph, Don Reddy (CFI Color); m, Euel Box.

Adventure   **Cas.**   **(MPAA:G)**

FOREVER YOUNG, FOREVER FREE

(1976, South Africa) 87m Film Trust-Milton Okun/UNIV c

Jose Ferrer *(Father Alberto),* Karen Valentine *(Carol Anne),* Bess Finney *(Sister Marguerita),* Muntu Ndebele *(Tsepo),* Norman Knox *(Jannie),* Bingo Mbonjeni *(Cash General),* Simon Sabela *(Rakwaba).*

Jannie (Norman Knox), a white boy, and Tsepo (Muntu Ndebele), a black youngster, are brought up in a South African mission by a priest (Jose Ferrer), a nun (Bess Finney), and a Peace Corps volunteer (Karen Valentine). Overcoming racial tensions, the boys become close friends, but tragedy strikes when Jannie becomes very ill and must be flown to New York City for special treatment. Tsepo follows but winds up lost and alone in Harlem; however, the boys are reunited for a happy ending.

p, Andre Pieterse; d&w, Ashley Lazarus (based on a story by Andre Pieterse); ph, Arthur J. Ornitz; m, Lee Holdridge.

Drama   **(MPAA:NR)**

FOUR HUNDRED BLOWS, THE

(1959) 93m SEDIF, Les Films du Carosse/JANUS bw (LES QUATRES CENTS COUPS)

Jean-Pierre Leaud *(Antoine Doinel),* Claire Maurier *(Mme. Doinel),* Albert Remy *(Mon. Doinel),* Guy Decomble *(Teacher),* Patrick Auffay *(Rene Bigey),* Georges Flamant *(Mon. Bigey),* Yvonne Claudie *(Mme. Bigey),* Robert Beauvais *(Director of the School),* Claude Mansard *(Examining Magistrate),* Jacques Monod *(Commissioner),* Henri Virlojeux *(Nightwatchman),* Jeanne Moreau *(Woman with Dog),* Jean-Claude Brialy *(Man in Street),* Jacques Demy *(Policeman).*

This extraordinary film was Francois Truffaut's first major work and the start of a cycle that included LOVE AT TWENTY, STOLEN KISSES, BED AND BOARD, and LOVE ON THE RUN, all starring the same actor, Jean-Pierre Leaud, in a continuing tale stretching across 20 years that reflected much of Truffaut's own life. Twelve-year-old Antoine Doinel (Leaud), more or less left to his own devices by his mother (Claire Maurier) and father (Albert Remy), gets into trouble at school, runs away from home, and eventually ends up in an observation center for juvenile delinquents. THE FOUR HUNDRED BLOWS—an idiomatic French expression for raising hell in protest—is a nonjudgmental film about injustice, pain, and the events in a young boy's life that make him the person he is. Neither good nor bad, Antoine is just an average child caught up in a maelstrom not of his making, and the situations in which he finds himself make us wonder how *we* might have acted under the same circumstances. Truffaut's favorite film, THE FOUR HUNDRED BLOWS was originally conceived as a 20-minute short titled "Antoine Runs Away" that was to have appeared in a compilation film that included an earlier sketch by Truffaut called "The Mischief Makers." (In French; English subtitles.)

p&d, Francois Truffaut; w, Francois Truffaut, Marcel Moussy (story by Francois Truffaut); ph, Henri Decae; m, Jean Constantin.

Drama   **Cas.**   **(MPAA:NR)**

FOX AND THE HOUND, THE

(1981) 83m BV c

Voices of: Mickey Rooney *(Tod)*, Kurt Russell *(Copper)*, Pearl Bailey *(Big Mamma)*, Jack Albertson *(Amos Slade)*, Sandy Duncan *(Vixey)*, Jeanette Nolan *(Widow Tweed)*, Pat Buttram *(Chief)*, John Fiedler *(Porcupine)*, John McIntire *(Badger)*, Dick Bakalyan *(Dinky)*, Paul Winchell *(Boomer)*, Keith Mitchell *(Young Tod)*, Corey Feldman *(Young Copper)*.

This charming Disney animated outing details the lives of a young fox and a puppy who become close friends one summer. When the dog's owner, a mean hunter, takes him away for the winter, the fox and the hound expect to renew their friendship the following spring. When the hunter and the hound return, the fox's former friend has become the man's favorite hunting dog. The dog saves the fox's life once, but warns him to stay away if he doesn't want to be killed. Meanwhile, the fox has fallen for another young fox, Vixey. The hunter is determined to catch the fox, and there is a terrifying chase, but the tables turn when the dog is cornered by a large bear. Friends to the finish, the fox and hound each get a chance to show their loyalty to the other by the picture's end. The animation here is better than average (veteran Disney animators Wolfgang Reitherman and Art Stevens supervised the talents of a new crop of artists that developed during a 10-year program at the studio), though not quite of the quality of the heyday of Disney Studios. Still, this is wonderful entertainment.

p, Wolfgang Reitherman, Art Stevens; d, Art Stevens, Ted Berman, Richard Rich; w, Laury Clemmons, Ted Berman, Peter Young, Steve Hulett, David Michener, Burny Mattinson, Earl Kress, Vance Gerry (based on the book by Daniel P. Mannix); m, Buddy Baker.

Animation   **Cas.**   **(MPAA:G)**

FRANCIS

(1949) 91m UNIV bw

Donald O'Connor *(Peter Stirling)*, Patricia Medina *(Maureen Gelder)*, ZaSu Pitts *(Valerie Humpert)*, Ray Collins *(Col. Hooker)*, John McIntire *(Gen. Stevens)*, Eduard Franz *(Col. Plepper)*, Howland Chamberlin *(Maj. Nadel)*, James Todd *(Col. Saunders)*, Robert Warwick *(Col. Carmichel)*, Frank Faylen *(Sgt. Chillingbacker)*, Anthony Curtis [Tony Curtis] *(Capt. Jones)*, Mikel Conrad *(Maj. Garber)*, Loren Tindall *(Maj. Richards)*, Charles Meredith *(Banker Munroe)*, Chill Wills *(Voice of Francis the Talking Mule)*, Judd Holdren *(1st Ambulance Man)*, Al Ferguson *(Capt. Dean)*, Roger Moore *(M.C. Major)*, Harry Harvey, Peter Prouse, Howard Negley *(Correspondents)*, Duke York *(Sgt. Poor)*, Joseph Kim *(Japanese Lieutenant)*, Robert Anderson *(Capt. Grant)*, Jack Shutta *(Sgt. Miller)*, Robert Blunt *(2nd Ambulance Man)*, Tim Graham *(Lt. Bremm)*, Jim Hayward *(Capt. Norman)*, Marvin Kaplan *(1st M.C. Lieutenant)*, Harold Fong *(Japanese Soldier)*, Mickey McCardle *(Capt. Addison)*.

This is the first in a series of amusing comedies starring

Donald O'Connor as Peter Stirling, a dim-witted GI who, while stationed in Burma, hooks up with a talking mule named Francis. With Francis' help, Peter performs a series of heroic deeds. Peter insists on telling others that the mule talks to him, though Francis stubbornly refuses to communicate with anyone else. Peter's commanding officer thinks he's nuts, of course, and keeps sending the poor sap to the psycho ward. These goofy comedies made more money than anyone expected and director Lubin went on to create another successful talking equine for television in "Mr. Ed."

p, Robert Arthur; d, Arthur Lubin; w, David Stern (based on his novel); ph, Irving Glassberg; m, Frank Skinner.

Comedy   **(MPAA:NR)**

FRANCIS IN THE HAUNTED HOUSE

(1956) 80m UNIV bw

Mickey Rooney *(David Prescott)*, Virginia Welles *(Loma MacLeod)*, James Flavin *(Chief Martin)*, Paul Cavanagh *(Neil Frazer)*, Mary Ellen Kaye *(Lorna Ann)*, David Janssen *(Lt. Hopkins)*, Ralph Dumke *(Mayor Hargrove)*, Richard Gaines *(District Attorney Reynold)*, Richard Deacon *(Jason)*, Dick Winslow *(Sgt. Arnold)*, Charles Horvath *(Malcolm)*, Timothy Carey *(Hugo)*, Helen Wallace *(Mrs. MacPherson)*, Edward Earle *(Howard Grisby)*, John Maxwell *(Edward Ryan)*, Glen Kramer *(Ephraim Biddle)*, Paul Frees *(Voice of Francis the Talking Mule)*.

After making six "Francis the Talking Mule" comedies, the team of Donald O'Connor, Chill Wills (Francis' voice), and director Arthur Lubin left the series, leaving Mickey Rooney to take over the role of the none-too-smart pal of the vocal jackass (spoken for here by Paul Frees). In this installment, Francis rescues the hapless David Prescott (Rooney) from a haunted house where he is trapped with a group of crooks who are trying to replace genuine works of art with forgeries.

p, Robert Arthur; d, Charles Lamont; w, Herbert Margolis, William Raynor (based on the "Francis" character created by David Stern); ph, George Robinson.

Comedy   **(MPAA:NR)**

FRASIER, THE SENSUOUS LION

(1973) 97m Shuster-Sandler/LCS c

Michael Callan *(Marvin Feldman)*, Katherine Justice *(Allison Stewart)*, Victor Jory *(Frasier's Voice)*, Frank de Kova *(The Man)*, Malachi Throne *(Bill Windsor)*, Marc Lawrence *(Chiarelli)*, Peter Lorre, Jr. *(Boscov)*, Patrick O'Moore *(Worcester)*, Arthur Space *(Dredge)*, Lori Saunders *(Minerva Dolly)*, Joe E. Ross *(Kuback)*, Fritzi Burr *(Marvin's Mother)*, A. E. Gould-Porter *(Motel Manager)*, Ralph James *(Newspaper Reporter)*, Jerry Kobrin *(Newspaper Editor)*, John Qualen *(Old Man on Porch)*, Florence Lake *(Old Woman on Porch)*, Maryesther Denver *(Nurse)*, Allison McKay *(Wife in Kitchen)*, Charles Woolf *(Man in Kitchen)*, John J. Fox *(Heavyset Man)*, Paul "Mousie"

Garner *(Man in Bar)*, Frank Biro *(Host at Cocktail Party)*, Frasier the Lion.

Michael Callan plays a young zoologist who goes to the California Lion Country Safari preserve to study Frasier, an incredibly potent and amorous lion who has fathered 37 cubs with seven different lionesses. To the zoologist's surprise, the lion talks (or, at least, Victor Jory does), and confides his secrets to his newfound friend. A billionaire (Frank de Kova) wants to slaughter Frasier for his glands, hoping to attain the lion's powers (a step up from the old monkey-gland scenario). Soon there are run-ins with criminals, chases galore, and plenty of words of wisdom from Frasier.

p, Allan Sandler; d, Pat Shields; w, Jerry Kobrin (based on a story by Sandy Dore); ph, David L. Butler (Deluxe Color); m, Robert Emenegger.

Comedy (MPAA:PG)

FREAKY FRIDAY

(1976) 95m Disney/BV c

Barbara Harris *(Ellen Andrews)*, Jodie Foster *(Annabel Andrews)*, John Astin *(Bill Andrews)*, Patsy Kelly *(Mrs. Schmauss)*, Vicki Schreck *(Virginia)*, Dick Van Patten *(Harold Jennings)*, Sorrell Booke *(Mr. Dilk)*, Alan Oppenheimer *(Mr. Joffert)*, Kaye Ballard *(Coach Betsy)*, Ruth Buzzi *(Opposing Coach)*, Marc McClure *(Boris Harris)*, Marie Windsor *(Mrs. Murphy)*, Sparky Marcus *(Ben Andrews)*, Ceil Cabot *(Miss McGuirk)*, Brooke Mills *(Mrs. Gibbons)*, Karen Smith *(Mary Kay Gilbert)*, Marvin Kaplan *(Carpet Cleaner)*, Al Molinaro *(Drapery Man)*, Iris Adrian *(Bus Passenger)*, Barbara Walden *(Mrs. Benson)*, Shelly Juttner *(Hilary Miller)*, Charlene Tilton *(Bambi)*, Lori Rutherford *(Jo-Jo)*, Jack Shelton *(Lloyd)*, Laurie Main *(Mills)*, Don Carter *(Delivery Boy)*, Fuddle Bagley *(Bus Driver)*, Fritz Feld *(Jackman)*, Dermott Downs *(Harvey Manager)*, Jimmy Van Patten *(Cashier)*.

A forerunner of the 1980s place-changing comedies (LIKE FATHER, LIKE SON; 18 AGAIN; VICE VERSA), this offbeat live-action Disney film stars Barbara Harris and Jodie Foster as a bickering mother and daughter who wish they could switch places for one whole day. Magically, their wish is granted, and in no time Ellen Andrews (Harris) is running around the neighborhood playing pranks, while her daughter Annabel (Foster) is wearing make-up and acting like an adult. Of course, all these experiences help Annabel to acquire some maturity and Ellen to gain some insight into her daughter's actions. The film is filled with sight gags and features a wonderful performance by Harris.

p, Ron Miller; d, Gary Nelson; w, Mary Rodgers (based on her book); ph, Charles F. Wheeler (Technicolor); m, Johnny Mandel.

Comedy Cas. (MPAA:G)

FULLER BRUSH GIRL, THE

(1950) 87m COL bw (GB: THE AFFAIRS OF SALLY)

Lucille Ball *(Sally Elliot)*, Eddie Albert *(Humphrey Briggs)*, Carl Benton Reid *(Christy)*, Gale Robbins *(Ruby Rawlings)*, Jeff Donnell *(Jane Bixby)*, John Litel *(Watkins)*, Fred Graham *(Rocky Mitchell)*, Lee Patrick *(Claire Simpson)*, Arthur Space *(Inspector Rodgers)*, Sid Tomack *(Bangs)*, Billy Vincent *(Punchy)*, Lorin Raker *(Deval)*, Lelah Tyler *(Mrs. North)*, Sarah Edwards *(Mrs. East)*, Lois Austin *(Mrs. West)*, Isabel Randolph *(Mrs. South)*, Isabel Withers *(Mrs. Finley)*, Donna Boswell *(Sue/Lou)*, Gregory Marshall *(Alvin/Albert)*, Gail Bonney *(Baby Sitter)*, Joel Robinson, Shirley Whitney *(Dancers)*, Sumner Getchell *(Magazine Salesman)*, Red Skelton *(Fuller Brush Man)*, Jay Barney *(Fingerprint Man)*, John Doucette, Charles Hamilton, Cy Malis, Joseph Palma *(Cops)*, Jack Little, James L. Kelly *(Comics)*, Myron Healey *(Employee)*, Bud Osborne *(Old Sailor)*.

Lucille Ball stars as the title door-to-door salesgirl who gets tangled up in a murder. Forced to flee the cops, she and her boy friend (Eddie Albert) go on the lam. Lots of slapstick, plenty of chases, and some of the great comic bits that are Ball's specialty. Albert does a fine job as her not-too-bright beau, and Red Skelton makes a brief appearance as an in-joke reference to his own film THE FULLER BRUSH MAN.

d, Lloyd Bacon; w, Frank Tashlin; ph, Charles Lawton, Jr.; m, Heinz Roemheld.

Comedy (MPAA:NR)

FULLER BRUSH MAN

(1948) 92m COL bw (GB: THAT MAN MR. JONES)

Red Skelton *(Red Jones)*, Janet Blair *(Ann Elliot)*, Don McGuire *(Keenan Wallick)*, Hillary Brooke *(Mrs. Trist)*, Adele Jergens *(Miss Sharmley)*, Ross Ford *(Freddie Trist)*, Trudy Marshall *(Sara)*, Nicholas Joy *(Commissioner Trist)*, Donald Curtis *(Gregory Crackston)*, Arthur Space *(Lt. Quint)*, Selmer Jackson *(Henry Seward)*, Roger Moore *(Detective Foster)*, Stanley Andrews *(Detective Ferguson)*, Bud Wolfe *(Jiggers)*, David Sharpe *(Skitch)*, Chick Collins *(Blackie)*, Billy Jones *(Herman)*, Jimmy Lloyd *(Chauffeur)*, Jimmy Logan *(Butler)*, Jimmy Hunt *(Junior)*.

Red Skelton is at his best in this slapstick tale of a Fuller Brush salesman who is implicated in a murder mystery. (Sound familiar? See THE FULLER BRUSH GIRL, above.) Aided by Ann Elliot (Janet Blair), Red Jones (Skelton) undertakes a little sleuthing to clear himself of the murder rap. They follow the clues to a war surplus factory where the final scene is thoroughly madcap, ranking with the early Mack Sennett silents. Coscripted by Frank Tashlin (THE GIRL CAN'T HELP IT; WILL SUCCESS SPOIL ROCK HUNTER?), one of Hollywood's most gifted comic screenwriter-directors.

p, Edward Small; d, S. Sylvan Simon; w, Frank Tashlin,

Devery Freeman (based on a story by Roy Huggins); ph, Lester White; m, Heinz Roemheld.

Comedy　　　　**Cas.**　　　　**(MPAA:NR)**

FUN AND FANCY FREE

(1947) 73m RKO c

Edgar Bergen, Luana Patten; voices of: Dinah Shore *(Narrator)*, Anita Gordon *(The Singing Harp)*, Cliff Edwards *(Jiminy Cricket)*, Billy Gilbert *(The Giant)*, Clarence Nash *(Donald Duck)*, The King's Men, The Dinning Sisters, The Starlighters.

This Disney feature is comprised of two shorts brought together by the unifying presence of Jiminy Crickett. The first episode, adapted from a Sinclair Lewis story and narrated by Dinah Shore, tells the tale of Bongo, a circus bear who escapes to the wilderness. He meets a female bear and her bear boy friend, as well as an early version of Chip and Dale. Eventually, the sappy Bongo becomes brave and wins over the she-bear. The second and more ambitious episode combines live action and animation, bringing together Edgar Bergen and his dummies Charlie McCarthy and Mortimer Snerd with Mickey Mouse, Donald Duck, and Goofy. One of the highlights of this version of "Jack and the Beanstalk" is Billy Gilbert, as the voice of Willie the Giant, performing his familiar sneezing-fit bit.

p, Walt Disney; d, Jack Kinney, W.O. Roberts, Hamilton Luske, William Morgan; w, Homer Brightman, Harry Reeves, Ted Sears, Lance Nolley, Eldon Dedini, Tom Oreb ("Bongo" segment based on a story by Sinclair Lewis); ph, Charles P. Boyle (Technicolor); m, Paul J. Smith, Oliver Wallace, Eliot Daniel.

Animation/Fantasy　　　**Cas.**　　　**(MPAA:NR)**

G

GAY PURR-EE

(1962) 85m UPA/WB c

Voices of: Judy Garland *(Mewsette)*, Robert Goulet *(Jaune-Tom)*, Red Buttons *(Robespierre)*, Hermione Gingold *(Mme. Rubens-Chatte)*, Paul Frees *(Meowrice)*, Morey Amsterdam, Mel Blanc, Julie Bennett, Joan Gardiner.

Produced by the man who gave us "Mr. Magoo," this full-length cartoon is the story of Mewsette, a country cat who longs for the excitement of Paris. She flees the farm to seek fame and Friskies in the big town. Her presumed lover, Jaune-Tom, follows her there with his amusing sidekick, Robespierre, to keep an eye on her and make sure she doesn't fall in with bad company. Once in Paris, Mewsette is catnaped by Meowrice, who takes her off to

Rubens-Chatte's beauty school. They intend to marry her off to some fat cat in Pittsburgh. Meanwhile, Jaune-Tom and Robespierre are sent to Alaska by Meowrice, but they turn the tables and come back rich, paws laden with gold, ready to win back Mewsette. The songs are by E.Y. "Yip" Harburg and Harold Arlen, who contributed so many wonderful tunes to THE WIZARD OF OZ (1939).

p, Henry G. Saperstein; d, Abe Levitow; w, Dorothy Jones, Chuck Jones, Ralph Wright; ph, Roy Hutchcroft, Jack Stevens, Dan Miller, Duane Keegan (Technicolor).

Animation　　　　　　　　　　**(MPAA:NR)**

GENTLE GIANT

(1967) 93m PAR c

Dennis Weaver *(Tom Wedloe)*, Vera Miles *(Ellen Wedloe)*, Clint Howard *(Mark Wedloe)*, Ralph Meeker *(Fog Hanson)*, Huntz Hall *(Dink)*, Charles Martin *(Mike)*, Rance Howard *(Tater)*, Frank Schuller *(Charlie)*, Robertson White *(Swenson)*, Ric O'Feldman *(Mate)*, James Riddle *(Skipper)*, Jerry Newby *(1st Townsman)*, Frank Logan *(2nd Townsman)*, Alfred Metz *(1st Fisherman)*, Levirne DeBord *(2nd Fisherman)*, Ben the Bear.

The "Gentle Giant" of the title is a big, friendly bear, which 7-year-old Mark Wedloe (Clint Howard) and his parents (Dennis Weaver and Vera Miles) befriend and come to own, much to their neighbors' horror. After a number of adventures with the lovable and curious bear, Mark leads Ben back to the wilds and frees him, but their farewell is only temporary in this sweet movie. This film later spawned the television series "Gentle Ben."

p, Ivan Tors; d, James Neilson; w, Edward J. Lakso, Andy White (based on the novel *Gentle Ben* by Walt Morey); ph, Howard Winner (Eastmancolor); m, Samuel Matlovsky.

Drama　　　　　**Cas.**　　　　**(MPAA:NR)**

GHOST AND MRS. MUIR, THE

(1942) 104m FOX bw

Gene Tierney *(Lucy)*, Rex Harrison *(The Ghost of Capt. Daniel Gregg)*, George Sanders *(Miles Fairley)*, Edna Best *(Martha)*, Vanessa Brown *(Anna)*, Anna Lee *(Mrs. Fairley)*, Robert Coote *(Coombe)*, Natalie Wood *(Anna as a Child)*, Isobel Elsom *(Angelica)*, Victoria Horne *(Eva)*, Whitford Kane *(Sproule)*, Brad Slaven *(Enquiries)*, William Stelling *(Bill)*, Helen Freeman *(Author)*, David Thursby *(Sproggins)*, Heather Wilde *(Maid)*, Stuart Holmes *(Man on Train)*, Houseley Stevenson.

There's really nothing scary about this wonderful fantasy-romance, in which the beautiful widow Lucy (Gene Tierney) buys a remote seacoast house that was once occupied by a dashing merchant captain. Shortly after Lucy moves in with her little daughter, Anna (Natalie Wood), she encounters some strange doings, but is not alarmed even though her neighbors have already warned the headstrong woman that the cottage is haunted. Lucy is more curious than apprehensive and she demands that the ghost (Rex Harrison) show himself. He does, in all his handsome, bearded glory, and not only befriends Lucy and her daughter, but falls in love with the lovely lady. This fragile story would immediately collapse into implausibility were it not for the fine performances of Harrison and Tierney, whose wonderful interaction is materially brought forth by director Joseph L. Mankiewicz. Bernard Herrmann's score is both whimsical and full of other-world lyricism. In this, his second American film, Harrison is superb as the sharp-tongued, affectionate ghost and Tierney shines as his earthbound object of love. Remade in 1955 as STRANGER IN THE NIGHT and as a 1968-70 TV series.

p, Fred Kohlmar; d, Joseph L. Mankiewicz; w, Philip Dunne (based on the novel by R.A. Dick); ph, Charles Lang; m, Bernard Herrmann.

Fantasy/Romance   Cas.   (MPAA:NR)

GHOST BREAKERS, THE

(1940) 83m PAR bw

Bob Hope *(Larry Lawrence)*, Paulette Goddard *(Mary Carter)*, Richard Carlson *(Geoff Montgomery)*, Paul Lukas *(Parada)*, Willie Best *(Alex)*, Pedro De Cordoba *(Havez)*, Virginia Brissac *(Mother Zombie)*, Noble Johnson *(The Zombie)*, Anthony Quinn *(Ramon/Francisco Maderos)*, Tom Dugan *(Raspy Kelly)*, Paul Fix *(Frenchy Duval)*, Lloyd Corrigan *(Martin)*, Emmett Vogan *(Announcer)*, Grace Hayle *(Screaming Woman)*, Herbert Elliott *(Lt. Murray)*, James Blaine *(Police Sergeant)*, Jack Hatfield *(Elevator Boy)*, David Durand *(Bellhop)*, James Flavin *(Hotel Porter)*, Leonard Sues *(Newsboy)*, Jack Edwards *(Ship Bellboy)*, Max Wagner *(Ship Porter)*, Paul Newlan *(Baggage Man)*, Francisco Maran *(Headwaiter)*, Jack Norton *(Drunk)*, Blanca Vischer *(Dolores)*, Douglas Kennedy, Robert Ryan *(Internes)*, Kay Stewart *(Telephone Girl)*.

Looking for a follow-up to its successful Bob Hope-Paulette Goddard 1939 comedy thriller THE CAT AND THE CANARY, Paramount dusted off an old haunted house film called THE GHOST BREAKERS that had been made twice in the silent days—once in 1914 with H.B. Warner, and again in 1922 with Wallace Reid. The result was a stylish, frequently funny little scare show that was even better than THE CAT AND THE CANARY. Larry Lawrence (Hope) is a radio commentator known for his crime exposes (obviously inspired by Walter Winchell) who inadvertently becomes involved with a murder and winds up in Havana after hiding in a steamer trunk owned by Mary Carter (Goddard). A romance soon develops between Mary and Larry, and they both become worried when they are greeted by repeated warnings that the house she has inherited is haunted. Though really a comedy, THE GHOST BREAKERS has its fair share of effective and spooky horror scenes, directed with an atmospheric flavor by Marshall. The balance between laughs and chills is expertly handled, making the film a pleasure to watch. In 1953 the film was remade as SCARED STIFF with Dean Martin and Jerry Lewis. THE GHOST BREAKERS was listed, along with the Bowery Boys film GHOST

CHASERS, as a principal source of inspiration for the phenomenally successful 1984 film GHOSTBUSTERS.

p, Arthur Hornblow, Jr.; d, George Marshall; w, Walter De Leon (based on the play by Paul Dickey and Charles Goddard); ph, Charles Lang; m, Ernst Toch.

Comedy   (MPAA:NR)

GIDGET

(1959) 95m COL c

Sandra Dee *(Francie)*, James Darren *(Moondoggie)*, Cliff Robertson *(Kahoona)*, Arthur O'Connell *(Russell Lawrence)*, The Four Preps *(Themselves)*, Mary LaRoche *(Dorothy Lawrence)*, Joby Baker *(Stinky)*, Tom Laughlin *(Lover Boy)*, Sue George *(B.L.)*, Robert Ellis *(Hot Shot)*, Jo Morrow *(Mary Lou)*, Yvonne Craig *(Nan)*, Doug McClure *(Waikiki)*, Burt Metcalfe *(Lord Byron)*, Richard Newton, Ed Hinton *(Cops)*, Patti Kane *(Patty)*.

The all-American ideal is wholesomely embodied in happy-go-lucky Sandra Dee, who became a model for countless teenagers in the late 1950s. Dee plays Gidget (a nickname meaning "girl midget"), a sad-faced youngster who doesn't quite measure up to the chesty, bikinied girls on the beach. Her mom's reassurances come true when the two grooviest surfers in town, Moondoggie (James Darren) and Kahoona (Cliff Robertson), start paying Gidget some attention. The first and best of the series, GIDGET benefits from a fine cast; Sandra Dee had just appeared in Douglas Sirk's IMITATION OF LIFE, and Robertson, who turned in a commendable performance as Kahoona, was later praised for his role in CHARLY. Also hanging ten was Tom Laughlin, who much later made BILLY JACK.

p, Lewis J. Rachmil; d, Paul Wendkos; w, Gabrielle Upton (based on the novel by Frederick Kohner); ph, Burnett Guffey (CinemaScope, Eastmancolor); m, Morris Stoloff.

Comedy   Cas.   (MPAA:NR)

GIRL CRAZY

(1943) 97m MGM bw (AKA: WHEN THE GIRLS MEET THE BOYS)

Mickey Rooney *(Danny Churchill, Jr.)*, Judy Garland *(Ginger Gray)*, Gil Stratton *(Bud Livermore)*, Robert E. Strickland *(Henry Lathrop)*, Rags Ragland *(Rags)*, June Allyson *(Specialty)*, Nancy Walker *(Polly Williams)*, Guy Kibbee *(Dean Phineas Armour)*, Tommy Dorsey and His Band *(Themselves)*, Frances Rafferty *(Marjorie Tait)*, Howard Freeman *(Gov. Tait)*, Henry O'Neill *(Mr. Churchill, Sr.)*, Sidney Miller *(Ed)*, Eve Whitney *(Brunette)*, Carol Gallagher, Kay Williams *(Blondes)*, Jess Lee Brooks *(Buckets)*, Roger Moore *(Cameraman)*, Charles Coleman *(Maitre d'Hotel)*, Harry Depp *(Nervous Man)*, Richard Kipling *(Dignified Man)*, Henry Roquemore *(Fat Man)*, Alphonse Martel *(Waiter)*, Frances MacInerney, Sally Cairns *(Checkroom Girls)*, Barbara Bedford *(Churchill's Secretary)*, Victor Potel *(Stationmaster)*, Joseph Geil, Jr., Ken Stewart *(Students)*, William Beaudine, Jr. *(Tom)*, Irving

Bacon *(Reception Clerk)*, George Offerman, Jr. *(Messenger)*, Mary Elliott *(Southern Girl)*, Katharine Booth *(Girl)*.

A fast-moving, funny film, GIRL CRAZY was the eighth pairing of Judy Garland and Mickey Rooney and surely one of their best. In this picture based on a play by Guy Bolton and Jack McGowan (with music by George and Ira Gershwin), Rooney stars as Danny Churchill, Jr., the rich son of a newspaper publisher (Henry O'Neill). He is sent to an all-boys mining school where wake-up time is 6 a.m., which is usually the hour he goes to sleep. Stuck out in the desert, Danny finds it hard to exercise his girl-craziness, as the only woman of any consequence nearby is Ginger Gray (Garland), the granddaughter of the school's dean (Guy Kibbee). Although Danny originally hates the school, his love for Ginger eventually prompts him to help save the financially imperiled institution. The movie was originally to be directed by Busby Berkeley, but he and MGM musical maven Roger Edens didn't get along; nor did Garland care for him, after friction arose between them on FOR ME AND MY GAL the year before. Berkeley was, however, brought in to stage the spectacular "I Got Rhythm" number, leaving the rest of the musical work to Charles Walters, who did a splendid job. Other songs included are "Embraceable You," "Fascinating Rhythm," "Treat Me Rough," "Bidin' My Time," "But Not for Me," "Do," and "Barbary Coast," all by the Gershwins, and Edens' "Happy Birthday, Ginger."

p, Arthur Freed; d, Norman Taurog; w, Fred Finklehoffe, (uncredited) Dorothy Kingsley, Sid Silvers, William Ludwig (based on the musical play by George and Ira Gershwin, Guy Bolton, and Jack McGowan); ph, William Daniels, Robert Planck.

Comedy/Musical   **Cas.**   **(MPAA:NR)**

GLITTERBALL, THE

(1977, Brit.) 56m Children's Film Foundation c

Ben Buckton, Keith Jayne, Ron Pember, Marjorie Yates, Barry Jackson, Andrew Jackson.

This compelling children's film predates Steven Spielberg's E.T. by five years. Essentially, the story is the same: a little alien named Glitterball is abandoned on Earth and two kids (Ben Buckton and Keith Jayne) help it get home. In the finale, the alien's mother ship comes to the rescue. THE GLITTERBALL has some commendable special effects, and is short enough to hold the little ones' attention.

p, Mark Forstater; d, Harley Cokliss; w, Howard Thompson; ph, Alan Hall.

Science Fiction   **(MPAA:NR)**

GNOME-MOBILE, THE

(1967) 84m BV c

Walter Brennan *(D.J. Mulrooney/Knobby)*, Tom Lowell *(Jasper)*, Matthew Garber *(Rodney Winthrop)*, Ed Wynn *(Rufus)*, Karen Dotrice *(Elizabeth Winthrop)*, Richard Deacon *(Ralph Yarby)*, Sean McClory *(Horatio Quaxton)*,

Jerome Cowan *(Dr. Conrad Ramsey)*, Charles Lane *(Dr. Scroggins)*, Norman Grabowski, Hay Baylor *(Male Nurses)*, Gil Lamb *(Gas Station Attendant)*, Maudie Prickett *(Katie Barrett)*, Cami Sebring *(Violet)*, Ellen Corby *(Etta Pettibone)*, Frank Cady *(Charlie Pettibone)*, Karl Held *(Paul)*, Charles Smith *(Airport Attendant)*, Byron Foulger *(Hotel Clerk)*, Susan Flannery *(Airline Stewardess)*, Ernestine Barrier *(Nell)*, Dee Carroll *(2nd Secretary)*, William Fawcett *(Chauffeur)*, Robert S. Carson *(Twin Oaks Attendant)*, Jack Davis *(Manson)*, John Cliff *(Night Watchman)*, Mickey Martin *(Bellboy)*, Alvy Moore *(Gas Station Mechanic)*, Dale Van Sickel *(Uniformed Guard)*, Parley Baer *(Voice of Owl)*, Jimmy Murphy *(Voice of Raccoon)*, Jesslyn Fax, Dee Carroll *(Voices of Bluejays)*, Pamela Gail *(Snapdragon)*.

Based on a novel by social reformer Upton Sinclair, author of *The Jungle*, this charming Disney film features Walter Brennan as D.J. Mulrooney, a conservative, elderly timber tycoon who takes his grandchildren (Matthew Garber and Karen Dotrice) for a drive in his prized 1930 Rolls Royce. When the trio stops to picnic they meet Jasper (Tom Lowell), a youthful, tiny gnome, and his 943-year-old ailing grandfather (Brennan again, playing the role as a stereotypical leprechaun, brogue and all). Because he's isolated from other gnomes, Jasper seems fated to be the last of his line, a situation that depresses his grandfather to the point of illness. Enlisting the humans' aid, the gnomes therefore set out in the Rolls Royce (now a "Gnome-Mobile") to find others of their kind. While the fact that lumber tycoon Mulrooney is responsible for the destruction of the gnomes' forest causes some initial tension, the businessman soon becomes dedicated to their cause. Highly reminiscent of Disney's DARBY O'GILL AND THE LITTLE PEOPLE, this wonderfully entertaining fantasy, complete with talking animals, is propelled by the terrific dual-role performance from Brennan.

p, Walt Disney, James Algar; d, Robert Stevenson; w, Ellis Kadison (based on the novel *The Gnomobile, a Gnice Gnew Gnarrative With Gnonsense, But Gnothing Gnaughty* by Upton Sinclair); ph, Edward Coleman (Technicolor); m, Buddy Baker.

Fantasy   **Cas.**   **(MPAA:NR)**

GOING MY WAY

(1944) 130m PAR bw

Bing Crosby *(Father Chuck O'Malley)*, Rise Stevens *(Genevieve Linden)*, Barry Fitzgerald *(Father Fitzgibbon)*, Frank McHugh *(Father Timothy O'Dowd)*, Gene Lockhart *(Ted Haines, Sr.)*, William Frawley *(Max Dolan)*, James Brown *(Ted Haines, Jr.)*, Jean Heather *(Carol James)*, Porter Hall *(Mr. Belknap)*, Fortunio Bonanova *(Tomasso Bozzani)*, Eily Malyon *(Mrs. Carmody)*, George Nokes *(Pee Wee)*, Tom Dillon *(Officer McCarthy)*, Stanley Clements *(Tony Scaponi)*, Carl "Alfalfa" Switzer *(Herman Langerhanke)*, Hugh Maguire *(Pitch Pipe)*, Sybil Lewis *(Maid at Metropolitan Opera House)*, George McKay *(Mr. Van Heusen)*, Jack Norton *(Mr. Lilley)*, Anita Bolster *(Mrs.*

Quimp), Jimmie Dundee *(Fireman)*, Adeline De Walt Reynolds *(Mother Fitzgibbon)*, Gibson Gowland *(Church-goer)*, Julie Gibson *(Taxi Driver)*, Bill Henry *(Intern)*, Robert Tafur *(Don Jose)*, Martin Garralaga *(Zuniga)*, Robert Mitchell Boy Choir.

A warm and moving film, GOING MY WAY was a sleeper that turned into an enormous box-office hit. Father Chuck O'Malley (Bing Crosby) is an easy-going, trouble-shooting priest who arrives at St. Dominic's Church, a Catholic institution that has seen better days, as has its curate, the elderly Father Fitzgibbon (Barry Fitzgerald). The old and stubborn priest has led the parish for 45 years, but recently the church has gotten heavily in debt, disillusioning even the parishioners. Through the magic of music, however, Father O'Malley brings Father Fitzgibbon out of the doldrums and saves the parish. Leo Mc-Carey's direction is masterful, stopping the sentiment just short of the maudlin. It all works like magic, especially the unbeatable chemistry between Crosby and Fitzgerald. The film was box-office dynamite and swept the Oscars, winning for Best Picture (Paramount had not gotten this award since WINGS, 16 years earlier), Best Director, Best Screenplay, Best Song ("Swingin' on a Star"), Best Actor (Crosby), and Best Supporting Actor (Fitzgerald). GOING MY WAY and its equally wonderful sequel, THE BELLS OF ST. MARY'S, were also popular with the Catholic Church and Pope Pius XII, who later gave a private audience to Crosby in thanks for the latter's priestly portrayal. Besides "Swingin' on a Star," the songs include "The Day After Forever," "Too-ra-loo-ra-loo-a," and "Going My Way."

p&d, Leo McCarey; w, Frank Butler, Frank Cavett (based on a story by Leo McCarey); ph, Lionel Lindon.

Drama/Musical   **Cas.**   **(MPAA:NR)**

GOLDEN VOYAGE OF SINBAD, THE

(1974, Brit.) 105m COL c

John Phillip Law *(Sinbad)*, Caroline Munro *(Margiana)*, Tom Baker *(Koura)*, Douglas Wilmer *(Vizier)*, Martin Shaw *(Rachid)*, Gregoire Aslan *(Hakim)*, Kurt Christian *(Haroun)*, Takis Emmanuel *(Achmed)*, John D. Garfield *(Abdul)*, Aldo Sambrell *(Omar)*.

This sequel to the terrific THE SEVENTH VOYAGE OF SINBAD (1958) is great fun, with a minimum of plot and a maximum of wonderful Ray Harryhausen special effects. John Phillip Law is the famed sailor here, in search of a gold tablet that will restore a deposed ruler (Douglas Wilmer) to the throne. En route Sinbad encounters a one-eyed centaur, a winged griffin, a six-armed statue, and a host of other fantastic creatures. Fast-paced and exciting, the film features some of Harryhausen's best stop-motion animation work, and Tom ("Dr. Who") Baker makes a marvelous villain. The surprising box-office success of THE GOLDEN VOYAGE OF SINBAD led to yet another sequel, the relatively disappointing SINBAD AND THE EYE OF THE TIGER (1977).

p, Charles H. Schneer, Ray Harryhausen; d, Gordon

Hessler; w, Brian Clemens; ph, Ted Moore (Dynarama); m, Miklos Rozsa.

Adventure/Fantasy   **Cas.**   **(MPAA:G)**

GOODBYE MR. CHIPS

(1939, Brit.) 114m MGM bw

Robert Donat *(Charles Chipping)*, Greer Garson *(Katherine Ellis)*, Terry Kilburn *(John Colley/Peter Colley)*, John Mills *(Peter Colley as a Young Man)*, Paul Henreid *(Max Staefel)*, Judith Furse *(Flora)*, Lyn Harding *(Dr. Wetherby)*, Milton Rosmer *(Charteris)*, Frederick Leister *(Marsham)*, Louise Hampton *(Mrs. Wickett)*, Austin Trevor *(Ralston)*, David Tree *(Jackson)*, Edmund Breon *(Col. Morgan)*, Jill Furse *(Helen Colley)*, Guy Middleton *(McCulloch)*, Nigel Stock *(John Forrester)*, Scott Sunderland *(Sir John Colley)*, Ronald Ward, Patrick Ludlow, Simon Lack, Caven Watson, Cyril Raymond, John Longden.

Robert Donat gives a smashing performance in this superlative production as the shy, retiring British school-teacher who guides several generations of young boys to manhood. Set at Brookfield Boys School in the late 1800s, the film follows the career of Charles Chipping, nicknamed "Mr. Chips," from his first days as an unpopular novice instructor through the marriage that brings him out of his shell to his final years as the school's beloved elder statesman. So moving was Donat's performance that he beat out the most popular American candidate for the Best Actor Oscar, Clark Gable, who was nominated for his work in GONE WITH THE WIND. Greer Garson, as Mrs. Chips, also shines in this, the film that introduced her to American audiences. The script is bright and the direction crisp, but it is Donat who captivates. James Hilton wrote the original story as a novella in four days to meet a 1934 magazine deadline. A 1969 musical remake of the film starred Peter O'Toole but was lackluster, aside from O'Toole's charming Chips, from beginning to end.

p, Victor Saville; d, Sam Wood; w, R.C. Sherriff, Claudine West, Eric Maschwitz, Sidney Franklin (based on the novella by James Hilton); ph, Frederick A. Young; m, Richard Addinsell.

Drama   **Cas.**   **(MPAA:NR)**

GOODBYE, MY LADY

(1956) 94m Batjac/WB bw

Walter Brennan *(Uncle Jesse)*, Phil Harris *(Cash)*, Brandon de Wilde *(Skeeter)*, Sidney Poitier *(Gates)*, William Hopper *(Grover)*, Louise Beavers *(Bonnie Drew)*.

This rite-of-passage childhood drama stars Brandon de Wilde as Skeeter, a 14-year-old orphan living in the Mississippi swamps with his elderly uncle (Walter Brennan). One day Skeeter finds a stray dog and adopts her; after he has become attached to the animal, however, he discovers that the dog's original owner has posted a large reward for her return. Torn between his love for the dog and his conscience, which tells him to return her, Skeeter makes his first mature decision in bringing the dog back to its rightful owner. An appealing family film with some tender moments.

d, William A. Wellman; w, Sid Fleischman (based on a novel by James Street); ph, William H. Clothier; m, Laurindo Almeida, George Field.

Drama (MPAA:NR)

GREAT AMERICAN BUGS BUNNY-ROAD RUNNER CHASE

(1979) 97m WB c (AKA: THE BUGS BUNNY-ROAD RUNNER MOVIE)

Mel Blanc (Voice Characterizations).

This outstanding compilation of some of Chuck Jones' finest Bugs Bunny cartoons was released on the irrepressible rabbit's 40th birthday. Some 20 minutes of new animated footage showing Bugs in his Beverly Hills home reminiscing over his past triumphs provide the structure for this nostalgic look at Daffy Duck, Elmer Fudd, and Porky Pig from the years 1939 to 1962. Also making a brief appearance are Road Runner and Wile E. Coyote, in a montage of scenes culled from 16 different cartoons. Good fun.

p&d, Chuck Jones; w, Mike Maltese, Chuck Jones; m, Carl Stalling, Milt Franklyn, Dean Elliott.

Animation (MPAA:G)

GREAT ESCAPE, THE

(1963) 169m UA c

Steve McQueen ("Cooler King" Hilts), James Garner ("The Scrounger" Hendley), Richard Attenborough ("Big X" Bartlett), James Donald (Senior Officer Ramsey), Charles Bronson (Danny Velinski), Donald Pleasence ("The Forger" Blythe), James Coburn ("The Manufacturer" Sedgwick), David McCallum (Ashley-Pitt), Gordon Jackson (MacDonald), John Leyton (Willie), Angus Lennie ("The Mole" Ives), Nigel Stock (Cavendish), Jud Taylor (Goff), William Russell (Sorren), Robert Desmond ("The Tailor" Griffith), Tom Adams (Nimmo), Lawrence Montaigne (Haynes), Hannes Messemer (Von Luger), Robert Graf (Werner), Harry Riebauer (Strachwitz), Hans Reiser (Kuhn), Robert Freitag (Posen), Heinz Weiss (Kramer), Til Kiwe (Frick), Ulrich Beiger (Preissen), George Mikell (Dietrich), Karl Otto Alberty (Steinach).

This classic escape picture concerns hundreds of the toughest Allied prisoners of WW II, thrown together into a special "escape-proof" German prison camp. The collected prisoners, all of whom have made so many escape attempts that they are deemed incorrigible by the Nazis, include "Big X" Bartlett (Richard Attenborough), the British master escape planner; Danny Velinski (Charles Bronson), a Polish officer in charge of tunnel digging; Blythe, "The Forger" (Donald Pleasence), responsible for fake passports and papers; and Americans Hendley, "The Scrounger" (James Garner), in charge of

assembling needed supplies, and "Cooler King" Hilts (Steve McQueen), a maverick who has his own ideas of escape. Big X plans to dig three tunnels and move out not just a few prisoners, but hundreds, which will cause havoc and keep numbers of German troops busy searching for the escapees rather than at the front line. Based on a book detailing a real-life mass escape of Allied troops in 1942, the film is beautifully directed, well written, and superbly enacted by the entire cast. Director-producer John Sturges was in great form here and, although the film is long, it's done with such a hearty pace that viewers won't feel it drag. THE GREAT ESCAPE was a box-office smash and went down well with the critics, joining the ranks of such similarly themed productions as THE BRIDGE ON THE RIVER KWAI (1957), GRAND ILLUSION (1937), and STALAG 17 (1953).

p&d, John Sturges; w, James Clavell, W.R. Burnett (based on the book by Paul Brickhill); ph, Daniel L. Fapp (Deluxe Color); m, Elmer Bernstein.

Prison/War **Cas.** (MPAA:NR)

GREAT EXPECTATIONS

(1946, Brit.) 118m Cineguild/UNIV bw

John Mills (Pip Pirrip), Valerie Hobson (Estella/Her Mother), Bernard Miles (Joe Gargery), Francis L. Sullivan (Jaggers), Martita Hunt (Miss Havisham), Finlay Currie (Abel Magwitch), Anthony Wager (Pip as a Child), Jean Simmons (Estella as a Child), Alec Guinness (Herbert Pocket), Ivor Barnard (Wemmick), Freda Jackson (Mrs. Gargery), Torin Thatcher (Bentley Drummle), Eileen Erskine (Biddy), Hay Petrie (Uncle Pumblechook), George Hayes (Compeyson), O.B. Clarence (Aged Parent), Richard George (Sergeant), Everley Gregg (Sarah Pocket), John Burch (Mr. Wopsle), Grace Denbigh-Russell (Mrs. Wopsle), John Forrest (Pale Young Gentleman), Anne Holland (A Relation), Frank Atkinson (Mike), Gordon Begg (Night Porter), Edie Martin (Mrs. Whimple), Walford Hyden (Dancing Master), Roy Arthur (Galley Steersman).

A masterful realization of Charles Dickens' novel, this may be the best cinematic translation of the author's work, as well as director David Lean's greatest achievement. Beginning in 1830, the film follows the life of orphan Pip Pirrip (Anthony Wager as a child, John Mills as an adult), from his humble beginnings as a blacksmith's apprentice to his days as the wealthy beneficiary of an escaped convict (Finlay Currie) he once helped. Wonderfully directed by Lean—especially the childhood passages—GREAT EXPECTATIONS is brimming with unforgettable images and characters. Although literature students may have problems with major scenes and the excision of some of the novel's characters, the film captures the spirit of Dickens, translating his prose into flawless cinema. Cinematographer Guy Green and production designer John Bryan were awarded Academy Awards for their memorable work. A must see.

p, Ronald Neame; d, David Lean; w, David Lean, Ronald Neame, Anthony Havelock-Allan, Cecil McGivern, Kay

Walsh (based on the novel by Charles Dickens); ph, Guy Green; m, Walter Goehr.

Drama   **Cas.**   **(MPAA:NR)**

GREAT MUPPET CAPER, THE

(1981) 95m UNIV c

Jim Henson *(Kermit/Rowlf/Dr. Teeth/Waldorf/Swedish Chef)*, Frank Oz *(Miss Piggy/Fozzie Bear/Animal/Sam the Eagle)*, Dave Goelz *(The Great Gonzo/Beauregard/Zoot/ Dr. Bunsen/Honeydew)*, Jerry Nelson *(Floyd/Pops/Lew Zealand)*, Richard Hunt *(Scooter/Statler/Sweetums/Janice/Beaker)*, Charles Grodin *(Nicky Holiday)*, Diana Rigg *(Lady Holiday)*, John Cleese, Robert Morley, Peter Ustinov, Jack Warden *(Guest Stars)*, Steve Whitmore *(Rizzo the Rat/Lips)*, Carroll Spinney *(Oscar the Grouch)*, Erica Creer *(Marla)*, Kate Howard *(Carla)*, Della Finch *(Darla)*, Michael Robbins *(Guard)*, Joan Sanderson *(Dorcas)*, Peter Hughes *(Maitre D')*, Peggy Aitchison *(Prison Guard)*, Tommy Godfrey *(Bus Conductor)*, Katia Borg, Valli Kemp, Michele Ivan-Zadeh, Chai Lee *(Models)*, Peter Falk.

The Muppet menagerie cavorts in the middle of London in this, their second film. Kermit, Fozzie Bear, and Gonzo are reporters investigating the theft of fashion queen Lady Holiday's (Diana Rigg) jewels. Lady Holiday's brother, Nicky (Charles Grodin), frames Miss Piggy for the theft, but the other Muppets save the day by exposing Nicky as the real criminal. The film boasts fewer guest-star cameo appearances than the Muppets' first movie, but those who are here do a good job, and Miss Piggy's Busby Berkeley-type dance and the Esther Williams-ish water ballet are fun to watch.

p, David Lazer, Frank Oz; d, Jim Henson; w, Tom Patchett, Jay Tarses, Jerry Juhl, Jack Rose; ph, Oswald Morris (Technicolor).

Comedy/Musical   **Cas.**   **(MPAA:G)**

GREAT RUPERT, THE

(1950) 86m Eagle Lion bw

Jimmy Durante *(Mr. Amendola)*, Terry Moore *(Rosalinda)*, Tom Drake *(Peter Dingle)*, Frank Orth *(Mr. Dingle)*, Sarah Haden *(Mrs. Dingle)*, Queenie Smith *(Mrs. Amendola)*, Chick Chandler *(Phil Davis)*, Jimmy Conlin *(Joe Mahoney)*, Hugh Sanders *(Mulligan)*, Donald T. Beddoe *(Mr. Haggerty)*, Cindy Candido *(Molineri)*, Clancy Cooper *(Policeman)*, Harold Goodwin *(FBI Man)*, Frank Cady *(Tax Investigator)*.

This entertaining fluff stars Jimmy Durante and a squirrel (which is actually a puppet) in renowned animator George Pal's producing debut in feature film. Durante, as Mr. Amendola, heads a hard-luck family of acrobats who suddenly find gobs of money stashed throughout their house. The squirrel has been stealthily taking the money from a miserly neighbor. The family's bubble bursts when a suspicious FBI agent starts snooping around in order to discover the source of their riches. Terry Moore and

Tom Drake provide the romance, while Durante wonderfully mugs his way through the film.

p, George Pal; d, Irving Pichel; w, Laslo Vadnay (based on a story by Ted Allen); ph, Lionel Lindon; m, Fred Spielman, Buddy Kaye.

Comedy   **(MPAA:NR)**

GREATEST SHOW ON EARTH, THE

(1952) 153m PAR c

Betty Hutton *(Holly)*, Cornel Wilde *(Sebastian)*, Charlton Heston *(Brad)*, Dorothy Lamour *(Phyllis)*, Gloria Grahame *(Angel)*, James Stewart *(Buttons, a Clown)*, Henry Wilcoxon *(Detective)*, Lyle Bettger *(Klaus)*, Lawrence Tierney *(Henderson)*, John Kellogg *(Harry)*, John Ridgely *(Jack Steelman, Assistant Manager)*, Frank Wilcox *(Circus Doctor)*, Bob Carson *(Ringmaster)*, Lillian Albertson *(Buttons' Mother)*, Julia Faye *(Birdie)*, Emmett Kelly, Cucciola, Antoinette Concello, John Ringling North *(Themselves)*, Gloria Drew *(Ann)*, Anthony Marsh *(Tony)*, Bruce Cameron *(Bruce)*, Noel Neill *(Noel)*, Charmienne Harker *(Charmienne)*, Dorothy Crider *(Dorothy)*, Patricia Michon *(Patricia)*, Vicki Bakken *(Vicki)*, Gay McEldowney *(Gay)*, Hugh Prosser *(Hugh)*, Rus Conklin *(Rus)*, John Crawford *(Jack)*, Claude Dunkin *(Claude)*, Keith Richards *(Keith)*, Rosemary Dvorak *(Rosemary)*, Lorna Jordan *(Lorna)*, Mona Knox *(Mona)*, Gertrude Messinger *(Gertrude)*, John Parrish *(Jack Lawson)*, William Hall *(Bill)*, Brad Johnson *(Reporter)*, William J. Riley, Robert W. Rushing *(Policemen)*, Adele Cook Johnson *(Mabel)*, Lane Chandler *(Lane)*, Ross Bagdasarian *(Man)*, Edmond O'Brien *(Midway Barker)*, Dale Van Sickel *(Man in Train Wreck)*, William Boyd *(Himself)*, Bing Crosby, Bob Hope, Mona Feeman *(People in Grandstands)*, Liberty Horses, The Flying Concellos, Paul Jung, The Maxellos *(Circus Acts)*.

It's big, it's garish, it's loud, and most of all, it's wonderful. This is Cecil B. DeMille's superlative salute to the circus world, and all its glamour and flashy hoopla suits perfectly the director whose middle name was epic. An episodic soap opera set under the big top, the film is almost like a documentary in its meticulous detailing of circus life. Charlton Heston plays the head of the sprawling ensemble and the entire cast is outstanding, particularly James Stewart as the clown hiding from his past. Since the early 1920s, DeMille had planned on producing a spectacular circus film, but his biblical epics got in the way. Finally, in 1949, after Paramount paid Ringling Brothers $250,000 for the right to use the circus' name, equipment, and talent, DeMille began elaborate preparations. The film is authentic and awesome and earned an Oscar as Best Picture. DeMille got an Oscar for the first time in his life, an Irving Thalberg Academy Award for the role of producer.

p&d, Cecil B. DeMille; w, Fredric M. Frank, Barre Lyndon, Theodore St. John (based on a story by Fredric M. Frank, Theodore St. John, Frank Cavett); ph, George Barnes, J. Peverell Marley, Wallace Kelly (Technicolor); m, Victor Young.

Drama   **Cas.**   **(MPAA:NR)**

GREYFRIARS BOBBY

(1961, Brit.) 91m BV c

Donald Crisp *(John Brown)*, Laurence Naismith *(Mr. Traill)*, Alexander Mackenzie *(Old Jock)*, Kay Walsh *(Mrs. Brown)*, Andrew Cruickshank *(Lord Provost)*, Vincent Winter *(Tammy)*, Moultrie Kelsall *(Magistrate)*, Gordon Jackson *(Farmer)*, Rosalie Crutchley *(Farmer's Wife)*, Freda Jackson *(Old Woman Caretaker)*, Jameson Clark *(Constable)*, Duncan Macrae *(Constable Maclean)*, Joan Buck *(Allie)*, Jennifer Nevinson *(Farmer's Daughter)*, Joyce Carey *(1st Lady)*, Jack Lambert *(Doctor)*, Bruce Seton, Hamish Wilson, Sean Keir.

A typically well-done Disney picture guaranteed to melt the heart of any animal lover. Set in Edinburgh at the turn of the century, the film follows the adventures of a cute little Skye terrier named Bobby. When his elderly master dies, the loyal dog refuses to leave the grave. Eventually Bobby is persuaded to venture into town and play with the local children, but at night he runs back to the cemetery and his master's grave. Word of the dog's odd behavior spreads throughout Edinburgh and Bobby becomes quite a local celebrity. Based on a true story.

p, Walt Disney; d, Don Chaffey; w, Robert Westerby (from the novel by Eleanor Atkinson); ph, Paul Beeson; m, Francis Chagrin.

Drama   **Cas.**   **(MPAA:NR)**

GULLIVER'S TRAVELS

(1939) 75m PAR c

Lanny Ross *(Singing Voice of the Prince)*, Jessica Dragonette *(Singing Voice of the Princess)*.

With the success of Walt Disney's SNOW WHITE AND THE SEVEN DWARFS in 1937, the Fleisher brothers, of POPEYE and BETTY BOOP fame, decided to try their hands at a full-length animated feature. They used Jonathan Swift's famed satire as their source, cutting some episodes and trimming the remaining original material to its bare bones. What's left is the story of Gulliver's shipwreck on the island of Lilliput, where the inhabitants are only a few inches tall. When Gulliver washes up on the beach of their kingdom, the terrified little people tie him down. He easily escapes, however, and surprises his would-be captors by proving to be friendly rather than fearsome. While no SNOW WHITE, GULLIVER'S TRAVELS nonetheless has some fine animation. The opening storm sequence is especially excellent. Gulliver was rotoscoped (animated from live footage) and the technique worked well, making the giant remarkably realistic and a nice contrast to the little people. Although it lacks Swift's biting satire, the film is of great historical value for its technique, and, of course, the kids will love it.

p, Max Fleischer; d, Dave Fleischer; w, Dan Gordon, Ted Pierce, Izzy Sparber, Edmond Seward (based on a story by Seward from the book by Jonathan Swift); ph, Charles Schettler; m, Victor Young.

Animation   **Cas.**   **(MPAA:NR)**

H

HANS CHRISTIAN ANDERSEN ✓

(1952) 120m RKO c

Danny Kaye *(Hans Christian Andersen)*, Farley Granger *(Niels)*, [Renee] Jeanmaire *(Doro)*, Joey [Joseph] Walsh *(Peter)*, Philip Tonge *(Otto)*, Erik Bruhn *(The Hussar)*, Roland Petit *(The Prince)*, John Brown *(Schoolmaster)*, John Qualen *(Burgomaster)*, Jeanne Lafayette *(Celine)*, Robert Malcolm *(Stage Doorman)*, George Chandler *(Farmer)*, Fred Kelsey *(1st Gendarme)*, Gil Perkins *(2nd Gendarme)*, Peter Votrian *(Lars)*, Betty Uitti *(The Princess)*, Jack Klaus *(Sea Witch)*.

This delightful children's film stars Danny Kaye as the beloved Danish author whose rise to literary prominence is detailed here in an admittedly fanciful manner. This movie was something of an obsession for producer Samuel Goldwyn, who had been announcing production of the project for nearly 15 years, only to have it delayed time and time again. After paying a king's ransom for 16 different screenplays, Goldwyn finally found one he liked, and production began. Luckily, Goldwyn's dream paid off big at the box office, as HANS CHRISTIAN ANDERSEN grossed $6 million and eventually ranked as Goldwyn's third biggest moneymaker (behind THE BEST YEARS OF OUR LIVES, 1946, and GUYS AND DOLLS, 1955). Not only was the film popular with the public, but the Motion Picture Academy nominated it for six awards: Best Cinematography, Best Score of a Musical Film, Best Song ("Thumbelina"), Best Art/Set Design for a Color Film, Best Costume Design, and Best Sound Recording. Kaye is wonderful and the enjoyable songs include "Inchworm" and "Wonderful Wonderful Copenhagen."

p, Samuel Goldwyn; d, Charles Vidor; w, Moss Hart (based on a story by Myles Connolly); ph, Harry Stradling (Technicolor); m, Frank Loesser.

Biography   **Cas.**   **(MPAA:NR)**

HAPPY TIME, THE

(1952) 94m Kramer/COL bw

Charles Boyer *(Jacques Bonnard)*, Louis Jourdan *(Uncle Desmonde)*, Marsha Hunt *(Susan Bonnard)*, Kurt Kasznar *(Uncle Louis)*, Linda Christian *(Mignonette Chappuis)*, Bobby Driscoll *(Bibi)*, Marcel Dalio *(Grandpere Bonnard)*, Jeanette Nolan *(Felice)*, Jack Raine *(Mr. Frye)*, Richard Erdman *(Alfred Grattin)*, Marlene Cameron *(Peggy O'Hare)*, Gene Collins *(Jimmy Bishop)*, Ann Faber *(Yvonne)*, Kathryn Sheldon *(Miss Tate)*, Maurice Marsac *(The Great Gaspari)*, Will Wright *(Dr. Marchaud)*, Eugene Borden *(Mons. Lafayette)*.

This fine film version of a stage hit captures the world opening before the eyes of an innocent, beguiling 12-

year-old boy, Bibi (Bobby Driscoll), who lives in Ottawa with his warm, fun-loving largely French-Canadian family. His father, Jacques (Charles Boyer), is a kindly man who sees him through his first romantic crisis. His Scots-born mother (Marsha Hunt) provides balance for a family that is more carefree than responsible, more capricious than pragmatic. The dialog is charming and witty, and the entire cast—particularly Boyer—play their roles with aplomb. This was Boyer's last starring role, and it remained one of his favorite films. Driscoll, who was one of the most versatile child actors in Hollywood, having appeared in such fine films as THE SULLIVANS (1944) and THE WINDOW (1949), is terrific as the young boy suddenly jolted by emotions he never knew existed. He would die tragically of a heart attack from a drug overdose at age 30. Richard Fleischer directs with elan and provides a zippy pace. A rare film with plenty of vitality that never misses a beat, except for a few in Driscoll's fluttering heart.

p, Stanley Kramer; d, Richard Fleischer; w, Earl Felton (based on the play by Samuel A. Taylor and the book by Robert Fontaine); ph, Charles Lawton, Jr.; m, Dmitri Tiomkin.

Comedy (MPAA:NR)

HARVEY

(1950) 104m UNIV bw

James Stewart *(Elwood P. Dowd)*, Josephine Hull *(Veta Louise Simmons)*, Peggy Dow *(Miss Kelly)*, Charles Drake *(Dr. Sanderson)*, Cecil Kellaway *(Dr. Chumley)*, Victoria Horne *(Myrtle Mae)*, Jesse White *(Wilson)*, William Lynn *(Judge Gaffney)*, Wallace Ford *(Lofgren)*, Nana Bryant *(Mrs. Chumley)*, Grace Mills *(Mrs. Chauvenet)*, Clem Bevans *(Herman)*, Ida Moore *(Mrs. McGiff)*, Richard Wessel *(Cracker)*, Pat Flaherty *(Policeman)*, Norman Leavitt *(Cab Driver)*, Maudie Prickett *(Elvira)*, Ed Max *(Salesman)*, Minerva Urecal *(Nurse Dunphy)*, Almira Sessions *(Mrs. Halsey)*, Anna O'Neal *(Nurse)*, Sally Corner *(Mrs. Cummings)*, Sam Wolfe *(Minninger)*, Polly Bailey *(Mrs. Krausmeyer)*, Grayce Hampton *(Mrs. Strickleberger)*, Ruth Elma Stevens *(Miss LaFay)*, Eula Guy *(Mrs. Johnson)*, William Val *(Chauffeur)*, Gino Corrado *(Eccentric Man)*, Don Brodie *(Mailman)*, Harry Hines *(Meegels)*, Aileen Carlyle *(Mrs. Tewksbury)*.

Elwood P. Dowd (Jimmy Stewart) is the whimsical inebriate whose kindness spills over into the lives of all around him as he tries to help those in need. Elwood lurches home one night to see a six-foot rabbit named Harvey leaning against a lamppost. This invisible "Pooka" becomes his friend and follows him everywhere, much to the chagrin of Elwood's social-climbing family, who think he has finally flipped and should be put in an asylum. Faithfully adapted by Mary Chase from her popular Broadway play, HARVEY is a delightful fantasy. Jimmy Stewart, in one of his best-loved roles, is wonderful as the gentle, sweet soul who befriends the invisible rabbit. His performance earned him an Oscar nomination, and Josephine Hull, as Stewart's harried sister, was honored

as Best Supporting Actress. Henry Koster's direction is sharp and moves along at a rapid clip. This is a happy movie and leaves a long, lingering warm glow.

p, John Beck; d, Henry Koster; w, Mary Chase, Oscar Brodney (based on a play by Mary Chase); ph, William Daniels; m, Frank Skinner.

Comedy (MPAA:NR)

HARVEY GIRLS, THE

(1946) 101m MGM c

Judy Garland *(Susan Bradley)*, John Hodiak *(Ned Trent)*, Ray Bolger *(Chris Maule)*, Preston Foster *(Judge Sam Purvis)*, Virginia O'Brien *(Alma)*, Angela Lansbury *(Em)*, Marjorie Main *(Sonora Cassidy)*, Chill Wills *(H.H. Hartsey)* Kenny Baker *(Terry O'Halloran)*, Selena Royle *(Miss Bliss)*, Cyd Charisse *(Deborah)*, Ruth Brady *(Ethel)*, Catherine McLeod *(Louise)*, Jack Lambert *(Marty Peters)*, Edward Earle *(Jed Adams)*, Virginia Hunter *(Jane)*, William "Bill" Phillips, Norman Leavitt *(Cowboys)*, Morris Ankrum *(Rev. Claggett)*, Ben Carter *(John Henry)*, Mitchell Lewis *(Sandy)*, Stephen McNally *(Goldust McClean)*, Bill Hall *(Big Joe)*, Ray Teal, Robert Emmett O'Connor *(Conductors)*, Vernon Dent *(Engineer)*, Jim Toney *(Mule Skinner)*, Dorothy Gilmore, Lucille Casey, Mary Jo Ellis, Mary Jean French, Joan Thorson, Jacqueline White, Daphne Moore, Dorothy Tuttle, Gloria Hope *(Harvey Girls)*.

THE HARVEY GIRLS is a lighthearted musical comedy with some terrific tunes by Harry Warren and Johnny Mercer, including the Oscar-winning "On the Atchison, Topeka and the Santa Fe." Susan Bradley (Judy Garland) is a 19th-century mail-order bride who goes out west to work as a waitress at one of Fred Harvey's new restaurants. Ned Trent (John Hodiak) owns the local saloon and his girl friend is Em (Angela Lansbury), a Mae West type who runs a bawdy house in the small New Mexico town. THE HARVEY GIRLS has a little of everything: songs, dance, action, romance, and the triumph of virtue and chastity over the forces of saloondom. Hodiak is suave and sophisticated as the gambler, and Garland was never more vibrant as the female lead. There is also some excellent supporting work by Ray Bolger, Marjorie Main, and Virginia O'Brien. Lenny Hayton received an Oscar nomination for his musical direction.

p, Arthur Freed; d, George Sidney; w, Edmund Beloin, Nathaniel Curtis, Harry Crane, James O'Hanlon, Samson Raphaelson (based on a story by Eleanore Griffin and William Rankin, from the novel by Samuel Hopkins Adams); ph, George Folsey (Technicolor).

Comedy/Musical (MPAA:NR)

HEAVENS ABOVE!

(1963, Brit.) 118m Charter/BL-Romulus-Janus bw

Peter Sellers *(Rev. John Smallwood)*, Cecil Parker *(Archdeacon Aspinall)*, Isabel Jeans *(Lady Despard)*, Eric Sykes *(Harry Smith)*, Bernard Miles *(Simpson)*, Brock Peters *(Matthew)*, Ian Carmichael *(The Other Smallwood)*,

Irene Handl *(Rene Smith)*, Miriam Karlin *(Winnie Smith)*, Joan Miller *(Mrs. Smith-Gould)*, Eric Barker *(Bank Manager)*, Roy Kinnear *(Fred Smith)*, Kenneth Griffith *(Rev. Owen Smith)*, Miles Malleson *(Rockerby)*, William Hartnell *(Maj. Fowler)*, Joan Hickson *(Garrulous Housewife)*, Harry Locke *(Shop Steward)*, Nicholas Phipps *(Director General)*, Thorley Walters *(Tranquilax Executive)*, George Woodbridge *(Bishop)*, Basil Dignam *(Prisoner Governor)*, Colin Gordon *(Prime Minister)*, Joan Heal *(Disgruntled Housewife)*, Malcolm Muggeridge *(Cleric)*, Conrad Phillips *(PRO)*, Cardew Robinson *(Tramp)*, Billy Milton *(Fellowes)*, Howard Pays *(Astronaut)*.

John Smallwood (Peter Sellers) is a prison chaplain who is appointed in error as the pastor of a wealthy church in an English industrial city. The man who was to have been given this plum parish (Ian Carmichael) is a fawning toady who would be quite content to mirror the desires of the rich parishioners. Instead, they get Smallwood, a man with progressive social convictions and the courage to carry them out. This British comedy makes its satirical points gently without belaboring the issue, and Sellers is totally believable as the simple, guileless man who only wants the best for his flock. Just about every supporting role is perfectly cast, with special kudos to Miles Malleson as a deranged psychiatrist and Cecil Parker as an archdeacon. The film's message seems to be that charity, no matter how Christian, is difficult to bestow and even more difficult to accept in the 20th century.

p, Roy Boulting; d, John Boulting; w, Frank Harvey, John Boulting (based on an idea by Malcolm Muggeridge); ph, Max Greene; m, Richard Rodney Bennett.

Comedy   **Cas.**   **(MPAA:NR)**

HEIDI

(1937) 87m Darryl F. Zanuck/FOX bw

Shirley Temple *(Heidi)*, Jean Hersholt *(Adolph Kramer)*, Arthur Treacher *(Andrews)*, Helen Westley *(Blind Anna)*, Pauline Moore *(Elsa)*, Thomas Beck *(Pastor Schultz)*, Mary Nash *(Fraulein Rottenmeier)*, Sidney Blackmer *(Herr Sesemann)*, Mady Christians *(Aunt Dete)*, Sig Rumann *(Police Captain)*, Marcia Mae Jones *(Klara Sesemann)*, Delmar Watson *(Peter the Goat Boy)*, Egon Brecher *(Innkeeper)*, Christian Rub *(Baker)*, George Humbert *(Organ Grinder)*.

Johanna Spyri's novel provided an excellent vehicle for the young Shirley Temple, and the public did the casting, as the studio received tons of fan mail demanding her in the title role. She plays Heidi, a Swiss orphan who is sent to live with her reclusive grandfather (Jean Hersholt), a bitter man because his son has left him. Heidi quickly breaks through the old man's cold exterior; however, she is taken away by an evil aunt, who sells her as a servant girl. She works at the home of a wealthy man with an invalid daughter and brightens up their lives while her grandfather struggles to find her. This classic children's film, expertly directed by Allan Dwan, is wonderfully en-

tertaining, with moppet Shirley Temple at her adorable best.

p, Raymond Griffith; d, Allan Dwan; w, Walter Ferris, Julien Josephson (based on a novel by Johanna Spyri); ph, Arthur Miller.

Drama   **Cas.**   **(MPAA:NR)**

HELLO, DOLLY!

(1969) 129m Chenault/FOX c

Barbra Streisand *(Dolly Levi)*, Walter Matthau *(Horace Vandergelder)*, Michael Crawford *(Cornelius Hackl)*, Louis Armstrong *(Orchestra Leader)*, Marianne McAndrew *(Irene Molloy)*, E.J. Peaker *(Minnie Fay)*, Danny Lockin *(Barnaby Tucker)*, Joyce Ames *(Ermengarde)*, Tommy Tune *(Ambrose Kemper)*, Judy Knaiz *(Gussie Granger)*, David Hurst *(Rudolph Reisenweber)*, Fritz Feld *(Fritz, German Waiter)*, Richard Collier *(Vandergelder's Barber)*, J. Pat O'Malley *(Policeman in Park)*.

HELLO, DOLLY! is a huge galumph of a movie based on Thornton Wilder's wildly successful play "The Matchmaker." Barbra Streisand was only 26 when she made this, considerably younger than the character she plays, a widow who earns her living in turn-of-the-century New York as a professional matchmaker, while trying to romance disinterested grain merchant Horace Vandergelder (Walter Matthau). Although it's a very pleasant musical with lots of catchy songs, HELLO, DOLLY! bombed at the box office and was one of three financially disastrous musicals on which Fox spent all of its SOUND OF MUSIC profits (STAR and DR. DOLITTLE were the others). The sure-fire combination of Streisand, Matthau, director Gene Kelly, and producer-writer Ernest Lehman isn't as flawless as one might hope it would be, but they hit much more than they miss, and HELLO, DOLLY! will elicit smile after smile. The tuneful score is by Jerry Herman, who wrote two new songs for the feature, "Just Leave Everything to Me" and "Love Is Only Love," which was originally intended to be used in "Mame." Other tunes in the film include "It Only Takes a Moment," "It Takes a Woman," "Put on Your Sunday Clothes," "Before the Parade Passes By," and the title song, which, as sung by Louis Armstrong, is the highlight of the movie.

p, Ernest Lehman; d, Gene Kelly; w, Ernest Lehman (based on the play "The Matchmaker" by Thornton Wilder); ph, Harry Stradling, Sr. (Todd-AO, Deluxe Color); m, Lenny Hayton, Lionel Newman.

Comedy/Musical   **Cas.**   **(MPAA:G)**

HENRY ALDRICH FOR PRESIDENT

(1941) 73m PAR bw

Jimmy [James] Lydon *(Henry Aldrich)*, Charles Smith *(Dizzy Stevens)*, June Preisser *(Geraldine Adams)*, Mary Anderson *(Phyllis Michael)*, Martha O'Driscoll *(Mary Aldrich)*, Dorothy Peterson *(Mrs. Aldrich)*, John Litel *(Mr. Aldrich)*, Rod Cameron *(Ed Calkins)*, Frank Coghlan, Jr.

(Marvin Bagshaw), Lucien Littlefield *(Mr. Crosley)*, Kenneth Howell *(Irwin Barrett)*, Buddy Pepper *(Johnny Beal)*, Vaughan Glaser *(Mr. Bradley)*, Dick Paxton *(Red MacGowan)*, Paul Matthews *(Tubby Gibbons)*, Bob Pittard *(Elmer Pringle)*, Bud [Lon] McCallister, Carmen Johnson, Helen Westcott, Rosita Butler, Georgia Lee Settle *(Students)*.

Henry Aldrich (Jimmy Lydon) runs for high-school class president in one of the best films of the "Aldrich" series—the first to star Lydon, who had replaced Jackie Cooper. Henry is nominated by a conniving rich kid whose intention is to split the votes and insure his own election. That plan backfires when the female candidate (Mary Anderson) falls for Henry and drops from the race. Complications arise as Henry is accused of stealing his opponent's speech, and someone tries to stuff the ballot boxes. Paramount created the "Henry Aldrich" series to compete with the "Andy Hardy" films that were mopping up at the box office. By purchasing the rights to the popular radio show "The Aldrich Family," the studio had a built-in audience, but they spent little money on the series, and it never rose above "B" picture status. Jimmy Lydon became so typecast in the Henry Aldrich role that when he appeared in films other than the series about the bumbling youth, members of the audience would shout "There's Henry Aldrich."

p, Sol C. Siegel; d, Hugh Bennett; w, Val Burton (based on the character created by Clifford Goldsmith); ph, John Mescall.

Comedy (MPAA:NR)

HERBIE RIDES AGAIN

(1974) 88m BV c

Helen Hayes *(Mrs. Steinmetz)*, Ken Berry *(Willoughby Whitfield)*, Stefanie Powers *(Nicole)*, John McIntire *(Mr. Judson)*, Keenan Wynn *(Alonzo Hawk)*, Huntz Hall *(Judge)*, Ivor Barry *(Chauffeur)*, Dan Tobin *(Lawyer)*, Vito Scotti *(Taxi Driver)*, Raymond Bailey *(Lawyer)*, Liam Dunn *(Doctor)*, Elaine Devry *(Secretary)*, Chuck McCann *(Loostgarten)*, Richard X. Slattery *(Traffic Commissioner)*, Hank Jones *(Sir Lancelot)*, Rod McCary *(Red Knight)*.

This sequel to THE LOVE BUG was one of Disney's most successful films of the 1970s. Herbie, the heroic Volkswagen, comes to the rescue of Mrs. Steinmetz (Helen Hayes) and Nicole (Stefanie Powers), who are trying to prevent villains Judson (John McIntire) and Hawk (Keenan Wynn, playing the same character he portrayed in THE ABSENT-MINDED PROFESSOR) from building a skyscraper where their house stands. Willoughby Whitfield (Ken Berry), Hawk's lawyer nephew, also joins with Herbie in the fight to stop the construction. Herbie enlists the help of all the VWs in San Francisco, and they arrive like the cavalry to fight off the imposing bulldozers. The "Herbie" films proved to be so popular that the Germans produced a ripoff of them in 1971 titled EIN KAEFER GEHT AUFS GANZE (their VW was called Dudu).

p, Bill Walsh; d, Robert Stevenson; w, Bill Walsh (based on a story by Gordon Buford); ph, Frank Phillips (Technicolor); m, George Bruns.

Comedy **Cas.** (MPAA:G)

HERE COME THE CO-EDS

(1945) 88m UNIV bw

Bud Abbott *(Slats)*, Lou Costello *(Oliver Quackenbush)*, Peggy Ryan *(Patty)*, Martha O'Driscoll *(Molly)*, June Vincent *(Diane)*, Lon Chaney, Jr. *(Johnson)*, Donald Cook *(Benson)*, Charles Dingle *(Jonathan Kirkland)*, Richard Lane *(Nearsighted Man)*, Joe Kirk *(Honest Dan)*, Bill Stern *(Announcer)*, Anthony Warde *(Timekeeper)*, Dorothy Ford *(Bertha)*, Sammy Stein *(Tiger McGurk)*, Carl Knowles *(Basketball Coach)*, Martha Garotto, Naomi Stout, June Cuendet, Muriel Stetson, Marilyn Hoeck, Margaret Eversole, Lorna Peterson *(Amazon Basketball Players)*, Ruth Lee *(Miss Holford)*, Don Costello *(Diamond)*, Rebel Randall, Maxine Gates, Dorothy Granger, Marie Osborn *(Women)*, Milt Bronson *(Ring Announcer)*, Phil Spitalny and His Band.

This amusing Abbott and Costello vehicle features the duo as caretakers at a women's college that is in deep financial trouble. To raise money to help keep the school open, Oliver (Costello) gets in the wrestling ring with "The Masked Marvel" (Lon Chaney, Jr.), who, sans his grappling disguise, is the man who is trying to close down the college. There are many hilarious moments in this consistently funny film, including a silent classic bit originally developed by Billy Bevan in which Costello is served a bowl of stew containing a live oyster. The oyster squirts his face, bites his fingers, and devours his necktie when he tries to catch it, yanking his face into the bowl. (This routine appeared three years earlier in a Three Stooges short, "Dutiful but Dumb," with Curly Howard as the victim, and a variation of the gag was employed in THE WISTFUL WIDOW OF WAGON GAP.)

p, John Grant; d, Jean Yarbrough; w, Arthur T. Horman, John Grant (based on a story by Edmund L. Hartmann); ph, George Robinson.

Comedy (MPAA:NR)

HERE COMES SANTA CLAUS

(1984) 78m NW c

Emeric Chapuis *(Simon)*, Armand Meffre *(Santa Claus)*, Karen Cheryl *(Teacher/Magic Fairy)*, Alexia *(Elodie)*, Dominique Hulin *(The Ogre)*, Jeanne Herviale *(Simon's Grandmother)*, Helene Zidi *(Simon's Mother)*, Jean-Louis Foulquier *(Simon's Father)*, Bouake *(Baye-Fall)*.

Simon (Emeric Chapuis) is a 7-year-old whose parents have mysteriously disappeared somewhere in Africa. After telling his teacher (Karen Cheryl), he heads to the North Pole with his friend Elodie (Alexia), in hopes of enlisting the help of Santa Claus (Armand Meffre). En route Simon must pass through the forest of an evil ogre (Dominique Hulin), but eventually he makes it to St. Nick's home. Of course, the jolly fat man is more than willing to help. Great fun for the kids. The special effects were created by George Lucas' Industrial Light & Magic company.

p&d, Christian Gion; w, Christian Gion, Didier Kaminka; ph, Jacques Assuerus; m, Francis Lai.

Fantasy   **Cas.**   **(MPAA:G)**

HILDUR AND THE MAGICIAN

(1969) 95m Canyon Cinema Cooperative bw

John Graham *(The Magician/Narrator)*, Hildur Mahl *(Hildur)*, Patricia Jordon *(Companion)*, Jim Yensan *(Gnome)*, Jani Novak *(Driad)*, Roy Berger *(Woodcutter)*, Shelby Sache *(His Wife)*, Tres Berger *(Arabelle)*, Sydney Droshin *(Wicked Queen)*, Tito Patri *(Huckster)*, Cook Ruddick *(King)*, Gael Knepfer *(Maid)*, Bunny Kirsch, Gina Batchelder, Sally Berger, Cathy Seitz, Mark Batchelder *(Fairies)*, Joel Andrews, Julie Iger, Avery Faulkner, Paula White *(Musicians)*, Sandra Della Valle.

This charming, well-photographed fairy tale will please kids while still holding adults' interest. The story, filmed in black and white, is about a princess who is kidnaped by an evil gnome. Armed with a magic potion, Hildur (Hildur Mahl), a fairy queen, sets out to rescue her. In addition to some excellent animation sequences, the tale is played out in mime, with John Graham, who plays the film's bumbling wizard, providing a voice-over narration. The cast also served as set constructors and costume makers, giving this independent 16mm feature a nice family feeling. Its only defect is the running time. An hour and a half is a little long for the material.

p,d&w, Larry Jordan (based on an idea by John Graham and Patricia Jordan); ph, Larry Jordan; m, Joel Andrews, Julie Iger.

Fantasy   **(MPAA:NR)**

HILLS OF HOME

(1948) 97m MGM c (AKA: MASTER OF LASSIE)

Edmund Gwenn *(Dr. William MacLure)*, Donald Crisp *(Drumsheugh)*, Tom Drake *(Tammas Milton)*, Janet Leigh *(Margit Mitchell)*, Rhys Williams *(Mr. Milton)*, Reginald Owen *(Hopps)*, Edmond Breon *(Jaimie Soutar)*, Alan Napier *(Sir George)*, Hugh Green *(Geordie)*, Lumsden Hare *(Lord Kilspindle)*, Eileen Erskine *(Belle Saunders)*, Victor Wood *(David Mitchell)*, David Thursby *(Burnbrae)*, Frederick Worlock *(Dr. Weston)*, Lassie the Dog.

One of the most enjoyable films of the very successful "Lassie" series, this finds the famous collie suffering from a psychological fear of water. In between tending to the medical needs of the area, her owner, a Scottish doctor (Edmund Gwenn), works with the dog to rid her of her phobia. When he is badly injured in an accident, Lassie overcomes her fears and swims a raging river to bring help to him. Tom Drake plays a young student doctor, Janet Leigh, in one of her early roles, plays his sweetheart, and Donald Crisp plays Gwenn's rich friend. Twenty-five years earlier, Crisp directed a British film based on the same Ian McLaren story.

p, Robert Sisk; d, Fred M. Wilcox; w, William Ludwig (based on "Doctor of the Old School" by Ian MacLaren); ph, Charles Schoenbaum (Technicolor); m, Herbert Stothart, Albert Sendrey, Robert Franklyn.

Drama   **(MPAA:NR)**

HIT THE DECK

(1955) 112m Metro c

Jane Powell *(Susan Smith)*, Tony Martin *(Chief Boatswain's Mate William F. Clark)*, Debbie Reynolds *(Carol Pace)*, Walter Pidgeon *(Rear Adm. Daniel Xavier Smith)*, Vic Damone *(Rico Ferrari)*, Gene Raymond *(Wendell Craig)*, Ann Miller *(Ginger)*, Russ Tamblyn *(Danny Xavier Smith)*, J. Carrol Naish *(Mr. Peroni)*, Kay Armen *(Mrs. Ottavio Ferrari)*, Richard Anderson *(Lt. Jackson)*, Jane Darwell *(Jenny)*, Alan King, Henry Slate *(Shore Patrol)*, Jubalaires *(Themselves)*, Frank Reynolds *(Dancer)*.

The familiar "three sailors on leave" plot line gets a big shot in the arm in this musical due to HIT THE DECK's outstanding cast, good production numbers, and nice visuals. Tony Martin, Russ Tamblyn, and Vic Damone play the three swabbies who venture into San Francisco in search of romance. Although Danny (Tamblyn) and Rico (Damone) must fulfill family obligations (Danny visits his father, an admiral, and Rico goes to see his mother), they all find time to fall in love.

p, Joe Pasternak; d, Roy Rowland; w, Sonya Levien, William Ludwig (based on the musical play by Herbert Fields and "Shore Leave" by Hubert Osborne); ph, George Folsey (CinemaScope, Eastmancolor).

Musical   **(MPAA:NR)**

HOLD THAT GHOST

(1941) 85m UNIV bw (AKA: OH, CHARLIE)

Bud Abbott *(Chuck Murray)*, Lou Costello *(Ferdinand Jones)*, Richard Carlson *(Dr. Jackson)*, Evelyn Ankers *(Norma Lind)*, Joan Davis *(Camille Brewster)*, Ted Lewis *(Himself)*, Mischa Auer *(Maitre D')*, Marc Lawrence *(Charlie Smith)*, Milton Parsons *(Harry Hoskins)*, Frank Penny *(Snake-Eyes)*, Edgar Dearing *(Irondome)*, Don Terry *(Strangler)*, Edward Pawley *(High Collar)*, Nestor Paiva *(Glum)*, Russell Hicks *(Lawyer Bannister)*, William B. Davidson *(Moose Matson)*, Paul Fix *(Lefty)*, Howard Hickman *(Judge)*, Harry Hayden *(Jenkins)*, William Forrest *(State Trooper)*, Paul Newlan *(Big Fink)*, Joe LaCava *(Little Fink)*, Bobby Barker *(Waiter)*, Shemp Howard *(Soda Jerk)*, Thurston Hall *(Alderman)*, Janet Shaw *(Alderman's Girl)*, Frank Richards *(Gunman)*, William Ruhl *(Customer)*, Mrs. Gardner Crane *(Mrs. Gitledge)*, The Andrews Sisters, Ted Lewis and his Orchestra.

Bud Abbott and Lou Costello inherit a haunted house where a gangster was murdered. There are all sorts of strange goings on and, of course, Costello sees the ghostly pranks and Abbott does not. Costello performs some brilliant pantomime as his terror-wracked form bumbles and bounces about the house and the sight gags run rampant. The routines in this film so impressed comics Olsen and Johnson that they used some of them in their own GHOST CATCHERS (1944). Fans of 1940s swing will enjoy the musical numbers, which include the Andrews Sisters performing "Sleepy Serenade" and "Aurora," and Ted Lewis and his Orchestra doing "When My Baby Smiles at Me" and "Me and My Shadow."

p, Alex Gottlieb; d, Arthur Lubin; w, Robert Lees, Frederic I. Rinaldo, John Grant (based on a story by Robert Lees and Frederic I. Rinaldo); ph, Elwood Bredell, Joseph Valentine.

Comedy   **Cas.**   **(MPAA:NR)**

HOME IN INDIANA

(1944) 103m FOX c

Walter Brennan *(J.P. "Thunder" Bolt)*, Lon McCallister *(Sparke Thorton)*, Jeanne Crain *(Char)*, June Haver *(Cri-Cri)*, Charlotte Greenwood *(Penny)*, Ward Bond *(Jed Bruce)*, Charles Dingle *(Godaw Boole)*, Robert Condon *(Gordon Bradley)*, Charles Saggau *(Jitterbug)*, Willie Best *(Mo' Bum)*, George H. Reed *(Tuppy)*, Noble "Kid" Chissell *(Fleaflit Dryer)*, Walter Baldwin *(Ed)*, George Cleveland *(Sam)*, Arthur Aylesworth *(Blacksmith)*, Libby Taylor *(Maid)*, Roger Imhof *(Old Timer)*, Matt McHugh *(Dave)*, Eddy Waller *(Bill)*, Billy Mitchell *(Waiter)*, Tom Dugan *(Soft Drink Man)*, Sam McDaniel, Emmett Smith *(Swipes)*, Hobart Condon *(Gordon)*.

Heartfelt story about Sparke Thorton (Lon McCallister), a city kid who goes to live in the country with his aunt and uncle (Charlotte Greenwood and Walter Brennan), a pair of semi-retired horse breeders with only one trotter left on their farm. Char (Jeanne Crain) and Cri-Cri (June Haver) are the two local lovelies who show Sparke another side of country living (swimming holes and jitterbugging, primarily—this *is* the 1940s). With the help of his uncle and the handyman (Willie Best), Sparke decides to raise a filly and become a champion sulky racer himself. This is a cheerful, upbeat film with some nice location work on the racetracks of Kentucky, Indiana, and Ohio. The sequence wherein the filly is born is sensitively handled and quite effective. The young actors handle their roles well, while the seasoned performers give nice support in their background roles, and Henry Hathaway's direction keeps things rolling along nicely.

p, Andre Daven; d, Henry Hathaway; w, Winston Miller (based on the novel *The Phantom Filly* by George Agnew Chamberlain); ph, Edward Cronjager (Technicolor); m, Hugo Freidhofer.

Drama   **(MPAA:NR)**

HOPE AND GLORY

(1987, Brit.) 113m COL c

Sebastian Rice-Edwards *(Bill Rohan)*, Geraldine Muir *(Sue Rohan)*, Sarah Miles *(Grace Rohan)*, David Hayman *(Clive Rohan)*, Sammi Davis *(Dawn Rohan)*, Derrick O'Connor *(Mac)*, Susan Wooldridge *(Molly)*, Jean-Marc Barr *(Cpl. Bruce Carey)*, Ian Bannen *(George)*, Annie Leon *(Bill's Grandmother)*, Jill Baker *(Faith)*, Amelda Brown *(Hope)*, Katrine Boorman *(Charity)*, Colin Higgins *(Clive's Friend)*, Shelagh Fraser *(WVS Woman)*, Gerald James *(Headmaster)*, Barbara Pierson *(Teacher)*, Nicky Taylor *(Roger)*, Sara Langton *(Pauline)*, Imogen Cawrse *(Jennifer)*, Susan Brown *(Mrs. Evans)*, Charley Boorman *(Luftwaffe Pilot)*, Peter Hughes *(Policeman)*, Christine Crowshaw *(Pianist)*, William Armstrong *(Canadian Sergeant)*, Arthur Cox *(Fireman)*, Ann Thornton, Andrew Bicknell *(Honeymoon Couple)*, Jodie Andrews, Nicholas Askew, Jamie Bowman, Colin Dale, David Parkin, Carlton Taylor *(Roger's Gang)*, John Boorman *(Narrator)*.

A wonderful film—an intelligent, heartfelt, personal, and marvelously entertaining look at growing up in England during WW II. A semiautobiographical project from British director John Boorman, the film concerns 9-year-old Bill (Sebastian Rice-Edwards) as he experiences the wonders of war from his suburban London home. While Americans may find it somewhat disconcerting to see the Blitz and its horrors made the setting for a nostalgic comedy, the fact is that for a young boy the war was a particularly exciting and vivid time, and a joyous feeling permeates the film. The total upheaval of the staid family order, the lack of normal restrictions and discipline, and the wholly liberating effect the war had on women are all brilliantly conveyed by Boorman, because he views the war from a child's perspective. Told in a series of vignettes, HOPE AND GLORY unfolds in a surprisingly nonchalant manner, tossing out its vividly realized observations at every turn. Boorman skillfully combines nuggets of truth with moments of mirth and is always prepared to surprise and amuse without sentimentalizing. Of all the WW II movies featuring children that were released in 1987-88 (EMPIRE OF THE SUN, AU REVOIR LES ENFANTS, RADIO DAYS), HOPE AND GLORY is the best.

p, John Boorman, Michael Dryhurst; d&w, John Boorman; ph, Philippe Rousselot, John Harris (Eastmancolor); m, Peter Martin.

Comedy/Drama   **Cas.**   **(MPAA:PG-13)**

HORN BLOWS AT MIDNIGHT, THE

(1945) 78m WB bw

Jack Benny *(Athanael)*, Alexis Smith *(Elizabeth)*, Dolores Moran *(Fran)*, Allyn Joslyn *(Osidro)*, Reginald Gardiner *(Archie Dexter)*, Guy Kibbee *(The Chief)*, John Alexander *(Doremus)*, Franklin Pangborn *(Sloan)*, Margaret Dumont *(Miss Rodholder)*, Bobby [Robert] Blake *(Junior)*, Ethel Griffies *(Lady Stover)*, Paul Harvey *(Thompson)*, Truman Bradley *(Radio Announcer)*, Mike Mazurki *(Humphrey Rafferty)*, John Brown *(Lew)*, Murray Alper *(Tony)*, Pat O'Moore *(Clerk)*, Isobel Elsom, James Burke, Harry Morgan, Monte Blue, Jack J. Ford, Emma Dunn, Harry Rosenthal.

In this delightful, if lightweight, screwball comedy, great

comedian Jack Benny plays an inept third-chair trumpet player in a band. He falls asleep and dreams that he is an archangel named Athanael, ordered to go to earth and blow his horn at midnight—signalling the end of this world and bringing about Judgment Day, as decreed by the heavenly Chief (Guy Kibbee), who is fed up with the way humans have been conducting themselves. Elizabeth (Alexis Smith), another heavenly type, is enamored of the scatterbrained Athanael, but knows he's a lost cause. Athanael arrives on earth and is about to blast it to eternity when he gets mixed up with a con man (Reginald Gardiner), and his efforts are further spoiled by two fallen angels (Allyn Joslyn and John Alexander) who do all in their power to prevent the final trumpeting. Although Benny used this film as a running gag on his radio show for years (claiming it had ruined his movie career), there are some comic gems here, especially in the smash finale.

p, Mark Hellinger; d, Raoul Walsh; w, Sam Hellman, James V. Kern (based on an idea by Aubrey Wisberg); ph, Sid Hickox; m, Franz Waxman.

Comedy (MPAA:NR)

HOW GREEN WAS MY VALLEY

(1941) 118m FOX bw

Walter Pidgeon *(Mr. Gruffydd)*, Maureen O'Hara *(Angharad)*, Donald Crisp *(Mr. Morgan)*, Anna Lee *(Bronwyn)*, Roddy McDowall *(Huw)*, John Loder *(Ianto)*, Sara Allgood *(Mrs. Morgan)*, Barry Fitzgerald *(Cyfartha)*, Patric Knowles *(Ivor)*, Morton Lowry *(Mr. Jonas)*, Arthur Shields *(Parry)*, Ann Todd *(Cienwen)*, Frederic Worlock *(Dr. Richards)*, Richard Fraser *(Davy)*, Rhys Williams *(Dai Bando)*, Clifford Severn *(Mervyn)*, Lionel Pape *(Mr. Evans)*, Ethel Griffies *(Mrs. Nicholas)*, Eve March *(Meillyn Lewis)*, Marten Lamont *(Iestyn Evans)*, Irving Pichel *(Narrator)*, Mary Field *(Eve)*, Evan S. Evans *(Gwinlyn)*, James Monks *(Owen)*, Mary Gordon.

Emotionally majestic, visually awesome, and spiritually uplifting in every scene, this was one of John Ford's undisputed masterpieces, a film that neither fades nor fails after repeated viewings. The mining area in South Wales and its hard-working miners and their families are seen through the eyes of Huw (Roddy McDowall), the youngest of six children in a family headed by a stern father (Donald Crisp) and loving mother (Sara Allgood). Set at the turn of the century and told in flashback, the film shows an unspoiled valley, full of love and warmth, wherein the trials and hardships of the community are told through a series of moving vignettes. Everything about this film is touching; master director John Ford (he won an Oscar for this film, one of four as Best Director) builds one simple scene upon another with very little plot, using incidents in the life of one family to tell the general tale, demonstrating changes and recording milestones. None but Ford could take such a simple tale and convert it into such a wonderful film. Beautifully assisted by cameraman Arthur Miller, who also won an Oscar, Ford received strong support from studio chief Darryl Zanuck, who personally produced the film. In addition to Ford and Miller, Oscars went to Fox for Best Picture, Richard Day and Nathan Juran for Best Art Direction, Thomas Little for Best Interior (set) Decoration, and Donald Crisp for Best Supporting Actor.

p, Darryl F. Zanuck; d, John Ford; w, Philip Dunne (based on the novel by Richard Llewellyn); ph, Arthur Miller; m, Alfred Newman.

Drama (MPAA:NR)

HOW THE WEST WAS WON

(1962) 165m MGM/Cinerama c

Spencer Tracy *(Narrator)*, Carroll Baker *(Eve Prescott)*, Lee J. Cobb *(Lou Ramsey)*, Henry Fonda *(Jethro Stuart)*, Carolyn Jones *(Julie Rawlings)*, Karl Malden *(Zebulon Prescott)*, Gregory Peck *(Cleve Van Valen)*, George Peppard *(Zeb Rawlings)*, Robert Preston *(Roger Morgan)*, Debbie Reynolds *(Lilith Prescott)*, James Stewart *(Linus Rawlings)*, Eli Wallach *(Charlie Gant)*, John Wayne *(Gen. William T. Sherman)*, Richard Widmark *(Mike King)*, Brigid Bazlen *(Dora Hawkins)*, Walter Brennan *(Col. Hawkins)*, David Brian *(Attorney)*, Andy Devine *(Cpl. Peterson)*, Raymond Massey *(Abraham Lincoln)*, Agnes Moorehead *(Rebecca Prescott)*, Harry Morgan *(Gen. Ulysses S. Grant)*, Thelma Ritter *(Agatha Clegg)*, Mickey Shaughnessy *(Deputy Marshall)*, Russ Tamblyn *(Reb Soldier)*, Tudor Owen *(Scotsman)*, Barry Harvey, Jamie Ross *(His Sons)*, Willis Bouchey *(Surgeon)*, Kim Charney *(Sam Prescott)*, Bryan Russell *(Zeke Prescott)*, Claude Johnson *(Jeremiah Rawlings)*, Jerry Holmes *(Railroad Clerk)*, Rudolfo Acosta *(Desperado)*, Chief Weasel, Red Cloud, Ben Black Elk *(Indians)*, Mark Allen *(Colin)*, Lee Van Cleef *(Marty)*, Charles Briggs *(Barker)*, Jay C. Flippen *(Huggins)*, Clinton Sundberg *(Hylan Seabury)*.

A great epic, a wonderful western, and a thrilling and poignant motion picture by any standard, HOW THE WEST WAS WON is so jam-packed with action and stars it's difficult to keep the events and personalities straight. Yet it is forthright movie-making at its best and is one of the few giant episodic adventures that holds viewer interest throughout. The film is basically a family picture, showing the growth of one family and how its descendants fared over three generations through the momentous events of 19th-century America. As such it becomes living, colorful history of the kind that could be made from many an American family tree. This mammoth film, beautifully narrated by Spencer Tracy, was directed by three Hollywood stalwarts, all action western directors of the first rank. Henry Hathaway handled the segments titled "The Rivers," "The Plains," and "The Outlaws"; George Marshall directed "The Railroad"; and the venerable John Ford did "The Civil War." Transitional sequences were directed by the uncredited Richard Thorpe. All handle their segments well, with Hathaway carrying most of the directorial burden. Though the story is lengthy, it is well written, with the emphasis correctly on action, yet the characters are infused with enough personality to make each distinctive. The Cinerama photography—which loses much on TV and on cassette—is beautifully done as the cameras recorded the vast American frontier. Unwieldy as it might have been, the film works, chiefly because Hollywood brought its finest technical talent to bear in this most memorable epic.

p, Bernard Smith; d, Henry Hathaway, John Ford, George Marshall, (uncredited) Richard Thorpe; w, James R. Webb (based on articles in *Life Magazine)*; ph, Joseph LaShelle, Charles Lang, Jr., William Daniels, Milton Krasner, Harold Wellman (Cinerama, Technicolor); m, Alfred Newman, Ken Darby.

Western   **Cas.**   **(MPAA:NR)**

HUCKLEBERRY FINN

(1939) 88m MGM bw (AKA: THE ADVENTURES OF HUCKLEBERRY FINN)

Mickey Rooney *(Huckleberry Finn)*, Walter Connolly *(The "King")*, William Frawley *(The "Duke")*, Rex Ingram *(Jim)*, Lynn Carver *(Mary Jane)*, Jo Ann Sayers *(Susan)*, Minor Watson *(Capt. Brandy)*, Elisabeth Risdon *(Widow Douglass)*, Victor Kilian *("Pap" Finn)*, Clara Blandick *(Miss Watson)*.

The second of four versions of *The Adventures of Huckleberry Finn* by Mark Twain, this is the best to date. The story is the same one America grew up on but director Richard Thorpe, producer Joseph L. Mankiewicz, and screenwriter Hugo Butler managed to put more fun into this remake than all the others combined. With Mickey Rooney as the irrepressible Huck, the fast-moving story grabs the audience from the start and never ceases to amuse. Huck resists the efforts of Widow Douglass (Elisabeth Risdon) and Miss Watson (Clara Blandick) to "civilize" him and flees to the Mississippi, where he hooks up with escaped slave Jim (Rex Ingram). The two float down the "Mighty Miss" on a raft, discovering much about the country and each other. Although the studio kept the budget to a minimum, the film is a great success due to Thorpe's imaginative direction and the excellent cast, with Rooney and Ingram especially memorable.

p, Joseph L. Mankiewicz; d, Richard Thorpe; w, Hugo Butler (based on the novel by Mark Twain); ph, John Seitz; m, Franz Waxman.

Comedy/Drama   **Cas.**   **(MPAA:NR)**

HUGO THE HIPPO

(1976, Hung./US) 78m Brut/FOX c

Voices of: Robert Morley, Paul Lynde, Jesse Emmet, Lance Taylor, Sr., Ronny Cox, Len Maxwell, Percy Rodrigues, Burl Ives, Marie Osmond, Jimmy Osmond.

Well animated, HUGO THE HIPPO is a charming children's film that tells the tale of a small hippo trying to escape death at the hands of angry Africans who are out to get him. The little hippo has run away from his captors after the Africans have drafted his fellow hippos into

service to scare off shark attacks. When the shark menace is gone, the Africans have no use for the hippos, so they let them starve. Hugo flees, and with the aid of a young African boy, he manages to call attention to the slaughter of his species. Marie and Jimmy Osmond and Burl Ives handle the singing chores.

p, Robert Halmi; d, Bill Feigenbaum; w, Tom Baum; m, Burt Keyes.

Animation   **Cas.**   **(MPAA:G)**

I

I REMEMBER MAMA

(1948) 134m RKO bw

Irene Dunne *(Mama)*, Barbara Bel Geddes *(Katrin)*, Oscar Homolka *(Uncle Chris)*, Philip Dorn *(Papa)*, Sir Cedric Hardwicke *(Mr. Hyde)*, Edgar Bergen *(Mr. Thorkelson)*, Rudy Vallee *(Dr. Johnson)*, Barbara O'Neil *(Jessie Brown)*, Florence Bates *(Florence Dana Moorhead)*, Peggy McIntyre *(Christine)*, June Hedin *(Dagmar)*, Steve Brown *(Nels)*, Ellen Corby *(Aunt Trina)*, Hope Landin *(Aunt Jenny)*, Edith Evanson *(Aunt Sigrid)*, Tommy Ivo *(Cousin Arne)*, Lela Bliss, Constance Purdy *(Nurses)*, Stanley Andrews *(Minister)*, Franklyn Farnum *(Man)*, Cleo Ridgley *(Schoolteacher)*, George Atkinson *(Postman)*, Howard Keiser *(Bellboy)*, Ruth Tobey, Alice Kerbert, Peggy McKim, Peggy Kerbert *(Girls)*.

Based on Kathryn Forbes' collection of autobiographical short stories *Mama's Bank Account*, this meticulously directed George Stevens film tells the heartwarming story of a Norwegian immigrant family making a go of it in turn-of-the-century San Francisco. Katrin (Barbara Bel Geddes), one of the daughters, narrates from her diary as the family's trials, tribulations, and triumphs are shown in flashback. At the center of the proceedings is the indefatigable Mama (Irene Dunne, giving one of her finest performances), keeping the house and her head while a dizzying parade of offbeat relatives and friends come and go, including Oscar Homolka, Cedric Hardwicke, Rudy Vallee, Edgar Bergen, and Philip Dorn as Papa. Forbes' nostalgic tale had earlier been brought to Broadway by Richard Rodgers and Oscar Hammerstein II (adapted by John Van Druten), and Peggy Wood later appeared in a long-running (1946 to 1957) TV series based on the story.

p, George Stevens, Harriet Parsons; d, Stevens; w, DeWitt Bodeen (based on the musical play by Richard Rodgers, Oscar Hammerstein II, and John Van Druten and the novel *Mama's Bank Account* by Kathryn Forbes); ph, Nick Musuraca; m, Roy Webb.

Drama   **Cas.**   **(MPAA:NR)**

IN SEARCH OF THE CASTAWAYS

(1962, Brit.) 100m BV c

Maurice Chevalier *(Prof. Jacques Paganel)*, Hayley Mills *(Mary Grant)*, George Sanders *(Thomas Ayerton)*, Wilfrid Hyde-White *(Lord Glenarvan)*, Michael Anderson, Jr. *(John Glenarvan)*, Antonio Cifariello *(Thalcave)*, Keith Hamshere *(Robert Grant)*, Wilfrid Brambell *(Bill Gaye)*, Jack Gwillim *(Capt. Grant)*, Ronald Fraser *(Guard)*, Inia Te Wiata *(Maori Chief)*, Norman Bird, Michael Wynne, Milo Sperber, Barry Keegan, George Murcell, Mark Dignam, Roger Delgado, Maxwell Shaw, Andreas Malandrinos, David Spenser.

A message in a bottle sends Prof. Jacques Paganel (Maurice Chevalier) on a globetrotting search for a missing sea captain (Jack Gwillin) in this Disney adventure. Accompanied by the captain's children (Hayley Mills and Keith Hamshere), Paganel embarks on a perilous journey that leads from South America to Australia and confronts the searchers with earthquakes, giant condors, cannibals, and the rascal responsible for the mutiny that led to the captain's disappearance.

p, Walt Disney; d, Robert Stevenson; w, Lowell S. Hawley (based on a story by Jules Verne); ph, Paul Beeson (Technicolor); m, William Alwyn.

Adventure/Fantasy   **Cas.**   **(MPAA:NR)**

IN THE GOOD OLD SUMMERTIME

(1949) 102m MGM c

Judy Garland *(Veronica Fisher)*, Van Johnson *(Andrew Larkin)*, S.Z. Sakall *(Otto Oberkugen)*, Spring Byington *(Nellie Burke)*, Clinton Sundberg *(Rudy Hansen)*, Buster Keaton *(Hickey)*, Marcia Van Dyke *(Louise Parkson)*, Lillian Bronson *(Aunt Addie)*.

Judy Garland and Van Johnson star in this music-filled remake of THE SHOP AROUND THE CORNER (1940) as antagonistic coworkers in a Chicago music store at the turn of the century who don't realize that they are pen pals. She plays piano and sells music; he pushes musical instruments. The cooler they are to each other at work, the hotter their letters become, and by the end they are in each other's arms, but not before a mix-up occurs involving a priceless Stradivarius and a more common fiddle, which ends up broken. Eighteen-month-old Liza Minnelli made her second screen appearance as the (finally married) couple's child at the film's end. (Her first appearance was in EASTER PARADE a year earlier.)

p, Joe Pasternak; d, Robert Z. Leonard; w, Samson Raphaelson, Francis Goodrich, Ivan Tors, Albert Hackett (based on the play "The Shop Around the Corner" by Miklos Laszlo); ph, Harry Stradling (Technicolor); m, George Stoll.

Comedy/Musical   **Cas.**   **(MPAA:NR)**

INCREDIBLE JOURNEY, THE

(1963) 86m Disney-Cangary/BV c

Emile Genest *(John Longridge)*, John Drainie *(Prof. Jim Hunter)*, Tommy Tweed *(The Hermit)*, Sandra Scott *(Mrs. Hunter)*, Syme Jago *(Helvi Nurmi)*, Marion Finlayson *(Elizabeth Hunter)*, Ronald Cohoon *(Peter Hunter)*, Robert Christie *(James MacKenzie)*, Beth Lockerbie *(Nell MacKenzie)*, Jan Rubes *(Carl Nurmi)*, Irena Mayeska *(Mrs. Nurmi)*, Beth Amos *(Mrs. Oakes)*, Eric Clavering *(Bert Oakes)*, Rex Allen *(Narrator)*, Muffey *(Bodger the Bull Terrier)*, Syn Cat *(Tao the Siamese Cat)*, Rink *(Luath the Labrador Retriever)*.

When a family goes abroad, leaving their two dogs and cat with a friend who lives 250 miles away, the pets get homesick and undertake the long journey home, encountering kindness from a little girl and an old hobo, as well as great danger. Returning from their foreign trip, Prof. Jim Hunter (John Drainie) and his family are heartbroken to learn of their beloved pets' disappearance, but the Disney folks were not about to let this one end unhappily. Featuring some astonishing *acting* from the highly trained animal stars and some beautiful shots of the Canadian high country, this simply told, episodic tale is great for kids and not too bad for big people either.

p, Walt Disney, James Algar; d, Fletcher Markle; w, James Algar (based on the book by Sheila Burnford); ph, Kenneth Peach (Technicolor); m, Oliver Wallace.

Adventure   **Cas.**   **(MPAA:NR)**

INN OF THE SIXTH HAPPINESS, THE

(1958) 158m FOX c

Ingrid Bergman *(Gladys Aylward)*, Curt Jurgens *(Capt. Lin Nan)*, Robert Donat *(Mandarin)*, Ronald Squire *(Sir Francis Jamison)*, Noel Hood *(Miss Thompson)*, Joan Young *(Cook)*, Moultrie Kelsall *(Dr. Robinson)*, Edith Sharpe *(Secretary)*, Richard Wattis *(Mr. Murfin)*, Athene Seyler *(Mrs. Lawson)*, Peter Chong *(Yang)*, Michael David *(Ho Ka)*, Zed Zakari *(Prison Guard)*, Burt Kwouk *(Li)*, Frank Blaine *(Madman)*, Ronald Kyaing *(Young Lin)*, Tsai Chin *(Sui-Lan)*, Louise Lin *(Mai-Da)*, Michael Wee *(Mandarin's Aide)*, Lian-Shin Yang *(Woman with Baby)*, Ye-Min *(Bai Boa)*, Judith Lai *(Sixpence)*, Frank Goh *(Timothy)*, Andre Mikhelson *(Russian Commissar)*, Stanislaw Mikula *(Russian Conductor)*, Lin Chen *(Innkeeper's Wife)*, Ronald Lee *(Chief Muleteer)*, Christopher Chen *(Tax Collector)*, Aung Min *(Buddhist Priest)*.

Set in pre-WW II China and based on the true story of Gladys Aylward, THE INN OF THE SIXTH HAPPINESS is an inspiring film. Aylward (Ingrid Bergman), an English domestic, ventures to an inn high in the mountains of northern China, where she helps a British missionary (Athene Seyler) save souls. In the process Aylward earns the grudging respect of an old mandarin (Robert Donat), who does his best to see that she is occupied with do-gooding and out of his hair. When invasion by the Japanese is imminent, Capt. Lin Nan (Curt Jurgens), a Chinese army officer, appears and enlists Aylward's help in informing the locals of the coming danger. The captain and Aylward fall in love, but when the invasion begins, he rejoins his unit and she leads the villagers on an arduous journey to the safety of a mission located in the country's interior. Shot in north Wales, this film marked the last screen appearance for gifted actor Donat.

p, Buddy Adler; d, Mark Robson; w, Isobel Lennart (based on the novel *The Small Woman* by Alan Burgess); ph, Frederick A. Young (CinemaScope, Deluxe Color); m, Malcolm Arnold.

Drama **Cas.** **(MPAA:NR)**

INSPECTOR GENERAL, THE

(1949) 102m WB c (AKA: HAPPY TIMES)

Danny Kaye *(Georgi)*, Walter Slezak *(Yakov)*, Barbara Bates *(Leza)*, Elsa Lanchester *(Maria)*, Gene Lockhart *(The Mayor)*, Alan Hale *(Kovatch)*, Walter Catlett *(Col. Castine)*, Rhys Williams *(Inspector General)*, Benny Baker *(Telecki)*, Norman Leavitt *(Laszlo)*, Sam Hearn *(Gizzick)*, Lew Hearn *(Izzick)*, Byron Foulger *(Burbis)*, Lennie Bremen *(Lieutenant)*, Nestor Paiva *(Gregor)*.

This loose musical-comedy adaptation of the famous Gogol play is primarily a showcase for the many talents of Danny Kaye. Mistaken for an emissary of the Czar, Georgi (Kaye), an illiterate medicine show sideman, is welcomed by a group of corrupt small-town Russian officials with all the respect due a royal inspector. Kaye sings, dances, and mugs his way through the film in his inimitable fashion, particularly shining on "The Gypsy Drinking Song," a wonderful comic piece cowritten by his wife, Silvia Fine, and Johnny Mercer.

p, Jerry Wald; d, Henry Koster; w, Philip Rapp, Harry Kurnitz (based on the play by Nikolai Gogol); ph, Elwood Bredell; m, Johnny Green.

Comedy/Musical **Cas.** **(MPAA:NR)**

INVISIBLE BOY, THE

(1957) 90m Pan/MGM bw

Richard Eyer *(Timmie Merrinoe)*, Philip Abbott *(Dr. Merrinoe)*, Diane Brewster *(Mary Merrinoe)*, Harold J. Stone *(Gen. Swayne)*, Robert H. Harris *(Prof. Allerton)*, Dennis McCarthy *(Col. Macklin)*, Alexander Lockwood *(Arthur Kelvaney)*, John O'Malley *(Dr. Baine)*, Gage Clark, Than Wyenn, Jefferson Dudley Searles, Alfred Linder, Ralph Votrian, Michael Miller.

An underrated science-fiction film about young Timmie Merrinoe (Richard Eyer) and his relationship with the robot that becomes a kind of surrogate father for him. Dr. Merrinoe (Philip Abbott), the genius who is Timmie's actual father, invents a supercomputer that soon begins to act on its own, taking over the "conscience" of Robby the Robot (a refugee from FORBIDDEN PLANET). Timmie puts an end to the chaos by smashing the machine that his father can't bring himself to destroy. The picture's strength lies in its point of view, as—a la Steven Spielberg's E.T.—it sympathetically observes events

from Timmie's perspective, showing the film's adults to be nearly as insensitive as the machines.

p, Nicholas Nayfack; d, Herman Hoffman; w, Cyril Hume (based on a story by Edmund Cooper); ph, Harold Wellman; m, Les Baxter.

Science Fiction **(MPAA:NR)**

ISLAND AT THE TOP OF THE WORLD, THE

(1974) 95m Disney/BV c

David Hartman *(Prof. Ivarsson)*, Donald Sinden *(Sir Anthony Ross)*, Jacques Marin *(Capt. Brieux)*, Mako *(Oomiak)*, David Gwillim *(Donald Ross)*, Agneta Eckemyr *(Freyja)*, Gunnar Ohlund *(The Godi)*, Lasse Kolstad *(Erik)*, Erik Silju *(Torvald)*, Rolf Soder *(Lawspeaker)*, Torsten Wahlund *(Sven)*, Sverre [Anker] Ousdal *(Gunnar)*, Niels Hinrichsen *(Sigurd)*, Denny Miller *(Town Guard)*, Brendan Dillon *(The Factor)*, James Almanzar *(French Engineer)*, Ivor Barry *(The Butler)*, Lee Paul *(Chief of Boat Archers)*.

Reminiscent of Jules Verne fantasies, this Disney adventure sends a team of Arctic explorers into an uncharted area at the turn of the century. Sir Anthony Ross (Donald Sinden), a wealthy Englishman, organizes the team in an attempt to locate his missing son. With a professor of Nordic history (David Hartman) along to provide expert counsel, they venture into a mysterious valley that borders on a massive volcano. There they soon encounter a Viking settlement, making their search even more dangerous. Stunningly photographed scenery and convincing visual effects make this film one of Disney's more believable efforts.

p, Winston Hibler; d, Robert Stevenson; w, John Whedon (based on the novel *The Lost Ones* by Ian Cameron); ph, Frank Phillips (Technicolor); m, Maurice Jarre.

Adventure/Science Fiction **Cas.** **(MPAA:NR)**

ISLAND OF THE BLUE DOLPHINS

(1964) 93m UNIV c

Celia Kaye *(Karana)*, Larry Domasin *(Ramo)*, Ann Daniel *(Tutok)*, George Kennedy *(Aleut Captain)*, Carlos Romero *(Chowig)*, Hal Jon Norman *(Kimki)*, Martin Garralaga *(The Priest)*, Alex Montoya *(Spanish Captain)*, Julie Payne *(Lurai)*, Jon Alvar *(Tainer)*, Junior the Dog *(Rontu)*, Manchester Tribe of the Poma Nation, Kashia Tribe of the Poma Nation.

Based on the popular children's novel by Scott O'Dell, this adventure is a sort of female, children's *Robinson Crusoe* set in the Aleutian Islands. Karana (Celia Kaye) is a young native girl who is forced to flee her island home with the rest of her tribe in the early 1800s when white hunters threaten. Realizing her young brother has been left behind, she jumps ship and swims back. The two remain on the island and endure solitude for nearly 20 years. She learns to hunt and fish, make a home, and domesticate a wild dog, although her brother is not so resourceful and falls victim to a pack of wild animals. Distrustful, she passes up a chance to be rescued when another group of white hunters arrives on the island. Years later, after her trusty canine companion has died, she gets a second chance to be saved. She goes with the hunters, bringing her collection of pets along for the ride. A well-made film with a lead character with whom kids will easily empathize.

p, Robert B. Radnitz, Edward Mull; d, James B. Clark; w, Ted Sherdeman, Jane Klove, Robert B. Radnitz (based on the novel by Scott O'Dell); ph, Leo Tover (Eastmancolor); m, Paul Sawtell.

Drama   Cas.   (MPAA:NR)

IT HAPPENS EVERY SPRING

(1949) 87m FOX bw

Ray Milland (Vernon Simpson), Jean Peters (Deborah Greenleaf), Paul Douglas (Monk Lanigan), Ed Begley (Stone), Ted de Corsia (Dolan), Ray Collins (Prof. Greenleaf), Jessie Royce Landis (Mrs. Greenleaf), Alan Hale, Jr. (Schmidt), Bill Murphy (Isbell), William E. Green (Prof. Forsythe), Edward Keane (Bell), Gene Evans (Mueller), Al Eben (Parker), Ruth Lee (Miss Collins), John Butler (Fan), Jane Van Duser (Miss Mengalstein), Ray Teal (Mac), Don Hicks (Assistant to Announcer), Mickey Simpson (Policeman), Johnny Calkins (Boy), Harry Cheshire (Doctor), Ward Brant, John McKee (Baseball Players), Debra Paget (Alice), Mae Marsh (Maid), Tom Hanlon (St. Louis Broadcaster), Sam Hayes (New York Announcer), Douglas Spencer (Conductor), Pat Combs (Messenger Boy), Robert Patten (Cab Driver).

Superb actor Ray Milland, at home with drama or comedy, shines as Vernon Simpson, a chemistry professor who stumbles onto a formula that repels any kind of wood that gets near it. Needing some extra cash so that he can marry his sweetheart (Jean Peters), Vernon, a big baseball fan, gets a tryout with a major league team and, applying his special solution to the baseballs, transforms himself into an unhittable pitcher. Not only does he make the team, but he wins 38 games and almost single-handedly wraps up the World Series as his doctored screwballs hop, bounce, jerk, and flit around mightily swung bats. One of the funniest moments in this side-splitting comedy comes when Vernon's catcher roommate (Paul Douglas) mistakes the solution for hair tonic and tries to take a brush to his head. Featuring a marvelous script by Valentine Davies and ably directed by Lloyd Bacon, IT HAPPENS EVERY SPRING is one of the most entertaining films ever made about the national pastime.

p, William Perlberg; d, Lloyd Bacon; w, Valentine Davies (based on a story by Davies, Shirley W. Smith); ph, Joe MacDonald; m, Leigh Harline.

Comedy/Sports   (MPAA:NR)

IT'S A GIFT

(1934) 73m PAR bw

W.C. Fields (Harold Bissonette, Proprietor), Jean Rouverol (Mildred Bissonette, Lovesick Daughter), Julian Mad-

ison (John Durston, Salesman), Kathleen Howard (Amelia Bissonette), Tom Bupp (Norman Bissonette, Skate-Wearing Son), Tammany Young (Everett Ricks, Clerk), Baby LeRoy (Baby Ellwood Dunk), Morgan Wallace (Jasper Fitchmueller, Kumquats Customer), Charles Sellon (Mr. Muckle/Blind Man/House Detective), Josephine Whittell (Mrs. Dunk), Diana Lewis (Miss Dunk), T. Roy Barnes (Insurance Salesman), Spencer Charters (Gate Guard), Guy Usher (Harry Payne Bosterly, Promoter), Jerry Mandy (Vegetable Man), Patsy O'Byrne (Mrs. Frobisher, Doing Her Wash), Edith Kingdom (Old Woman in Limousine), James Burke (Iceman), William Tooker (Old Man in Limousine), Billy Engle (Bit), Jack Mulhall (Butler), Bud Fine (Driver), Eddie Baker (Yard Attendant), Chill Wills and the Avalon Boys (Campfire Rustics/Singers), Jane Withers (Hopscotch Girl), Buster the Dog.

This is not only the finest, funniest movie W.C. Fields ever made, it's one of the greatest comedies ever put on the screen, thanks to the performance of the great Fields. A rollicking spoof of middle-class marriage and mainstream ambitions, it casts Fields as a henpecked, harassed small-town shopowner with selfish children and a nagging wife. When his family isn't making his life miserable, his customers and neighbors are. He dreams of the good life and a California orange grove he's purchased with an inheritance, but the hostile world won't even let him get a decent night's sleep. When he and his family finally make it to California, they learn he's been swindled, but, predictably, he gets the last laugh. IT'S A GIFT is nonstop humor, loaded with Fields' patented sight gags, slapstick, and routines. Fields resurrected much of this material from other sources, such as his silent film IT'S THE OLD ARMY GAME and the 1925 play "The Comic Supplement," and also drew on his memories as the son of a Philadelphia pushcart vendor for some of the story, which he wrote under the name of Charles Bogle. Though Norman McLeod was the nominal director, Fields picked his own cast and essentially ran the film, and his wonderful, caustic humor comes through on every frame. It was during this film that Fields pulled his infamous prank on Baby LeRoy, loading the two-and-a-half-year-old's bottle with gin when the child star acted up on the set.

p, William LeBaron; d, Norman Z. McLeod; w, Jack Cunningham (uncredited) W.C. Fields (based on "The Comic Supplement" by J.P. McEvoy, [uncredited] W.C. Fields, and a story by Charles Bogle [W.C. Fields]); ph, Henry Sharp.

Comedy   Cas.   (MPAA:NR)

IT'S A MAD, MAD, MAD, MAD WORLD

(1963) 192m Casey/UA c

Spencer Tracy (Capt. C.G. Culpeper), Milton Berle (J. Russell Finch), Sid Caesar (Melville Crump), Buddy Hackett (Benjy Benjamin), Ethel Merman (Mrs. Marcus), Mickey Rooney (Ding Bell), Dick Shawn (Sylvester Marcus), Phil Silvers (Otto Meyer), Terry-Thomas (J. Algernon Hawthorne), Jonathan Winters (Lennie Pike), Edie Adams (Monica Crump), Dorothy Provine (Emmeline Finch), Jim Backus (Tyler Fitzgerald), Ben Blue (Airplane Pilot), Alan Carney (Police Sergeant), Barrie Chase (Mrs. Haliburton), William Demarest (Chief of Police), Eddie "Rochester" Anderson, Leo Gorcey, Peter Falk (Cab Drivers), Paul Ford (Col. Wilberforce), Edward Everett Horton (Dinckler), Buster Keaton (Jimmy the Crook), Don Knotts (Nervous Man), Carl Reiner (Tower Control), The Three Stooges (Firemen), Joe E. Brown (Union Official), Andy Devine (Sheriff Mason), Sterling Holloway (Fire Chief), Marvin Kaplan (Irwin, Gas Station Attendant), Arnold Stang (Ray, Gas Station Attendant), Howard Da Silva (Airport Officer), ZaSu Pitts (Switchboard Operator), Madlyn Rhue (Police Secretary), Jesse White (Radio Tower Operator), Selma Diamond (Voice of Culpeper's Wife), Stan Freberg (Deputy Sheriff), Mike Mazurki (Miner), Sammee Tong (Chinese Laundryman), Jimmy Durante (Smiler Grogan), Harry Lauter (Radio Operator), Doodles Weaver (Stuntman), Jack Benny (Man on Road), Jerry Lewis (Mad Driver), Chick Chandler, Barbara Pepper, Cliff Norton, Roy Roberts.

Designed to be the biggest, most lavish comedy ever made (its $7-million budget was a heavy one at the time), IT'S A MAD, MAD, MAD, MAD WORLD is a mirthful, star-studded pageant of Keystone Kops-style slapstick. With his dying breath, a gangster recently released from prison (Jimmy Durante) tells the motorists who come upon him after an auto accident that $350,000 is buried under "the big W," instigating a greedy, madcap dash for the cash. Among the lunatic treasure seekers who will stop at nothing to get to the loot first are Milton Berle, Dorothy Provine (who plays his wife), Ethel Merman (as his mother-in-law), Sid Caesar and Edie Adams (as husband and wife), Buddy Hackett, Mickey Rooney, and Jonathan Winters, playing a truck driver. Phil Silvers, Terry-Thomas, Peter Falk, Dick Shawn, and Spencer Tracy also become involved, and the film is a who's who of Hollywood comedians in cameo appearances. Director-producer Kramer spared no expense on the spectacular stunts, using 39 stunt men and paying them $252,000 for some of the most incredible feats on film.

p&d, Stanley Kramer; w, William and Tania Rose; ph, Ernest Laszlo (UltraPanavision, Technicolor); m, Ernest Gold.

Comedy   **Cas.**   **(MPAA:NR)**

IT'S A WONDERFUL LIFE

(1946) 129m Liberty Films/RKO bw

James Stewart (George Bailey), Donna Reed (Mary Hatch), Lionel Barrymore (Mr. Potter), Thomas Mitchell (Uncle Billy), Henry Travers (Clarence), Beulah Bondi (Mrs. Bailey), Frank Faylen (Ernie), Ward Bond (Bert), Gloria Grahame (Violet Bick), H.B. Warner (Mr. Gower), Frank Albertson (Sam Wainwright), Samuel S. Hinds (Pa Bai-

ley), Todd Karns (Harry Bailey), Mary Treen (Cousin Tilly), Virginia Patton (Ruth Dakin), Charles Williams (Cousin Eustace), Sarah Edwards (Mrs. Hatch), William Edmunds (Mr. Martini), Lillian Randolph (Annie), Argentina Brunetti (Mrs. Martini), Bobby Anderson (Little George), Ronnie Ralph (Little Sam), Jean Gale (Little Mary), Jeanine Anne Roose (Little Violet), Danny Mummert (Little Marty Hatch), George Nokes (Little Harry Bailey), Sheldon Leonard (Nick), Frank Hagney (Potter's Bodyguard), Ray Walker (Joe at Luggage Shop), Charles Lane (Real Estate Salesman), Edward Keane (Tom), Carol Coomes (Janie Bailey), Karolyn Grimes (Zuzu Bailey), Jimmy Hawkins (Tommy Bailey), Larry Simms (Pete Bailey), Carl "Alfalfa" Switzer (Freddie), Hal Landon (Marty Hatch), Harry Holman (High School Principal), Bobby Scott (Mickey), Harry Cheshire (Dr. Campbell), Charles Halton (Bank Examiner), Ed Featherstone (Bank Teller), Stanley Andrews (Mr. Welch), J. Farrell MacDonald (House Owner), Marion Carr (Mrs. Wainwright), Garry Owen (Bill Poster), Lane Chandler, Ellen Corby, Almira Sessions, Lee Frederick, Bert Moorehouse.

This heartwarming fantasy, one of the most popular films ever made, begins as angels discuss George Bailey (James Stewart), a small-town resident so beset with problems that he contemplates a Christmastime suicide. In flashback, we review George's life, learning that he has always wanted to leave his hometown to see the world, but that circumstances and his own good heart have kept him in Bedford Falls, sacrificing his own education for his brother's, keeping the family-run savings and loan afloat, protecting the town from the avarice of banker Potter (Lionel Barrymore), marrying his childhood sweetheart (Donna Reed), and raising a family. Back in the present, George prepares to jump from a bridge, but ends up rescuing his guardian angel, Clarence Oddbody (Henry Travers), who has come to earn his wings. Clarence shows him how badly Bedford Falls would have turned out without George and his good deeds. Filled with renewed joy in life, George goes home to his loving family and friends, who pitch in to put his worries behind him. Few filmmakers have rivaled director Frank Capra when it comes to examining the human heart, and IT'S A WONDERFUL LIFE is a masterfully crafted exercise in sentiment, augmented by Capra's undying faith in community. Reed and Barrymore give excellent performances, as does a superb cast of character players, but this is Stewart's film, and he is stirring as the dreamer who sacrifices all for his fellow man. The bright, funny screenplay is based on "The Greatest Gift," a story that Philip Van Doren Stern originally sent to his friends as a Christmas card.

p&d, Frank Capra; w, Frances Goodrich, Albert Hackett, Frank Capra, Jo Swerling (based on the story "The Greatest Gift" by Philip Van Doren Stern); ph, Joseph Walker, Joseph Biroc; m, Dimitri Tiomkin.

Comedy/Fantasy   **Cas.**   **(MPAA:NR)**

JACK FROST

(1966, USSR) 79m Gorky/EM c (MOROZKO)

Aleksandr Khvylya *(Jack Frost)*, Natasha Sedykh *(Nastenka)*, Eduard Izotov *(Ivan)*, Inna Churikova *(Marfushka)*, Pavel Pavlenko *(Father)*, Vera Altayskaya *(Stepmother)*, Georgiy Millyar *(Witch)*, M. Yanshin, G. Borisova *(Old Mushrooms)*, Anatoliy Kubatskiy *(Bandit Chieftain)*, Valentin Bryleyev *(Eligible Bachelor)*, T. Pelttser *(Eligible Bachelor's Mother)*, T. Barysheva *(Matchmaker)*, V. Popova *(Old Woman)*, Z. Vorkul *(Ivan's Mother)*, A. Zuyeva *(Storyteller, Russian Version)*.

This enchanting children's film from Russia is filled with interesting characters and contains enough visual excitement to keep restless eyes attentive. The fairy tale plot concerns an emotionally neglected young girl whose wicked stepmother forces her to work, while her sister gets to enjoy life. The girl falls in love with a handsome village boy, but a gremlin turns the boy's head into that of a bear. He must prove his worth by performing a good deed, and only then will he be returned to his normal state. An unbroken string of adventures makes this fantasy a joy for all ages.

d, Aleksandr Rou; w, Mikhail Volpin, Nikolay Erdman (based on the fairy tale "Morozko"); ph, Dmitriy Surenskiy; m, Nikolay Budashkin.

Fantasy **(MPAA:NR)**

JACK THE GIANT KILLER

(1962) 94m Zenith/UA c

Kerwin Mathews *(Jack)*, Judi Meredith *(Princess Elaine)*, Torin Thatcher *(Pendragon)*, Walter Burke *(Garna)*, Roger Mobley *(Peter)*, Barry Kelley *(Sigurd)*, Don Beddoe *(Imp in Bottle)*, Dayton Lummis *(King Mark)*, Anna Lee *(Lady Constance)*, Helen Wallace *(Jack's Mother)*, Tudor Owen *(Chancellor)*, Robert Gist *(Capt. McFadden)*, Ken Mayer *(Boatswain)*.

Nearly a carbon copy of THE SEVENTH VOYAGE OF SINBAD, this medieval fantasy concerns an evil wizard (Torin Thatcher) who attempts to regain lost magical powers by abducting a princess (Judi Meredith). The hardy Jack (Kerwin Mathews), a farmer's son, kills the wizard's giant servant and rescues her, whereupon he is asked to escort the damsel to safety at a faraway convent. Over the course of the trip Jack must battle an assortment of witches, dragons, sea monsters, and other fantastic creatures, with the aid of a magic leprechaun, a dog, and even a chimpanzee. The wizard tries to stop the crew one last time when he turns himself into a dragon, but is promptly slain for a happy ending. The live animation was created by Jim Danforth, who earlier worked on the popular "Gumby" shorts with Art Clokey. Despite the

borrowed plot line, the film carries its own share of thrills, making for a fun outing. Kids will love it.

p, Edward Small; d, Nathan Juran; w, Orville H. Hampton, Nathan Juran (based on story by Orville H. Hampton); ph, David S. Horsley (Fantascope, Technicolor); m, Paul Sawtell, Bert Shefter.

Adventure/Fantasy **(MPAA:NR)**

JALOPY

(1953) 62m AA bw

Leo Gorcey *(Terrence Aloysius "Slip" Mahoney)*, Huntz Hall *(Horace Debussy "Sach" Jones)*, David Condon *(Chuck)*, Bennie Bartlett *(Butch)*, Bernard Gorcey *(Louie Dumbrowski)*, Robert Lowery *(Skid Wilson)*, Jane Easton *(Bobbie Lane)*, Leon Belasco *(Prof. Bosgood Elrod)*, Richard Benedict *(Tony Lango)*, Murray Alper *(Red Baker)*, Tom Hanlon *(Race Announcer)*, Mona Knox *("Invented" Girl)*, Conrad Brooks *(Party Guest)*, Robert Rose, George Dockstader, George Barrows, Fred Lamont, Teddy Mangean, Bud Wolfe, Carey Loftin, Louis Tomei, Dude Criswell, Dick Crockett, Pete Kellett, Carl Saxe *(Jalopy Drivers)*.

By 1953, the "Bowery Boys" series was beginning to drag. Its near-middle-aged stars, Leo Gorcey and Huntz Hall, who had been with the series since DEAD END (1937), felt foolish playing the same juvenile delinquent characters. Gorcey and Hall pushed for a new producer, Ben Schwalb, and a new director, William Beaudine, who had the cast "grow up" and play adults—or rather the befuddled parodies of adults to which the films' mainly youthful audience could relate. The new approach revitalized the series for five more years. In JALOPY, the boys are desperate for a way to bail a pal (Bernard Gorcey) out of his financial troubles. Slip Mahoney (Leo Gorcey) decides to enter his junky car in a race to win some quick cash, and when Sach Jones (Hall) discovers a superfuel that will transform any normal vehicle into an unbelievable speed machine, Slip's car is able to whip around the track in just over 10 seconds. (In another deviation from the conventions of the series, Sach's potion apparently has the further power of causing beautiful young women to appear from nowhere!) A crooked gambler finds out about the fuel and tries to steal it, but the boys manage to keep it out of his hands—although the day of the big race is not without its slapstick complications.

p, Ben Schwalb; d, William Beaudine; w, Tim Ryan, Jack Crutcher, Edmond Seward, Jr., Bert Lawrence (based on a story by Tim Ryan and Jack Crutcher); ph, Harry Neumann; m, Marlin Skiles.

Comedy **(MPAA:NR)**

JASON AND THE ARGONAUTS

(1963, Brit.) 104m COL c (AKA: JASON AND THE GOLDEN FLEECE)

Todd Armstrong *(Jason)*, Nancy Kovack *(Medea)*, Gary Raymond *(Acastus)*, Laurence Naismith *(Argus)*, Niall

MacGinnis (Zeus), Michael Gwynn (Hermes), Douglas Wilmer (Pelias), Jack Gwillim (King Aeetes), Honor Blackman (Hera), John Cairney (Hylas), Patrick Troughton (Phineas), Andrew Faulds (Phalerus), Nigel Green (Hercules), Gernando Poggi (Castor), John Crawford (Polydeuces), Douglas Robinson (Euphemus).

This film, along with THE SEVENTH VOYAGE OF SINBAD, contains special effects master Ray Harryhausen's finest work, evoking a world of dragons, living statues, harpies, and gods. Pelias (Douglas Wilmer) murders the king of Thessaly and steals his throne, but the infant prince, Jason, survives. Years later, aided by the goddess Hera (Honor Blackman), Jason (Todd Armstrong) begins a search for the Golden Fleece, which will finally instate him as rightful king. With a crew of brave men (including Hercules, in a fine performance by Nigel Green), he sets out on his glorious quest in his ship, the Argo. At one point, the Argo is menaced by a giant living statue, but Jason defeats it and, after further adventures in which Jason battles harpies, encounters the gigantic Neptune, and discovers Medea (Nancy Kovack) on an empty ship, the crew finally finds the Fleece. They kill the seven-headed hydra that guards it, but are halted again when the hydra's teeth grow into seven sword-brandishing living skeletons. In a stunning display of technical wizardry, the Argonauts fight the skeletons to the death. Harryhausen is at his most creative and brilliant, the film is well directed (by Don Chaffey) and acted, the photography of the Mediterranean is beautiful, and Bernard Herrmann's score is one of his best, making this a great film for kids that will also please even the most discriminating adult viewer. A must see.

p, Charles H. Schneer; d, Don Chaffey; w, Jan Reed, Beverly Cross; ph, Wilkie Cooper (Dynamation 90, Eastmancolor); m, Bernard Herrmann.

Adventure/Fantasy   **Cas.**   **(MPAA:NR)**

JOHN AND JULIE

(1957, Brit.) 83m Group 3/BL c

Colin Gibson (John Pritchett), Lesley Dudley (Julie), Noelle Middleton (Miss Stokes), Moira Lister (Dora), Wilfrid Hyde-White (Sir James), Sidney James (Mr. Pritchett), Megs Jenkins (Mrs. Pritchett), Constance Cummings (Mrs. Davidson), Joseph Tomelty (Mr. Davidson), Patric Doonan (Jim Webber), Andrew Cruickshank (Uncle Ben), Colin Gordon (Mr. Swayne), Winifred Shotter (Mrs. Swayne), Peter Jones (Jeremy), Peter Sellers (Police Constable Diamond), Vincent Ball (Digger), Peter Coke (Captain), Richard Dimbleby, Wynford Vaughan Thomas, Mona Washbourne.

Two children (Colin Gibson and Lesley Dudley) decide to make a 150-mile journey to London to see Elizabeth II's coronation in Westminster Abbey. They travel via foot, bicycle, train, and automobile and meet several characters along the way, including a police constable (an early appearance by Peter Sellers). This is a charming little film, featuring some nice stock footage of the actual coronation.

p, Herbert Mason; d&w, William Fairchild; ph, Arthur Grant (Eastmancolor); m, Philip Green.

Adventure/Comedy   **Cas.**   **(MPAA:NR)**

JOHN WESLEY

(1954, Brit.) 77m Radio & Film Commission of Methodist Church c

Leonard Sachs (John Wesley), Gerald Loham (Wesley as a Child), Neil Heayes (Wesley as a Student), Keith Pyott (Rev. Samuel Wesley), Curigwen Lewis (Susannah Wesley), John Witty (Peter Bohler, a Moravian), Derek Aylward (Charles Wesley), Patrick Barton (George Whitefield), John Slater (Condemned Man), Philip Lever (Beau Nash), Joss Ambler, Col. Oglethorpe, Andrew Cruickshank, Horace Sequiera, Sidney Monckton, Erik Chitty, George Bishop, Milton Rosmer (Trustees for Georgia), Henry Hewitt (Bishop of Bristol), Patrick Holt (Thomas Maxfield), Arthur Young (King George II), Vincent Holman (Beaumont, a Quaker), Edward Jewesbury (James Hutton), Julian Mitchell (Tom Dekkar), Harry Towb (Michael O'Rory), Neil Arden (William Holland), F.B.J. Sharp (Vicar), Roger Maxwell (Gen. Holt), Rodney Hughes (Mr. Bligh).

This handsomely mounted biography of the title Methodist leader was originally conceived as a short black-and-white film, but was expanded to include more of Wesley's life and work. The film was financed by J. Arthur Rank, a prominent Methodist layman, and produced through the church. The plot is minimal, focusing on the young Wesley's studies and the development of his principles, but the production values are excellent and Leonard Sachs' Wesley is superb. The initial release of the film went to some 500 churches that contributed to the $200,000 budget in return for first rights on viewing.

d, Norman Walker; w, Lawrence Barrett; ph, Hone Glendinning, Stanley Grant (Eastmancolor); m, Henry Reed.

Biography   **(MPAA:NR)**

JOHNNY ON THE RUN

(1953, Brit.) 68m International Realist-Children's Film Foundation/ABF bw

Eugeniusz Chylek (Johnny), Sydney Tafler (Harry), Michael Balfour (Fingers), Jean Anderson (Mrs. MacIntyre), Moultrie Kelsall (Mr. MacIntyre), Mona Washbourne (Mrs. MacGregor), Margaret McCourt (Janet MacGregor), Edna Wynn, David Coote, Cleopatra Sylvestre, Louis Alexander, Elizabeth Saunders, Keith Faulkner, John Levitt.

Eugeniusz Chylek plays Johnny, an orphaned child who dreams of returning to his native Poland, but whose attempts to accomplish this feat only get him into a great deal of hot water. Jewel thieves decide to put him to use in several robberies, and the lad doesn't see through their schemes until it's almost too late. Luckily, he happens upon a small village filled with people from all over the world who take him in and protect him against the evil forces that are after him. This well-paced film is particularly strong in its realistic depiction of children who are quite capable of individual thought.

p, Victor Lyndon; d, Lewis Gilbert, Vernon Harris; w, Patricia Latham; ph, Gerald Gibbs.

Adventure (MPAA:NR)

JOHNNY TREMAIN

(1957) 80m BV c

Hal Stalmaster *(Johnny Tremain)*, Luana Patten *(Cilla Lapham)*, Jeff York *(James Otis)*, Sebastian Cabot *(Jonathan Lyte)*, Dick [Richard] Beymer *(Rab Silsbee)*, Walter Sande *(Paul Revere)*, Rusty Lane *(Samuel Adams)*, Whit Bissell *(Josiah Quincy)*, Will Wright *(Ephraim Lapham)*, Virginia Christine *(Mrs. Lapham)*, Walter Coy *(Dr. Joseph Warren)*, Geoffrey Toone *(Maj. Pitcairn)*, Ralph Clanton *(Gen. Gage)*, Gavin Gordon *(Col. Smith)*, Lumsden Hare *(Adm. Montagu)*, Anthony Ghazlo, Jr. *(Jehu)*, Charles Smith *(Horse Tender)*.

This fine adaptation of Esther Forbes' novel opens in 1773 as Johnny Tremain (Hal Stalmaster), a silversmith's apprentice, becomes involved with revolutionary colonists, though he is at first uncommitted to their cause. His views change when he takes a silver cup his mother gave him, embellished with his family crest, to a nobleman (Sebastian Cabot) as proof that he is the nobleman's relative. The noble accuses him of theft and, though he is later cleared of the charge, the incident turns him into a revolutionary. Tremain then participates in the Boston Tea Party, followed by a torchlight parade in which the rebels sing "The Liberty Tree." The patriots' continued refusal to cooperate with the British sets the stage for an armed confrontation at Lexington Green. Both sides have been ordered not to fire, but when a shot rings out from an unknown source, the American Revolution—symbolized by the bonfire around which the rebels gather in the final scene—begins. JOHNNY TREMAIN makes history come alive. Stalmaster is very good as an average young man caught up in tumultuous times, and the film offers a balanced portrayal of both sides of the conflict, with characters presented as human beings first, historical figures second.

p, Walt Disney; d, Robert Stevenson; w, Tom Blackburn (based on the novel by Esther Forbes); ph, Charles P. Boyle (Technicolor); m, George Bruns.

Historical **Cas.** (MPAA:NR)

JOURNEY FOR MARGARET

(1942) 81m MGM bw

Robert Young *(John Davis)*, Laraine Day *(Nora Davis)*, Fay Bainter *(Trudy Strauss)*, Signe Hasso *(Anya)*, Margaret O'Brien *(Margaret)*, Nigel Bruce *(Herbert V. Allison)*, William Severn *(Peter Humphreys)*, G.P. Huntley, Jr. *(Rugged)*, Doris Lloyd *(Mrs. Barrie)*, Halliwell Hobbes *(Mr. Barrie)*, Jill Esmond *(Susan Fleming)*, Charles Irwin *(Fairoaks)*, Elisabeth Risdon *(Mrs. Bailey)*, Lisa Golm *(Frau Weber)*, Herbert Evans *(Man)*, Clare Sandars *(Child)*, Leyland Hodgson *(Censor)*, Anita Bolster *(Woman)*, Matthew Boulton *(Warden)*, Lilyan Irene *(Nurse)*, Olaf Hytten *(Manager)*, Ottola Nesmith *(Nurse)*, John Burton *(Surgeon)*, Colin Kenny *(Steward)*, Jimmy Aubrey *(Porter)*, Heather Thatcher *(Mrs. Harris)*, Joan Kemp *(Isabel)*, Norbert Muller *(Hans)*, Al Ferguson *(Policeman)*, Bea Nigro *(Nora's Mother)*, Cyril Delevanti *(Stage Manager)*, Jody Gilbert *(Mme. Bornholm)*, Crauford Kent *(Everton)*, Keye Luke *(Japanese Statesman)*, David Thursby *(Air Raid Warden)*, Henry Guttman *(Polish Captain)*, Doris Stone *(Mother)*, Eric Snowden *(Porter)*, Clive Morgan *(Father)*.

An unabashed three-hanky movie, JOURNEY FOR MARGARET was the final film of director W.S. Van Dyke II's distinguished career. John and Nora Davis (Robert Young and Laraine Day) are an American couple in London during the Blitz. Nora is awaiting their first child while John, a journalist, covers the war for US readers. During an air raid, John meets young Peter Humphreys (William Severn) and takes him to a home for orphans; his wife, meanwhile, is injured, loses the child, and has to return to the States. John remains in London, promising to join her as soon as he can. After visiting Peter and meeting the boy's sister, Margaret (Margaret O'Brien), a child who seems to fear everything, John becomes the siblings' surrogate father. He and Nora plan to adopt them, but, on the brink of leaving England, John is told he cannot take both kids with him on the plane. Eventually the trio does depart for the US and Nora's open arms. The cast is excellent, with Young especially believable, while O'Brien—considered by many to be one of the best, if not the greatest, child actresses ever—is heartwringing. The movie was a big success and movingly depicts the personal tragedy of war through the eyes of children, its most innocent victims.

p, B.P. Fineman; d, W.S. Van Dyke II; w, David Hertz, William Ludwig (based on the book by William L. White); ph, Ray June; m, Franz Waxman.

Drama/War (MPAA:NR)

JOURNEY OF NATTY GANN, THE

(1985) 100m Disney-Silver Screen Partners II/BV c

Meredith Salenger *(Natty Gann)*, John Cusack *(Harry)*, Ray Wise *(Sol Gann)*, Lainie Kazan *(Connie)*, Scatman Crothers *(Sherman)*, Barry Miller *(Parker)*, Verna Bloom *(Farm Woman)*, Bruce M. Fischer *(Charlie Linfield)*, John Finnegan *(Logging Boss)*, Jack Rader *(Employment Agent)*, Matthew Faison *(Buzz)*, Jordan Pratt *(Frankie)*, Zachary Ansley *(Louis)*, Campbell Lane *(Chicago Moderator)*, Max Trumpower, Doug MacLeod, Gary Chalk, Dwight McFee *(Chicago Workers)*, Peter Anderson *(Unemployed Worker)*, Corliss M. Smith, Jr. *(Bus Driver)*, Hagan Beggs *(Policeman)*, Ian Black, Ray Michal *(Hoboes)*, Clint Rowe *(Bullwhip)*, Frank C. Turner *(Farmer)*, Jack Ackroyd *(Grocery Clerk)*, Grant Heslov, Gary Riley, Scott Anderson, Ian Tracey, Jennifer Michas *(Parker's Gang)*, Wally Marsh *(Interrogator)*, Kaye Grieve *(Matron)*, Hannah Cutronal *(Twinky)*, Gabrielle Rose *(Exercise Matron)*, Marie Klingenberg *(Dormitory Matron)*.

A boy and his dog, a girl and her wolf . . . what does it matter? The folks at Disney know what to do with a child and an animal in a film. Natty Gann (Meredith Salenger) is a young girl living with her father (Ray Wise) in Depression-era Chicago. He badly needs work and takes a job in the Northwest, leaving Natty in the care of a hotel manager, promising to send for her. But Natty can't bear the separation and runs away, making her way across the country to reunite with her father. The story of her journey is a good, often exciting road adventure in which a wolf becomes Natty's protector and traveling companion. Their trip takes them through various hardships and dangers, which they surmount by learning the tricks of survival with help from a youthful hobo (John Cusack) and a teenager who leads a pack of juvenile drifters (Barry Miller). It's a totally engaging, well-written story (although someone thought it wise to give Salenger some four-letter dialog, probably to avoid the box-office-poison G rating) that ends with daughter and father reunited and the wolf allowed to trot off to a life of freedom in the wild. Excellent cinematography on the road and particularly good camerawork for the dismal gray 1930s Chicago settings. Salenger is wonderful, and so is the wolf.

p, Mike Lobell; d, Jeremy Kagan; w, Jeanne Rosenberg; ph, Dick Bush; m, James Horner.

Adventure   **Cas.**   **(MPAA:PG)**

JOURNEY TO THE CENTER OF THE EARTH

(1959) 132m FOX c

Pat Boone (*Alec McEwen*), James Mason (*Prof. Oliver Lindenbrook*), Arlene Dahl (*Carla*), Diane Baker (*Jenny*), Thayer David (*Count Saknussemm*), Peter Ronson (*Hans*), Robert Adler (*Groom*), Alan Napier (*Dean*), Alex Finlayson (*Prof. Bayle*), Ben Wright (*Paisley*), Mary Brady (*Kirsty*), Frederick Halliday (*Chancellor*), Alan Caillou (*Rector*).

Half-camp, half-serious, and all fun, this is an excellent combination of witty scripting and fine acting. James Mason plays Oliver Lindenbrook, an Edinburgh geologist who travels with student Alec McEwen (Pat Boone) to Iceland as part of a planned descent to the center of the earth via volcano. In Iceland, they meet Carla (Arlene Dahl), whose husband has been killed in a similar attempt and who joins the expedition, along with a young Icelander (Peter Ronson) and his pet duck. They begin the descent, imperiled by prehistoric beasts, rock slides, and the evil Count Saknussemm (Thayer David), who murdered Carla's husband and who is determined to be the first to reach the earth's core. Eventually they reach a subterranean ocean and the lost city of Atlantis; however, they appear to be trapped there, until the film's explosive finale provides them with an escape. A well-photographed film, with location footage shot in Carlsbad Caverns, featuring great special effects and a Bernard Herrmann score that heightens the excitement. Mason is charming, caustic, and debonair, and the whole affair is captivating, silly fun.

p, Charles Brackett; d, Henry Levin; w, Brackett, Walter Reisch (based on the novel by Jules Verne); ph, Leo Tover (CinemaScope, Deluxe Color); m, Bernard Herrmann.

Science Fiction   **Cas.**   **(MPAA:NR)**

JUDGE HARDY AND SON

(1939) 88m MGM bw

Lewis Stone (*Judge Hardy*), Mickey Rooney (*Andy Hardy*), Cecilia Parker (*Marian Hardy*), Ann Rutherford (*Polly Benedict*), Fay Holden (*Mrs. Hardy*), Sara Haden (*Aunt Milly*), Maria Ouspenskaya (*Mrs. Volduzzi*), June Preisser (*Euphrasia Clark*), Martha O'Driscoll (*Elvie Norton*), Leona Maricle (*Mrs. Norton*), Margaret Early (*Clarabelle Lee*), Egon Brecher (*Mr. Volduzzi*), Edna Holland (*Nurse Trowbridge*), Jack Mulhall (*Intern*), Henry Hull (*Dr. Jones*), George Breakston (*"Beezy"*), Marie Blake (*Augusta*), Joe Yule.

This is the eighth film in MGM's profitable and entertaining "Andy Hardy" series, starring Mickey Rooney as the brash youth with a heart of gold. This time Andy gets in trouble with girls and money when he tries to manipulate the results of an essay contest with a cash prize. His wise father (Lewis Stone) steps in to give the mixed-up but well-meaning fellow some sage advice, and the family is also drawn closer when Mrs. Hardy (Fay Holden) comes down with a life-threatening case of pneumonia. Ann Rutherford is back as Andy's girl pal, Polly Benedict, though she gets some competition this time from June Preisser as Euphrasia Clark. MGM mogul Louis B. Mayer took special interest in the popular Hardy series and kept a careful eye on the production of each one of these lucrative films; it was Mayer who "scripted" Andy's prayer for his mother's return to health. With this film George B. Seitz went back to directing the series, after the brief lapse of ANDY HARDY GETS SPRING FEVER. The results are excellent, making this a fine addition to the series.

p, Lou Ostrow; d, George B. Seitz; w, Carey Wilson (based on characters created by Aurania Rouverol); ph, Lester White; m, David Snell.

Drama   **(MPAA:NR)**

JUDGE HARDY'S CHILDREN

(1938) 78m MGM bw

Lewis Stone (*Judge Hardy*), Mickey Rooney (*Andy Hardy*), Cecilia Parker (*Marian Hardy*), Fay Holden (*Mrs. Hardy*), Ann Rutherford (*Polly Benedict*), Betsy Ross Clarke (*Aunt Milly*), Robert Whitney (*Wayne Trenton*), Ruth Hussey (*Margaret Bee*), Leonard Penn (*Steve Prentiss*), Jacqueline Laurent (*Suzanne Cortot*), Janet Beecher (*Miss Budge*), Boyd Crawford (*Radio Announcer*), Don Douglas (*J.O. Harper*), Edward Earle (*Peniwill*).

Mickey Rooney grabbed the "Andy Hardy" series with this film and never let go. In this, the series' third entry, the Hardy family travels to Washington, DC, where Judge Hardy (Lewis Stone) is to sit in on important utilities hearings (echoing 1938 headlines involving the Tennessee Valley Authority and contemporary Supreme Court rulings). But the film is not all official business—Andy, as usual, has girl troubles, and at one point teaches a marvelously energetic dance, "The Big Apple," to the daughter of a French ambassador (Jacqueline Laurent). Betsy Ross Clarke plays Aunt Milly in this film, temporarily replacing Sara Haden. It's good innocent fun, with Rooney a delight to watch.

d, George B. Seitz; w, Kay Van Riper (based on characters created by Aurania Rouverol); ph, Lester White; m, David Snell.

Drama   **(MPAA:NR)**

JUNGLE BOOK, THE

(1942) 108m UA c (AKA: RUDYARD KIPLING'S JUNGLE BOOK)

Sabu *(Mowgli)*, Joseph Calleia *(Buldeo)*, John Qualen *(The Barber)*, Frank Puglia *(The Pundit)*, Rosemary De Camp *(Messua)*, Patricia O'Rourke *(Mahala)*, Ralph Byrd *(Durga)*, John Mather *(Rao)*, Faith Brook *(English Girl)*, Noble Johnson *(Sikh)*.

This loose adaptation of Rudyard Kipling's *Jungle Books* stars Sabu as Mowgli, a young man raised by wolves who returns to his native village with no idea of human language or customs. Once he acquires speech, he captivates Mahala (Patricia O'Rourke), the daughter of the aged Buldeo (Joseph Calleia), with tales of the jungle and his animal friends. Mowgli and Mahala trek into the jungle and discover ruins of a lost civilization, filled with treasures. When Mahala returns to the village with a gold coin, her father tries to get Mowgli to divulge the gold's location, but the boy refuses, fearing the village will be corrupted. Buldeo then turns others against the lad, who is sentenced to be burned at the nearest convenient stake. He escapes and is pursued into the jungle by a pack of fortune seekers, all of whom die for their troubles, except Buldeo, who lives on to become the film's narrator. Shot outside Los Angeles, the film features dazzling photography, expressive animals, and a brilliant Miklos Rozsa score, with individual themes for each animal. An enchanting film for viewers of all ages, JUNGLE BOOK received Oscar nominations for cinematographer Lee Garmes and Rozsa, and was later remade as a cartoon by Disney. The soundtrack was made into a record—the first time that was ever done—with narration by Sabu, a real elephant boy from Mysore, India, who was discovered by Robert Flaherty.

p, Alexander Korda; d, Zoltan Korda; w, Laurence Stallings (based on the books by Rudyard Kipling); ph, Lee Garmes (Technicolor); m, Miklos Rozsa.

Adventure   **Cas.**   **(MPAA:NR)**

JUNGLE BOOK, THE

(1967) 78m Disney/BV c

Voices of: Phil Harris *(Baloo the Bear)*, Sebastian Cabot *(Bagheera the Panther)*, Louis Prima *(King Louie of the Apes)*, George Sanders *(Shere Khan the Tiger)*, Sterling Holloway *(Kaa the Snake)*, J. Pat O'Malley *(Col. Hathi the Elephant)*, Bruce Reitherman *(Mowgli the Man Cub)*, Verna Felton, Clint Howard *(Elephants)*, Chad Stuart Lord, Tim Hudson *(Vultures)*, John Abbott, Ben Wright *(Wolves)*, Darleen Carr *(The Girl)*.

A fine animated feature from the Disney camp based on the famous Rudyard Kipling stories. Abandoned as a child, Mowgli is raised by wolves, then befriended by a panther who attempts to return him to civilization, until the beast realizes that the wolf-boy doesn't want to leave the jungle. Mowgli's happy-go-lucky trail leads to a meeting with a lazy bear, a kidnaping by monkeys, and an encounter with a fire-fearing tiger. In the finale, Mowgli sees a beautiful young girl with whom he falls in love, finally forsaking his jungle ways to be with her. The last animated film to be directly overseen by Walt Disney himself, this contains some of the studio's most vividly cinematic animation techniques. Well-known personalities are particularly effective in providing the voices, notably Phil Harris, Louis Prima, and George Sanders. Released 10 months after Disney's death, the film went on to be one of Disney's most successful pictures, was nominated for Best Song Oscar ("The Bare Necessities" by Terry Gilkyson), and received nearly unanimous critical acclaim.

p, Walt Disney; d, Wolfgang Reitherman; w, Larry Clemmons, Ralph Wright, Ken Anderson, Vance Gerry (based on the books by Rudyard Kipling); m, George Bruns.

Animation   **(MPAA:G)**

K

KARATE KID, THE

(1984) 126m COL c

Ralph Macchio *(Daniel)*, Noriyuki "Pat" Morita *(Miyagi)*, Elisabeth Shue *(Ali)*, Martin Kove *(Kreese)*, Randee Heller *(Lucille)*, William Zabka *(Johnny)*, Ron Thomas *(Bobby)*, Rob Garrison *(Tommy)*, Chad McQueen *(Dutch)*, Tony O'Dell *(Jimmy)*, Israel Juarbe *(Freddy)*, William H. Bassett *(Mr. Mills)*, Larry B. Scott *(Jerry)*, Juli Fields *(Susan)*, Dana Andersen *(Barbara)*, Frank Burt Avalon *(Chucky)*, Jeff Fishman *(Billy)*, Ken Daly *(Chris)*, Tom Fridley *(Alan)*, Pat E. Johnson *(Referee)*, Bruce Malmuth *(Ring Announcer)*, Darryl Vidal *(Karate Semi-Finalist)*, Frances Bay *(Lady with Dog)*, Christopher Kriesa *(Official)*, Bernard Kuby *(Mr. Harris)*, Joan Lemmo *(Restaurant Manager)*, Helen J. Siff *(Cashier)*, Molly Basler *(Cheerleading Coach)*, Larry Drake, David Abbott *(Yahoos)*, Brian Davis *(Boy in Bathroom)*, David De Lange *(Waiter)*, Erik Felix *(Karate Student)*, Peter Jason *(Soccer Coach)*, Todd Lookinland *(Chicken Boy)*, Clarence McGee, Jr., Sam Scarber *(Referees)*, William Norren *(Doctor)*, Scott Strader *(Eddie)*.

Totally irresistible, THE KARATE KID treads the same path as ROCKY, and with good reason, as it was directed by John Avildsen, who also helmed Sylvester Stallone's star-making movie. Daniel (Ralph Macchio) and his mother (Randee Heller) move from Newark, New Jersey, to southern California, where the whole world seems to be blond and brutal. Daniel is immediately bullied by his schoolmates, lead by Johnny (William Zabka). The boy grows increasingly unhappy until he meets Miyagi (Pat Morita), a Japanese janitor. Miyagi takes Daniel under his wing and begins to teach him about life and karate. Made for a pittance, the way the first ROCKY was (less than a million for that Oscar winner), THE KARATE KID reaped a bonanza at the box office. It offers some genuine moments of warmth, humor, and excitement. Naturally, the movie gave birth to a sequel, and, not surprisingly, the sequel wasn't as good as the original.

p, Jerry Weintraub; d, John G. Avildsen; w, Robert Mark Kamen; ph, James Crabe (Metrocolor); m, Bill Conti.

Sports   **Cas.**   **(MPAA:PG)**

KENTUCKY

(1938) 95m FOX c

Loretta Young (Sally Goodwin), Richard Greene (Jack Dillon), Walter Brennan (Peter Goodwin), Douglas Dumbrille (John Dillon, 1861), Karen Morley (Mrs. Goodwin, 1861), Moroni Olsen (John Dillon, II 1937), Russell Hicks (Thad Goodwin, Sr., 1861), Willard Robertson (Bob Slocum), Charles Waldron (Thad Goodwin, 1937), George Reed (Ben), Bobs Watson (Peter Goodwin, 1861), Delmar Watson (Thad Goodwin, Jr., 1861), Leona Roberts (Grace Goodwin), Charles Lane (Auctioneer), Charles Middleton (Southerner), Harry Hayden (Racing Secretary), Robert Middlemass (Track Official), Billy McClain (Zeke), Madame Sul-Te-Wan (Lily), Cliff Clark (Melish), Meredith Howard (Susie May), Charles Trowbridge (Doctor), Eddie Anderson (Groom), Stanley Andrews (Presiding Judge), Fred Burton (Presiding Officer), John Nesbitt (Commentator), Joan Valerie (Lucy Pemberton), Chick Chandler (Clerk), Thaddeus Jones (Zeb).

This bright, entertaining showcase for Kentucky—whose picturesque blue grass really shines here, thanks to Technicolor—could justifiably be called "Romeo and Juliet at the Derby." Richard Greene is Jack, and Loretta Young plays Sally, lovers from families that have been feuding since the Civil War, when Jack's family took over the stables run by Sally's grandfather. Keeping his lineage a secret, Jack begins training Sally's horse. But just before the Kentucky Derby, as their love affair is heating up, Sally discovers his identity, and orders him out of the stable. When race day arrives, it's basically a contest between the rival families' horses. Walter Brennan won his second Best Supporting Actor Oscar in as many years (he'd already won for COME AND GET IT, 1936) for his strong performance as Sally's uncle, Peter Goodwin, who was there when the feud began and does his best to keep it going.

p, Darryl F. Zanuck, Gene Markey; d, David Butler; w, La-

mar Trotti, John Taintor Foote (based on the book The Look of Eagles by John Taintor Foote); ph, Ernest Palmer, Ray Rennahan (Technicolor).

Romance   **Cas.**   **(MPAA:NR)**

KID FROM BROOKLYN, THE

(1946) 114m Goldwyn/RKO c

Danny Kaye (Burleigh Sullivan), Virginia Mayo (Polly Pringle), Vera-Ellen (Susie Sullivan), Walter Abel (Gabby Sloan), Eve Arden (Ann Westley), Steve Cochran (Speed MacFarlane), Lionel Stander (Spider Schultz), Fay Bainter (Mrs. E. Winthrop LeMoyne), Clarence Kolb (Wilbur Austin), Victor Cutler (Photographer), Charles Cane (Willard), Jerome Cowan (Fight Ring Announcer), Don Wilson, Knox Manning (Radio Announcers), Kay Thompson (Matron), Johnny Downs (M.C.), Pierre Watkin (Mr. LeMoyne), Frank Riggi (Killer Kelly), Karen X. Gaylord, Ruth Valmy, Shirley Ballard, Virginia Belmont, Betty Cargyle, Jean Cronin, Vonne Lester, Diana Mumby, Mary Simpson, Virginia Thorpe, Tyra Vaughn, Kismi Stefan, Betty Alexander, Martha Montgomery, Joyce MacKenzie, Helen Kimball, Jan Bryant, Donna Hamilton (The Goldwyn Girls), Frank Moran (Fight Manager), John Indrisano (Boxing Instructor), Almeda Fowler (Bystander), Snub Pollard (Man Who Reacts to Lion), Robert Wade Chatterton (Man Who Lifts Up Susie), Torben Meyer, William Forrest, Jack Norton (Guests), Billy Nelson, Ralph Dunn (Seconds), Billy Wayne, George Chandler (Reporters), Betty Blythe, James Carlisle (Mrs. LeMoyne's Friends).

Based on the 1936 Harold Lloyd film THE MILKY WAY, THE KID FROM BROOKLYN overcomes its hokey story with great songs and plenty of style, and the result is a happy amalgam of nonsense and laughter. Danny Kaye, starring in his third film, plays Burleigh Sullivan, a wimpy milkman who inadvertently becomes a champion prizefighter. Although the premise is patently absurd, Kaye's intricate performance pulls it off with good humor and verve. The songs were done by everyone but Kaye, save for "Pavlova," a ballet satire written especially for him by Max Liebman and Sylvia Fine, Kaye's wife.

p, Samuel Goldwyn; d, Norman Z. McLeod; w, Don Hartman, Melville Shavelson (based on a screenplay by Grover Jones, Frank Butler, and Richard Connell from the play "The Milky Way" by Lynn Root and Harry Clork); ph, Gregg Toland (Technicolor); m, Carmen Dragon.

Comedy/Musical   **Cas.**   **(MPAA:NR)**

KID FROM SPAIN, THE

(1932) 118m Goldwyn/UA bw

Eddie Cantor (Eddie Williams), Lyda Roberti (Rosalie), Robert Young (Ricardo), Ruth Hall (Anita Gomez), John Miljan (Pancho), Noah Beery, Sr. (Alonzo Gomez), J. Carrol Naish (Pedro), Robert Emmett O'Connor (Detective Crawford), Stanley Fields (Jose), Paul Porcasi (Gonzales, Border Guard), Sidney Franklin (American Matador), Julian Rivero (Dalmores), Theresa Maxwell Conover (Mar-

tha Oliver), Walter Walker *(The Dean)*, Ben Hendricks, Jr. *(Red)*, Grace Poggi *(Specialty Dancer)*, Edgar Connor *(Black Bull Handler)*, Leo Willis *(Thief)*, Harry Gribbon *(Traffic Cop)*, Eddie Foster *(Patron)*, Harry C. Bradley *(Man on Line at Border)*, Jean Allen, Loretta Andrews, Consuelo Baker, Betty Bassett, Lynn Browning, Maxie Cantway, Hazel Craven, Dorothy Rae Coonan, Shirley Chambers, Patricia Farnum, Sarah Jane Fulks [Jane Wyman], Betty Grable, Paulette Goddard, Jeannie Gray, Ruth Hale, Pat Harper, Margaret La Marr, Adele Lacey, Bernice Lorimer, Nancy Lynn, Vivian Mathison, Nancy Nash, Edith Roark, Marian Sayers, Renee Whitney, Diana Winslow, Toby Wing *(The 1932 Goldwyn Girls)*.

Samuel Goldwyn wanted to become the Flo Ziegfeld of movies by producing opulent, entertaining musicals for which he could charge a fortune. He succeeded far beyond his dreams with THE KID FROM SPAIN, which cost more than $2 to see in an era when 75 cents was the top ticket price for a first-run movie. College roommates Eddie (Eddie Cantor) and Ricardo (Robert Young) are tossed out of school after being caught in the girls' dorm. Ricardo invites Eddie to accompany him to his home in Mexico, and their trip becomes a necessity when bank robbers mistake Eddie for their getaway driver, the only person who can identify them. This leads to many sticky situations as Eddie avoids both the crooks and the cops. Chock-full of laughs, THE KID FROM SPAIN also boasts some fine songs, written mostly by Bert Kalmar and Harry Ruby (who also cowrote the screenplay). Leo McCarey's wonderful direction here brought him enough recognition to put him at the helm of the Marx Brothers' DUCK SOUP. Famed choreographer Busby Berkeley was not yet in top form (that came later at MGM), but he showed enough inventiveness in THE KID FROM SPAIN to prove to everyone that he was a comer. A very pleasant way to spend two hours.

p, Samuel Goldwyn; d, Leo McCarey; w, William Anthony McGuire, Bert Kalmar, Harry Ruby; ph, Gregg Toland.

Comedy/Musical **(MPAA:NR)**

KIDNAPPED

(1938) 93m FOX bw

Warner Baxter *(Alan Breck)*, Freddie Bartholomew *(David Balfour)*, Arleen Whelan *(Jean MacDonald)*, C. Aubrey Smith *(Duke of Argyle)*, Reginald Owen *(Capt. Hoseason)*, John Carradine *(Gordon)*, Nigel Bruce *(Neil MacDonald)*, Miles Mander *(Ebenezer Balfour)*, Ralph Forbes *(James)*, H. B. Warner *(Rankeiller)*, Arthur Hohl *(Riach)*, E. E. Clive *(Minister MacDougall)*, Halliwell Hobbes *(Dominie Campbell)*, Montagu Love *(English Officer)*, Donald Haines *(Ransome)*, Moroni Olsen *(Douglas)*, Leonard Mudie *(Red Fox)*, Mary Gordon *(Mrs. MacDonald)*, Forrester Harvey *(Innkeeper)*, Clyde Cook *(Cook)*, Russell Hicks *(Bailiff)*, Billy Watson *(Bobby MacDonald)*, Eily Malyon *(Mrs. Campbell)*, Kenneth Hunter *(Capt. Frazer)*, Charles Irwin *(Sgt. Ellis)*, John Burton *(Lt. Stone)*, David Clyde *(Blacksmith)*, Holmes Herbert *(Judge)*, Bran-

don Hurst *(Donnelly)*, Vernon Steele *(Captain)*, C. Montague Shaw *(Scotch Statesman)*, R.T. Noble *(Warden)*.

Robert Louis Stevenson would turn over, nay, spin in his grave if he were to see the liberties taken with his classic novel; however, this is one of those rare times when the adaptation does the original justice. Just about every British actor living in Hollywood was used in the picture and their presence lent credibility to the story. In the final years of the 18th century, with the British cruelly subduing the forces of Scottish rebellion, David Balfour (Freddie Bartholomew), the young heir to a fortune, is set up by his evil uncle to be kidnaped and sent to sea. However, David meets Alan Breck (Warner Baxter), a fugitive from the British authorities and a rebel against the crown. The two join forces, and after a series of adventures, David is restored to his true position. With its convoluted story and abundance of derring-do, KIDNAPPED is reminiscent of THE PRINCE AND THE PAUPER, in which the relationship between Errol Flynn's Miles and the prince is similar to the one between David and Breck. Unfortunately, KIDNAPPED isn't quite as exciting or humorous as that classic, but it is a fine film in its own right. Though it was shot in California, the studio's art directors managed to successfully evoke the feeling of Scotland, right down to the heather and the fog.

p, Kenneth MacGowan; d, Alfred Werker; w, Sonya Levien, Eleanor Harris, Ernest Pascal, Edwin Blum (based on the novel by Robert Louis Stevenson); ph, Gregg Toland; m, Arthur Lange.

Adventure **Cas.** **(MPAA:NR)**

KIM

(1950) 113m MGM c

Errol Flynn *(Mahbub Ali, the Red Beard)*, Dean Stockwell *(Kim)*, Paul Lukas *(Lama)*, Robert Douglas *(Col. Creighton)*, Thomas Gomez *(Emissary)*, Cecil Kellaway *(Hurree Chunder)*, Arnold Moss *(Lurgan Sahib)*, Reginald Owen *(Father Victor)*, Laurette Luez *(Laluli)*, Richard Hale *(Hassan Bey)*, Roman Toporow, Ivan Triesault *(Russians)*, Hayden Rorke *(Maj. Ainsley)*, Walter Kingsford *(Dr. Bronson)*, Henry Mirelez *(Wanna)*, Frank Lackteen *(Shadow)*, Frank Richards *(Abul)*, Henry Corden, Peter Mamakos *(Conspirators)*, Donna Martell *(Haikun)*, Jeanette Nolan *(Foster Mother)*, Rod Redwing *(Servant)*, Michael Ansara *(Guard)*, Stanley Price *(Water Carrier)*, Movita Castenada *(Woman with Baby)*, Edgar Lansbury *(Young Officer)*, Francis McDonald *(Letter Writer)*, Adeline DeWalt Reynolds *(Old Maharanee)*, Mike Tellegan *(Policeman)*, Richard Lupino *(Sentry)*, Olaf Hytten *(Mr. Fairlee)*, George Khoury *(Little Man)*.

This adaptation of the classic Rudyard Kipling novel features a young, bright-eyed Dean Stockwell in the title role as the rebellious, adventure-seeking son of an English envoy living in 1880s India. Fed up with his school's rigid rules, Kim assumes the role of a turbaned peasant boy and wanders through the Indian marketplace. He is befriended by a philosophical lama (Paul Lukas) who treats him with fatherly warmth and offers him invaluable advice. From Mahbub Ali (Errol Flynn), a flamboyant horse thief who doubles as a British agent, Kim learns the finer points of espionage. The adventure and fun continue as the three get involved in an explosive political situation when the Russians prepare an invasion of the Khyber Pass. Luxuriously photographed in Technicolor, KIM offers countless panoramic views of India even though a large portion of the film was shot in California and 13-year-old Stockwell never set foot in India. KIM kicked around MGM for some time before it finally went into production. Freddie Bartholomew and Robert Taylor were cast in 1938, but WW II halted the production; later, Mickey Rooney, Conrad Veidt, and Basil Rathbone were to star, but the tenuous situation brought about by the Indian struggle for independence led to another shutdown. When independence was achieved in 1948, MGM finally thought it safe to begin. Although it's a bit long for some viewers, KIM is a fine family picture that allows younger viewers to identify with Stockwell's adventurous character.

p, Leon Gordon; d, Victor Saville; w, Leon Gordon, Helen Deutsch, Richard Schayer (based on the novel by Rudyard Kipling); ph, William V. Skall (Technicolor); m, Andre Previn.

Adventure   **Cas.**   **(MPAA:NR)**

KING AND I, THE

(1956) 133m FOX c

Deborah Kerr (*Anna Leonowens*), Yul Brynner (*The King*), Rita Moreno (*Tuptim*), Martin Benson (*Kralahome*), Terry Saunders (*Lady Thiang*), Rex Thompson (*Louis Leonowens*), Carlos Rivas (*Lun Tha*), Patrick Adiarte (*Prince Chulalongkorn*), Alan Mowbray (*British Ambassador*), Geoffrey Toone (*Ramsay*), Yuriko (*Eliza*), Marion Jim (*Simon Legree*), Robert Banas (*Keeper of the Dogs*), Dusty Worrall (*Uncle Thomas*), Gemze de Lappe (*Specialty Dancer*), Thomas and Dennis Bonilla (*Twins*), Michiko Iseri (*Angel in Ballet*), Charles Irwin (*Ship's Captain*), Leonard Strong (*Interpreter*), Irene James (*Siamese Girl*), Jadin and Jean Wong (*Amazons*), Fuji, Weaver Levy (*Whipping Guards*), William Yip (*High Priest*), Eddie Luke (*Messenger*), Josephine Smith (*Guest at Palace*), Jocelyn New (*Princess Ying Yoowalak*).

Phenomenally successful on both the stage and screen, this delightful musical stars Deborah Kerr as Anna Leonowens, a British schoolteacher who has been engaged to teach the many children of the king of Siam (Yul Brynner). The male chauvinist king clings to the old ways, but as the picture unspools, he becomes appreciative of this "mere woman." Realizing that he must accept new customs, he strives to overcome a lifetime of arrogance to become a man of today. The two principals spar until a grudging love emerges between them. Even without the music, the well-written story elicits a full range of emotions. But the music, that glorious score by Rodgers and Hammerstein, is what makes this so special, and many of the songs have gone into the musical lexicon, including "Shall We Dance?" "Getting to Know You," "Hello,

Young Lovers," and "I Whistle a Happy Tune." THE KING AND I won Oscars for Brynner and musical directors Alfred Newman and Ken Darby, and garnered a host of technical awards. The story first came to the screen in 1946 as ANNA AND THE KING OF SIAM, starring Rex Harrison and Irene Dunne; however, Yul Brynner was born to play the king and would forever be associated with the role. By the time of his death in 1985, he had been the king for more than 4,000 performances, and he breathed new life into the character every night.

p, Charles Brackett; d, Walter Lang; w, Ernest Lehman (based on the musical play by Oscar Hammerstein II and Richard Rodgers, from the book *Anna and the King of Siam* by Margaret Landon); ph, Leon Shamroy (Cinema-Scope, Deluxe Color); m, Richard Rodgers.

Musical   **Cas.**   **(MPAA:NR)**

KING KONG

(1933) 100m RKO bw

Fay Wray (*Ann Darrow*), Robert Armstrong (*Carl Denham*), Bruce Cabot (*John Driscoll*), Frank Reicher (*Capt. Englehorn*), Sam Hardy (*Charles Weston*), Noble Johnson (*Native Chief*), Steve Clemento (*Witch King*), James Flavin (*2nd Mate Briggs*), Victor Wong (*Charley*), Paul Porcasi (*Socrates*), Russ Powell (*Dock Watchman*), Ethan Laidlaw, Blackie Whiteford, Dick Curtis, Charles Sullivan, Harry Tenbrook, Gil Perkins (*Sailors*), Vera Lewis, LeRoy Mason (*Theatre Patrons*), Frank Mills, Lynton Brent (*Reporters*), Jim Thorpe (*Native Dancer*), George MacQuarrie (*Police Captain*), Madame Sulte-wan (*Handmaiden*), Etta MacDaniel (*Native Woman*), Ray Turner (*Native*), Dorothy Gulliver (*Girl*), Carlotta Monti (*Girl*), Barney Capehart, Bob Galloway, Eric Wood, Dusty Mitchell, Russ Rogers (*Pilots*), Reginald Barlow (*Engineer*), Merian C. Cooper (*Flight Commander*), Ernest B. Schoedsack (*Chief Observer*).

One of the greatest adventure films ever made, KING KONG is one of a handful of films that have become enduring icons of American popular culture and it is justly praised as a true motion picture classic. Hollywood filmmaker Carl Denham (Robert Armstrong) takes starlet Ann Darrow (Fay Wray) to a mysterious prehistoric island in search of the legendary King Kong, a giant ape that is worshiped as a god by the local natives. To their amazement, the two find the giant beast, and it falls in love with Ann. Denham manages to capture the monster and bring it back to New York City for display, but Kong breaks loose and wreaks havoc on Manhattan in his search for his beloved Ann. To this day children and adults alike thrill to the mastery of KING KONG and most feel sorry for the gorilla. In reality, an 18-inch-tall stop-motion-animation model, Kong came to life through the genius of special effects wizard Willis O'Brien, who was able to create a unique and memorable character from an inanimate object. Although it is often edited severely for television, an uncut version of the film (which restored several minutes trimmed by the studio) is available on videotape. KING KONG remains an outstanding achievement in motion picture history and a moving testament to the human imagination that will endure as long as there is an audience to thrill to its unparalleled mastery of the medium. Avoid the 1976 remake and its 1986 sequel.

p&d, Merian C. Cooper, Ernest B. Schoedsack; w, James Creelman, Ruth Rose (based on a story by Merian C. Cooper and Edgar Wallace); ph, Edward Linden, Vernon L. Walker, J.O. Taylor; m, Max Steiner.

Adventure   Cas.   (MPAA:NR)

KING OF KINGS

(1961) 168m MGM c

Jeffrey Hunter *(Jesus Christ)*, Siobhan McKenna *(Mary)*, Hurd Hatfield *(Pontius Pilate)*, Ron Randell *(Lucius, the Centurion)*, Viveca Lindfors *(Claudia)*, Rita Gam *(Herodias)*, Carmen Sevilla *(Mary Magdalene)*, Brigid Bazlen *(Salome)*, Harry Guardino *(Barabbas)*, Rip Torn *(Judas)*, Frank Thring *(Herod Antipas)*, Guy Rolfe *(Caiphas)*, Maurice Marsac *(Nicodemus)*, Gregoire Aslan *(King Herod)*, Royal Dano *(Peter)*, Edric Connor *(Balthazar)*, Robert Ryan *(John the Baptist)*, George Coulouris *(Camel Driver)*, Conrado San Martin *(Gen. Pompey)*, Gerard Tichy *(Joseph)*, Jose Antonio *(Young John)*, Luis Prendes *(Good Thief)*, David Davies *(Burly Man)*, Jose Nieto *(Caspar)*, Ruben Rojo *(Matthew)*, Fernando Sancho *(Madman)*, Michael Wager *(Thomas)*, Felix de Pomes *(Joseph of Arimathea)*, Adriano Rimoldi *(Melchior)*, Barry Keegan *(Bad Thief)*, Rafael Luis Calvo *(Simon of Cyrene)*, Tino Barrero *(Andrew)*, Francisco Moran *(Blind Man)*, Orson Welles *(Narrator)*.

This excellent biblical epic was produced by the legendary Samuel Bronston and directed with a skillful mix of spiritual reverence and cinematic imagination by Nicholas Ray. The film covers the 33 years from Jesus Christ's birth in Bethlehem through the Crucifixion, Resurrection, and Ascension. Included are His relationship with John, the 40 days in the desert, the choosing of the Apostles, the Sermon on the Mount, and Judas' betrayal at the Passover seder that was Jesus' Last Supper. Although Ray Bradbury is not credited, the narration by Orson Welles was supposedly written by him. Jeffrey Hunter is excellent as Jesus, and Robert Ryan is superb as John, but Hurd Hatfield, who made his mark in THE PICTURE OF DORIAN GRAY, goes a bit over the top as Pilate. Other outstanding performances are contributed by Royal Dano, Harry Guardino, Viveca Lindfors, and Rip Torn. KING OF KINGS is an epic of great scope, filled with broad vistas, yet there are enough intimate moments for the audience to realize that these were real people.

p, Samuel Bronston; d, Nicholas Ray; w, Philip Yordan; ph, Franz F. Planer, Milton Krasner, Manuel Berenguer (Technirama 70, Technicolor); m, Miklos Rozsa.

Religious   Cas.   (MPAA:NR)

KING OF THE COWBOYS

(1943) 67m REP bw

Roy Rogers *(Roy)*, Smiley Burnette *(Frog Millhouse)*, Peggy Moran *(Judy Mason)*, Bob Nolan and The Sons of the Pioneers *(Themselves)*, Gerald Mohr *(Maurice)*, Dorothea Kent *(Ruby Smith)*, Lloyd Corrigan *(William Kraly)*, James Bush *(Dave Mason)*, Russell Hicks *(Gov. Shuville)*, Irving Bacon *(Deputy Alf Cluckus)*, Stuart Hamblen *(Duke Wilson)*, Emmett Vogan *(Saboteur)*, Eddie Dean *(Tex)*, Forrest Taylor *(Cowhand)*, Dick Wessel *(Hershel)*, Jack Kirk *(Bartender)*, Edward Earle *(Manufacturer)*, Yakima Canutt, Charles King, Jack O'Shea *(Henchmen)*, Trigger the Horse.

Roy Rogers plays a rodeo performer-cum-government agent who is appointed by the governor (Russell Hicks) to discover who has been blasting military warehouses filled with the hardware needed to win WW II. The sabotage appears to be related to the presence of a traveling tent show, so Rogers joins the show and discovers that the saboteurs receive their cryptic instructions through messages coded by the show's spiritualist, transmitted during performances. Rogers had recently been the subject of a cover story in the enormously popular *Life* magazine, which accorded him the appellation "King of the Cowboys." Consequently, studio chiefs upped production budgets for Rogers' features following this aptly titled film. The tent-show setting affords ample opportunities for musical numbers from both the star and the Sons of the Pioneers, and the songs include "I'm an Old Cowhand," "Gay Ranchero," "Roll Along Prairie Moon," and "Red River Valley."

p, Harry Grey; d, Joseph Kane; w, Olive Cooper, J. Benton Cheney (based on a story by Hal Long); ph, Reggie Lanning.

Western   (MPAA:NR)

KING SOLOMON'S MINES

(1950) 102m MGM c

Deborah Kerr *(Elizabeth Curtis)*, Stewart Granger *(Allan Quatermain)*, Richard Carlson *(John Goode)*, Hugo Haas *(Van Brun)*, Lowell Gilmore *(Eric Masters)*, Kimursi *(Khiva)*, Siriaque *(Umbopa)*, Sekaryongo *(Chief Gagool)*, Baziga *(King Twala)*, Cpl. Munto Anampio *(Chief Bilu)*, Gutare *(Kafa, Double for Umbopa)*, Ivargwema *(Blue Star)*, Benempinga *(Black Circle)*, John Banner *(Austin)*, Henry Rowland *(Traum)*.

For those who love thrilling, large-scale adventure films loaded with action and exotic scenery, KING SOLOMON'S MINES is a must. MGM spent $3.5 million—a fortune in those days—in producing this wonderful movie that has something for everyone. Great white hunter Allan Quatermain (Stewart Granger) is hired by the beautiful Elizabeth (Deborah Kerr) and her brother (Richard Carlson) to help find Elizabeth's husband, who disappeared while searching for the fabled diamond mines of King Solomon. Their party goes through swamps and forests, over mountains, across deserts, and flees bloodthirsty warriors and stampeding animals in their search. This is one of the most majestically filmed adventure tales ever put on celluloid, and cinematographer Robert Surtees won an Oscar for his photographic achievement. The production went first to Nairobi and then, by specially built trucks and airplanes, to Tanganyika and the Belgian Congo, covering more than 14,000 miles and contending with temperatures soaring between 140 and 152 degrees. Decimating their ranks were all manner of exotic diseases—amoebic dysentery, malaria, fever. And they were plagued by swarms of snakes and tsetse flies. There was so much excess footage of great quality that MGM used it in many other movies, including WATUSI (1959), TARZAN THE APE MAN (1959), DRUMS OF AFRICA (1963), TRADER HORN (1973), and even the 1977 remake of KING SOLOMON'S MINES.

p, Sam Zimbalist; d, Compton Bennett, Andrew Marton; w, Helen Deutsch (based on the novel by Sir Henry Rider Haggard); ph, Robert Surtees (Technicolor).

Adventure   **Cas.**   **(MPAA:NR)**

KNUTE ROCKNE—ALL AMERICAN

(1940) 98m WB bw (GB: A MODERN HERO)

Pat O'Brien *(Knute Rockne)*, Gale Page *(Bonnie Skilles Rockne)*, Ronald Reagan *(George Gipp)*, Donald Crisp *(Father Callahan)*, Albert Basserman *(Father Julius Nieuwland)*, John Litel *(Chairman of Committee of Educators)*, Henry O'Neill *(Doctor)*, Owen Davis, Jr. *(Gus Dorais)*, John Qualen *(Lars Knutson Rockne)*, Dorothy Tree *(Martha Rockne)*, John Sheffield *(Knute Rockne as a boy)*, Nick Lukats *(Harry Stuhldreher)*, Kane Richmond *(Elmer Laydon)*, William Marshall *(Don Miller)*, William Byrne *(James Crowley)*, John Ridgely *(Reporter)*, George Reeves *(Player)*, Dutch Hendrian *(Hunk Anderson)*, Gaylord [Steve] Pendleton *(Player)*, Richard Clayton *(Student)*, Howard Jones, Glenn "Pop" Warner, Alonzo Stagg, Bill Spaulding *(Themselves)*, Robert O. Davis [Rudolph Anders], Egon Brecher, Fred Vogeding *(Elders)*, Phil Thorpe *(Boy Center)*, Dickie Jones *(Boy Captain)*, George Billings *(Boy Quarterback)*, Cliff Clark *(Post Office Paymaster)*, William Haade, Eddy Chandler, Pat Flaherty *(Workers)*, Creighton Hale *(Secretary)*, Lee Phelps *(Army Coach)*, Peter B. Goode *(Bill Rockne, Age 2)*, Bunky Fleischman *(Bill Rockne, Age 5)*, David Dickson *(Bill Rockne, Age 10)*, Jack Grant, Jr. *(Bill Rockne, Age 14)*, David Wade *(Knute Rockne, Jr., Age 7)*, Billy Dawson *(Knute Rockne, Jr., Age 12)*, Bill Gratton *(Jackie Rockne, Age 4)*, Patricia Hayos *(Joanne Rockne, Age 10)*, Bill Sheffield *(Knute Rockne, Age 4)*.

Pat O'Brien gives a brilliant performance as the great Notre Dame football coach Knute Rockne in this fond biography that features Ronald Reagan as Rockne's most famous player, George Gipp. The film follows Rockne from his Norwegian immigrant beginnings through his playing days at Notre Dame (when he helped invent the forward pass) and on to his glorious tenure as head coach at his alma mater. With the support of Father Callahan (Donald Crisp), Rockne rises from assistant coach

and chemistry teacher to the top spot and revolutionizes the game as he turns out winning team after winning team, blessed with great players like the "Four Horsemen" and Gipp, who dies young of pneumonia and exhorts his teammates to "win one for the Gipper." Along the way Rockne even finds time to romance and marry Bonnie Skilles (Gale Page). Four of Rockne's contemporaries play themselves—the grandfather of all coaches, Amos Alonzo Stagg, Howard Jones of USC, William Spaulding, and "Pop" Warner—and much of the football action is culled from newsreel footage.

p, Jack Warner, Hal B. Wallis; d, Lloyd Bacon; w, Robert Buckner (based on the private papers of Mrs. Knute Rockne); ph, Tony Gaudio; m, Ray Heindorf.

Biography/Sports   **Cas.**   **(MPAA:NR)**

KONGA, THE WILD STALLION

(1939) 62m COL bw

Fred Stone *(Calhoun)*, Rochelle Hudson *(Judith Hadley)*, Richard Fiske *(Steve Calhoun)*, Eddy Waller *(Gloomy)*, Robert Warwick *(Hadley)*, Don Beddoe *(Martin)*, Carl Stockdale *(Mason)*, George Cleveland *(Tabor)*, Burr Caruth *(Breckenridge)*.

Fred Stone plays an aging rancher whose love for horses is threatened by the encroachment of civilization, whereby grassland becomes farmland. A feud develops between Calhoun (Stone) and his farmer neighbor, Hadley (Robert Warwick), when horses knock down the farmer's fences and trample his wheat fields. Hadley shoots several horses, including Calhoun's favorite stallion, Konga, and the rancher retaliates by shooting Hadley. The love affair that develops between Calhoun's son (Richard Fiske) and Warwick's daughter (Rochelle Hudson) offers some hope for a peaceful future, though. Good performances highlight this competently made film.

p, Wallace MacDonald; d, Sam Nelson; w, Harold Shumate; ph, Benjamin Kline.

Western   **(MPAA:NR)**

LABYRINTH

(1986) 101m Tri-Star c

David Bowie *(Jareth)*, Jennifer Connelly *(Sarah)*, Toby Froud *(Toby)*, Shelley Thompson *(Stepmother)*, Christopher Malcolm *(Father)*, Natalie Finland *(Fairy)*, Brian Henson *(Voice of Hoggle)*, Shari Weiser *(Hoggle)*, Ron Mueck *(Voice of Ludo)*, Rob Mills *(Ludo)*, David Shaughnessy *(Voice of Didymus)*, Dave Goelz, David Barclay *(Didymus)*, Timothy Bateson *(Voice of the Worm)*, Karen Prell

(The Worm), Michael Hordern *(Voice of the Wiseman)*, Frank Oz *(The Wiseman)*, David Shaughnessy *(Voice of the Hat)*, Dave Goelz *(The Hat)*, Denise Bryer, Karen Prell *(The Junk Lady)*, Anthony Jackson, Douglas Blackwell, David Shaughnessy, Timothy Bateson *(Voices of the Four Guards)*, Steve Whitmire, Kevin Clash, Anthony Asbury, Dave Goelz *(The Four Guards)*, David Healy *(Voice of Right Door Knocker)*, Anthony Asbury *(Right Door Knocker)*, Robert Beatty, Dave Goelz *(Left Door Knocker)*, Kevin Clash, Charles Augins, Danny John-Jules, Richard Bodkin *(Voices of the Fireys)*, Kevin Clash, David Barclay, Karen Prell, Ian Thom, Dave Goelz, Rob Mills, Steve Whitmire, Cheryl Henson, Toby Philpot, Sherry Amott, Kevin Bradshaw, Anthony Asbury, Alistair Fullarton, Rollin Krewson *(Fireys)*, Percy Edwards, Steve Whitmire, Kevin Clash *(Ambrosius)*.

Muppet creator Jim Henson, who previously directed THE DARK CRYSTAL (1984), special-effects master George Lucas, screenwriter Terry Jones (of Monty Python fame), and rock star/actor David Bowie combined their talents to produce this fantasy reminiscent of THE WIZARD OF OZ, ALICE IN WONDERLAND, and Maurice Sendak's "Outside over There." While baby-sitting, Sarah (Jennifer Connelly), a suburban teenager, lets her imagination run wild and goes on a magical adventure to rescue her brother from Jareth (Bowie), the Goblin King, who is holding the boy in his castle on the other side of an intricate maze. Along the way she meets an array of charming creatures and overcomes great danger, as well as Jareth's deceptions, to learn that the surest route to her brother is both simple and direct. The finest work that Henson has yet produced, LABYRINTH packs enough surprises to captivate an audience of children and provides enough wisecracking to keep adults laughing. Besides acting in the role of the Goblin King, Bowie (who was chosen for the role from a group of other rock stars that included Mick Jagger, Sting, and Michael Jackson) composed and performed a number of songs for the film.

p, Eric Rattray; d, Jim Henson; w, Terry Jones (based on a story by Dennis Less and Jim Henson); ph, Alex Thomson; m, Trevor Jones.

Fantasy   **Cas.**   **(MPAA:PG)**

LADDIE

(1935) 70m RKO bw

John Beal *(Laddie Stanton)*, Gloria Stuart *(Pamela Pryor)*, Virginia Weidler *(Little Sister)*, Charlotte Henry *(Shelly Stanton)*, Donald Crisp *(Mr. Pryor)*, Gloria Shea *(Sally Stanton)*, Willard Robertson *(Mr. Stanton)*, Dorothy Peterson *(Mrs. Stanton)*, Jimmy Butler *(Leon Stanton)*, Greta Meyer *(Candace)*, Mary Forbes *(Mrs. Pryor)*, Grady Sutton *(Peter Dover)*.

George Stevens' remake of the 1925 silent film about life on a farm in Indiana features John Beal in the title role as a youngster in love with the daughter of a neighboring country gentleman. Of course, the old fellow doesn't think too much of the young clodhopper. Stevens' strong direction here can be seen as a sign of things to come in SHANE (1953) and GIANT (1956). Recognizing talent when he saw it, producer Pandro S. Berman signed Stevens to direct ALICE ADAMS (1935), which garnered an Academy Award Best Picture nomination.

p, Pandro S. Berman; d, George Stevens; w, Ray Harris, Dorothy Yost (based on the novel by Gene Stratton-Porter); ph, Harold Wenstrom.

Drama   **(MPAA:NR)**

LADY AND THE TRAMP

(1955) 75m BV c

Voices of: Peggy Lee *(Darling/Peg/Si/Am)*, Barbara Luddy *(Lady)*, Larry Roberts *(Tramp)*, Bill Thompson *(Jock/Bull/Dachsie)*, Bill Baucon *(Trusty)*, Stan Freberg *(Beaver)*, Verna Felton *(Aunt Sarah)*, Alan Reed *(Boris)*, George Givot *(Tony)*, Dallas McKennon *(Toughy/Professor)*, Lee Millar *(Jim Dear)*, The Mello Men.

This animated Disney classic tells the tale of Lady, a prim and proper cocker spaniel who falls in love with Tramp, a ragged mutt. When Lady runs away from her owner and is pursued by tough dogs in a bad neighborhood, Tramp rescues her. The two pups spend a night on the town, which includes the memorable spaghetti-eating scene in which both Lady and Tramp eat the same strand, their mouths drawn closer and closer until at last . . . they kiss. Lady is furious with Tramp when they end up in the pound after being caught raiding a chicken coup, but by the finale they are happily raising their own litter of pups. Disney's first CinemaScope cartoon, LADY AND THE TRAMP cost $4,000,000 and took three years to complete, but it grossed over $25,000,000, making more money than any film from the 1950s except THE TEN COMMANDMENTS (1956) and BEN-HUR (1959).

p, Walt Disney; d, Hamilton Luske, Clyde Geronimi, Wilfred Jackson; w, Erdman Penner, Joe Rinaldi, Ralph Wright, Donald DaGradi (based on the novel by Ward Greene); ph, (CinemaScope, Technicolor); m, Oliver Wallace.

Animation   **Cas.**   **(MPAA:NR)**

LASSIE, COME HOME

(1943) 90m MGM c

Roddy McDowall *(Joe Carraclough)*, Donald Crisp *(Sam Carraclough)*, Edmund Gwenn *(Rowlie)*, Dame May Whitty *(Dolly)*, Nigel Bruce *(Duke of Rudling)*, Elsa Lanchester *(Mrs. Carraclough)*, Elizabeth Taylor *(Priscilla)*, J. Patrick O'Malley *(Hynes)*, Ben Webster *(Dan'l Fadden)*, Alec Craig *(Snickers)*, John Rogers *(Buckles)*, Arthur Shields *(Jock)*, Alan Napier *(Andrew)*, Roy Parry *(Butcher)*, George Broughton *(Allen)*, Howard Davies *(Cobbler)*, John Power *(Miner)*, Nelson Leigh *(Teacher)*, May Beatty *(Fat Woman)*, Charles Irwin *(Tom)*, Pal the Dog *(Lassie)*, Larry Kert *(Stunt Boy for Roddy McDowall)*.

This low-budget effort wasn't expected to do much at the box office, but moviegoers fell in love with the title collie, and many sequels, a radio program, and a long-running TV show followed. In Yorkshire in the dark days after WW I, young Joe Carraclough (Roddy McDowall) is forced to give up Lassie when his parents (Donald Crisp and Elsa Lanchester) can no longer afford to keep the dog. After escaping once from her new owner, the Duke of Rudling (Nigel Bruce), Lassie is taken by him to Scotland, and, freed by the duke's sympathetic granddaughter (Elizabeth Taylor), makes a long, eventful journey back to Joe. This Lassie, actually a male dog named Pal, was bought for $10 by trainer Rudd Weatherwax, who had worked for MGM training animals for PECK'S BAD BOY and THE CHAMP. The studio wanted a female dog and Weatherwax was chosen to find a good one, but when shooting began the female shed heavily and was replaced by Pal. Contrary to popular belief, this was not Taylor's first film. She had been signed to a brief contract by Universal and appeared in THERE'S ONE BORN EVERY MINUTE. It is, however, as good a boy-and-his-dog story as you'll ever see.

p, Samuel Marx; d, Fred M. Wilcox; w, Hugo Butler (based on the novel by Eric Knight); ph, Leonard Smith (Technicolor); m, Daniele Amfitheatrof.

Drama (MPAA:NR)

LASSIE'S GREAT ADVENTURE

(1963) 103m Wrather/FOX c

June Lockhart (Ruth Martin), Hugh Reilly (Paul Martin), Jon Provost (Timmy Martin), Robert Howard (Sgt. Sprague), Will J. White (Constable MacDonald), Richard Kiel (Chinook Pete), Walter Stocker (John Stanley), Walter Kelley (Control Tower Operator), Patrick Waltz (Pilot), Leo Needham (Ranger Henty), Richard Simmons, Patrick Westwood, Lassie the Dog.

Little Timmy Martin (Jon Provost) and faithful pup Lassie are carried off in a hot air balloon that is being used as a promotional display at a country fair. After drifting to Canada, they are befriended by a giant mute Indian (Richard Kiel). Timmy's parents (June Lockhart and Hugh Reilly) are frantic, as a Mountie-organized helicopter search attempts to locate the missing pair. LASSIE'S GREAT ADVENTURE was originally presented as a four-part television program titled "The Journey."

p, Robert Golden; d, William Beaudine, Sr.; w, Monroe Manning, Charles O'Neal (based on a story by Sumner Arthur Long); ph, Ed Fitzgerald (Eastmancolor).

Adventure **Cas.** (MPAA:NR)

LAST ROUND-UP, THE

(1947) 77m COL bw

Gene Autry (Himself), Jean Heather (Carol), Ralph Morgan (Mason), Carol Thurston (Lydia Henry), Mark Daniels (Matt Mason), Bobby Blake (Mike), Russ Vincent (Jeff Henry), George "Shug" Fisher (Marvin), Trevor Bardette (Indian Chief), Lee Bennett (Goss), John Halloran (Taylor), Sandy Sanders (Jim), Roy Gordon (Smith),

Silverheels Smith [Jay Silverheels] (Sam Luther), Frances Rey (Cora Luther), Bob Cason (Carter), Dale Van Sickle, Don Kay Reynolds, Nolan Leary, Ted Adams, Jack Baxley, Steve Clark, Chuck Hamilton, Bud Osborne, Frankie Marvin, Kernan Cripps, Jose Alvarado, J.W. Cody, Iron Eyes Cody, Blackie Whiteford, Robert Walker, Virginia Carroll, Arline Archuletta, Louis Crosby, Brian O'Hara, Rodd Redwing, Alex Montoya, The Texas Rangers, Ed Piel, Sr., George Carleton, Billy Wilkinson, Champion, Jr., the Horse.

Gene Autry is given the task of rounding up and relocating an Indian tribe living on a plot of barren land where an aqueduct is to be constructed. Not surprisingly, the Indians aren't particularly thrilled with the prospect of moving, but Gene, playing himself (well, not exactly), is up to the challenge and, as usual, ready to burst into song at a moment's notice. The first film produced by Gene Autry Productions, THE LAST ROUND-UP is reportedly Autry's personal favorite. Fans of the "Singing Cowboy" shouldn't miss this well-written, fast-paced entry that includes a number of good tunes.

p, Armand Schaefer; d, John English; w, Jack Townley, Earle Snell; ph, William Bradford.

Western (MPAA:NR)

LET'S GO NAVY

(1951) 68m MON bw

Leo Gorcey (Terrence Aloysius "Slip" Mahoney/Dalton B. Dalton), Huntz Hall (Horace Debussy "Sach" Jones/Hobenocker), Billy Benedict (Whitey/Schwartz), David Gorcey (Chuck/Merriweather), Buddy Gorman (Butch/Stevenson), Bernard Gorcey (Louie Dumbrowski), Allen Jenkins (Mervin Longnecker), Charlita (Princess Papoola), Paul Harvey (Cmdr. Tannen), Tom Neal (Joe), Richard Benedict (Red), Emory Parnell (Sgt. Mulloy), Douglas Evans (Lt. Smith), Frank Jenks (Shell Game Operator), Tom Kennedy (Donovan), Dorothy Ford (Kitten), Harry Lauter (Dalton B. Dalton), Dave Willock (Horatio Hobenocker), Peter Mamakos (Nuramo), Ray Walker (Lt. Bradley), Jonathan Hale (Captain), Paul Bryar (Policeman), Richard Monahan (Merriweather), William Lechner (Stevenson), George Offerman, Jr. (Harry Schwartz), Mike Lally (Detective Snyder), Russ Conway (Lt. Moss), Harry Strang (Petty Officer Grompkin), William Vincent (Sailor).

One of the best films in the "Bowery Boys" series, LET'S GO NAVY sends Slip Mahoney (Leo Gorcey) and the fellas on a high seas adventure when they enlist in the Navy to catch two sailors who've stolen $1,600 in charity funds the boys were holding. After a year on the sea, they still haven't caught up with the thieves, but when Sach Jones (Huntz Hall) wins $2,000 gambling, the boys leave the Navy (they'd joined under assumed names so they would be able to go AWOL as soon as they were ready). Unfortunately, Sach's winnings are stolen by the same two crooks who robbed them earlier, but their commanding officer manages to retrieve the money and through a bureaucratic mistake the boys are re-enlisted. This was the

LIFE WITH FATHER—

23rd film in the "Bowery Boys" series and the last to be produced by Jan Grippo.

p, Jan Grippo; d, William Beaudine; w, Max Adams, Bert Lawrence; ph, Marcel Le Picard.

Comedy (MPAA:NR)

LIFE WITH FATHER

(1947) 118m WB c

William Powell *(Clarence Day)*, Irene Dunne *(Vinnie Day)*, Elizabeth Taylor *(Mary)*, Edmund Gwenn *(Rev. Dr. Lloyd)*, ZaSu Pitts *(Cora)*, Jimmy Lydon *(Clarence)*, Emma Dunn *(Margaret)*, Moroni Olsen *(Dr. Humphries)*, Elisabeth Risdon *(Mrs. Whitehead)*, Derek Scott *(Harlan)*, Johnny Calkins *(Whitney)*, Martin Milner *(John)*, Heather Wilde *(Annie)*, Monte Blue *(Policeman)*, Nancy Evans *(Delia)*, Mary Field *(Nora)*, Queenie Leonard *(Maggie)*, Clara Blandick *(Mrs. Wiggins)*, Frank Elliott *(Dr. Somers)*, Clara Reid *(Scrub Woman)*, Philo McCullough *(Milkman)*, Loie Bridge *(Corsetierre)*, George Meader *(Salesman)*, Douglas Kennedy *(Mr. Morley)*, Phil Van Zandt *(Clerk)*, Russell Arms *(Stock Quotation Operator)*, Faith Kruger *(Hilda)*, Jean De Val *(Francois)*, Michael and Ralph Mineo *(Twins)*, Creighton Hale *(Father of Twins)*, Jean Andren *(Mother of Twins)*, Elaine Lange *(Ellen)*, Jack Martin *(Chef)*, Arlene Dahl *(Girl in Delmonico's)*, Gertrude Valerie, David Cavendish, Henry Sylvester, Hallene Hill, Laura Treadwell *(Churchgoers)*, John Beck *(Perkins the Clerk)*, James Metcalf *(Customer)*, Joe Bernard *(Cashier)*, Lucille Shamberger *(Nursemaid)*.

Based on an autobiographical book by Clarence Day, Jr., and a play that ran for 3,224 performances on Broadway (a total that was only eclipsed by "Fiddler on the Roof"), LIFE WITH FATHER is a son's fond remembrance of his Victorian youth spent in the home of his authoritarian but lovable father (William Powell). There's really not much of a plot, just a lot of alternately quiet and raucous moments of love and laughter as the family goes about its urban, urbane life. Irene Dunne, playing the mother of the red-headed Day clan, is frequently rankled by Father's sexist ways, but, like the rest of the family, she loves dear old Dad anyway. When she becomes deathly ill, Father promises he will finally be baptized if she recovers. She does, and he makes good on his promise, reluctantly. Powell is nothing less than magnificent as the mustached philosophizing patriarch, and his performance won him an Academy Award. Elizabeth Taylor, Martin Milner, Jimmy Lydon, and Edmund Gwenn all contribute strong supporting performances; Michael Curtiz (CASABLANCA; YANKEE DOODLE DANDY; THE ADVENTURES OF ROBIN HOOD) provides his usual surehanded direction; Peverell Marley and William V. Skall earned Oscar nominations for Best Black-and-White Cinematography; and Max Steiner's score was also nominated.

p, Robert Buckner; d, Michael Curtiz; w, Donald Ogden Stewart (based on the play by Howard Lindsay and Rus-

sel Crouse and the book by Clarence Day, Jr.); ph, Peverell Marley, William V. Skall (Technicolor); m, Max Steiner.

Comedy　　　**Cas.**　　　(MPAA:NR)

LIGHT IN THE FOREST, THE

(1958) 93m BV c

James MacArthur *(Johnny Butler/True Son)*, Carol Lynley *(Shenandoe Hastings)*, Fess Parker *(Del Hardy)*, Wendell Corey *(Wilse Owens)*, Joanne Dru *(Milly Elder)*, Jessica Tandy *(Myra Butler)*, Joseph Calleia *(Chief Cuyloga)*, John McIntire *(John Elder)*, Rafael Campos *(Half Arrow)*, Frank Ferguson *(Harry Butler)*, Norman Fredric *(Niskitoon)*, Marian Seldes *(Kate Owens)*, Stephen Bekassy *(Col. Henry Bouquet)*, Sam Buffington *(George Owens)*.

True Son (James MacArthur), a white raised by Indians, is forced to return to white society after the signing of a peace treaty, and Army scout Del Hardy (Fess Parker) oversees his readjustment. Johnny experiences great difficulty in trying to adapt to the white man's ways, with his cruel uncle Wilse Owens (Wendell Corey) making life especially miserable for the youth. Shenandoe Hastings (Carol Lynley) is Wilse's indentured servant, who at first despises Johnny because her parents were killed by Indians, but who grows to love him and help him put his life back together. The "young-man-at-odds-with-his-surroundings" theme was typical of Disney films of the 1950s, and this is an intelligent, well-characterized treatment. Lynley (in her first film) and MacArthur have a nice chemistry as the young lovers. This was the start of a long relationship between the studio and MacArthur, but it was the end of Parker's work for Disney, as he'd grown weary of playing what he felt was the same character over and over. Iron Eyes Cody, who had filled Indian roles in several films, served as a technical director on THE LIGHT IN THE FOREST.

p, Walt Disney; d, Herschel Daugherty; w, Lawrence Edward Watkin (based on the novel by Conrad Richter); ph, Ellsworth Fredericks (Technicolor); m, Paul J. Smith.

Drama　　　**Cas.**　　　(MPAA:NR)

LI'L ABNER

(1959) 113m PAR c

Peter Palmer *(Li'l Abner)*, Leslie Parrish *(Daisy Mae)*, Stubby Kaye *(Marryin' Sam)*, Julie Newmar *(Stupefyin' Jones)*, Howard St. John *(General Bullmoose)*, Stella Stevens *(Appassionata Von Climax)*, Billie Hayes *(Mammy Yokum)*, Joe E. Marks *(Pappy Yokum)*, Bern Hoffman *(Earthquake McGoon)*, Al Nesor *(Evil Eye Fleagle)*, Robert Strauss *(Romeo Scragg)*, William Lanteau *(Available Jones)*, Ted Thurston *(Sen. Jack S. Phogbound)*, Carmen Alvarez *(Moonbeam McSwine)*, Alan Carney *(Mayor Dawgmeat)*, Stanley Simmonds *(Rasmussen T. Finsdale)*, Joe Ploski, Diki Lerner.

In this faithful adaptation of the Broadway musical comedy based on Al Capp's famous comic strip, the town of Dogpatch is deemed "the most useless town in all of

America," making it the perfect site for an A-bomb test. The enraged citizens fight back and search for something that will prove that their town is important. Finally they decide that "Yokumberry Tonic" the wonder elixir concocted by Mammy Yokum (Billie Hayes), will raise a few eyebrows in Washin'ton. Naturally, the government is interested and all ends happily. The cast, nearly all from the original show, are wonderful, bringing lots of energy and yokel innocence to their cartoonish roles. The costumes are excellent, the music is lively, and the well-edited dance sequences prove that there's more to movie dance numbers than just fancy footwork. Though LI'L ABNER shows its age a bit, it's still plenty of fun.

p, Norman Panama; d, Melvin Frank; w, Norman Panama, Melvin Frank (based on the musical play and characters from the comic strip created by Al Capp); ph, Daniel L. Fapp (VistaVision, Technicolor); m, Nelson Riddle.

Comedy/Musical   **Cas.**   **(MPAA:NR)**

LILI

(1953) 81m MGM c

Leslie Caron *(Lili Daurier)*, Mel Ferrer *(Paul Berthalet)*, Jean Pierre Aumont *(Marc)*, Zsa Zsa Gabor *(Rosalie)*, Kurt Kasznar *(Jacquot)*, Amanda Blake *(Peach Lips)*, Alex Gerry *(Proprietor)*, Ralph Dumke *(Mons. Corvier)*, Wilton Graff *(Mons. Tonit)*, George Baxter *(Mons. Enrique)*, Eda Reiss Merin *(Fruit Peddler)*, George Davis *(Workman)*, Mitchell Lewis *(Concessionaire)*, Fred Walton *(Whistler)*, Richard Grayson *(Flirting Vendor)*, Dorothy Jarnac *(Specialty Dancer)*.

Leslie Caron plays the title role in this charming film. Sixteen-year-old Lili Daurier runs off to work as a waitress with a carnival and falls in love with Marc (Jean Pierre Aumont), a magician who is more amused by the young innocent than anything else. Fired for paying too much attention to Marc, Lili is comforted by a group of puppets operated by Paul Berthalet (Mel Ferrer), a bitter ex-dancer crippled by a war injury. Though Paul is insanely jealous of Lili's affection for Marc, he is only able to show his tender side through his puppets (in the film's nicest moment, as Lili and the dancing figures sing the famous "Hi-Lili, Hi-Lo"), and Lili thinks of him as a cruel man. When Lili learns that Rosalie (Zsa Zsa Gabor, in a surprisingly good performance) is Marc's wife as well as his assistant, she packs her bags to leave, but love wins out in the end, though it's not the magician who has the final trick up his sleeve. Caron is wonderful as Lili and was nominated for an Academy Award, as were Charles Walters for his direction and Helen Deutsch for her adaptation of Paul Gallico's short story. Bronislau Kaper won an Oscar for his music. LILI was the basis for a hit Broadway musical in 1961 called "Carnival," with Anna Maria Alberghetti in the Caron role.

p, Edwin H. Knopf; d, Charles Walters; w, Helen Deutsch (based on the story by Paul Gallico); ph, Robert Planck (Technicolor); m, Bronislau Kaper.

Musical   **Cas.**   **(MPAA:NR)**

LITTLE ARK, THE

(1972) 100m NG c

Theodore Bikel *(Captain)*, Genevieve Ambas *(Adinda)*, Philip Frame *(Jan)*, Max Croiset *(Father Grijpma)*, Johan De Slaa *(Cook, U.K. 516)*, Lo Van Hensbergen *(Mr. Tandema)*, Truss Dekker *(Mother Grijpma)*, Edda Barends *(Miss Winter)*, Lex Schoorel *(Sparks)*, Heleen Van Meurs *(Nurse)*, Guus Verstraete *(Pieters)*, Heleen Pimentel *(Mrs. Ool)*, Riek Schagen *(Vrouu Brodfelder)*, Martin Brozius *(Farmer)*, Maurits Koek *(Farmer's Son)*, John Soer *(Man with Dog)*, Tim Beekman *(Launch Officer)*, Jos Knipscheer *(Doctor)*, Jeroen Krabbe *(1st Man)*, Jos Bergman *(Young Man)*, Renier Heidemann *(1st Photographer)*, Manfred De Graff *(2nd Photographer)*, Wik Jongsma *(2nd Man)*, Monica Achterberg *(Little Girl)*, Bussy, Noisette, Ko, Prince.

A pair of adopted children, one Caucasian and the other Malaysian, are separated from their parents during the 1953 flood that devastated Holland. The captain of a houseboat (Theodore Bikel) rescues the kids and takes care of them and their pets. In the end, the children are reunited with their father, but, sadly, their mother has drowned. The mother's death and some of the flood sequences may be a bit intense for very young children, but, beyond this, THE LITTLE ARK is an outstanding family film. Bikel is wonderful as the pseudogruff boatman, and there is an enthralling animated sequence, narrated by Bikel, that dramatizes the old Dutch legend of a maiden who gives up her soul to save her true love. The production values are first rate—especially the photography of the Dutch landscape—and the film's song, "Come Follow Me," was nominated for an Oscar.

p, Robert B. Radnitz; d, James B. Clark; w, Joanna Crawford (based on the novel by Jan De Hartog); ph, Austin Dempster, Denys Coop (Panavision, Technicolor); m, Fred Karlin.

Adventure   **(MPAA:NR)**

LITTLE KIDNAPPERS, THE

(1954, Brit.) 93m UA bw (GB: THE KIDNAPPERS)

Duncan Macrae *(Granddaddy)*, Jean Anderson *(Grandma)*, Adrienne Corri *(Kirsty)*, Theodore Bikel *(Willem Bloem)*, Jon Whiteley *(Harry)*, Vincent Winter *(Davy)*, Francis de Wolff *(Jan Hooft, Sr.)*, James Sutherland *(Aaron McNab)*, John Rae *(Andrew McCleod)*, Jack Stewart *(Dominie)*, Jameson Clark *(Tom Cameron)*, Eric Woodburn *(Sam Howie)*, Christopher Beeny *(Jan Hooft, Jr.)*, Howard Connell *(Archibald Jenkins)*.

In turn-of-the-century Nova Scotia, a stern, bigoted grandfather (Duncan Macrae) tries to pass on his own prejudices against the Boers to his orphaned grandsons (Vincent Winter and Jon Whiteley). When the boys ask for a dog, the grandfather forbids it, but their desire to express love is so overwhelming that they adopt a baby. This is a warm, human film that conveys its message without being heavy-handed. At the film's heart are the delightfully natural performances of Winter and White-two fine child actors who make their young characters extraordinarily believable. The direction by Philip Leacock is sensitive and caring. This one ought to please everyone in the family.

p, Sergei Nolbandov, Leslie Parkyn; d, Philip Leacock; w, Neil Paterson; ph, Eric Cross; m, Bruce Montgomery.

Drama (MPAA:NR)

LITTLE LORD FAUNTLEROY

(1936) 98m UA bw

C. Aubrey Smith *(Earl of Dorincourt)*, Freddie Bartholomew *(Ceddie)*, Dolores Costello Barrymore *("Dearest," Mrs. Errol)*, Henry Stephenson *(Havisham)*, Guy Kibbee *(Mr. Hobbs)*, Mickey Rooney *(Dick)*, Eric Alden *(Ben)*, Jackie Searl *(The Claimant)*, Reginald Barlow *(Newick)*, Ivan Simpson *(Rev. Mordaunt)*, E.E. Clive *(Sir Harry Lorridaile)*, Constance Collier *(Lady Lorridaile)*, Una O'Connor *(Mary)*, May Beatty *(Mrs. Mellon)*, Joan Standing *(Dawson)*, Jessie Ralph *(Apple Woman)*, Lionel Belmore *(Higgins)*, Gilbert Emery *(Purvis)*, Joseph Tyzack *(Thomas)*, Alex Pollard *(Footman)*, Daisy Belmore *(Mrs. Baines)*, Walter Kingsford *(Mr. Snade)*, Eric Alden, Helen Flint, Tempe Pigott, Lawrence Grant, Walter Kingsford, Eily Malyon, Fred Walton, Robert Emmett O'Connor, Elsa Buchanan, "Prince."

Ceddie (Freddie Bartholomew), is a nice young Brooklyn boy whose mother (Dolores Costello Barrymore) is the widow of an Englishman. Her late husband's father (C. Aubrey Smith) hates Americans simply because they are Americans. When it's discovered that Ceddie is the heir to a fortune and a title, he has to go to England and claim his inheritance, win the heart of his grumpy grandfather, and deal with the efforts of an impostor bent on claiming the title. The expression "Little Lord Fauntleroy" has come to be associated with prissy types, but that's not the case here, as Ceddie proves his mettle against a bunch of Brooklyn toughs. Mickey Rooney does a small bit as a shoeshine boy and, as always, stands out. Guy Kibbee, as a Brooklyn grocer, is also excellent in a role that could have been a parody in the hands of a lesser actor. The technical work is terrific and the script goes right for the heart. This was the third of four versions of the durable Frances Hodgson Burnett story. Done as a silent in 1914 and 1922, it was also made as a TV movie with Ricky Schroder and Alec Guinness.

p, David O. Selznick; d, John Cromwell; w, Hugh Walpole (based on the book by Frances Hodgson Burnett); ph, Charles Rosher; m, Max Steiner.

Drama **Cas.** (MPAA:NR)

LITTLE MISS MARKER

(1934) 78m PAR bw (GB: GIRL IN PAWN)

Adolphe Menjou *(Sorrowful Jones)*, Dorothy Dell *(Bangles Carson)*, Charles Bickford *(Big Steve)*, Shirley Temple *(Miss Marker)*, Lynne Overman *(Regret)*, Frank McGlynn, Sr. *(Doc Chesley)*, Jack Sheehan *(Sun Rise)*, Garry Owen *(Grinder)*, Willie Best *(Dizzy Memphis)*, Puggy White *(Eddie White)*, Tammany Young *(Buggs)*, Sam Hardy *(Bennie the Gouge)*, Edward Earle *(Marky's Father)*, John Kelly *(Sore Toe)*, Warren Hymer *(Canvas-Back)*, Frank Conroy *(Dr. Ingalls)*, James Burke *(Detective Reardon)*, Mildred Gover *(Sarah)*, Lucille Ward *(Mrs. Walsh)*, Crauford Kent *(Doctor)*, Nora Cecil *(Head of Home Finding Society)*, Ernie Adams, Don Brodie *(Bettors)*, Stanley Price *(Bookie)*.

This was the first of several versions of Damon Runyon's charming and durable story, but none of others (SORROWFUL JONES, 1949; 40 POUNDS OF TROUBLE, 1963; LITTLE MISS MARKER, 1980) compared with the original, because none of them had the amazing Shirley Temple. This was the picture that sent her career soaring. Temple plays an adorable little tyke whose father leaves her as a marker for a $20 bet with bookie Sorrowful Jones (Adolphe Menjou), then kills himself. Jones has no idea of what to do with her, but gradually he and "Marky" grow closer as Jones finds religion, marries longtime amour nightclub singer Bangles Carson (Dorothy Dell), and becomes generous—much to the surprise of his cronies, whom the little girl thinks of as Knights of the Round Table. There are plenty of plot twists, including a running battle with Jones' gangster enemy (Charles Bickford) and a thrilling climax. The scene in which Jones' buddies don medieval garb is hysterical. Menjou holds his own opposite 5-year-old Temple (a difficult task), and Dell—whose career ended in a fatal car accident at the time of the film's release—also gives a fine performance. This is the sort of yarn that Runyon told well and often: hard-hearted wise guys melt when they have to put aside tough talk and show their true emotions. It'll have you showing your emotions, too.

p, B.P. Schulberg; d, Alexander Hall; w, William R. Lipman, Sam Hellman, Gladys Lehman (based on the story by Damon Runyon); ph, Alfred Gilks; m, Ralph Rainger.

Musical (MPAA:NR)

LITTLE PRINCESS, THE

(1939) 91m FOX c

Shirley Temple *(Sara Crewe)*, Richard Greene *(Geoffrey Hamilton)*, Anita Louise *(Rose)*, Ian Hunter *(Capt. Crewe)*, Cesar Romero *(Ram Dass)*, Arthur Treacher *(Bertie Minchin)*, Mary Nash *(Amanda Minchin)*, Sybil Jason *(Becky)*, Miles Mander *(Lord Wickham)*, Marcia Mae Jones *(Lavinia)*, Beryl Mercer *(Queen Victoria)*, Deidre Gale *(Jessie)*, Ira Stevens *(Ermengarde)*, E.E. Clive *(Mr. Barrows)*, Keith Kenneth *(Bobbie)*, Will Stanton, Harry Allen *(Grooms)*, Holmes Herbert, Evan Thomas, Guy Bellis *(Doctors)*, Kenneth Hunter *(General)*, Lionel Braham *(Colonel)*, Eily Malyon *(Cook)*, Clyde Cook *(Attendant)*, Olaf Hytten *(Man)*, Rita Page *(Girl)*.

In this top-flight Shirley Temple charmer, the lovable moppet is placed in a boarding school by her father (Ian Hunter) when he ships out with his regiment to fight in the Boer War. When he is reportedly killed, the wicked headmistress (Mary Nash) forces young Sara Crewe

(Temple) to work as a servant, but she gets away long enough to search the military hospitals for her father. This is the sort of film that made Temple a legend.

p, Darryl F. Zanuck; d, Walter Lang; w, Ethel Hill, Walter Ferris (based on the novel *The Fantasy* by Frances Hodgson Burnett); ph, Arthur Miller, William Skall (Technicolor); m, Walter Bullock, Samuel Pokrass.

Drama **Cas.** **(MPAA:NR)**

LITTLE ROMANCE, A

(1979, US/Fr.) 108m Pan Arts-Trinacra/Orion c

Laurence Olivier *(Julius)*, Diane Lane *(Lauren)*, Thelonious Bernard *(Daniel)*, Arthur Hill *(Richard King)*, Sally Kellerman *(Kay King)*, Broderick Crawford *(Brod)*, David Dukes *(George de Marco)*, Andrew Duncan *(Bob Duryea)*, Claudette Sutherland *(Janet Duryea)*, Graham Fletcher-Cook *(Londet)*, Ashby Semple *(Natalie)*, Claude Brosset *(Michel Michon)*, Jacques Maury *(Inspector Leclerc)*, Anna Massey *(Mrs. Siegel)*, Peter Maloney *(Martin)*, Dominique Lavanant *(Mme. Corier)*, Mike Marshall *(1st Assistant Director)*, Michel Bardinet *(French Ambassador)*, Alain David Gabison *(French Representative)*, Isabelle Duby *(Monique)*, Jeffrey Carey *(Makeup Man)*, John Pepper *(2nd Assistant Director)*, Denise Glaser *(Woman Critic)*, Jeanne Herviale *(Woman in Metro)*, Carlo Lastricati *(Tour Guide)*, Judy Mullen *(Secretary)*, Philippe Briguad *(Theater Manager)*, Lucienne Legrand *(Cashier)*.

Completely charming, this teenage romantic comedy tells the innocent tale of a pair of 13-year-olds who fall in love in Paris. Lauren (Diane Lane) is living in Paris with her understanding stepfather (Arthur Hill) and her floozy mother (Sally Kellerman). While visiting the set of a movie production, Lauren meets Daniel (Thelonious Bernard), a lower-class youngster with a system for playing the horses and a fascination with both Robert Redford and Humphrey Bogart. Daniel becomes "Bogie" to Lauren's "Bacall," and before long they've fallen for each other in the most innocent of ways. Their attachment strengthens when they discover they both have extremely high IQ's and interests in philosophy, qualities that usually embarrass them. Their adventures begin when they meet Julius (Laurence Olivier), a friendly old scoundrel informs them of an ages-old romantic legend—if two lovers kiss under Venice's Bridge of Sighs in a gondola at sunset when the bells toll, their love will last forever. The two youngsters are determined to try out the legend for themselves, but cannot travel without a guardian and must bring along Julius, who isn't quite what he appears to be. This sweet and innocent movie about teen romance won't fail to bring a tear and a smile in its heart-tugging finale. The Oscar-winning score by Georges Delerue is magnificent.

p, Robert L. Crawford, Yves Rousset-Rouard; d, George Roy Hill; w, Allan Burns (based on the novel *E = MC², Mon Amour* by Patrick Cauvin); ph, Pierre William Glenn (Panavision, Technicolor); m, Georges Delerue.

Comedy/Romance **Cas.** **(MPAA:PG)**

LITTLE WOMEN

(1933) 117m RKO bw

Katharine Hepburn *(Jo)*, Joan Bennett *(Amy)*, Paul Lukas *(Prof. Fritz Bhaer)*, Edna May Oliver *(Aunt March)*, Jean Parker *(Beth)*, Frances Dee *(Meg)*, Henry Stephenson *(Mr. Laurence)*, Douglass Montgomery *(Laurie)*, John Davis Lodge *(Brooke)*, Spring Byington *(Marmee)*, Samuel S. Hinds *(Mr. March)*, Mabel Colcord *(Hannah)*, Marion Ballou *(Mrs. Kirke)*, Nydia Westman *(Mamie)*, Harry Beresford *(Dr. Bangs)*, Marina Schubert *(Flo King)*, Dorothy Gray, June Filmer *(Girls at Boarding House)*, Olin Howland *(Mr. Davis)*.

Nominated for a Best Picture Oscar, this unabashedly sentimental adaptation of Louisa May Alcott's novel remains, to this day, an example of Hollywood's best filmmaking as it tells the captivating Civil War-era story of four independent New England sisters—Jo (Katharine Hepburn), Amy (Joan Bennett), Meg (Frances Dee), and Beth (Jean Parker) March. Jo, who wants to leave home and become a writer, stays on for the good of the family, but when Meg plans to marry, Jo leaves for New York, fearing that the family will disintegrate. There she meets a professor who helps her with both her anger and her writing. Meanwhile, Amy falls in love with and marries Jo's old sweetheart (Douglass Montgomery). Beth, however, is dying, and Jo returns to be with her during her last days. Sarah Mason and Victor Heerman's Oscar-winning script called for great production values, and RKO provided them, foreshadowing David O. Selznick's opulent treatment of life on the southern side of the Civil War, GONE WITH THE WIND. The sets, costumes, lighting, and Oscar-nominated direction by George Cukor all contribute greatly to this magnificent film, but the performances, especially Hepburn's, are what make the simple story so moving. There are laughs and tears aplenty in this movie, which presents a slice of American history in a way that children will find palatable. Released during the depths of the Depression, LITTLE WOMEN buoyed Americans' spirits. It still does.

p, Kenneth Macgowan; d, George Cukor; w, Sarah Y. Mason, Victor Heerman (based on the novel by Louisa May Alcott); ph, Henry Gerrard; m, Max Steiner.

Drama **Cas.** **(MPAA:NR)**

LITTLEST HORSE THIEVES, THE

(1977) 104m Disney/BV c (GB: ESCAPE FROM THE DARK)

Alastair Sim *(Lord Harrogate)*, Peter Barkworth *(Richard Sandman)*, Maurice Colbourne *(Luke Armstrong)*, Susan Tebbs *(Violet Armstrong)*, Geraldine McEwan *(Miss Coutt)*, Joe Gladwin *(Bert)*, Andrew Harrison *(Dave Sadler)*, Benjie Bolgar *(Tommy Sadler)*, Chloe Franks *(Alice Sandman)*, Prunella Scales *(Mrs. Sandman)*, Leslie Sands *(Foreman Sam Carter)*, Jeremy Bulloch *(Ginger)*, Derek Newark, Duncan Lamont, Ian Hogg, Richard Warner, Don Henderson, Tommy Wright, John Hartley, Ken Kitson, Peter Geddis, Roy Evans, Gordon Kaye, James

Marcus, Donald Bisset, Gordon Christie, Walter Hall, Grimethorpe Colliery Band.

This is a well-done Disney period piece set in turn-of-the-century England about three youngsters who attempt to rescue a herd of pit ponies from their hazardous and cruel duties in Yorkshire coal mines. Aided by the mine manager's spirited daughter (Chloe Franks), two boys (Andrew Harrison and Benjie Bolgar) join forces with an old groom to hoist the ponies from the depths of the mine. When the animals are at last discovered in the abandoned chapel where the children have hidden them, they are prepared for slaughter. It's then up to the boys' stepfather to plead their case and he succeeds to such an extent that the miners vote to strike if the animals are killed. Financial troubles and a mine explosion follow, giving the youngsters and one special pony, the blind Flash, the chance to show their mettle.

p, Ron Miller; d, Charles Jarrott; w, Rosemary Anne Sisson (based on a story by Rosemary Anne Sisson, Burt Kennedy); ph, Paul Beeson (Technicolor); m, Ron Goodwin.

Drama   Cas.   (MPAA:G)

LITTLEST OUTLAW, THE

(1955) 73m BV c

Pedro Armendariz *(Gen. Torres)*, Joseph Calleia *(Padre)*, Rodolfo Acosta *(Chato)*, Andres Velasquez *(Pablito)*, Matador Pepe Ortiz *(Himself)*, Laila Maley *(Celita)*, Gilberto Gonzales *(Tiger)*, Jose Torvay *(Vulture)*, Ferrusquilla *(Senor Garcia)*, Enriqueta Zazueta *(Senora Garcia)*, Senor Lee *(Gypsy)*, Carlos Ortigoza *(Doctor)*, Margarito Luna *(Silvestre)*, Ricardo Gonzales *(Marcos)*, Maria Eugenia *(Bride)*, Pedrito Vargas *(Groom)*.

Disney Studios employed a neo-realist filmmaking approach in this enjoyable little film, casting Spanish nonactors (with the exception of Joseph Calleia) and shooting entirely on location. The story is simple but effective: Pablito (Andres Velasquez), a young boy, grows fond of a horse his nasty stepfather is training through torture. The horse's owner, a general, orders that it be destroyed after it throws his daughter. Pablito steals the animal and runs away, seeking refuge with a padre (Calleia). Through numerous travails, which include the horse's life being threatened in a bull ring and the ongoing efforts of the general to have the horse destroyed, boy and beast continue to show their devotion to each other. Filmed in both Spanish and English, THE LITTLEST OUTLAW includes one scene that doesn't fit the Disney mold—in footage taken from real life, bullfighter Pepe Ortiz is gored by a wild bull. That scene notwithstanding, this is a fine film for kids and a top-notch example of what Disney could do on a limited budget.

p, Larry Lansburgh; d, Roberto Gavaldon; w, Bill Walsh (based on a story by Larry Lansburgh); ph, Alex Phillips, J. Carlos Carbajal (Technicolor); m, William Lava.

Drama   Cas.   (MPAA:NR)

LITTLEST REBEL, THE

(1935) 73m FOX bw

Shirley Temple *(Virginia Houston Cary)*, John Boles *(Confederate Capt. Herbert Cary)*, Jack Holt *(Union Col. Morrison)*, Karen Morley *(Mrs. Cary)*, Bill Robinson *(Uncle Billy)*, Guinn "Big Boy" Williams *(Sgt. Dudley)*, Willie Best *(James Henry)*, Frank McGlynn, Sr. *(President Lincoln)*, Bessie Lyle *(Mammy)*, Hannah Washington *(Sally Ann)*, James Flavin *(Guard)*.

In this wonderful Shirley Temple picture set in the South during the Civil War, little Virginia (Temple) tries to keep the plantation afloat with the help of Uncle Billy (played by legendary tap dancer Bill "Bojangles" Robinson). When her mother takes ill, Virginia's father, Capt. Herbert Cary (John Boles), tries to sneak through enemy lines to see her. Union troops capture him and arrest him as a spy. A Yankee colonel (Jack Holt) helps Cary escape, but the captain is caught again and sentenced to die. Virginia takes her appeal all the way to the top, and drops in on President Lincoln. In one of the film's most captivating scenes, Virginia appeals to "Honest Abe" while sharing an apple with him. THE LITTLEST REBEL features a great duet by Temple and Robinson on "Polly Wolly Doodle."

p, Darryl F. Zanuck, B.G. DeSylva; d, David Butler; w, Edwin Burke, Harry Tugend (based on the play by Edward Peple); ph, John Seitz.

Drama   Cas.   (MPAA:NR)

LIVE WIRES

(1946) 64m MON bw

Leo Gorcey *(Terrence "Slip" Mahoney)*, Huntz Hall *(Sach)*, Bobby Jordan *(Bobby)*, Billy Benedict *(Whitey)*, William Frambes *(Homer)*, Claudia Drake *(Jeanette)*, Pamela Blake *(Mary Mahoney)*, Patti Brill *(Mabel)*, Mike Mazurki *(Patsy Clark)*, John Eldredge *(Herbert L. Sayers)*, Pat Gleason *(John Stevens)*, William Ruhl *(Construction Foreman)*, Rodney Bell *(George)*, Bill Christy *(Boy Friend)*, Nancy Brinkman *(Girl Friend)*, Robert Emmett Keane *(Barton)*, Earle Hodgins *(Barker)*, Bernard Gorcey *(Jack Kane)*, Frank Marlowe *(Red)*, Gladys Blake *(Ann Clark)*, Eddie Borden *(Shill)*, Charlie Sullivan, Henry Russell *(Ditch Diggers)*, John Indrisano, Steve Taylor *(Bouncers)*, Beverly Hawthorne *(1st Pretty Girl)*, Jack Chefe *(Head Waiter)*, Malcolm McClean *(MC/Announcer)*, George Eldredge *(Cop)*.

LIVE WIRES was the first in the series of "Bowery Boys" films that continued until 1957. It's practically Leo Gorcey's film, however, with the rest of the gang in subordinate roles. Terrence "Slip" Mahoney (Gorcey), a tough guy who still answers to his even tougher sister, Mary (Pamela Blake), loses his job at a construction firm when he punches out the foreman. Slip soon finds himself working with Sach (Huntz Hall) at the district attorney's office. The two get themselves into hot water when they try to bring in a gangster (Mike Mazurki) on their own. Their amateur investigation leads them to an even rougher gangster (John Eldredge) who runs the construction company where Slip worked. Setting a pattern from which the series wouldn't deviate, Slip and the boys bring their nemesis to justice. Bernard Gorcey, who would become familiar as drugstore owner Louie in subsequent series entries, plays a small-time bookie here.

p, Lindsley Parsons, Jan Grippo; d, Phil Karlson; w, Tim Ryan, Josef Mischel (based on a story by Jeb [Dore] Schary); ph, William Sickner.

Comedy (MPAA:NR)

LOUISIANA STORY

(1948) 77m Flaherty/Lopert bw

Joseph Boudreaux *(Boy)*, Lionel Le Blanc *(Father)*, Mrs. E. Bienvenu *(Mother)*, Frank Hardy *(Driller)*, C.T. Guedry *(Boileman)*.

In 1948, Standard Oil persuaded noted documentarist Robert Flaherty (NANOOK OF THE NORTH; MAN OF ARAN) to make a film about oil exploration, and this brilliantly photographed treat was the result. Given an initial budget of $175,000, total creative freedom, and the distribution rights, Flaherty took his crew to the Bayou country of Louisiana and filmed this simple but sincere story about the effect of the oncoming oil derricks and modern technology on the local Cajun population and on one family in particular. Flaherty's camera lovingly records daily Bayou life, focusing on the activities of a young boy, Joseph Boudreaux (one of the nonactors who contribute to the film's wholly natural feel), as he traps raccoons and fights off an alligator. Friendly oil workers try to peacefully coexist with the Cajuns, and when an oil rig blows (an event that actually occurred near the main shooting site), the workers are able to cap the rig, saving the environment. Unlike many corporate-sponsored films, LOUISIANA STORY is not propaganda but an honest story with realistic situations. The fine score by Virgil Thomson was performed by Eugene Ormandy and the Philadelphia Orchestra. Flaherty's cameraman was Richard Leacock, who would become a noted filmmaker in his own right.

p&d, Robert J. Flaherty; w, Robert J. Flaherty, Frances Flaherty; ph, Richard Leacock; m, Virgil Thomson.

Documentary Cas. (MPAA:NR)

LOVE BUG, THE

(1968) 108m Disney/BV c

Dean Jones *(Jim Douglas)*, Michele Lee *(Carole)*, David Tomlinson *(Thorndyke)*, Buddy Hackett *(Tennessee Steinmetz)*, Joe Flynn *(Havershaw)*, Benson Fong *(Mr. Wu)*, Joe E. Ross *(Detective)*, Barry Kelley *(Police Sergeant)*, Iris Adrian *(Carhop)*, Andy Granatelli *(Himself)*, Dale Van Sickel, Regina Parton, Bob Drake, Hal Brock, Rex Ramsey, Lynn Grate, Richard Warlock, Everett Creach, Bill Couch, Robert Hoy, Jack Mahoney, Richard Brill, Rudy Doucette, Jim McCullough, Glenn Wilder, Robert James, Bob Harris, Richard Geary, Jack Perkins,

Ronnie Rondell, Reg Parton, Tom Bamford, Marion J. Playan, Bill Hickman, Hal Grist, Larry Schmitz, Dana Derfus, Gerald Jann, Ted Duncan, Gene Roscoe, Charles Willis, Roy Butterfield, J.J. Wilson, Bud Ekins, Gene Curtis, John Timanus, Fred Krone, Jesse Wayne, Fred Stromsoe, Kim Brewer *(The Drivers)*.

One of the most successful Disney productions ever, this was the first in the series of films that starred Herbie, a cute little Volkswagen with a mind of its own. In this installment, unsuccessful race car driver Jim Douglas (Dean Jones) rescues Herbie from Thorndyke (David Tomlinson), a slick driver who mistreats the little car. The car takes to Jim and begins winning races for him without the man behind the steering wheel ever realizing Herbie's special attributes. Thorndyke becomes jealous of Jim's success and continually tries to buy Herbie back. No way. The entire cast give standout performances, but Herbie steals the show in this well-directed, funny picture.

p, Bill Walsh; d, Robert Stevenson; w, Don DaGradi, Bill Walsh (based on a story by Gordon Buford); ph, Edward Colman (Technicolor); m, George Bruns.

Comedy Cas. (MPAA:NR)

LOVE FINDS ANDY HARDY

(1938) 90m MGM bw

Lewis Stone *(Judge James Hardy)*, Mickey Rooney *(Andrew Hardy)*, Judy Garland *(Betsy Booth)*, Cecilia Parker *(Marian Hardy)*, Fay Holden *(Mrs. Hardy)*, Ann Rutherford *(Polly Benedict)*, Betty Ross Clarke *(Aunt Milly)*, Lana Turner *(Cynthia Potter)*, Marie Blake *(Augusta)*, Don Castle *(Dennis Hunt)*, Gene Reynolds *(Jimmy MacMahon)*, Mary Howard *(Mrs. Tompkins)*, George Breakston *(Beezy)*, Raymond Hatton *(Peter Dugan)*, Frank Darien *(Bill Collector)*, Rand Brooks *(Judge)*, Erville Alderson *(Court Attendant)*.

Another entry in the "Andy Hardy" series extolling the small-town American virtues that movie mogul Louis B. Mayer loved so much, this picture proved to be one of the highest grossing films for MGM in 1938 and also marked Judy Garland's first appearance in the series. In this episode, Andy (Mickey Rooney) angers his girl friend, Polly Benedict (Ann Rutherford), when he agrees to escort his buddy's "dishy" girl, Cynthia Potter (Lana Turner, in her first MGM appearance), for a fee, so that he can pay off the car he just bought. When Betsy Booth (Judy Garland) pops up to visit her aunt and uncle, Andy quickly dismisses her as nothing but a kid—until he hears her sing at a local dance. She quickly becomes another girl problem for Andy, but she sets him straight pronto. The entire cast give excellent performances under the skilled direction of George B. Seitz. The wholesome script was written by William Ludwig, a young lawyer from New York who moved west for his health and got a job in MGM's Junior Writing Department. In 1942 the "Andy Hardy" series won an award certificate at the Oscar ceremonies for "Achievement in Representing an American Way of Life."

p, Carey Wilson; d, George B. Seitz; w, William Ludwig (based on stories by Vivian B. Bretherton and characters by Aurania Rouverol); ph, Lester White; m, David Snell.

Comedy/Drama (MPAA:NR)

MA AND PA KETTLE

(1949) 76m UNIV bw

Marjorie Main *(Ma Kettle)*, Percy Kilbride *(Pa Kettle)*, Richard Long *(Tom Kettle)*, Meg Randall *(Kim Parker)*, Patricia Alphin *(Secretary)*, Esther Dale *(Mrs. Birdie Hicks)*, Barry Kelley *(Mr. Tomkins)*, Harry Antrim *(Mayor Swiggins)*, Isabel O'Madigan *(Mrs. Hicks's Mother)*, Ida Moore *(Emily)*, Emory Parnell *(Billy Reed)*, Boyd Davis *(Mr. Simpson)*, O.Z. Whitehead *(Mr. Billings)*, Ray Bennett *(Sam Rogers)*, Alvin Hammer *(Alvin)*, Lester Allen *(Geoduck)*, Chief Yowlachie *(Crowbar)*, Rex Lease *(Sheriff)*, Dale Belding *(Danny Kettle)*, Teddy Infuhr *(George Kettle)*, George McDonald *(Henry Kettle)*, Robin Winans *(Billy Kettle)*, Gene Persson *(Ted Kettle)*, Paul Dunn *(Donny Kettle)*, Margaret Brown *(Ruthie Kettle)*, Beverly Wook *(Eve Kettle)*, Diane Florentine *(Sara Kettle)*, Gloria Moore *(Rosie Kettle)*, Melinda Plowman *(Susie Kettle)*, Harry Tyler *(Ticket Agent)*, Dewey Robinson *(Giant Man)*, Sam McDaniel *(Waiter)*, Ted Stanhope *(Steward)*, Harry Cheshire *(Fletcher)*, Eddy C. Waller *(Mr. Green)*, John Wald *(Dick Palmer)*, Donna Leary *(Salty Kettle)*, Elena Schreiner *(Nancy Kettle)*, George Arglen *(Willie Kettle)*.

Percy Kilbride and Marjorie Main star as Ma and Pa Kettle in this spin-off of THE EGG AND I (1947), in which they played the Kettles as supporting characters and spawned the lengthy comedic series that lasted well into the 1950s. The Kettles, down-and-out parents of 15 kids, are on the verge of being evicted from their ramshackle home. Things begin to look up when Pa wins the grand prize in a tobacco slogan contest and the family is awarded a brand-new, fully automated house. The house and its modern conveniences provide the setting for some very funny sequences, while the Kettles also do battle with a local grouch (Esther Dale) who is jealous of their new fortune and accuses Pa of plagiarizing the slogan.

p, Leonard Goldstein; d, Charles Lamont; w, Herbert Margolis, Louis Morheim, Al Lewis (based on characters from the novel *The Egg and I* by Betty MacDonald); ph, Maury Gertsman; m, Milton Schwarzwald.

Comedy (MPAA:NR)

MA AND PA KETTLE ON VACATION

(1953) 79m UNIV bw (GB: MA AND PA KETTLE GO TO PARIS)

Marjorie Main *(Ma Kettle)*, Percy Kilbride *(Pa Kettle)*, Ray Collins *(Jonathan Parker)*, Bodil Miller *(Inez Kraft)*, Sig Ruman *(Cyrus Kraft)*, Barbara Brown *(Elizabeth Parker)*, Peter Brocco *(Adolph Wade)*, Sherry Jackson *(Susie Kettle)*, Gary Lee Jackson *(Billy Kettle)*, Billy Clark *(George Kettle)*, Jackie Jackson *(Henry Kettle)*, Elana Schreiner *(Nancy Kettle)*, Ronnie Rondell *(Dannie Kettle)*, Margaret Brown *(Ruthie Kettle)*, Jon Gardner *(Benjamin Kettle)*, Jenny Linder *(Sara Kettle)*, Beverly Mook *(Eve Kettle)*, Donna Leary *(Sally Kettle)*, Robert Scott *(Teddy Kettle)*, George Arglen *(Willie Kettle)*, Gloria Pall *(French Girl)*, Major Sam Harris *(Plane Passenger)*, Carli Elinor *(Orchestra Leader)*, Eddie Le Baron *(Wine Steward)*, Dave Willock *(Franklin)*.

This entry in the "Ma and Pa Kettle" series follows the country couple (Percy Kilbride and Marjorie Main) as they vacation in Paris, accompanied by their daughter-in-law's wealthy parents (Ray Collins and Barbara Brown). Between ogling racy postcards and cancan girls, Pa finds himself unwittingly involved in espionage when a spy gives him a letter to be delivered to one Adolph Wade (Peter Brocco). To complicate matters, Wade is knocked off by rival spies, and soon the chase through the streets of Paris is on.

p, Leonard Goldstein; d, Charles Lamont; w, Jack Henley; ph, George Robinson.

Comedy (MPAA:NR)

MADAME CURIE

(1943) 124m MGM bw

Greer Garson *(Mme. Marie Curie)*, Walter Pidgeon *(Pierre Curie)*, Robert Walker *(David LeGros)*, Dame May Whitty *(Mme. Eugene Curie)*, Henry Travers *(Eugene Curie)*, C. Aubrey Smith *(Lord Kelvin)*, Albert Basserman *(Prof. Jean Perot)*, Victor Francen *(President of University)*, Reginald Owen *(Dr. Henri Becquerel)*, Van Johnson *(Reporter)*, Elsa Basserman *(Mme. Perot)*, Lumsden Hare *(Prof. Reget)*, James Hilton *(Narrator)*, Charles Trowbridge, Edward Fielding, James Kirkwood, Nestor Eristoff *(Board Members)*, Moroni Olsen *(President of Businessmen's Board)*, Miles Mander, Arthur Shields, Frederic Worlock *(Businessmen)*, Alan Napier *(Dr. Bladh)*, Almira Sessions *(Mme. Michaud)*, Margaret O'Brien *(Irene, Age 5)*, Dorothy Gilmore *(Nurse)*, Gigi Perreau *(Eva, Age 18 Months)*, Ruth Cherrington *(Swedish Queen)*, Wyndham Standing *(King Oscar)*, Harold de Becker, Guy D'Ennery *(Professors)*, George Davis, William Edmunds *(Cart Drivers)*, Michael Visaroff *(Proud Papa)*, George Meader *(Singing Professor)*, Franz Dorfler *(Assistant Seamstress)*, Ray Teal *(Driver)*, Noel Mills *(Wedding Guest)*, Teddy Infuhr *(Son)*.

This fine film stirs the heart and stays closer to the facts of its subject's life than might be expected for its time. Greer Garson plays Marie, a Polish student studying in

Paris near the turn of the century, who shares a lab with scientist Pierre Curie (Walter Pidgeon). The shy Pierre grows not only to respect Marie's scientific knowledge, but also falls in love with her, and the two become engaged. They have been observing some pitchblende that has been behaving oddly in the course of experiments, eventually leading, after five years of marriage and study, to Marie's discovery of radium. Years pass as the Curies struggle to continue financing their work, until finally they extract one decigram of radium from thousands of pounds of pitchblende. The breakthrough makes the couple famous, but shortly thereafter, Pierre is killed in an auto accident. Marie continues her work as the film concludes. Nominated for Best Picture, Best Actor, Best Actress, Best Cinematography, and Best Music Oscars (but winning no awards in a heavily competitive field), MADAME CURIE is an intelligent, interesting, and unusually faithful screen biography.

p, Sidney Franklin; d, Mervyn LeRoy; w, Paul Osborn, Paul H. Rameau (based on the book by Eve Curie); ph, Joseph Ruttenberg; m, Herbert Stothart.

Biography   **(MPAA:NR)**

MAGIC BOX, THE

(1952, Brit.) 118m Festival/BL c

Renee Asherson (*Miss Tagg*), Richard Attenborough (*Jack Carter*), Robert Beatty (*Lord Beaverbrook*), Martin Boddey (*Sitter in Bath Studio*), Edward Chapman (*Father in Family Group*), John Charlesworth (*Graham Friese-Greene*), Maurice Colbourne (*Bride's Father*), Roland Culver (*1st Company Promoter*), John Howard Davies (*Maurice Friese-Greene*), Michael Denison (*Connaught Rooms Reporter*), Robert Donat (*William Friese-Greene*), Joan Dowling (*Friese-Green Maid*), Henry Edwards (*Butler*), Mary Ellis (*Mrs. Collings*), Marjorie Fielding (*Elderly Viscountess*), Robert Flemyng (*Doctor in Surgery*), Leo Genn (*Maida Vale Doctor*), Marius Goring (*House Agent*), Everly Gregg (*Bridegroom's Mother*), Joyce Grenfell (*Mrs. Clare*), Robertson Hare, Sybil Thorndike, Googie Withers (*Sitters in Bath Studio*), Kathleen Harrison (*Mother*), Joan Hickson (*Mrs. Stukely*), Stanley Holloway (*Broker's Man*), Michael Hordern (*Official Receiver*), Glynis Johns (*May Jones*), Mervyn Johns (*Pawnbroker*), Margaret Johnston (*Edith Friese-Greene*), Ann Lancaster (*Bridesmaid*), Herbert Lomas (*Warehouse Manager*), John Longdon (*Speaker in Connaught Rooms*), Bessie Love (*Bride's Mother*), Miles Malleson (*Orchestra Conductor*), Muir Mathieson (*Sir Arthur Sullivan*), A.E. Matthews (*Old Gentleman*), Laurence Olivier (*2nd Holborn Policeman*), Michael Redgrave (*Mr. Lege*), Margaret Rutherford (*Lady Pond*), Maria Schell (*Helena Friese-Greene*), Peter Ustinov (*Industry Man*), Emlyn Williams (*Bank Manager*).

Nearly every living actor who ever appeared in British movies worked in this feature, it seems. Robert Donat plays William Friese-Greene, the pioneer who patented the first motion picture camera. The film shows his beginnings as a photographer's assistant, then his days as a society lenser in London spending all his resources on his new invention (patented two years before Edison). His first wife (Maria Schell) shares his triumphs while his second wife (Margaret Johnston) shares his failures. In between, viewers are treated to the sight of at least 50 of England's finest actors, all playing tiny bits, moving the story along. Friese-Greene is hardly remembered now and had already been dead more than 30 years when THE MAGIC BOX was made, but the filmmakers' conviction that his story should be told convinced all of the actors (who agreed to alphabetical billing) to devote their talents to this good-looking, well-directed film. Donat is excellent, holding his own among the industry's finest.

p, Ronald Neame; d, John Boulting; w, Eric Ambler (based on *Friese-Greene, Close-up of an Inventor* by Ray Allister); ph, Jack Cardiff (Technicolor); m, Wiliam Alwyn.

Biography   **(MPAA:NR)**

MAGNIFICENT YANKEE, THE

(1950) 89m MGM bw (GB: THE MAN WITH THIRTY SONS)

Louis Calhern (*Oliver Wendell Holmes, Jr.*), Ann Harding (*Fanny Bowditch Holmes*), Eduard Franz (*Judge Louis Brandeis*), Philip Ober (*Mr. Owen Wister*), Ian Wolfe (*Mr. Adams*), Edith Evanson (*Annie Gough*), Richard Anderson (*Baxter*), Guy Anderson (*Baxter*), James Lydon (*Clinton*), Robert Sherwood (*Drake*), Hugh Sanders (*Parker*), Harlan Warde (*Norton*), Charles Evans (*Chief Justice Fuller*), John R. Hamilton (*Justice White*), Dan Tobin (*Dixon*), Robert E. Griffin (*Court Crier*), Stapleton Kent (*Court Clerk*), Robert Malcolm (*Marshall*), Everett Glass (*Justice Peckham*), Hayden Rorke (*Graham*), Marshall Bradford (*Head Waiter*), Holmes Herbert (*Justice McKenna*), Selmer Jackson (*Lawyer*), George Spaulding (*Justice Hughes*), Todd Karns (*Secretary*), Freeman Lusk (*Announcer*), David McMahon (*Workman*), Sherry Hall, Jack Gargan, Dick Cogan, Tony Merrill (*Reporters*), Robert Board, Wilson Wood, James Horne, Gerald Pierce, Lyle Clark, David Alpert, Tommy Kelly, Bret Hamilton, Jim Drum (*Secretaries*), Wheaton Chambers, Gayne Whitman (*Senators*), William Johnstone (*Lawyer*).

An excellent cinematization of Emmet Lavery's long-running Broadway play (which also starred Louis Calhern), THE MAGNIFICENT YANKEE is the story of Oliver Wendell Holmes, Jr. (Calhern), and his rise to the top of American jurisprudence. In following his career, the movie charts the contemporary history, but without neglecting Holmes' personal life, particularly his touching relationship with his wife, Fanny (Ann Harding). Also portrayed are Louis Brandeis (Eduard Franz) and Holmes' close friend, author Owen Wister (Philip Ober), whose literate narration never intrudes upon the drama. MGM producers were not surprised at the film's critical success, but it also appealed to an unexpectedly large audience and turned a mild profit.

p, Armand Deutsch; d, John Sturges; w, Emmet Lavery (based on the book *Mr. Justice Holmes* by Francis Biddle

MAKE MINE MUSIC—

and the play by Emmet Lavery); ph, Joseph Ruttenberg; m, David Raksin.

Biography　　　　　　　　　　　　　**(MPAA:NR)**

MAKE MINE MUSIC

(1946) 74m Disney/RKO c

Voices of: Nelson Eddy, Dinah Shore, Benny Goodman and His Orchestra, The Andrews Sisters, Jerry Colonna, Andy Russell, Sterling Holloway, The Pied Pipers, The King's Men, The Ken Darby Chorus, Tatiana Riabouchinska, David Lichine.

A musical pastiche that's a sort of pop FANTASIA, MAKE MINE MUSIC has excellent animation and fine music, with 10 separate sequences having little in common except their high entertainment value. The segments include "The Whale Who Wanted to Sing at the Met," with Nelson Eddy singing as the title whale; "The Martins and the Coys," about feuding mountain people; "A Jazz Interlude," with Benny Goodman on the number "All the Cats Join In" (in which teenagers dance at the malt shop); "Peter and the Wolf," "A Ballad in Blue," and many, many more. The picture took two years to make and the resulting colors and animation are superb. The film will delight children who have only been exposed to the Saturday morning TV animation and not the infinitely lovelier work of the Disney studios.

p, Joe Grant; d, Jack Kinney, Clyde Geronimi, Hamilton Luske, Robert Cormack, Joshua Meador; w, Homer Brightman, Dick Huemer, Dick Kinney, John Walbridge, Tom Oreb, Dick Shaw, Eric Gurney, Sylvia Holland, T. Hee, Dick Kelsey, Jesse Marsh, Roy Williams, Ed Penner, James Bodrero, Cap Palmer, Erwin Graham.

Animation　　　　　　　　　　　　　**(MPAA:NR)**

MAN CALLED FLINTSTONE, THE

(1966) 90m COL c (AKA: THAT MAN FLINTSTONE)

Voices of: Alan Reed, Sr. *(Fred Flintstone)*, Mel Blanc *(Barney Rubble)*, Jean Vanderpyl *(Wilma Flintstone)*, Gerry Johnson *(Betty Rubble)*, Don Messick, Janet Waldo, Paul Frees, Harvey Korman, John Stephenson, June Foray.

This full-length cartoon featuring the stone-age Fred Flintstone and family was brought into theaters during the TV show's sixth season. In this spy spoof aimed at the younger set, Fred is the doppelganger of master spy Rock Slag, and when Slag is put out of commission, the Stone Age Secret Service puts Fred in his place. Fred, wife Wilma, and neighbors Barney and Betty Rubble go to Paris, where Fred is to find the Green Goose, head of SMIRK, and his accomplice. From Paris, the group goes on to Rome, where Fred and Barney are taken prisoners by the Goose until the real Rock Slag arrives to save them. An enjoyable animated film for the kids, featuring Mel Blanc, who provides the voices of Bugs Bunny, Daffy Duck, and other Warner Bros. cartoon characters, this time doing Barney Rubble.

p&d, Joseph Barbera, William Hanna; w, Harvey Bullock, R.S. Allen (based on a story by Harvey Bullock, R.S. Allen, and story material by Joseph Barbera, William Hanna, Warren Foster, Alex Lovy); ph, Charles Flekal, Roy Wade, Gene Borghi, Bill Kotler, Norman Stainback, Dick Blundell, Frank Parrish, Hal Shiffman, John Pratt (Eastmancolor); m, Marty Paich, Ted Nichols.

Animation　　　　　　　　　　　　　**(MPAA:NR)**

MAN CALLED PETER, A

(1955) 119m FOX c

Richard Todd *(Peter Marshall)*, Jean Peters *(Catherine Marshall)*, Marjorie Rambeau *(Miss Fowler)*, Jill Esmond *(Mrs. Findlay)*, Les Tremayne *(Sen. Harvey)*, Robert Burton *(Mr. Peyton)*, Gladys Hurlburt *(Mrs. Peyton)*, Gloria Gordon *(Barbara)*, Billy Chapin *(Peter John Marshall)*, Sally Corner *(Mrs. Whiting)*, Voltaire Perkins *(Sen. Wiley)*, Betty Caulfield *(Jane Whitney)*, Marietta Canty *(Emma)*, Edward Earle *(Sen. Prescott)*, Mimi Hutson *(College Girl)*, Agnes Bartholomew *(Grandmother)*, Peter Votrian *(Peter Marshall, Ages 7 to 14)*, Janet Stewart *(Nancy)*, Ann B. Davis *(Ruby Coleman)*, Arthur Tovay *(Usher)*, Sam McDaniel *(Maitre d')*, Dorothy Neumann *(Miss Crilly)*, Oliver Hartwell *(Janitor)*, Doris Lloyd *(Miss Hopkins)*, William Forrest *(President)*, Barbara Morrison *(Miss Standish)*, Carlyle Mitchell *(Dr. Black)*, Amanda Randolph *(Willie)*, Rick Kelman *(Peter, Age 51)*, Louis Torres, Jr. *(Peter, Age 61)*, Emmett Lynn *(Mr. Briscoe)*, William Walker *(Butler)*, Charles Evans *(President of Senate)*, Alexander Campbell, Jonathan Hole *(Elders)*, Larry Kent *(Chaplain)*.

A MAN CALLED PETER is a fine biography of Peter Marshall, the Scotsman who became the US Senate's chaplain. Marshall appealed to young and old in his sermons, as will this picture, a good yarn combining firm ideals and solid production values. Richard Todd is captivating as Marshall, as is Jean Peters as his wife, upon whose memoirs the film was based. She must cope with Marshall's tuberculosis and derives her strength from his sermons, as does Sen. Harvey (Les Tremayne), who resolves to clean up politics in his home state. There are struggles along the way, most of which arise from Marshall's unconventional treatment of religion as a living thing, rather than as a repository of dead tradition. The message is never blatant, however, even in Marshall's fascinating sermons, and the performances are all excellent under Henry Koster's direction. Shot in and around Washington, DC, the movie looks as good as it sounds, with preachiness put aside in favor of the very down-to-earth story of two people who are devoted to each other.

p, Samuel G. Engel; d, Henry Koster; w, Eleanore Griffin (based on the book by Catherine Marshall); ph, Harold Lipstein (CinemaScope, Deluxe Color); m, Alfred Newman.

Biography　　　　　　　　　　　　　**(MPAA:NR)**

MANHATTAN PROJECT, THE

(1986) 120m Gladden Entertainment/FOX c (AKA: MANHATTAN PROJECT: THE DEADLY GAME)

John Lithgow *(John Mathewson)*, Christopher Collet *(Paul Stephens)*, Cynthia Nixon *(Jenny Anderman)*, Jill Eikenberry *(Elizabeth Stephens)*, John Mahoney *(Lt. Col. Conroy)*, Sully Boyar *(Night Guard)*; University Lab: Richard Council *(Government)*, Robert Schenkkan *(Government Aide)*, Paul Austin *(General)*, Adrian Sparks, Curt Dempster *(Scientists)*, Bran Ferren *(Lab Assistant)*; Ithaca: Greg Edelman *(Science Teacher)*, Abe Unger *(Roland)*, Robert Leonard *(Max)*, David Quinn *(Tennis)*, Geoffrey Nauffts *(Craig)*, Katherine Hiler *(Emma)*, Trey Cummins *(Terry)*, Steve Borton, Harlan Cary Poe *(Local FBI)*, Ned Schmidtke, Sarah Burke *(Jenny's Parents)*, Allan DeCheser, Arthur DeCheser *(Jenny's Brother)*; Science Fair: Fred G. Smith *(Conroy's Lieutenant)*, John David Cullum *(Eccles)*, Manny Jacobs *(Moore)*, Charlie Fields *(Price)*, Eric Hsiao *(Saito)*, Trevor Bolling *(Halley's Comet Kid)*, Richard Cardona *(Laser Efficiency Kid)*, Heather Dominic, Bruce Smolanoff *(Flirting Kids)*, Joan Kendall *(Registrar)*, John Doumanian *(Cabbie)*, Tom Tarpey *(Injection Doctor)*, Alec Massey, Edward D. Murphy, Dee Ann McDavid *(FBI)*, Joan Harris *(TV Reporter Barbara Collins)*, Kerry Donovan *(Himself)*; Nuclear Emergency Search Team: Ken Chapin *(Command)*, Peter McRobbie *(Electronics)*, Warren Keith *(Computer)*, Bruce Jarchow, Stephen Markle *(Interrogators)*.

What would happen if a private citizen, on his own, were able to construct a nuclear bomb capable of mass annihilation? This familiar, but fascinating, premise is explored here through the eyes of Paul Stephens (Christopher Collet), a sensitive teenager. Paul meets scientist John Mathewson (John Lithgow), who takes the gifted youth on a tour of his "research firm," which, Paul realizes, is a government front for developing nuclear weapons. Determined to expose the operation, Paul sets out to steal some plutonium which will enable him to build his own nuclear device. The movie features a number of fascinating sequences, particularly Paul's clever methods for infiltrating plant security to gain the needed plutonium. It also benefits from a thrilling and action-packed climax. An exciting, if conventional, teen thriller, effectively making its points about the dangers of the nuclear age. Lithgow is very good as the brilliant yet troubled scientist and writer-director Marshall Brickman does a nice job of emphasizing human values.

p, Jennifer Ogden, Marshall Brickman; d, Marshall Brickman; w, Marshall Brickman, Thomas Baum; ph, Billy Williams (Technicolor); m, Philippe Sarde.

Drama   Cas.   **(MPAA:PG-13)**

MARY POPPINS

(1964) 140m Disney/BV c

Julie Andrews *(Mary Poppins)*, Dick Van Dyke *(Bert/Mr. Dawes, Sr.)*, David Tomlinson *(Mr. Banks)*, Glynis Johns *(Mrs. Banks)*, Hermione Baddeley *(Ellen)*, Reta Shaw *(Mrs. Brill)*, Karen Dotrice *(Jane Banks)*, Matthew Garber *(Michael Banks)*, Elsa Lanchester *(Katie Nanna)*, Arthur Treacher *(Constable Jones)*, Reginald Owen *(Adm. Boom)*, Ed Wynn *(Uncle Albert)*, Jane Darwell *(The Bird Woman)*, Arthur Malet *(Mr. Dawes, Jr.)*, Cyril Delevanti *(Mr. Grubbs)*, Lester Matthews *(Mr. Tomes)*, Clive L. Halliday *(Mr. Mousely)*, Donald Barclay *(Mr. Binnacle)*, Marjorie Bennett *(Miss Lark)*, Alma Lawton *(Mrs. Corry)*, Marjorie Eaton *(Miss Persimmon)*, Doris Lloyd *(Depositor)*, Major Sam Harris *(Citizen)*, James Logan.

One of the greatest children's films ever, MARY POPPINS is as perfect and inventive a musical as anyone could see, with a timeless story, excellent performances, a flawless blend of live action and animation, wonderful songs, and a superb script with all the charm of the P.L. Travers books upon which it is based. The film begins when a remote father and mother (David Tomlinson and Glynis Johns) decide to advertise for a nanny to care for their rowdy children, Michael and Jane Banks (Matthew Garber and Karen Dotrice). The children write their own ad, and when their father tears it up and burns it in the fireplace, the pieces miraculously reassemble and go up the flue. Next day, Mary Poppins (Julie Andrews) appears, gliding down from on high with an umbrella as her parachute. As the children soon learn, this is no ordinary nanny, as she leads them on a series of delightful escapades, all the while teaching them lessons in proper behavior. Among the wonderful new friends Mary introduces the children to are Bert the chimney sweep (Dick Van Dyke), who accompanies them on a holiday in another world containing the famous animated penguins who serve them tea on a carousel with strangely willful horses, and Uncle Albert (Ed Wynn), whose infectious laughter leads to strange consequences. Nominated for 13 Academy Awards (winning for Best Actress, Best Film Editing, Best Original Score, Best Song, and Best Special Visual Effects), MARY POPPINS was producer Walt Disney's crowning achievement in a career that had earned him more Oscars than anyone else. The memorable songs by Disney writers Richard and Robert Sherman include "Supercalifragilisticexpialidocious" "Chim Chim Cheree," and "A Spoonful of Sugar."

p, Walt Disney, Bill Walsh; d, Robert Stevenson; w, Bill Walsh, Don DaGradi (based on the Mary Poppins books by P.L. Travers); ph, Edward Colman (Technicolor); m, Irwin Kostal.

Comedy/Musical   Cas.   **(MPAA:NR)**

MEET ME IN ST. LOUIS

(1944) 113m MGM c

Judy Garland *(Esther Smith)*, Margaret O'Brien *("Tootie" Smith)*, Mary Astor *(Mrs. Anne Smith)*, Lucille Bremer *(Rose Smith)*, June Lockhart *(Lucille Ballard)*, Tom Drake *(John Truett)*, Marjorie Main *(Katie)*, Harry Davenport *(Grandpa)*, Leon Ames *(Mr. Alonzo Smith)*, Hank Daniels *(Lon Smith, Jr.)*, Joan Carroll *(Agnes Smith)*, Hugh Marlowe *(Col. Darly)*, Robert Sully *(Warren Sheffield)*, Chill Wills *(Mr. Neely)*, Donald Curtis *(Dr. Terry)*, Mary Jo Ellis

(Ida Boothby), Ken Wilson *(Quentin)*, Robert Emmett O'Connor *(Motorman)*, Darryl Hickman *(Johnny Tevis)*, Leonard Walker *(Conductor)*, Victor Kilian *(Baggage Man)*, John Phipps *(Mailman)*, Major Sam Harris *(Mr. March)*, Mayo Newhall *(Mr. Braukoff)*, Belle Mitchell *(Mrs. Braukoff)*, Sidney Barnes *(Hugo Borvis)*, Myron Tobias *(George)*, Victor Cox *(Driver)*, Kenneth Donner, Buddy Gorman, Joe Cobbs *(Clinton Badgers)*, Helen Gilbert *(Girl on Trolley)*.

The 22-year-old Judy Garland shines under the stylish direction of her future husband, Vincente Minnelli, in this wonderful period musical. It opens in 1903 in St. Louis, where Alonzo Smith (Leon Ames), a well-to-do businessman, lives with his wife (Mary Astor), daughters (Garland, Lucille Bremer, Joan Carroll, and Margaret O'Brien), son (Hank Daniels), capricious Grandpa (Harry Davenport), and maid (Marjorie Main). Daughter Rose (Bremer) is courted by one beau at home and corresponds with another away at college, while Esther (Garland) becomes engaged to the new boy next door. Constantly flitting in and out is Tootie, the precocious youngest child, as O'Brien steals scene after scene and duets with Garland on "I Was Drunk Last Night" and "Under the Bamboo Tree." Trouble arises when Alonzo is promoted and ordered to New York, a move no one in the family wants to make. Tootie registers her despair by burying her dolls in the backyard and destroying a snowman on the lawn (this just after Garland sings "Have Yourself a Merry Little Christmas"). This is a sensitive portrayal of America at the turn of the century and one family's struggles to deal with progress, symbolized by the 1904 World's Fair in St. Louis (beautifully re-created for the film). Minnelli proves his eye for detail and captures the era and its values in richly colored, gentle images, displaying a startling balance of emotions from scene to scene, song to song. Among the songs included in this triumph of Americana are "The Boy Next Door," "Meet Me in St. Louis," "Little Brown Jug," and the marvelous production number "The Trolley Song."

p, Arthur Freed; d, Vincente Minnelli; w, Irving Brecher, Fred F. Finklehoffe (based on the stories by Sally Benson); ph, George Folsey (Technicolor).

Musical   **Cas.**   **(MPAA:NR)**

MELODY

(1971, Brit.) 103m Hemdale-Sagittarius/Levitt-Pickman c (AKA: S.W.A.L.K.)

Jack Wild *(Ornshaw)*, Mark Lester *(Daniel Latimer)*, Tracy Hyde *(Melody Perkins)*, Colin Barrie *(Chambers)*, Billy Franks *(Burgess)*, Ashley Knight *(Stacey)*, Craig Marriott *(Dadds)*, William Vanderpuye *(O'Leary)*, Peter Walton *(Fensham)*, Camille Davies *(Muriel)*, Dawn Hope *(Maureen)*, Kay Skinner *(Peggy)*, Sheila Steafel *(Mrs. Latimer)*, Kate Williams *(Mrs. Perkins)*, Roy Kinnear *(Mr. Perkins)*, Hilda Barry *(Grandma Perkins)*, James Cossins *(Headmaster)*, Ken Jones *(Mr. Dicks)*, June Jago *(Miss Fairfax)*, June Ellis *(Miss Dimkins)*, Tim Wylton *(Mr. Fellows)*, John Gorman *(Boys' Brigade Captain)*, Petal Young *(Betty)*,

Robin Hunter *(George)*, Neil Hallett, Tracy Reed *(Man and Woman in Hospital, TV Film)*, Deborah Childs, Heather Gibson, Susan Hassell, Sara Maddern, Stephanie Muldenhall, Jacqueline Pullen, Leslie Roach, Caroline Stratford, Gill Wain, Karen Williams *(Girls' Group)*, Leonard Brockwell, Billy Ferguson, Robin Hopwood, Nigel Kingsley, Peter Lewis, Stephen Mallett, Kenny Robson, Tommy Skipp, Wayne Thistleton, Roy Wain, Ricky Wales *(Boys' Group)*.

OLIVER! star Mark Lester plays Daniel Latimer, a preteen who falls in love with and decides to marry a young girl his age (Tracy Hyde). They inform their parents of their plans, despite the pleas of an older friend (Jack Wild, another OLIVER! veteran). The plot isn't very convincing, but the actors' charming innocence more than makes up for it, and a plus for Bee Gees fans is a fine score performed by the group that sounds nothing like SATURDAY NIGHT FEVER and includes "Teach Your Children," "To Love Somebody," and "Working on It Night and Day." Scriptwriter Alan Parker would go on to direct MIDNIGHT EXPRESS and PINK FLOYD—THE WALL, while producer David Puttnam would later deliver CHARIOTS OF FIRE.

p, David Puttnam; d, Waris Hussein, Andrew Birkin; w, Alan Parker; ph, Peter Suschitzky (Technicolor); m, The Bee-Gees, Richard Hewson.

Drama   **Cas.**   **(MPAA:G)**

MELODY TIME

(1948) 75m Disney/RKO c

Roy Rogers, Luana Patten, Bobby Driscoll, Ethel Smith, Bob Nolan, Sons of the Pioneers; the voices of: Buddy Clark, The Andrews Sisters, Fred Waring and His Pennsylvanians, Frances Langford, Dennis Day, Freddy Martin and His Orchestra, Jack Fina, The Dinning Sisters.

This last musical compilation film from the Disney studios was also one of the best, and Disney's animators display their entire creative range, from the irrepressible comedy of Donald Duck to more refined work reminiscent of FANTASIA. The sequences include the story of a young couple's quarrel, told in flashback after they are a long-married pair; a marvelously surreal piece, dubbed "an instrumental nightmare," in which a befuddled bee buzzes about in a frenzied effort to escape a variety of musical perils to the accompaniment of a jazzy "Flight of the Bumble Bee"; a retelling of the Johnny Appleseed folktales; the charming "Little Toot," in which the title tugboat is always getting into trouble in its attempts to emulate its father; "Trees," a version of Joyce Kilmer's poem that is Disney animation at its best; "Blame It on the Samba," which once more teams Donald Duck with his pal Joe Carioca from the popular cartoon "The Three Caballeros"; and a final segment featuring cowboy king Roy Rogers and the Sons of the Pioneers crooning "Blue Shadows on the Trail" against a series of desert night scenes. Essentially a compendium of unrelated shorts, the delightful MELODY TIME incorporates visual styles as varied as the subjects of its segments.

p, Walt Disney; d, Clyde Geronimi, Wilfred Jackson, Hamilton Luske, Jack Kinney; w, Winston Hibler, Erdman Penner, Harry Reeves, Homer Brightman, Ken Anderson, Ted Sears, Joe Rinaldi, Art Scott, Bill Cottrell, Bob Moore, Jesse Marsh, John Walbridge, Hardie Gramatky.

Animation/Musical (MPAA:NR)

MIDSUMMER NIGHT'S DREAM, A

(1961, Czech.) 74m Ceskoslovensky/Showcorporation c

Voices of: Richard Burton (Narrator), Tom Criddle (Lysander), Ann Bell (Hermia), Michael Meacham (Demetrius), John Warner (Egeus), Barbara Leigh-Hunt (Helena), Hugh Manning (Theseus), Joss Ackland (Quince), Alec McCowen (Bottom), Stephen Moore (Flute), Barbara Jefford (Titania), Jack Gwillim (Oberon), Roger Shepherd (Puck), Laura Graham (Hippolyta).

This wonderfully executed, beautifully photographed version of the famous play boasts a cast of puppets. A winner of the Grand Prix at the Cannes Film Festival, the film provides a great way to introduce younger audiences to Shakespeare's classic fantasy.

p, Jiri Trnka; d, Jiri Trnka, Howard Sackler; w, Jiri Trnka, Jiri Brdecka, Howard Sackler (based on the play by William Shakespeare); ph, Jiri Vojta (CinemaScope, Eastmancolor); m, Vaclav Trojan.

Drama (MPAA:NR)

MIGHTY MOUSE IN THE GREAT SPACE CHASE

(1983) 87m Filmation-Viacom/Miracle c

In this entertaining animated feature starring the Superman of mice, Mighty saves the entire universe from certain destruction at the paws of malevolent feline Harry the Heartless. Good kid stuff.

p, Lou Scheimer, Norm Prescott, Don Christensen; d, Ed Friedman, Lou Kachivas, Marsh Lamore, Gwen Wetzler, Kay Wright, Lou Zukor; ph, R.W. Pope (Technicolor); m, Yvette Blais, Jeff Michael.

Animation (MPAA:NR)

MILKY WAY, THE

(1936) 83m PAR bw

Harold Lloyd (Burleigh "Tiger" Sullivan), Adolphe Menjou (Gabby Sloan), Verree Teasdale (Ann Westley), Helen Mack (Mae Sullivan), William Gargan (Elwood "Speed" MacFarland), George Barbier (Wilbur Austin), Dorothy Wilson (Polly Pringle), Lionel Stander (Spider Schultz), Charles Lane (Willard, Reporter), Marjorie Gateson (Mrs. E. Winthrop LeMoyne), Bull Anderson (Oblitsky), Jim Marples (O'Rourke), Larry McGrath (Referee), Bonita (Landlady), Milburn Stone (1st Reporter), Paddy O'Flynn (2nd Reporter), Henry Roquemore (Doctor), Arthur S. "Pop" Byron (Cop), Eddie Dunn (Barber), Larry McGrath (Referee, Todd Fight), Jack Clifford (Announcer, Todd Fight), Jack Perry ("Tornado" Todd), Phil Tead (Radio An-

nouncer, Todd Fight), Jack Murphy (Newsboy), Bob Callahan (Onion), Eddie Fetherston (Cameraman), Leonard Carey (Butler), Antrim Short (Photographer), Melville Ruick (Austin's Secretary), Harry Bowen (Bartender), James Farley (Fight Promoter), Harry Bernard (Cop-Tenant).

This very funny film shows the great Harold Lloyd making the transition from silent to sound films with no problems. Lloyd plays milquetoast milkman Burleigh Sullivan, who happens to be in the right place at the right time. When a middleweight champion (William Gargan) throws a punch his way, Sullivan ducks, and the punch is returned by bruiser Spider Schultz (Lionel Stander). The champ is knocked senseless and "Tiger" Sullivan gets the credit. The champ's manager (Adolphe Menjou) then decides to take the milkman on as a boxer-client, with predictable comedic results. Lloyd (who almost always did his own spectacular stunts) stepped aside from producing chores on THE MILKY WAY, and was thus able to concentrate on his comedy without worrying about finances and other woes. He gives a superb performance in his patented role of the bespectacled, naive everyman who triumphs over ironic perils every time. Remade as THE KID FROM BROOKLYN (1946), starring Danny Kaye.

p, E. Lloyd Sheldon; d, Leo McCarey; w, Grover Jones, Frank Butler, Richard Connell (based on the play by Lynn Root and Harry Clork); ph, Alfred Gilks.

Comedy **Cas.** (MPAA:NR)

MIRACLE ON 34TH STREET, THE

(1947) 96m FOX bw (GB: THE BIG HEART)

Maureen O'Hara (Doris Walker), John Payne (Fred Gailey), Edmund Gwenn (Kris Kringle), Gene Lockhart (Judge Henry X. Harper), Natalie Wood (Susan Walker), Porter Hall (Mr. Sawyer), William Frawley (Charles Halloran), Jerome Cowan (Thomas Mara), Philip Tonge (Mr. Shellhammer), James Seay (Dr. Pierce), Harry Antrim (Mr. Macy), Thelma Ritter, Mary Field (Mothers), Theresa Harris (Cleo), Alvin Greenman (Albert), Anne Staunton (Mrs. Mara), Robert Hyatt (Thomas Mara, Jr.), Richard Irving, Jeff Corey (Reporters), Anne O'Neal (Secretary), Lela Bliss (Mrs. Shellhammer), Anthony Sydes (Peter), William Forrest (Dr. Rogers), Alvin Hammer (Mara's Assistant), Joseph McInerney (Bailiff), Ida McGuire (Drum Majorette), Percy Helton (Santa Claus), Jane Green (Mrs. Harper), Marlene Lyden (Dutch Girl), Jack Albertson, Guy Thomajan (Post Office Employees), Robert Lynn (Macy's Salesman), Jean O'Donnell (Secretary), Snub Pollard (Mail-Bearing Court Officer), Robert Karnes, Basil Walker (Interns), Herbert Heyes (Mr. Gimbel), Stephen Roberts (Guard), Teddy Driver (Terry), Robert Gist (Window Dresser), Patty Smith (Alice).

This beloved film is shown every Christmas, and rightly so. MIRACLE ON 34TH STREET opens during Manhattan's Christmas Parade as Macy's executive Doris Walker (Maureen O'Hara) finds the Santa Claus for the store float so drunk he can't stand up. Chiding Doris for employing such a derelict is a kindly, white-bearded man who, when she asks his name, tells her it's "Kris Kringle." Ignoring this, she pleads with him to replace the drunk, and he proves such a crowd-pleaser that she hires him as Macy's resident Santa for the holiday rush. This sets in a motion a series of events in which Kris touches the lives of many, teaching them a lot about faith and the true meaning of Christmas. Among those touched are Doris, her sophisticated little girl, Susan (Natalie Wood), who thinks the very idea of Santa Claus is ridiculous, Doris' suitor Fred Gailey (John Payne), and dozens of Macy's customers who are pleasantly surprised when Kris directs them to competitors to get the gifts they seek. Unfortunately all are not smitten with this kindly man, particularly the store's amateur psychologist whose contention that Kris is unbalanced leads to a trial in which the court must decide the weighty matter of whether or not there is a Santa Claus. Gwenn won an Oscar for his role, and for many, his charming, endearing performance has been identified with the spirit of the Christmas season ever since the completion of this superb production.

p, William Perlberg; d&w, George Seaton (based on a story by Valentine Davies); ph, Charles Clarke, Lloyd Ahern; m, Cyril Mockridge.

Fantasy   **Cas.**   **(MPAA:NR)**

MIRACLE WORKER, THE

(1962) 106m Playfilms/UA bw

Anne Bancroft *(Annie Sullivan)*, Patty Duke *(Helen Keller)*, Victor Jory *(Capt. Keller)*, Inga Swenson *(Kate Keller)*, Andrew Prine *(James Keller)*, Kathleen Comegys *(Aunt Ev)*, Beah Richards *(Viney)*, Jack Hollander *(Mr. Anagnos)*, Peggy Burke *(Helen, Age 7)*, Mindy Sherwood *(Helen, Age 5)*, Grant Code *(Doctor)*, Michael Darden *(Percy, Age 10)*, Dale Ellen Bethea *(Martha, Age 10)*, Walter Wright, Jr. *(Percy, Age 8)*, Donna Bryan *(Martha, Age 7)*, Diane Bryan *(Martha, Age 5)*, Keith Moore *(Percy, Age 6)*, Michele Farr *(Young Annie, Age 10)*, Allan Howard *(Young Jimmie, Age 8)*, Judith Lowry *(1st Crone)*, William F. Haddock *(2nd Crone)*, Helen Ludlum *(3rd Crone)*, Belle the Dog.

THE MIRACLE WORKER is the powerful and uplifting story of Annie Sullivan and Helen Keller. The film begins as the deaf, dumb, and blind Helen (Patty Duke) appears helpless and unreachable in her silent world. Annie (Anne Bancroft) then arrives, determined to teach the girl how to communicate through sign language. The task seems impossible, although Annie, herself partially blind and for many years institutionalized, has greater insight into Helen's condition than the girl's family. In addition to Helen's seemingly hopeless condition, Annie also has to contend with her parents, who are appalled by her stringent methods for reaching the daughter they love. The film is a masterful display of technique from all involved, especially Bancroft, Duke, and director Arthur Penn. Most spectacular is a lengthy battle between Annie and Helen as the teacher attempts to teach her pupil some table manners—a battle of wills in which Annie is

determined to defeat Helen's stubbornness. In 1979 a TV version of the story was made, with Duke taking the role of Sullivan this time and Melissa Gilbert as Keller.

p, Fred Coe; d, Arthur Penn; w, William Gibson (based on his play and the book, *The Story of My Life* by Helen Keller); ph, Ernesto Caparros; m, Laurence Rosenthal.

Drama   **Cas.**   **(MPAA:NR)**

MR. BUG GOES TO TOWN

(1941) 78m PAR c (AKA: HOPPITY GOES TO TOWN)

Voices of: Kenny Gardner, Gwen Williams, Jack Mercer, Ted Pierce, Mike Meyer, Stan Freed, Pauline Loth.

This was the last cartoon feature that the Fleischer brothers, Max and Dave, released before going their separate ways. The story concerns an insect community threatened by problems within their society, in addition to pressures from the human race. Unfortunately, this expensive production was a financial failure, causing the animators, who had been the Disney's chief rivals, to close up shop. While MR. BUG GOES TO TOWN falls short of such earlier Fleischer features as GULLIVER'S TRAVELS, it features animation that was well ahead of its time.

p, Max Fleischer; d, Dave Fleischer; w, Dave Fleisher, Dan Gordon, Ted Pierce, Isidore Sparber, William Turner, Mike Meyer, Graham Place, Bob Wickersham, Cal Howard; ph, Charles Schnettler (Technicolor).

Animation   **Cas.**   **(MPAA:NR)**

MISTER 880

(1950) 90m FOX bw

Burt Lancaster *(Steve Buchanan)*, Dorothy McGuire *(Ann Winslow)*, Edmund Gwenn *(Skipper Miller)*, Millard Mitchell *(Mac)*, Minor Watson *(Judge O'Neil)*, Howard St. John *(Chief)*, Hugh Sanders *(Thad Mitchell)*, James Millican *(Olie Johnson)*, Howland Chamberlin *(Duff)*, Larry Keating *(Lee)*, Kathleen Hughes *(Secretary)*, Geraldine Wall *(Miss Gallagher)*, Mervin Williams *(US Attorney)*, Norman Field *(Bailiff)*, Helen Hatch *(Maggie)*, Robert B. Williams *(Sergeant)*, Ed Max *(Mousie)*, Frank Wilcox *(Mr. Beddington)*, George Adrian *(Carlos)*, Michael Lally *(George)*, Joe McTurk *(Gus)*, Minerva Urecal *(Rosie)*, George Gastine *(Waiter)*, Ray De Ravenne, Paul Bradley, Arthur Dulac *(Men)*, Curt Furberg *(German)*, Joan Valerie *(Cashier)*, Jack Daly *(Court Clerk)*, Dick Ryan *(US Marshal)*, William J. O'Leary *(Junk Man)*, Billy Gray *(Mickey)*, Billy Nelson *(Taxi Driver)*, Bill McKenzie *(Jimmy)*, Herbert Vigran *(Barker)*.

This enchanting comedy stars Edmund Gwenn as the cheery Skipper Miller, an aging counterfeiter who prints dollar bills to support himself. Although he breaks the law, he is such a harmless, whimsical criminal that he defies censure, counterfeiting bills because he needs money to live and out of love for his old-fashioned printing press, which he calls "Cousin Henry." Miller proves an embarrassment to the federal agents who have been after him for 10 years, but a new man on the case, Steve Buchanan (Burt Lancaster), comes closer than any other agent to nabbing Miller. He traces one of the bills to an apartment where he meets a pretty United Nations translator (Dorothy McGuire) with whom he falls in love, and soon afterwards he discovers that the elusive counterfeiter is his girl friend's neighbor. But identifying the "crook" proves to be only half the battle as Buchanan and his colleagues find it difficult to prosecute this charming little man. Lancaster and McGuire perform admirably, but Gwenn, who earned a Best Supporting Actor Oscar nomination for his work, steals the show with one of his most memorable performances (along with his role in MIRACLE ON 34TH STREET and his endearing presence in THE TROUBLE WITH HARRY).

p, Julian Blaustein; d, Edmund Goulding; w, Robert Riskin (based on *The New Yorker* article "Old Eight Eighty" by St. Clair McKelway); ph, Joseph LaShelle; m, Sol Kaplan.

Comedy/Drama **(MPAA:NR)**

MR. HOBBS TAKES A VACATION

(1962) 115m FOX c

James Stewart *(Mr. Hobbs)*, Maureen O'Hara *(Peggy Hobbs)*, Fabian *(Joe)*, Lauri Peters *(Katey)*, Lili Gentle *(Janie)*, John Saxon *(Byron)*, John McGiver *(Martin Turner)*, Marie Wilson *(Emily Turner)*, Reginald Gardiner *(Reggie McHugh)*, Valerie Varda *(Marika)*, Natalie Trundy *(Susan Carver)*, Josh Peine *(Stan Carver)*, Michael Burns *(Danny Hobbs)*, Minerva Urecal *(Brenda)*, Richard Collier *(Mr. Kagle)*, Peter Oliphant *(Peter Carver)*, Thomas Lowell *(Freddie)*, Stephen Mines *(Carl)*, Dennis Whitcomb *(Dick)*, Michael Sean *(Phil)*, Sherry Alberoni, True Ellison *(Girls in Dormitory)*, Ernie Gutierrez *(Pizza Maker)*, Barbara Mansell *(Receptionist)*, Maida Severn *(Secretary)*, Darryl Duke *(Boy)*, Doris Packer *(Hostess)*.

James Stewart plays Mr. Hobbs, a midwestern banker who rents a cottage at the seashore for a relaxing vacation with his family. Things get off to a bad start when their hideaway turns out to be a spooky dump that drives their live-in cook out of the kitchen permanently. Moreover, despite the miles of beach outside, couch potato son Danny (Michael Burns) remains transfixed before the TV set, and young Katey (Lauri Peters) refuses to be seen in public with her new braces. Two other daughters (Natalie Trundy and Lili Gentle) show up with their deadbeat husbands in tow, while the attractive Mrs. Peggy Hobbs (Maureen O'Hara) is kept busy fending off a local yachtsman's advances. Disaster piles upon disaster in this satire of family togetherness, though Mr. Hobbs, in another of Stewart's solid, humane characterizations, manages to pull his family through the nightmare holiday. Whirlwind direction, witty quips from screenwriter Nunnally Johnson, and the seasoned Stewart's likability insure that the laughs keep coming in this fun film.

p, Jerry Wald; d, Henry Koster; w, Nunnally Johnson (based on the book *Hobbs' Vacation* by Edward Streeter);

ph, William C. Mellor (CinemaScope, Deluxe Color); m, Henry Mancini.

Comedy **(MPAA:NR)**

MR. SCOUTMASTER

(1953) 87m FOX bw

Clifton Webb *(Robert Jordan)*, Edmund Gwenn *(Dr. Stone)*, George "Foghorn" Winslow *(Mike)*, Frances Dee *(Helen Jordan)*, Orley Lindgren *(Ace)*, Veda Ann Borg *(Blonde)*, Jimmy Moss *(Vernon)*, Sammy Ogg *(Harold Johnson)*, Jimmy Hawkins *(Herbie)*, Skip Torgerson *(Christy Kerns)*, Dee Aaker *(Arthur)*, Mickey Little *(Chick)*, Jon Gardner *(Larry)*, Sarah Selby *(Mrs. Weber)*, Amanda Randolph *(Savannah)*, Otis Garth *(Swanson)*, Teddy Infuhr *(Lew Blodges)*, Harry Seymour *(Customer)*, Bill McKenzie *(Andy)*, Steve Brent *(Sammy)*, Robert B. Williams *(Motorcycle Policeman)*, Bob Sweeney *(Hackett)*, Tina Thompson *(Little Sister)*, Billy Nelson *(Chauffeur)*, Stan Malotte *(Mr. Weber)*, Gordon Nelson *(Scout Executive)*, Dabbs Greer *(Fireman)*, Dee Pollock *(Scout No. 1)*, Martin Dean *(Scout No. 2)*, Robert Winans *(Bookworm Scout)*, Dick Fortune *(Page Boy)*, Ralph Gamble *(Executive)*, Tom Greenway *(Doorman)*, Ned Glass *(News Dealer)*, Mary Alan Hokanson, Kay Stewart, Elizabeth Flournoy *(Den Mothers)*.

Television star Robert Jordan (Clifton Webb) wants to attract more juvenile viewers to his show, and to get into the proper spirit he becomes involved with the Boy Scouts. Since Jordan is the type of man who values order and propriety above all else, trying to handle a troop of unruly scouts is courting disaster and leads to numerous complications. While struggling to cope with his charges, Jordan and his wife (Frances Dee) find they become the focus of attention of little Mike (George "Foghorn" Winslow), who is too young to be a Boy Scout, but nevertheless always seems to hanging around Jordan and his troop. Jordan camps and hikes his way through his unwanted assignment, and in the process reveals a warm side which had been hidden most of his life. Webb made a career out of playing one part, that of the cooly efficient professional man with no time for emotions. Nobody ever played the part better, and here his screen persona is put to good use as he struggles mightily to maintain his calm exterior while dealing with the unpredictable youths. The material features a good humorous touch, which, though sentimental, is well paced and convincing.

p, Leonard Goldstein; d, Henry Levin; w, Leonard Praskins, Barney Slater (based on the book by Rice E. Cochran); ph, Joseph La Shelle; m, Cyril Mockridge.

Comedy/Drama **(MPAA:NR)**

MR. SMITH GOES TO WASHINGTON

(1939) 125m COL bw

Jean Arthur *(Saunders)*, James Stewart *(Jefferson Smith)*, Claude Rains *(Sen. Joseph Paine)*, Edward Arnold *(Jim Taylor)*, Guy Kibbee *(Gov. Hubert Hopper)*, Thomas Mitchell *(Diz Moore)*, Eugene Pallette *(Chick McGann)*, Beulah Bondi *(Ma Smith)*, H.B. Warner *(Sen. Fuller)*, Harry Carey *(President of the Senate)*, Astrid Allwyn *(Susan Paine)*, Ruth Donnelly *(Mrs. Emma Hopper)*, Grant Mitchell *(Sen. MacPherson)*, Porter Hall *(Sen. Monroe)*, Pierre Watkin *(Sen. Barnes)*, Charles Lane *(Nosey)*, William Demarest *(Bill Griffith)*, Dick Elliott *(Carl Cook)*, H.V. Kaltenborn *(Broadcaster)*, Kenneth Carpenter *(Announcer)*, Jack Carson *(Sweeney)*, Maurice Costello *(Diggs)*, Allan Cavan *(Ragner)*, Frederick Hoose *(Senator)*, Joe King *(Summers)*, Paul Stanton *(Flood)*, Russell Simpson *(Allen)*, Stanley Andrews *(Sen. Hodges)*, Walter Soderling *(Sen. Pickett)*, Frank Jaquet *(Sen. Byron)*, Ferris Taylor *(Sen. Carlisle)*, Carl Stockdale *(Sen. Burdette)*, Alan Bridge *(Sen. Dwight)*, Edmund Cobb *(Sen. Gower)*, Frederick Burton *(Sen. Dearhorn)*, Vera Lewis *(Mrs. Edwards)*, Dora Clemant *(Mrs. McGann)*, Laura Treadwell *(Mrs. Taylor)*, Ann Doran *(Paine's Secretary)*, Douglas Evans *(Francis Scott Key)*, Lloyd Whitlock *(Schultz)*, Myonne Walsh *(Jane Hopper)*, Billy Watson, Delmar Watson, John Russell, Harry Watson, Garry Watson, Baby Dumpling, *(The Hopper Boys)*.

This great film works on the premise that all that is necessary for evil to triumph is the inaction of good men. Against this danger, director Frank Capra shows a naive everyman to be the true guardian of democratic ideals. James Stewart gives the performance that made him a star as Jefferson Smith, an innocent bumpkin selected by cynical politicians to replace a recently deceased senator in the belief that he can be manipulated by the state's esteemed senior senator, Joseph Paine (Claude Rains). Smith sets off for Washington full of ideals and dreams of working with his idol, Paine, little realizing that he is expected to be a rubber stamp for a crooked scheme to finance a new dam that will profit only Paine and his cronies. The Washington press immediately sizes Smith up as a gullible novice, getting him off to a rocky start, but his idealism captivates Saunders (Jean Arthur), his cynical new secretary. Saunders proves to be a valuable mentor as the innocent Smith slowly comes to realize that his altruistic view of world doesn't necessarily jibe with reality and he sets out to expose those who make a mockery of the country he loves so dearly. While MR. SMITH GOES TO WASHINGTON is the most moral of films, it is so artfully filled with real emotion that it never becomes heavy-handed. Capra supervised every element of the production and used a variety of techniques to accelerate the story line without disrupting it, making every move by every player meaningful and illustrating his credo of "one man, one film." This inspiring masterpiece received 11 Oscar nominations—including Best Actor, Best Director, Best Picture, and Best Supporting Player (for Rains and Harry Carey)—but won only for Best Original Story. Stewart is terrific and the rest of the cast, featuring such familiar veterans as Thomas Mitchell, Edward Arnold, and William Demarest, provides solid support.

p&d, Frank Capra; w, Sidney Buchman (based on the book *The Gentleman from Montana* by Lewis R. Foster); ph, Joseph Walker; m, Dimitri Tiomkin.

Drama   **Cas.**   **(MPAA:NR)**

MISTY

(1961) 93m FOX c

David Ladd *(Paul Beebe)*, Arthur O'Connell *(Grandpa Beebe)*, Pam Smith *(Maureen Beebe)*, Anne Seymour *(Grandma Beebe)*, Duke Farley *(Eba Jones)*, People of Chincoteague, Virginia.

Set on an island off the coast of Virginia, this charming film stars 12-year-old David Ladd and his young sister, Pam Smith, as an orphaned pair living with their grandparents. When the locals engage in their annual Pony-Penning Day activities, the children joyfully go along, traveling to a nearby island, where they round up a herd of wild ponies that are then put up for auction. The children are able to capture a mare, named Phantom, that has eluded the pony-penners for some time, and also catch her colt, which they name Misty. They've saved $100 in order to purchase a pony, but when Phantom and Misty are put to auction, a stranger ends up as the owner. The heartbroken children then must find a way to get the pony they so treasure.

p, Robert B. Radnitz; d, James B. Clark; w, Ted Sherdeman (based on the novel *Misty of Chincoteague* by Marguerite Henry); ph, Leo Tover, Lee Garmes (CinemaScope, Deluxe Color); m, Paul Sawtell, Bert Shefter.

Adventure   **(MPAA:NR)**

MOBY DICK

(1956, Brit.) 116m Moulin/WB c

Gregory Peck *(Capt. Ahab)*, Richard Basehart *(Ishmael)*, Leo Genn *(Starbuck)*, Harry Andrews *(Stubb)*, Bernard Miles *(Man of Man)*, Orson Welles *(Father Mapple)*, Mervyn Johns *(Peleg)*, Noel Purcell *(Carpenter)*, Friedrich Ledebur *(Queequeg)*, James Robertson Justice *(Capt. Boomer)*, Edric Connor *(Daggoo)*, Seamus Kelly *(Flask)*, Philip Stainton *(Bildad)*, Joseph Tomelty *(Peter Coffin)*, Royal Dano *(Elijah)*, Francis De Wolff *(Capt. Gardiner)*, Tamba Alleney *(Pip)*, Ted Howard *(Blacksmith)*, Tom Clegg *(Tashtego)*, Iris Tree *(Lady with Bibles)*.

John Huston gives a passionate and faithful rendering of Herman Melville's novel in MOBY DICK, aided by a stellar cast. The film opens as a man (Richard Basehart) enters the whaling town of New Bedford in 1840, and, in voice-over, makes the famous declaration, "Call me Ishmael." He signs on board the *Pequod*, commanded by peg-legged Capt. Ahab (Gregory Peck). Once under way, the wild-eyed, stony, horribly scarred Ahab assembles his crew to tell them that this will be no routine whaling expedition but a mission of vengeance against the great white whale Moby Dick, which tore off his leg and scarred him for life. He whips them into a frenzy, and when Moby Dick is finally sighted, the crew is as obsessed with killing it as Ahab is. Filmed at considerable danger to cast and crew, MOBY DICK, under Huston's superb direction, is one of the most historically authentic, visually stunning, and powerful adventures ever made. Inevitably, many critics disagreed with Huston's interpretation of Melville's classic. But the film is splendid; Peck and the supporting actors who play Ahab's mesmerized crew are all superb, and Huston received the New York Film Critics Best Director Award.

p, John Huston, Vaughan N. Dean; d, John Huston; w, John Huston, Ray Bradbury (based on the novel by Herman Melville); ph, Oswald Morris (Technicolor); m, Philip Stainton.

Adventure/Drama   **Cas.**   **(MPAA:NR)**

MOON PILOT

(1962) 98m Disney/BV c

Tom Tryon *(Capt. Richmond Talbot)*, Brian Keith *(Maj. Gen. John Vanneman)*, Edmond O'Brien *(McClosky)*, Dany Saval *(Lyrae)*, Tommy Kirk *(Walter Talbot)*, Bob Sweeney *(Sen. McGuire)*, Kent Smith *(Secretary of the Air Force)*, Simon Scott *(Medical Officer)*, Bert Remsen *(Agent Brown)*, Sarah Selby *(Mrs. Celia Talbot)*, Bob Hastings *(Air Force Officer)*, Dick Whittinghill *(Col. Briggs)*, Nancy Kulp *(Nutritionist)*, Muriel Landers *(Fat Lady)*, Cheeta *(Charlie the Chimp)*, William Hudson, Robert Brubaker.

MOON PILOT is an uproarious satirical comedy from the Disney folks, who aren't generally known for their social criticism. Here the space program gets the treatment when a mischievous monkey volunteers Capt. Richmond Talbot (Tom Tryon) to be the first man in orbit. On a trip to tell his mother the news, Talbot notices that a mysterious woman (Dany Saval) seems to be following him. She shows up in his mother's town, and when the NASA officials lock him in a hotel, she shows up again, and reveals some surprising facts about her background. In throwing a monkey into the proceedings, Disney—as always—guaranteed that kids will love the film.

p, Bill Anderson; d, James Neilson; w, Maurice Tombragel (based on a serialized story by Robert Buckner); ph, William Snyder (Technicolor); m, Paul Smith.

Science Fiction   **Cas.**   **(MPAA:NR)**

MOON-SPINNERS, THE

(1964) 118m Disney/BV c

Hayley Mills *(Nikky Ferris)*, Eli Wallach *(Stratos)*, Pola Negri *(Mme. Habib)*, Peter McEnery *(Mark Camford)*, Joan Greenwood *(Aunt Frances Ferris)*, Irene Papas *(Sophia)*, Sheila Hancock *(Cynthia Gamble)*, Michael Davis *(Alexis)*, Paul Stassino *(Lambis)*, John Le Mesurier *(Anthony Gamble)*, Andre Morell *(Yacht Captain)*, George Pastell *(Police Lieutenant)*, Tutte Lemkow *(Orestes)*, Steve Plytas *(Hearse Driver)*, Harry Tardios *(Bus Driver)*, Pamela Barrie *(Ariadne)*.

Illogical but suspenseful, THE MOON-SPINNERS focuses on the adventures of Nikky Ferris (Hayley Mills) and her Aunt Frances (Joan Greenwood). While staying at the Moon-Spinners Hotel on Crete, Nikky meets young Mark Camford (Peter McEnery) and later discovers him, wounded, in a deserted church after he is shot by an associate of the hotel's owner, Stratos (Eli Wallach). She learns that Mark, who lost his job as a London bank messenger after a jewel robbery, believes Stratos is the true culprit, and has come to Crete to investigate. The pair sets out to gather evidence, falling in love in the process, and getting into a number of scrapes and encounters with shady characters. Silly fun, with a special plus in the performance of silent film siren Pola Negri as an exotic jewel fancier.

p, Bill Anderson, Hugh Attwooll; d, James Neilson; w, Michael Dyne (based on the novel by Mary Stewart); ph, Paul Beeson, John Wilcox, Michael Reed (Technicolor); m, Ron Grainer.

Mystery   **Cas.**   **(MPAA:NR)**

MOUSE THAT ROARED, THE

(1959, Brit.) 83m Open Road/COL c

Peter Sellers *(Tully Bascombe/Grand Duchess Gloriana XII/Prime Minister Count Mountjoy)*, Jean Seberg *(Helen)*, David Kossoff *(Prof. Kokintz)*, William Hartnell *(Will)*, Timothy Bateson *(Roger)*, MacDonald Parke *(Snippet)*, Monty Landis *(Cobbley)*, Leo McKern *(Benter)*, Harold Kasket *(Pedro)*, Colin Gordon *(BBC Announcer)*, George Margo *(O'Hara)*, Robin Gatehouse *(Mulligan)*, Jacques Cey *(Ticket Collector)*, Stuart Sanders *(Cunard Captain)*, Ken Stanely *(Cunard 2nd Officer)*, Bill Nagy *(US Policeman)*, Mavis Villiers *(Telephone Operator)*, Charles Clay *(British Ambassador)*, Harry de Bray *(French Ambassador)*, Bill Edwards *(Army Captain)*, Austin Willis *(US Secretary of Defense)*, Guy Deghy *(Soviet Ambassador)*, Robert O'Neill *(Reporter)*.

THE MOUSE THAT ROARED is the outlandish, very funny tale of the fortunes of the Duchy of Grand Fenwick, a mythical land on the verge of bankruptcy because their one export, a fine wine, has been copied and undercut by a US company. Grand Fenwick's prime minister (Peter Sellers) and queen (Sellers again) cook up a scheme to solve the problem: they will declare war on the States, lose immediately, then get back in the black with all the aid that the US usually bestows upon beaten foes. They send out an "army" of 20, clad in armor and carrying bows and arrows, led by Tully Bascombe (Sellers once more). Of course, the arrival of these ragtag warriors in New York leads to a series of very funny situations, which includes the group's inadvertent acquisition of a weapon that makes them a genuine threat. In the meantime, Bascomb meets and falls in love with Helen (Jean Seberg), the daughter of a scientist. Besides the wonderful Sellers, there are fine performances from all, especially Leo McKern as the pompous leader of Grand Fenwick's "loyal opposition." An inferior sequel, MOUSE ON THE MOON (1963), was directed by Richard Lester.

p, Jon Pennington, Walter Shenson; d, Jack Arnold; w, Roger MacDougall, Stanley Mann (based on the novel

MUPPET MOVIE, THE—

The Wrath of the Grapes by Leonard Wibberley); ph, John Wilcox (Eastmancolor); m, Edwin Astley.

Comedy　　　　**Cas.**　　　　**(MPAA:NR)**

MUPPET MOVIE, THE

(1979) 98m ITC Entertainment/Associated Film Distribution c

Muppet Performers: Jim Henson (Kermit the Frog/Rowlf/Dr. Teeth/Waldorf), Frank Oz (Miss Piggy/Fozzie Bear/Animal/Sam the Eagle), Jerry Nelson (Floyd Pepper/Crazy Harry/Robin the Frog/Lew Zealand), Richard Hunt (Scooter/Statler/Janice/Sweetums/Beaker), Dave Goelz (The Great Gonzo/Zoot/Dr. Bunsen Honeydew); Charles Durning (Doc Hopper), Austin Pendleton (Max), Scott Walker (Frog Killer), Mel Brooks (Prof. Krassman), Edgar Bergen, Milton Berle, James Coburn, Dom DeLuise, Elliott Gould, Bob Hope, Madeline Kahn, Carol Kane, Cloris Leachman, Steve Martin, Richard Pryor, Telly Savalas, Orson Welles, Paul Williams, Carroll Spinney, Steve Whitmire, Kathryn Mullen, Bob Payne, Eren Ozker, Carolyn Wilcox, Olga Felgemacher, Bruce Schwartz, Michael Davis, Buz Suraci, Tony Basilicato, Adam Hunt.

This charming children's film was the first to star the successful television puppets (two sequels followed). The loose plot follows Kermit the Frog and Fozzie Bear as they travel cross-country on their way to fame and fortune in Hollywood. On the road they pick up a variety of passengers (muppet and human) and sing a dozen songs. The special effects are handled very well; highlights feature Kermit riding a bicycle and rowing a boat. Cute without being insipid, funny without being childish, THE MUPPET MOVIE contains enough magic to please all ages.

p, Jim Henson; d, James Frawley; w, Jerry Juhl, Jack Burns; ph, Isidore Mankofsky (CFI color); m, Paul Williams.

Comedy/Musical　　　**Cas.**　　　**(MPAA:G)**

MUPPETS TAKE MANHATTAN, THE

(1984) 94m Tri-Star c

Muppet Performers: Jim Henson (Kermit/Rowlf/Dr. Teeth/Swedish Chef, Waldorf), Frank Oz (Miss Piggy/Fozzie/Animal), Dave Goelz (Gonzo/Chester/Rat/Bill/Zoot), Steve Whitmire (Rizzo the Rat/Gil), Richard Hunt (Scooter/Janice/Statler), Jerry Nelson (Camilla/Lew Zealand/Floyd); Steve Burnett, Mary Lou Harris (College Students), Cheryl McFadden (Mr. Price's Secretary), Nancy Kirsch (Screaming Woman), John Bentley (Train Conductor), Dorothy Baxter, Stephen Sherrard Hicks, Susan Miller-Kovens, John Maguire, Sinead MaGuire, Trish Noel (Elevator Passengers), Ron Foster, Michael Hirsch (Men in Winesop's Office), Vic Polizos, Kenneth MacGregor, Chet Washington (Construction Workers), Graham Brown (Mr. Wrightson), James Bryson, Chico Kasinoir (Customers in Pete's), Viola Borden (Bingo Caller), Paul Stolarsky (Aquacade Announcer), Maree Dow (Woman in Bleachers), Don Quigley (Man in Bleachers), Michael Connolly (Maitre d' at Sardi's), Wade Barnes (Customer at Sardi's), Joe Jamrog (Cop in Central Park), Mark Marrone (Chauffeur), Cyril Jenkins (The Minister), Karen Prell (Yolanda), Brian Muehl (Tatooey Rat), Bruce Edward Hall (Masterson/Beth), Juliana Donald (Jenny), Lonny Price (Ronnie), Louis Zorich (Pete), Art Carney, James Coco, Dabney Coleman, Gregory Hines, Linda Lavin, Joan Rivers, Elliott Gould, Liza Minnelli, Brooke Shields, Francis Bergen, Mayor Edward I. Koch, John Landis, Vincent Sardi.

This follow-up to THE MUPPET MOVIE and THE GREAT MUPPET CAPER is not as good or as hip as its predecessors, but the Muppet gang remains charming. The plot follows the old "Hey kids, let's put on a show" story line—except that this time the barn is Broadway and the "kids" are a frog, a chicken, a pig, and other assorted creations of executive producer and Muppet master Jim Henson. Kermit and the gang are presenting a revue called "Manhattan Melodies" at a college campus and they feel that the show is good enough to take to New York, so everyone goes off to conquer the Big Apple. There they find the doors of all the reputable producers firmly closed, although one unsavory character (Dabney Coleman) is interested, providing they kick in $300 each. Crestfallen, they all go off in different directions to raise money for their show, with various adventures and encounters with the film's guest stars (making for some fun celebrity-spotting) on the way.

p, David Lazer; d, Frank Oz; w, Frank Oz, Tom Patchett, Jay Tarses (based on a story by Tom Patchett and Jay Tarses); ph, Robert Paynter (Technicolor, Metrocolor); m, Ralph Burns.

Comedy　　　　**Cas.**　　　　**(MPAA:G)**

MUSIC MAN, THE

(1962) 151m WB c

Robert Preston (Harold Hill), Shirley Jones (Marian Paroo), Buddy Hackett (Marcellus Washburn), Hermione Gingold (Eulalie MacKechnie Shinn), Paul Ford (Mayor Shinn), Ewart Dunlop, Oliver Hix, Jacey Squires, Olin Britt (The Buffalo Bills), Pert Kelton (Mrs. Paroo), Timmy Everett (Tommy Djilas), Susan Luckey (Zaneeta Shinn), Ronny [Ron] Howard (Winthrop Paroo), Harry Hickox (Charlie Cowell), Charles Lane (Constable Locke), Mary Wickes (Mrs. Squires), Monique Vermont (Amaryllis), Ronnie Dapo (Norbert Smith), Jesslyn Fax (Avis Grubb), Patty Lee Hilka (Gracie Shinn), Garry Potter (Dewey), J. Delos Jewkes (Harley MacCauley), Ray Kellogg (Harry Joseph), William Fawcett (Lester Lonnergan), Rance Howard (Oscar Jackson), Roy Dean (Gilbert Hawthorne), David Swain (Chet Glanville), Arthur Mills (Herbert Malthouse), Rand Barker (Duncan Shyball), Jeannine Burnier (Jessie Shyball), Shirley Claire (Amy Dakin), Natalie Core (Truthful Smith), Therese Lyon (Dolly Higgins), Penelope Martin (Lila O'Brink), Barbara Pepper (Feril Hawkes), Anne Loos (Stella Jackson), Peggy Wynne (Ada Nutting), Hank Worden (Undertaker), Milton Parsons

(Farmer), Natalie Masters (Farmer's Wife), Peggy Mondo, Sarah Seegar, Adnia Rice (Townswomen), Casey Adams, Charles Perchesky (Salesmen), Percy Helton (Conductor).

THE MUSIC MAN is a nostalgic mix of corn, laughs, exuberance, and infectious songs. Robert Preston reprises his greatest Broadway role as Prof. Harold Hill, a traveling salesman/con man who arrives in River City, Iowa, in 1912 and persuades its citizens that the town is headed for moral ruin because of its new pool room. The way to keep the town youth from being corrupted is to start a band, says Hill, adding that he will sell them the instruments and teach the kids how to play. His real plan is to take the money and run before the instruments arrive. Prim Marian Paroo (Shirley Jones) questions Hill's credentials, but he sells her on his revolutionary "Think System," by which all one has to do is think a tune to be able to play it. As he attempts to swindle the townsfolk, Hill alternately charms and exasperates its citizens, including Mayor Shinn (Paul Ford), his wife (Hermione Gingold), and the members of town council (played by the barbershop quartet the Buffalo Bills). In a gross oversight, Preston was not nominated for an Oscar, though the film was nominated for Best Picture and won for Musical Direction. Jones is excellent and in glorious voice—but this is, and will always be, Preston's picture. Meredith Willson's songs, which are among the best ever to grace a musical production, include "Trouble," "Gary, Indiana," "Till There Was You," and the stirring "76 Trombones" which provides an unforgettable climax for the movie.

p&d, Morton DaCosta; w, Marion Hargrove (based on the musical play by Meredith Willson and Franklin Lacey); ph, Robert Burks (Technirama, Technicolor); m, Meredith Willson.

Comedy/Musical   Cas.   (MPAA:NR)

MY BROTHER TALKS TO HORSES

(1946) 93m MGM bw

"Butch" Jenkins (Lewis Penrose), Peter Lawford (John S. Penrose), Beverly Tyler (Martha), Edward Arnold (Mr. Bledsoe), Charlie Ruggles (Richard Pennington Roeder), Spring Byington (Mrs. Penrose), O.Z. Whitehead (Mr. Puddy), Paul Langton (Mr. Gillespie), Ernest Whitman (Mr. Mordecai), Irving Bacon (Mr. Piper), Lillian Yarbo (Psyche), Howard Freeman (Hector Damson), Harry Hayden (Mr. Gibley).

Nine-year-old Butch Jenkins plays Lewis Penrose, a kid with psychic powers that enable him to converse with racehorses. The horses give him "inside" information on races, prompting gamblers to try to exploit the young prognosticator for their own wicked purposes. This was Fred Zinnemann's third film with Jenkins, and he directs well, overdoing neither sentimentality nor comedy. The film looks good, with fine art decoration and photography. The kids will eat it up.

p, Samuel Marx; d, Fred Zinnemann; w, Morton Thompson; ph, Harold Rosson; m, Rudolph G. Kopp.

Comedy   (MPAA:NR)

MY FAIR LADY

(1964) 170m WB c

Audrey Hepburn (Eliza Doolittle), Rex Harrison (Prof. Henry Higgins), Stanley Holloway (Alfred P. Doolittle), Wilfrid Hyde-White (Col. Hugh Pickering), Gladys Cooper (Mrs. Higgins), Jeremy Brett (Freddy Eynsford-Hill), Theodore Bikel (Zoltan Karpathy), Isobel Elsom (Mrs. Eynsford-Hill), Mona Washbourne (Mrs. Pearce), John Alderson (Jamie), John McLiam (Harry), Marni Nixon (Singing Voice of Eliza), Bill Shirley (Singing Voice of Freddie), Ben Wrigley, Clive Halliday, Richard Peel, Eric Heath, James O'Hara (Costermongers), Kendrick Huxham, Frank Baker (Elegant Bystanders), Walter Burke (Main Bystander), Queenie Leonard (Cockney Bystander), Laurie Main (Hoxton Man), Maurice Dallimore (Selsey Man), Owen McGiveney (Man at Coffee Stand), Jack Raine (Male Member), Marjorie Bennett (Cockney with Pipe), Britannia Beatey (Daughter of Elegant Bystander), Beatrice Greenough (Grand Lady), Hilda Plowright (Bystander), Dinah Anne Rogers, Lois Battle (Maids), Jacqueline Squire (Parlor Maid), Gwen Watts (Cook), Eugene Hoffman, Kai Farrelli (Jugglers), Jack Greening (George), Ron Whelan (Algernon/Bartender), John Holland (Butler), Roy Dean (Footman), Charles Fredericks (King), Lily Kemble-Cooper (Lady Ambassador), Barbara Pepper (Doolittle's Dance Partner).

This film version of the classic Richard Lerner and Frederick Loewe musical made a fortune at the box office and took Oscars in almost every category—with the exception of Best Actress, which ironically went to MARY POPPINS' Julie Andrews, who costarred with Rex Harrison in the Broadway hit "My Fair Lady" but was passed over for the movie role in favor of Audrey Hepburn. Prof. Henry Higgins (Harrison) bets fellow linguist Col. Hugh Pickering (Wilfrid Hyde-White) that he can turn Cockney flower girl Eliza Doolittle (Hepburn) into a lady with elocution so pure no one will suspect her origins. The two men work hard with Eliza until they feel she is ready to be tested at Ascot, where she meets and charms the handsome young Freddy Eynsford-Hill (Jeremy Brett). Then they take her to a huge ball where even a famous linguist takes her for royalty. Back home, Higgins and Pickering congratulate each other but disregard Eliza, who departs in anger to carry on with Freddy. Only then does confirmed bachelor Higgins realize that he has fallen in love with his "creation." The movie suffers in comparison with the Broadway original, in part because the patrician Hepburn (whose singing voice is dubbed by Marni Nixon) is an unconvincing, if beautiful, guttersnipe. Nonetheless, Harrison is wonderful, the Lerner and Loewe songs are glorious, and the film is a delight. The songs include "The Rain in Spain," "I Could Have Danced all Night," "On the Street Where You Live," "Get Me to the Church on Time," and "I've Grown Accustomed to Her Face."

p, Jack L. Warner; d, George Cukor; w, Alan Jay Lerner (based on the musical play by Alan Jay Lerner and Frederick Loewe and the play "Pygmalion" by George Bernard Shaw); ph, Harry Strading (Super Panavision, Technicolor); m, Frederick Loewe.

Comedy/Musical   **Cas.**   **(MPAA:NR)**

MY FRIEND FLICKA

(1943) 89m FOX c

Roddy McDowall *(Ken McLaughlin)*, Preston Foster *(Rob McLaughlin)*, Rita Johnson *(Nell)*, James Bell *(Gus)*, Jeff Corey *(Tim Murphy)*, Diana Hale *(Hildy)*, Arthur Loft *(Charley Sargent)*, Jimmy Aubrey.

A wonderful story, beautifully photographed and sensitively told. Ken (Roddy McDowall) is a young boy who longs for a colt of his own. His rancher father finally gives in, but is displeased when the boy chooses the foal from an unruly mare. Through painstaking work by Ken, the colt is trained and nurtured, eventually growing to become a fine mare and a loyal companion. The performances and direction are as fine as they come. The humanistic qualities within the film come through well, without being the least bit overbearing or overly sentimental. The color photography is wonderful, capturing all the grandeur of the Rocky Mountains. Perfect for the whole family. A 1945 sequel was made with almost the same cast: THUNDERHEAD, SON OF FLICKA.

p, Ralph Dietrich; d, Harold Schuster; w, Lillie Hayward, Frances Edwards Faragoh (based on the novel by Mary O'Hara); ph, Dewey Wrigley (Technicolor); m, Alfred Newman.

Drama   **(MPAA:NR)**

MY PAL TRIGGER

(1946) 79m REP bw

Roy Rogers *(Roy Rogers)*, George "Gabby" Hayes *(Gabby Kendrick)*, Dale Evans *(Susan)*, Jack Holt *(Brett Scoville)*, LeRoy Mason *(Carson)*, Roy Barcroft *(Hunter)*, Sam Flint *(Sheriff)*, Kenne Duncan *(Croupier)*, Ralph Sanford *(Auctioneer)*, Francis McDonald *(Storekeeper)*, Harlan Briggs *(Dr. Bentley)*, William Haade *(Davis)*, Alan Bridge *(Wallace)*, Paul E. Burns *(Walling)*, Frank Reicher *(Magistrate)*, Bob Nolan and the Sons of the Pioneers, Fred Graham, Ted Mapes, Trigger the Horse.

Roy Rogers named this as his favorite of all his films, and one can see why. It's well plotted, with lively direction and much better camerawork than most of the Singing Cowboy's films. Rogers plays a horse trader planning to mate a prize mare with a stallion belonging to his pal Gabby Kendrick (Gabby Hayes). A gambler (Jack Holt) with similar plans for his own mare tries to steal the stallion, which escapes and mates with Rogers' mare. When the gambler catches up to the horse, he shoots it. Rogers is blamed, but he and his now-pregnant mare escape capture and leave town, with Roy determined to return to clear his name and unmask the real villain. This is the

quintessential Rogers film, with some fine acting (undoubtedly some of the best the genre would produce) and, of course, musical numbers by the Sons of the Pioneers and duets by Rogers and Dale Evans.

p, Armand Schaefer; d, Frank McDonald; w, Jack Townley, John K. Butler (based on a story by Paul Gangelin); ph, William Bradford.

Western   **Cas.**   **(MPAA:NR)**

MY SIDE OF THE MOUNTAIN

(1969) 100m PAR c

Teddy Eccles *(Sam Gribley)*, Theodore Bikel *(Bando)*, Tudi Wiggins *(Miss Turner)*, Frank Perry *(Mr. Gribley)*, Peggi Loder *(Mrs. Gribley)*, Gina Dick *(Daughter No. 1)*, Karen Pearson *(Daughter No. 2)*, Danny McIlravey *(Little Boy)*, Cosette Lee *(Mrs. Fielder)*, Larry Reynolds *(Hunter No. 1)*, Tom Harvey *(Hunter No. 2)*, Paul Hebert *(Hunter No. 3)*, Ralph Endersby *(1st Boy)*, George Allan *(2nd Boy)*, Patrick Pervion *(Ranger)*, Ed Persons, Max Rosenbloom, Gus the Raccoon, Frightful the Falcon.

MY SIDE OF THE MOUNTAIN stars 13-year-old Teddy Eccles as Sam Gribley, a young man who admires Henry David Thoreau. Emulating his hero, Sam runs away to live in the Canadian woodlands, leaving a note telling his parents that he will return in one year. Taking some equipment and his pet raccoon, Sam builds a home in a hollow tree, learns various survival methods, and teaches himself about falconry. He also meets a wandering folk singer (delightfully played by Theodore Bikel) who teaches the boy more woodland lore. While the boy learns much about life in the wilderness, he also learns much about himself and his relationship with his family in the process. The film is both entertaining and educational; Sam's daily life in the woods, inventiveness, and pluck are nicely portrayed and completely believable. Bikel and Tudi Wiggins lend good support, although the raccoon definitely steals the show. Intelligently made, with respect for its subject, MY SIDE OF THE MOUNTAIN is good family viewing that will delight kids and interest grown-ups as well.

p, Robert B. Radnitz; d, James B. Clark; w, Ted Sherdeman, Jane Klove, Joanna Crawford (based on the novel by Jean Craighead George); ph, Denys Coop (Panavision, Technicolor); m, Wilfred Josephs.

Adventure   **Cas.**   **(MPAA:G)**

MY SISTER EILEEN

(1942) 96m COL bw

Rosalind Russell *(Ruth Sherwood)*, Brian Aherne *(Robert Baker)*, Janet Blair *(Eileen Sherwood)*, George Tobias *(Appopolous, Landlord)*, Allyn Joslyn *(Chick Clark)*, Elizabeth Patterson *(Grandma Sherwood)*, Grant Mitchell *(Walter Sherwood)*, Richard Quine *(Frank Lippincott)*, June Havoc *(Effie Shelton)*, Donald MacBride *(Officer Lonigan)*, Gordon Jones *("The Wreck")*, Jeff Donnell *(Helen Loomis)*, Clyde Fillmore *(Ralph Craven)*, Minna

Phillips *(Mrs. Wade)*, Frank Sully *(Jansen, Janitor)*, Charles La Torre *(Capt. Anadato)*, Danny Mummert *(Boy)*, Almira Sessions *(Prospective Tenant)*, Kirk Alyn, George Adrian, Tom Lincir *(Cadets)*, Ann Doran *(Receptionist)*, Bob Kellard *(Bus Driver)*, Forrest Tucker *(Sand Hog)*, The Three Stooges *(Bus Passengers)*, Walter Sande, Pat Lane, Ralph Dunn *(Policemen)*, Arnold Stang *(Jimmy)*.

When Ruth McKenney and her sister came to New York's Greenwich Village from Columbus, Ohio, the older sister took many notes about their experiences and wrote stories that eventually were the basis for a hit Broadway comedy. This film version is much like the stage show, following sisters Ruth (Rosalind Russell) and Eileen Sherwood (Janet Blair) after they move into a basement apartment in the Village. Their neighbors are a nutty group, including "the Wreck" (Gordon Jones), a former Georgia Tech football player forever recounting his days as one of the "Rambling Wrecks," his wife (Jeff Donnell), and his mother (Minna Phillips). The sisters' apartment is as busy as a train station, with hot and cold running subplots, including Eileen's flirtation with a journalist (Allyn Joslyn) and Ruth's attempts to sell her stories to an editor (Brian Aherne). The Three Stooges appear briefly as workmen digging a new subway in the area who come up through the basement floor. The film presents an entertaining series of incidents and character sketches, all of which are funny and true to life.

p, Max Gordon; d, Alexander Hall; w, Joseph Fields, Jerome Chodorov (based on the play by Joseph Fields and Jerome Chodorov, from the stories by Ruth McKenney); ph, Joseph Walker.

Comedy **(MPAA:NR)**

MY SISTER EILEEN

(1955) 108m COL c

Janet Leigh *(Eileen Sherwood)*, Betty Garrett *(Ruth Sherwood)*, Jack Lemmon *(Bob Baker)*, Robert [Bob] Fosse *(Frank Lippencott)*, Kurt Kasznar *(Appopolous)*, Richard [Dick] York *("Wreck")*, Lucy Marlow *(Helen)*, Tommy Rall *(Chick Clark)*, Barbara Brown *(Helen's Mother)*, Horace McMahon *(Lonigan)*, Henry Slate, Hal March *(Drunks)*, Alberto Morin *(Brazilian Consul)*, Queenie Smith *(Alice)*, Richard Deacon *(George)*, Ken Christy *(Police Sergeant)*.

This musical version of the hit Broadway play has virtually the same story as the 1942 film (see above). The actors this time include Bob Fosse, who also choreographs and dances, and Jack Lemmon, charming in the first of several films he was to do with director Richard Quine. The plot once again follows a series of incidents and complications in the lives of a pair of sisters (Betty Garrett and Janet Leigh) who come to New York from Ohio and wind up in what must be the busiest apartment in the city. It's a fast-moving version of the play with songs that add greatly to the fun provided by the crackling dialog and good performances.

p, Fred Kohlmar; d, Richard Quine; w, Blake Edwards, Richard Quine (based on the play by Joseph Fields and Jerome Chodorov, from the stories by Ruth McKenney);

ph, Charles Lawton, Jr. (CinemaScope, Technicolor); m, George Duning.

Comedy/Musical **(MPAA:NR)**

MY UNCLE

(1958, Fr.) 110m Specta-Gray-Alter-Cady Film del Centauro/Continental c (MON ONCLE)

Jacques Tati *(Mons. Hulot)*, Jean-Pierre Zola *(Mons. Arpel)*, Adrienne Servantie *(Mme. Arpel)*, Alain Becourt *(Gerald Arpel)*, Lucien Fregis *(Mons. Pichard)*, Betty Schneider *(Betty, Landlord's Daughter)*, Yvonne Arnaud *(Georgette, Arpel's Maid)*, Dominique Marie *(Neighbor)*, J.F. Martial *(Walter)*, Andre Dino *(Sweep)*, Claude Badolle *(Rag Picker)*, Nicolas Bataille *(Worker)*, Regis Fontenay *(Suspenders Seller)*, Adelaide Danielli *(Mme. Pichard)*, Denise Peronne *(Mlle. Fevier)*, Michel Goyot *(Car Seller)*, Dominique Derly *(Arpel's Secretary)*, Max Martel, Francomme, Claire Rocca, Jean Remoleux, Rene Lord, Nicole Regnault, Loriot, Mancini, Jean Meyet, Suzanne Franck.

France's beloved director Jacques Tati follows MR. HULOT'S HOLIDAY (1953) with this impressive satire on technology and its worshipers. Tati himself plays disheveled, hapless Mons. Hulot. Hulot, content in his run-down quarters, is contrasted with his brother-in-law, Mons. Arpel (Jean-Pierre Zola), who resides in a modernized, desensitized suburban house cluttered with gadgets that are meant to save time but only serve to waste it and that fill the rooms with clanking noises. Arpel's young son (Alain Becourt) prefers his uncle's back-street environment, although even Hulot cannot completely escape technology (the film's most precious scenes are those in which he battles with modern appliances). Life becomes more complex for Hulot when he is employed by Arpel and sent away on business. The interchange teaches him something about modern living, while Arpel and son are once again able to communicate. MY UNCLE is less a condemnation of technology than of those who become its slaves. Tati has described his own comedy as "laughter born of a certain fundamental absurdity. Some things are not funny of themselves but become so on being dissected." It is this quality that Tati's films share which such satires as Rene Clair's A NOUS LA LIBERTE (1931), Charles Chaplin's MODERN TIMES (1936), and even Albert Brooks' LOST IN AMERICA (1985).

p&d, Jacques Tati; w, Jacques Tati, Jacques Lagrange, Jean L'Hote; ph, Jean Bourgoin (Eastmancolor); m, Franck Barcellini, Alains Romans.

Comedy **(MPAA:NR)**

MYSTERIOUS ISLAND

(1961, US/Brit.) 100m Ameran/COL c

Michael Craig *(Capt. Cyrus Harding)*, Joan Greenwood *(Lady Mary Fairchild)*, Michael Callan *(Herbert Brown)*, Gary Merrill *(Gideon Spilettt)*, Herbert Lom *(Capt. Nemo)*, Beth Rogan *(Elena)*, Percy Herbert *(Sgt. Pencroft)*, Dan Jackson *(Neb)*, Nigel Green *(Tom)*.

Jules Verne's sequel to *20,000 Leagues Under the Sea* was the subject of several films, and this 1961 version is probably the most popular. Capt. Cyrus Hardin (Michael Craig) is the leader of some Union soldiers (and one Confederate deserter) who escape by balloon from a Confederate jail. They descend into the sea and wash up on the shores of a strange island. There they encounter the marvelous creations of special effects great Ray Harryhausen, including giant bees and crabs and other oversized monstrosities. In addition, they suffer an attack by pirates and meet the mysterious Capt. Nemo (Herbert Lom) and learn of his strange plan to solve the world's food shortage problems. The direction is spirited, but the film's best features are Harryhausen's effects and the score by the great film composer Bernard Herrmann, energetically rendered by the London Symphony Orchestra.

p, Charles H. Schneer; d, Cy Endfield; w, John Prebble, Daniel Ullman, Crane Wilbur (based on the novel *The Mysterious Island* by Jules Verne); ph, Wilkie Cooper, Egil Woxholt (Eastmancolor); m, Bernard Herrmann.

Science Fiction Cas. (MPAA:NR)

NATIONAL VELVET

(1944) 125m MGM c

Mickey Rooney *(Mi Taylor)*, Donald Crisp *(Mr. Brown)*, Elizabeth Taylor *(Velvet Brown)*, Anne Revere *(Mrs. Brown)*, Angela Lansbury *(Edwina Brown)*, Juanita Quigley *(Malvolia Brown)*, Jackie "Butch" Jenkins *(Donald Brown)*, Reginald Owen *(Farmer Ede)*, Terry Kilburn *(Ted)*, Alec Craig *(Tim)*, Eugene Loring *(Mr. Taski)*, Norma Varden *(Miss Sims)*, Arthur Shields *(Mr. Hallam)*, Dennis Hoey *(Mr. Greenford, Farmer)*, Aubrey Mather *(Entry Official)*, Frederic Worlock *(Stewart)*, Arthur Treacher *(Man with Umbrella)*, Harry Allen *(Van Driver)*, Billy Bevan *(Constable)*, Barry Macollum *(Townsman)*, Matthew Boulton *(Entry Clerk)*, Leyland Hodgson *(1st Pressman)*, Leonard Carey *(2nd Pressman)*, Colin Campbell *(Cockney)*, Frank Benson *(Englishman)*, Wally Cassell *(Jockey)*, Alec Harford *(Valet)*, William Austin *(Reporter)*, Gerald Oliver Smith *(Cameraman)*, Olaf Hytten *(1st Villager)*, George Kirby *(Second Villager)*, Moyna MacGill *(Woman)*, Donald Curtis *(American)*.

One of MGM's most beloved children's films, NATIONAL VELVET was the picture that made a matinee idol of Elizabeth Taylor. The place is Sussex, England, where radiant Velvet Brown (Taylor) wins a horse that she names Pie and plans to enter in the famous Grand National. She and Mi Taylor (Mickey Rooney) train the animal, despite the fact that the entrance fee is more than her family can afford. However, Velvet's mother (Anne Revere, who won a Best Supporting Actress Oscar for this performance) pays the fee with money she'd won years before for swimming the English Channel. That's not an end to their problems, however, as Velvet must overcome more obstacles in her quest to win the Grand National. The movie features one of the best horse-racing sequences ever filmed, as well as a host of winning performances. Although Taylor had already appeared in four films, this is the one that made her a shining star. Surprisingly, she was not the first choice for the role, which had been bandied about since the novel's publication 10 years previously. Katharine Hepburn, Margaret Sullavan, and Shirley Temple were among those considered, but the role belonged to Taylor and she was unforgettable in it. The story came to the screen again in 1977 as INTERNATIONAL VELVET, starring Tatum O'Neal.

p, Pandro S. Berman; d, Clarence Brown; w, Theodore Reeves, Helen Deutsch (based on the novel by Enid Bagnold); ph, Leonard Smith (Technicolor); m, Herbert Stothart.

Drama Cas. (MPAA:NR)

NEVER CRY WOLF

(1983) 91m Amarok/BV c

Charles Martin Smith *(Tyler)*, Brian Dennehy *(Rosie)*, Zachary Ittimangnaq *(Ootek)*, Samson Jorah *(Mike)*, Hugh Webster *(Drunk)*, Martha Ittimangnaq *(Woman)*, Tom Dahlgren, Walker Stuart *(Hunters)*.

This is the haunting story of a scientist who is sent to the Arctic to study the behavior of wolves. Unfamiliar with the wilderness, Tyler (Charles Martin Smith) finds himself unprepared for his stay in the desolate area of frozen land and icy winds. Near death, he is rescued by a mysterious Eskimo, who builds him a shelter, then leaves without waiting for thanks. Forced to rely on his ingenuity and common sense, Tyler survives until the spring and sets up camp near a small pack of wolves, building mutual trust with the head male. His now-idyllic surroundings are threatened, however, when a group of caribou hunters arrives. Based on Farley Mowat's study of wolves for the Ottawa Wildlife Service, this beautifully photographed wilderness film is matched only by another of director Carroll Ballard's films, THE BLACK STALLION. Capturing the changes a man goes through as he learns about life in the wilds, NEVER CRY WOLF is as informative as any public television nature program, but it is Smith's performance as the civilized man discovering his baser instincts that makes the film a resounding success. The scene in which Tyler, surviving like the wolves, eats field mice may disgust some viewers, but, most likely, it will be the adults who are grossed out and not the kids.

p, Lewis Allen, Jack Couffer, Joseph Strick; d, Carroll Ballard; w, Curtis Hanson, Sam Hamm, Richard Kletter, C.M. Smith, Eugene Corr, Christina Luescher (based on the book by Farley Mowat); ph, Hiro Narita (Technicolor); m, Mark Isham.

Adventure Cas. (MPAA:PG)

NEWS HOUNDS

(1947) 68m MON bw

Leo Gorcey *("Slip" Mahoney)*, Huntz Hall *(Sach)*, Bobby Jordan *(Bobby)*, Gabriel Dell *(Gabe)*, Billy Benedict *(Whitey)*, David Gorcey *(Chuck)*, Christine McIntyre *(Jane Ann Connelly)*, Tim Ryan *(John Burke)*, Anthony Caruso *("Dapper Dan"Greco)*, Bill Kennedy *(Mark Morgan)*, Ralph Dunn *(Dutch Miller)*, Nita Bieber(Mame), John Hamilton *(Big Tim Donlin)*, Terry Goodman *(Little Boy)*, Robert Emmett Keane *(Mack Snide Lawyer)*, Bernard Gorcey *(Louie)*, Buddy Gorman (Copyboy), Russ Whiteman *(Jimmy Gale)*, Emmett Vogan Jr. *(Johnny Gale)*, John H.Elliott *(Judge)*, Meyer Grace *(Sparring Partner)*, Leo Kaye *(Red Kane)*, Emmett Vogan, Sr. *(Defense Attorney)*, Gene Stutenroth *(Dutch's Henchman)*, Terry Goodman.

The Bowery Boys try to make a name for themselves in the world of journalism by getting the goods on an underworld figure. Slip (Leo Gorcey) is a copyboy and would-be reporter, and Satch (Huntz Hall) is a photographer for the same paper. Acting on a tip from a buddy (Gabriel Dell) and claiming to be friends of a friend, they visit the gangster, get the story, and then publish it under another writer's name. Naturally, Slip and Satch are walking on thin ice, but they manage to save their skins and deliver the mobster to justice by the film's end. There's plenty of action packed into NEWS HOUNDS' slight 68 minutes, and, as usual, Gorcey's mutilation of the English language and Hall's cretinous antics lead to lots of laughs.

p, Jan Grippo; d, William Beaudine; w, Edmond Seward, Tim Ryan (based on a story by Edmond Seward, Tim Ryan, and George Cappy); ph, Marcel Le Picard.

Comedy/Crime **(MPAA:NR)**

NEXT VOICE YOU HEAR, THE

(1950) 82m MGM bw

James Whitmore *(Joe Smith, American)*, Nancy Davis *(Mrs. Joe Smith)*, Gary Gray *(Johnny Smith)*, Lillian Bronson *(Aunt Ethel)*, Art Smith *(Mr. Brannan)*, Tom D'Andrea *(Hap Magee)*, Jeff Corey *(Freddie)*, George Chandler *(Traffic Cop)*.

Mr. and Mrs. Joe Smith (James Whitmore and Nancy Davis [Reagan]) are happily married and eagerly awaiting the birth of their second child when they, and the rest of the world, are shaken by the voice of God emanating from the radio one night. Skepticism and fear grip the globe, but, returning to the airwaves for six nights, the voice persuades listeners not to be afraid of His pronouncements. The lives of the Smiths, and those of their neighbors, are forever changed as they realize the direction they must now take. Despite a seemingly ludicrous concept, this is a sincere drama handled with care under William Wellman's direction. Rather than projecting a heavy-handed message, the film concentrates on the effect these broadcasts have on the characters' everyday lives. Whitmore and Davis are especially believa-

ble as the changed couple, conveying an honest warmth that adds to the spirit of the picture. Producer Dore Schary intended to create a film about God that emphasized His effects on the common man and not a biblical spectacle like those Hollywood was so adept at producing. Gossip monger Hedda Hopper called THE NEXT VOICE YOU HEAR a film "for every member of the family. In fact, for America."

p, Dore Schary; d, William A. Wellman; w, Charles Schnee (based on a story by George Sumner Albee); ph, William Mellor; m, David Raksin.

Drama **(MPAA:NR)**

NIGHT AT THE OPERA, A

(1935) 90m MGM bw

Groucho Marx *(Otis B. Driftwood)*, Chico Marx *(Fiorello)*, Harpo Marx *(Tomasso)*, Kitty Carlisle *(Rosa Castaldi)*, Allan Jones *(Riccardo Baroni)*, Walter Woolf King *(Rodolfo Lassparri)*, Siegfried "Sig" Rumann *(Herman Gottlieb)*, Margaret Dumont *(Mrs. Claypool)*, Edward Keane *(Captain)*, Robert Emmett O'Connor *(Detective Henderson)*, Gino Corrado *(Steward)*, Purnell Pratt *(Mayor)*, Frank Yaconelli *(Engineer)*, Billy Gilbert *(Engineer's Assistant/ Peasant)*, Sam Marx *(Extra on Ship and at Dock)*, Claude Peyton *(Police Captain)*, Rita and Rubin *(Dancers)*, Luther Hoobyar *(Ruiz)*, Rodolfo Hoyos *(Count di Luna)*, Olga Dane *(Azucena)*, James J. Wolf *(Ferrando)*, Inez Palange *(Maid)*, Jonathan Hale *(Stage Manager)*, Otto Fries *(Elevator Man)*, William Gould *(Captain of Police)*, Leo White, Jay Eaton, Rolfe Sedan *(Aviators)*.

In what is arguably the Marx Brothers' finest film (many critics favor DUCK SOUP, but Groucho himself called this his favorite), Groucho, Chico, and Harpo join forces to disrupt the stuffy opera world by wreaking havoc on the music, stage, and audience. Otis B. Driftwood (Groucho) trying to con rich Mrs. Claypool (Margaret Dumont) into investing her money in an opera company, while Tomasso (Harpo) and Fiorello (Chico) join the fray and they take it upon themselves to help advance the careers of two struggling young singers (Allan Jones and Kitty Carlisle). It was the Marx Brothers' first film for MGM after they were dropped by Paramount and the first one without Zeppo. Producer Irving Thalberg had faith in the boys and thought that their other films for Paramount lacked cohesive stories and enough time to work out the routines, so he prevailed upon them to take a 50-minute precis of the best scenes on the road. They toured four cities with writers George S. Kaufman and Morrie Ryskind in the audience for 24 days and polished the gags until they were ready to film. The result was a huge success and the picture was a hit. Today it is fondly remembered for such classic comedy bits as Groucho and Chico drafting a contract, the stateroom scene, and the hilarious climax where the brothers make a shambles of "Il Trovatore."

p, Irving Thalberg; d, Sam Wood; w, George S. Kaufman, Morrie Ryskind, Al Boasberg, Bert Kalmar, Harry Ruby (based on a story by James Kevin McGuinness); ph, Merritt B. Gerstad; m, Herbert Stothart.

Comedy   **(MPAA:NR)**

NIKKI, WILD DOG OF THE NORTH

(1961, US/Can.) 74m Disney-Cangary-WEST/BV c

Jean Coutu *(Andre Dupas)*, Emile Genest *(Jacques Lebeau)*, Uriel Luft *(Makoki)*, Robert Rivard *(Durante)*, Taao the Dog *(Old Champion Fighting Dog)*, Jacques Fauteux *(Narrator)*, The Nomads *(Performers of French-Canadian Folk Songs)*, Neewa the Bear, Nikki the Dog.

Andre Dupas (Jean Coutu) is a trapper in the Canadian wilderness whose dog Nikki runs off and returns with a new friend, Neewa, a bear cub. Andre ties the two animals together, loads them into his canoe, and heads downstream; however, they are separated from him when the canoe overturns in the rapids. The animals, still leashed together, have to learn to fend for themselves under their unusual constraint. The rope finally breaks, but Nikki and Neewa stick together for further adventures. Unlike many films of this type, NIKKI, WILD DOG OF THE NORTH is a well-made and exciting animal-action piece. Nikki and Neewa are quite a team, and some sequences will have the viewer wondering how the Disney folks ever got these surprising animal actors to behave so naturally. Perfect for the kids (though one fight scene may be a little too much for the youngest in the family), and the adults will be charmed as well.

p, Walt Disney, Winston Hibler; d, Jack Couffer, Donald Haldane; w, Winston Hibler, Ralph Wright, Dwight Hauser (based on the novel *Nomads of the North* by James Oliver Curwood); ph, Lloyd Beebe, Couffer, Ray Jewell, William V. Bacon III, Donald Wilder (Technicolor); m, Oliver Wallace.

Adventure   **Cas.**   **(MPAA:NR)**

NOOSE HANGS HIGH, THE

(1948) 77m EL bw

Bud Abbott *(Ted Higgins)*, Lou Costello *(Homer Hinchcliffe)*, Cathy Downs *(Carol Scott)*, Joseph Calleia *(Mike Craig)*, Leon Errol *(Julius Caesar McBride)*, Mike Mazurki *(Chuck)*, Jack Overman *(Joe)*, Fritz Feld *(Psychiatrist)*, Vera Martin *(Elevator Girl)*, Joe Kirk, Matt Willis *(Gangsters)*, Ben Welden *(Stewart)*, Jimmy Dodd , Ben Hall *(Messengers)*, Ellen Corby *(Maid)*, Isabel Randolph *(Miss Van Buren)*, Frank O'Connor *(Postman)*, Bess Flowers *(Patient)*, Pat Flaherty *(Tough Driver)*, Elvia Allman *(Bit Woman)*, Lois Austin *(Woman on Street)*, Herb Vigran *(Man with Coat)*, James Flavin *(Traffic Cop)*, Minerva Urecal *(Husky Woman)*, Russell Hicks *(Manager)*, Arno Frey *(Headwaiter)*, Lyle Latell *(Workman)*, Irmgard Dawson *(Girl)*, Joan Myles *(Secretary)*, Harry Brown *(Upson)*, Benny Rubin *(Chinaman)*, Murray Leonard *(Crazy Dentist)*, Sandra Spence *(Dentist's Assistant)*, Alvin Hammer *(Tipster)*, Jerry Marlowe *(Cashier)*, Paul Maxey *(Jewel Proprietor)*, Fred Kelsey

(Cop), James Logan *(Valet)*, Oscar Otis *(Race Track Announcer)*, Fred M. Browne, Ralph Montgomery *(Waiters)*, Tim Wallace, Chalky Williams *(Cab Drivers)*.

Abbott and Costello play a pair of window washers who are mistaken for gamblers and get mixed up with gangsters. This minimal plot, however, is really just an excuse for the great comedy team to strut its patented stuff. The bits are as old as movies, but the boys give the material an invigorating spin. There's a well-timed bit with a pair of pants that is an excellent display of physical comedy, and the fellas also engage in some snappy wordplay (in the same vein as the famous "Who's on first?" routine) as they fool around with the phrase "You can't be here." A good supporting cast, fine comedy direction, and, of course, the irrepressible Abbott and Costello combine for some very funny moments.

p&d, Charles Barton; w, John Grant, Howard Harris (based on a story by Daniel Taradash, Julian Blaustein and Bernard Fins); ph, Charles Van Enger; m, Walter Schumann.

Comedy   **(MPAA:NR)**

NOW YOU SEE HIM, NOW YOU DON'T

(1972) 88m Disney/BV c

Kurt Russell *(Dexter Riley)*, Cesar Romero *(A.J. Arno)*, Joe Flynn *(Dean Higgins)*, Jim Backus *(Timothy Forsythe)*, William Windom *(Prof. Lufkin)*, Michael McGreevey *(Richard Schuyler)*, Joyce Menges *(Debbie Dawson)*, Richard Bakalyan *(Cookie)*, Alan Hewitt *(Dean Collingsgood)*, Kelly Thordsen *(Sgt. Cassidy)*, Neil Russell *(Alfred)*, George O'Hanlon *(Ted)*, John Myhers *(Golfer)*, Pat Delany *(Secretary)*, Robert Rothwell *(Driver)*, Frank Aletter *(TV Announcer)*, Dave Willock *(Mr. Burns)*, Edward Andrews *(Mr. Sampson)*, Jack Bender *(Slither Roth)*, Frank Welker *(Myles)*, Mike Evans *(Henry Fathington)*, Ed Begley, Jr. *(Druffle)*, Paul Smith *(Road Block Officer)*, Billy Casper, Dave Hill *(Themselves)*.

Kurt Russell repeats his role as college student Dexter Riley in this follow-up to Disney's THE COMPUTER WORE TENNIS SHOES (1969). This time Dexter finds an invisibility serum that he uses to keep his financially troubled alma mater, Medfield College, from falling into the hands of gangster A.J. Arno (Cesar Romero). One of the film's funniest and most exciting scenes features a wild car chase involving invisible cars. Benefitting from some fine special effects, this fast-moving comedy ought to please any family.

p, Ron Miller; d, Robert Butler; w, Joseph McEveety (based on a story by Robert L. King); ph, Frank Phillips (Technicolor); m, Robert F. Brunner.

Comedy   **(MPAA:G)**

NUTCRACKER: THE MOTION PICTURE

(1986) 84m Hyperion Kushner-Locke/Atlantic Releasing c

Hugh Bigney *(Herr Drosselmeier)*, Vanessa Sharp *(Young*

Clara), Patricia Barker (Dream Clara), Wade Walthall (Nutcracker); Act I, Party Scene: Maia Rosal (Frau Stahlbaum), Carey Homme (Dr. Stahlbaum), Patricia Barker (Ballerina Doll), Courtland Weaver (Sword Dancer), Alejandra Bronfman, Kevin Kaiser, Reid Olson (Pas de Trois), Russell Burnett (Fritz), Emerald Stacy (Little Girl), Cary Stidham (Little Boy); Fight Scene: Jacob Rice (Nutcracker), Banjamin Houk (Mouse Captain), Deborah Inkster (Mother Mouse); Act II: Heather Boe, Tracy Carboneau, Charina Dimaano, Nicole Fiset, Joey-Lynn Mann, Erin Sokol (Scrim Mice), Maia Rosal (Peacock), Erik Cederlund, Jeffrey Plourde (Slaves), Jeffery N. Bullock (Chinese Tiger), Rachel Harrison, Lee Johnson, Jennifer Owen, Nicole Wolgamott (Chinese Girls), Benjamin Houk, Jacob Rice, Courtland Weaver (Dervishes), Alejandra Bronfman, Sterling Kekoa, Carron Donaldson (Commedia); Snow Scene: Carol Anderson, Martha Boyle, Dianne Brace, Irene Damestoy, Carron Donaldson, Susan Gladstone, Amy Greene, Jennifer Homans, Stephanie Irwin, Elizabeth McCarthy, Ann Renhard, Angela Sterling, Laura Schwenk, Lisa Stolzy, Julie Tobiason, Lisl Vaillant, Clara Wilson (Snowflakes).

Transferring ballet to film has always been a difficult task. Part of its beauty comes in witnessing the dance unfold before one's eyes, and such elements as close-ups and editing intrude on the dancer's and the choreographer's art. This version of the Christmas classic directed by Carroll Ballard attempts to rework a highly praised stage production for the screen, and while it is not entirely successful as a dance film, Ballard does capture the uniqueness of the Pacific Northwest Ballet's revolutionary production. The story follows Clara (played by both Vanessa Sharp and Patricia Barker), a 12-year-old whose real world becomes magical one Christmas, when her toys come alive and she becomes enamored of the Nutcracker, her dream lover. The unusual sets by Maurice Sendak transfer well to screen and add a remarkable visual element to this adaptation.

p, Willard Carroll, Donald Kushner, Peter Locke, Thomas L. Wilhite; d, Carroll Ballard; w, Kent Stowell, Maurice Sendak (based on the fairy tale "The Nutcracker and the Mouse King" by E.T.A. Hoffman); ph, Stephen H. Burum (MGM Color); m, Peter Ilyich Tchaikovsky.

Dance/Fantasy   Cas.   (MPAA:G)

O. HENRY'S FULL HOUSE
(1952) 117m FOX bw (GB: FULL HOUSE)

"The Gift of the Magi": Jeanne Crain (Della), Farley Granger (Jim), Sig Rumann (Menkie), Harry Hayden (Mr. Crump), Fred Kelsey (Santa Claus), Richard Hylton (Bill), Richard Allen (Pete), Fritz Feld (Maurice), Frank Jaquet (Butcher); "The Last Leaf": Anne Baxter (Joanna), Jean Peters (Susan), Gregory Ratoff (Behrman), Richard Garrick (Doctor), Steven Geray (Radolf), Warren Stevens (Druggist), Martha Wentworth (Mrs. O'Brien), Ruth Warren (Neighbor), Bert Hicks (Sheldon Sidney), Beverly Thompson (Girl), Hal J. Smith (Dandy); "The Cop and the Anthem": Charles Laughton (Soapy), Marilyn Monroe (Streetwalker), David Wayne (Horace), Philip Tonge (Man with Umbrella), Thomas Browne Henry (Manager), Richard Karlan (Headwaiter), Erno Verebes (Waiter), William Vedder (Judge), Billy Wayne (Bystander), Nico Lek (Owner), Marjorie Holliday (Cashier), James Flavin (Cop); "The Clarion Call": Dale Robertson (Barney Woods), Richard Widmark (Johnny Kernan), Joyce MacKenzie (Hazel), Richard Rober (Chief of Detectives), Will Wright (Manager), House Peters Sr. (Bascom), Tyler McVey (O. Henry), Phil Tully (Guard), Frank Cusack (Waiter), Stuart Randall (Detective), Abe Dinovitch (Bartender); "The Ransom of Red Chief": Fred Allen (Sam), Oscar Levant (Bill), Lee Aaker (J.B.), Kathleen Freeman (J.B.'s Mother), Alfred Mizner (J.B.'s Father), Irving Bacon (Mr. Dorset), Gloria Gordon (Ellie Mae), Robert Easton, Robert Cherry, Norman Leavitt (Yokels), John Steinbeck (Narrator).

This hearty and entertaining compendium of O. Henry's best stories features some energetic performances and, in a few cases, marvelous direction. The first tale, "The Cop and the Anthem," is about a haughty tramp who, with the onset of winter, tries to get arrested so he can enjoy the warmth of a jail cell. But, try as he might, he simply cannot offend the law. "The Clarion Call" is a terse slice of life in which a decent cop must arrest an old friend. In "The Last Leaf," a dying woman watches autumn leaves wither, and comes to believe that when the last leaf blows away, she, too, will die. Winter comes and the leaves vanish, one by one, until a single leaf remains, stubbornly clinging to the wall and giving the woman hope. There's a laugh a minute in "The Ransom of Red Chief," the story of a boy so bad that his parents couldn't care less when he's kidnaped. The rowdy kid makes life so miserable for his abductors that they bribe the parents to take the insufferable brat back. In the famous "The Gift of the Magi," a pair of impoverished young newlyweds sacrifice their most cherished possessions to buy each other Christmas gifts. The direction and writing in all these sequences are good and the entire film is a great treat, enhanced by John Steinbeck's narration—an homage to the mysterious O. Henry.

p, Andre Hakim; d, Henry Hathaway, Henry Koster, Henry King, Howard Hawks, Jean Negulesco; w, Lamar Trotti, Richard Breen, Ben Roberts, Ivan Goff, Walter Bullock, Nunnally Johnson (based on the stories by O. Henry); ph, Lloyd Ahern, Lucien Ballard, Joe MacDonald, Milton Krasner; m, Alfred Newman.

Comedy/Drama   (MPAA:NR)

OF STARS AND MEN
(1961) 53m Storyboard c

Voices of: Dr. Harlow Shapley, Mark Hubley, Hamp Hubley.

Evolution and man's place in the universe are explored in this charming animated fable created by John and Faith Hubley. Using Dr. Harlow Shapley's book *Of Stars and Men* as a basis (a volume written "to tell the people in simple language what man is and where he is in the universe of atoms, protoplasm, stars, and galaxies"), the Hubleys begin by showing the evolution of the earth and animal life. Man is introduced in the form of an arrogant boy who slowly comes to realize he's not alone in the universe. Though the ideas expressed in the story are familiar, the presentation is pure visual delight. The stylized pictures are brimming with humor and also carry a touch of pathos. The soundtrack is well suited to the images, using Hubley's children, Mark and Hamp, along with Dr. Shapley, as commentators on the action. OF STARS AND MEN is another standout in John Hubley's productive career. He worked with Disney on such films as SNOW WHITE and DUMBO before leaving to help form UPA Productions, where he created such memorable cartoon characters as Gerald McBoing Boing and the irrepressible Mr. Magoo.

p, John Hubley, Faith Hubley; d, John Hubley; w, John Hubley, Faith Hubley, Harlow Shapley (based on the book *Of Stars and Men* by Harlow Shapley); ph, John Buehre (Eastmancolor).

Animation   **(MPAA:NR)**

OKLAHOMA!

(1955) 145m Magna Theatres c

Gordon MacRae *(Curly)*, Gloria Grahame *(Ado Annie)*, Gene Nelson *(Will Parker)*, Charlotte Greenwood *(Aunt Eller)*, Shirley Jones *(Laurey)*, Eddie Albert *(Ali Hakim)*, James Whitmore *(Carnes)*, Rod Steiger *(Jud Fry)*, Barbara Lawrence *(Gertie)*, J.C. Flippen *(Skidmore)*, Roy Barcroft *(Marshal)*, James Mitchell *(Dream Curly)*, Bambi Linn *(Dream Laurey)*, Jennie Workman, Kelly Brown, Marc Platt, Lizanne Truex, Virginia Bosler, Evelyn Taylor, Jane Fischer *(Dancers)*, Ben Johnson *(Cowboy at Train Depot)*.

This paean to Oklahoma's "Sooner" pioneers is one of Hollywood's most inventive musicals despite its rudimentary plot: Boys (Gordon MacRae and Gene Nelson) meet Girls (Shirley Jones and Gloria Grahame), Boys almost lose Girls, and Boys get Girls, all complicated by the antiromantic efforts of villainous Jud Fry (Rod Steiger). Until the stage version of "Oklahoma!" dared to be different, the traditional Broadway opening had a line of high-stepping chorus girls with razzle-dazzle outfits. Here the set is quiet until MacRae extols the pleasures of "Oh, What a Beautiful Morning," and we realize right away that we're in for something special. Although the score is, by now, deeply imbedded in the minds of anyone who has ears, it is the creative and, in some cases, offbeat casting that makes OKLAHOMA! so constantly surprising. Despite the huge success it rightfully had when first released and which now continues whenever it's shown in revival houses, OKLAHOMA! received only one Oscar, for Best Score. The unforgettable Rodgers and Hammerstein tunes include "Surrey with the Fringe on Top," "Many a New Day," "People Will Say We're in Love," and the exuberant title song.

p, Arthur Hornblow, Jr.; d, Fred Zinnemann; w, Sonya Levien, William Ludwig (based on the musical play by Richard Rodgers and Oscar Hammerstein II, from the play "Green Grow the Lilacs" by Lynn Riggs); ph, Robert Surtees (Todd-AO, Eastmancolor); m, Richard Rodgers.

Musical   **Cas.**   **(MPAA:G)**

OLD YELLER

(1957) 83m Disney/BV c

Dorothy McGuire *(Katie Coates)*, Fess Parker *(Jim Coates)*, Tommy Kirk *(Travis Coates)*, Kevin Corcoran *(Arliss Coates)*, Jeff York *(Bud Searcy)*, Beverly Washburn *(Lisbeth Searcy)*, Chuck Connors *(Burn Sanderson)*, Spike the Dog *(Old Yeller)*.

Set in Texas in 1869, Disney Studios' first and best attempt at a boy-and-his-dog film tells the story of a farm family whose head, Jim Coates (Fess Parker), must go on a cattle drive for three months, leaving his 15-year-old son, Travis (Tommy Kirk), in charge. When Travis' younger brother, Arliss (Kevin Corcoran), finds a stray yellow dog and decides to adopt him, Travis is frustrated by this breach of his authority. But his mother (Dorothy McGuire) approves of the dog's presence and reminds Travis that his little brother is lonely. Soon the dog, Old Yeller, has won the hearts of the whole family. Their attachment to the dog will serve as a test for their strength and love in this powerful and moving film. The movie is not afraid to confront issues that all children must eventually face—the loss of a pet and the transformation from child into adult. It is a film which will undoubtedly sadden children (and adults), but its redemptive and educational qualities will also lead young viewers to think about things that have previously gone unnoticed. Sequel: SAVAGE SAM.

p, Walt Disney; d, Robert Stevenson; w, Fred Gipson, William Tunberg (based on the novel by Fred Gipson); ph, Charles P. Boyle (Technicolor); m, Oliver Wallace.

Drama   **Cas.**   **(MPAA:NR)**

OLIVER!

(1968, Brit.) 153m Warwick-Romulus/COL c

Ron Moody *(Fagin)*, Shani Wallis *(Nancy)*, Oliver Reed *(Bill Sikes)*, Harry Secombe *(Mr. Bumble)*, Mark Lester *(Oliver Twist)*, Jack Wild *(The Artful Dodger)*, Hugh Griffith *(The Magistrate)*, Joseph O'Conor *(Mr. Brownlow)*, Peggy Mount *(Widow Corney)*, Leonard Rossiter *(Mr. Sowerberry)*, Hylda Baker *(Mrs. Sowerberry)*, Kenneth Cranham *(Noah Claypole)*, Megs Jenkins *(Mrs. Bedwin)*, Sheila White *(Bet)*, Wensley Pithey *(Dr. Grimwig)*, James Hayter *(Mr. Jessop)*, Elizabeth Knight *(Charlotte)*, Fred Emney *(Chairman of Workhouse Governors)*, Edwin Finn, Foy Evans *(Workhouse Paupers)*, Norman Mitchell *(Arresting Policeman)*, Robert Bartlett, Graham Buttrose, Jeffrey Chandler, Kirk Clugeston, Dempsey Cook,

Christopher Duff, Nigel Grice, Ronnie Johnson, Nigel Kingsley, Robert Langley, Brian Lloyd, Peter Lock, Ian Ramsey, Peter Renn, Bill Smith, Kim Smith, Freddie Stead, Raymond Ward, John Watters *(Fagin's Boys)*, Clive Moss *(Charlie Bates)*, Veronica Page *(Oliver's Mother)*, Henry Kay *(Doctor)*, Jane Peach *(Rose the Maid)*, Keith Roberts *(Policeman in Magistrate's Court)*, Peter Hoar *(Court Clerk)*, John Baskcombe, Norman Pitt, Arnold Locke, Frank Crawshaw *(Workhouse Governors)*.

An energetic celebration of musicals, childhood, and Charles Dickens, OLIVER! is one of the finest films of the 1960s and, despite its length, a movie from which it is nearly impossible to walk away. It's the familiar story of young Oliver Twist (played superbly by Mark Lester), an orphan who prefers life on the streets to the hard labor of a foster family or living in a vile orphanage. One day he meets another street urchin, the Artful Dodger (Jack Wild, in an equally superb performance), who tells him of a group of young hooligans that will consider him "part of the family." All Oliver has to do is learn to pickpocket and give his earnings to Fagin (Ron Moody), the crusty criminal gang leader; in return he'll have a "family" and a place to stay. OLIVER! (using only one exclamation point is a gross understatement) is a thoroughly entertaining picture with wonderful performances, fantastic sets, awesome camerawork, unrelenting direction by Carol Reed, and a nonstop assault of outstanding songs, including "Consider Yourself," "Food, Glorious Food," "Who Will Buy?" and "I'd Do Anything." Although there are few opportunities to see OLIVER! on the big screen any more, it has such a grand, breathtaking scale that one should make every effort to see it in a theater.

p, John Woolf; d, Carol Reed; w, Vernon Harris (based on the musical play by Lionel Bart, from the novel *Oliver Twist* by Charles Dickens); ph, Oswald Morris (Panavision, Technicolor); m, Lionel Bart.

Musical   **Cas.**   **(MPAA:G)**

OLIVER TWIST

(1951, Brit.) 105m Cineguild/RANK-UA bw

Robert Newton *(Bill Sikes)*, Alec Guinness *(Fagin)*, Kay Walsh *(Nancy)*, Francis L. Sullivan *(Mr. Bumble)*, Henry Stephenson *(Mr. Brownlow)*, Mary Clare *(Mrs. Corney)*, John Howard Davies *(Oliver Twist)*, Josephine Stuart *(Oliver's Mother)*, Henry Edwards *(Police Official)*, Ralph Truman *(Monks)*, Anthony Newley *(The Artful Dodger)*, Hattie Jacques, Betty Paul *(Singers)*, Kenneth Downey *(Workhouse Master)*, Gibb McLaughlin *(Mr. Sowerberry)*, Kathleen Harrison *(Mrs. Sowerberry)*, Amy Veness *(Mrs. Bedwin)*, W.G. Fay *(Bookseller)*, Maurice Denham *(Chief of Police)*, Frederick Lloyd *(Mr. Grimwig)*, Ivor Barnard *(Chairman of the Board)*, Deidre Doyle *(Mrs. Thingummy)*, Edie Martin *(Annie)*, Fay Middleton *(Martha)*, Diana Dors *(Charlotte)*, Michael Dear *(Noah Claypole)*, Graveley Edwards *(Mr. Fang)*, Peter Bull *(Landlord of "Three Cripples")*, John Potter *(Charlie Bates)*, Maurice Jones *(Workhouse Doctor)*.

David Lean's version of Charles Dickens' *Oliver Twist* is

not as enthralling as Carol Reed's subsequent musical (see above), but it is a fine film in its own right. This time Alec Guinness plays Fagin, Anthony Newley is the Artful Dodger, and the then-unknown and now-forgotten John Howard Davies is Oliver Twist. (Actually, some may recognize Davies as the British television producer responsible for "Monty Python's Flying Circus" and "Fawlty Towers.") Many of the novel's characters have been excised or compressed to fit the time frame of the film, but only the most die-hard Dickensians will protest. The sets are as much a part of the story as the dialog, and set designer John Bryan's accomplishment should not go unnoticed. All the acting is first-rate and there is not a false move from the cast.

p, Ronald Neame, Anthony Havelock-Allan; d, David Lean; w, David Lean, Stanley Haynes (based on the novel by Charles Dickens); ph, Guy Green; m, Sir Arnold Bax.

Drama   **Cas.**   **(MPAA:NR)**

ONE FOOT IN HEAVEN

(1941) 106m WB bw

Fredric March *(William Spence)*, Martha Scott *(Hope Morris Spence)*, Beulah Bondi *(Mrs. Lydia Sandow)*, Gene Lockhart *(Preston Thurston)*, Grant Mitchell *(Clayton Potter)*, Moroni Olsen *(Dr. John Romer)*, Harry Davenport *(Elias Samson)*, Elisabeth Fraser *(Eileen Spence, Age 17)*, Frankie Thomas *(Hartzell Spence, Age 18)*, Laura Hope Crews *(Mrs. Thurston)*, Jerome Cowan *(Dr. Horrigan)*, Ernest Cossart *(John E. Morris)*, Nana Bryant *(Mrs. Morris)*, Mary Field *(Louella Digby)*, Hobart Bosworth *(Richard Hardy Case)*, Roscoe Ates *(George Reynolds)*, Clara Blandick *(Mrs. Watkins)*, Charles Halton *(Haskins)*, Paula Trueman *(Miss Peabody)*, Virginia Brissac *(Mrs. Jellison)*, Casey Johnson *(Fraser Spence, Age 10)*, Carlotta Jelm *(Eileen Spence, Age 11)*, Peter Caldwell *(Hartzell Spence, Age 10)*, Milt Kibbee *(Alf McAfee)*, Harlan Briggs *(Druggist MacFarlan)*, Olin Howland *(Zeke Harris)*, Frank Mayo *(Drummer)*, Fred Kelsey *(Conductor)*, Vera Lewis *(Mrs. Simpson)*, Dorothy Vaughan *(Mrs. Erlich)*, Tempe Pigott *(Mrs. Dibble)*, Sarah Edwards *(Mrs. Spicer)*, Herbert Heywood *(Storekeeper)*, Dick Elliott *(Casper Cullenbaugh)*, Charlotte Treadway *(Ella Hodges)*, Ann Edmonds *(Bride)*, Byron Barr [Gig Young] *(Groom)*, Ruth Robinson, Cathy Lipps.

In one of his finest performances, Fredric March plays Rev. William Spence, a Methodist minister who devotes his life to transforming wavering parishes into strong pillars of faith. Episodic in form, ONE FOOT IN HEAVEN begins in Canada in 1904. After listening to an evangelist, Spence and his devoted wife, Hope (Martha Scott), decide to move to a small Iowa community desperately in need of spiritual guidance. Trying to fit in, Spence and Hope live at poverty level, forgoing the luxuries to which they are accustomed. After their work in one parish is complete, they move on to the next, adding to their family in the process. Over the next 20 years, Spence and Hope fight a number of uphill battles, and when it finally appears as if the Spence family is going to settle down, word reaches them of another troubled parish. A huge audience pleaser, ONE FOOT IN HEAVEN was based on the real-life exploits of Rev. William Spence, whose story was told in a book written by his son. Adding to its authenticity was the presence of Rev. Dr. Norman Vincent Peale as technical advisor. What makes the film so enjoyable, however, isn't its religious message, but March's portrayal of Spence as a real man—one with morals and common sense, who can also be aggressive when necessary. ONE FOOT IN HEAVEN received an Oscar nomination for Best Picture.

p, Jack L. Warner, Hal B. Wallis; d, Irving Rapper; w, Casey Robinson (based on the biography of William Spence by Hartzell Spence); ph, Charles Rosher; m, Max Steiner.

Biography (MPAA:NR)

ONE HUNDRED AND ONE DALMATIANS

(1961) 79m Disney/BV c

Voices of: Rod Taylor *(Pongo)*, Lisa Davis *(Anita)*, Cate Bauer *(Perdita)*, Ben Wright *(Roger Radcliff)*, Frederick Worlock *(Horace)*, J. Pat O'Malley *(Jasper/Miscellaneous Dogs)*, Betty Lou Gerson *(Cruella De Vil/Miss Birdwell)*, Martha Wentworth *(Nani/Goose/Cow)*, Tom Conway *(Collie)*, George Pelling *(Great Dane)*, Micky Maga *(Patch the Puppy)*, Barbara Beaird *(Holly the Puppy)*, Queenie Leonard, Marjorie Bennett *(Cows)*, Tudor Owen, Mimi Gibson, Sandra Abbott, Paul Wexler, Mary Wickes, Barbara Luddy, Lisa Daniels, David Frankham, Ramsay Hill, Sylvia Marriott, Thurl Ravenscroft, Bill Lee, Max Smith, Bob Stevens, Helene Stanley, Donald Barclay, Dal McKennon, Jeanne Bruns.

Three hundred artists worked on this project for three years and came up with one of the best feature cartoons ever produced by Disney Studios. The story, a romance with an interesting detective twist, is combined with exquisite caricatures of both humans and dogs. The plot revolves around a dog, Pongo, and his master, Roger, who fall for Anita and her dog, Perdita. Roger and Anita marry, allowing Pongo and Perdita to be together and produce an offspring of 15 Dalmatian puppies. Wicked Cruella De Vil is overly persistent in her desire to have all 15 puppies, but Roger refuses her, prompting the wealthy woman to hire a pair of cockney crooks to steal the pups. Roger and Anita try everything to locate them, but to no avail, so Pongo resorts to the "twilight bark," a system of dog signals that locates the puppies in a deserted mansion on the outskirts of London. Pongo, assisted by a dog named the Colonel, a horse, and a cat, then sets out to rescue the puppies, discovering in the process a total of 99 Dalmatians that the evil Cruella has gathered to make herself a rare coat. Throughout the story are subtle visual elements creating an atmosphere that transcends mere cartoon reality. The characters are also evocatively voiced by a cast that includes Rod Taylor as Pongo. For fun, note the physical resemblance between many of the dogs and their masters.

p, Walt Disney; d, Wolfgang Reitherman, Hamilton S. Luske, Clyde Geronimi; w, Bill Peet (based on a book by Dodie Smith); m, George Bruns.

Animation (MPAA:NR)

ONE NIGHT IN THE TROPICS

(1940) 82m UNIV bw

Allan Jones *(Jim Moore)*, Robert Cummings *(Steve Harper)*, Nancy Kelly *(Cynthia)*, Mary Boland *(Aunt Kitty)*, Bud Abbott *(Abbott)*, Lou Costello *(Costello)*, Peggy Moran *(Mickey Fitzgerald)*, William Frawley *(Roscoe)*, Leo Carrillo *(Senor Escobar)*, Don Alvarado *(Rudolfo)*, Theodore Rand, Mina Farragut *(The Theodores)*, Nina Orla *(Nina)*, Richard Carle *(Mr. Moore)*, Edgar Dearing *(Man)*, Barnett Parker *(Thompson)*, Francis McDonald *(Escobar's Aide)*, Jerry Mandy *(Vendor)*, Eddie Dunn *(Edwards)*, Vivian Fay *(Dancer)*, Eddie Acuff *(Steward)*, Frank Penny *(Waiter)*, William Alston *(Orchestra Leader)*, Charles B. Murphy *(Drunk)*, Charlie Hall *(Steward)*, Kathleen Howard, Tyler Brooke, Sally Payne, Cyril Ring, Barry Norton.

Abbott and Costello made their film debut in this picture and are, unquestionably, the best thing in it. Using some of the routines they had already made popular through their radio show, the two add very effective comedy relief to the story of insurance salesman Jim Moore (Allan Jones), who sells a policy to soon-to-be-wed Steve Harper (Robert Cummings), but elopes with his bride (Nancy Kelly). Most memorable is a small portion of Abbott and Costello's famous "Who's On First?" routine.

p, Leonard Spigelgass; d, A. Edward Sutherland; w, Gertrude Purcell, Charles Grayson, Kathryn Scola, Francis Martin (based on the novel *Love Insurance* by Earl Derr Biggers); ph, Joseph Valentine.

Comedy/Musical (MPAA:NR)

1001 ARABIAN NIGHTS

(1959) 76m UPA/COL c

Voices of: Jim Backus *(Uncle Abdul Azziz Magoo)*, Kathryn Grant *(Princess Yasminda)*, Dwayne Hickman *(Aladdin)*, Hans Conried *(The Wicked Wazir)*, Herschel Bernardi *(The Jinni)*, Alan Reed *(The Sultan)*, Daws Butler *(Omar the Rug Maker)*, Clark Sisters *(Three Maids from Damascus)*.

Mr. Magoo—called Abdul Azziz Magoo here—is a lamp seller from Old Baghdad whose life changes drastically when he finds a genie in one of his lamps. This discovery gets the near-sighted bumbler into a number of unusual situations as he helps his nephew marry a beautiful princess. Actor Jim Backus supplies Magoo's voice. This was the first animated feature film for Mr. Magoo. The kids will love it.

p, Stephen Bosustow; d, Jack Kinney; w, Czeni Ormonde (based on a story by Dick Shaw, Dick Kinney, Leo Salkin, Pete Burness, Lew Keller, Ed Nofziger, Ted Allan, Margaret Schneider and Paul Schneider); ph, Jack Eckes (Technicolor); m, George Duning.

Animation   Cas.   (MPAA:NR)

PAINTED HILLS, THE

(1951) 65m MGM

Paul Kelly *(Jonathan Harvey)*, Bruce Cowling *(Lin Taylor)*, Gary Gray *(Tommy Blake)*, Art Smith *(Pilot Pete)*, Ann Doran *(Martha Blake)*, Chief Yowlachie *(Bald Eagle)*, Andrea Virginia Lester *(Mita)*, "Brown Jug" Reynolds *(Red Wing)*, Lassie the Dog *(Shep)*.

Jonathan Harvey (Paul Kelly) is Lassie's master, a gold miner in the 1870s. His mining partner, Lin Taylor (Bruce Cowling), gets a bad case of gold fever and, because he wants Harvey's share of the gold, tries to arrange his partner's death in such a manner that Lassie will be blamed. It's up to the canine heroine to avert this disaster and outsmart the villain. The story is played with too much sentiment; nonetheless, THE PAINTED HILLS is a good adventure that's perfect for the kids, with some fine color photography of the picturesque mountain scenery. This was the famous collie's last film for MGM.

p, Chester M. Franklin; d, Harold F. Kress; w, True Boardman (based on the novel *Shep of the Painted Hills* by Alexander Hull); ph, Alfred Gilks, Harold Lipstein (Technicolor); m, Daniele Amfitheatrof.

Adventure   (MPAA:NR)

PALOOKA

(1934) 86m Reliance/UA bw (GB: THE GREAT SCHNOZZLE; AKA: JOE PALOOKA)

Jimmy Durante *(Knobby Walsh)*, Lupe Velez *(Nina Madero)*, Stuart Erwin *(Joe Palooka)*, Marjorie Rambeau *(Mayme Palooka)*, Robert Armstrong *(Pete Palooka)*, Mary Carlisle *(Anne)*, William Cagney *(Al McSwatt)*, Thelma Todd *(Trixie)*, Franklyn Ardell *(Doc Wise)*, Tom Dugan *(Whitey)*, Guinn "Big Boy" Williams *(Slats)*, Stanley Fields *(Blacky)*, Louise Beavers *(Crystal)*, Fred "Snowflake" Toones *(Smokey)*, Al Hill *(Dynamite Wilson)*, Gordon De Main *(Photographers' Official)*, Gus Arnheim and His Orchestra.

Jimmy Durante plays the great fight manager Knobby Walsh of Ham Fisher's famed comic strip, who finds young pugster Joe Palooka (Stuart Erwin) knocking things around a gym. He trains the kid for the "big fight" against Al McSwatt, played by William Cagney, the younger brother of Jimmy. This is a fun comedy with all the right elements for a good time at the movies. Durante is wonderful in his first big role, and he even has an op-

portunity to sing his trademark "Ink-a-Dinka-Do!" There is no connection between this film and the "Joe Palooka" series made in the late 1940s.

d, Benjamin Stoloff; w, Ben Ryan, Murray Roth, Gertrude Purcell, Jack Jevne, Arthur Kober (based on the comic strip by Ham Fisher); ph, Arthur Edeson.

Comedy/Sports   Cas.   (MPAA:NR)

PARENT TRAP, THE

(1961) 124m Disney/BV c

Hayley Mills *(Sharon McKendrick/Susan Evers)*, Maureen O'Hara *(Maggie McKendrick)*, Brian Keith *(Mitch Evans)*, Charlie Ruggles *(Charles McKendrick)*, Una Merkel *(Verbena)*, Leo G. Carroll *(Rev. Mosby)*, Joanna Barnes *(Vicky Robinson)*, Cathleen Nesbitt *(Louise McKendrick)*, Ruth McDevitt *(Miss Inch)*, Crahan Denton *(Hecky)*, Linda Watkins *(Edna Robinson)* Nancy Kulp *(Miss Grunecker)*, Frank DeVol *(Mr. Eaglewood)*.

Hayley Mills plays twins in this innocent, fast-paced comedy, a favorite of countless youngsters in the 1960s. The twins are separated at birth when their parents divorce—one goes off with the father, and the other with the mother. Reunited at a summer camp, they discover their relationship and, despite the extreme differences in their personalities, begin a scheme to get their parents back together by switching places when camp is over. They discover that their father is about to marry a gold digger and decide to put a stop to it, making her life miserable with all kinds of tricks and pranks. An enjoyable, corny Disney picture with a memorable soundtrack featuring tunes sung by Tommy Sands and Annette Funicello.

p, George Golitzen; d&w, David Swift (based on the novel *Das Doppelte Lottchen* by Erich Kastner); ph, Lucien Ballard (Technicolor); m, Paul J. Smith.

Comedy   Cas.   (MPAA:NR)

PETER PAN

(1953) 76m Disney/RKO c

Voices of: Bobby Driscoll *(Peter Pan)*, Kathryn Beaumont *(Wendy)*, Hans Conried *(Capt. Hook/Mr. Darling)*, Bill Thompson *(Mr. Smee)*, Heather Angel *(Mrs. Darling)*, Paul Collins *(Michael Darling)*, Tommy Luske *(John)*, Candy Candido *(Indian Chief)*, Tom Conway *(Narrator)*.

PETER PAN is a wonderful movie. Patriarch Mr. Darling (whose voice is provided by Hans Conried) is annoyed that daughter Wendy (voiced by Kathryn Beaumont) insists on telling stories to the other children about a mythical boy known as Peter Pan. When Mr. and Mrs. Darling leave for a night on the town, Peter Pan (voiced by Bobby Driscoll) and fairy sidekick Tinker Bell magically appear in Wendy's room. They all take a magical trip to Never Never Land, where they get involved in a series of adventures that include a confrontation with the evil Captain Hook (Conried, in a dual role). Lots of laughs, fabulous animation, and excellent voicing by the actors. The picture cost more than $4 million to make, a huge amount for a film in 1953. Lest you wonder why it came in so high, you should know that Disney filmed a live-action version of the movie first in order to give his artists something to base their sketches upon.

p, Walt Disney; d, Hamilton Luske, Clyde Geronimi, Wilfred Jackson; w, Ted Sears, Bill Peet, Joe Rinaldi, Erdman Penner, Winston Hibler, Milt Banta, Ralph Wright (based on the play by Sir James M. Barrie); ph, (Technicolor); m, Oliver Wallace, Edward H. Plumb.

Animation (MPAA:NR)

PETER RABBIT AND TALES OF BEATRIX POTTER

(1971, Brit.) 90m EMI/MGM c (GB: TALES OF BEATRIX POTTER)

Frederick Ashton *(Mrs. Tiggy-Winkle)*, Alexander Grant *(Pigling Bland/Peter Rabbit)*, Julie Wood *(Mrs. Tittlemouse)*, Keith Martin *(Johnny Town Mouse)*, Ann Howard *(Jemima Puddle-Duck)*, Robert Mead *(Fox)*, Gary Grant *(Alexander Town Mouse)*, Sally Ashby *(Mrs. Pettitoes/Tabitha Twitchit)*, Brenda Last *(Black Berkshire Pig)*, Wayne Sleep *(Tom Thumb/Squirrel Nutkin)*, Michael Coleman *(Jeremy Fisher)*, Lesley Collier *(Hunca Munca)*, Leslie Edwards *(Owl/Mr. Brown)*, Carole Ainsworth, Avril Bergen, Jill Cooke, Graham Fletcher, Bridget Goodricke, Suzanna Raymond, Rosemary Taylor, Anita Young *(Squirrels/Country Mice)*, Erin Geraghty *(Beatrix Potter)*, Joan Benham *(The Nurse)*, Wilfred Babbage *(Cox the Butler)*, The Royal Ballet Corps.

This film is based on the stories of Beatrix Potter, creator of the memorable Peter Rabbit and his friends, with the stories set to music and performed by the Royal Ballet. The film follows the withdrawn Potter and the way in which she blossoms when the toy animals in her room come to life. The film was a tremendous success in Britain, hitting it big with the younger set and with adults who grew up reading Potter's books. The costumes steal the show, particularly the humanlike masks created by Rostislav Douboujinsky. Frederick Ashton's choreography is also a standout.

p, Richard Goodwin; d, Reginald Mills; w, Richard Goodwin, Christine Edzard (based on stories and characters created by Beatrix Potter); ph, Austin Dempster (Technicolor).

Dance/Fantasy Cas. (MPAA:G)

PETE'S DRAGON

(1977) 134m Disney/BV c

Helen Reddy *(Nora)*, Jim Dale *(Dr. Terminus)*, Mickey Rooney *(Lampie)*, Red Buttons *(Hoagy)*, Shelley Winters *(Lena Gogan)*, Sean Marshall *(Pete)*, Jean Kean *(Miss Taylor)*, Jim Backus *(The Mayor)*, Charles Tyner *(Merle)*, Gary Morgan *(Grover)*, Jeff Conway *(Willie)*, Cal Bartlett *(Paul)*, Charlie Callas *(Voice of Elliott)*, Walter Barnes

(Captain), Robert Easton *(Store Proprietor)*, Roger Price *(Man with Visor)*, Robert Foulk *(Old Sea Captain)*, Ben Wrigley *(Egg Man)*, Joe Ross *(Cement Man)*, Al Checco, Henry Slate, Jack Collins *(Fishermen)*.

Set in turn-of-the-century Maine, PETE'S DRAGON tells the tale of an orphan boy named Pete (Sean Marshall) who runs away from his nasty foster family and encounters a charming animated dragon named Elliott (Charlie Callas provides the voice). Eventually Pete finds happiness in the company of Nora (Helen Reddy), a lighthouse keeper's daughter. Elliott is a clever creation, sure to delight audiences with his ability to disappear at will, and the Disney sets and production values are as fine as ever, but the film lacks the emotional complexity and classic status of previous Disney films. This was in 1977, however, and in less then a decade Disney Studios and its offshoot, Touchstone Pictures, would be among the most successful in Hollywood. A half-hour was trimmed off the running time for a 1984 re-release of PETE'S DRAGON.

p, Ron Miller, Jerome Courtland; d, Don Chaffey; w, Malcolm Marmorstein (based on a story by Seton I. Miller and S.S. Field); ph, Frank Phillips (Technicolor); m, Irwin Kostal.

Fantasy Cas. (MPAA:G)

PHANTOM TOLLBOOTH, THE

(1970) 90m MGM c

Butch Patrick *(Milo)*, Voices of: Mel Blanc, Daws Butler, Candy Candido, Hans Conried, June Foray, Patti Gilbert, Shep Menken, Cliff Norton, Larry Thor, Les Tremayne.

This fine adaptation of the children's book by Norton Juster was Chuck Jones' and MGM's first animated feature. Butch Patrick stars (in the live-action sequences) as Milo, a bored youngster who cannot maintain an interest in anything. One day the "phantom tollbooth" appears in his bedroom and Milo drives his toy car into it. He is then transported through the magic of animation into a strange and wonderful world broken up into two camps, letters and numbers. Unfortunately letters and numbers are at war with each other (each thinking they are more important to society) and Milo soon finds himself caught in the middle. Aided by a dog called Tock, Milo strives mightily to restore the land to peace, in a charming film that combines some fairly sophisticated ideas (demons from the "Mountains of Ignorance" cause much of the trouble, and Milo tries to restore "Rhyme and Reason" to the land) with cute and likable characters that are sure to grab a child's attention.

p, Chuck Jones, Abe Levitow, Les Goldman; d, Chuck Jones, Abe Levitow, David Monahan; w, Chuck Jones, Sam Rosen (based on the book by Norton Juster); ph, Lester Shorr (Metrocolor); m, Dean Elliott.

Animation/Fantasy Cas. (MPAA:G)

PHAR LAP

(1984, Aus.) 108m FOX c (AKA:PHAR LAP—HEART OF A NATION)

Tom Burlinson *(Tommy Woodcock)*, Ron Leibman *(Dave Davis)*, Martin Vaughan *(Harry Telford)*, Judy Morris *(Bea Davis)*, Celia De Burgh *(Vi Telford)*, Richard Morgan *("Cashy" Martin)*, Robert Grubb *(William Neilsen)*, Georgia Carr *(Emma)*, James Steele *(Jim Pike)*, Vincent Ball *(Lachlan McKinnon)*, Peter Whitford *(Bert Wolfe)*, John Stanton *(Eric Connolly)*, Roger Newcombe *(James Crofton)*, Len Kaserman *(Baron Long)*, Tom Woodcock *(Trainer)*, Steven Bannister, Richard Terrill, Warwick Moss, Henry Duvall, Pat Thompson, Redmond Phillips, Maggie Miller, Anthony Hawkins, Brian Anderson, Paul Riley, Brian Adams, Alan Wilson.

Another story of a boy and his horse, this time a factual one set in Australia in the early 1930s. The film opens as the horse lies dying in a Mexican stable after winning the biggest race of its career, the Agua Caliente, in April 1932. The cause of Phar Lap's death goes unexplained, as it has to this day, although blame is clearly directed toward the gamblers who consistently lost money as the horse won race after race. From this point the narrative moves backward, showing how the young horse was purchased in New Zealand by Harry Telford (Martin Vaughan), a trainer whose experienced eye spots potential in the animal despite its lack of pedigree. His partner in the purchase is Dave Davis (Ron Leibman), a fast-talking American Jew who suffers greatly at the hands of anti-Semites in Australia as his horse triumphs over their horses. The horse is extremely skittish, though, and loses its first four races, even as Telford tries ever more brutal methods of snapping it into line. Finally Tommy Woodcock (Tom Burlinson), a stable boy, establishes a bond with the horse through kindness, and from that time on it wins every race. Phar Lap today is remembered in Australia in the same way as Man O' War in the US or Red Rum in Britain—as the greatest horse of its day, and a symbol of national pride. While the film plays a little too heavily on this patriotic theme, its simple boy-and-his-horse story is beautifully effective.

p, John Sexton; d, Simon Wincer; w, David Williamson (based on the book *The Phar Lap Story* by Michael Wilkinson); ph, Russell Boyd (Panavision); m, Bruce Rowland.

Sports   **Cas.**   **(MPAA:PG)**

PICKWICK PAPERS, THE

(1952, Brit.) 109m REN/Mayer-Kingsley bw

James Hayter *(Samuel Pickwick)*, James Donald *(Mr. Winkle)*, Alexander Gauge *(Mr. Tupman)*, Lionel Murton *(Mr. Snodgrass)*, Nigel Patrick *(Mr. Jingle)*, Kathleen Harrison *(Rachael Wardle)*, Joyce Grenfell *(Mrs. Leo Hunter)*, Hermione Gingold *(Miss Tomkins)*, Donald Wolfit *(Sgt. Buzfuz)*, Hermione Baddeley *(Mrs. Bardell)*, Harry Fowler *(Sam Weller)*, Diane Hart *(Emily Wardle)*, Joan Heal *(Isabel Wardle)*, William Hartnell *(Irate Cabman)*, Athene Seyler *(Miss Witherfield)*, Sam Costa *(Job Trotter)*, George Robey *(Tony Weller)*, Gerald Campion *(Fat Boy)*, Walter Fitzgerald *(Mr. Wardle)*, Mary Merrall *(Grandma Wardle)*, Raymond Lovell *(Surgeon)*, Cecil Trouncer *(Mr. Justice Stareleigh)*, June Thorburn *(Arabella)*, D.A. Clarke-Smith *(Mr. Dodson)*, Alan Wheatley *(Mr. Fogg)*, Felix Fenton *(Dr. Slammer)*, Max Adrian *(Aide)*, Barry MacKay *(Mr. Snubbins)*, Hattie Jacques *(Mrs. Nupkins)*, Noel Purcell *(Roker)*, Gibb McLaughlin *(Foreman)*, Dandy Nichols, Helen Goss, Jack MacNaughton, Noel Willman, Helen Burls, May Hallatt, Raf de la Torre, David Hannaford, Jessie Evans, Linda Gray, Joan Benham, Pamela Deeming, John Vere, John Kelly, William Strange.

If ever a Dickens novel shouted to be filmed, it was *The Pickwick Papers,* and a jolly good job was done with this version. The Pickwick club is a group of middle-class, middle-aged men chaired by Samuel Pickwick (James Hayter). Their sole mission in life is to study English life, and to that end they set out on a series of episodic adventures more strictly humorous than found in other Dickens novels or film adaptations. They meet Mr. Jingle (Nigel Patrick), a very cavalier Casanova who gets them into several hassles—including a duel, a hilariously funny fancy dress breakfast, a breach of promise suit brought against Pickwick, and a sojourn in debtor's prison. In the end, Pickwick, who turns phrases mightily but doesn't have a farthing to his name, manages to make enough money to begin his life anew. It's a very funny film with some of England's best light comedians and comediennes.

p, Noel Langley, George Minter; d&w, Noel Langley (based on the novel by Charles Dickens); ph, Wilkie Cooper; m, Antony Hopkins.

Comedy   **Cas.**   **(MPAA:NR)**

PINOCCHIO

(1940) 88m Disney/RKO c

Voices of: Dickie Jones *(Pinocchio)*, Christian Rub *(Geppetto)*, Cliff Edwards *(Jiminy Cricket)*, Evelyn Venable *(The Blue Fairy)*, Walter Catlett *(J. Worthington Foulfellow)*, Frankie Darro *(Lampwick)*, Charles Judels *(Stromboli the Coachman)*, Don Brodie *(Barker)*.

This was Disney's second full-length animated feature and it remains one of his greatest classics, brilliantly (and, in some scenes, terrifyingly) created, with awesome detail and images so startling that generations of children have been enthralled by its gripping and unforgettable tale. PINOCCHIO is a technical masterpiece far exceeding most of what Disney did earlier or during the remainder of his life. The timeless story focuses on a wooden puppet that wants nothing more than to be a real boy, a wish echoed by his creator, Geppetto. One night, the Blue Fairy descends from the skies and promises to turn Pinocchio into a flesh-and-blood little boy if he swears to be brave and unselfish and to learn right from wrong. The Blue Fairy even assigns Pinocchio a conscience, in the form of Jiminy Cricket. This is, of course, the film that features what would become the Disney theme song, "When You Wish upon a Star," sung by the inimitable Cliff Edwards, the voice of Jiminy Cricket. Everything about this film is wonderful, with imaginative scene after imaginative scene amazing any and all viewers, regardless of age.

p, Walt Disney; d, Ben Sharpsteen, Hamilton Luske; w, Ted Sears, Otto Englander, Webb Smith, William Cottrell, Joseph Sabo, Erdman Penner, Aurelius Battaglia (based on the story by Collodi [Carlo Lorenzini]); m, Paul J. Smith.

Animation   Cas.   (MPAA:NR)

PINOCCHIO AND THE EMPEROR OF THE NIGHT

(1987) 88m Filmation/NW c

Voices of: Edward Asner (Scalawag), Tom Bosley (Geppetto), Lana Beeson (Twinkle), James Earl Jones (Emperor of the Night), Rickie Lee Jones (Fairy Godmother), Don Knotts (Gee Willikers), Scott Grimes (Pinocchio), Linda Gary (Beeatrice), Jonathan Harris (Lt. Grumblebee), William Windom (Puppetino), Frank Welker (Igor).

Although this animated feature has some impressive sequences, coupled with an extremely varied voice cast, it duplicates much from Disney's 1940 PINOCCHIO. The film opens as a mysterious carnival, which travels by ship, settles down in a quiet meadow, disturbing the tranquility of an insect named Grumblebee. From this ominous beginning, we switch to the idyllic life of Geppetto and his son, the former puppet and now living boy Pinocchio. It is Pinocchio's birthday and to celebrate, his old pal the Blue Fairy shows up to sing a song. She tells Pinocchio that the greatest gift of all is free will, thus setting up the possibility that this could turn into a philosophical kiddie picture. Instead, Pinocchio pesters Geppetto until the kindly old woodcarver allows his son to deliver an important jewel box to the mayor. To Pinocchio's surprise, his toy glowbug, dubbed "Gee Willikers," comes to life thanks to the Blue Fairy's magic and beseeches Pinocchio not to get sidetracked from his mission. There wouldn't be much of a story if Pinocchio didn't get into trouble, though, so the lad hooks up with Scalawag, a shyster raccoon with a monkey assistant, Igor, and gets into a load of trouble. Artistically inferior to Disney, but fun for the kids.

p, Lou Scheimer; d, Hal Sutherland; w, Robby London, Barry O'Brien, Dennis O'Flaherty (based on a story by Dennis O'Flaherty, from The Adventures of Pinocchio by Collodi [Carlo Lorenzini]); ph, Ervin L. Kaplan (CFI Color); m, Anthony Marinelli, Brian Banks.

Animation   (MPAA:G)

PLAYTIME

(1973, Fr.) 108m Specta/Continental c

Jacques Tati (Mons. Hulot), Barbara Dennek (Young Tourist), Jacqueline Lecomte (Her Friend), Valerie Camille (Mons. Luce's Secretary), France Romilly (Woman Selling Eyeglasses), France Delahalle (Shopper in Department Store), Laure Paillette, Colette Proust (Two Women at the Lamp), Erika Dentzler (Mme. Giffard), Yvette Ducreux (Hat Check Girl), Rita Maiden (Mr. Schultz's Companion), Nicole Ray (Singer), Jack Gauthier (The Guide), Henri Piccoli (An Important Gentleman), Leon Doyen (Doorman), Billy Kearns (Mons. Schultz), Francois Viaur, Reinhart Kolldehoff, Michel Francini.

French director-comedian Jacques Tati's fourth feature was 10 years in the making and he risked everything on it, going so far as to sell off rights to his previous films in order to raise the money for the immense modernistic set used in this picture. As in other Tati movies, there is no plot to speak of but a series of incidents that Tati gets into and out of with no comment, just boundless energy and incurable optimism. Tati is again Mons. Hulot, the gangly, pipe-smoking innocent who wanders about, wreaks havoc, and goes on. The film is a satire of the glass-and-steel world that was coming into being in the 1960s in which Tati plays complex, carefully calculated games with sound and composition that appear onscreen as pure and simple sight gags, appealing to everyone. People bump into glass doors and get lost in a maze of corridors, a herd of American tourists descends on Paris with predictable comic antics, and a nightclub is inadvertently destroyed by the careless Hulot in this plotless and completely unpredictable film. A few lines in English, written by Washington columnist-humorist Art Buchwald, are the only verbal gags in an almost totally visual movie. For the uninitiated, Tati's films are not "laugh-riots" in which the humor hits you over the head, but slowly paced films of comic subtlety. You will discover, however, that the longer you watch a Tati film the more you will find yourself laughing uncontrollably at even the smallest things.

p, Rene Silvera; d, Jacques Tati; w, Jacques Tati, Jacques Lagrange, Art Buchwald; ph, Jean Badal, Andreas Winding (Eastmancolor); m, Francis Lemarque, James Campbell.

Comedy   Cas.   (MPAA:NR)

POCKETFUL OF MIRACLES

(1961) 136m Franton/UA c

Glenn Ford (Dave "the Dude" Conway), Bette Davis (Apple Annie, "Mrs. E. Worthington Manville"), Hope Lange (Elizabeth "Queenie" Martin), Arthur O'Connell (Count Alfonso Romero), Peter Falk (Joy Boy), Thomas Mitchell (Judge Henry G. Blake), Edward Everett Horton (Hutchins, the Butler), Mickey Shaughnessy (Junior), David Brian (Governor), Sheldon Leonard (Steve Darcey), Peter Mann (Carlos Romero), Ann-Margret (Louise), Barton MacLane (Police Commissioner), John Litel (Police Inspector McCrary), Jerome Cowan (Mayor), Jay Novello (Cortega, the Spanish Consul), Frank Ferguson, Willis Bouchey (Editors), Fritz Feld (Pierre), Ellen Corby (Soho Sal), Gavin Gordon (Mr. Cole, the Hotel Manager), Benny Rubin (Flyaway), Jack Elam (Cheesecake), Mike Mazurki (Big Mike), Hayden Rorke (Capt. Moore), Doodles Weaver sitto *(Angie)*, Edgar Stehli *(Gloomy)*, George E. Stone *(Shimley)*, William F. Sauls *(Smiley)*, Tom Fadden *(Herbie)*, Snub Pollard *(Knuckles)*, Byron Foulger *(Lloyd, the Assistant Hotel Manager)*, Betty Bronson *(The Mayor's Wife)*, Romo Vincent *(Kidnaped Reporter)*.

This was Frank Capra's swan song as a producer-director, and although it was not well received upon initial release, it's still a good movie with some outstanding performances. New York gangster Dave "the Dude" Conway (Glenn Ford) is a superstitious type who believes he can't come to any harm as long as he continues to buy his daily apple from Apple Annie (Bette Davis), a drunken fruit vendor. In essence, Dave's belief is that "an apple a day keeps the Mafia away," and although his bodyguard, Joy Boy (Peter Falk), and chauffeur, Junior (Mickey Shaughnessy), think it's a lot of hooey, his girl friend (Hope Lange) goes along with whatever Dave wants. When Apple Annie isn't at her usual street corner one morning, Dave goes looking for her. He finds her in deep depression because her daughter, Louise (Ann-Margret, in her first role), who thinks her mother is a wealthy matron, is coming to pay a visit. With Dave's help, Apple Annie is able to pull off her charade as "Mrs. E. Worthington Manville," even receiving help from the mayor, the governor, and a horde of real socialites. A remake of Capra's 1933 picture LADY FOR A DAY.

p&d, Frank Capra; w, Hal Kanter, Harry Tugend, Jimmy Cannon (based on the story "Madame La Gimp" by Damon Runyon and the screenplay LADY FOR A DAY by Robert Riskin); ph, Robert Bronner (Panavision, Technicolor); m, Walter Scharf, Petr Ilyich Tchaikovsky.

Comedy/Crime   **Cas.**   **(MPAA:NR)**

POLLYANNA

(1960) 134m BV c

Hayley Mills *(Pollyanna)*, Jane Wyman *(Aunt Polly Harrington)*, Richard Egan *(Dr. Edmund Chilton)*, Karl Malden *(Rev. Paul Ford)*, Nancy Olson *(Nancy Furman)*, Adolphe Menjou *(Mr. Pendergast)*, Donald Crisp *(Mayor Karl Warren)*, Agnes Moorehead *(Mrs. Snow)*, Kevin Corcoran *(Jimmy Bean)*, James Drury *(George Dodds)*, Reta Shaw *(Tillie Lagerlof)*, Leora Dana *(Mrs. Paul Ford)*, Anne Seymour *(Mrs. Amelia Tarbell)*, Edward Platt *(Ben Tarbell)*, Mary Grace Canfield *(Angelica)*, Jenny Egan *(Mildred Snow)*, Gage Clark *(Mr. Murg)*, Ian Wolfe *(Mr. Neely)*, Nolan Leary *(Mr. Thomas)*, Edgar Dearing *(Mr. Gorman)*, Harry Harvey *(Editor)*, William "Billy" Newell *(Mr. Hooper)*.

Ever since Mary Pickford filmed the silent version of this book in 1920, the name "Pollyanna" has become English vernacular meaning someone who is a die-hard optimist. This time Pollyanna (Hayley Mills) is an orphan who comes to live with her Aunt Polly (Jane Wyman), a wealthy woman in a small 1912 town. The village is filled with nay-sayers and depressing townsfolk, but Pollyanna soon changes matters by always managing to find something good in every situation, seeing the bright side of even the blackest occurrences. Although the towns-

people are initially reluctant to share in her optimism, they are eventually won over, even coming to Pollyanna's aid when she is temporarily paralyzed and can no longer find any good in life. Another fine Disney entry, this one earning Hayley Mills a special Oscar for Outstanding Juvenile Performance.

p, Walt Disney; d&w, David Swift (based on the novel by Eleanor H. Porter); ph, Russell Harlan (Technicolor); m, Paul Smith.

Comedy   **Cas.**   **(MPAA:NR)**

PRIDE OF ST. LOUIS, THE

(1952) 93m FOX bw

Dan Dailey *(Dizzy Dean)*, Joanne Dru *(Patricia Nash Dean)*, Richard Hylton *(Johnny Kendall)*, Richard Crenna *(Paul Dean)*, Hugh Sanders *(Horst)*, James Brown *(Moose)*, Leo T. Cleary *(Manager Ed Monroe)*, Kenny Williams *(Castleman)*, John McKee *(Delaney)*, Stuart Randall *(Frankie Frisch)*, William Frambes *(Herbie)*, Damian O'Flynn *(Johnnie Bishop)*, Cliff Clark *(Pittsburgh Coach)*, Fred Graham *(Alexander)*, Billy Nelson *(Chicago Manager)*, Pattee Chapman *(Ella)*, Richard Reeves *(Connelly)*, Bob Nichols *(Eddie)*, John Duncan *(Western Union Boy)*, Clyde Trumbull *(Mike)*, John Butler *(Waiter)*, Freeman Lusk *(Doctor)*, Jack Rice *(Voorhees)*, Al Green *(Joe)*, Phil Van Zandt *(Louis)*, Victor Sutherland *(Kendall, Sr.)*, Kathryn Carl *(Mrs. Martin)*, George MacDonald *(Roscoe)*, Joan Sudlow *(Miss Johnson)*, Frank Scannell *(Chicago 3rd Base Coach)*, Larry Thor, John Wald, Hank Weaver, William Forman, Jack Sherman, Tom Hanlon *(Announcers)*, Chet Huntley *(Tom Weaver)*, John Doucette *(Benny)*, Harris Brown *(Hotel Clerk)*.

Dizzy Dean was one of the most wonderful legends in the history of baseball, and this film captures the spirit and color of the great St. Louis hurler, thanks to a fine performance by Dan Dailey. The story starts with Dean's days as an Ozark hillbilly with a lightning delivery, then follows him as he struggles up from poverty and works his way to semipro ball, where he is discovered while playing for the Houston Buffaloes, more as a lark than a profession. He goes to work for the St. Louis Cardinals, pitching his heart out and, with his brother Paul (well played by Richard Crenna), leads his team to a World Series championship. A warm and humorous subplot showing Dizzy's courtship of his wife, Patricia (played expertly by Joanne Dru), adds depth and feeling to this good-natured story. Director Harmon Jones, who does a commendable job of mixing fact with a little fiction, does not fail to include the wonderful Dizzy Dean pranks, like the time he had his team sit down on the playing field while he struck out all three opposing hitters, much to his manager's consternation.

p, Jules Schermer; d, Harmon Jones; w, Herman J. Mankiewicz (based on a story by Guy Trosper); ph, Leo Tover; m, Arthur Lange.

Biography/Sports   **(MPAA:NR)**

PRIDE OF THE YANKEES, THE

(1942) 127m RKO bw

Gary Cooper *(Lou Gehrig)*, Teresa Wright *(Eleanor Gehrig)*, Walter Brennan *(Sam Blake)*, Dan Duryea *(Hank Hanneman)*, Babe Ruth *(Himself)*, Elsa Janssen *(Mom Gehrig)*, Ludwig Stossel *(Pop Gehrig)*, Virginia Gilmore *(Myra)*, Bill Dickey *(Himself)*, Ernie Adams *(Miller Huggins)*, Pierre Watkin *(Mr. Twitchell)*, Harry Harvey *(Joe McCarthy)*, Addison Richards *(Coach)*, Robert W. Meusel, Mark Koenig, Bill Stern *(Themselves)*, Hardie Albright *(Van Tuyl)*, Edward Fielding *(Clinic Doctor)*, George Lessey *(Mayor of New Rochelle)*, Vaughan Glaser *(Doctor in Gehrig Home)*, Douglas Croft *(Lou Gehrig as a Boy)*, Rip Russell *(Laddie)*, Frank Faylen *(3rd Base Coach)*, Jack Shea *(Hammond)*, George MacDonald *(Wally Pip)*, Gene Collins *(Billy)*, David Holt *(Billy, Age 17)*, David Manley *(Mayor Fiorello La Guardia)*, Max Willenz *(Colletti)*, Jimmy Valentine *(Sasha)*, Anita Bolster *(Sasha's Mother)*, Robert Winkler *(Murphy)*, Spencer Charters *(Mr. Larsen)*, Rosina Galli *(Mrs. Fabini)*, Billy Roy *(Joe Fabini)*, Sarah Padden *(Mrs. Robert)*, Janet Chapman *(Tessie)*, Eva Dennison *(Mrs. Worthington)*, Montague Shaw *(Mr. Worthington)*, Jack Stewart *(Ed Burrow)*, Fay Thomas *(Christy Mathewson)*, Lane Chandler *(Player in Locker Room)*.

Eloquently written, stunningly photographed, and directed with sensitivity and care, THE PRIDE OF THE YANKEES is the sweet, sentimental, and utterly American story of Lou Gehrig, the "Iron Man" first baseman for the indefatigable New York Yankees of the 1920s and 1930s. Gary Cooper is exceptional as Gehrig and Teresa Wright marvelous as his sweetheart (and later wife) Eleanor. Gehrig is first shown as a university student, playing baseball whenever possible. He refuses a contract with the Yankees, intending to become an engineer to please his mother (Elsa Janssen), who has slaved to pay his tuition. When she requires surgery, however, Gehrig signs with the team to pay for medical expenses, beginning his spectacular career in June 1925 and meeting his future wife during his first game. Soon Gehrig has helped the team make it to the World Series, becoming one of the best to ever play the game, until, in 1939, he learns that he has a lethal neurological disease (amyotrophic lateral sclerosis, since known as Lou Gehrig's disease), and has only a short time to live. He resigns from the team and makes a dramatic farewell at Yankee Stadium, standing at home plate and stating, "Some people say I've had a bad break, but I consider myself to be the luckiest man on the face of the earth." As the crowd gives him a deafening ovation, Gehrig walks from the field, into the dugout, and up a passageway, exiting into legend. THE PRIDE OF THE YANKEES is the story of a simple man with extraordinary talent and a soaring spirit that made him the idol of every American schoolboy. The film is star-studded with real-life baseball greats, including Babe Ruth.

p, Samuel Goldwyn; d, Sam Wood; w, Jo Swerling, Herman J. Mankiewicz (based on a story by Paul Gallico); ph, Rudolph Mate; m, Leigh Harline.

Biography/Romance/Sports   **Cas.**   **(MPAA:NR)**

PRINCE AND THE PAUPER, THE

(1937) 120m FN-WB bw

Errol Flynn *(Miles Hendon)*, Claude Rains *(Earl of Hertford)*, Henry Stephenson *(Duke of Norfolk)*, Barton MacLane *(John Canty)*, Billy Mauch *(Tom Canty)*, Bobby Mauch *(Prince Edward)*, Alan Hale *(Captain of the Guard)*, Eric Portman *(1st Lord)*, Montagu Love *(Henry VIII)*, Robert Warwick *(Lord Warwick)*, Halliwell Hobbes *(Archbishop)*, Lionel Pape, Leonard Willey *(Lords)*, Elspeth Dudgeon *(Grandmother Canty)*, Fritz Leiber *(Father Andrews)*, Murray Kinnell *(Hugo)*, Ivan F. Simpson *(Clemens)*, Lionel Braham *(Ruffler)*, Helen Valkis *(Jane Seymour)*, Phyllis Barry *(Barmaid)*, Rex Evans *(Rich Man)*, Lester Matthews *(St. John)*, Robert Adair, Harry Cording *(Guards)*, Mary Field *(Tom Canty's Mother)*, Noel Kennedy, Billy Maguire, Clifford Severn *(Urchins)*, Gwendolyn Jones *(Lady Elizabeth)*, Leyland Hodgson *(Watchman)*, Holmes Herbert, Ian MacLaren *(Doctors)*, Forrester Harvey *(Meaty Man)*, Sidney Bracey *(Man in Window)*, Ernie Stanton *(Guard)*, Tom Wilson *(One-Eyed Beggar)*, Lionel Belmore *(Innkeeper)*, Ian Wolfe *(Proprietor)*, Harry Beresford *(The Watch)*, St. Luke's Choristers.

This Mark Twain doppelganger tale of rags and royalty in 16th-century England is sumptuously produced and full of high drama and adventure, with Errol Flynn swashbuckling between the precocious Mauch twins—Billy and Bobby. The look-alikes decide that they will switch roles as a lark, one being Prince Edward (later King Edward VI), the other a beggar boy. Despite the beggar boy's outlandish behavior in his new station, the royal court and advisors accept him as the heir to the throne. The true Edward, however, is submerged in low-life London and, when he decides he's had enough of the game, asserts that he is the real prince. Miles Hendon (Flynn), a soldier of fortune, meets the real Edward and is amused by his claims to the throne, thinking him mad until he begins to believe the emphatic urchin just as the impostor is about to be crowned king. Enemies at court send an assassin (Alan Hale) after the boy, but he is prevented from carrying out his evil task by Miles, who saves the real king-to-be at the last moment.

p, Hal B. Wallis; d, William Keighley; w, Laird Doyle (based on the novel by Mark Twain and the play by Catherine Chishold Cushing); ph, Sol Polito; m, Erich Wolfgang Korngold.

Adventure   **Cas.**   **(MPAA:NR)**

PRINCESS BRIDE, THE

(1987) 98m Act III Communications/FOX c

Cary Elwes *(Westley)*, Mandy Patinkin *(Inigo Montoya)*, Chris Sarandon *(Prince Humperdinck)*, Christopher Guest *(Count Rugen)*, Wallace Shawn *(Vizzini)*, Andre the Giant *(Fezzik)*, Fred Savage *(The Grandson)*, Robin Wright *(Buttercup)*, Peter Falk *(The Grandfather)*, Peter Cook *(The Impressive Clergyman)*, Billy Crystal *(Miracle Max the Wizard)*, Carol Kane *(Valerie, the Wizard's Wife)*,

Mel Smith *(The Albino)*, Willoughby Gray *(The King)*, Malcolm Storry *(Yellin)*.

A hilarious mixture of Errol Flynn swashbuckler and Monty Python send-up, THE PRINCESS BRIDE works as love story, as adventure, and as satire. In the framing story, a sick 10-year-old (Fred Savage) is visited by his grandfather (Peter Falk), who reads him *The Princess Bride*, a "kissing" story set in a medieval make-believe land. In it, the beautiful Buttercup (Robin Wright) reluctantly becomes engaged to a prince (Chris Sarandon) when her true love, Westley (Cary Elwes), disappears. Soon, however, she is kidnaped by a crafty Sicilian (Wallace Shawn) and his hirelings, Spanish swordsman Inigo Montoya (Mandy Patinkin) and gargantuan Fezik (Andre the Giant). Buttercup is rescued by a mysterious man in black, who turns out to be Westley, but after surviving the Dreaded Fireswamp, they are apprehended by the prince. Buttercup agrees to marry the prince when he promises to free Westley, but the dashing lad is actually tortured to death—or is he? With the help of a wizened miraclemaker (Billy Crystal), Inigo and Fezik join forces with Westley to make sure this story ends very happily ever after. With tongues in cheeks and hearts on sleeves, director Rob Reiner and scripter William Goldman have created a dazzling adventure for younger viewers, while at the same time hilariously sending up the same genre. Goldman's screenplay, adapted from his own novel, which was in turn based on a children's book by "S. Morgenstern," made the rounds for 14 years before finally making it to the screen. The wait was worth it. When it comes to pleasing both kids and adults, you can't do much better than THE PRINCESS BRIDE.

p, Arnold Scheinman, Rob Reiner; d, Rob Reiner; w, William Goldman (based on his novel); ph, Adrian Biddle (Deluxe Color); m, Mark Knopfler.

Adventure/Comedy   **Cas.**   **(MPAA:PG)**

R

RASCAL

(1969) 85m Disney/BV c

Steve Forrest *(Willard North)*, Bill Mumy *(Sterling North)*, Pamela Toll *(Theo North)*, Elsa Lanchester *(Mrs. Satterfield)*, Henry Jones *(Garth Shadwick)*, Bettye Ackerman *(Miss Whalen)*, Jonathon Daly *(Rev. Thurman)*, John Fiedler *(Cy Jenkins)*, Richard Erdman *(Walter Dabbitt)*, Herbert Anderson *(Mr. Pringle)*, Robert Emhardt *(Constable Stacey)*, Steve Carlson *(Norman Bradshaw)*, Maudie Prickett *(Miss Pince-nez)*, Walter Pidgeon *(Voice of Sterling North)*.

RASCAL is the delightful autobiographical story of young Sterling North (Billy Mumy) and a pet raccoon, aptly named Rascal, that he saves from the jaws of a

lynx. The film is set in the summer of 1918 in northern Wisconsin, where Sterling lives with his widowed father. The father is often away on business, leaving Sterling and Rascal to entertain each other, and they manage to get into a fair amount of mischief. At the end of the summer the two must part company for good, but Sterling feels better about saying goodbye knowing that Rascal now has a female raccoon to watch over him. This very simple depiction of a past era manages to be warmhearted without wallowing in sentiment. The reassuring narration by Walter Pidgeon, as the voice of the adult Sterling North, helps guide viewers along.

p, James Algar; d, Norman Tokar; w, Harold Swanton (based on the novel *Rascal, Memoir of a Better Era* by Sterling North); ph, William Snyder; m, Buddy Baker.

Drama   **(MPAA:G)**

RESCUERS, THE

(1977) 76m Disney c

Voices of: Bob Newhart *(Bernard)*, Eva Gabor *(Miss Bianca)*, Geraldine Page *(Mme. Medusa)*, Joe Flynn *(Mr. Snoops)*, Jeanette Nolan *(Ellie Mae)*, Pat Buttram *(Luke)*, Jim Jordan *(Orville)*, John McIntire *(Rufus)*, Michelle Stacy *(Penny)*, Bernard Fox *(Chairman)*, Larry Clemmons *(Gramps)*, James MacDonald *(Evinrude)*, George Lindsey *(Rabbit)*, Bill McMillan *(TV Announcer)*, Dub Taylor *(Digger)*, John Fiedler *(Owl)*.

Four years in the making, costing nearly $8 million, THE RESCUERS is a beautifully animated film that showed the Disney studio still knew a lot about making quality children's fare even as their track record was weakening. The story concerns two mice, Bernard and Miss Bianca (their voices provided by Bob Newhart and Eva Gabor), who set out to rescue a girl named Penny (Michelle Stacy) from the evil Mme. Medusa (Geraldine Page). The girl is held captive in a swamp, which offers the setting for some genuinely frightening action. Comic relief is provided by a bird named Orville, who transports the mice as they search for the girl. The voices are all well suited to the characters, and the film is a delight for children, as well as for adults who appreciate good animation and brisk storytelling.

p, Wolfgang Reitherman; d, Wolfgang Reitherman, John Lounsbery, Art Stevens; w, Ken Anderson, Vance Gerry, Larry Clemmons, David Michener, Burny Mattinson, Frank Thomas, Fred Lucky, Ted Berman, Dick Sebast (based on the stories "The Rescuers" and "Miss Bianca" by Margery Sharp); ph, (Technicolor); m, Artie Butler.

Animation   **(MPAA:G)**

RETURN OF THE JEDI

(1983) 133m Lucasfilm/FOX c

Mark Hamill *(Luke Skywalker)*, Harrison Ford *(Han Solo)*, Carrie Fisher *(Princess Leia)*, Billy Dee Williams *(Lando Calrissian)*, Anthony Daniels *(See Threepio [C-3PO])*, Peter Mayhew *(Chewbacca)*, Sebastian Shaw *(Anakin*

Skywalker), Ian McDiarmid (Emperor Palpatine), Frank Oz (Yoda), David Prowse (Darth Vader), James Earl Jones (Voice of Darth Vader), Alec Guinness (Ben "Obi-Wan" Kenobi), Kenny Baker (Artoo-Detoo [R2-D2]/Paploo), Michael Pennington (Moff Jerjerrod), Kenneth Colley (Adm. Piett), Michael Carter (Bib Fortuna), Denis Lawson (Wedge), Tim Rose (Adm. Ackbar), Dermot Crowley (Gen. Madine), Caroline Blakiston (Mon Mothma), Warwick Davis (Wicket), Jeremy Bulloch (Boba Fett), Femi Taylor (Oola), Annie Arbogast (Sy Snootles), Claire Davenport (Fat Dancer), Jack Purvis (Teebo), Mike Edmonds (Logray), Jane Busby (Chief Chirpa), Malcom Dixon, Mike Cottrell (Ewok Warriors), Nicki Reade (Nicki), Adam Bareham (1st Stardestroyer Controller), Jonathan Oliver (2nd Stardestroyer Controller), Pip Miller (1st Stardestroyer Captain), Tom Mannion (2nd Stardestroyer Captain).

This final segment of the trilogy that began with STAR WARS and THE EMPIRE STRIKES BACK is the most spectacular of the trio in terms of the special effects mastery of George Lucas and his cohorts at the Industrial Light and Magic Company. Darth Vader (acted by David Prowse, with a breathy voice by James Earl Jones) is up to no good again. He's building a new Death Star vehicle that cannot be destroyed. Han Solo (Harrison Ford) has been placed in carbonite by the heinous Jabba, a toad with elephantiasis, a combination of a space Godfather and something you'd dissect in biology class. Luke Skywalker (Mark Hamill) has sent pals C-3PO (Anthony Daniels) and R2-D2 (Kenny Baker) to rescue Solo. Princess Leia (Carrie Fisher) arrives, masquerading as a bounty hunter, bringing Chewbacca (Peter Mayhew) along. Since Lando Calrissian (Billy Dee Williams) has been disguised as a palace guard, Solo has a chance to escape and the fight between good and evil rages. There is also the adorable Yoda (Frank Oz) and a collection of cuddly critters called Ewoks. The sensational effects include floating barges, amazing creatures, airborne cycles, death-ray machines, light-swords, and more and more. The space battles are overwhelming photographically and every technical credit is first rate, although dialog and characterization are minimal. The film won the 1983 Oscar for Special Visual Effects.

p, Howard Kazanjian, Robert Watts, Jim Bloom; d, Richard Marquand; w, Lawrence Kasdan, George Lucas (based on a story by George Lucas); ph, Alan Hume, Jack Lowin, Jim Glennon (Panavision, Rank Color); m, John Williams.

Science Fiction   **Cas.**   **(MPAA:PG)**

RIDE 'EM COWBOY

(1942) 86m UNIV bw

Bud Abbott (Duke), Lou Costello (Willoughby), Anne Gwynne (Anne Shaw), Samuel S. Hinds (Sam Shaw), Dick Foran (Robert "Bronco Bob" Mitchell), Richard Lane (Peter Conway), Judd McMichael (Tom), Ted McMichael (Dick), Joe McMichael (Harry), Mary Lou Cook (Dotty Davis), Johnny Mack Brown (Alabam), Ella Fitzgerald (Ruby), Douglas Dumbrille (Jake Rainwater), Jody Gilbert (Moonbeam), Morris Ankrum (Ace Anderson), Charles Lane (Martin Manning), Russell Hicks, Tom Hanlon (Announcers), Wade Boteler (Rodeo Manager), James Flavin (Railroad Detective), Boyd Davis (Doctor), Eddie Dunn (2nd Detective), Isabel Randolph (Lady), James Seay (Ranger Captain), Harold Daniels (Reporter), Ralph Peters (1st Henchman), Linda Brent (Sunbeam), Lee Sunrise (2nd Indian Girl), Chief Yowlachie (Chief Tomahawk), Harry Monty (Midget), Sherman E. Sanders (Square Dance Caller), Carmela Cansino (1st Indian Girl), The Hi-Hatters, The Buckaroos Band, The Ranger Chorus of Forty, The Congoroos.

Abbott and Costello play two peanut and hot dog vendors who end up as cowhands on a dude ranch for some typical comedic fare, with the pair going through their usual antics. What separates RIDE 'EM, COWBOY from their other films is the unusual quality of the musical talent. Ella Fitzgerald, of all people, is a featured singer, doing some marvelous numbers, including a rousing version of "A Tisket, a Tasket." If you look closely, you'll also see Dorothy Dandridge doing the jitterbug as one of the Congoroos. In one of the film's most riotous scenes, the boys, dressed in loud checkered shirts, play cards with some western toughs, making a mockery of the game and getting themselves in a heap of trouble with almost no effort at all.

p, Alex Gottlieb; d, Arthur Lubin; w, True Boardman, John Grant, Harold Shumate (based on a story by Edmund L. Hartmann); ph, John W. Boyle.

Comedy/Musical   **(MPAA:NR)**

ROAD TO MOROCCO

(1942) 83m PAR bw

Bing Crosby (Jeff Peters), Bob Hope (Turkey Jackson), Dorothy Lamour (Princess Shalmar), Anthony Quinn (Mullay Kasim), Dona Drake (Mihirmah), Mikhail Rasumny (Ahmed Fey), Vladimir Sokoloff (Hyder Khan), George Givot (Neb Jolla), Andrew Tombes (Oso Bucco), Leon Belasco (Yusef), Monte Blue, Jamiel Hanson (Aides to Mullay Kasim), Louise La Planche, Theo de Voe, Brooke Evans, Suzanne Ridgeway, Yvonne De Carlo, Patsy Mace, Poppy Wilde (Handmaidens), George Lloyd, Sammy Stein (Guards), Ralph Penney (Arabian Waiter), Dan Seymour (Arabian Buyer), Pete G. Katchenaro (Philippine Announcer), Brandon Hurst (English Announcer), Richard Loo (Chinese Announcer), Leo Mostovoy (Russian Announcer), Vic Groves, Joe Jewett (Knife Dancers), Michael Mark (Arab Pottery Vendor), Nestor Paiva (Arab Sausage Vendor), Stanley Price (Idiot), Rita Christiana (Specialty Dancer), Robert Barron (Gigantic Bearded Arab), Cy Kendall (Fruit Stand Proprietor), Sara Berner (Voice for Female Camel), Kent Rogers (Voice for Male Camel), Edward Emerson (Bystander), Sylvia Opert (Dancer), Blue Washington (Nubian Slave), Harry Cording, Dick Botiller (Warriors).

The third, and best, in the "Road" series, ROAD TO MOROCCO has everything going for it. Bob Hope and Bing

Crosby were not yet tired of the formula, and their breezy acting wafts the picture along in a melange of gags, songs, thrills, and calculated absurdities. The duo had already sent up adventure movies in ROAD TO SINGAPORE and jungle films in ROAD TO ZANZIBAR—the next target was the Arabian Nights. Jeff Peters (Crosby) and Turkey Jackson (Hope) are the lone survivors of a Mediterranean shipwreck. They land on a beach, mount a passing camel, and go off toward Morocco, where they learn that things aren't swell. The area is parched, the people poor, and foreigners looked upon with scorn. The two are penniless and hungry when a local merchant offers Jeff money to sell Turkey into slavery as the personal plaything of Princess Shalmar (Dorothy Lamour). Jeff makes the deal, Turkey is forcibly removed to the palace, and life in Morocco gets increasingly difficult for everyone thereafter. The picture is filled with great gags and one-liners, including Hope's lament for the Oscar he might have won; the camel's complaint that "this is the screwiest picture I've ever been in!"; Hope's appearance in drag; and the backfire of the "patty cake" routine, after which it's remarked, "Hmmm. That gag sure got around." And there are countless more, delivered at a pace that never lets up.

p, Paul Jones; d, David Butler; w, Frank Butler, Don Hartman; ph, William Mellor.

Comedy/Musical (MPAA:NR)

ROAD TO RIO

(1947) 100m PAR bw

Bing Crosby (Scat Sweeney), Bob Hope (Hot Lips Barton), Dorothy Lamour (Lucia Maria De Andrade), Gale Sondergaard (Catherine Vail), Frank Faylen (Trigger), Joseph Vitale (Tony), Frank Puglia (Rodrigues), Nestor Paiva (Cardoso), Robert Barrat (Johnson), Jerry Colonna (Cavalry Captain), Wiere Brothers (Musicians), Andrews Sisters, Carioca Boys, Stone-Baron Puppeteers (Themselves), George Meeker (Sherman Malley), Stanley Andrews (Capt. Harmon), Harry Woods (Ship's Purser), Tor Johnson (Samson), Donald Kerr (Steward), Stanley Blystone (Assistant Purser), George Sorel (Prefeito), John "Skins" Miller (Dancer), Alan Bridge (Ship's Officer), Arthur Q. Bryan (Mr. Stanton), Babe London (Woman), Gino Corrado (Barber), George Chandler (Valet), Paul Newlan, George Lloyd (Butchers), Fred Zendar (Stevedore), Ralph Gomez, Duke York, Frank Hagney (Roustabouts), Ralph Dunn (Foreman), Pepito Perez (Dignified Gentleman), Ray Teal (Buck), Brandon Hurst (Barker), Barbara Pratt (Airline Hostess), Tad Van Brunt (Pilot), Patsy O'Bryne (Charwoman), Raul Roulien (Cavlary Officer), Charles Middleton (Farmer), Albert Ruiz, Laura Corbay (Specialty Dancers).

The fifth "Road" picture was a more standard comedy than most of the others and paid off at the box office, becoming the top-grossing film of the year. Gone were the talking animals and some of the zany humor of the earlier entries. In their place was a more conventional story, sans Hollywood in-jokes, in which Hot Lips Barton

(Bob Hope) and Scat Sweeney (Bing Crosby) are musicians who accidentally cause a fire at a carnival. To avoid being arrested for arson, they jump on an ocean liner headed for Rio and stow away. On the ship, they meet Lucia Maria De Andrade (Dorothy Lamour), who is friendly, then chilly, smiling, then frowning, so that the boys can't figure her out. Upon investigation, they discover she has been hypnotized by the evil Catherine Veil (Gale Sondergaard) and is to marry a man she doesn't love once they reach Rio. Of course, the pair decide they must interfere and prevent the marriage, going so far as to crash the wedding party dressed as a pirate (Crosby) and a Latin American bombshell (Hope in drag) in order to expose the hypnotist's deceit. Lots of laughs.

p, Daniel Dare; d, Norman Z. McLeod; w, Edmund Beloin, Jack Rose; ph, Ernest Laszlo.

Comedy/Musical (MPAA:NR)

ROAD TO UTOPIA

(1945) 90m PAR bw

Bing Crosby (Duke Johnson/Junior Hooton), Bob Hope (Chester Hooton), Dorothy Lamour (Sal Van Hoyden), Hillary Brooke (Kate), Douglas Dumbrille (Ace Larson), Jack LaRue (LeBec), Robert Barrat (Sperry), Nestor Paiva (McGurk), Robert Benchley (Narrator), Will Wright (Mr. Latimer), Jimmy Dundee (Ringleader of Henchmen), Jim Thorpe (Passenger), William Benedict (Newsboy), Art Foster (Husky Sailor), Arthur Loft (Purser), Stanley Andrews (Official at Boat), Alan Bridge (Boat Captain), Lee Shumway, Al Ferguson (Policemen), Romaine Callender (Top Hat), George Anderson (Townsman), Edgar Dearing, Charles C. Wilson (Official Cops), Brandon Hurst, Don Gallaher, Bud Harrison (Men at Zambini's), Edward Emerson (Master of Ceremonies), Ronnie Rondell (Hotel Manager), Allen Pomeroy, Jack Stoney (Henchmen), Frank Moran, Bobby Barber, Pat West (Bartenders), Larry Daniels (Ring-leader), Ferdinand Munier (Santa Claus), Ethan Laidlaw (Saloon Extra), Jimmy Lono (Eskimo), Charles Gemora (Bear), Paul Newlan (Tough Ship's Purser), Claire James, Maxine Fife (Girls), Jack Rutherford (1st Man), Al Hill (2nd Man), George McKay (Waiter).

This addition to the "Road" series is told in flashback, as a wealthy couple, Chester Hooton (Bob Hope) and Sal Van Hoyden (Dorothy Lamour), recall how they got rich. They'd gained control of a Klondike gold mine but lost their best friend, Duke Johnson (Bing Crosby), in the process. While they reminisce, he suddenly pops in, very much alive. The three begin to talk about the old days, and the film goes back in time to show Chester and Duke as a couple of failed vaudevillians who try to make a shady deal in San Francisco and then must flee the city. They board a northbound ship and purloin the deed to a gold mine in Alaska from a pair of vicious murderers. Considering this theft and the fact that they are running from the cops, the vaudevillians pretend to be the tough guys they just scammed. But, in keeping with tradition, the duo get in deep trouble and find themselves vying for the affections of Sal before the final credits roll. Lots of excellent gags punctuate the story, including one in which Hope and Crosby are in the boiler room of the steamer when a formally dressed gentleman walks in looking for a match. Hope and Crosby want to know if he's supposed to be in the movie, and the man replies with a shrug, "Nope, I'm taking a shortcut to stage 10." Once again, animals talk, sight gags abound, and the complementing temperaments of Hope and Crosby are mined to great advantage.

p, Paul Jones; d, Hal Walker; w, Norman Panama, Melvin Frank; ph, Lionel Lindon; m, Leigh Harline.

Comedy/Musical **(MPAA:NR)**

ROAD TO ZANZIBAR

(1941) 92m PAR bw

Bing Crosby *(Chuck Reardon)*, Bob Hope *(Fearless [Hubert] Frazier)*, Dorothy Lamour *(Donna Latour)*, Una Merkel *(Julia Quimby)*, Eric Blore *(Charles Kimble)*, Iris Adrian *(French Soubrette in Cafe)*, Lionel Royce *(Mons. Lebec)*, Buck Woods *(Thonga)*, Leigh Whipper *(Scarface)*, Ernest Whitman *(Whiteface)*, Noble Johnson *(Chief)*, Leo Gorcey *(Boy)*, Joan Marsh *(Dimples)*, Luis Alberni *(Proprietor of Native Booth)*, Robert Middlemass *(Police Inspector)*, Norma Varden *(Clara Kimble)*, Paul Porcasi *(Turk at Slave Mart)*, Ethel Loreen Greer *(Fat Lady)*, Georges Renavent *(Saunders)*, Jules Strongbow *(Solomon)*, Priscilla White, LaVerne Vess *(Curzon Sisters)*, Harry C. Johnson, Harry C. Johnson Jr. *(Acrobats)*, Alan Bridge *(Policeman)*, Henry Roquemore *(Cafe Proprietor)*, James B. Carson *(Waiter)*, Eddy Conrad *(Barber)*, Charlie Gemora *(Aqua the Gorilla)*, Ken Carpenter *(Commentator)*, Richard Keene *(Clerk)*, Douglas Dumbrille *(Slave Trader)*.

Tarzan movies had been around for years when ROAD TO ZANZIBAR, the second of the "Road" pictures, took the opportunity to satirize every jungle picture lensed up to that time. The script was funny, although much of the humor reportedly derived from on-set improvisations. Connivers Fearless Frazier (Bob Hope) and Chuck Reardon (Bing Crosby) must blow town because they sold a bogus diamond mine to Mons. Lebec (Lionel Royce), a criminal type who doesn't take well to being fleeced. Rather than face Lebec, Chuck and Hubert (as Fearless is known) light out for Zanzibar, where they meet a pair of Brooklynite entertainers, Donna Latour (Dorothy Lamour) and Julia Quimby (Una Merkel), who are in Africa to find Donna's brother. The girls convince Chuck and Hubert to put up the money for a safari into the interior, but the boys soon realize that they've been duped. It's not Donna's brother they're after, but a British millionaire she hopes to marry. Things only get worse after that, but that's as expected. The lyrics of "On the Road to Zanzibar" are banal compared to Sammy Cahn's words for "Road to Morocco," but it's a funny routine, with cannibals chanting a nonsense background.

p, Paul Jones; d, Victor Schertzinger; w, Frank Butler, Don Hartman (based on the story "Find Colonel Fawcett" by Don Hartman, Sy Bartlett); ph, Ted Tetzlaff; m, Victor Young.

Comedy/Musical **(MPAA:NR)**

ROBIN HOOD

(1973) 83m Disney-BV c

Voices of: Roger Miller *(Allan-A-Dale)*, Brian Bedford *(Robin Hood)*, Monica Evans *(Maid Marian)*, Phil Harris *(Little John)*, Andy Devine *(Friar Tuck)*, Carole Shelley *(Lady Kluck)*, Peter Ustinov *(Prince John)*, Terry-Thomas *(Sir Hiss)*, Pat Buttram *(Sheriff of Nottingham)*, George Lindsay *(Trigger)*, Ken Curtis *(Nutsy)*.

This enjoyable animated feature from the people at Disney retells the Robin Hood legend with animal characters. Robin Hood becomes a fox, Allan-A-Dale a rooster, Friar Tuck a badger, Little John a bear, and the Sheriff of Nottingham a wolf. Maid Marian remains a compatible fox for her loving hero. An inventive, well-animated, appropriately cast film.

p&d, Wolfgang Reitherman; w, Larry Clemmons (based on characters and a story by Ken Anderson); m, George Bruns.

Animation **Cas.** **(MPAA:G)**

ROOM FOR ONE MORE

(1952) 98m WB bw (AKA: THE EASY WAY)

Cary Grant *("Poppy" Rose)*, Betsy Drake *(Anna Rose)*, Lurene Tuttle *(Miss Kenyon)*, Randy Stuart *(Mrs. Foreman)*, John Ridgely *(Harry Foreman)*, Irving Bacon *(The Mayor)*, Mary Lou Treen *(Mrs. Roberts)*, Hayden Rorke *(The Doctor)*, Iris Mann *(Jane)*, George "Foghorn" Winslow *(Teensie)*, Clifford Tatum Jr. *(Jimmy-John)*, Gay Gordon *(Trot)*, Malcolm Cassell *(Tim)*, Larry Olsen *(Ben)*, Mary Newton, Ezelle Poule, Dorothy Kennedy, Marcorita Hellman, Karen Hale, Doris Kemper, Mary Alan Hokanson Felice Richmond *(Women)*, Ray Page *(Gas Station Attendent)*, Charles Meredith *(Mr. Thatcher)*, Oliver Blake *(Mr. Doran)*, Frank Ferguson *(Steve)*, Don Beddoe *(School Principal)*, Lilliam Bronson *(Teacher)*, William Bakewell *(Milkman)*, Douglas Fowley *(Ice Man)*, John McGovern *(Senior Patrol Leader)*, Gretchen Hartman *(Chairwoman)*, Tony Taylor *(Joey)*, Dabbs Greer *(Scoutmaster)*, Stevie Wooten *(Little Brother)*.

This warmhearted comedy stars Cary Grant and Betsy Drake as Poppy and Anna Rose, middle-class parents of three children. Anna's generosity crowds the house when she agrees to take in withdrawn 13-year-old Jane (Iris Mann) for two weeks. Poppy balks at the idea, but consents at Anna's insistence, and by the end of the two weeks, Jane has become a permanent member of the household. Anna then hears of Jimmy-John (Clifford Tatum, Jr.), an emotionally scarred, lame boy who has only received abuse from previous foster parents. Through love and sincerity, Anna gains Jimmy-John's trust and also wins over Poppy, whose resistance to the new additions is overcome. ROOM FOR ONE MORE is based on the experiences of an actual couple, Poppy and Anna Perrott Rose, whose good deeds were recorded in a book by Anna. The story's authenticity was enhanced by the real-life marriage of Grant and Drake and their resulting on-screen rapport. Grant found a part not only for Drake in the film, but also for George "Foghorn" Winslow. He saw Winslow on Art Linkletter's "People Are Funny" show and quickly signed the boy who, at the tender age of five, gained fame and the nickname "Foghorn" for his basso profundo voice. The film's fond and honest treatment of children won special mention from the Venice International Film Festival.

p, Henry Blanke; d, Norman Taurog; w, Jack Rose, Melville Shavelson (based on the book by Anna Perrott Rose); ph, Robert Burks; m, Max Steiner.

Comedy (MPAA:NR)

ROSEANNA McCOY

(1949) 100m RKO bw

Farley Granger *(Johnse Hatfield)*, Joan Evans *(Roseanna McCoy)*, Charles Bickford *(Devil Anse Hatfield)*, Raymond Massey *(Old Randall McCoy)*, Richard Basehart *(Mounts Hatfield)*, Gigi Perreau *(Allifair McCoy)*, Aline MacMahon *(Sarie McCoy)*, Marshall Thompson *(Tolbert McCoy)*, Lloyd Gough *(Phamer McCoy)*, Peter Miles *(Young Randall McCoy)*, Arthur Franz *(Thad Wilkins)*, Frank Ferguson *(Ellison Hatfield)*, Elisabeth Fraser *(Bess McCoy)*, Hope Emerson *(Levisa Hatfield)*, Dan White *(Abel Hatfield)*, Mabel Paige *(Grandma Sykes)*, Almira Sessions *(Cousin Zinny)*, William Mauch *(Cap Hatfield)*, Alan Bridge *(Medicine Seller)*, Sherman Saunders *(Dance Caller)*, Bert Goodrich *(Strong Man)*, Pat Flaherty *(Joe McCoy)*.

ROSEANNA McCOY departs from Hollywood convention to tell a love story set against a Blue Ridge Mountain backdrop without resorting to "Li'l Abner" hillbilly stereotypes. Taking liberties with the facts of the infamous Hatfield-McCoy feud, the story concentrates on a romance between two young members of the clans, Johnse Hatfield (Farley Granger) and Roseanna McCoy (Joan Evans), who meet at a country fair. She tries to put him out of her mind, but can't stop herself from falling in love, and one night Johnse comes to her house and carries her off. They end up back at the Hatfields' house, where the clan greets her with mixed reactions. Devil Anse (Charles Bickford), the Hatfield patriarch, sends Roseanna home in an attempt to keep peace between the two families, but the gesture fails and the two sides once again wage war. Meanwhile, the lovers are reunited and run off together. Their path takes them right through the gunfire, however, forcing both sides to cease warring, presumably for good. Although ROSEANNA McCOY did poorly at the box office, producer Sam Goldwyn seems to have been more concerned with rendering an honest sketch of mountain life than with profit. Great attention is paid to detail and atmosphere, giving a better sense of locale and history than was usual in Hollywood pictures.

p, Samuel Goldwyn; d, Irving Reis; w, John Collier (based on the novel by Alberta Hannum); ph, Lee Garmes; m, David Buttolph.

Romance (MPAA:NR)

S

SAND CASTLE, THE

(1961) 70m Noel/Louis de Rochemont

Barry Cardwell *(Boy)*, Laurie Cardwell *(Girl)*, George Dunham *(Artist)*, Alec Wilder *(Fisherman)*, Maybelle Nash *(Shade Lady)*, Erica Speyer *(Sun Lady)*, Charles Rydell *(Young Man)*, Allegra Ahern *(Young Girl)*, Lester Judson *(Fat Man)*, Martin Russ *(Frogman)*, Ghislain Dussart *(Priest)*, Mabel Mercer *(Voice of the Shell)*.

This highly imaginative exercise in filmmaking is set at the beach, where a brother and sister (Barry and Laurie Cardwell) wait while their mother goes shopping. The boy builds a sand castle, and his work attracts a horde of visitors ranging from a drunk to a bunch of softball-playing nuns. When it rains the children seek the shelter of a beach umbrella, and the boy, falling asleep, dreams of the people who visited his castle. (The visitors appear as paper cutouts that are stop-motion animated against a real model of the castle.) The dream is interrupted by his mother's call, the children head home, and the sand castle is washed away by the tide. Director Jerome Hill handles the material nicely, wisely underplaying the story. The live-action sequences are shot in black and white, with the dream portrayed in wonderful contrasting color. The well-animated cutouts were inspired by the paper cutout theater presented for children in the 19th century.

p,d&w, Jerome Hill; ph, Lloyd Ahern (Eastmancolor); m, Alec Wilder.

Fantasy (MPAA:NR)

SANDS OF IWO JIMA

(1949) 110m REP bw

John Wayne *(Sgt. John M. Stryker)*, John Agar *(Pfc Peter Conway)*, Adele Mara *(Allison Bromley)*, Forrest Tucker *(Pfc Al Thomas)*, Wally Cassell *(Pfc Benny Regazzi)*, James Brown *(Pfc Charlie Bass)*, Richard Webb *(Pfc Shipley)*, Arthur Franz *(Cpl. Robert Dunne/Narrator)*, Julie Bishop *(Mary)*, James Holden *(Pfc Soames)*, Peter Coe *(Pfc Hellenpolis)*, Richard Jaeckel *(Pfc Frank Flynn)*, Bill Murphy *(Pfc Eddie Flynn)*, George Tyne *(Pfc Harris)*, Hal Fieberling [Hal Baylor] *(Pvt. "Ski" Choynski)*, John McGuire *(Capt. Joyce)*, Martin Milner *(Pvt. Mike McHugh)*, Leonard Gumley *(Pvt. Sid Stein)*, William Self *(Pvt. L.D. Fowler, Jr.)*, Dick Wessel *(Grenade Instructor)*, I. Stanford Jolley *(Forrestal)*, David Clarke *(Wounded Marine)*, Gil Herman *(Lt. Baker)*, Dick Jones *(Scared Marine)*, Don Haggerty *(Colonel)*, Bruce Edwards *(Marine)*, Dorothy

Ford *(Tall Girl)*, John Whitney *(Lt. Thompson)*, Col. D.M. Shoup, USMC, Lt. Col. H.P. Crowe, USMC, Capt. Harold G. Schrier, USMC, Pfc Rene A. Gagnon, Pfc Ira H. Hayes, PM 3/C John H. Bradley.

Unlike many of John Wayne's WW II films, in which he single-handedly destroys whole Japanese battalions, SANDS OF IWO JIMA presents him as a believable, vulnerable human being. As Sgt. John M. Stryker, a battle-toughened Marine, he prepares a group of recruits for combat, driving them hard, not worried about making friends. Nonetheless, he is hurt when Pfc Peter Conway (John Agar) says he hopes his newborn son won't be anything like Stryker. Once in combat, on Tarawa, the men are furious when Stryker refuses to rescue a Marine who has been separated from the squad, because to do so would give away their position. After Tarawa, they go to Hawaii for some R & R, and there Stryker shows his heart of gold to a young mother forced into prostitution. The Marines' biggest test comes on Iwo Jima. Stryker's men perform magnificently as they inch their way up Mount Suribachi, but their leader is killed, and Conway, now his disciple, tries to fill Stryker's big shoes. This is one of Wayne's finest performances and it earned him an Oscar nomination. Directed with marvelous restraint by old hand Allan Dwan, SANDS OF IWO JIMA features appearances by three of the Marines who actually participated in the famous flag-raising on Mt. Suribachi—Ira Hayes, Rene Gagnon, and John Bradley.

p, Edmund Grainger; d, Allan Dwan; w, Harry Brown, James Edward Grant (based on a story by Harry Brown); ph, Reggie Lanning; m, Victor Young.

War   **Cas.**   **(MPAA:NR)**

SCHOOL FOR SCOUNDRELS

(1960, Brit.) 94m Guardsman/CD bw

Ian Carmichael *(Henry Palfrey)*, Terry-Thomas *(Raymond Delauney)*, Alastair Sim *(Stephen Potter)*, Janette Scott *(April Smith)*, Dennis Price *(Dunstan Dorchester)*, Peter Jones *(Dudley Dorchester)*, Edward Chapman *(Gloatbridge)*, John Le Mesurier *(Headwaiter)*, Irene Handl *(Mrs. Stringer)*, Kynaston Reeves *(General)*, Hattie Jacques *(1st Instructress)*, Hugh Paddick *(Instructor)*, Barbara Roscoe *(2nd Instructress)*, Gerald Campion *(Proudfoot)*, Monty Landis *(Fleetsnod)*, Jeremy Lloyd *(Dingle)*, Charles Lamb *(Carpenter)*, Anita Sharp-Bolster *(Maid)*.

Reminiscent of HOW TO SUCCEED IN BUSINESS WITHOUT REALLY TRYING, this nonstop British comedy, subtitled "How to Win Without Cheating," is a delicious satire of self-improvement strategies. Henry Palfrey (Ian Carmichael) is one of life's real losers. He'd like to win the heart of April Smith (Janette Scott), but she's already spoken for by boorishly successful Raymond Delauney (Terry-Thomas). Determined to change his fortunes, Henry enrolls in the College of Lifesmanship, run by Stephen Potter (Alistair Sim). After immersing himself in such courses as "womanship," "partymanship," and "oneupmanship," Henry returns to London to get the best of those who have taken advantage of him in the

past, most notably—and hilariously—Delauney. Not surprisingly, Henry also ends up with April. Based on the satirical how-to-get-ahead books written by the real Stephen Potter, SCHOOL FOR SCOUNDRELS features a terrific cast of comic actors who play the whole affair straight, netting laugh after laugh.

p, Hal E. Chester, Douglas Rankin, d, Robert Hamer; w, Hal E. Chester, Patricia Moyes, Peter Ustinov (based on the books *Theory and Practice Gamesmanship*, *Some Notes on Lifemanship* and *Oneupmanship* by Stephen Potter); ph, Edwin Hillier; m, John Addison.

Comedy   **(MPAA:NR)**

SCROOGE

(1935, Brit.) 72m Twickenham/PAR bw

Sir Seymour Hicks *(Ebenezer Scrooge)*, Donald Calthrop *(Bob Cratchit)*, Robert Cochran *(Fred)*, Mary Glynne *(Belle)*, Garry Marsh *(Belle's Husband)*, Oscar Asche *(Spirit of Christmas Present)*, Marie Ney *(Spirit of Christmas Past)*, C.V. France *(Spirit of Christmas Future)*, Athene Seyler *(Scrooge's Charwoman)*, Maurice Evans *(A Poor Man)*, Mary Lawson *(His Wife)*, Barbara Everest *(Mrs. Cratchit)*, Eve Grey *(Fred's Wife)*, Morris Harvey *(Poulterer)*, Philip Frost *(Tiny Tim)*, D.J. Williams *(Undertaker)*, Margaret Yarde *(Scrooge's Laundress)*, Hugh E. Wright *(Old Joe)*, Charles Carson *(Middlemark)*, Hubert Harben *(Worthington)*.

This well-executed adaptation of the classic Dickens tale remains brilliantly faithful to the original. The familiar story this time features Seymour Hicks as the greedy old man Ebenezer Scrooge, who has a change of heart on Christmas Eve when he looks into his lonely past and future. Hicks had played this role many times in the previous quarter-century, and by the time this was made in 1935, he had become Scrooge.

p, Julius Hagen, Hans [John] Brahm; d, Henry Edwards; w, Seymour Hicks, H. Fowler Mear (based on Charles Dickens' *A Christmas Carol*); ph, Sydney Blythe, William Luff.

Fantasy   **Cas.**   **(MPAA:NR)**

SCROOGE

(1970, Brit.) 118m Waterbury/NG c

Albert Finney *(Ebenezer Scrooge)*, Alec Guinness *(Jacob Marley's Ghost)*, Edith Evans *(Ghost of Christmas Past)*, Kenneth More *(Ghost of Christmas Present)*, Laurence Naismith *(Fezziwig)*, Michael Medwin *(Nephew)*, David Collings *(Bob Cratchit)*, Anton Rodgers *(Tom Jenkins)*, Suzanne Neve *(Isabel)*, Frances Cuka *(Mrs. Cratchit)*, Derek Francis, Roy Kinnear *(Portly Gentlemen)*, Mary Peach *(Nephew's Wife)*, Paddy Stone *(Ghost of Christmas Yet to Come)*, Kay Walsh *(Mrs. Fezziwig)*, Gordon Jackson *(Nephew's Friend)*, Richard Beaumont *(Tiny Tim)*, Geoffrey Bayldon *(Toy Shop Owner)*, Molly Weir, Helena Gloag *(Women Debtors)*, Reg Lever *(Punch and Judy*

Man), Keith Marsh *(Well Wisher)*, Marianne Stone *(Party Guest)*.

At the center of this musical adaptation of Charles Dickens' *A Christmas Carol* is Albert Finney, singing, dancing, and "Bah, humbug"-ing his way through the familiar title role. Guiding him on his journey to moral reawakening are Edith Evans as the Ghost of Christmas Past, Kenneth More as the Ghost of Christmas Present, and Paddy Stone as the Ghost of Christmas Yet to Come. Director Ronald Neame's well-paced film captures the period beautifully, and the acting is superb, with Finney and Alec Guinness, as Marley's ghost, real standouts. Richard Harris was originally slated to star, then was replaced by Rex Harrison, who also dropped out, and Finney stepped in just three weeks before shooting began. SCROOGE received Oscar nominations for Best Song ("Thank You Very Much"), Best Art Direction, Best Score, and Best Costumes. If you like your Dickens set to music, this (like OLIVER!) is just the ticket; if you prefer the story played a little straighter, see A CHRISTMAS CAROL (1938) or the 1935 version of SCROOGE.

p, Robert H. Solo; d, Ronald Neame; w, Leslie Bricusse (based on the novel *A Christmas Carol* by Charles Dickens); ph, Oswald Morris (Panavision, Technicolor); m, Leslie Bricusse.

Musical	**Cas.**	**(MPAA:G)**

SEA GYPSIES, THE

(1978) 101m WB c (GB: SHIPWRECK?)

Robert Logan *(Travis)*, Mikki Jamison-Olsen *(Kelly)*, Heather Rattray *(Courtney)*, Cjon Damitri Patterson *(Jesse)*, Shannon Saylor *(Samantha)*.

This satisfying family adventure was produced independently, with kids in mind. Ready to set sail for Jamaica, Travis (Robert Logan) and his two daughters anxiously await the arrival of a writer from the magazine that is partially financing the trip. When it turns out that the journalist is a beautiful woman, Travis is initially miffed, but eventually the two fall in love. Disaster strikes when the crew—including an orphaned boy who has stowed away—is shipwrecked off the coast of Alaska, with a variety of animals, including a killer whale, some Kodiak bears, and a pack of wolves, threatening their existence. Of course, rescue is imminent. Great fun for the young ones, with some excellent nature footage.

p, Joseph C. Rafill; d&w, Stewart Rafill; ph, Thomas McHugh (CFI Color); m, Fred Steiner.

Adventure	**Cas.**	**(MPAA:G)**

SECRET GARDEN, THE

(1949) 92m MGM bw-c

Margaret O'Brien *(Mary Lennox)*, Herbert Marshall *(Archibald Craven)*, Dean Stockwell *(Colin Craven)*, Gladys Cooper *(Mrs. Medlock)*, Elsa Lanchester *(Martha)*, Brian Roper *(Dickon)*, Reginald Owen *(Ben Weatherstaff)*, Aubrey Mather *(Dr. Griddlestone)*, George Zucco *(Dr. Fortescue)*, Lowell Gilmore *(British Officer)*, Billy Bevan *(Barney)*, Dennis Hoey *(Mr. Pitcher)*, Matthew Boulton *(Mr. Bromley)*, Isobel Elsom *(Governess)*, Norma Varden *(Nurse)*.

Twelve-year-old Margaret O'Brien stars in this strange, wonderful little film as an orphan sent to live in a spooky Victorian mansion with her grouchy uncle (Herbert Marshall). Uncle Archibald Craven has grown cold and uncaring ever since the death of his wife in the estate garden, and he refuses to allow anyone near the area. He also keeps his son, Colin (Dean Stockwell), a virtual prisoner upstairs, convinced that the paralysis of the boy's legs is incurable. The arrival of Mary Lennox (O'Brien), however, begins to change things. She finds the key to the locked garden and secretly tends to the long-dormant flower beds. Aided by a neighbor boy, she soon transforms the sickly brown garden into a lush, green hideaway, into which she and her pal sneak Colin for daily visits. Soon, the garden isn't alone in experiencing the life-giving magic of Mary's presence. Most of the film is in black and white, but the sequences in the revived garden are in Technicolor. This moving tale of the redemptive power of friendship is as touching for adults as it is for kids.

p, Clarence Brown; d, Fred M. Wilcox; w, Robert Ardrey (based on the novel by Frances Hodgson Burnett); ph, Ray June (Technicolor); m, Bronislau Kaper.

Drama		**(MPAA:NR)**

SECRET OF NIMH, THE

(1982) 82m MGM-UA c

Voices of: Derek Jacobi *(Nicodemus)*, Elizabeth Hartman *(Mrs. Brisby)*, Arthur Malet *(Mr. Ages)*, Dom DeLuise *(Jeremy)*, Hermione Baddeley *(Auntie Shrew)*, John Carradine *(Great Owl)*, Peter Strauss *(Justin)*, Paul Shenar *(Jennar)*, Tom Hattan *(Farmer Fitzgibbons)*, Shannen Doherty *(Teresa)*, Wil Wheaton *(Martin)*, Jodi Hicks *(Cynthia)*, Ian Fried *(Timmy)*, Lucille Bliss, Aldo Ray.

This superbly animated (but weakly scripted) tale was produced by Don Bluth, who left Disney Studios when he became dissatisfied with the quality of their animated films in the 1970s, taking a dozen of Disney's best animators with him. The result is a return to the lush, finely detailed animation seen in the best Disney features. This is the story of a mother mouse's desperate attempt move her family to a new location before they are killed by the farmer who is soon to plow his field. Although hindered by her son's illness, the mother mouse some help from some escaped laboratory rats with superior intelligence. Among the actors who lend their vocal talents to the proceedings are Dom DeLuise and the fine British stage actor Derek Jacobi.

p, Don Bluth, Gary Goldman, John Pomeroy; d, Don Bluth; w, Don Bluth, Gary Goldman, John Pomeroy, Will Finn (based on the novel *Mrs. Frisby and the Rats of*

N.I.M.H. by Robert C. O'Brien); ph, Joe Jiuliano, Charles Warren, Jeff Mellquist (Technicolor); m, Jerry Goldsmith.

Animation   **Cas.**   **(MPAA:G)**

SEE HERE, PRIVATE HARGROVE

(1944) 101m MGM bw

Robert Walker *(Pvt. Marion Hargrove)*, Donna Reed *(Carol Halliday)*, Robert Benchley *(Mr. Halliday)*, Keenan Wynn *(Pvt. Mulvehill)*, Bob Crosby *(Bob)*, Ray Collins *(Brody S. Griffith)*, Chill Wills *(Sgt. Cramp)*, Marta Linden *(Mrs. Halliday)*, Grant Mitchell *(Uncle George)*, George Offerman, Jr. *(Pvt. Orrin Esty)*, Edward Fielding *(Gen. Dillon)*, Donald Curtis *(Sgt. Heldon)*, William "Bill" Phillips *(Pvt. Bill Burk)*, Douglas Fowley *(Capt. Manville)*, Morris Ankrum *(Col. Forbes)*, Mickey Rentschler *(Sergeant)*, Frank Faylen *(MP)*, Jack Luden *(Doctor)*, Clarence Straight *(Capt. Hamilton)*, William "Billy" Newell *(Mr. Smith)*, Michael Owen *(Officer of Day)*, John Kelly *(Exercise Sergeant)*, Joe Devlin *(Mess Sergeant)*, Louis Mason *(Farmer)*, Connie Gilchrist *(Farmer's Wife)*, Harry Tyler *(Old Man)*, Mantan Moreland *(Porter)*, Mary McLeod *(Girl Clerk)*, Eddie Acuff *(Capt. Hammond)*, Ken Scott, Stephen Barclay *(Corporals)*, Dennis Moore, James Warren *(Executive Officers)*.

Robert Walker stars in this lively screen adaptation of Marion Hargrove's memoirs of life in boot camp. Walker plays Hargrove, a bumbling cub reporter who makes his editor crazy. When WW II breaks out, he finds himself in the Army, driving his commanders up the wall and doing a lot of KP duty. The goofy soldier sells a huckster (Keenan Wynn) a percentage of his future earnings as a writer to raise enough money to visit his girl friend (Donna Reed) in New York. This pleasant, well-cast wartime comedy originally had a fairly serious ending because the studio feared presenting a too flip view of WW II. Preview audiences disapproved of the mixture of seriousness and comedy, however, and the studio reconsidered. Since director Wesley Ruggles was engaged on a project in London, Tay Garnett was designated to direct a new upbeat, comic ending. The film's success resulted in a sequel the next year, WHAT NEXT, CORPORAL HARGROVE? Film director Blake Edwards (S.O.B., VICTOR/VICTORIA) can be seen in a bit role as a field operator.

p, George Haight; d, Wesley Ruggles, (uncredited) Tay Garnett; w, Harry Kurnitz (based on the book by Marion Hargrove); ph, Charles Lawton; m, David Snell.

Comedy   **(MPAA:NR)**

SERGEANT YORK

(1941) 134m WB bw

Gary Cooper *(Alvin C. York)*, Walter Brennan *(Pastor Rosier Pile)*, Joan Leslie *(Gracie Williams)*, George Tobias *(Michael T. "Pusher" Ross)*, Stanley Ridges *(Maj. Buxton)*, Margaret Wycherly *(Mother York)*, Ward Bond *(Ike Botkin)*, Noah Beery, Jr. *(Buck Lipscomb)*, June Lockhart *(Rose York)*, Dickie Moore *(George York)*, Clem Bevans *(Zeke)*, Howard Da Silva *(Lem)*, Charles Trowbridge *(Cordell Hull)*, Harvey Stephens *(Capt. Danforth)*, David Bruce *(Bert Thomas)*, Charles [Carl] Esmond *(German Major)*, Joseph Sawyer *(Sgt. Early)*, Pat Flaherty *(Sgt. Harry Parsons)*, Robert Porterfield *(Zeb Andrews)*, Erville Alderson *(Nate Tompkins)*, Joseph Girard *(Gen. Pershing)*, Frank Wilcox *(Sergeant)*, Donald Douglas *(Capt. Tillman)*, Lane Chandler *(Cpl. Savage)*, Frank Marlowe *(Beardsley)*, Jack Pennick *(Cpl. Cutting)*, James Anderson *(Eb)*, Guy Wilkerson *(Tom)*, Tully Marshall *(Uncle Lige)*, Lee "Lasses" White *(Luke the Target Keeper)*, Jane Isbell *(Gracie's Sister)*, Frank Orth *(Drummer)*, Arthur Aylesworth *(Bartender)*, Rita La Roy, Lucia Carroll, Kay Sutton *(Saloon Girls)*, Elisha Cook, Jr. *(Piano Player)*, William Haade *(Card Player)*, Jody Gilbert *(Fat Woman)*, Victor Kilian *(Andrews)*, Frank Faylen, Murray Alper *(Gunnery Spotters)*, Gaylord "Steve" Pendleton, Charles Drake *(Scorers)*, Theodore Von Eltz *(Prison Camp Commander)*.

Gary Cooper won his first Oscar for his brilliant portrayal of WW I hero Alvin C. York, who single-handedly captured 132 German soldiers during the Meuse-Argon offensive and became one of America's most decorated, most beloved heroes. Beginning in 1916, Howard Hawks' masterfully directed film follows the man from the hills of East Tennessee as he falls in love with Gracie Williams (Joan Leslie) and then struggles to hold onto his land. When lightning strikes his rifle, York decides that it's a sign from God and, becoming a pacifist, tries to avoid service in WW I. Eventually he does fight in France, and the rest is spectacular military history. Hawks brings the life of this incredible hero to the screen with forceful integrity, and Cooper is wonderful as the country fellow who gets religion and holds onto it, even through the nightmare of war. Technically, the film is faultless, with Hawks keeping his cameras fluid and employing Sol Polito's magnificent photographic skills at every turn. Jesse Lasky, who saw York in the 1919 Armistice Day Parade, spent years trying to convince the modest Tennessean to allow his story to be filmed, finally winning York's approval provided that the proceeds go to charity and that Gary Cooper play him. At first Cooper refused, but he changed his mind after visiting York. Warner Bros. had hoped to have Michael Curtiz direct, but Cooper wouldn't work with him, and when several others couldn't take the job, Hawks was hired, to the lasting pleasure of all who see this magnificent film.

p, Jesse L. Lasky, Hal B. Wallis; d, Howard Hawks; w, Abem Finkel, Harry Chandlee, Howard Koch, John Huston (based on *War Diary of Sergeant York* by Sam K. Cowan, *Sergeant York and His People* by Sam K. Cowan, and *Sergeant York—Last of the Long Hunters* by Tom Skeyhill); ph, Sol Polito, Arthur Edeson; m, Max Steiner.

Biography/War   **Cas.**   **(MPAA:NR)**

SEVEN BRIDES FOR SEVEN BROTHERS

(1954) 102m MGM c

Jane Powell *(Milly)*, Howard Keel *(Adam Pontabee)*, Jeff

Richards *(Benjamin Pontabee)*, Russ Tamblyn *(Gideon Pontabee)*, Tommy Rall *(Frank Pontabee)*, Howard Petrie *(Pete Perkins)*, Virginia Gibson *(Liza)*, Ian Wolfe *(Rev. Elcott)*, Marc Platt *(Daniel Pontabee)*, Matt Mattox *(Caleb Pontabee)*, Jacques d'Amboise *(Ephraim Pontabee)*, Julie Newmeyer [Julie Newmar] *(Dorcas)*, Nancy Kilgas *(Alice)*, Betty Carr *(Sarah)*, Ruta Kilmonis [Ruta Lee] *(Ruth)*, Norma Doggett *(Martha)*, Earl Barton *(Harry)*, Dante DiPaolo *(Matt)*, Kelly Brown *(Carl)*, Matt Moore *(Ruth's Uncle)*, Dick Rich *(Dorcas' Father)*, Marjorie Wood *(Mrs. Bixby)*, Russell Simpson *(Mr. Bixby)*, Anna Q. Nilsson *(Mrs. Elcott)*, Larry Blake *(Drunk)*, Phil Rich *(Prospector)*, Lois Hall *(Girl)*, Russ Saunders, Terry Wilson, George Robotham *(Swains)*, Walter Beaver *(Lem)*, Jarma Lewis *(Lem's Girl Friend)*, Sheila James *(Dorcas' Sister)*, I. Stanford Jolley, Tim Graham *(Fathers)*.

A magical blend of the right story, a great score, and the astonishing choreography of Michael Kidd, SEVEN BRIDES FOR SEVEN BROTHERS is one the big screen's most entertaining musicals. The action takes place in Oregon, where Adam (Howard Keel), the oldest of the Pontabee brothers, who live on a ranch high in the mountains, decides to find a bride. In town, he meets Milly (Jane Powell), a waitress, and woos, marries, and takes her back to the homestead, which is considerably less civilized than she'd expected. Soon Adam's brothers decide they, too, would like some female company, and, taking their inspiration from the story of the "Sobbin' Women" (Sabine women), they kidnap some local beauties, who have to winter at the ranch when an avalanche prevents the townspeople from rescuing them. Come spring, wedding bells ring for all. Based on Stephen Vincent Benet's "The Sobbin' Women," SEVEN BRIDES FOR SEVEN BROTHERS is a rollicking film with a breathless pace, well-defined characters, and incredible vitality under Stanley Donen's direction. Adolph Deutsch and Saul Chaplin's scoring won an Oscar, and the film was also nominated for Best Picture, Best Cinematography, and Best Script. Seldom have 104 minutes been packed with more effervescence.

p, Jack Cummings; d, Stanley Donen; w, Albert Hackett, Frances Goodrich, Dorothy Kingsley (based on the story "The Sobbin' Women" by Stephen Vincent Benet); ph, George Folsey (CinemaScope, Ansco Color).

Comedy/Musical   **Cas.**   **(MPAA:NR)**

SEVEN FACES OF DR. LAO

(1964) 100m Galaxy-Scarus/MGM c

Tony Randall *(Dr. Lao/Merlin the Magician/Pan/The Abominable Snowman/Medusa/The Giant Serpent/Apollonius of Tyana)*, Barbara Eden *(Angela Benedict)*, Arthur O'Connell *(Clint Stark)*, John Ericson *(Ed Cunningham)*, Noah Beery, Jr. *(Tim Mitchell)*, Lee Patrick *(Mrs. Howard T. Cassan)*, Minerva Urecal *(Kate Lindquist)*, John Qualen *(Luther Lindquist)*, Frank Kreig *(Peter Ramsey)*, Peggy Rea *(Mrs. Peter Ramsey)*, Eddie Little Sky *(George G. George)*, Royal Dano *(Carey)*, Argentina Brunetti *(Sarah Benedict)*, John Doucette *(Lucas)*, Dal McKennon *(Lean*

Cowboy)*, Frank Cady *(Mayor James Sargent)*, Chubby Johnson *(Fat Cowboy)*, Douglas Fowley *(Toothless Cowboy)*, Kevin Tate *(Mike Benedict)*.

Set in the Old West, this is a wonderful fantasy from puppeteer George Pal, whose futurist fancies have delighted many. When Dr. Lao (Tony Randall), an oriental magician, rides into Abalone with his strange circus, he finds the good citizens threatened by the land-grabbing activities of villainous Clint Stark (Arthur O'Connell). Calling upon his mysterious powers and the services of the bizarre characters who populate the strange circus (all played by Randall), Lao comes to the aid of the crusading young newspaper editor (John Ericson) who tries to prevent Stark's takeover of the town. In the film's most fantastic sequence, Lao's pet fish becomes a seven-headed monster to chase down one of Stark's henchmen. Randall gives a virtuoso multiple-character performance, and the special effects are dazzling, including a few scenes from Pal's ATLANTIS, THE LOST CONTINENT (1961). Makeup man William Tuttle won the first of only two special Academy Awards for his work on this film—before the category was permanently established in 1981.

p&d, George Pal; w, Charles Beaumont (based on the novel *The Circus of Dr. Lao* by Charles G. Finney); ph, Robert Bronner (Metrocolor); m, Leigh Harline.

Fantasy/Western   **Cas.**   **(MPAA:NR)**

SEVEN LITTLE FOYS, THE

(1955) 95m PAR c

Bob Hope *(Eddie Foy)*, Milly Vitale *(Madeleine Morando)*, George Tobias *(Barney Green)*, Angela Clarke *(Clara)*, Herbert Heyes *(Judge)*, Richard Shannon *(Stage Manager)*, Billy Gray *(Brynie)*, Lee Erickson *(Charley)*, Paul De Rolf *(Richard Foy)*, Lydia Reed *(Mary Foy)*, Linda Bennett *(Madeleine Foy)*, Jimmy Baird *(Eddie)*, James Cagney *(George M. Cohan)*, Tommy Duran *(Irving)*, Lester Matthews *(Father O'Casey)*, Joe Evans, George Boyce *(Elephant Act)*, Oliver Blake *(Santa Claus)*, Milton Frome *(Driscoll)*, King Donovan *(Harrison)*, Jimmy Conlin *(Stage Doorman)*, Marian Carr *(Soubrette)*, Harry Cheshire *(Stage Doorman at Iroquois)*, Renata Vanni *(Italian Ballerina Mistress)*, Betty Uitti *(Dance Specialty Double)*, Noel Drayton *(Priest)*, Jack Pepper *(Theater Manager)*, Dabbs Greer *(Tutor)*, Billy Nelson *(Customs Inspector)*, Joe Flynn *(2nd Priest)*, Jerry Mathers *(Brynie, Age 5)*, Lewis Martin *(Presbyterian Minister)*, Eddie Foy, Jr. *(Narrator)*.

Funny and heartwarming, though a little on the cute side, this engaging musical biography of vaudevillian Eddie Foy, Sr., features a socko cameo by multitalented James Cagney, reprising his Oscar-winning role as George M. Cohan. Bob Hope plays Foy, who declares that he'll always do a "single," both onstage and in life, but who, in short order, is married and has seven kids. When his wife (Milly Vitale) dies, Foy has problems adjusting to single parenthood, but before long the kids are not only in the act, but stealing the show. With Eddie, Jr., Foy's real-life son, doing the narrating, we are taken through the various episodes of the family's life. The highlight of the film comes at a Friars Club dinner for Foy when he and his great pal Cohan get on stage, throw some fast and furious jokes back and forth, and wind up in a splendid dance routine. Cagney reportedly did the role for no pay, even though he and Hope rehearsed their dancing for 10 days. Melville Shavelson (making his directorial debut) and Jack Rose were Oscar-nominated for the script. A must see for Hope and Cagney fans.

p, Jack Rose; d, Melville Shavelson; w, Melville Shavelson, Jack Rose; ph, John F. Warren (VistaVision, Technicolor).

Biography/Musical (MPAA:NR)

SEVENTH VOYAGE OF SINBAD, THE

(1958) 87m Morningside/COL c

Kerwin Mathews *(Capt. Sinbad)*, Kathryn Grant *(Princess Parisa)*, Richard Eyer *(Baronni the Genie)*, Torin Thatcher *(Sokurah the Magician)*, Alec Mango *(Caliph)*, Danny Green *(Karim)*, Harold Kasket *(Sultan)*, Alfred Brown *(Harufa)*, Nana de Herrera *(Sadi)*, Nino Falanga *(Gaunt Sailor)*, Luis Guedes *(Crewman)*, Virgilio Teixeria *(Ali)*.

Stop-motion animation master Ray Harryhausen's first color film is also one of the greatest achievements in fantasy filmmaking since KING KONG (1933). For the first time Harryhausen ventures into the realm of myth and legend (his previous films were the modern-day giant monster variety), resuscitating the Sinbad adventure, long thought to be box-office poison. The film opens as Sinbad (Kerwin Mathews) sails to Baghdad, accompanied by Princess Parisa (Kathryn Grant), his future bride. A violent storm blows the ship off course and the travelers land on the island of Colossa, where they find the sorcerer Sokurah (Torin Thatcher) being chased by a monstrous cyclops from whom he has stolen a magic lamp. Sinbad fends off the cyclops, but only with help from the lamp's genie are they able to escape. During their retreat, the lamp falls into the sea and is recovered by the angry cyclops. Despite the sorcerer's pleas to return for the lamp, Sinbad sails for Baghdad. Sokurah, however, shrinks the princess to miniature size to force Sinbad to see things his way. The rest of the film is an assault of the visually fantastic: Sinbad and his crew battle a baby roc and its giant mother, another cyclops, a fire-breathing dragon, and in the most memorable scene of all, Sinbad has a thrilling sword fight with a living skeleton. Harryhausen would make more magic in such outstanding fantasy features as MYSTERIOUS ISLAND, JASON AND THE ARGONAUTS, and CLASH OF THE TITANS.

p, Charles H. Schneer; d, Nathan Juran; w, Kenneth Kolb; ph, Wilkie Cooper (Dynamation, Technicolor); m, Bernard Herrmann.

Fantasy Cas. (MPAA:NR)

SHAGGY D.A., THE

(1976) 91m Walt Disney/BV c

Dean Jones *(Wilby Daniels)*, Suzanne Pleshette *(Betty Daniels)*, Tim Conway *(Tim)*, Keenan Wynn *(District Attorney John Slade)*, Jo Anne Worley *(Katrinka Muggelberg)*, Dick Van Patten *(Raymond)*, Shane Sinutko *(Brian Daniels)*, Vic Tayback *(Eddie Roschak)*, John Myhers *(Adm. Brenner)*, Dick Bakalyan *(Freddie)*, Warren Berlinger *(Dip)*, Ronnie Schell *(TV Director)*, Jonathan Daly *(TV Interviewer)*, John Fiedler *(Howie Clemmings)*, Hans Conried *(Prof. Whatley)*, Michael McGreevey *(Sheldon)*, Richard O'Brien *(Desk Sergeant)*, Dick Lane *(Roller Rink Announcer)*, Benny Rubin *(Waiter)*, Ruth Gillette *(Song Chairman)*, Hank Jones *(Policeman)*, Iris Adrian *(Manageress)*, Pat McCormick *(Bartender)*, George Kirby *(Dog Character Voices)*.

Made nearly 20 years after THE SHAGGY DOG, this sequel is every bit as bit as good as its predecessor. Dean Jones plays Wilby Daniels, a lawyer who comes across an ancient ring that changes him into a large sheep dog (the same fate that befell Tommy Kirk in the original). Wilby is running for district attorney against John Slade (Keenan Wynn), a villainous sort who gets his comeuppance when he turns into a bulldog. Though at times the film relies a bit too much on slapstick humor, skilled director Robert Stevenson (working on his 19th Disney film) keeps the action from getting *too* out of hand.

p, Bill Anderson; d, Robert Stevenson; w, Don Tait (based on the novel *The Hound Of Florence* by Felix Salten); ph, Frank Phillips (Technicolor); m, Buddy Baker.

Comedy/Fantasy Cas. (MPAA:G)

SHAGGY DOG, THE

(1959) 101m Walt Disney/BV bw

Fred MacMurray *(Wilson Daniels)*, Jean Hagen *(Frieda Daniels)*, Tommy Kirk *(Wilby Daniels)*, Annette Funicello *(Allison D'Allessio)*, Tim Considine *(Buzz Miller)*, Kevin Corcoran *(Moochie Daniels)*, Cecil Kellaway *(Prof. Plumcutt)*, Alexander Scourby *(Dr. Mikhail Andrassy)*, Roberta Shore *(Franceska Andrassy)*, James Westerfield *(Officer Hanson)*, Jacques Aubochon *(Stefano)*, Strother Martin *(Thurm)*, Forrest Lewis *(Officer Kelly)*, Ned Wever *(E.P. Hackett)*, Gordon Jones *(Capt. Scanlon)*, John Hart *(Police Broadcaster)*, Jack Albertson *(Reporter)*, Mack Williams *(Betz)*, Paul Frees *(Psychiatrist)*, Shaggy the dog.

This was the first so-called "live-action comedy" from the Disney studios, and it was extremely successful at the box office. It not only marked the return of Fred MacMurray to comedy—in which he got his start in the 1930s—but it also convinced the Disney folks that the combination of situation comedy and fantasy was an idea worth pursuing. In this particular shaggy dog story, an ancient ring falls in the pants cuff of Wilby Daniels (Tommy Kirk) while he is visiting a museum. After reading the ring's inscription, Wilby finds himself transformed into a large sheep dog, identical to one owned by his next-door neighbors. This poses a problem for his father (MacMurray), who happens to be allergic to dogs. The dog/Wilby overhears a conversation that reveals the neighbor to be a spy, and he ends up chasing the spies when they attempt escape. Wilby's father and the neighbor's dog get all the credit, but younger viewers will delight at knowing who really performed the heroics.

p, Walt Disney, Bill Walsh; d, Charles Barton; w, Bill Walsh, Lillie Hayward (based on the novel *The Hound of Florence* by Felix Salten); ph, Edward Coleman; m, Paul J. Smith.

Comedy/Fantasy   Cas.   (MPAA:NR)

SHANE

(1953) 118m PAR c

Alan Ladd (*Shane*), Jean Arthur (*Marion Starrett*), Van Heflin (*Joe Starrett*), Brandon de Wilde (*Joey*), Jack Palance (*Wilson*), Ben Johnson (*Chris*), Edgar Buchanan (*Lewis*), Emile Meyer (*Ryker*), Elisha Cook, Jr. (*Torrey*), Douglas Spencer (*Shipstead*), John Dierkes (*Morgan*), Ellen Corby (*Mrs. Torrey*), Paul McVey (*Grafton*), John Miller (*Atkey*), Edith Evanson (*Mrs. Shipstead*), Leonard Strong (*Wright*), Ray Spiker (*Johnson*), Janice Carroll (*Susan Lewis*), Martin Mason (*Howell*), Helen Brown (*Mrs. Lewis*), Nancy Kulp (*Mrs. Howell*), Howard J. Negley (*Pete*), Beverly Washburn (*Ruth Lewis*), Charles Quirk (*Clerk*), George J. Lewis, Jack Sterling, Henry Wills, Rex Moore, Ewing Brown, Chester W. Hannan, Bill Cartledge, Steve Raines (*Ryker Men*).

This classic western stars Alan Ladd in the unforgettable title role of the gunslinger who becomes a young boy's idol. Joe and Marion Starrett (Van Heflin and Jean Arthur) and their adventurous young son Joey (Brandon de Wilde) are struggling to survive on their Wyoming frontier homestead. One day, Shane (Alan Ladd) approaches on horseback and asks for water for himself and his mount. Joe obliges and before long Shane is helping the family protect their land from villainous cattle baron Ryker (Emile Meyer). Shane stays on as a ranch hand and, in the process, becomes a friend and hero to young Joey. Shane's presence, however, proves to be too much of an obstacle for Ryker and the inevitable showdown occurs. SHANE is a powerful drama in which the Old West of gunslingers and cattle barons bows to the new era of the homesteader and the family. Ladd, who was never better as the doomed hero, and who gives one of the best performances ever seen in *any* western, knows he is a creature of the past and that he cannot escape his reputation as a hired gun. Although the film is often brutal (especially when the wholly evil Jack Palance appears), there is such a positive sense of morality displayed here SHANE should be seen be the whole family.

p&d, George Stevens; w, A.B. Guthrie, Jr., Jack Sher (based on the novel by Jack Schaefer); ph, Loyal Griggs (Technicolor); m, Victor Young.

Western   Cas.   (MPAA:NR)

SHUT MY BIG MOUTH

(1942) 71m COL bw

Joe E. Brown (*Wellington Holmes*), Adele Mara (*Conchita Montoya*), Victor Jory (*Buckskin Bill*), Fritz Feld (*Robert Oglethorpe*), Don Beddoe (*Hill*), Will Wright (*Long*), Russell Simpson (*Mayor Potter*), Pedro de Cordoba (*Don Carlos Montoya*), Joan Woodbury (*Maria*), Ralph Peters (*Butch*), Joe McGuinn (*Hank*), Lloyd Bridges (*Skinny*), Forrest Tucker (*Red*), Noble Johnson (*Chief Standing Bull*), Chief Thunder-Cloud (*Indian Interpreter*), Art Mix, Blackjack Ward (*Bandits*), Hank Bell (*Stage Coach Driver*), Earle Hodgins (*Stage Coach Guard*), Eddy Waller (*Happy*), Fern Emmett (*Maggie*), Lew Kelly (*Westerner*), Dick Curtis (*Joe*), Edmund Cobb (*Stage Agent*), Bob Folkerson (*Boy*), Clay De Roy (*Spanish Driver*), Ed Peil, Sr. (*Hotel Proprietor*), Al Ferguson (*Pursuer*), John Tyrell (*Man*), Georgia Backus (*Woman*).

Enjoyable Joe E. Brown vehicle finds him as an easterner out West. He unwittingly becomes the sheriff and must fight off blackhearted villain Buckskin Bill (Victor Jory). He does this in drag of all things, with marvelous comic effect. Lots of laughs and some good direction that never overplays its hand.

p, Robert Sparks; d, Charles Barton; w, Oliver Drake, Karen De Wolf, Francis Martin (based on a story by Oliver Drake); ph, Henry Freulich.

Comedy/Western   (MPAA:NR)

SIDEWALKS OF LONDON

(1940, Brit.) 84m Mayflower/PAR bw (GB: ST. MARTIN'S LANE)

Charles Laughton (*Charles Saggers*), Vivien Leigh (*Libby*), Rex Harrison (*Harley Prentiss*), Larry Adler (*Constantine*), Tyrone Guthrie (*Gentry*), Gus McNaughton (*Arthur Smith*), Bart Cormack (*Strang*), Edward Lexy (*Mr. Such*), Maire O'Neill (*Mrs. Such*), Basil Gill (*Magistrate*), Claire Greet (*Old Maud*), David Burns (*Hackett*), Cyril Smith (*Blackface*), Ronald Ward (*Temperley*), Romilly Lunge (*Duchesi*), Helen Haye (*Lady Selina*), Phyllis Stanley (*Della Fordingbridge*), Jerry Verno (*Drunk*), Polly Ward (*Frankie*), Alf Goddard (*Doggie*), Carroll Gibbons and His Orchestra, The Luna Boys.

Charles Laughton plays Charles Saggers, a London street entertainer who befriends Lilly (Vivien Leigh), a street urchin. She engages in minor theft to keep herself alive, but Charles—after catching her in the act—takes pity on Lilly and makes her part of his act. Lilly is spotted by impresario Harley Prentiss (Rex Harrison) and is catapulted to fame in the British music hall. But unable to forget the man who saved her, she seeks out Charles, wanting to help him get into the big time. He, however, declines her offer; the busker's life is the only life for him. The film evocatively captures the gaiety of London street life and the direction carries the story along nicely, carefully drawing out characters.

p, Eric Pommer; d, Tim Whelan; w, Clemence Dane

(based on her story "St. Martin's Lane"); ph, Jules Kruger; m, Arthur Johnson.

Comedy   **Cas.**   **(MPAA:NR)**

SINBAD AND THE EYE OF THE TIGER

(1977, US/Brit.) 112m Morningside/COL c

Patrick Wayne *(Sinbad)*, Taryn Power *(Dione)*, Margaret Whiting *(Zenobia)*, Jane Seymour *(Princess Farah)*, Patrick Troughton *(Melanthius)*, Kurt Christian *(Rafi)*, Nadim Sawaiha *(Hassan)*, Damien Thomas *(Prince Kassim)*, Bruno Barnabe *(Balsora)*, Bernard Kay *(Zabid)*, Salami Coker *(Maroof)*, David Sterne *(Aboo-Seer)*.

In this adventure based on the exploits of the famed mythical sailor from *A Thousand and One Nights*, Sinbad (Patrick Wayne, son of John) is enlisted by Princess Farah (Jane Seymour) to help rid her brother of a curse that is gradually turning him into an ape. He is about to ascend to the throne, but an evil sorceress has cast the spell in the hope that her own son might become ruler. The plot and performances are definitely aimed at the younger set, but the film boasts terrific effects by the inimitable master animator Ray Harryhausen. His creations here include a saber-toothed tiger, a chess-playing baboon, a giant walrus, and three nasty ghouls.

p, Charles H. Schneer, Ray Harryhausen; d, Sam Wanamaker; w, Beverley Cross (based on a story by Beverley Cross and Ray Harryhausen, from *A Thousand and One Nights*); ph, Ted Moore (Metrocolor); m, Roy Budd.

Fantasy   **Cas.**   **(MPAA:G)**

SINBAD THE SAILOR

(1947) 117m RKO c

Douglas Fairbanks, Jr. *(Sinbad)*, Maureen O'Hara *(Shireen)*, Walter Slezak *(Melik)*, Anthony Quinn *(Emir)*, George Tobias *(Abbu)*, Jane Greer *(Pirouze)*, Mike Mazurki *(Yusuf)*, Sheldon Leonard *(Auctioneer)*, Alan Napier *(Aga)*, John Miljan *(Moga)*, Barry Mitchell *(Muallin)*, Glenn Strange *(Slave Master)*, George Chandler *(Commoner)*, Louis-Jean Heydt *(Mercenary)*, Cy Kendall *(Kahn of Basra)*, Hugh Prosser *(Captain of the Guard)*, Harry Harvey *(Crier at Execution)*, George Lloyd *(Lancer Guard)*, Paul Guifoyle *(Camel Drover)*, Jean Lind, Mary Bradley, Norma Creiger, Vonne Lester *(Dancing Girls)*, Nick Thompson *(Beggar on Street)*, Billy Bletcher *(Crier)*, Max Wagner *(Assistant Overseer)*, Norbert Schiller *(Timekeeper)*, Wade Crosby *(Soldier)*, Ben Welden *(Porter)*, Charles Soldani, Mikandor Dooraff, Joe Garcio, Chuck Hamilton *(Merchants)*, Phil Warren, Lida Durova, Dolores Costelli, Milly Reauclaire, Teri Toy, Joan Webster, Leslie Charles, Norma Brown, Ann Cameron, Jamiel Hasson, Al Murphy, Bill Shannon, Dave Kashner, Eddie Abdo, Charles Stevens, Gordon Clark.

In this lengthy, purely escapist swashbuckling adventure, Douglas Fairbanks, Jr., conjures up images of his heroic father from such films as THE THIEF OF BAGDAD (1924) and THE BLACK PIRATE (1926). An Arabian Nights tale, SINBAD THE SAILOR casts Fairbanks as Sinbad, sailing the seas in search of a hidden treasure. He makes a stop in Daibul, where his ship is put up for auction. Shireen (Maureen O'Hara), a wealthy and beautiful adventuress, makes a bid for the ship, but Sinbad, stealing money from the auctioneer's pocket, bids higher. When Sinbad becomes enamored of Shireen, the sword-wielding Emir of Daibul (Anthony Quinn) prepares to kill him, but he is stopped by the love-stricken Shireen, who passes Sinbad off as royalty. Sinbad and Shireen soon team with the Emir and Melik (Walter Slezak), a Mongolian sailor who concocts a scheme to hunt for the treasure. Soon enough, Sinbad realizes that he is the victim of an elaborate double cross. Although boasting ornate sets and a collection of glittering Arabian fashions, SINBAD THE SAILOR badly needs a cohesive plot, but somehow that just doesn't matter. Kids and adults will be swept along by the excitement anyway.

p, Stephen Ames; d, Richard Wallace; w, John Twist (based on a story by John Twist, George Worthing Yates); ph, George Barnes (Technicolor); m, Roy Webb.

Adventure/Fantasy   **Cas.**   **(MPAA:NR)**

SING YOU SINNERS

(1938) 88m PAR bw

Bing Crosby *(Joe Beebe)*, Fred MacMurray *(David Beebe)*, Donald O'Connor *(Mike Beebe)*, Elizabeth Patterson *(Mrs. Beebe)*, Ellen Drew *(Martha)*, John Gallaudet *(Harry Ringmer)*, William Haade *(Pete)*, Paul White *(Filter)*, Irving Bacon *(Lecturer)*, Tom Dugan *(Race Fan)*, Herbert Corthell *(Nightclub Manager)*.

Until this picture, Bing Crosby had been playing cliched light comedy roles that made him popular but did nothing to show his acting talent. Here he was able to present another side of his character and audiences loved it. Joe Beebe (Crosby) is a 35-year-old wastrel who spends most of his time concocting plans to make money without toil. His mother (Elizabeth Patterson) wishes he would be more like his brother David (Fred MacMurray), a hard-working garage mechanic. Mom also wants Joe to set a better example for her youngest son, 13-year-old Mike (Donald O'Connor, in only his second film role). The three brothers, all musicians, make a few extra bucks working at a small nightclub, but Joe, not content with barely squeezing out an existence, leaves for Los Angeles. He promises his poor but loving family that as soon as he gets a good job he'll send them money for the fare. Time passes and Mom hears from Joe that he's now in a new business and doing well. That's encouragement enough for her to sell the family home and go to Los Angeles—only to find that Joe has purchased a racehorse, and is hardly prosperous. They scrape by on almost nothing, and little David is pressed into service as a jockey for the Big Race that rounds off the film with a big finish.

p&d, Wesley Ruggles; w, Claude Binyon; ph, Karl Struss.

Comedy/Musical   **(MPAA:NR)**

SITTING PRETTY

(1948) 84m FOX bw

Robert Young *(Harry)*, Maureen O'Hara *(Tacey)*, Clifton Webb *(Lynn Belvedere)*, Richard Haydn *(Mr. Appleton)*, Louise Allbritton *(Edna Philby)*, Randy Stuart *(Peggy)*, Ed Begley *(Hammond)*, Larry Olsen *(Larry)*, John Russell *(Bill Philby)*, Betty Ann Lynn *(Ginger)*, Willard Robertson *(Mr. Ashcroft)*, Anthony Sydes *(Tony)*, Roddy McCaskill *(Roddy)*, Grayce Hampton *(Mrs. Appleton)*, Cara Williams, Marion Marshall *(Secretaries)*, Charles Arnt *(Mr. Taylor)*, Ken Christy *(Mr. McPherson)*, Ann Shoemaker *(Mrs. Ashcroft)*, Minerva Urecal *(Mrs. Maypole)*, Mira McKinney *(Mrs. Phillips)*, Syd Saylor *(Cab Driver)*, Ruth Warren *(Matron)*, Isabel Randolph *(Mrs. Frisbee)*, Ellen Lowe *(Effie)*, Dave Morris *(Mailman)*, Anne O'Neal *(Mrs. Gibbs)*, Albin Robeling *(Maitre d')*, Josephine Whittell *(Mrs. Hammond)*, Mary Field *(Librarian)*, Billy Wayne *(Newsreel Man)*, Charles Owens, Iris James, Robert Tidwell, Barbara Blaine *(Jitterbugs)*, Gertrude Astor *(Woman)*, Jane Nigh *(Mable)*, J. Farrell MacDonald *(Cop)*, Charles Tannen *(Director)*, Dorothy Adams *(Mrs. Goul)*.

If ever an actor was born to play a part, it was Clifton Webb in his Oscar-nominated role as Lynn Belvedere, a prissy genius who takes a job as a babysitter. The scene is Hummingbird Hill, a typical suburban community where the three sons of Harry and Tacey (Robert Young and Maureen O'Hara) are so bratty that the family has lost a trio of maids, with little hope of finding another replacement. Tacey advertises in the local paper and in walks Mr. Belvedere, a self-proclaimed genius with definite ideas about raising children. He is stern but fair and it's not long before the boys knuckle under to his discipline. When the baby tosses oatmeal at Belvedere, his response is to toss the goop right back at the baby, thereby establishing his superiority. The neighborhood is filled with gossips and busybodies, and they are all shocked when the real reason for Belvedere's presence is unveiled: he's a writer (besides being a doctor, lawyer, philosopher, and everything else) who has been researching the community. The town is then exposed when Belvedere's book is published and becomes a best-seller. The two sequels to this successful film, MR. BELVEDERE GOES TO COLLEGE and MR. BELVEDERE RINGS THE BELL, were not nearly as witty or biting as the original. In 1985, a TV series was also attempted based on the Webb character.

p, Samuel G. Engel; d, Walter Lang; w, F. Hugh Herbert (based on the novel *Belvedere* by Gwen Davenport); ph, Norbert Brodine; m, Alfred Newman.

Comedy **(MPAA:NR)**

SKIPPY

(1931) 85m PAR bw

Jackie Cooper *(Skippy Skinner)*, Robert Coogan *(Sooky Wayne)*, Mitzie Green *(Eloise)*, Jackie Searl *(Sidney)*, Willard Robertson *(Dr. Herbert Skinner)*, Enid Bennett *(Mrs. Ellen Skinner)*, David Haines *(Harley Nubbins)*, Helen Jerome Eddy *(Mrs. Wayne)*, Jack Clifford *(Dogcatcher Nubbins)*, Guy Oliver *(Dad Burkey)*.

A charming children's picture that doesn't neglect adults, SKIPPY was good enough to merit Oscar nominations for Best Picture, Best Director, Best Story, and for Jackie Cooper as Best Actor. Based on a comic strip by Percy Crosby, it's a simple, adorable tale of boys and girls and their dogs. When a dog belonging to Sooky Wayne (Robert Coogan, younger brother of Jackie Coogan) is captured by the local dogcatcher, Sooky and his friend Skippy Skinner (Jackie Cooper) try to raise money to buy a license for the pooch. In order to get the necessary $3, they try everything. One of their plans is to stage a show, for which they sell tickets, lemonade, etc. They also try smashing Skippy's unbreakable bank by putting it under the wheels of a truck. There are many wonderful moments in the picture, and watching Cooper cry is worth the price of admission. There have been few child actors who have been as convincing as he could be. The sequel was SOOKY.

p, Louis D. Lighton; d, Norman Taurog; w, Joseph L. Mankiewicz, Norman McLeod, Don Marquis, Percy Crosby, Sam Mintz (based on the comic strip by Percy Crosby); ph, Karl Struss.

Comedy/Drama **(MPAA:NR)**

SLEEPING BEAUTY

(1959) 75m Disney/BV c

Voices of: Eleanor Audley *(Maleficent)*, Verna Felton *(Flora)*, Barbara Jo Allen [Vera Vague] *(Fauna)*, Barbara Luddy *(Merryweather)*, Taylor Holmes *(King Stefan)*, Bill Thompson *(King Hubert)*, Candy Candido *(Goons)*, Mary Costa *(Princess Aurora)*, Bill Shirley *(Prince Phillip)*.

One of the most ambitious projects ever undertaken by Disney, SLEEPING BEAUTY opens as the king and queen decide to throw a gala celebration announcing the birth of their daughter, Aurora, and her immediate betrothal to the infant Prince Phillip. Unfortunately, the overjoyed parents neglect to invite the evil fairy Maleficent, causing the angry denizen of the forest to place a curse on the infant girl that ensures she will prick her finger on a spindle upon her 16th birthday and die. The curse, however, is altered by a good fairy who changes the promise of death to sleep. Hoping to circumvent this prophecy, three good fairies named Flora, Fauna, and Merryweather take the baby into the forest where they can raise her away from the prying eyes of Maleficent. The fairies keep the girl's royal identity a secret from her, and she grows up to be a normal young woman. One day she meets Prince Phillip in the forest, and though both are unaware that they have been betrothed since birth, they fall in love. Tragedy soon strikes despite the three good fairies' precautions; on Aurora's 16th birthday the curse is enacted and she falls into a deep sleep which can only be broken by the kiss of a brave prince. This was the most expensive animated film to date, and every penny was on the screen. The attention to movement and detail is stunning, with multiple layers of action filling the frame. The highlight of the film, the fight with the dragon, is terrifying, exciting, and brilliantly executed, though some youngsters may find it a bit too scary.

p, Walt Disney; d, Clyde Geronimi, Eric Larson, Wolfgang Reitherman, Les Clark; ph, (Technirama, Technicolor); m, George Bruns, from Petr Illich Tchaikovsky's "Sleeping Beauty Ballet".

Animation (MPAA:G)

SLIPPER AND THE ROSE, THE

(1976, Brit.) 146m Paradine/UNIV c (AKA: THE STORY OF CINDERELLA)

Richard Chamberlain (Prince Edward), Gemma Craven (Cinderella), Annette Crosbie (Fairy Godmother), Edith Evans (Dowager Queen), Christopher Gable (John), Michael Hordern (King), Margaret Lockwood (Stepmother), Kenneth More (Lord Chamberlain), Julian Orchard (Montague), Lally Bowers (Queen), Sherrie Hewson (Palatine), Rosalind Ayres (Isobella), John Turner (Major Domo), Keith Skinner (Willoughby), Polly Williams (Lady Caroline), Norman Bird (Dress Shop Proprietor), Peter Graves (General), Gerald Sim (First Lord of the Navy), Elizabeth Mansfield, Ludmilla Nova (Ladies in Waiting), Roy Barraclough (Tailor), Geoffrey Bayldon (Archbishop), Valentine Dyall (2nd Major Domo), Tim Barrett (Minister), Vivienne McKee (Bride), Andre Morell (Bride's Father), Myrtle Reed (Bride's Mother), Peter Leeming (Singing Guard).

This modernized version of the fairy tale "Cinderella" stars Richard Chamberlain as the suave prince and Gemma Craven as the young servant girl with whom he falls in love. The dialog is translated into more up-to-date language, and an undercurrent of wit should keep adults as engaged as youngsters will be. The scenic Austrian background, for the outdoor sequences, adds the appropriate atmosphere.

p, Stuart Lyons; d, Bryan Forbes; w, Bryan Forbes, Richard M. Sherman, Robert B. Sherman; ph, Tony Imi (Panavision, Technicolor); m, Richard M. Sherman, Robert B. Sherman.

Musical (MPAA:G)

SMALL CHANGE

(1976, Fr.) 105m Les Films du Carrosse-Les Artistes Associes/NW c (L'ARGENT DE POCHE)

Geory Desmouceaux (Patrick), Philippe Goldman (Julien), Claudio Deluca (Mathieu Deluca), Franck Deluca (Franck Deluca), Richard Golfier (Richard), Laurent Devlaeminck (Laurent Riffle), Bruno Staab (Bruno Rouillard), Sebastien Marc (Oscar), Sylvie Grezel (Sylvie), Pascale Bruchon (Martine), Corinne Boucart (Corinne), Eva Truffaut (Patricia), Jean-Francois Stevenin (Jean-Francois Richet), Chantal Mercier (Chantal Petit), Francis Devlaeminck (Mons. Riffle), Tania Torrens (Nadine Riffle), Virginie Thevenet (Lydia Richel), Laura Truffaut (Made-

leine Doinel), Francois Truffaut (Martine's Father), Le Petit Gregory (Gregory).

Chiefly a collection of vignettes, this sentimental homage to children and their innocent ways focuses on two young boys, Patrick (Geory Desmouceaux) and Julien (Philippe Goldman). Patrick is a shy, slightly plump boy who looks after his paralyzed father and is infatuated with a schoolmate's mother. His desire for romance is finally satisfied by the film's end, when he gets his first kiss from schoolgirl Martine (Pascale Bruchon). Julien's life is the polar opposite of Patrick's. Long-haired and neglected, he is a present-day "wild child" (see Truffaut's 1972 film, THE WILD CHILD) living in a hovel with his hateful mother and grandmother, who are not beyond physically abusing him. At the center of the children's lives is a schoolteacher (Jean-Francois Stevenin), a thoughtful, fatherly man who eventually becomes a parent himself. The film is filled with adorable youngsters: Sylvie, a 7-year-old with two pet fish and a fuzzy elephant purse that her parents won't let her bring to a restaurant; the Deluca brothers, who offer to play barber to save a classmate some money; and little Gregory, a mischievous tyke who is too charming to arouse anger. Director Francois Truffaut worked his screenplay around the children, using them as his inspiration rather than forcing his screenplay on them. The result is a collection of some of the most natural sequences ever filmed. Although the cast is made up of children, SMALL CHANGE is a film which parents will appreciate far more than kids will. (In French; English subtitles.)

d, Francois Truffaut; w, Francois Truffaut, Suzanne Schiffmann; ph, Pierre-William Glenn (Eastmancolor); m, Maurice Jaubert.

Comedy/Drama **Cas.** (MPAA:PG)

SNOOPY, COME HOME

(1972) 80m Cinema Center/NG c

Voices of: Chad Webber (Charlie Brown), Robin Kohn (Lucy Van Pelt), Stephen Shea (Linus Van Pelt), David Carey (Schroeder), Johanna Baer (Lila), Hilary Momberger (Sally), Chris De Faria (Peppermint Patty), Linda Ercoli (Clara), Linda Mendelson (Frieda), Bill Melendez (Snoopy).

The adventures of America's favorite beagle are brought to the big screen for the second time (following A BOY NAMED CHARLIE BROWN), with the famous cartoon's creator, Charles M. Schulz, acting as the screenwriter. Snoopy packs his bowl and faithful bird Woodstock, and heads off to find Lila, his original owner, who has written him from a hospital. When she invites Snoopy to move in with her family, he returns to say his goodbyes to Charlie Brown and the gang. Where this film towers above the first one is in the music, written by Disney stalwarts Richard M. and Robert B. Sherman.

p, Lee Mendelson, Bill Melendez; d, Bill Melendez; w, Charles M. Schulz (based on the cartoon characters created by Charles M. Schulz); ph, Nick Vasu (Technicolor); m, Donald Ralke.

Animation   Cas.   (MPAA:G)

SNOW WHITE AND THE SEVEN DWARFS

(1937) 83m Disney/RKO c

Voices of: Adriana Caselotti *(Snow White)*, Harry Stockwell *(Prince Charming)*, Lucille LaVerne *(The Queen)*, Moroni Olsen *(Magic Mirror)*, Billy Gilbert *(Sneezy)*, Pinto Colvig *(Sleepy/Grumpy)*, Otis Harlan *(Happy)*, Scotty Mattraw *(Bashful)*, Roy Atwell *(Doc)*, Stuart Buchanan *(Humbert)*, Marion Darlington *(Bird Sounds and Warbling)*, The Fraunfelder Family, Jim Macdonald *(Yodeling)*.

Dubbed "Disney's Folly" by its detractors, this masterpiece was a personal success for Walt Disney—the fulfillment of his dream to pioneer animation of unimagined scope. The film opens on a storybook, and as "Some Day My Prince Will Come" plays in the background, the turning pages explain how the orphaned Snow White has been brought up as a servant of a wicked queen. The queen, an icily beautiful woman with piercing eyes, stands before her Magic Mirror and poses her vain, oft-asked question: "Mirror, mirror, on the wall, who is the fairest of them all?" She is shocked when the mirror gives an unexpected answer: "Snow White." The nasty queen then orders that the innocent young woman be killed. Snow White, however, has eight things going for her—Prince Charming and seven dwarfs named Doc, Happy, Sleepy, Sneezy, Bashful, Grumpy, and Dopey. The familiar story, adapted from the Grimm brothers' tale, pulls in the audience with its imaginative development. This is animation as it had never before been experienced, with images both engaging and terrifying. Disney wisely realized the film could only work if it was full of believable characters, and each personality is distinct, from the purity of Snow White to the absolute evil of the queen. This film classic also features some unforgettable songs, including "Whistle While You Work," "Heigh Ho," and "Some Day My Prince Will Come."

p, Walt Disney; d, David Hand, Perce Pearce, Larry Morey, William Cottrell, Wilfred Jackson, Ben Sharpsteen; w, Ted Sears, Otto Englander, Earl Hurd, Dorothy Ann Blank, Richard Creedon, Dick Richard, Merrill De Maris, Webb Smith (based on the fairy tale "Sneewittchen" in the collection *Children's and Household Tales* by Jacob Grimm, Wilhelm Grimm); m, Frank Churchill, Leigh Harline, Paul Smith.

Animation   Cas.   (MPAA:G)

SO DEAR TO MY HEART

(1949) 82m Disney/RKO c

Burl Ives *(Uncle Hiram)*, Beulah Bondi *(Granny Kincaid)*, Harry Carey *(Judge)*, Luana Patten *(Tildy)*, Bobby Driscoll *(Jeremiah Kincaid)*, Raymond Bond *(Storekeeper)*, Daniel Haight *(Storekeeper's Son)*, Walter Soderling *(Villager)*, Matt Willis *(Horse Trainer)*.

SO DEAR TO MY HEART is a lovely, heartwarming live-action film with several superb animation sequences perfectly blended in. Set around the turn of the century in Indiana, the film is the story of young Jeremiah Kincaid (Bobby Driscoll), who yearns to own a horse. Jeremiah lives with his grandmother (Beulah Bondi) and lovingly raises a pet lamb, although the adventurous animal is sometimes a problem. Uncle Hiram (Burl Ives), the local blacksmith, supports Jeremiah's love for his pet, and thinks the lamb just might be championship calibre, encouraging the boy to enter it in the county fair. It will cost a few bucks to get to the fair and pay the entry fee, but Jeremiah is determined to showcase his lamb, so he takes a job gathering honey. This simple tale is often funny, always intelligent, and never overly sentimental. The animated sequences illustrate Jeremiah's fantasies as he pores over his scrapbook and a wise owl comes to life to demonstrate the importance of following one's dream; in another animated scene, a souvenir program from the fair comes to life.

p, Walt Disney, Perce Pearce; d, Harold Schuster, Hamilton Luske; w, John Tucker Battle, Maurice Rapf, Ted Sears (based on the book *Midnight and Jeremiah* by Sterling North); ph, Winton C. Hoch; m, Paul J. Smith.

Musical   Cas.   (MPAA:NR)

SO THIS IS NEW YORK

(1948) 79m Enterprise/UA bw

Henry Morgan *(Ernie Finch)*, Rudy Vallee *(Herbert Daley)*, Bill Goodwin *(Jimmy Ralston)*, Hugh Herbert *(Mr. Trumbull)*, Leo Gorcey *(Sid Mercer)*, Virginia Grey *(Ella Finch)*, Dona Drake *(Kate Goff)*, Jerome Cowan *(Francis Griffin)*, Dave Willock *(Willis Gilbey)*, Frank Orth *(A.J. Gluskoter)*, Arnold Stang *(Western Union Clerk)*, William Bakewell *(Hotel Clerk)*.

A side-splitting look at the experiences of a group of country folk who visit bustling New York City. They encounter all types of city slickers, including cabbies whose delivery is so exotic that their lines are subtitled on the screen. Henry Morgan takes his radio act to the big screen this time, rarely failing to score with his humor. Dead End Kid/Bowery Boy Leo Gorcey is in top form as a drunken jockey.

p, Stanley Kramer; d, Richard O. Fleischer; w, Carl Foreman, Herbert Baker (based on the novel *The Big Town* by Ring Lardner); ph, Jack Russell; m, Dimitri Tiomkin.

Comedy   (MPAA:NR)

SON OF FLUBBER

(1963) 102m Disney/BV bw

Fred MacMurray *(Prof. Ned Brainard)*, Nancy Olson *(Betsy Brainard)*, Keenan Wynn *(Alonzo Hawk)*, Tommy Kirk *(Biff Hawk)*, Elliott Reid *(Shelby Ashton)*, Joanna Moore *(Desiree de la Roche)*, Leon Ames *(President Rufus Daggett)*, Ed Wynn *(A.J. Allen)*, Ken Murray *(Mr. Hur-*

ley), Charlie Ruggles *(Judge Murdock)*, William Demarest *(Mr. Hummel)*, Bob Sweeney *(Mr. Harker)*, Paul Lynde *(Sportscaster)*, Stuart Erwin *(Coach Wilson)*, Edward Andrews *(Defense Secretary)*, Alan Hewitt *(Prosecutor)*, Leon Tyler *(Humphrey Harker)*, Forrest Lewis *(Officer Kelly)*, James Westerfield *(Officer Hanson)*, Alan Carney *(1st Referee)*, Lee Giroux *(Newscaster)*, Jack Albertson *(Mr. Barley)*, Eddie Ryder *(Mr. Osborne)*, Harriet MacGibbon *(Edna Daggett)*, Beverly Wills *(Mother)*, Wally Boag *(Father)*, Walter Elias Miller *(Baby Walter in TV Commercial)*, Robert Shayne *(Assistant to Defense Secretary)*, Henry Hunter *(Admiral)*, Hal Smith *(Bartender)*, J. Pat O'Malley *(Sign Painter)*, Norman Grabowski *(Rutland Football Player No. 33)*, Gordon Jones *(Rutland Coach)*.

So great were the potential for fun with new inventions and the success of THE ABSENT-MINDED PROFESSOR that this sequel appeared two years later. Backed by almost the same cast as appeared in the first film, Fred MacMurray reprises his role as Prof. Ned Brainard, who becomes so entangled in red tape that his latest invention, some antigravity goop, goes unsold. Meanwhile, young Biff Hawk (Tommy Kirk) uses the professor's tools and helps create a flubber gas that, when pumped into a football uniform, makes a player practically unstoppable. It's all makes for a goofy and enjoyable time before the screen.

p, Bill Walsh, Ron Miller; d, Robert Stevenson; w, Bill Walsh, Don DaGradi (based on the story "A Situation of Gravity" by Samuel W. Taylor and the Danny Dunn books by Jay Williams and Raymond Abrashkin); ph, Edward Colman; m, George Bruns.

Comedy   **Cas.**   **(MPAA:G)**

SON OF LASSIE

(1945) 102m MGM c

Peter Lawford *(Joe Carraclough)*, Donald Crisp *(Sam Carraclough)*, June Lockhart *(Priscilla)*, Nigel Bruce *(Duke of Rudling)*, William "Billy" Severn *(Henrik)*, Leon Ames *(Anton)*, Donald Curtis *(Sgt. Eddie Brown)*, Nils Asther *(Olav)*, Robert Lewis *(Sgt. Schmidt)*, Fay Helm *(Joanna)*, Peter Helmers *(Willi)*, Otto Reichow *(Karl,* Patricia Prest *(Hedda)*, Helen Koford [Terry Moore] *(Thea)*, Leon Tyler *(Arne)*, Lotta Palfi *(Old Woman)*, Eily Malyon *(Washwoman)*, Lester Matthews *(Major)*, Pedro de Cordoba *(Village Priest)*, Hans Schumm *(German Command Officer)*, Lassie the Dog, Laddie the Dog.

In this sequel to the classic LASSIE COME HOME, Lassie's son, Laddie, follows his master all over Europe as he fights the Germans during WW II. The story gets going when Laddie sneaks onto a plane piloted by Joe Carraclough (Peter Lawford). When they are shot down over Norway, Joe parachutes to safety with Laddie in his arms. Joe is hurt and Laddie takes off to get help, unwittingly fetching two German soldiers. Joe manages to escape, but each time he reaches safe territory Laddie keeps coming after his master, with the Germans in pursuit, although eventually, of course, dog and master

make it to safety. The suspenseful action and pretty European scenery make this a pleasant collie adventure.

p, Samuel Marx; d, S. Sylvan Simon; w, Jeanne Bartlett (based on characters by Eric Knight); ph, Charles Schoenbaum; m, Herbert Stothart.

War   **(MPAA:NR)**

SONG OF BERNADETTE, THE

(1943) 156m FOX bw

Jennifer Jones *(Bernadette Soubirous)*, William Eythe *(Antoine)*, Charles Bickford *(Peyremaie)*, Vincent Price *(Dutour)*, Lee Cobb *(Dr. Dozous)*, Gladys Cooper *(Sister Vauzous)*, Anne Revere *(Louise Soubirous)*, Roman Bohnen *(Francois Soubirous)*, Mary Anderson *(Jeanne Abadie)*, Patricia Morison *(Empress Eugenie)*, Aubrey Mather *(Lacade)*, Charles Dingle *(Jacomet)*, Edith Barrett *(Croisine)*, Sig Rumann *(Louis Bouriette)*, Blanche Yurka *(Bernarde Casterot)*, Ermadean Walters *(Marie Soubirous)*, Marcel Dalio *(Callet)*, Pedro de Cordoba *(Le Crampe)*, Jerome Cowan *(Emperor Napoleon)*, Charles Waldron *(Bishop of Tarbes)*, Moroni Olsen *(Chaplain)*, Nana Bryant *(Convent Mother Superior)*, Manart Kippen *(Charles Bouhouhorts)*, Merrill Rodin *(Jean Soubirous)*, Nino Pipitone, Jr. *(Justin Soubirous)*, John Maxwell Hayes *(Father Pomian)*, Jean Del Val *(Estrade)*, Tala Birell *(Mme. Bruat)*, Eula Morgan *(Mme. Nicolau)*, Frank Reicher *(Dr. St. Cyr)*, Charles La Torre *(Duran)*, Linda Darnell *(Blessed Virgin)*, Nestor Paiva *(Baker)*, Dorothy Shearer *(Mother Superior)*, Nino Pipitone, Sr. *(Mayor's Secretary)*, Edwin Stanley *(Mr. Jones)*, Lionel Braham *(Baron Massey)*, Ian Wolfe *(Minister of the Interior)*, Andre Charlot *(Bishop)*.

This film depicts the stirring true story of the woman who had a vision of the Virgin Mary in a grotto at Lourdes in 1858. Jennifer Jones is Bernadette Soubirous, a peasant girl whose family lives in the town jail because they have no place of their own. One morning, Bernadette is gathering sticks of wood near the grotto when she is visited by the Virgin (Linda Darnell). Bernadette is directed to dig at the grotto for a healing water with curative power for the lame and the halt. Everyone scoffs at her except her devout mother and, eventually, Peyremaie (Charles Bickford), a local priest. He helps her get into a convent, and, after many years of defending her vision, Bernadette is canonized by the Catholic Church. Since that time, millions have flocked to Lourdes to bathe in the Holy Water. Jones is touching in an Oscar-winning performance.

p, William Perlberg; d, Henry King; w, George Seaton (based on the novel by Franz Werfel); ph, Arthur Miller; m, Alfred Newman.

Biography   **Cas.**   **(MPAA:NR)**

SONG OF THE SOUTH

(1946) 94m Disney/RKO c

Ruth Warrick *(Sally)*, James Baskett *(Uncle Remus/Voice*

of Brer Fox), Bobby Driscoll *(Johnny),* Luana Patten *(Ginny),* Lucile Watson *(Grandmother),* Hattie McDaniel *(Aunt Tempy),* Glenn Leedy *(Toby),* George Nokes, Gene Holland *(The Favers Boys),* Erik Rolf *(John),* Mary Field *(Mrs. Favers),* Anita Brown *(Maid),* Nicodemus Stewart *(Voice of Brer Bear),* Johnny Lee *(Voice of Brer Rabbit).*

This Disney charmer is also the studio's most controversial production. Set in the Reconstruction South, it stars Bobby Driscoll as Johnny, a white little boy who goes to live on his grandmother's plantation after his parents separate. Upset by things he can't understand, Johnny runs away and meets former slave Uncle Remus (James Baskett). Uncle Remus decides to trick Johnny into going home, telling the boy he would also like to run away, but must stop home for a few things. As Uncle Remus packs, he tells Johnny a story, and the film moves into a marvelous combination of live action and animation in a bright cartoon setting in which Brer Rabbit, too, has an adventure while running away from home. SONG OF THE SOUTH's cartoon sequences are as fine as anything produced by the Disney animators. The live action projected into a cartoon setting transcends gimmickry, the actors and caricatures carefully matched within the frame. Baskett's performance (for which received an honorary Oscar) makes the technique work that much better. The film's idyllic portrayal of the Reconstruction setting was controversial, however, particularly among black Americans. The NAACP and the National Urban League, among others, protested the stereotypes in the film, though Disney officials maintained the film was "...a sincere effort to depict American folklore, to put the Uncle Remus stories into pictures." Included is the well-known song "Zip A Dee Doo Dah."

p, Walt Disney; d, Harve Foster, Wilfred Jackson; w, Dalton Raymond, Morton Grant, Maurice Rapf (based on a story by Dalton Raymond and a cartoon story by William Peet, Ralph Wright and George Stallings, from *Tales of Uncle Remus* by Joel Chandler Harris); ph, Gregg Toland (Technicolor); m, Daniele Amfitheatrof, Paul J. Smith.

Animation/Fantasy (MPAA:NR)

SOUND OF MUSIC, THE

(1965) 174m FOX c

Julie Andrews *(Maria),* Christopher Plummer *(Capt. Von Trapp),* Eleanor Parker *(The Baroness),* Richard Haydn *(Max Detweiler),* Peggy Wood *(Mother Abbess),* Charmian Carr *(Liesl),* Heather Menzies *(Louisa),* Nicholas Hammond *(Friedrich),* Duane Chase *(Kurt),* Angela Cartwright *(Brigitta),* Debbie Turner *(Marta),* Kym Karath *(Gretl),* Anna Lee *(Sister Margaretta),* Portia Nelson *(Sister Berthe),* Ben Wright *(Herr Zeller),* Daniel Truhitte *(Rolfe),* Norma Varden *(Frau Schmidt),* Gil Stuart *(Franz),* Marni Nixon *(Sister Sophia),* Evadne Baker *(Sister Bernice),* Doris Lloyd *(Baroness Ebberfeld).*

THE SOUND OF MUSIC is one of the most loved movie musicals ever made, if not necessarily one of the best. Maria (Julie Andrews) is a young postulant at a nunnery who quickly realizes that the cloister is not for her. Yet she still believes in the values espoused by the church, so she goes out into the world and radiantly attempts to bring what she's learned to the lay world. Soon Maria is hired by Austrian widower Capt. Von Trapp (Christopher Plummer) as a governess for his seven singing children. Noting that the children seem cowed by their disciplinarian father, she strives to open their lives to joy. They live in one of the most beautiful sections of the Alps, but only learn to appreciate the surrounding vistas when Maria, with her fresh outlook, shows them what they have. All that is soon threatened by Nazi rule in Austria, forcing the Von Trapps to flee while en route to Salzburg for a musical festival in which they are to perform. A staple of 1960s Hollywood films, THE SOUND OF MUSIC earned an Oscar for Best Picture, delivered an unforgettable Julie Andrews performance, and presented a most picturesque view of Austria. The songs, too, are hard to forget, especially "The Sound of Music," "Do Re Mi," "My Favorite Things," and "Edelweiss."

p&d, Robert Wise; w, Ernest Lehman (based on the musical play by Richard Rodgers, Oscar Hammerstein II, Howard Lindsay and Russel Crouse); ph, Ted McCord (Todd-AO, DeLuxe Color); m, Rodgers.

Biography/Musical **Cas.** **(MPAA:G)**

SOUNDER

(1972) 105m Radnitz-Mattel/FOX c

Cicely Tyson *(Rebecca Morgan),* Paul Winfield *(Nathan Lee Morgan),* Kevin Hooks *(David Lee Morgan),* Carmen Mathews *(Mrs. Boatwright),* Taj Mahal *(Ike),* James Best *(Sheriff Young),* Yvonne Jarrell *(Josie Mae Morgan),* Eric Hooks *(Earl Morgan),* Sylvia "Kuumba" Williams *(Harriet),* Janet MacLachlan *(Camille Johnson),* Teddy Airhart *(Mr. Perkins),* Rev. Thomas N. Phillips *(Preacher),* Judge William Thomas Bennett *(Judge),* Inez Durham *(Court Clerk),* Spencer Bradford *(Clarence),* Myrl Sharkey *(Mrs. Clay).*

"Heartwarming," "heart-tugging," and "heartbreaking" are all words that can describe SOUNDER, a film that celebrates a family's dedication to one another through whatever travails befall them. It's the 1930s in Louisiana, where Nathan Lee and Rebecca Morgan (Paul Winfield and Cicely Tyson) are sharecroppers raising their three children and their dog, Sounder, as best they can in the poverty of the Depression. Nathan Lee farms and supplements meals by hunting for game, Rebecca takes in washing, and the trio of children take an equal part in doing the other tasks. There's not much game to be had, however, and when Nathan Lee is arrested for stealing a ham, the family is torn apart. Rebecca and the children now begin a backbreaking schedule as they strive to work the land, make their quota, and keep body and soul together. Adapted from a slim book that won the 1970 Newberry Award for children's literature, SOUNDER is one of the truest examples of a "family film" ever made and a triumph for all concerned. A sequel, SOUNDER, PART 2, followed in 1976, with Harold Sylvester and Ebony Wright taking over the roles of Nathan Lee and Rebecca.

p, Robert B. Radnitz; d, Martin Ritt; w, Lonne Elder III (based on the novel by William H. Armstrong); ph, John Alonzo (Panavision, DeLuxe Color); m, Taj Mahal.

Drama   **Cas.**   **(MPAA:G)**

SOUTHERN YANKEE, A

(1948) 90m MGM bw (AKA: MY HERO!)

Red Skelton (*Aubrey Filmore*), Brian Donlevy (*Curt Devlynn*), Arlene Dahl (*Sallyann Weatharby*), George Coulouris (*Maj. Jack Drumman*), Lloyd Gough (*Capt. Steve Lorford*), John Ireland (*Capt. Jed Calbern*), Minor Watson (*Gen. Watkins*), Charles Dingle (*Col. Weatharby*), Art Baker (*Col. Clifford M. Baker*), Reed Hadley (*Fred Munsey*), Arthur Space (*Mark Haskins*), Addison Richards (*Dr. Clayton*), Joyce Compton (*Hortense Dobson*), Paul Harvey (*Mr. Twitchell*), Jeff Corey (*Union Cavalry Sergeant*), Cliff Clark (*Dr. Cooper*), Dick Wessel, Ian MacDonald, John Hilton (*Orderlies*), Ed Gargan (*Male Nurse*), David Sharp (*Confederate Officer*), Frank McGrath (*Dispatch Rider*), David Newell (*Sentry*), William Tannen, Stanley Andrews, Roger Moore, Dick Simmons *(SS Men)*, Susan Simon (*Jenny*), Byron Foulger (*Mr. Duncan*), Paul Newlan (*Man with Saber*), Howard Mitchell, Paul Krueger, Vic Zimmerman, Chris Frank, James Logan *(Men)*, Marcus Turk, Ralph Montgomery, Walter Merrill (*Confederate Soldiers*), Ralph Volkie, Steve Bennett, Allen Mathews, William "Bill" Phillips (*Soldiers*), Ann Staunton (*Nurse*), Henry Hall (*Thadeus Drumman*), Lane Chandler, Carl Saxe (*Sentries*).

A SOUTHERN YANKEE's chief assets are its star, Red Skelton, and the unheralded contributions of silent comedy genius Buster Keaton. Skelton plays Aubrey Filmore, a not-so-bright St. Louis bellboy during the Civil War who ends up becoming a spy for Union forces when an infamous Confederate agent, "The Gray Spider," is captured. Filmore fills in for the Southerner and is sent behind enemy lines to obtain important information. While squirreling about below the Mason-Dixon line he meets Southern belle Sallyann Weatharby (Arlene Dahl), and tries to romance her without blowing his cover. The film has fine moments, chiefly because of the genuine earnestness Skelton gives to his character. Keaton had seen this quality in Skelton's previous work and was convinced it would shine in the right material. Then working as a gag man for MGM, Keaton went to studio chief Louis Mayer and made an offer to work exclusively with Skelton. The offer was declined, but Keaton was assigned as gag man for A SOUTHERN YANKEE and came up with the film's funniest moments. Most memorable is a sequence in which Filmore, walking a direct line between fighting Yankee and Confederate forces, wears a uniform that is half-blue and half-gray, with the appropriate side facing each army.

p, Paul Jones; d, Edward Sedgwick; w, Harry Tugend (based on a story by Melvin Frank and Norman Panama); ph, Ray June; m, David Snell.

Comedy   **(MPAA:NR)**

SPIRIT OF ST. LOUIS, THE

(1957) 135m WB c

James Stewart (*Charles A. Lindbergh*), Murray Hamilton (*Bud Gurney*), Patricia Smith (*Mirror Girl*), Bartlett Robinson (*B.F. Mahoney*), Robert Cornthwaite (*Knight*), Sheila Bond (*Model/Dancer*), Marc Connelly (*Father Hussman*), Arthur Space (*Donald Hall*), Harlan Warde (*Boedecker*), Dabbs Greer (*Goldsborough*), Paul Birch (*Blythe*), David Orrick (*Harold Bixby*), Robert Burton (*Maj. Lambert*), James L. Robertson, Jr. (*William Robertson*), Maurice Manson (*E. Lansing Ray*), James O'Rear (*Earl Thompson*), David McMahon (*Lane*), Griff Barnett (*Old Farmer*), John Lee (*Jess the Cook*), Herb Lytton (*Casey Jones*), Roy Gordon (*Associate Producer*), Aaron Spelling (*Mr. Pearless*), Charles Watts (*O.W. Schultz*), Virginia Christine (*Secretary*), Syd Saylor, Lee Roberts (*Photographers*), Richard Deacon (*Levine*), Ann Morrison (*Mrs. Pearless*), William Neff, William White (*Cadets*), Nelson Leigh (*Director*), Jack Daly (*Louie*), Carleton Young (*Captain*), Eugene Borden (*French Gendarme*), Erville Alderson (*Burt*), Olin Howlin [Olin Howland] (*Surplus Dealer*), Robert B. Williams (*Editor*), Percival Vivian (*Professor*), George Selk [Budd Buster] (*Mechanic*), Paul Brinegar (*Okie*), Chief Yowlachie (*Indian*), Ray Walker (*Barker*).

Billy Wilder's re-creation of Charles A. Lindbergh's 1927 solo flight from New York to Paris is an intelligent piece, marked by James Stewart's strong performance as the brave pilot. The story, based on Lindbergh's autobiography, opens as Lindbergh is working as an airmail pilot. His flying goals go well beyond his mail route, however, and he begins to think about a solo voyage across the Atlantic, something no single pilot has ever accomplished. Lindbergh tries to find financial backers for his dream and, after much struggle, finds a willing group in St. Louis, Missouri. He has a special plane built for the trip, dubbing it *The Spirit of St. Louis* in honor of his backers. On the day he is to take off from New York, Lindbergh is forced to spend some time on the ground while waiting for the rain to stop and, in flashback, reflects on his career. This is a well-told story, capturing the thoughts and feelings of a man alone in the most extraordinary conditions. Stewart is sincere and thoughtful in his depiction of the 1920s' greatest hero, and Wilder's direction shows the monotony of the flight without making his story tedious. The film gives a complete picture of Lindbergh, one that shows this dangerous journey to be the fulfillment of a devotion to and pure love of flying.

p, Leland Hayward; d, Billy Wilder; w, Billy Wilder, Wendell Mayes, Charles Lederer (based on the book by Charles A. Lindbergh); ph, Robert Burks, J. Peverell Marley (CinemaScope, Warner Color); m, Franz Waxman.

Biography   **Cas.**   **(MPAA:NR)**

STANLEY AND LIVINGSTONE

(1939) 101m FOX bw

Spencer Tracy *(Henry M. Stanley)*, Nancy Kelly *(Eve Kingsley)*, Richard Greene *(Gareth Tyce)*, Walter Brennan *(Jeff Slocum)*, Charles Coburn *(Lord Tyce)*, Sir Cedric Hardwicke *(Dr. David Livingstone)*, Henry Hull *(James Gordon Bennett)*, Henry Travers *(John Kingsley)*, Miles Mander *(Sir John Gresham)*, David Torrence *(Mr. Cranston)*, Holmes Herbert *(Frederick Holcomb)*, Montague Shaw *(Sir Oliver French)*, Paul Stanton *(Capt. Webb)*, Brandon Hurst *(Sir Henry Forrester)*, Hassan Said *(Hassan)*, Paul Harvey *(Col. Grimes)*, Russell Hicks, Frank Dae *(Commissioners)*, Clarence Derwent *(Sir Francis Vane)*, Joseph Crehan *(Morehead)*, Robert Middlemass *(Carmichael)*, Frank Jaquet *(Senator)*, William Williams *(Mace)*, Ernest Baskett *(Zucco)*, Emmett Vogan *(Bennett's Secretary)*, James McNamara *(Committeeman)*, William Dunn *(Chuma)*, Emmett Smith *(Susi)*, Jack Clisby *(Mombay)*, Dick Stanley *(Lieutenant)*, Thomas A. Coleman *(Corporal)*, William E. "Red" Blair *(Sergeant)*, Frank Orth *(Man with Pills)*, Billy Watson *(Copy Boy)*, Harry Harvey *(Man)*, Vernon Dent *(Newspaperman)*, Everett Brown *(Bongo)*.

An intelligent, if not strictly factual, retelling of the Stanley and Livingstone legend, this hardy adventure succeeds largely because of Spencer Tracy's fine, subdued performance as American journalist Henry Stanley, who searches for the missing Dr. David Livingstone (Sir Cedric Hardwicke). The film opens as Stanley returns to New York after filing reports from the West. His editor next wants the reporter to head into the African jungle and find Livingstone, a Scottish missionary who has disappeared. Stanley accepts the assignment, taking along Jeff Slocum (Walter Brennan) to accompany him on the search. The trip proves full of dangers hidden within the jungle. Stanley comes down with jungle fever, yet will not let this stop the mission. Finally he encounters the missionary in a remote jungle settlement and utters the famous line, "Dr. Livingstone, I presume?" Tracy gives a dignified portrait of a man who is profoundly changed as a result of his experience. The drama is well constructed, adroitly combining adventure with the humane values Livingstone espouses. The story is romanticized, with characters added to suit Hollywood conventions and the truth about Stanley's life after his encounter with Livingstone fictionalized.

p, Darryl F. Zanuck; d, Henry King; w, Philip Dunne, Julien Josephson (based on historical research and a story outline by Hal Long and Sam Hellman); ph, George Barnes, Otto Brower; m, Robert R. Bennett, David Buttolph, Louis Silvers, R.H. Bassett, Cyril Mockridge, Rudy Schrager.

Adventure   **Cas.**   **(MPAA:NR)**

STAR TREK: THE MOTION PICTURE

(1979) 132m PAR c

William Shatner *(Capt. James T. Kirk)*, Leonard Nimoy *(Mr. Spock)*, DeForest Kelley *(Dr. Leonard "Bones" McCoy)*, James Doohan *(Chief Engineer Montgomery "Scotty" Scott)*, George Takei *(Sulu)*, Majel Barrett *(Dr. Christine Chapel)*, Walter Koenig *(Chekov)*, Nichelle Nichols *(Uhura)*, Persis Khambatta *(Ilia)*, Stephen Collins *(Comdr. Willard Decker)*, Mark Lenard *(Klingon Captain)*, Billy Van Zandt *(Alien Boy)*, Grace Lee Whitney *(Janice Rand)*, Roger Aaron Brown *(Epsilon Technician)*, Gary Faga *(Airlock Technician)*, David Gautreaux *(Comdr. Branch)*, John D. Gowans *(Assistant to Rand)*, Jon Rashad Kamal *(Ltd. Comdr. Sonak)*, Howard Itzkowitz *(Cargo Deck Ensign)*, Marcy Lafferty *(Chief DiFalco)*, Jeri McBride *(Technician)*, Michele Ameen Billy *(Lieutenant)*, Terrence O'Conner *(Chief Ross)*, Michael Rougas *(Lt. Cleary)*.

It finally happened. The characters loved by millions, preserved in reruns even though the TV series was canceled nearly 10 years previously, were born again. The plot of this $40-million film sometimes gets lost amid technical gadgetry, but a generation of young adults that grew up watching one of the most successful television programs ever found, and still find, it fascinating to see what has become of the crew members of the starship *Enterprise*. Capt. James T. Kirk (William Shatner), now an admiral, is called upon one last time to take over the command of his old ship and halt a strange alien craft that is gobbling up everything in its path and is headed directly for Earth. To undertake this mission he calls upon the assistance of all the old crew members, and some new ones as well.

p, Gene Roddenberry; d, Robert Wise; w, Harold Livingston, Gene Roddenberry (based on a story by Alan Dean Foster, and on the TV program "Star Trek" created by Gene Roddenberry); ph, Richard H. Kline (Panavision, Metrocolor); m, Jerry Goldsmith.

Science Fiction   **Cas.**   **(MPAA:G)**

STAR TREK II: THE WRATH OF KHAN

(1982) 113m PAR c

William Shatner *(Adm. James T. Kirk)*, Leonard Nimoy *(Mr. Spock)*, DeForest Kelley *(Dr. Leonard "Bones" McCoy)*, James Doohan *(Chief Engineer Montgomery "Scotty" Scott)*, Walter Koenig *(Chekov)*, George Takei *(Sulu)*, Nichelle Nichols *(Comdr. Uhura)*, Bibi Besch *(Dr. Carol Marcus)*, Merritt Butrick *(David)*, Paul Winfield *(Starship Reliant Captain Terrell)*, Kirstie Alley *(Saavik)*, Ricardo Montalban *(Khan)*, Ike Eisenmann, John Vargas, John Winston, Paul Kent, Nicholas Guest, Russell Takaki, Kevin Sullivan, Joel Marstan, Teresa E. Victor, Dianne Harper, David Ruprecht, Marcy Vosburgh.

Of the first three "Star Trek" films, this second entry comes closest to the spirit of the television series. Adm. James T. Kirk (William Shatner) is still in charge of a space fleet, but his desk job doesn't allow him to do the kind of work for which he was born. When cajoled by Mr. Spock (Leonard Nimoy) and "Bones" McCoy (DeForest Kelley), Kirk agrees to take command of a mission that seems simple enough, but the sudden appearance of the evil Khan (Ricardo Montalban) makes for a very sticky situation. An interesting aspect of this film, ignored in the television series, is the focus on Kirk's family life back on Earth.

p, Robert Sallin; d, Nicholas Meyer; w, Jack B. Sowards (based on a story by Harve Bennett and Jack B. Sowards and on the TV program "Star Trek" created by Gene Roddenberry); ph, Gayne Rescher (Panavision, Movielab Color); m, James Horner.

Science Fiction   **Cas.**   **(MPAA:PG)**

STAR TREK III: THE SEARCH FOR SPOCK

(1984) 105m PAR c

William Shatner *(Kirk)*, Leonard Nimoy *(Spock)*, DeForest Kelley *(McCoy)*, James Doohan *(Scotty)*, Walter Koenig *(Chekov)*, George Takei *(Sulu)*, Michelle Nichols *(Uhura)*, Robin Curtis *(Saavik)*, Merritt Butrick *(David)*, Phil Morris *(Trainee Foster)*, Scott McGinnis *("Mr. Adventure")*, Robert Hooks *(Adm. Morrow)*, Carl Steven *(Spock, Age 9)*, Vadia Potenza *(Spock, Age 13)*, Stephen Manley *(Spock, Age 17)*, Joe W. Davis *(Spock, Age 25)*, Paul Sorensen *(Captain, Merchant Ship)*, Cathie Shirriff *(Valkris)*, Christopher Lloyd *(Kurge)*, Stephen Liska *(Torg)*, John Larroquette *(Maltz)*, Dave Cadiente *(Sergeant)*, Bob Cummings *(Gunner No. 1)*, Branscombe Richmond *(Gunner No. 2)*, Phillip Richard Allen *(Capt. Esteban)*, Jeanne Mori *(Helmsman)*, Mario Marcelino *(Communications, USS Grissom)*, Allan Miller *(Alien)*, Sharon Thomas *(Waitress)*, Conroy Gedeon *(Civilian Agent)*, James B. Sikking *(Capt. Styles)*, Miguel Ferrer *(1st Officer, USS Excelsior)*, Mark Lenard *(Sarek)*.

The third "Star Trek" film is not as good as the second, but it is still a very entertaining movie. Directed by Leonard Nimoy, the picture begins where the STAR TREK II: THE WRATH OF KHAN left off. The crew of the *Enterprise* is coming home when they learn that their beloved ship is slated to be put into the futuristic equivalent of mothballs. Mr. Spock, who apparently died in the last feature, is now kept alive in spirit, and Adm. James T. Kirk (William Shatner) must find Spock's body and bring it to the planet Vulcan, along with a crew member who is possessed by Spock's thoughts. But how can Kirk complete his mission when his ship is due for the junk heap? Never say die; the fearless Kirk and his loyal crew prevail.

p, Harve Bennett; d, Leonard Nimoy; w, Harve Bennett (based on the TV program "Star Trek" created by Gene Roddenberry); ph, Charles Correll (Panavision, Movielab Color); m, James Horner.

Science Fiction   **Cas.**   **(MPAA:PG)**

STAR TREK IV: THE VOYAGE HOME

(1986) 119m Paramount Pictures c

William Shatner *(Capt. James T. Kirk)*, Leonard Nimoy *(Mr. Spock)*, DeForest Kelley *(Dr. Leonard "Bones" McCoy)*, James Doohan *(Chief Engineer Montgomery "Scotty" Scott)*, George Takei *(Sulu)*, Walter Koenig *(Chekov)*, Nichelle Nichols *(Commander Uhura)*, Majel

Barrett *(Dr. Christine Chapel)*, Jane Wyatt *(Amanda, Spock's Mother)*, Catherine Hicks *(Dr. Gillian Taylor)*, Mark Lenard *(Sarek)*, Robin Curtis *(Lt. Saavik)*, Robert Ellenstein *(Federation Council President)*, John Schuck *(Klingon Ambassador)*, Brock Peters *(Cartwright)*, Scott DeVenney *(Bob Briggs)*, Madge Sinclair *(Capt. of the USS Saratoga)*, Jane Wiedlin *(Trillya)*.

The fourth STAR TREK film is, so far, the best. Its silliest of all STAR TREK movie plots is all the more satisfying, allowing us to laugh along with the characters who have lived for more than two decades in America's imagination. When the crew of the *Enterprise* was last seen, Mr. Spock (Leonard Nimoy, who directed this film) had been resurrected, but his fabulous mind was wiped clean of memory. The ship had been destroyed, its crew dejected. Now they respond to an eerie sound emanating from a space probe near 23rd-century Earth. The crew identifies the sound as a duplication of a humpback whale's cry, eventually realizing that the huge probe is looking for a whale to chat with and will destroy the Earth if it doesn't find one. But centuries of hunters have killed all the whales, and to save the Earth the crew must get back to the 20th century, find a pair of the sweet-voiced mammals, and transport them to the future. They therefore drop into San Francisco, 1986, concealing their ship under a cloak of invisibility while Spock and fearless Capt. James T. Kirk (William Shatner) carry out the task. Even in the unlikely instance that you have never seen a STAR TREK movie or TV episode, you will still enjoy this film. Shatner and Nimoy's comedic byplay goes beyond Hope and Crosby and sometimes into Cheech and Chong. They've gained years and pounds, but the film makes no attempt to present them as perpetually youthful. A thoroughly enjoyable film, preceded by STAR TREK: THE MOTION PICTURE; STAR TREK II: THE WRATH OF KHAN; and STAR TREK III: THE SEARCH FOR SPOCK.

p, Harve Bennett; d, Leonard Nimoy; w, Harve Bennett, Steve Meerson, Peter Krikes, Nicholas Meyer (based on a story by Leonard Nimoy and Harve Bennett and the TV series created by Gene Roddenberry); ph, Don Peterman (Panavision, Technicolor); m, Leonard Rosenman.

Science Fiction   **Cas.**   **(MPAA:PG)**

STAR WARS

(1977) 121m FOX c

Mark Hamill *(Luke Skywalker)*, Harrison Ford *(Han Solo)*, Carrie Fisher *(Princess Leia Organa)*, Peter Cushing *(Grand Moff Tarkin)*, Alec Guinness *(Ben "Obi-Wan" Kenobi)*, Anthony Daniels *(See Threepio [C-3PO])*, Kenny Baker *(Artoo-Detoo [R2-D2])*, Peter Mayhew *(Chewbacca)*, David Prowse *(Lord Darth Vader)*, Phil Brown *(Uncle Owen Lars)*, Shelagh Fraser *(Aunt Beru Lars)*, Jack Purvis *(Chief Jawa)*, Alex McCrindle *(Gen. Dodonna)*, Eddie Byrne *(Gen. Willard)*, Drewe Henley *(Red Leader)*, Dennis Lawson *(Red Two)*, Garrick Hagon *(Red Three)*, Jack Klaff *(Red Four)*, William Hootkins *(Red Six)*, Angus McInnis *(Gold Leader)*, Jeremy Sinden *(Gold Two)*, Graham Ashley *(Gold Five)*, Don Henderson *(Gen. Taggi)*, Richard LeParmentier *(Gen. Motti)*, Leslie Schoffield *(Commander No. 1)*.

"A long, long time ago, in a galaxy far away," reads the opening crawl of STAR WARS, introducing not only the film, but, in effect, a whole new generation of films and filmgoers. From this point on film was changed, and so were audience expectations. Like Steven Spielberg's JAWS, STAR WARS left the average viewer wanting more, more, more—and more is what they got, although much that has followed has paled by comparison. The cast of this phenomenal blockbuster is familiar to anyone who has walked the Earth in the past decade: pretty boy Mark Hamill is Luke Skywalker, rugged Harrison Ford is Han Solo, and attractive Carrie Fisher is Princess Leia. Also along for the ride are a pair of robots, R2-D2 (Kenny Baker) and C-3PO (Anthony Daniels); an oversized stuffed animal, Chewbacca (Peter Mayhew); and the mysterious force of good, Obi-Wan Kenobi (Alec Guinness). The far-off galaxy is ruled by a vicious tyrant (Peter Cushing) and his cruel masked aide, Darth Vader (David Prowse). A titanic battle between good and evil ensues, with thundering spaceships, exploding planets, and dueling lasers—the whole glorious affair presented with a maximum of adventure and humor. Whether or not you like science fiction, you will enjoy STAR WARS; this excellent piece of entertainment transcends genre pigeonholes. Try to see it on a big screen with a loud sound system to get the "you are there" feeling. Of the nine films planned for the STAR WARS series, only two others have been completed—THE RETURN OF THE JEDI and THE EMPIRE STRIKES BACK.

p, Gary Kurtz; d&w, George Lucas; ph, Gilbert Taylor (Panavision, Technicolor); m, John T. Williams.

Science Fiction   Cas.   **(MPAA:PG)**

STARS AND STRIPES FOREVER

(1952) 89m FOX c (GB: MARCHING ALONG)

Clifton Webb *(John Philip Sousa)*, Debra Paget *(Lily)*, Robert Wagner *(Willie)*, Ruth Hussey *(Jennie)*, Finlay Currie *(Col. Randolph)*, Benay Venuta *(Mme. Bernsdorff-Mueller)*, Roy Roberts *(Maj. Houston)*, Tom Browne Henry *(David Blakely)*, Lester Matthews *(Mr. Pickering)*, Maude Prickett *(Maid)*, Erno Verebes *(Organ Grinder)*, Richard Garrick *(Secretary of the Navy)*, Romo Vincent *(Music Professor)*, Roy Gordon *(President Harrison)*, Florence Shirley *(Navy Nurse)*, Delos Jewkes *(Bass Singer)*, Norman Leavitt *(Purvis)*, Hellen Van Tuyl *(Mrs. Harrison)*, Walter Woolf King, Roger Moore *(President's Aides)*, Thomas E. Jackson *(Senator)*, Maude Wallace *(Nora)*, Lenee Martin *(Priscilla)*, Sharon Jan Altman *(Helen)*, Nicholas Koster *(John Philip Sousa, Jr.)*, William Vedder *(Prof. Estaban)*, Olan Soule *(Glove Salesman)*, Aileen Carlyle *(Mme. Liebling)*, Paul Maxey *(Mr. McCaull)*, Frank Ferguson, Jack Rice, The Atlanta Stone Mountain Choir.

This lively and colorful biography of John Philip Sousa preserves the spirit of his music with entertaining verve. The film opens with Sousa (Clifton Webb) as leader of the Marine Corps band. He then leaves the military to form his own band, taking the group all over the world to perform. One band member (Robert Wagner) helps create the Sousa legend by devising a giant horn he dubs the "Sousaphone." The plot is thin, but the film is full of energy, music, and color. The 1890s are faithfully re-created, including some wonderful period costumes. The cast gives the story everything it needs to work, with Webb giving an engaging, eccentric performance. Based on Sousa's autobiography, *Marching Along*, the film points out some little-known facts about the composer's life, such as his secret dream to write ballads rather than marches. It was the marches, however, that made him famous, and the film is packed with them, including "Stars and Stripes Forever," "El Capitan," and "Washington Post."

p, Lamar Trotti; d, Henry Koster; w, Lamar Trotti, Ernest Vajda (based on *Marching Along* by John Philip Sousa); ph, Charles G. Clarke (Technicolor).

Biography/Musical   Cas.   **(MPAA:NR)**

STORM BOY

(1976, Aus.) 88m South Australian Film c

Greg Rowe *(Storm Boy)*, Peter Cummins *(Hide-Away Tom)*, David Gulpilil *(Fingerbone Bill)*, Judy Dick *(Miss Walker)*, Tony Allison *(Ranger)*, Michael Moody *(Boat Master)*, Graham Dow *(Edwards)*, Frank Foster-Brown *(Lynch)*, Eric Mack *(Jones)*, Michael Caulfield, Paul Smith *(Hunters)*, Hedley Cullen *(Marina Manager)*, Schoolchildren from the Port Elliot Primary School.

Filled with many a tearful moment, this coming-of-age tale deals with a young Australian boy (Greg Rowe) who lives with his father in an uninhabited coastal area, learning all he can about life just by living it. The boy befriends an old aborigine, finds a nest of abandoned pelicans, and begins to care for them at the old man's urging. As the picture progresses, the boy's relationships with his father and the aborigine deepen.

p, Matt Carroll; d, Henri Safran; w, Sonia Berg (based on the novel by Colin Thiele); ph, Geoff Burton; m, Michael Carlos.

Drama   Cas.   **(MPAA:NR)**

STORY OF ALEXANDER GRAHAM BELL, THE

(1939) 97m FOX bw (GB: THE MODERN MIRACLE)

Don Ameche *(Alexander Graham Bell)*, Loretta Young *(Mrs. Bell)*, Henry Fonda *(Tom Watson)*, Charles Coburn *(Gardner Hubbard)*, Spring Byington *(Mrs. Hubbard)*, Gene Lockhart *(Thomas Sanders)*, Sally Blane *(Gertrude Hubbard)*, Polly Ann Young *(Grace Hubbard)*, Georgiana Young *(Berta Hubbard)*, Bobs Watson *(George Sanders)*, Russell Hicks *(Barrows)*, Paul Stanton *(Chauncey Smith)*, Jonathan Hale *(President of Western Union)*, Harry Davenport *(Judge)*, Beryl Mercer *(Queen Victoria)*, Elizabeth Patterson *(Mrs. McGregor)*, Charles Trowbridge *(George Pollard)*, Claire DuBrey *(Landlady)*, Ralph Remley

(D'Arcy), Zeffie Tilbury (Mrs. Sanders), Jan Duggan (Mrs. Winthrop), Harry Tyler (Doc Elliott), Lillian West (Nurse), Warren Jackson, Tyler Brooke (Singers), George Guhl (Mr. Winthrop), Mary Field (Piano Player), William Wagner (Bit), Dave Morris (Telegrapher), Jack Kelly (Banker's Son), Edmund Elton (Banker), Jarold Clifford Lyons (Infant), Landers Stevens (Manager of North Eastern Telephone Exchange), John Spacey (Sir John Cowell), Dick Elliott (Man Who Laughs), Jack Walsh (James J. Starrow), Charles Tannen (Court Clerk), Otto Hoffman (Pawnbroker).

THE STORY OF ALEXANDER GRAHAM BELL is the film for which Don Ameche will be best remembered, despite his Oscar-winning performance in COCOON more than 40 years later. The film opens in 1873 with Alexander Graham Bell (Ameche) trying to earn his living by working with deaf-mutes while spending his off-hours inventing. Bell is soon enamored of a pretty young Scot (Loretta Young) whom he has been asked to teach. They fall in love, and she asks her father to unbuckle his copious money belt to back one of Bell's inventions. Bell hopes to perfect a process whereby he can use the same kind of wires Western Union uses for sending dots and dashes to transmit the sound of a human voice. After much trial and error, he succeeds and, in doing so, becomes one of the most famous inventors in history. Not even remotely factual, this Hollywood-invented story is an enjoyable feature nonetheless, especially when Ameche is on-screen.

p, Darryl F. Zanuck, Kenneth MacGowan; d, Irving Cummings; w, Lamar Trotti (based on a story by Ray Harris); ph, Leon Shamroy.

Biography   **Cas.**   **(MPAA:NR)**

STORY OF G.I. JOE, THE

(1945) 109m UA bw (AKA: WAR CORRESPONDENT)

Burgess Meredith (Ernie Pyle), Robert Mitchum (Lt. Walker), Freddie Steele (Sgt. Warnicki), Wally Cassell (Pvt. Dondaro), Jimmy Lloyd (Pvt. Spencer), Jack Reilly (Pvt. Murphy), Bill Murphy (Pvt. Mew), William Self (Cookie Henderson), Dick Rich (Sergeant at Showers), Billy Benedict (Whitey), Tito Renaldo (Lopez), Michael Browne (Sergeant), Yolanda Lacca (Amelia), Dorothy Coonan (Nurse), Don Whitehead, George Lait, Chris Cunningham, Hal Boyle, Sgt. Jack Foisie, Bob Landry, Lucien Hubbard, Clete Roberts, Robert Reuben (Themselves, Correspondents).

This story of the greatest of America's WW II combat correspondents, Ernie Pyle, immortalizes the man who celebrated the common soldier in his dispatches and books (Brave Men and Here Is Your War). As the film begins, Pyle (Burgess Meredith) catches up with a tired platoon of infantrymen in Italy, observing and comforting them as they fight through town after town, enduring death, misery, boredom, and fear. Leading the platoon is Lt. Walker (Robert Mitchum), a tough but likable officer who is respected and admired by his men. The film has no real story, only the consistent wearing down of the men

through combat and fatigue. Meredith is superb, conveying the humanity and caring of Pyle, but it is Mitchum who steals the show. This great picture had the full cooperation of Pyle, who was killed in the South Pacific before seeing THE STORY OF G.I. JOE.

p, Lester Cowan; d, William A. Wellman; w, Leopold Atlas, Guy Endore, Philip Stevenson (based on the book Here Is Your War by Ernie Pyle); ph, Russell Metty; m, Ann Ronell, Louise Applebaum.

War   **Cas.**   **(MPAA:NR)**

STORY OF LOUIS PASTEUR, THE

(1936) 85m WB bw

Paul Muni (Louis Pasteur), Josephine Hutchinson (Mme. Pasteur), Anita Louise (Annette Pasteur), Donald Woods (Jean Martel), Fritz Leiber, Sr. (Dr. Charbonnet), Henry O'Neill (Roux), Porter Hall (Dr. Rosignol), Ray Brown (Dr. Radisse), Akim Tamiroff (Dr. Zaranoff), Walter Kingsford (Napoleon III), Iphigenie Castiglioni (Empress Eugenie), Herbert Heywood (Boncourt), Frank Reicher (Dr. Pheiffer), Halliwell Hobbes (Dr. Joseph Lister), Dickie Moore (Phillip Meister), Herbert Corthell (President Louis-Adolphe Thiers), Frank Mayo (President Sadi Carnot), William Burress (Doctor), Robert Strange (Magistrate), Mabel Colcord (A Lady), Niles Welch (Courier), Leonard Mudie (Coachman), Brenda Fowler (Midwife), Eric Mayne (Lord Chamberlain), Alphonze Ethier (Finance Minister), Edward Van Sloan (Chairman), George Andre Beranger (Assistant), Montague Shaw (British Reporter), Otto Hoffman (Farmer), Tempe Pigott (Woman), Richard Alexander (Burly Farmer).

This film biography stars Paul Muni as Louis Pasteur, the French scientist who worked to find a cure for anthrax and hydrophobia. His colleagues at the Medical Academy are convinced his experiments are a waste of time and ridicule his research, so he and his family move to the French countryside, where he can conduct his experiments in peace. Authorities soon learn that the sheep in Pasteur's area are disease-free as a result of his efforts, a finding which causes some stir in the Medical Academy, as Pasteur is now praised for his ground-breaking work by his former critics. THE STORY OF LOUIS PASTEUR is well told, with an intelligent script, excellent performances, and careful attention to scientific accuracy. Muni's performance, which won him a Best Actor Oscar, is a fine characterization that shows the famed scientist as a man faced with extraordinary obstacles.

p, Henry Blanke; d, William Dieterle; w, Sheridan Gibney, Pierre Collins (based on the story by Sheridan Gibney, Pierre Collins); ph, Tony Gaudio.

Biography   **Cas.**   **(MPAA:NR)**

STORY OF ROBIN HOOD, THE

(1952, Brit.) 84m RKO-Disney/RKO c (GB: THE STORY OF ROBIN HOOD AND HIS MERRIE MEN)

Richard Todd (Robin Hood), Joan Rice (Maid Marian), Peter Finch (Sheriff of Nottingham), James Hayter (Friar Tuck), James Robertson Justice (Little John), Martita Hunt (Queen Eleanor), Hubert Gregg (Prince John), Bill Owen (Stutely), Reginald Tate (Hugh Fitzooth), Elton Haytes (Allan-a-Dale), Antony Eustrel (Archbishop of Canterbury), Patrick Barr (King Richard), Anthony Forwood (Will Scarlett), Hal Osmond (Midge the Miller), Michael Hordern (Scathelock), Clement McCallin (Earl of Huntingdon), Louise Hampton (Tyb), Archie Duncan (Red Gill), Julian Somers (Posse Leader), Bill Travers (Posse Man), David Davies (Forester).

After the success of Disney's first live-action feature, TREASURE ISLAND, the studio decided to make another, again in Britain, this time based on the legend of Robin Hood. Unfairly dismissed today as merely a Disney adventure, this version holds up nearly as well as Michael Curtiz's THE ADVENTURES OF ROBIN HOOD (1938), but doesn't offer a cast that can compare with Errol Flynn, Olivia de Havilland, Basil Rathbone, and Claude Rains. The story is a familiar one—Robin Hood and his band of merry men trying to save the poor folks of Nottingham from Prince John's greedy ways—but, given the Disney treatment, the legendary heroes and events seem even more romantic.

p, Perce Pearce; d, Ken Annakin; w, Lawrence E. Watkin; ph, Guy Green (Technicolor); m, Clifton Parker.

Adventure (MPAA:NR)

STORY OF WILL ROGERS, THE

(1952) 109m WB c

Will Rogers, Jr. (Will Rogers), Jane Wyman (Mrs. Will Rogers), Carl Benton Reid (Clem Rogers), Eve Miller (Cora Marshall), James Gleason (Bert Lynn), Slim Pickens (Dusty Donovan), Noah Beery, Jr. (Wiley Post), Mary Wickes (Mrs. Foster), Steve Brodie (Dave Marshall), Pinky Tomlin (Orville James), Margaret Field (Sally Rogers), Virgil S. Taylor (Art Frazer), Richard Kean (Mr. Cavendish), Jay Silverheels (Joe Arrow), William Forrest (Flo Ziegfeld), Earl Lee (President Wilson), Brian Daly (Tom McSpadden), Eddie Cantor (Himself), Robert Scott Correll (Younger Will), Carol Ann Gainey (Younger Mary), Michael Gainey (Younger Jimmy/Young Will), Carol Nugent (Young Mary), Jack Burnette (Young Jimmy), Paul McWilliam (Dead-Eye Dick), Dub Taylor (Actor), Olan Soule (Secretary).

A charming tribute Will Rogers, this Michael Curtiz-directed film offers a simple, reverent recapitulation of the great American humorist's life. It follows Rogers from his birth in 1879 in Oologah, Oklahoma, through his marriage and experiences with a Wild West show, and on to his fateful Alaska-bound plane crash in 1935. Will Rogers, Jr., skillfully essays the role of his father.

p, Robert Arthur; d, Michael Curtiz; w, Frank Davis, Stanley Roberts, John C. Moffitt (based on the story "Uncle Clem's Boy," by Betty Blake Rogers); ph, Wilfrid M. Cline (Technicolor); m, Victor Young.

Biography (MPAA:NR)

STOWAWAY

(1936) 86m FOX bw

Shirley Temple (Ching-Ching), Robert Young (Tommy Randall), Alice Faye (Susan Parker), Eugene Pallette (The Colonel), Helen Westley (Mrs. Hope), Arthur Treacher (Atkins), J. Edward Bromberg (Judge Booth), Astrid Allwyn (Kay Swift), Allan Lane (Richard Hope), Robert Greig (Captain), Jayne Regan (Dora Day), Julius Tannen (First Mate), Willie Fung (Chang), Phillip Ahn (Sun Lo), Paul McVey (Second Mate), Helen Jerome Eddy (Mrs. Kruikshank), William Stack (Alfred Kruikshank), Honorable Wu (Latchee Lee).

In this pleasing Shirley Temple vehicle, the child star plays Ching-Ching, the ward of a group of murdered missionaries. She finds refuge in a car belonging to American Tommy Randall (Robert Young), which is then loaded onto an ocean liner. When Tommy gets married, he and his new bride (Alice Faye) adopt Ching-Ching. The once-happy lovers soon separate, however, and file for divorce, but Ching-Ching turns on the charm and persuades them to remain husband and wife. Temple's most memorable scene comes when she impersonates Al Jolson, Eddie Cantor, and Ginger Rogers (dancing with a Fred Astaire doll). STOWAWAY is worth watching just to hear Shirley speak Chinese.

p, Buddy G. DeSylva; d, William A. Seiter; w, William Conselman, Arthur Sheekman, Nat Perrin (based on a story by Samuel G. Engel); ph, Arthur Miller.

Comedy/Musical Cas. (MPAA:NR)

STRATTON STORY, THE

(1949) 106m MGM bw

James Stewart (Monty Stratton), June Allyson (Ethel Stratton), Frank Morgan (Barney Wile), Agnes Moorehead (Ma Stratton), Bill Williams (Gene Watson), Bruce Cowling (Ted Lyons), Eugene Bearden (Western All-Stars Pitcher), Bill Dickey, Jimmy Dykes (Themselves), Cliff Clark (Higgins), Mary Lawrence (Dot), Dean White (Luke Appling), Robert Gist (Larnie), Mervyn Shea (White Sox Catcher), Mitchell Lewis (Conductor), Michael Ross (Pitcher), James Nolan, Peter Crouse (Reporters), Florence Lake (Mrs. Appling), Anne Nagel (Mrs. Piet), Barbara Woodell (Mrs. Shea), Alphonse Martel (Headwaiter), Holmes Herbert (Doctor), Robert Graham, Eugene Persson (Boys), Lee Tung Foo (Waiter), Roy Partee (Western Pitcher), Kenneth Tobey (Detroit Player), Pat Flaherty (Western Manager), Capt. F.G. Somers (Giants Manager), Fred Millican (All-Star Catcher), Pat Orr, John "Ziggy" Sears, Jack Powell, Joe Rue (Umpires), John Kerr (Yankee Coach).

This is the true story of pitcher Monty Stratton's heroic return to professional baseball after his leg had been amputated as the result of a hunting accident. Although some liberties are taken with the story to make it play on-screen, the film doesn't stray too far from the facts. Stratton (James Stewart) is pitching in a semipro game in Texas when Barney Wile (Frank Morgan), a one-time baseball player but now a jobless hobo, recognizes his raw talent. Stratton likes the idea of hurling in the majors, and Barney offers to instruct him in the fine points that separate sandlotters from stars. The pair hitchhikes to California, where the White Sox are holding their training camp. White Sox manager Jimmy Dykes (playing himself) lets Stratton try out and the lanky right-hander is so impressive that he's given a contract. After a couple of superb years, it looks as though a great future is in store for the pitcher, until he accidentally shoots himself in the leg. With a prosthesis, Stratton learns to walk again, and then gets back into form on the pitching mound. An inspiring picture about a man who wouldn't give up.

p, Jack Cummings; d, Sam Wood; w, Douglas Morrow, Guy Trosper (based on a story by Douglas Morrow); ph, Harold Rosson.

Biography/Sports   **Cas.**   **(MPAA:NR)**

STRIKE UP THE BAND

(1940) 120m MGM bw

Mickey Rooney (*Jimmy Connors*), Judy Garland (*Mary Holden*), Paul Whiteman and Orchestra (*Themselves*), June Preisser (*Barbara Frances Morgan*), William Tracy (*Phillip Turner*), Ann Shoemaker (*Mrs. Connors*), Larry Nunn (*Willie Brewster*), George Lessey (*Mr. Morgan*), Francis Pierlot (*Mr. Judd*), Harry McCrillis (*Booper Barton*), Margaret Early (*Annie*), Sarah Edwards (*Miss Hodges*), Elliot Carpenter (*Henry*), Virginia Brissac (*Mrs. May Holden*), Howard Hickman (*The Doctor*), Virginia Sale (*Music Teacher*), Milton Kibbee (*Mr. Holden*), Mickey Martin, Charles Smith (*Boys*), Sherrie Overton, Margareet Marquis, Maxine Cook (*Girls*), Phil Silvers (*Pitch Man*), Billy Wayne (*Clown*), Joe Devlin (*Attendant*), Don Castle (*Charlie*), Enid Bennett (*Mrs. Morgan*), Helen Jerome Eddy (*Mrs. Brewster*), Harlan Briggs (*Doctor*), Dick Allen (*Policeman*), Jimmie Lucas, Jack Albertson (*Barkers*).

Mickey Rooney and Judy Garland, two of the great young stars of their day, team up in this musical comedy as a pair of high school students. Mary (Garland) works in the library after school, and Jimmy (Rooney) spends his free time practicing the drums. He wants to smack the skins in a dance band, but his widowed mother yearns for him to become a doctor. Jimmy and a bunch of his pals form an orchestra with the intention of entering a contest sponsored by big band "King of Jazz" Paul Whiteman. The kids manage to scrape together the money for their trip to the coast, but when one of them needs an emergency operation, Jimmy decides to pay for it and sacrifice his big chance. Luckily, Paul Whiteman is in town and Jimmy and his boys get a chance to play for him anyway. Rooney and Garland deliver their usual energy-packed performances, but one unexpected scene is a standout: as Jimmy uses a bowl of fruit to illustrate an idea he has for a musical number, the fruit transforms into little animated puppet models (masterminded by George Pal) that perform "Do the Conga." Also included is the big band classic "Sing, Sing, Sing."

p, Arthur Freed; d, Busby Berkeley; w, John Monks, Jr., Fred Finklehoffe, (uncredited) Herbert Fields, Kay Van Riper; ph, Ray June.

Comedy/Musical   **Cas.**   **(MPAA:NR)**

SUMMER HOLIDAY

(1948) 92m MGM c

Mickey Rooney (*Richard Miller*), Gloria DeHaven (*Muriel McComber*), Walter Huston (*Nat Miller*), Frank Morgan (*Uncle Sid*), Jackie "Butch" Jenkins (*Tommy Miller*), Marilyn Maxwell (*Belle*), Agnes Moorehead (*Cousin Lily*), Selena Royle (*Mrs. Miller*), Michael Kirby (*Arthur Miller*), Shirley Johns (*Mildred Miller*), Hal Hackett (*Wint*), Anne Francis (*Elsie Rand*), John Alexander (*Mr. McComber*), Virginia Brissac (*Miss Hawley*), Howard Freeman (*Mr. Peabody*), Alice MacKenzie (*Mrs. McComber*), Don Garner (*Gilbert Ralston*), Ruth Brady (*Crystal*), Emory Parnell (*Bartender*), Wally Cassell (*Salesman*), Terry Moore (*Hatcheck Girl*), Francis Stevens, Budd Fine (*Farmers*), Louise Colombet, Blanche Rose, Margaret Fealey, Nell Spaugh (*Old Painting Characters*), Oliver Blake (*Scorekeeper*), Margaret Bert (*Mrs. Nichols*).

This ~~fine musical~~ version of Eugene O'Neill's "Ah, Wilderness" stars Mickey Rooney as a boy struggling with the pitfalls of adolescence. In early 1900s New England we meet the Miller clan: Nat (Walter Huston), a newspaper editor and staunch upholder of Yankee tradition; his wife (Selena Royle), ever the doting mother; Richard (Rooney), their oldest son; and Tommy ("Butch" Jenkins), their youngest. Also living in their comfortable household are an old maid cousin (Agnes Moorehead) and a bachelor uncle (Frank Morgan). Richard is extraordinarily bright and has big ideas about changing the world. He adores neighbor Muriel McComber (Gloria DeHaven), but has been forbidden to see her by her conservative father. Peeved at his inability to see the girl he loves, Richard goes off on a drunk, meets a dance-hall girl, spends every cent he has, and gets kicked out of the bar. Naturally, he catches hell from his dad, but by the end he and Muriel are finally allowed to be together. A sweet movie with good work by all the actors. An earlier version of the O'Neill play appeared in 1935 as AH, WILDERNESS, with Rooney playing the role of the younger brother.

p, Arthur Freed; d, Rouben Mamoulian; w, Frances Goodrich, Albert Hackett, Irving Brecher, Jean Holloway (based on the play "Ah, Wilderness" by Eugene O'Neill); ph, Charles Schoenbaum (Technicolor); m, Harry Warren.

Comedy/Musical   **(MPAA:NR)**

SUMMER MAGIC

(1963) 109m Disney/BV c

Hayley Mills (*Nancy Carey*), Burl Ives (*Osh Popham*), Dorothy McGuire (*Margaret Carey*), Deborah Walley (*Cousin Julia*), Eddie Hodges (*Gilly Carey*), Jimmy Mathers (*Peter Carey*), Michael J. Pollard (*Digby Popham*), Wendy Turner (*Lallie Joy Popham*), Una Merkel (*Maria Popham*), Peter

Brown *(Tom Hamilton)*, James Stacy *(Charles Bryant)*, O.Z. Whitehead *(Mr. Perkins)*, Eddie Quillan *(Mailman)*, Norman Leavitt *(Barber)*, Paul E. Burns *(Drinker)*, Harry Holcombe *(Henry Lord)*, Jan Stine *(Mr. Perkins' Son)*, Hilda Plowright *(Mary)*, Marcy McGuire *(Ellen)*.

Almost but not *too cute*, this light, unpretentious Disney fare provides 109 minutes of escapist entertainment. Margaret Carey (Dorothy McGuire) is a recent widow forced to move from her expensive Boston home to a small town in Maine, dragging along her teenage daughter (Hayley Mills) and her young sons. Their new place is old and broken down, but through hard work, they transform it into very pleasant country home. Willing to go out of his way to lend a hand is the local postmaster (Burl Ives), who must be the sweetest man ever to grace the giant screen.

p, Walt Disney, Ron Miller; d, James Neilson; w, Sally Benson (based on the novel *Mother Carey's Chickens* by Kate Douglas Wiggin); ph, William Snyder (Technicolor); m, Buddy Baker.

Comedy   **Cas.**   **(MPAA:NR)**

SUN COMES UP, THE

(1949) 93m MGM c

Jeanette MacDonald *(Helen Lorfield Winter)*, Lloyd Nolan *(Thomas I. Chandler)*, Claude Jarman, Jr. *(Jerry)*, Percy Kilbride *(Mr. Willie B. Williegoode)*, Lewis Stone *(Arthur Norton)*, Nicholas Joy *(Victor Alvord)*, Margaret Hamilton *(Mrs. Golightly)*, Hope Landin *(Mrs. Pope)*, Esther Somers *(Susan)*, Dwayne Hickman *(Hank Winter)*, Teddy Infuhr *(Junebug)*, Barbara Billingsley *(Nurse)*, Charles Trowbridge *(Dr. Gage)*, John A. Butler *(Doorman)*, Ida Moore *(Sally)*, Paul E. Burns *(Dr. Sample)*, Guy Wilkerson *(Man)*, Peter Roman *(Love)*, Mickey McGuire *(Cleaver)*, Lassie the Dog.

Time to take out the handkerchiefs again as Jeanette MacDonald plays a war widow whose recent loss of her son has forced her to a retreat in the backwoods of Georgia. When a boy from the local orphanage (Claude Jarman) comes to help her with chores—accompanied by Lassie —the widow's motherly instincts resurface. Despite her efforts to remain detached from the youth, after he narrowly escapes being killed in a fire at the orphanage, she ultimately takes in the boy as her own. A fine cast of character actors adds strong support to this effective blend of drama, comedy, and action.

p, Robert Sisk: d, Richard Thorpe; w, William Ludwig, Margaret Fitts (based on short stories by Marjorie Kinnan Rawlings); ph, Ray June (Technicolor); m, Andre Previn.

Drama   **(MPAA:NR)**

SUPERMAN

(1978) 143m WB c

Marlon Brando *(Jor-El)*, Gene Hackman *(Lex Luthor)*, Christopher Reeve *(Superman/Clark Kent)*, Ned Beatty *(Otis)*, Jackie Cooper *(Perry White)*, Glenn Ford *(Pa Kent)*, Trevor Howard *(1st Elder)*, Margot Kidder *(Lois Lane)*, Jack O'Halloran *(Non)*, Valerie Perrine *(Eve Teschmacher)*, Maria Schell *(Vond-Ah)*, Terence Stamp *(Gen. Zod)*, Phyllis Thaxter *(Ma Kent)*, Susannah York *(Lara)*, Jeff East *(Young Clark Kent)*, Marc McClure *(Jimmy Olsen)*, Sarah Douglas *(Ursa)*, Harry Andrews *(2nd Elder)*, Lee Quigley *(Baby Kal-El)*, Aaron Smolinski *(Baby Clark Kent)*, Diane Sherry *(Lana Lang)*, Jeff Atcheson *(Coach)*, Jill Ingham *(Perry's Secretary)*, Rex Reed *(Himself)*, Weston Gavin *(Mugger)*, George Harris II *(Patrolman Mooney)*, Rex Everhardt *(Desk Sergeant)*, Jayne Tottman *(Little Girl)*, Larry Hagman *(Major)*, Paul Tuerpe *(Sgt. Hayley)*, Chief Tug Smith *(Indian Chief)*, Roy Stevens *(Warden)*, Kirk Alyn, Noel Neill *(Couple on Train)*, Bob Dahdah *(Newspaper Customer)*.

"You'll believe a man can fly," the ads said, and by SUPERMAN's end that's just about true. Christopher Reeve essays the title role and makes it his own, combining correctly chiseled features with a likable comic humanity, while the film itself nicely balances special effects with the romance of Superman and Lois Lane (Margot Kidder). The story opens on the planet Krypton, where Superman's father (Marlon Brando) sends his son off to Earth, where he grows up to be "mild-mannered reporter" Clark Kent. Flying around in tights and cape, Superman-alias-Clark saves the day—and Lois—a number of times. Eventually, he rescues all mankind from the evil Lex Luthor (Gene Hackman) and his assistants (Ned Beatty and Valerie Perrine, in an excellent bit of comic caricature) as they plot to take over the world. Lois is killed in the course of events, but Superman circles the globe at such terrific speed that its rotation is reversed, bringing his beloved back to life. The film burdens itself with too many story lines and an overlong (though beautifully photographed) prolog, but things really get moving when Reeve takes the screen. A worldwide hunt was conducted to find the right man for the role, with Robert Redford, Burt Reynolds, Nick Nolte, Kris Kristofferson, Sylvester Stallone, Ryan O'Neal, Clint Eastwood, and Charles Bronson among the candidates. So excellent is Reeve, however, that it is nearly impossible to think of anyone else as the "Man of Steel."

p, Pierre Spengler; d, Richard Donner; w, Mario Puzo, David Newman, Leslie Newman, Robert Benton (based on the story by Mario Puzo, from the comic strip created by Jerry Siegel and Joel Shuster); ph, Geoffrey Unsworth (Panavision, Technicolor); m, John Williams.

Science Fiction   **Cas.**   **(MPAA:PG)**

SUPERMAN II

(1980) 127m WB c

Gene Hackman *(Lex Luthor)*, Christopher Reeve *(Clark Kent/Superman)*, Ned Beatty *(Otis)*, Jackie Cooper *(Perry White)*, Sarah Douglas *(Ursa)*, Margot Kidder *(Lois Lane)*, Jack O'Halloran *(Non)*, Valerie Perrine *(Eve Teschmacher)*, Susannah York *(Lara)*, Clifton James *(Sheriff)*, E.G. Marshall *(The President)*, Marc McClure *(Jimmy Ol-*

sen), Terence Stamp *(Gen. Zod)*, Leueen Willoughby *(Leueen)*, Robin Pappas *(Alice)*, Roger Kemp *(Spokesman)*, Roger Brierley, Anthony Milner, Richard Griffiths *(Terrorists)*, Melissa Wiltsie *(Nun)*, Alain DeHay *(Gendarme)*, Marc Boyle *(CRS Man)*, Alan Stuart *(Cab Driver)*, John Ratzenberger, Shane Rimmer *(Controllers)*, John Morton *(Nate)*, Jim Dowdell *(Boris)*, Angus McInnes *(Warden)*, Antony Sher *(Bellboy)*, Elva May Hoover *(Mother)*, Hadley Kay *(Jason)*, Todd Woodcroft *(Father)*, John Hollis *(Krypton Elder)*, Gordon Rollings *(Fisherman)*, Peter Whitman *(Deputy)*, Bill Bailey *(J.J.)*, Dinny Powell *(Boog)*, Hal Galili *(Man at Bar)*, Marcus D'Amico *(Willie)*, Jackie Cooper *(Dino)*, Richard Parmentier *(Reporter)*, Don Fellows *(General)*, Michael J. Shannon *(President's Aide)*, Tony Sibbald *(Presidential Impostor)*, Tommy Duggan *(Diner Owner)*.

Poking fun at its American mythos, but never descending into camp comedy, this superior sequel to the original SUPERMAN makes for a wonderful time. Christopher Reeve reprises his role as the bumbling reporter/Man of Steel with marvelous success. The film opens with a fury as terrorists who have taken over the Eiffel Tower threaten to blow it up with a nuclear bomb. Lois Lane (Margot Kidder), ever the inquisitive reporter, tries to interview the terrorists and finds herself in more trouble than she bargained for. Fortunately, Superman comes to save the day, rescuing Lois and flinging the bomb into outer space. But this sets off a nuclear explosion that frees some bad guys (Terence Stamp, Sarah Douglas, and Jack O'Halloran) from the cosmic prison they were sentenced to in SUPERMAN. The sequel hits full stride as the villains come to take over Earth, not knowing their fellow Kryptonian is that planet's hero. The result is an especially fun movie and a rare instance of a sequel that not only equals, but even betters, its original. The same cannot be said for SUPERMAN III or SUPERMAN IV: THE QUEST FOR PEACE, despite Reeve's continued command of the role.

p, Pierre Spengler; d, Richard Lester; w, Mario Puzo, David Newman, Leslie Newman (based on a story by Mario Puzo, from characters created by Jerry Siegel, Joe Shuster); ph, Geoffrey Unsworth, Robert Paynter (Technicolor); m, Ken Thorne.

Science Fiction   Cas.   (MPAA:PG)

SWALLOWS AND AMAZONS

(1977, Brit.) 92m EMI/LDS c

Virginia McKenna *(Mrs. Walker)*, Ronald Fraser *(Uncle Jim)*, Brenda Bruce *(Mrs. Dixon)*, Jack Woolgar *(Old Billy)*, John Franklyn-Robbins *(Young Billy)*; The Swallows: Simon West *(John)*, Zanna Hamilton *(Susan)*, Sophie Neville *(Titty)*, Stephen Grendon *(Roger)*; The Amazons: Kit Seymour *(Nancy)*, Lesley Bennett *(Peggy)*.

Set in the 1920s, this pleasant children's tale follows four kids called the "Swallows" as they go on holiday in England's Lake District. There they meet two tomboys known as the "Amazons" and together experience a number of adventures. A simple, well-made film that uses its cast and locations to good effect.

p, Richard Pilbrow; d, Claude Whatham; w, David Wood (based on the book by Arthur Ransome); ph, Denis Lewiston (Technicolor); m, Wilfred Josephs.

Adventure   (MPAA:NR)

SWAN LAKE, THE

(1967) 111m United Productions of America-Seven Arts c

Rudolf Nureyev, Dame Margot Fonteyn, The Vienna State Opera Ballet.

This excellent adaptation of the famous ballet differs from other ballet films in its imaginative cinematic technique. Unlike many such films, this is not a heavy-handed or somber work; instead, it shows a group of people dancing for the sheer joy of the art and clearly having a good time. The production, said to have cost more than $1 million, includes the participation of the Vienna Symphony Orchestra and 60 dancers from the Vienna State Opera Ballet.

d, Truck Branss; w, Peter Ilyich Tchaikovsky; ph, Gunther Anders (Eastmancolor); m, Peter Ilyich Tchaikovsky.

Dance   (MPAA:NR)

SWISS FAMILY ROBINSON

(1960) 126m Disney/BV c

John Mills *(Father)*, Dorothy McGuire *(Mother)*, James MacArthur *(Fritz)*, Janet Munro *(Roberta)*, Sessue Hayakawa *(Pirate Chief)*, Tommy Kirk *(Ernst)*, Kevin Corcoran *(Francis)*, Cecil Parker *(Capt. Moreland)*, Andy Ho *(Auban)*, Milton Reid *(Big Pirate)*, Larry Taylor *(Battoo)*.

Disney's version of the famous novel is a superior adventure following the exploits of the title family. Father and Mother Robinson (John Mills and Dorothy McGuire) and their three sons, Fritz, Francis, and Ernst (James MacArthur, Kevin Corcoran, and Tommy Kirk), flee Napoleon and look for someplace to live in the South Seas, but in the course of the search they are chased by pirates and their ship is pounded by an angry sea. After the ship's crew deserts the sinking vessel with only the family on board, the Robinsons crash along a rocky shore and emerge to find a tropical island Eden. Since the ship, which is only half-submerged, is filled with food and gear, they prepare to settle in. Numerous adventures follow in this exciting and humorous picture filled with classic Disney touches. It's a tongue-in-cheek movie that avoids the sappy sentiment of so many "family" films and concentrates on sheer entertainment instead. The scenery is lush and colorful; the film's success made Tobago a tourist haven for many years afterward.

p, Bill Anderson; d, Ken Annakin; w, Lowell S. Hawley (based on the novel by Johann Wyss); ph, Harry Waxman (Panavision, Technicolor); m, William Alwyn.

Adventure   Cas.   (MPAA:G)

SYLVESTER

(1985) 103m Rastar/COL c

Richard Farnsworth *(Foster)*, Melissa Gilbert *(Charlie)*, Michael Schoeffling *(Matt)*, Constance Towers *(Muffy)*, Pete Kowanko *(Harris)*, Yankton Hatten *(Grant)*, Shane Serwin *(Seth)*, Chris Pedersen *(Red)*, Angel Salazar *(Tommy John)*, Arliss Howard *(Peter)*, Shizuko Hoshi *(Mrs. Daniels)*, Richard Jamison *(Capt. Marsh)*, James Gammon *(Steve)*, Ariane de Vogue *(Ariane)*, Norman Bennett *(Lenny)*, Sam Laws *(Sammy)*, Victoria Gallegos *(Sandy)*, Nigel Casserley *(Announcer)*, Barbara Brumley *(Secretary)*, Dabney Garrett Munson *(Judge)*, Helmut Graetz *(Dressage Official)*, Earl John McElroy *(Auctioneer)*, Brian T. O'Connor, Stuart Silbar *(Broadcasters)*, Maggie Wise Riley, Linda Snead *(Stewards)*, J.P. Robertson *(Trucker)*, Michael Osborne *(Irish Trainer)*, Dan Lufkin *(Starter)*.

The "girl-meets-horse" formula is a creaky one, but SYLVESTER is a surprisingly fresh reworking of a standard tale best told in NATIONAL VELVET (1944). Charlie (Melissa Gilbert of TV's "Little House on the Prarie," in her theatrical film debut) is an orphaned teenager trying to raise two younger brothers by herself. She wants to be a horse trainer, and decides to break in a seemingly uncontrollable animal she comes to love. Dubbing the horse "Sylvester," she sets out to make the nag a steeplechase competitor. She hooks up with Foster (Richard Farnsworth), an old horseman who has clearly seen better days and who, initially, wants nothing to do with Charlie, her brothers, or Sylvester. Eventually he succumbs, however, and the story builds to the all-important horse show. Gilbert gives her character an assured spunkiness and is well matched by Farnsworth, creating a fine on-screen rapport. The horse gets his name from Charlie as a tribute to one of her favorite actors, Sylvester Stallone.

p, Martin Jurow; d, Tim Hunter; w, Carol Sobieski; ph, Hiro Narita (Metrocolor); m, Lee Holdridge.

Drama   **Cas.**   **(MPAA:PG)**

T

TAIL OF THE TIGER

(1984, Aus.) 82m Producer's Circle/Roadshow c

Grant Navin *(Orville Ryan)*, Gordon Poole *(Harry)*, Caz Lederman *(Lydia Ryan)*, Gayle Kennedy *(Beryl)*, Peter Feeley *(Spike)*, Dylan Lyle *(Rabbit)*, Walter Sullivan *(Stan)*, Basil Clarke *(Jack)*.

Ten-year-old Orville Ryan (Grant Navin) is a Sydney youngster with a passion for old airplanes. The neighborhood gang won't let him join in when they fly their model airplanes, so he hangs around with cantankerous old Harry (Gordon Poole), who is restoring an ancient

DeHavilland Tiger Moth in an abandoned warehouse. The ghosts of three pilots turn up at times to encourage the pair, and even help them fight off a gang of ruffians who want to wreck the biplane. When the restoration is complete the duo fly above Sydney, in an exhilarating sequence. This is a good children's story that adults will enjoy, too.

p, James M. Vernon; d&w, Rolf de Heer; ph, Richard Michalak; m, Steve Arnold, Graham Tardif.

Adventure   **(MPAA:NR)**

TAKE ME OUT TO THE BALL GAME

(1949) 93m MGM c (GB: EVERYBODY'S CHEERING)

Frank Sinatra *(Dennis Ryan)*, Esther Williams *(K.C. Higgins)*, Gene Kelly *(Eddie O'Brien)*, Betty Garrett *(Shirley Delwyn)*, Edward Arnold *(Joe Lorgan)*, Jules Munshin *(Nat Goldberg)*, Richard Lane *(Michael Gilhuly)*, Tom Dugan *(Slappy Burke)*, Murray Alper *(Zalinka)*, Wilton Graff *(Nick Donford)*, Mack Gray, Charles Regan *(Henchmen)*, Saul Gorss *(Steve)*, Douglas Fowley *(Karl)*, Eddie Parkes *(Dr. Winston)*, James Burke *(Cop in Park)*, The Blackburn Twins *(Specialty)*, Gordon Jones *(Sen. Catcher)*, Virginia Bates, Joi Lansing *(Girls on Train)*, Mitchell Lewis *(Fisherman)*, Esther Michaelson *(Fisherman's Wife)*, Frank Scannell *(Reporter)*, Henry Kulky *(Burly Acrobat)*, Dorothy Abbott *(Girl Dancer)*, Jackie Jackson *(Kid)*, Si Jenks *(Sam)*, Jack Rice *(Room Clerk)*, Ed Cassidy *(Teddy Roosevelt)*, Dick Wessel *(Umpire)*, Sally Forrest *(Dancer)*.

This follow-up to ANCHORS AWEIGH (1945) teams Frank Sinatra and Gene Kelly again, this time as Dennis Ryan (Sinatra) and Eddie O'Brien (Kelly), a song-and-dance team who spend their summers playing semipro baseball. Beginning a new season, the two are surprised to find that K.C. Higgins (Esther Williams) is the new team owner and manager. Both are attracted to her, but she's only interested in fielding a good team, and when Eddie begins moonlighting as a dance director for a nightclub, she benches him for violating training rules. Eddie then falls under the spell of a seemingly benevolent man (Edward Arnold) who is, in reality, a big-time gambler who wants Eddie to help throw some games. Eventually Eddie catches on, helping the team take the pennant and winning his manager's heart as well. This amiable film has an enjoyable cast and lively music. Sinatra and Kelly are well matched, and Williams does a nice job with her tough-but-tender role, only getting near a pool once. Kelly and Stanley Donen came up with the original story and asked to direct, but it was decided to bring Busby Berkeley on for what was to be his last directorial effort. Kelly and Donen were allowed to direct the film's musical sequences, however, and turned in such good work that producer Arthur Freed let them direct the next Kelly-Sinatra film, ON THE TOWN, later that year.

p, Arthur Freed; d, Busby Berkeley; w, Harry Tugend, George Wells, (uncredited) Harry Crane (based on a story by Gene Kelly and Stanley Donen); ph, George Folsey (Technicolor); m, Robert Edens.

Musical/Sports (MPAA:NR)

TALE OF TWO CITIES, A

(1935) 120m MGM bw

Ronald Colman (*Sydney Carton*), Elizabeth Allan (*Lucie Manette*), Edna May Oliver (*Miss Pross*), Blanche Yurka (*Mme. DeFarge*), Reginald Owen (*Stryver*), Basil Rathbone (*Marquis St. Evremonde*), Henry B. Walthall (*Dr. Manette*), Donald Woods (*Charles Darnay*), Walter Catlett (*Barsad*), Fritz Leiber, Sr. (*Gaspard*), H.B. Warner (*Gabelle*), Mitchell Lewis (*Ernest DeFarge*), Claude Gillingwater (*Jarvis Lorry*), Billy Bevan (*Jerry Cruncher*), Isabel Jewell (*Seamstress*), Lucille La Verne (*La Vengeance*), Tully Marshall (*Woodcutter*), Fay Chaldecott (*Lucie the Daughter*), Eily Malyon (*Mrs. Cruncher*), E.E. Clive (*Judge in Old Bailey*), Lawrence Grant (*Prosecuting Attorney in Old Bailey*), John Davidson (*Morveau*), Tom Ricketts (*Tellson*, Donald Haines (*Jerry Cruncher*, Ralf Harolde (*Prosecutor*), Ed Piel, Sr. (*Cartwright*), Edward Hearn (*Leader*), Richard Alexander (*Executioner*), Cyril McLaglen (*Headsman*), Frank Mayo (*Jailer*), Walter Kingsford (*Victor the Jailer*), Barlowe Borland (*Jacques No. 116*), Rolfe Sedan (*Condemned Dandy*), Robert Warwick (*Tribunal Judge*), Dale Fuller, Tempe Piggott (*Old Hags*), Montague Shaw (*Chief Registrar*), Chappell Dossett (*English Priest*), Forrester Harvey (*Joe*), Jimmy Aubrey (*Innkeeper*), Billy House (*Border Guard*).

Probably the best film version of Charles Dickens' novel (there have been at least seven), A TALE OF TWO CITIES follows the turmoil and aftermath of the French Revolution. Sydney Carton (Ronald Colman) is a world-weary London barrister in love with Lucie Manette (Elizabeth Allan). She thinks of him only as a friend, however, and marries Charles Darnay (Donald Woods), a descendant of a noble French family who is also Carton's look-alike. Darnay's uncle, the Marquis St. Evremonde (Basil Rathbone), is a heartless tyrant who is killed at the Revolution's onset. As the nephew of the hated Marquis, Darnay is arrested in Paris and sentenced to death. Lucie is frantic with worry over her husband, and Carton, devoted to Lucie but seeing no hope of happiness, goes to Paris, where he frees Darnay and takes his place in prison. His last words as he ascends the scaffold have become so identified with Colman that they are almost impossible to say without slipping into his distinctive accent: "It is a far, far better thing that I do than I have ever done; it is a far, far better rest that I go to than I have ever known." This superb, lavish production features an MGM stock company playing every small role to perfection, while Colman gives one of the best performances of his life in a role he had long wanted to play. Equally memorable is Blanche Yurka as the sinister Mme. DeFarge. The film's huge success gave producer David O. Selznick the freedom to walk away from MGM (and his father-in-law, Louis B. Mayer) and set up Selznick International Pictures.

p, David O. Selznick; d, Jack Conway; w, W.P. Lipscomb,

S.N. Behrman (based on the novel by Charles Dickens); ph, Oliver T. Marsh; m, Herbert Stothart.

Drama **Cas.** (MPAA:NR)

TALES OF MANHATTAN

(1942) 118m FOX bw

Sequence A: Charles Boyer (*Paul Orman*), Rita Hayworth (*Ethel Halloway*), Thomas Mitchell (*John Halloway*), Eugene Pallette (*Luther*), Helene Reynolds (*Actress*), Robert Grieg (*Lazar*), Jack Chefe (*Tailor*), William Halligan (*Oliver Webb*), Charles Williams (*Paul's Agent*), Eric Wilton (*Halloway's Butler*); Sequence B: Ginger Rogers (*Diane*), Henry Fonda (*George*), Cesar Romero (*Harry Wilson*), Gail Patrick (*Ellen*), Roland Young (*Edgar the Butler*), Marion Martin (*Squirrel*), Frank Orth (*Secondhand Dealer*), Connie Leon (*Mary*); Sequence C: Charles Laughton (*Charles Smith*), Elsa Lanchester (*Elsa Smith*), Victor Francen (*Auturo Bellini*), Christian Rub (*Wilson*), Adeline DeWalt Reynolds (*Grandmother*), Sig Arno (*Piccolo Player*), Forbes Murray (*Dignified Man*), Buster Brodie (*Call Boy*), Frank Jaquet (*Musician*), Will Wright (*Skeptic*), Frank Dae (*Elderly Man*), Rene Austin (*Susan*), Frank Darien (*Grandpa*), Dewey Robinson (*Bar Proprietor*), Tom O'Grady (*Latecomer*), Curly Twyfford (*Bird Man*), Gino Corrado (*Spectator*); Sequence D: Edward G. Robinson (*Larry Browne*), George Sanders (*Williams*), James Gleason (*Father Joe*), Harry Davenport (*Prof. Lyons*), James Rennie (*Hank Bronson*), Harry Hayden (*Soupy Davis*), Morris Ankrum (*Judge Barnes*), Don Douglas (*Henderson*), Mae Marsh (*Molly*), Barbara Lynn (*Mary*), Paul Renay (*Spud Johnson*), Ted Stanhope (*Chauffeur*), Esther Howard (*Woman*), Joseph Bernard (*Postman*), Alex Pollard (*Waiter*), Don Brady (*Whistler*); Sequence E: Paul Robeson (*Luke*), Ethel Waters (*Esther*), Eddie "Rochester" Anderson (*Rev. Lazarus*), J. Carrol Naish (*Costello*), Clarence Muse (*Grandpa*), George Reed (*Christopher*), Cordell Hickman (*Nicodemus*), John Kelly (*Monk*), Lonnie Nichols (*Brad*), Charles Gray (*Rod*), Phillip Hurlie (*Jeff*), Archie Savage (*Man*), Charles Tannen (*Pilot*), Hall Johnson Choir (*Themselves*), Johnny Lee (*Carpenter*), Blue Washington (*Black Man*).

TALES OF MANHATTAN follows the adventures of a fancy tail coat as it goes from riches to rags. A famous actor (Charles Boyer) initially buys the coat, only to be told the garment carries a curse. Later, it winds up with a man (Cesar Romero) whose fiancee (Ginger Rogers) finds a love letter in one of the pockets. He insists the coat belongs to his pal (Henry Fonda), but his strategy backfires when, impressed by the letter's passion, she runs off with the friend. The cursed jacket then passes from a composer (Charles Laughton) to an impoverished lawyer (Edward G. Robinson), who wears it to a college reunion, where three former classmates decide to help him get back on his feet. Next to own the garment is a crook (J. Carrol Naish) who wears it while he pulls off a job. Pocketing the loot, he boards a plane, but during the flight he throws the coat out the window, forgetting it's stuffed with $40,000. The money flutters to the ground and is picked up by two sharecroppers (Paul Robeson and Ethel Waters) who take it to the local preacher, while the coat ends up on a scarecrow. TALES OF MANHATTAN unfolds with charm. Under the fine direction of Julien Duvivier (who directed the similarly episodic UN CARNET DU BAL, 1938), the episodes flow smoothly. It has, however, been criticized for its simplistic presentation of blacks in the final episode, and Robeson later denounced the film.

p, Boris Morros, S.P. Eagle [Sam Speigel]; d, Julien Duvivier; w, Ben Hecht, Ferenc Molnar, Donald Ogden Stewart, Samuel Hoffenstein, Alan Campbell, Ladislas Fodor, Laszlo Vadnai, Laslo Gorog, Lamar Trotti, Henry Blankford, (uncredited) Buster Keaton, Ed Beloin, Bill Morrow; ph, Joseph Walker; m, Sol Kaplan.

Comedy (MPAA:NR)

TARZAN, THE APE MAN

(1932) 99m MGM bw

Johnny Weissmuller (Tarzan), Neil Hamilton (Harry Holt), Maureen O'Sullivan (Jane Parker), C. Aubrey Smith (James Parker), Doris Lloyd (Mrs. Cutten), Forrester Harvey (Beamish), Ivory Williams (Riano), Cheta the Chimp.

A legend was born when MGM cast Johnny Weissmuller, a 28-year-old Olympic swimming champion, as Tarzan in this film. The Edgar Rice Burroughs character had been popular in silent films, but this was the first sound version. Jane Parker (Maureen O'Sullivan), her father (C. Aubrey Smith), and her boy friend (Neil Hamilton) venture into the African wilds in search of the ivory-laden Elephant's Graveyard and experience great danger in the process. Fears are heightened when Tarzan's jungle yell is heard, and before long, Jane is screaming and kicking as Tarzan carries her into the treetops. Her father and suitor threaten to shoot Tarzan, but after she is released, Jane defends the ape-man with whom she is falling in love. She is soon swinging through the trees under his arm, clowning around with the captivating chimp Cheta, and taking swims with Tarzan. Their happiness is threatened, however, when they are captured by pygmies and lowered into a pit with a giant ape. Cheta is thrown aside like a rag doll, but Tarzan lets out a thundering yell, and a herd of elephants comes crashing to the rescue. The first of six MGM Weissmuller-O'Sullivan "Tarzan" adventures, TARZAN, THE APE MAN suffers in technological comparison with today's Steven Spielbergian jungle adventures, but still has enough thrills to put most modern films to shame. The near-nonstop excitement holds up wonderfully, making this one of Hollywood's most memorable adventure films.

p, Irving Thalberg; d, W.S. Van Dyke; w, Cyril Hume, Ivor Novello (based on the characters created by Edgar Rice Burroughs); ph, Harold Rosson, Clyde DeVinna.

Adventure **Cas.** (MPAA:NR)

TEN COMMANDMENTS, THE

(1956) 219m PAR c

Charlton Heston (Moses), Yul Brynner (Rameses), Ann Baxter (Nefretiri), Edward G. Robinson (Dathan), Yvonne De Carlo (Sephora), Debra Paget (Lilia), John Derek (Joshua), Sir Cedric Hardwicke (Sethi), Nina Foch (Bithiah), Martha Scott (Yochabel), Judith Anderson (Memnet), Vincent Price (Baka), John Carradine (Aaron), Eduard Franz (Jethro), Olive Deering (Miriam), Donald Curtis (Mered), Douglas Dumbrille (Jannes), Lawrence Dobkin (Hur Ben Caleb), Frank DeKova (Abiram), H.B. Warner (Amminadab), Henry Wilcoxon (Pentaur), Julia Faye (Elisheba), Abbas El Boughdadly (Rameses' Charioteer), Fraser Heston (Infant Moses), Eugene Mazzola (Rameses' Son), John Miljan (The Blind One), Tommy Duran (Gershom), Francis J. McDonald (Simon), Ian Keith (Rameses I), Joan Woodbury (Korah's Wife), Ramsay Hill (Korah), Woody Strode (King of Ethiopia), Dorothy Adams (Hebrew at Golden Calf/Hebrew Woman at Rameses' Gate/Slave Woman), Eric Alden (High-Ranking Officer/Taskmaster/Slave Man/Officer), Henry Brandon (Commander of the Hosts), Touch [Mike] Connors (Amalekite Herder), Henry Corden (Sheik of Ezion), Edna May Cooper (Court Lady), Kem Dibbs (Corporal), Fred Kohler, Jr. (Foreman), Gail Kobe (Pretty Slave Girl), Onslow Stevens (Lugal), Clint Walker (Sardinian Captain), Frank Wilcox (Wazir), Luis Alberni (Old Hebrew at Moses' House), Michael Ansara (Taskmaster), Emmett Lynn (Old Slave Man/Hebrew at Golden Calf), Stanley Price (Slave Carrying Load), Robert Vaughn (Spearman/Hebrew at Golden Calf), Herb Alpert (Drum Player).

Director-producer Cecil B. DeMille ended his great career with this gigantic production, jam-packed with enormous crowd scenes, lavish spectacles, and wide-screen special effects orchestrated with dazzling brilliance. DeMille's Exodus (a tale he had also filmed in 1923) opens as the Egyptian pharaoh is told that the Deliverer of the enslaved Hebrews will soon be born. He orders the slaughter of all newborn Jewish males, but one is placed on a basket in the Nile, found by the pharaoh's sister, and brought up as her own. Years pass and the now-adult Moses (Charlton Heston) has become a beloved prince, much to the chagrin of Rameses (Yul Brynner), the pharaoh's son. When Moses' lineage is revealed, he is banished into the desert, but after several peaceful years, he learns of his destiny in his encounter with the burning bush. The film then depicts his return and his confrontation with Rameses, the mass exodus of the Hebrews, Moses' parting of the Red Sea, his receipt of the Ten Commandments, the Jews' worship of the idolatrous Golden Calf, and their 40 years of wandering as punishment. Finally, the aged Moses watches Joshua lead his people into the Promised Land. DeMille tells the biblical story on a scale no other filmmaker ever attempted, yet the fine cast is never overwhelmed by the epic production. Heston (cast in part because of his resemblance to Michelangelo's Moses) is magnificent in a role with which he will forever be identified. Brynner is also marvelous as his hard-hearted counterpart, and the many supporting performances (especially that of Edward G.

Robinson) are all fine. THE TEN COMMANDMENTS eventually grossed over $80 million, enjoying several re-releases, and DeMille's vision remains a powerful one, a testament to his inestimable talent as the master of the epic cinema.

p&d, Cecil B. DeMille; w, Aeneas MacKenzie, Jesse L. Lasky, Jr., Jack Gariss, Fredric M. Frank (based on the novels *The Prince of Egypt* by Dorothy Clarke Wilson, *Pillar of Fire* by the Rev. J.H. Ingraham, *On Eagle's Wings* by the Rev. G.E. Southon, and in accordance with the Holy Scripture, the ancient texts of Josephus, Eusebius, Philo, The Midrash); ph, Loyal Griggs, John Warren, Wallace Kelley, Peverell Marley (VistaVision, Technicolor); m, Elmer Bernstein.

Religious   **Cas.**   **(MPAA:NR)**

THAT DARN CAT

(1965) 116m Disney/BV c

Hayley Mills *(Patti Randall)*, Dean Jones *(Zeke Kelso)*, Dorothy Provine *(Ingrid Randall)*, Roddy McDowall *(Gregory Benson)*, Neville Brand *(Dan)*, Elsa Lanchester *(Mrs. MacDougall)*, William Demarest *(Mr. MacDougall)*, Frank Gorshin *(Iggy)*, Richard Eastham *(Supervisor Newton)*, Grayson Hall *(Margaret Miller)*, Ed Wynn *(Mr. Hofstedder)*, Tom Lowell *(Canoe)*, Richard Deacon *(Drive-in Manager)*, Iris Adrian *(Landlady)*, Liam Sullivan *(Graham)*, Don Dorrell *(Spires)*, Gene Blakely *(Cahill)*, Karl Held *(Kelly)*, Ben Lessy *(Candy Man)*, Larry J. Blake *(Police Officer)*.

This entertaining Disney picture details the exploits D.C., a Siamese cat owned by Patti and Ingrid Randall (Hayley Mills and Dorothy Provine). One night D.C. follows a pair of bank robbers to the apartment where they are holding a bank teller (Grayson Hall) prisoner. The robbers let the mischievous feline in long enough for the teller to scratch HEL (she doesn't have time to add the "P") on the back of her watch and attach it to the cat's collar. Patti finds the message and brings it to Zeke Kelso (Dean Jones), an FBI agent who, despite being allergic to cats, decides to follow the animal to the robbers. After running into a series of funny slapstick situations while trailing D.C. on its nocturnal wanderings, Zeke brings the crooks to justice. Silly, fun stuff, with a good supporting cast that includes Elsa Lanchester, William Demarest, and Roddy McDowall as nosy neighbors; Ed Wynn as a helpful jeweler; and Neville Brand and Frank Gorshin as the robbers.

p, Bill Walsh, Ron Miller; d, Robert Stevenson; w, Gordon Gordon, Mildred Gordon, Bill Walsh (based on the novel *Undercover Cat* by Gordon Gordon and Mildred Gordon); ph, Edward Colman (Technicolor); m, Bob Brunner.

Comedy   **Cas.**   **(MPAA:G)**

THIEF OF BAGHDAD, THE

(1940, Brit.) 106m LFP/UA c

Conrad Veidt *(Jaffar)*, Sabu *(Abu)*, June Duprez *(Princess)*, John Justin *(Ahmad)*, Rex Ingram *(Djinni)*, Miles Malleson *(Sultan)*, Morton Selten *(King)*, Mary Morris *(Halima)*, Bruce Winston *(Merchant)*, Hay Petrie *(Astrologer)*, Roy Emerton *(Jailer)*, Allan Jeayes *(Storyteller)*, Adelaide Hall *(Singer)*, Miki Hood, David Sharpe.

THE THIEF OF BAGHDAD is one of the best fantasy films ever made, with astounding special effects and wonderful performances. A host of directors worked on the spectacle under the meticulous eye of producer Alexander Korda. An assemblage of incidents from the Arabian Nights tales begins as the urchin Abu (Sabu) is thrown into a Baghdad dungeon for thievery. Soon, the city's ruler, Prince Ahmad (John Justin), joins him there, having been overthrown by the evil grand vizier, Jaffar (Conrad Veidt). The two escape and flee to exotic Basra, where Ahmad is smitten by Basra's princess (June Duprez). Learning that Jaffar is about to abduct the beauty, Ahmad and Abu try to thwart the plan, but the wicked magician turns them into a dog and a blind beggar. When the princess promises to wed Jaffar, he revokes his curse, and sails back to Baghdad with her. All seems lost until Abu, in a series of adventures involving an "All-Seeing Eye," a magic carpet, and a genie, saves the day. Although six directors worked on the film, it maintains such a consistent grandeur and even pace that it might well have been directed by one person. The marvelous set designs by Vincent Korda seem *truly* out of this world, and Miklos Rozsa has created a dynamic score. Duprez's stunning beauty is enhanced by the rich Technicolor; Justin is perfect in his part; and Korda's favorite actors, Veidt and Sabu, are splendid. THE THIEF OF BAGHDAD remains one of the most dazzling fantasies ever created for the screen.

p, Alexander Korda; d, Ludwig Berger, Michael Powell, Tim Whelan, Zoltan Korda, William Cameron Menzies, Alexander Korda; w, Lajos Biro, Miles Malleson; ph, Georges Perinal, Osmond Borrodaile (Technicolor); m, Miklos Rozsa.

Fantasy   **Cas.**   **(MPAA:NR)**

THIS IS THE ARMY

(1943) 120m WB c

Irving Berlin *(Himself)*, George Murphy *(Jerry Jones)*, Joan Leslie *(Eileen Dibble)*, George Tobias *(Maxie Stoloff)*, Alan Hale *(Sgt. McGee)*, Charles Butterworth *(Eddie Dibble)*, Rosemary DeCamp *(Ethel)*, Dolores Costello *(Mrs. Davidson)*, Una Merkel *(Rose Dibble)*, Stanley Ridges *(Maj. Davidson)*, Ruth Donnelly *(Mrs. O'Brien)*, Dorothy Peterson *(Mrs. Nelson)*, Kate Smith *(Herself)*, Frances Langford *(Cafe Singer)*, Gertrude Niesen *(Singer)*, Ronald Reagan *(Johnny Jones)*, Joe Louis *(Himself)*, Robert Shenley *(Ted Nelson)*, Herbert Anderson *(Danny Davidson)*, Sgt. Fisher *(Blake Nelson)*, Jackie Brown *(Mike Nelson)*, Patsy Moran *(Marie Twardofsky)*, James Conlin *(Doorman)*, Ilka Gruning *(Mrs. Twardofsky)*, Irving Bacon *(Waiter)*, Murray Alper *(Soldier)*, Pierre Watkin *(Stranger)*, Henry Jones *(Soldier-Singer)*, Doodles Weaver *(Soldier on Cot)*, Leah Baird *(Old Timer's Wife)*,

Warner Anderson *(Sports Announcer)*, Jack Young *(Franklin D. Roosevelt)*.

This is a star-studded musical salute to the Army filled with Irving Berlin's songs and radiant patriotism. It opens as Broadway star Jerry Jones (George Murphy) is drafted into the service at the beginning of WW I and given the job of putting on a big show, after which cast and crew go off to fight. Years later, Jones' son, Johnny (Ronald Reagan), is drafted for WW II service and given the same job his father had. He manages to write a terrific show that tours the country. For the final performance, Berlin (as himself) comes on stage to sing. Although two other parent-and-offspring tales also figure, the plot is scant, just enough to hang the musical numbers on. Michael Curtiz directs in a breezy style inspired by Berlin's original stage show (the profits of which went, along with $2 million made by the movie, to a relief fund for soldiers' families, so that it became a patriotic act to go see the film). There are lots of great Berlin songs, including "God Bless America" (performed by Kate Smith, of course), "This Is the Army, Mr. Jones," "Oh, How I Hate to Get Up in the Morning," and "The Army's Made a Man Out of Me." Berlin was given the US Medal of Merit for his work on the stage and screen versions of THIS IS THE ARMY, and received a Congressional Gold Medal for "God Bless America."

p, Jack L. Warner, Hal B. Wallis; d, Michael Curtiz; w, Casey Robinson, Claude Binyon (based on the musical play by Irving Berlin); ph, Bert Glennon, Sol Polito (Technicolor).

Musical   **Cas.**   **(MPAA:NR)**

THOSE CALLOWAYS

(1964) 131m Disney/BV c

Brian Keith *(Cam Calloway)*, Vera Miles *(Liddy Calloway)*, Brandon de Wilde *(Bucky Calloway)*, Walter Brennan *(Alf Simes)*, Ed Wynn *(Ed Parker)*, Linda Evans *(Bridie Mellot)*, Philip Abbott *(Dell Fraser)*, John Larkin *(Jim Mellot)*, Parley Baer *(Doane Shattuck)*, Frank De Kova *(Nigosh)*, Roy Roberts *(E.J. Fletcher)*, John Qualen *(Ernie Evans)*, Tom Skerritt *(Whit Turner)*, Paul Hartman *(Charley Evans)*, Russell Collins *(Nat Perkins)*, John Davis Chandler *(Ollie Gibbons)*, Chet Stratton *(Phil Petrie)*, Renee Godfrey *(Sarah Mellot)*, Frank Ferguson *(Doctor)*.

Brian Keith is Cam Calloway, an Irish trapper raised by Micmac Indians. He, his wife, and Bucky (Brandon de Wilde), their 19-year-old son, live in Swiftwater, Maine. Cam hopes to create a sanctuary for the large flocks of geese that fly through town each autumn, and spends so much money on land for the site that he can't make mortgage payments on his home. The family is evicted and moves near a lake, where their friends help them build a new home. Problems arise when a traveling salesman (Philip Abbott) decides to turn the area into a goose hunting haven. Pretending to be a conservationist, he gives Cam money to feed the geese and thereby lure them to Swiftwater regularly. Bucky learns of the plan, however, and the geese end up the big winners, but not before

Cam is shot and a big town meeting called. THOSE CALLOWAYS is moving film, presented without the naivete and sentimentality that marred the later Disney live-action features. Keith and the supporting players give strong performances, with Walter Brennan and Ed Wynn providing good comedy relief. The score and Vermont locations add to the film's charm.

p, Winston Hibler, Walt Disney; d, Norman Tokar; w, Louis Pelletier (based on the novel *Swiftwater* by Paul Annixter); ph, Edward Colman (Technicolor); m, Max Steiner.

Drama   **Cas.**   **(MPAA:NR)**

THOSE MAGNIFICENT MEN IN THEIR FLYING MACHINES; OR HOW I FLEW FROM LONDON TO PARIS IN 25 HOURS AND 11 MINUTES

(1965, Brit.) 133m FOX c (AKA: THOSE MAGNIFICENT MEN IN THEIR FLYING MACHINES)

Stuart Whitman *(Orvil Newton)*, Sarah Miles *(Patricia Rawnsley)*, James Fox *(Richard Mays)*, Alberto Sordi *(Count Emilio Ponticelli)*, Robert Morley *(Lord Rawnsley)*, Gert Frobe *(Col. Manfred von Holstein)*, Jean-Pierre Cassel *(Pierre Dubois)*, Eric Sykes *(Courtney)*, Terry-Thomas *(Sir Percival Ware-Armitage)*, Irina Demick *(Brigitte/ Ingrid/Marlene/Francoise/Yvette/Betty)*, Tony Hancock *(Harry Popperwell)*, Benny Hill *(Fire Chief Perkins)*, Yujiro Ishihara *(Yamamoto)*, Flora Robson *(Mother Superior)*, Karl Michael Vogler *(Capt. Rupelstrasse)*, Sam Wanamaker *(George Gruber)*, Eric Barker *(French Postman)*, Fred Emney *(Elderly Col. Willie)*, Gordon Jackson *(McDougal)*, Davy Kaye *(Jean)*, John Le Mesurier *(French Painter)*, Jeremy Lloyd *(Lt. Parsons)*, Zena Marshall *(Sophia Ponticelli)*, Millicent Martin *(Airline Hostess)*, Eric Pohlmann *(Italian Mayor)*, Marjorie Rhodes *(The Waitress)*, Norman Rossington *(Assistant Fire Chief)*, William Rushton *(Tremayne Gascoyne)*, Red Skelton *(The Neanderthal Man)*, Ferdy Mayne *(French Official)*, Bill Nagy *(American Journalist)*, James Robertson Justice *(Narrator)*, Cicely Courtneidge *(Muriel)*.

This rip-roaring comedy takes place in 1910, when English press bigwig Lord Rawnsley (Robert Morley) sets out to prove that Great Britain is No. 1 in the air. Putting up 10,000 pounds as a prize, he invites the world's best pilots to compete in an air race from London to Paris. All sorts of dandy planes arrive, but Rawnsley roots for his daughter's (Sarah Miles) fiance, Richard Mays (James Fox), a Royal Navy lieutenant. Other contenders include an Italian count (Alberto Sordi); a fanatical Prussian who will die before he lets anyone else win (Gert Frobe); a Frenchman (Jean-Pierre Cassel) followed by a sextet of women (all played by Irina Demick); a villainous Brit (Terry-Thomas); an inscrutable Japanese (Yujiro Ishihara); and American barnstormer Orvil Newton (Stuart Whitman), who decides that Rawnsley's daughter is the woman for him. After a series of slapstick mishaps, the competitors are winnowed until only the Italian and the two romantic rivals remain. Heroism and fair play are the order of the day in the big finish, but it's up to Rawnsley's daughter to decide which of the competitors has won her heart. Good, clean fun, with fast and furious action, good cinematography, Oscar-nominated dialog, wonderful planes, and a host of some of the funniest people in movies in the cast.

p, Stan Margulies; d, Ken Annakin; w, Jack Davies, Ken Annakin; ph, Christopher Challis (Todd-AO, Deluxe Color); m, Ron Goodwin.

Comedy   **Cas.**   **(MPAA:G)**

THREE CABALLEROS, THE

(1944) 70m Disney/RKO c

Aurora Miranda, Carmen Molina, Dora Luz, Nestor Amarale, Almirante, Trio Calaveras, Ascencio Del Rio Trio, Padua Hill Players; voices of: Sterling Holloway, Clarence Nash (Donald Duck), Jose Oliveira (Joe Carioca), Joaquin Garay (Panchito), Fred Shields, Frank Graham.

A smashing follow-up to SALUDOS AMIGOS, this is one of the most dazzling achievements of the cartoon genre. Donald Duck opens presents on his birthday, the first of which is a movie projector. He puts film on the projector and we are plunged into the tale of Pablo the Penguin, who is sick and tired of the Antarctic cold and wants to live in the tropics, and a story about a little Mexican boy who finds a donkey with wings. Donald's next present is a large book. The moment he opens it, up pops Joe Carioca (from SALUDOS AMIGOS), then we're off on one of the fastest-moving cartoon sequences ever devised, as the two travel to Brazil, where Donald meets and falls in love with Aurora Miranda (in a huge production number that's as elaborate as anything Busby Berkeley ever choreographed). A breakneck trip around Mexico follows, during which Donald, Joe, and Panchito the rooster cavort with beautiful women and dance with animated plants (as well as with Carmen Molina, who does her trademark "Jesusita" number). THREE CABALLEROS also includes the famous sequence in which Donald gets into the soundtrack, represented by a moving line. So much more happens on-screen that no synopsis of this fast and funny picture will begin to do it justice. A must for all ages.

p, Norman Ferguson; d, Ferguson, Clyde Geronimi, Jack Kinney, Bill Roberts, Harold Young; w, Homer Brightman, Ernest Terrazzas, Ted Sears, Bill Peet, Ralph Wright, Elmer Plymmer, Roy Williams, William Cottrell, Del Connell, James Bodrero; ph, Ray Rennahan (Technicolor).

Animation/Musical   **Cas.**   **(MPAA:G)**

THREE GODFATHERS, THE

(1948) 106m Argosy/MGM c

John Wayne (Robert Marmaduke Hightower), Pedro Armendariz (Pedro "Pete" Roca Fuerte), Harry Carey, Jr. (William Kearney "The Abilene Kid"), Ward Bond (Perley "Buck" Sweet), Mildred Natwick (The Mother), Charles Halton (Mr. Latham), Jane Darwell (Miss Florie), Mae Marsh (Mrs. Perley Sweet), Guy Kibbee (Judge), Dorothy Ford (Ruby Latham), Ben Johnson, Michael Dugan, Don Summers (Members of Posse), Fred Libby (Deputy Sheriff "Curly"), Hank Worden (Deputy Sheriff), Jack Pennick (Luke), Francis Ford (Drunken Old-Timer at Bar), Richard Hageman (Saloon Pianist), Cliff Lyons (Guard at Mojave Tanks).

John Ford's THE THREE GODFATHERS is a wonderful, heartfelt western about a bad man who redeems himself. It is also a tribute to Ford's mentor and friend, actor Harry Carey, who died in 1947. The film follows a trio of outlaws—Robert Marmaduke Hightower (John Wayne), "Pete" Roca Fuerte (Pedro Armendariz), and "The Abilene Kid" (Harry Carey, Jr.)—who flee a posse after robbing the bank at Welcome. After losing their horses in a desert sandstorm, they arrive at Terrapin Tanks, where they find an abandoned woman in labor but no water. After giving birth, the dying woman (Mildred Natwick) begs the men to save her baby, and they agree, deciding to bring it to the nearby town of New Jerusalem—a hazardous journey with a biblical analogy not lost on the outlaws. Only Hightower makes it, however, stumbling into New Jerusalem with the baby on Christmas Eve. Later, the sheriff of Welcome (Ward Bond) offers to drop the charges if the outlaw will give up custody of the baby, but Hightower's response shouldn't surprise anyone. Ford first filmed this story in 1919 as MARKED MEN with Harry Carey, who appeared in the first version of the story, THREE GODFATHERS, in 1916. This version, Ford's first color film, begins as a silhouetted cowboy astride Carey's favorite horse rides to the top of a hill, pushing his hat back on his head as the words "Dedicated to Harry Carey, a bright star in the early western sky" appear.

p, John Ford, Merian C. Cooper; d, John Ford; w, Laurence Stallings, Frank S. Nugent (based on the story by Peter B. Kyne); ph, Winton C. Hoch (Technicolor); m, Richard Hageman.

Western   **Cas.**   **(MPAA:NR)**

THREE LIVES OF THOMASINA, THE

(1963, US/Brit.) 87m Disney/BV c

Patrick McGoohan (Andrew MacDhui), Susan Hampshire (Lori MacGregor), Karen Dotrice (Mary MacDhui), Laurence Naismith (Rev. Angus Peddie), Jean Anderson (Mrs. MacKenzie), Wilfrid Brambell (Willie Bannock), Finlay Currie (Grandpa Stirling), Vincent Winter (Hughie Stirling), Denis Gilmore (Jamie McNab), Ewan Roberts (Constable McQuarrie), Oliver Johnston (Mr. Dobbie), Francis De Wolff (Targu), Charles Carson (Doctor), Nora Nicholson (Old Lady), Jack Stewart (Birnie), Matthew Garber (Geordie), Elspeth March (The Voice of Thomasina), Alex Mackenzie, Ruth Dunning, Gwen Nelson, Thomasina the Cat.

This is the charming tale of young Mary MacDhui (Karen Dotrice) and her cat, Thomasina. Mary lives in turn-of-the-century Scotland with her veterinarian father (Patrick McGoohan), who orders the family cat killed when it is diagnosed as having tetanus. Miraculously, Thomasina is saved by the mysterious Lori MacGregor (Susan Hampshire), who is thought to be a witch. As Thomasina is about to be buried, Lori brings her back to life, but not before the feline ventures through kitty heaven, filled with cat goddesses and sparkling stars. After chasing Thomasina in a thunderstorm, Mary contracts pneumonia, and is near death until, upon Lori's advice, her father brings her Thomasina and restores her will to live. A thoroughly enjoyable children's film, which will enchant the kids and leave them begging for their very own Thomasina.

p, Hugh Attwooll; d, Don Chaffey; w, Robert Westerby (based on the novel *Thomasina, the Cat Who Thought She Was God* by Paul Gallico); ph, Paul Beeson (Technicolor); m, Paul J. Smith.

Fantasy **Cas.** **(MPAA:NR)**

THREE MUSKETEERS, THE

(1948) 126m MGM c

Lana Turner *(Milady Countess Charlotte de Winter)*, Gene Kelly *(D'Artagnan)*, June Allyson *(Constance Bonacieux)*, Van Heflin *(Robert Athos)*, Angela Lansbury *(Queen Anne)*, Frank Morgan *(King Louis XIII)*, Vincent Price *(Richelieu the Prime Minister)*, Keenan Wynn *(Planchet)*, John Sutton *(George)*, Gig Young *(Porthos)*, Robert Coote *(Aramis)*, Reginald Owen *(De Treville)*, Ian Keith *(De Rochefort)*, Patricia Medina *(Kitty)*, Richard Stapley *(Albert)*, Byron Foulger *(Bonacieux)*, Sol Gorss *(Jussac)*, Robert Warwick *(D'Artagnan, Sr.)*, Marie Windsor *(Dark-Eyed Lady-in-Waiting)*, Ruth Robinson *(Mother of D'Artagnan)*, Tom Tyler *(Traveler)*, Fred Coby, Leonard Penn *(Musketeers)*, Kirk Alyn, John Holland *(Friends of Aramis)*, Francis McDonald *(Fisherman)*, Reginald Sheffield *(Subaltern)*, Wilson Benge, Alec Harford *(Valets)*, Harry Wilson *(Kidnaper)*, Mickey Simpson *(Executioner)*, Frank Hagney *(Executioner of Lyons)*, William Edmunds *(Landlord)*, Irene Seidner *(Landlord's Wife)*, Paul Maxey *(Major Domo)*, Arthur Hohl *(Dragon Rouge Host)*, Gil Perkins *(Guard)*, Albert Morin *(Bazin)*, Norman Leavitt *(Mousqueton)*, William "Bill" Phillips *(Grimaud)*, Richard Simmons *(Count DeWardes)*.

This is a rollicking version of the oft-filmed Dumas classic, with Gene Kelly essaying the role of D'Artagnan with great panache. The film opens as D'Artagnan leaves his country home for Paris, to join the famed Musketeers. He proves his ability in a duel with Athos (Van Heflin) and adopts the "one for all and all for one" motto, joining the Musketeers in serving King Louis XIII (Frank Morgan). Prime Minister Richelieu (Vincent Price, in a role that was toned down from the novel's religious Cardinal Richelieu) plots to end the king's reign, enlisting Louis' mistress, Lady de Winter (Lana Turner), in his evil scheme. The Musketeers, however, are not about to let that happen. Kelly is sheer delight, attacking the swashbuckling story with enormous zest. His acrobatics are a sight to behold, a marvelous extension of his much loved dancing skills. This was Kelly's favorite role of his non-

musical films, and he had hoped his performance here would convince MGM to let him do a musical version of "Cyrano de Bergerac." Alas, it didn't. The supporting cast is marvelous, especially Morgan in a wonderful portrayal of King Louis XIII.

p, Pandro S. Berman; d, George Sidney; w, Robert Ardrey (based on the novel by Alexandre Dumas, pere); ph, Robert Planck (Technicolor); m, Herbert Stothart.

Adventure/Comedy **Cas.** **(MPAA:NR)**

THREE SMART GIRLS

(1937) 86m UNIV bw

Deanna Durbin *(Penny Craig)*, Binnie Barnes *(Donna Lyons)*, Alice Brady *(Mrs. Lyons)*, Ray Milland *(Lord Michael Stuart)*, Charles Winninger *(Judson Craig)*, Mischa Auer *(Count Arisztid)*, Nan Grey *(Joan Craig)*, Barbara Read *(Kay Craig)*, Ernest Cossart *(Binns the Butler)*, Hobart Cavanaugh *(Wilbur Lamb)*, John King *(Bill Evans)*, Lucile Watson *(Trudel)*, Nella Walker *(Dorothy Craig)*, Dennis O'Keefe *(Club Extra)*, Gladden James *(Waiter)*, Wade Boteler, John Hamilton *(Sergeants)*, Lane Chandler *(Cop)*, Charles Coleman *(Butler)*, Franklin Pangborn *(Jeweler)*, Albert Conti *(Count's Friend)*, Selmer Jackson.

In her film debut, 14-year-old singing sensation Deanna Durbin is cast as Penny Craig, one of three sisters who try to keep their father from marrying a gold digger. Penny is the devoted matchmaker who tries everything to bring about her parent's reconciliation before her father exchanges vows with his new love. By the picture's finale, Penny's efforts have been all too successful—her sisters have found prospective husbands, and her mother and father have rekindled their romance. Penny is still single, however, though thoroughly content with everyone's newfound happiness. THREE SMART GIRLS spawned two sequels, THREE SMART GIRLS GROW UP, and HERS TO HOLD, both starring Durbin. There was also a remake, THREE DARING DAUGHTERS, which put Jane Powell in the Durbin role.

p, Joseph Pasternak; d, Henry Koster [Herman Kosterlitz]; w, Adele Comandini, Austin Parker (based on the story by Adele Comandini); ph, Joseph Valentine.

Comedy **(MPAA:NR)**

THUMBELINA

(1970) 62m Cinetron/R&S c

Shay Garner, Pat Morell, Bob O'Connell, Heather Grinter, Mike Yuenger, Sue Cable.

A well-done live-action version of Hans Christian Andersen's beloved fairy tale involving witches, royalty, magic, and kidnaping. As always in Andersen's tales, wisdom and whimsy combine to invest the story with symbolic significance.

p&d, Barry Mahon (based on the story "Tommelise" by Hans Christian Andersen); ph, Bill Tobin.

Fantasy **(MPAA:G)**

THUNDERHEAD-SON OF FLICKA

(1945) 78m FOX c

Roddy McDowall *(Ken McLaughlin)*, Preston Foster *(Rob McLaughlin)*, Rita Johnson *(Nelle)*, James Bell *(Gus)*, Diana Hale *(Hildy)*, Carleton G. Young *(Maj. Harris)*, Ralph Sanford *(Mr. Sargent)*, Robert Filmer *(Tim)*, Alan Bridge *(Dr. Hicks)*.

An enjoyable and engaging tale, this follow-up to MY FRIEND FLICKA (1943) is every bit as entertaining as the original. Ken McLaughlin (Roddy McDowall, returning from the original film) is trying to break in Thunderhead, the title horse. The all-white colt is trained for racing, and Ken enters him in competition. At a county race it appears Thunderhead is going to win when the horse suddenly pulls a tendon. Ken is content to restrict his use of Thunderhead to his father's ranch, but trouble brews when the albino horse who sired Thunderhead goes wild. That horse causes trouble for all the ranchers in the valley by stealing mares, but eventually it is challenged by Thunderhead. The brave colt saves Ken, then takes on the albino. The two horses engage in a terrific fight, with Thunderhead defeating his renegade father. Ken's horse returns to his master, but shows a desire to live free on the range. Though heartbroken, Ken understands what is best for his friend and allows the horse to go free. The film is well acted, though the players are really secondary to the real stars of the film: the horses and the beautiful Utah locations. Perfect family viewing.

p, Robert Bassler; d, Louis King; w, Dwight Cummins, Dorothy Yost (based on a novel by Mary O'Hara); ph, Charles Clarke (Technicolor); m, Cyril J. Mockridge.

Drama   **(MPAA:NR)**

TIGER BAY

(1959, Brit.) 105m Independent Artists/RANK-Continental bw

John Mills *(Superintendent Graham)*, Horst Buchholz *(Korchinsky)*, Hayley Mills *(Gillie)*, Yvonne Mitchell *(Anya)*, Megs Jenkins *(Mrs. Phillips)*, Anthony Dawson *(Barclay)*, George Selway *(Detective Sgt. Harvey)*, Shari *(Christine)*, George Pastell *(Poloma Captain)*, Marne Maitland *(Dr. Das)*, Paul Stassino *(1st Officer)*, Meredith Edwards *(Police Constable George Williams)*, Marianne Stone *(Mrs. Williams)*, Rachel Thomas *(Mrs. Parry)*, Brian Hammond *(Dai Parry)*, Kenneth Griffith *(Choirmaster)*, E. Eynon Evans *(Mr. Morgan)*, Christopher Rhodes *(Inspector Bridges)*, Edward Cast *(Detective Constable Thomas)*, David Davies *(Desk Sergeant)*.

A Polish sailor on leave, Korchinsky (Horst Buchholz), heads into Tiger Bay to visit his girl friend, Anya (Yvonne Mitchell). He finds that she is now living with another man and guns her down in a fit of anger. Their noisy argument attracts the attention of 12-year-old Gillie (Hayley Mills), a lonely tomboy who witnesses the murder through a mail slot. She gets hold of the murder weapon, convinced that having a gun will make her popular with

her peers when they play cowboys and Indians. In time, the precocious youngster is confronted by a police detective (Hayley's real-life father, John Mills), but she frustrates him by reciting a convincing string of lies that get her deeper into the situation than she ever imagined. TIGER BAY operates on several levels, creating a thriller of varying intensity with the warm relationship that develops between Gillie and Korchinsky at its center. Korchinsky's interest in the girl grows from a desperate need to keep his crime a secret into genuine affection. Likewise, Gillie sees this as an adventure which will make her popular with playmates, until she, too, develops strong feelings for the sailor. This was Hayley Mill's film debut, and she gives quite a performance for an actress of any age.

p, John Hawkesworth; d, J. Lee Thompson; w, John Hawkesworth, Shelley Smith (based on the novel *Rodolphe et le Revolver* by Noel Calef); ph, Eric Cross; m, Laurie Johnson.

Thriller   **Cas.**   **(MPAA:NR)**

TIKI TIKI

(1971, Can.) 71m Potterton-Commonwealth-United c

Voices of: Barrie Baldaro, Peter Cullan, Joan Stuart, Gayle Claitman, J. Shepard.

An offbeat, thoroughly enjoyable mixture of live action and animation, this Canadian feature is as much fun for adults as it is for children. It tells the story of a doctor who blasts off into space with two monkeys. They're on the run from some pirates and trying to rescue a colony of monkey children. Integrated with this adventure are some delightfully loopy animated sequences involving a Hollywood producer who is everything a hip, smarmy moviemaker should be. What makes him just a little different is that he's a monkey trying to produce the first all-people picture. The live-action sequences are culled from a Soviet children's feature, DR. ABOLIT.

d, Gerald Potterton; w, Gerald Potterton, Martin Hornstein, J. Chorodov; ph, Claude Lapierre; m, Jerry Blatt, L. Burnstein.

Animation/Comedy   **(MPAA:NR)**

TIME BANDITS

(1981, Brit.) 110m Handmade/AE c

John Cleese *(Robin Hood)*, Sean Connery *(King Agamemnon)*, Shelley Duvall *(Pansy)*, Katherine Helmond *(Mrs. Ogre)*, Ian Holm *(Napoleon)*, Michael Palin *(Vincent)*, Ralph Richardson *(Supreme Being)*, Peter Vaughan *(Ogre)*, David Warner *(Evil Genius)*, David Rappaport *(Randall)*, Kenny Baker *(Fidget)*, Jack Purvis *(Wally)*, Mike Edmunds *(Og)*, Malcolm Dixon *(Strutter)*, Tiny Ross *(Vermin)*, Craig Warnock *(Kevin)*, David Baker *(Kevin's Father)*, Sheila Fearn *(Kevin's Mother)*, Jim Broadbent *(Compere)*, John Young *(Reginald)*, Myrtle Devenish *(Beryl)*, Brian Bowes *(Stunt Knight/Hussar)*, Leon Lissek *(1st Refugee)*, Terence Bayler *(Lucien)*, Preston Lockwood *(Neguy)*, Charles McKeown *(Theater Man-*

ager), David Leland *(Puppeteer)*, John Hughman *(The Great Rumbozo)*, Derrick O'Connor *(Robber Leader)*, Peter Jonfield *(Arm Wrestler)*, Derek Deadman *(Robert)*, Jerold Wells *(Benson)*, Mark Holmes *(Troll Father)*, Andrew MacLachlan *(Fireman)*, Chris Grant *(Voice of TV Announcer)*, Tony Jay *(Voice of Supreme Being)*, Edwin Finn *(Supreme Being's Face)*, Neil McCarthy *(2nd Robber)*, Declan Mulholland *(3rd Robber)*, Frances De La Tour *(Salvation Army Major)*.

Terry Gilliam and Michael Palin, from Monty Python's Flying Circus, masterminded this madcap journey through history, in which a curious tot (Craig Warnock) is whisked out of his home by six mischievous dwarfs who possess a map that reveals gaps in the universe. They travel through history encountering the likes of Robin Hood (John Cleese), Greek warrior King Agamemnon (Sean Connery), Napoleon (Ian Holm), and the Supreme Being (Sir Ralph Richardson), the mastermind behind the structure of the universe. Beneath all the merriment is the message that the media, particularly television, are doing a good job of destroying human imagination. The story is delivered in the customary mayhemlike manner of Python features, resulting in an onslaught of witticisms and slapstick. It's probably a bit intense for the younger members of the family, but older kids may find its unorthodox view of a child living independently very appealing.

p&d, Terry Gilliam; w, Michael Palin, Terry Gilliam; ph, Peter Biziou (Technicolor); m, Mike Moran.

Comedy/Fantasy　　　　**Cas.**　　　　**(MPAA:PG)**

TIME MACHINE, THE

(1960, Brit./US) 103m Galaxy/MGM c

Rod Taylor *(George)*, Alan Young *(David Filby/James Filby)*, Yvette Mimieux *(Weena)*, Sebastian Cabot *(Dr. Philip Hillyer)*, Tom Helmore *(Anthony Bridewell)*, Whit Bissell *(Walter Kemp)*, Doris Lloyd *(Mrs. Watchell)*, Paul Frees *(Voice of the History Machine)*, Bob Barran *(Eloi Man)*.

This smashing science-fiction adaptation of H.G. Wells' famous novel has more creativity in every frame than most latter-day rip-offs have in their entirety. Rod Taylor plays George, an inventor who confounds his contemporaries in Victorian England by unveiling his new time machine. All believe him to be certifiable except for a Scotsman named Filby (Alan Young). In his little machine, decorated with red velvet upholstery, George whizzes through time, but not through space. Therefore, all of his adventures take place in the same general area of England, but at various points in history. He makes brief stops at both World Wars, the atomic confrontations of the future (1966 according to this film), and even as far ahead as the year 802,701. In this futuristic era, humanity has been divided into two opposing groups, and it's up to George to help straighten things out. He falls in love with Weena (Yvette Mimieux) and helps her people organize against the oppressors. Producer-director George Pal had already made quite a name for himself with his "Pup-

petoon" stop-motion animation techniques, and here he again delivers some amazing special effects. This time he received an Oscar for his efforts.

p&d, George Pal; w, David Duncan (based on the novel by H.G. Wells); ph, Paul C. Vogel (Metrocolor); m, Russell Garcia.

Science Fiction　　　　**Cas.**　　　　**(MPAA:NR)**

TIME OF THEIR LIVES, THE

(1946) 82m UNIV bw (AKA: THE GHOST STEPS OUT)

Bud Abbott *(Cuthbert/Dr. Greenway)*, Lou Costello *(Horatio Prim)*, Marjorie Reynolds *(Melody Allen)*, Binnie Barnes *(Mildred Prescott)*, John Shelton *(Sheldon Gage)*, Jess Barker *(Tom Danbury)*, Gale Sondergaard *(Emily)*, Robert Barrat *(Maj. Putnam)*, Donald MacBride *(Lt. Mason)*, Anne Gillis *(Nora)*, Lynne Baggett *(June Prescott)*, William Hall *(Connors)*, Rex Lease *(Sgt. Makepeace)*, Selmer Jackson *(Curator)*, Vernon Downing *(Leigh)*, Marjorie Eaton *(Bessie)*, George Carlton, Wheaton Chambers *(Guards)*, Harry Woolman *(Motorcycle Rider)*, Harry Brown *(2nd Sergeant)*, Walter Baldwin *(Bates)*, Boyd Irwin *(Cranwell)*.

A mansion serves as the setting for this funny outing, in which Lou Costello plays the ghost of Horatio Prim, who was wrongfully shot as a traitor during the Revolutionary War. He is joined in this plight by a beautiful ghost named Melody (Marjorie Reynolds), both of them confined to Earth until their innocence is proven. In a dual role, Bud Abbott plays a present-day psychologist and one of the men responsible for the ghosts' long-ago deaths. For a change, Costello has a chance to get his licks in against Abbott, as Horatio uses invisibility to play numerous tricks on the psychologist. In fact, most of the film's gags are derived from the fact that ghosts Horatio and Melody cannot be seen.

p, Val Burton; d, Charles Barton; w, Val Burton, Walter De Leon, Bradford Ropes, John Grant; ph, Charles Van Enger; m, Milton Rosen.

Comedy　　　　　　　　　　**(MPAA:NR)**

TO KILL A MOCKINGBIRD

(1962) 129m UNIV bw

Gregory Peck *(Atticus Finch)*, Mary Badham *(Jean Louise "Scout" Finch)*, Phillip Alford *(Jem Finch)*, John Megna *(Dill Harris)*, Frank Overton *(Sheriff Heck Tate)*, Rosemary Murphy *(Miss Maudie Atkinson)*, Ruth White *(Mrs. Dubose)*, Brock Peters *(Tom Robinson)*, Estelle Evans *(Calpurnia)*, Paul Fix *(Judge Taylor)*, Collin Wilcox *(Mayella Violet Ewell)*, James Anderson *(Bob Ewell)*, Alice Ghostley *(Stephanie Crawford)*, Robert Duvall *(Arthur "Boo" Radley)*, William Windom *(Gilmer)*, Crehan Denton *(Walter Cunningham)*, Richard Hale *(Mr. Radley)*, Steve Condit *(Walter Cunningham*, Bill Walker *(Rev. Sykes)*, Hugh Sanders *(Dr. Reynolds)*, Pauline Myers *(Jessie)*, Jester Hairston *(Spence Robinson)*, Jamie Forster *(Hiram Townsend)*, Nancy Marshall *(School Teacher)*, Kim

Hamilton *(Helen Robinson)*, Kelly Thordsen *(Burly Man)*, Kim Hector *(Cecil Jacobs)*, David Crawford *(Tom Robinson)*, Guy Wilkerson *(Jury Foreman)*, Charles Fredericks *(Court Clerk)*, Jay Sullivan *(Court Reporter)*, Barry Seltzer *(School Boy)*, Dan White, Tex Armstrong *(Men)*, Kim Stanley *(Narrator)*.

Based on Harper Lee's semiautobiographical, Pulitzer Prize-winning novel of 1960, TO KILL A MOCKINGBIRD is a hauntingly nostalgic portrayal of childhood mischief set in a racially divided Alabama town in the 1930s. Gregory Peck plays incorruptible lawyer Atticus Finch, a widower with two children, 10-year-old Jem (Phillip Alford) and tomboyish 6-year-old Scout (Mary Badham). During the summer, Jem and Scout amuse themselves by rolling each other down the street in a tire, or playing in a tree house. What occupies them most, however, is the creaky wooden house where Boo Radley (Robert Duvall) lives. According to neighborhood legend, Boo is crazy and chained to his bed by his father, though he has never been seen, at least by the children. While the kids play, Atticus agrees to represent a black man who is accused of raping a young white woman. A number of people try to pressure him into stepping down from the case, but his pursuit of justice is unwavering. As the trial proceeds, Atticus, Jem, and especially Scout learn as much about each other as they do about their own fears and prejudices. Since its release, this intelligent, atmospheric film has been warmly received by audiences responding not only to their own nostalgia, but also to the heroic image portrayed by Peck, a shining example of citizenship and fatherhood. There is also a superb score by Elmer Bernstein. The language, emotions, and general subject matter of the trial scenes may be a bit rough for some children, but in Peck's hands there is nothing to fear.

p, Alan J. Pakula; d, Robert Mulligan; w, Horton Foote (based on the novel by Harper Lee); ph, Russell Harlan; m, Elmer Bernstein.

Drama   **Cas.**   **(MPAA:NR)**

TOBY TYLER

(1960) 96m Disney/BV c

Kevin Corcoran *(Toby Tyler)*, Henry Calvin *(Ben Cotter)*, Gene Sheldon *(Sam Treat)*, Bob Sweeney *(Harry Tupper)*, Richard Eastham *(Col. Sam Castle)*, James Drury *(Jim Weaver)*, Barbara Beaird *(Mlle. Jeanette)*, Dennis Joel *(Mons. Ajax)*, Edith Evanson *(Aunt Olive)*, Tom Fadden *(Uncle Daniel)*, Ollie Wallace *(Bandleader)*, Mr. Stubbs *(Himself)*, The Flying Viennas, The Jungleland Elephants, The Marquis Family; The Ringling Brothers Clowns: "Eddie Spaghetti" Emerson, Abe "Korky" Goldstein, Duke Johnson, and Harry Johnson.

TOBY TYLER is one of those Disney pictures that has as much relevance today as it did when it was first released. The subject matter is every kid's dream (and probably that of many adults), running away to join the circus. Little Toby Tyler (Kevin Corcoran) goes through a period of rejection at the farm home of his aunt and uncle and

flees, hooking up with a traveling circus, where he experiences its exotic atmosphere, its eccentric characters, its excitement, and its wild animals. Toby even gets a chance to become a hero when he is called upon to perform a horseback trick. By the end, the lad discovers that his family really does care about him, and has, in fact, been trying to contact him. Juvenile star Corcoran had already earned a considerable following for his work in such Disney pictures as THE SHAGGY DOG and OLD YELLER.

p, Bill Walsh; d, Charles Barton; w, Bill Walsh, Lillie Hayward (based on the novel by James Otis Kaler); ph, William Snyder (Technicolor); m, Buddy Baker.

Drama   **Cas.**   **(MPAA:NR)**

TOM SAWYER

(1930) 85m PAR bw

Jackie Coogan *(Tom Sawyer)*, Junior Durkin *(Huckleberry Finn)*, Mitzi Green *(Becky Thatcher)*, Lucien Littlefield *(Teacher)*, Tully Marshall *(Muff Potter)*, Clara Blandick *(Aunt Polly)*, Mary Jane Irving *(Mary)*, Ethel Wales *(Mrs. Harper)*, Jackie Searl *(Sid)*, Dick Winslow *(Joe Harper)*, Jane Darwell *(Widow Douglass)*, Charles Stevens *(Injun Joe)*, Charles Sellon *(Minister)*, Lon Puff *(Judge Thatcher)*.

This entertaining adaptation of the Mark Twain classic succeeds chiefly because of Jackie Coogan's endearing performance. Tom Sawyer (Coogan) and his best pal, Huck Finn (Junior Durkin), dream of life away from their small Missouri town. Becky Thatcher (Mitzi Green) is the little girl who tags along with her more daring male companions. All of the famous scenes are handled well: Tom and Huck listening to themselves being eulogized when it's thought that they have drowned in the Mississippi, the moment when Tom persuades some other boys to whitewash a fence for him, and the boys' fright when they are menaced by Injun Joe. The following year, Paramount made HUCKLEBERRY FINN with the same cast, and, in 1938, they released a low-budget film called TOM SAWYER, DETECTIVE.

p, Louis D. Lighton; d, John Cromwell; w, Sam Mintz, Grover Jones, William Slavens McNutt (based on *The Adventures of Tom Sawyer* by Mark Twain); ph, Charles Lang.

Adventure   **(MPAA:NR)**

TOM SAWYER

(1973) 100m Reader's Digest/UA c

Johnny Whitaker *(Tom Sawyer)*, Celeste Holm *(Aunt Polly)*, Warren Oates *(Muff Potter)*, Jeff East *(Huckleberry Finn)*, Jodie Foster *(Becky Thatcher)*, Lucille Benson *(Widder Douglas)*, Henry Jones *(Mister Dobbins)*, Noah Keen *(Judge Thatcher)*, Dub Taylor *(Clayton)*, Richard Eastham *(Doc Robinson)*, Sandy Kenyon *(Constable Clemens)*, Joshua Hill Lewis *(Cousin Sidney)*, Susan Joyce *(Cousin Mary)*, Steve Hogg *(Ben Rogers)*, Sean Summers *(Billy Fisher)*, Kevin Jefferson *(Joe Jefferson)*,

Page Williams *(Saloon Girl)*, Kunu Hank *(Injun Joe)*, James A. Kuhn *(Blacksmith)*, Mark Lynch *(Prosecuting Attorney)*, Jonathan Taylor *(Small Boy)*, Anne Voss *(Girl)*.

This musical version of *Tom Sawyer* marked the fourth time Mark Twain's famous novel had been brought to the screen. Here the familiar story is augmented by a lilting score by the Sherman brothers, who also provided the screenplay. Shot entirely on location in Missouri, bathed in nostalgia, and boasting some good songs (though never managing to be quite as magical as one might hope), the film stars Johnny Whitaker, from TV's "Family Affair," as Tom Sawyer, and Jeff East, a young Missourian making his film debut, as Huck Finn. Thoroughly convincing as Becky Thatcher is 10-year-old Jodie Foster. While not as enjoyable as the Jackie Coogan version (see above), this more recent tale may be easier for some youngsters to watch. A disappointing sequel, HUCKLEBERRY FINN, followed in 1974.

p, Arthur P. Jacobs; d, Don Taylor; w, Robert B. Sherman, Richard M. Sherman (based on *The Adventures of Tom Sawyer)* by Mark Twain); ph, Frank Stanley (Panavision, Deluxe Color); m, Richard M. Sherman, Robert B. Sherman.

Adventure/Musical   **Cas.**   **(MPAA:G)**

TOM THUMB

(1958, Brit./US) 92m Galaxy/MGM c

Russ Tamblyn *(Tom Thumb)*, Alan Young *(Woody the Piper)*, Terry-Thomas *(Ivan)*, Peter Sellers *(Tony)*, Jessie Matthews *(Anna)*, June Thorburn *(The Forest Queen)*, Bernard Miles *(Jonathan)*, Ian Wallace *(The Cobbler)*, Peter Butterworth *(Kapellmeister)*, Stan Freberg *(Voice of Noveltoon Puppets)*, Peter Bull *(The Town Crier)*, Barbara Ferris *(Voice of Thumbelina)*, Stan Freberg *(Voice of Yawning Man)*, Dal McKennon *(Voice of Con-fu-shon)*, Norma Zimmer *(Singing Voice of Anna)*.

The makers of TOM THUMB put a lot of effort into providing a realistic and entertaining—for adults as well as children—adaptation of the famous Grimm brothers fairy tale, although their emphasis was almost totally on visuals and the song-and-dance routines rather than a well-developed script. Russ Tamblyn is a charmer as the five-inch-tall Tom Thumb, jumping about with unfailing grace and bringing joy to just about everyone's heart. The villainous Ivan and Tony (Terry-Thomas and Peter Sellers), however, plot to exploit his size for their own unsavory purposes. Their attempts to steal this little ball of energy from his woodcutter father's cottage and to sink him in a life of evil eventually fail, but not until a number of songs and adventures are delivered. The special effects that provide the illusion of the tiny boy's world are outstanding—good enough, in fact, to have received an Academy Award, yet another accolade for producer-director George Pal.

p&d, George Pal; w, Ladislas Fodor (based on a story

by The Brothers Grimm); ph, Georges Perinal (Eastmancolor); m, Douglas Gamley, Ken Jones.

Fantasy   **Cas.**   **(MPAA:G)**

TOPPER

(1937) 98m MGM bw

Constance Bennett *(Marion Kerby)*, Cary Grant *(George Kerby)*, Roland Young *(Cosmo Topper)*, Billie Burke *(Henrietta Topper)*, Alan Mowbray *(Wilkins)*, Eugene Pallette *(Casey)*, Arthur Lake *(Elevator Boy)*, Hedda Hopper *(Mrs. Stuyvesant)*, Virginia Sale *(Miss Johnson)*, Theodore Von Eltz *(Hotel Manager)*, J. Farrell MacDonald *(Policeman)*, Elaine Shepard *(Secretary)*, Doodles Weaver, Si Jenks *(Rustics)*, Three Hits and a Miss *(Themselves)*, Donna Dax *(Hat Check Girl at Rainbow Nightclub)*, Hoagy Carmichael *(Bill the Piano Player)*, Claire Windsor, Betty Blythe *(Ladies)*.

Low-budget comedy producer Hal Roach, who had made a fortune on his Laurel and Hardy shorts, finally decided to risk a big-budget, feature-length, sophisticated comedy, and he came up with a winner that spawned two sequels, a television series, and a made-for-TV remake. George and Marion Kerby (Cary Grant and Constance Bennett) are a young, wealthy, happy-go-lucky married couple whose main pursuit in life is having a good time. Though they are the chief stockholders in a bank, their minds are on anything but business. One night, while driving recklessly in their big car, they hit a tree and are killed. Their spirits walk out of the wreck, but are dismayed to learn that they have not ascended to the heavens but are still on Earth, albeit in a rather astral form (they can turn invisible at will). George and Marion then decide that they will probably be trapped on Earth forever unless they make amends for their frivolous lifestyle by doing something of value. TOPPER is an extremely enjoyable comedy that gets big laughs from its special effects—the invisible duo makes objects appear to move by themselves. The computer-colored version, which recently appeared on the market, adds nothing to the film's charm and humor, and should be avoided.

p, Hal Roach; d, Norman Z. McLeod; w, Jack Jevne, Eric Hatch, Eddie Moran (based on the novel *The Jovial Ghosts* by Thorne Smith); ph, Norbert Brodine; m, Edward Powell, Hugo Friedhofer.

Comedy   **Cas.**   **(MPAA:NR)**

TREASURE ISLAND

(1934) 109m MGM bw

Wallace Beery *(Long John Silver)*, Jackie Cooper *(Jim Hawkins)*, Lionel Barrymore *(Billy Bones)*, Otto Kruger *(Dr. Livesey)*, Lewis Stone *(Capt. Alexander Smollett)*, Nigel Bruce *(Squire Trelawney)*, Charles "Chic" Sale *(Ben Gunn)*, William V. Mong *(Pew)*, Charles McNaughton *(Black Dog)*, Dorothy Peterson *(Mrs. Hawkins)*, Douglas Dumbrille *("Ugly Israel" Hand)*, Edmund Breese *(Anderson)*, Olin Howland *(Dick)*, Charles Irwin *(Abraham Gray)*,

Edward Pawley *(O'Brien)*, Richard Powell *(William Post)*, James Burke *(George Merry)*, John Anderson *(Harry Sykes)*, Charles Bennett *(Dandy Dawson)*, J.M. Kerrigan *(Tom Morgan)*, Westcott Clark *(Allan)*, Yorke Sherwood *(Mr. Arrow)*, Harry Cording *(Henry)*, Tom Mahoney *(Redruth)*, Sidney D'Albrook *(Joyce)*, Frank Dunn *(Hunter)*, Robert Adair *(Tom)*, Cora Sue Collins *(Child at Inn)*, Harold Entwistle *(Ship's Chandler)*, Harold Wilson *(Oldster)*, Bernice Beatty *(Woman at Inn)*, Vernon Downing *(Boy at Inn)*, Bobby Bolder *(Mild Man at Inn)*, Edith Kingdon *(Wife at Inn)*, Wilson Benge *(Friend at Inn)*, Shirlee Simpson *(Woman Friend at Inn)*.

Robert Louis Stevenson's *Treasure Island* transfers easily from the page to the screen in this first sound version of the classic adventure tale. Wallace Beery plays the famous Long John Silver and Jackie Cooper takes the role of the doughty Jim Hawkins. The film opens at a rough-and-tumble coastal pub where young Jim meets the drunken Billy Bones (Lionel Barrymore) and learns that the old rummy has a secret map of an island in the Caribbean where a trove was left by a well-known pirate. When Billy Bones dies, Jim and two friends book passage on a ship run by Capt. Smollett (Lewis Stone). What they don't know, at first, is that practically all of the ship's men are one-time associates of the late pirate and one step from being cutthroats. What's more, all of them want their share of the booty. A beautiful production, a fine score, and a strong script all contribute to making this a respectful version of Stevenson's work.

p, Hunt Stromberg; d, Victor Fleming; w, John Lee Mahin, Leonard Praskins, John Howard Lawson (based on the novel by Robert Louis Stevenson); ph, Ray June, Harold Rosson, Clyde DeVinna; m, Herbert Stothart.

Adventure   **Cas.**   **(MPAA:NR)**

TREASURE ISLAND

(1950, Brit.) 96m Disney/RKO c

Bobby Driscoll *(Jim Hawkins)*, Robert Newton *(Long John Silver)*, Basil Sydney *(Capt. Smollett)*, Walter Fitzgerald *(Squire Trelawney)*, Denis O'Dea *(Dr. Livesey)*, Ralph Truman *(George Merry)*, Finlay Currie *(Capt. Bones)*, John Laurie *(Pew)*, Francis de Wolff *(Black Dog)*, Geoffrey Wilkinson *(Ben Gunn)*, David Davies *(Arrow)*, Andrew Blackett *(Gray)*, Paddy Brannigan *(Hunter)*, Ken Buckle *(Joyce)*, John Gregson *(Redruth)*, Howard Douglas *(Williams)*, Geoffrey Keen *(Israel Hand)*, William Devlin *(Tom Morgan)*, Diarmuid Kelly *(Bolen)*, Sam Kydd *(Cady)*, Eddie Moran *(Jack Bart)*, Harry Locke *(Haggott)*, Harold Jamieson *(Scully)*, Stephen Jack *(Job Anderson)*, Jack Arrow *(Norton)*, Jim O'Brady *(Wolfe)*, Chris Adcock *(Pike)*, Reginald Drummond *(Vane)*, Gordon Mulholland *(Durgin)*, Patrick Troughton *(Roach)*, Leo Phillips *(Spotts)*, Fred Clark *(Bray)*, Tom Lucas *(Upson)*, Bob Head *(Tardy)*.

This was Disney's first totally live-action movie and it is, by far, the best version of the familiar Stevenson story. Disney regular Bobby Driscoll takes on the coveted role of Jim Hawkins, and a number of reliable British actors round out the cast. This version has a marvelous full-bodied visual style that never appears to be studio-bound. When Disney wanted to rerelease the film in the 1970s, the MPAA rating system had arrived, and because of some rather graphic violence, the movie was given the dreaded (by Disney) "PG" rating. The offending scenes had to be snipped to acquire the desired "G" rating, depriving audiences of some excitement, but this remains an extremely satisfying film.

p, Perce Pearce; d, Byron Haskin; w, Lawrence E. Watkin (based on the novel by Robert Louis Stevenson); ph, F.A. Young (Technicolor); m, Clifton Parker.

Adventure   **Cas.**   **(MPAA:G)**

TRUE GRIT

(1969) 128m PAR c

John Wayne *(Reuben J. "Rooster" Cogburn)*, Glen Campbell *(La Boeuf)*, Kim Darby *(Mattie Ross)*, Jeremy Slate *(Emmett Quincy)*, Robert Duvall *(Ned Pepper)*, Dennis Hopper *(Moon)*, Alfred Ryder *(Goudy)*, Strother Martin *(Col. G. Stonehill)*, Jeff Corey *(Tom Chaney)*, Ron Soble *(Capt. Boots Finch)*, John Fiedler *(Lawyer J. Noble Daggett)*, James Westerfield *(Judge Parker)*, John Doucette *(Sheriff)*, Donald Woods *(Barlow)*, Edith Atwater *(Mrs. Floyd)*, Carlos Rivas *(Dirty Bob)*, Isabel Boniface *(Mrs. Bagby)*, H.W. Gim *(Chen Lee)*, John Pickard *(Frank Ross)*, Elizabeth Harrower *(Mrs. Ross)*, Ken Renard *(Yarnell)*, Jay Ripley *(Harold Parmalee)*, Kenneth Becker *(Farrell Parmalee)*, Myron Healey *(A Deputy)*, Hank Worden *(Undertaker)*, Guy Wilkerson *(The Hangman)*, Red Morgan *(Red the Ferryman)*, Robin Morse.

TRUE GRIT is a rollicking western, an enormously entertaining adventure that is as much about John Wayne's image as it is about a girl seeking revenge for her father's murder. Mattie Ross (Kim Darby) is a level-headed 14-year-old who goes to Rooster Cogburn (Wayne) after her father is killed. The murderer, Tom Chaney (Jeff Corey), has since fled into Indian territory, and Mattie wants a man of "true grit" to help bring him to justice. Cogburn, a potbellied US marshal with a patch over one eye, admires Mattie's spunk and agrees to take on the job. Joining them is La Boeuf (Glen Campbell), a Texas Ranger whom Mattie despises. He, too, is searching for Chaney, hoping to collect a reward offered by the family of a murdered Texas politician. Much of the film's entertainment comes from the obvious contrasts and subtle similarities between Cogburn and Mattie. Cogburn is fat, drunken, and not entirely honest, but has an underlying sense of honor, that "true grit" that Mattie demands. Though Wayne's performances in STAGECOACH and THE SEARCHERS are more complex, TRUE GRIT provides him with some of his most memorable screen moments, and he won an Oscar for his fine work. Wayne reprised the role in ROOSTER COGBURN (1975), costarring with Katharine Hepburn, and TRUE GRIT was redone as a made-for-television film in 1978, with Warren Oates in the lead role, but neither project approached this film in either quality or spirit.

p, Hal B. Wallis; d, Henry Hathaway; w, Marguerite Roberts (based on the novel by Charles Portis); ph, Lucien Ballard (Technicolor); m, Elmer Bernstein.

Western   **Cas.**   **(MPAA:G)**

TRUMAN CAPOTE'S TRILOGY

(1969) 100m AA c

"Miriam": Mildred Natwick *(Miss Miller)*, Susan Dunfee *(Miriam)*, Carol Gustafson *(Miss Lake)*, Robin Ponterio *(Emily)*, Beverly Ballard *(Nina)*, Jane Connell *(Mrs. Connolly)*, Frederick Morton *(Man in Theater)*, Richard Hamilton *(Man in Automat)*, Phyllis Eldridge *(Woman in Automat)*, Tony Ross *(Dwarf)*, Brooks Rogers *(Connolly)*, Niki Flacks *(Clerk in Shop)*; "Among the Paths to Eden": Maureen Stapleton *(Mary O'Meaghan)*, Martin Balsam *(Ivor Belli)*; "A Christmas Memory": Geraldine Page *(Woman)*, Donnie Melvin *(Buddy)*, Christine Marler, Lavinia Cassels *(Aunts)*, Josip Elic *(Haha)*, Lynn Forman *(Woman in Car)*, Win Forman *(Storekeeper)*, Truman Capote *(Narrator)*.

This three-part film, adapted by Truman Capote from his short stories, was originally intended as three different television specials. However, only one of the stories, "A Christmas Memory," was broadcast, winning both an Emmy and a Peabody Award. The three tales were then re-edited into a theatrical version that was given a limited release before being made available to its intended market, high schools and universities. Though each segment clearly suffers from its truncation, as a whole this is a strong, sensitive film blessed with some fine performances. "Miriam" features Mildred Natwick as a nanny who is slowly losing her mind. "Among the Paths to Eden" is a beautiful story about a spinster (Maureen Stapleton) who looks for a husband amongst widowers visiting their wives' graves. "A Christmas Memory," which Capote narrates, is a sensitive drama about a young child who watches a loved one slowly lose her memory as years go by.

p&d, Frank Perry; w, Truman Capote, Eleanor Perry (based on the stories "Miriam," "Among the Paths to Eden," and "A Christmas Memory" by Truman Capote); ph, Joseph Brun, Harry Sundby, Conrad Hall, Jordon Cronenweth (Eastmancolor); m, Meyer Kupferman.

Drama   **(MPAA:G)**

20,000 LEAGUES UNDER THE SEA

(1954) 120m Disney/BV c

Kirk Douglas *(Ned Land)*, James Mason *(Capt. Nemo)*, Paul Lukas *(Prof. Pierre Aronnax)*, Peter Lorre *(Conseil, His Assistant)*, Robert J. Wilke *(lst Mate of "Nautilus")*, Carleton Young *(John Howard)*, Ted De Corsia *(Capt. Farragut)*, Percy Helton *(Diver)*, Ted Cooper *(Mate of "Abraham Lincoln")*, Edward Marr *(Shipping Agent)*, Fred Graham *(Casey Moore)*, J.M. Kerrigan *(Billy)*, Harry Harvey *(Shipping Clerk)*, Herb Vigran *(Reporter)*, Esmeralda the Seal.

One of the best science-fiction movies ever made, this Disney picture recreates Jules Verne's prophetic tale (published in 1870) of submarines and atomic power. The time is 1868, and San Francisco is agog over reports of a sea-roving "monster" that devours any ship that ventures near it. Many voyages are canceled and the government is forced to send a warship to investigate and clear the sea lanes. That ship is sunk by the heinous "creature," and only three people survive the ordeal: a professional harpoonist (Kirk Douglas), a professor from the Nautical Museum in Paris (Paul Lukas), and his aide (Peter Lorre). They are picked up by the submarine *Nautilus,* the dreaded "monster." The sub is commanded by Capt. Nemo (James Mason), a strange, demented man who has been sinking ships in a misguided effort to end warfare at sea. This awesome adventure is so filled with fantastical elements that it's difficult to single out specific scenes, though the fight with the giant squid is a sight to behold. The unique sets alone are worth the price of admission, not to mention the excellent direction and special effects, and the memorable performance by James Mason.

p, Walt Disney; d, Richard Fleischer; w, Earl Felton (based on the novel *20,000 Leagues Under the Sea* by Jules Verne); ph, Franz F. Planer, Ralph Hammeras, Till Gabbani (CinemaScope, Technicolor); m, Paul J. Smith, J.S. Bach.

Science Fiction   **Cas.**   **(MPAA:NR)**

UV

VOYAGE TO THE BOTTOM OF THE SEA

(1961) 105m Windsor/FOX c

Walter Pidgeon *(Adm. Harriman Nelson)*, Joan Fontaine *(Dr. Susan Hiller)*, Barbara Eden *(Cathy Connors)*, Peter Lorre *(Commodore Lucius Emery)*, Robert Sterling *(Capt. Lee Crane)*, Michael Ansara *(Miguel Alvarez)*, Frankie Avalon *(Chip Romano)*, Regis Toomey *(Dr. Jamieson)*, John Litel *(Adm. Crawford)*, Howard McNear *(Congressman Parker)*, Henry Daniell *(Dr. Zucco)*, Mark Slade *(Smith)*, Charles Tannen *(Gleason)*, Delbert Monroe *(Kowski)*, Anthony Monaco *(Cookie)*, Robert Easton *(Sparks)*, Jonathan Gilmore *(Young)*, David McLean *(Ned Thompson)*, Larry Gray *(Dr. Newmar)*, George Diestel *(Lt. Hodges)*, Skip Ward, Michael Ford *(Crew Members)*, Art Baker *(UN Commentator)*, Kendrick Huxham *(UN Chairman)*, Dr. John Giovanni *(Italian Delegate)*.

VOYAGE TO THE BOTTOM OF THE SEA was the inspiration for the long-running television series of the same name. Its excellent cast, including Walter Pidgeon, Joan Fontaine, and Peter Lorre, play rather predictable characters, but the film boasts some captivating special effects and sets. Adm. Harriman Nelson (Pidgeon) is the inventor of a nuclear submarine designed to reach depths greater than man has ever reached before. This capacity is later required to evade submarines that are trying to blow it up. Against the wishes of the United Nations, Nelson decides to save the world by launching missiles against the Van Allen radiation belt, which has gone out of control and is threatening to melt the Earth. Nelson sees this mission through despite the other hostile subs and the efforts of Dr. Susan Hiller (Fontaine) to sabotage the project. In one of the most exciting scenes, the sub is attacked by a giant squid.

p&d, Irwin Allen; w, Irwin Allen, Charles Bennett (based on the story by Irwin Allen); ph, Winton C. Hoch (CinemaScope, Deluxe Color); m, Paul Sawtell, Bert Shefter.

Science Fiction   Cas.   (MPAA:NR)

WACKY WORLD OF MOTHER GOOSE, THE

(1967) 81m Videocraft/EM c

Voice of Margaret Rutherford *(Mother Goose)*.

A combination of secret agents and well-known storybook characters, from Sleeping Beauty to Tom Thumb, populates this animated children's feature. Good kids' fare.

p, Arthur Rankin, Jr.; d, Jules Bass; w, Romeo Muller (based on characters created by Charles Perrault in the book *Mother Goose Tales*); ph, (Pathe Color).

Animation   Cas.   (MPAA:NR)

WATER BABIES, THE

(1979, Brit.) 93m Ariadne/Pethurst International c

James Mason *(Grimes)*, Billie Whitelaw *(Mrs. Doasyouwouldbedoneby)*, Bernard Cribbins *(Masterman)*, Joan Greenwood *(Lady Harriet)*, David Tomlinson *(Sir John)*, Paul Luty *(Sladd)*, Tommy Pender *(Tom)*, Samantha Gates *(Ellie)*.

This enchanting children's film mixes live action and animated underwater sequences to tell the story of Tom (Tommy Pender), the 12-year-old apprentice to veteran chimney sweep Grimes (James Mason), who tends to hit the bottle. When the youngster is wrongly accused of stealing, he flees and leaps into a pool. There he encounters an assortment of underwater characters and rescues the water babies—children being held captive by an eel and a shark—before returning to dry land cleared of any wrongdoing. The animation is average, but kids will get a kick out of Tom's adventures.

p, Peter Shaw; d, Lionel Jeffries; w, Michael Robson (based on the novel by Charles Kingsley); ph, Ted Scaife.

Adventure/Animation   Cas.   (MPAA:NR)

WAY OUT WEST

(1937) 65m Hal Roach/MGM bw

Stan Laurel, Oliver Hardy *(Themselves)*, James Finlayson *(Mickey Finn)*, Sharon Lynne *(Lola Marcel)*, Stanley Fields *(Sheriff)*, Rosina Lawrence *(Mary Roberts)*, James Mason *(Anxious Patron)*, James C. Morton, Frank Mills, Dave Pepper *(Bartenders)*, Vivien Oakland *(Stagecoach Passenger/Molly)*, Harry Bernard *(Man Eating at Bar)*, Mary Gordon, May Wallace *(Cooks)*, Avalon Boys Quartet: [Chill Wills, Art Green, Walter Trask, Don Brookins] *(Themselves)*, Jack Hill *(Worker at Mickey Finn's)*, Sam Lufkin *(Stagecoach Baggage Man)*, Tex Driscoll *(Bearded Miner)*, Flora Finch *(Maw)*, Fred "Snowflake" Toones *(Janitor)*.

Laurel and Hardy's only western spoof, WAY OUT WEST, ranks among the best of their films, with more exuberant laughs crammed into its scant 65 minutes than can be found in a dozen modern comedies. With their faithful mule, the boys head into Brushwood Gulch to deliver a gold mine deed to their departed partner's daughter. But they get hopelessly lost, and make the mistake of asking bartender Mickey Finn (James Finlayson) for advice. Finn's scullery maid, Mary Roberts (Rosina Lawrence), is actually the woman they seek, but he deliberately steers them toward his wife, Lola Marcel (Sharon Lynne)—a brassy blonde who is so obviously not the right person that everyone can see she cries crocodile tears upon learning of her "father's" death. Everyone, that is, except Laurel and Hardy. Included is the song "Trail of the Lonesome Pine." A computer-colored version of this film also exists.

p, Stan Laurel; d, James W. Horne; w, Charles Rogers, Felix Adler, James Parrott (based on a story by Jack Jevne, Charles Rogers); ph, Art Lloyd, Walter Lundin; m, Marvin Hatley, LeRoy Shield, Egbert Van Alstyne, Leonard-Munson, J.L. Hill, Carroll-MacDonald, Nathaniel Shilkret, Irving Berlin, Franz von Suppe.

Comedy/Western   Cas.   (MPAA:NR)

WEE GEORDIE

(1956, Brit.) 93m Argonaut/Times c (GB: GEORDIE)

Alistair Sim *(The Laird)*, Bill Travers *(Geordie MacTaggart)*, Norah Gorsen *(Jean Donaldson)*, Molly Urquhart *(Geordie's Mother)*, Francis de Wolff *(Henry Samson)*, Jack Radcliffe *(Rev. McNab)*, Brian Reece *(Dick Harley)*, Raymond Huntley *(Rawlins)*, Miles Malleson *(Lord Paunceton)*, Jameson Clarke *(Geordie's Father)*, Doris Godard *(Helga*, Danish Shot-Putter), Stanley Baxter *(Postman)*, Duncan Macrae *(Schoolmaster)*, Paul Young *(Young Geordie)*, Anna Ferguson *(Young Jean)*, Margaret Boyd *(Laird's Housekeeper)*, Alex McCrindle *(Guard)*.

Set in the "past and present, with a wee glimpse into the future," this tender tale about a youngster's rise to fame is photographed against the picturesque Scottish highlands. Young Geordie MacTaggart (first played by Paul Young) is a frail lad who takes a ribbing from his schoolmates because of his size, or lack of it. After seeing a muscleman ad in a magazine, however, he begins to get himself into shape. His pains pay off when Geordie (now played by Bill Travers) is selected for Britain's Olympic squad in the hammerthrow. A plus is the characteristically fine performance from the top-billed Alastair Sim as the laird who employs Geordie's gamekeeper father.

p, Frank Launder, Sidney Gilliat; d, Frank Launder; w, Frank Launder, Sidney Gilliat (based on a novel by David Walker); ph, Wilkie Cooper (Technicolor); m, William Alwyn.

Drama (MPAA:NR)

WEE WILLIE WINKIE

(1937) 103m FOX bw

Shirley Temple (Priscilla Williams), Victor McLaglen (Sgt. MacDuff), C. Aubrey Smith (Col. Williams), June Lang (Joyce Williams), Michael Whalen (Lt. "Coppy" Brandes), Cesar Romero (Khoda Khan), Constance Collier (Mrs. Allardyce), Douglas Scott (Mott), Gavin Muir (Capt. Bibberbeigh), Willie Fung (Mohammet Dihn), Brandon Hurst (Bagby), Lionel Pape (Maj. Allardyce), Clyde Cook (Pipe Maj. Sneath), Lauri Beatty (Elsie Allardyce), Lionel Braham (Maj. Gen. Hammond), Mary Forbes (Mrs. MacMonachie), Cyril McLaglen (Cpl. Tummel), Jack Pennick (Soldier Guard), George Hassell (MacMonachie), Pat Somerset (Capt. Stuart), Hector V. Sarno (Coach Driver), Noble Johnson (Sikh Policeman), Scotty Mattraw (Merchant), Louis Vincenot (African Chieftain).

Little Shirley Temple works her charms on India in this starring vehicle, which is very loosely based on a Rudyard Kipling story and directed by, of all people, John Ford, best known for his classic westerns. At the turn of the century, Priscilla (Shirley Temple) and her widowed mother (June Lang) go to live with her grandfather, Col. Williams (C. Aubrey Smith), on a British army base in India. Priscilla goes through maneuvers with the troops, donning a darling pint-sized uniform and managing to win over everyone she comes in contact with, including rebel leader Khoda Khan (Cesar Romero). The entire political situation is solved when Priscilla asks why the two factions are mad at each other, thus bringing about a peaceful resolution!

p, Gene Markey; d, John Ford; w, Ernest Pascal, Julien Josephson (based on a story by Rudyard Kipling); ph, Arthur Miller; m, Louis Silvers.

Comedy/Drama (MPAA:NR)

WHAT'S UP, DOC?

(1972) 94m Saticoy/WB c

Barbra Streisand (Judy Maxwell), Ryan O'Neal (Prof. Howard Bannister), Madeline Kahn (Eunice Burns), Kenneth Mars (Hugh Simon), Austin Pendleton (Frederick Larrabe), Sorrell Booke (Harry), Stefan Gierasch (Fritz), Mabel Albertson (Mrs. Van Hoskins), Michael Murphy (Mr. Smith), Graham Jarvis (Bailiff), Liam Dunn (Judge), Phil Roth (Mr. Jones), John Hillerman (Mr. Kaltenborn),

George Morfogen (Rudy the Headwaiter), Randall R. [Randy] Quaid (Prof. Hosquith), M. Emmet Walsh (Arresting Officer), Eleanor Zee (Banquet Receptionist), Kevin O'Neal (Delivery Boy), Paul Condylis (Room Service Waiter), Fred Scheiwiller, Carl Saxe, Jack Perkins (Jewel Thieves), Paul B. Kililman (Druggist), Gil Perkins (Jones' Driver), Christa Lang (Mrs. Hosquith), Stan Ross, Peter Paul Eastman (Musicologists), John Byner (Head), Eric Brotherson (Larrabee's Butler), Elaine Partnow (Party Guest), George R. Burrafato (Eunice's Cabdriver), Jerry Summers (Smith's Cabdriver), Morton C. Thompson (Airport Cabdriver), John Allen Vick (Airport Driver), Donald T. Bexley (Skycap), Leonard Lookabaugh (Painter on Roof), Candace Brownell (Ticket Seller), Sean Morgan (Banquet Official), Patricia O'Neal (Elderly Lady on Plane), Joe Alfasa (Waiter in Hall), Chuck Hollom (Pizza Cook), William M. Niven (Painter).

Peter Bogdanovich's attempt to revive the screwball comedy genre is more an imitation than an hommage, especially if you've seen the Howard Hawks classic BRINGING UP BABY. Still, there's plenty of good 1930s slapstick and cartoon humor to hold attention and justify Bugs Bunny's famed opening line (which serves as the title) and Porky Pig's equally famed closing: "Th-th-that's all, folks!" Prof. Howard Bannister (Ryan O'Neal) is a clumsy, shy professor from Iowa who hopes to win a $20,000 fellowship in musicology. In a plaid suitcase, he carries some ancient rocks that demonstrate his theory on music's prehistoric origins. Bannister arrives at a San Francisco hotel with his fiancee, Eunice Burns (Madeline Kahn, in her film debut), while other guests with identical suitcases, including the breezy Judy Maxwell (Barbra Streisand), are also checking in. Naturally, the suitcases get hopelessly mixed up—a daffy coincidence leading to countless comic scenes. While WHAT'S UP, DOC? may not be as great as the classic screwball comedies of the 1930 and 1940s, director Bogdanovich has delivered a film with energy, wit, and a madcap pace that is well worth watching.

p&d, Peter Bogdanovich; w, Buck Henry, David Newman, Robert Benton (based on a story by Peter Bogdanovich); ph, Laszlo Kovacs (Technicolor); m, Artie Butler.

Comedy Cas. (MPAA:G)

WHERE'S CHARLEY?

(1952, Brit.) 97m WB c

Ray Bolger (Charley Wykeham), Allyn McLerie (Amy Spettigue), Robert Shackleton (Jack Chesney), Horace Cooper (Stephen Spettigue), Margaretta Scott (Dona Lucia), Howard Marion Crawford (Sir Francis Chesney), Mary Germaine (Kitty Verdun), Henry Hewitt (Brassett), H.G. Stoker (Wilkinson), Martin Miller (Photographer).

WHERE'S CHARLEY? is made extraordinary by its incredible star, Ray Bolger, a 48-year-old actor playing a college student at Oxford. Charley Wykeham (Bolger) and Jack Chesney (Robert Shackleton) are roommates in love with Amy Spettigue (Allyn McLerie) and Kitty Verdun (Mary Germaine) and would like to have a date with them, but dating without a chaperon isn't allowed. When Charley's wealthy, widowed aunt is delayed in her arrival to chaperon them, Charley dresses up as his aunt in order to prevent an embarrassing situation. Things get embarrassing enough, however, when Amy's elderly uncle becomes enamored of Charley's feminine persona. Eventually, the whole tempest in a teapot is calmed, but not before we've been treated to a tour de force performance by Bolger.

p, Ernest Martin, Cy Feuer; d, David Butler; w, John Monks, Jr. (based on the musical play by Frank Loesser and George Abbott, from the play "Charley's Aunt" by Brandon Thomas); ph, Erwin Hillier (Technicolor).

Comedy/Musical (MPAA:NR)

WHITE CHRISTMAS

(1954) 120m PAR c

Bing Crosby (Bob Wallace), Danny Kaye (Phil Davis), Rosemary Clooney (Betty), Vera-Ellen (Judy), Dean Jagger (Gen. Waverly), Mary Wickes (Emma), John Brascia (Joe), Anne Whitfield (Susan), Richard Shannon (Adjutant), Grady Sutton (General's Guest), Sig Rumann (Landlord), Robert Crosson (Albert), Herb Vigran (Novello), Dick Keene (Assistant Stage Manager), Johnny Grant (Ed Harrison), Gavin Gordon (Gen. Carlton), Marcel De La Brosse (Maitre d'), James Parnell (Sheriff), Percy Helton (Conductor), Elizabeth Holmes (Fat Lady), Barrie Chase (Doris), I. Stanford Jolley (Station Master), George Chakiris (Specialty Dancer).

This eagerly awaited musical comedy had all the ingredients for success: two of its day's biggest-box office draws, a solid director, and a score by America's treasure, Irving Berlin. And though it's not as satisfying as it might have been, it still boasts great stars and catchy songs in addition to a love story, and is a perennial holiday favorite. Bob Wallace (Bing Crosby) and Phil Davis (Danny Kaye) meet during the war and team up afterward to become the hottest song-and-dance duo around. After five years of heady success, they think it's about time to take a vacation, so they travel to a New England ski resort in the company of lovely sister entertainers Betty (Rosemary Clooney) and Judy (Vera-Ellen) for some rest and recuperation. They arrive to find the place in terrible financial condition and in desperate need of an infusion of money, because there hasn't been any snow for almost a year. The man who runs the inn is their old Army topkick, Gen. Waverly (Dean Jagger). Bob and Phil decide to aid Waverly by staging a benefit show that is, of course, a smash. Included is the title song, which Irving Berlin had written for HOLIDAY INN 12 years before. With that tune as the core, the script was fashioned, and several more Berlin tunes were added.

p, Robert Emmett Dolan; d, Michael Curtiz; w, Norman Krasna, Norman Panama, Melvin Frank; ph, Loyal Griggs (VistaVision, Technicolor).

Musical Cas. (MPAA:NR)

WHO FRAMED ROGER RABBIT?

(1988) 103m Touchstone-Amblin/BV c

Bob Hoskins (Eddie Valiant), Christopher Lloyd (Judge Doom), Joanna Cassidy (Dolores), Stubby Kaye (Marvin Acme), Alan Tilvern (R.K. Maroon), Richard Le Parmentier (Lt. Santino), Joel Silver (Raoul Raoul), Betsy Brantley (Jessica Performance Model), Charles Fleischer (Roger Rabbit/Greasy/Psycho), Lou Hirsch (Baby Herman), Paul Springer (Augie), Richard Ridings (Angelo), Edwin Craig (Arthritic Cowboy), Lindsay Holiday (Soldier), Mike Edmonds (Midget), Morgan Deare (Editor), Danny Capri, Christopher Hollosy, John-Paul Sipla (Kids), Laura Frances (Blonde Starlet), Joel Cutrara, Billy J. Mitchell (Forensics), Ed Herlihy (Newscaster), Mel Blanc (Daffy Duck/Tweety Bird/Bugs Bunny/Sylvester/Porky Pig), Tomy Anselmo (Donald Duck), Russi Taylor (Birds/Minnie Mouse), Wayne Allwine (Mickey Mouse), Pat Buttram, Jim Cummings (Bullets), Frank Sinatra (Singing Sword).

A startling combination of live-action and animation, WHO FRAMED ROGER RABBIT? was instantly catapulted into the ranks of cinema classics. Set in Los Angeles circa 1947, the film takes place in a universe where cartoon characters really exist and work alongside human beings. Disdainfully referred to as "Toons" by humans, the cartoon characters are underpaid by human standards and are forced to live in a segregated ghetto known as Toontown. When Maroon Cartoons studio chief R.K. Maroon (Stubby Kaye) is found murdered, it appears that the studio's biggest star, Roger Rabbit, is the culprit. Desperate to clear his name, Roger hires down-on-his-luck private detective Eddie Valiant (Bob Hoskins) to crack the case. A human, Eddie is reluctant to take the case for he hates Toons because his brother was killed by one. As the mystery deepens, however, Roger begins to grow on Eddie and the pair team up to solve the mystery of Toontown, battling the sinister (Christopher Lloyd) in the process. Mere words cannot describe the technical brilliance of this movie. A small army of animators led by Richard Williams and assisted by Industrial Light and Magic performed the meticulous task of matching animation with camera movement and film noir lighting to give the cartoon characters a 3-D effect. Kudos must be heaped upon the human actors, especially Bob Hoskins, whose job it was to interact with thin air and floating props (the Toons handle real objects) because the animation was added to the frame months after principal photography had been completed. Director Bob Zemeckis deserves a Purple Heart for taking on the monumental technical headaches involved in the production and somehow managing to deliver a film that works wonderfully both on the technical and entertainment levels. A must see for all ages.

p, Robert Watts, Frank Marshall; d, Robert Zemeckis; w, Jeffrey Price, Peter S. Seamon (based on the book Who Censored Roger Rabbit? by Gary K. Wolf); ph, Dean Cundey (Rank Color); m, Alan Silvestri.

Animation/Comedy (MPAA:PG)

WHO SAYS I CAN'T RIDE A RAINBOW?

(1971) 85m Transvue c

Jack Klugman *(Barney Marcovitz)*, Norma French *(Mary Lee)*, Reuben Figueroa *(Angel)*, David Mann *(David)*, Kevin Riou *(Kevin)*, Val Avery *(The Marshal)*, Morgan Freeman *(Afro)*, Skitch Henderson, Heather MacRae, Otis Stephens *(Themselves)*, Ed Crowley, Nancy Davison, Lee Dowell, Dan Drake, Frank Durk, Laura Figueroa, Frances Foster, Roy Hill, Florence Kennedy, Virginia Kiser, Leib Lensky, Rick Moss, Bob Nielsen, Mervyn Nelson, David Polinger, Rod Rogers, Antonia Rey, Elliot Robins, Esther Rolle, Jack Strauss, Don Smith, Lee Steele, Douglas Watson, Barney Marovitz, Chichi Bonilla, Joey Vonilla, Nicky Brooks, Todd Hammer, Dara Mann, Eloy Mesa.

This charming children's film features Jack Klugman as Barney Marcovitz, who is convinced that the hope of the world lies with its young people. Barney runs a pony farm/petting zoo on a small plot of land in Manhattan so that city kids can encounter animals they might otherwise see only on television. His plans are upset when the real estate company that owns the property wants to put up a housing complex. The neighborhood rallies around him to no avail, so Barney gives his animals to the neighborhood kids with some amusing results (two youngsters have the unusual experience of trying to keep a pony hidden from their parents), until finally he is able to relocate to the Bronx. The film's potential for sentimentality is high, but luckily the filmmakers never stoop to the obvious, resulting in a warm-hearted (if rather slow-moving) tale.

p, Jerry Hammer; d, Edward Mann; w, Edward Mann, Daniel Hauer; ph, (Deluxe Color); m, Bobby Scott.

Comedy/Drama　　　　　　　　　　　**(MPAA:G)**

WILD CHILD, THE

(1970, Fr.) 90m Films du Carrosse-Les Productions Artistes Associes/UA bw (L'ENFANT SAUVAGE)

Jean-Pierre Cargol *(Victor the Boy)*, Francois Truffaut *(Dr. Jean Itard)*, Jean Daste *(Prof. Philippe Pinel)*, Francoise Seigner *(Mme. Guerin)*, Paul Ville *(Remy)*, Claude Miller *(Mons. Lemeri)*, Annie Miler *(Mme. Lemeri)*, Pierre Fabre *(Orderly at Institute)*, Rene Levert *(Police Offical)*, Jean Mandaroux *(Itard's Doctor)*, Nathan Miler *(Lemeri Baby)*, Mathieu Schiffman *(Mathieu)*, Jean Gruault *(Visitor at Institute)*, Robert Cambourakis, Gitt Magrini, Jean-Francois Stevenin *(Peasants)*, Laura Truffaut, Eva Truffaut, Guillaume Schiffman, Frederique Dolbert, Eric Dolbert, Tounet Cargol, Dominique Levert, Mlle. Theaudiere *(Children at Farm)*.

As in Francois Truffaut's THE 400 BLOWS (1959) and SMALL CHANGE (1976), THE WILD CHILD is devoted to the perceptual honesty and education of children. In this case, director and star Truffaut has made a clear, basic picture on the classic subject (Romulus and Remus, Tarzan) of the socialization of a boy discovered in the forest. Based on an actual case study published in 1806, THE WILD CHILD stars Jean-Pierre Cargol as Victor, a long-haired nature boy who, apparently abandoned in the woods by his parents years earlier, is found and placed in the Institute for the Deaf and Dumb in Paris. The boy is treated as a perverse outcast and freak, but Jean Itard (Truffaut), a patient and enlightened doctor, intervenes and cares for the child in his country home rather than allow him to be sent to an asylum. Truffaut, himself raised in an orphanage, had an affinity for children expressed in nearly all his pictures, consistently finding appropriate roles for them to play. "Even as a child," Truffaut said, "I loved children. I have very strong ideas about the world they inhabit. Morally, the child is like a wolf—outside society." In THE WILD CHILD (which feels more like a documentary or educational film than it does fiction) Truffaut displays this belief again and again. It is not necessarily a children's film, however, and will be best appreciated by mature youngsters. (In French; English subtitles.)

p, Marcel Berbeet; d, Francois Truffaut; w, Francois Truffaut, Jean Gruault (based on the journals by Jean-Marc Gaspard Itard); ph, Nestor Almendros; m, Antonio Vivaldi.

Drama　　　　　　　　　　　**(MPAA:G)**

WILLIE MCBEAN AND HIS MAGIC MACHINE

(1965, US/Jap.) 94m Dentsu-Videocraft International/Magna c

Willie McBean; voices of Larry D. Mann, Billie Richards, Alfred Scopp, Paul Kligman, Bunny Cowan, Paul Soles, Pegi Loder.

A delightful and technically superior puppet film about a mad scientist who travels in his time machine back to the days of Christopher Columbus, King Tut, King Arthur, Buffalo Bill, and the cavemen to rewrite history. A schoolboy gets in his own time machine and prevents disaster by making the scientist promise to be good.

p,d&w, Arthur Rankin, Jr.; ph, (AniMagic, Eastmancolor).

Fantasy　　　　　**Cas.**　　　　　**(MPAA:NR)**

WILLY WONKA AND THE CHOCOLATE FACTORY

(1971) 98m PAR c

Gene Wilder *(Willy Wonka)*, Jack Albertson *(Grandpa Joe)*, Peter Ostrum *(Charlie Bucket)*, Michael Bollner *(Augustus Gloop)*, Ursula Reit *(Mrs. Gloop)*, Denise Nickerson *(Violet Beauregarde)*, Leonard Stone *(Mr. Beauregarde)*, Julie Dawn Cole *(Veruca Salt)*, Roy Kinnear *(Mr. Salt)*, Paris Themmen *(Mike Teevee)*, Dodo Denny *(Mrs. Teevee)*, Diana Sowle *(Mrs. Bucket)*, Aubrey Wood *(Mr. Bill)*, David Battley *(Mr. Turkentine)*, Gunter Meissner *(Mr. Slugworth)*, Peter Capell *(Tinker)*, Werner J. Heyking *(Jopeck)*, Ernest Ziegler *(Grandpa George)*, Dora Altmann *(Grandma Georgina)*, Franziska Liebing *(Grandma Josephine)*.

Willy Wonka (Gene Wilder) is a legendary candy maker who hides five Golden Tickets in his candy bars. Whoever finds the precious tickets will get a tour of Wonka's top secret Chocolate Factory, plus a lifetime supply of inimitable Wonka chocolate, providing he or she follows the tour's strict rules. Young, impoverished Charlie Bucket (Peter Ostrum), one of the lucky winners, brings along his Grandpa Joe (Jack Albertson) on the tour. Wonka's archenemy asks Charlie to purloin the "Everlasting Gobstopper"—a sucker that literally lasts forever—from the factory, but the lad can't bring himself to steal. The other four winners, all nasty children, have also been approached. Inside the factory, they and their guests are awestruck by Wonka's operation, which contains such wonders as a chocolate river and tiny workers called "Oompa Loompas." It's a dream tour, but each of the kids except Charlie breaks Wonka's rules, and, in the end, the good Charlie receives a reward far greater than he could ever imagine. Adapted (with some changes) by Roald Dahl from his famous children's book, WILLY WONKA creates a marvelous world as close to heaven as any kid can imagine, a candy playland, and never talks down to its young audience. The film is sometimes dark in its tone, but by the end (when Wonka's motives and true nature are revealed) it is fabulously uplifting.

p, David L. Wolper, Stan Margulies; d, Mel Stuart; w, Roald Dahl (based on his book *Charlie and the Chocolate Factory*); ph, Arthur Ibbetson (Technicolor); m, Walter Scharf.

Fantasy/Musical　　　　**Cas.**　　　　**(MPAA:G)**

WINGS OF MYSTERY

(1963, Brit.) 55m Rayant/Children's Film Foundation bw

Judy Geeson *(Jane)*, Hennis Scott *(Don)*, Patrick Jordan *(McCarthy)*, Francesca Bertorelli *(Yvette)*, Graham Aza *(Antoine)*, Anthony Jacobs *(Agent)*, John Gabriel *(Father)*, Richard Carpenter *(Ted)*, Arnold Ridley *(Mr. Bell)*.

An entertaining children's film featuring a group of British youngsters flying to Belgium in pursuit of some stolen steel alloy plans. A fast-moving story is augmented by the nice location photography of Belgium.

p, Anthony Gilkison; d&w, Gilbert Gunn (based on a story by H.K. Lewenhak).

Adventure　　　　　　　　　**(MPAA:NR)**

WISHING MACHINE

(1971, Czech.) 75m Studio Gottwaldow/Xerox c (AUTOMAT NA PRANI)

Vit Weingaertner, Milan Zerman, Frantisek Filipovsky, Josef Hlinomaz, Miloslav Holub, Rudolf Deyl, Jr., Karel Effa, Jana Rendlova, Marketa Rauschgoldova.

Two boys see their fantasies come true when they encounter a wishing machine at a carnival. They build a similar machine, and their overactive imaginations take them on a perilous journey to the moon. Heedless of such responsible matters as how they will return home, the two are given a good lesson in discovering the limitations of their dreams. The children are presented in a realistic and winning fashion, without the romantic

notions of most Hollywood depictions. Likewise, their journey is a moral lesson designed to draw differences between fantasy and reality. The English dubbing is outstanding.

d, Josef Pinkava; w, Josef Pinkava, Jiri Blazek; ph, Jiri Kolin; m, William Bukovy.

Fantasy　　　　　　　　　　**(MPAA:G)**

WIZARD OF OZ, THE

(1939) 101m MGM c-bw

Judy Garland *(Dorothy)*, Ray Bolger *(Hunk/The Scarecrow)*, Bert Lahr *(Zeke/The Cowardly Lion)*, Jack Haley *(Hickory/The Tin Woodsman)*, Billie Burke *(Glinda)*, Margaret Hamilton *(Miss Gulch/The Wicked Witch)*, Charles Grapewin *(Uncle Henry)*, Clara Blandick *(Auntie Em)*, Pat Walsh *(Nikko)*, Frank Morgan *(Prof. Marvel/The Wizard/ Guard/Coachman)*, The Singer Midgets *(Munchkins)*, Mitchell Lewis *(Monkey Officer)*, Terry the Dog *(Toto)*.

One of the world's most beloved films, THE WIZARD OF OZ presents a dazzling fantasy musical, a treat for all. It is so beautifully directed and acted that is has rightly remained a classic since its initial release in 1939; in fact, the film has become so identified with moviedom that it's nearly impossible to think of a time when there wasn't a WIZARD OF OZ. Dorothy (Judy Garland) is a schoolgirl living in Kansas with family and her little dog, Toto. One afternoon, a twister sucks up Dorothy's house and she and Toto are dropped beyond the rainbow into Munchkinland. With a pair of magical red slippers and some advice from Glinda the Good Witch (Billie Burke), Dorothy, Toto and three new friends—the Scarecrow (Ray Bolger), Tin Man (Jack Haley), and Cowardly Lion (Bert Lahr)—follow the yellow brick road to the Emerald City, where they must ask the all-powerful Wizard of Oz (Frank Morgan) to get Dorothy and Toto back home. The Wicked Witch (Margaret Hamilton), however, is determined to get her hands on the slippers, and sends out her flying monkeys to capture the group. This marvelous film is as magical as Dorothy's red slippers, as much a part of growing up as homework or your first crush. Curiously, Garland, forever to be identified with the wide-eyed Dorothy, was not the first choice for the part; both Shirley Temple and Deanna Durbin were considered for the role. Some of Hollywood's most loved songs are included, namely "Somewhere over the Rainbow," "Ding Dong, the Witch Is Dead," "If I Only Had a Brain/a Heart/ the Nerve," "Follow the Yellow Brick Road," and "We're Off to See the Wizard." Just as "There's no place like home," there's no film like THE WIZARD OF OZ. Variations on this classic include the animated JOURNEY BACK TO OZ and THE WIZARD OF OZ, the overblown musical THE WIZ, and the intriguing RETURN TO OZ.

p, Mervyn LeRoy; d, Victor Fleming, (uncredited) King Vidor; w, Noel Langley, Florence Ryerson, Edgar Allen Woolf (based on the novel by L. Frank Baum); ph, Harold Rosson (Technicolor); m, Herbert Stothart.

Fantasy/Musical　　　　**Cas.**　　　　**(MPAA:NR)**

WOLFPEN PRINCIPLE, THE

(1974, Can.) 96m Image Flow c

Vladimir Valenta *(Henry Manufort)*, Doris Chillcot *(His Wife)*, Alica Ammon *(Her Mother)*, Tom Snelgrove *(Her Father)*, Lawrence Brown *(Indian Smith)*, Janet Wright *(Miss Mervin)*, Lee Taylor *(Sailor)*, Ivor Harries *(Watchman)*, Bullus Hutton *(Clergyman)*.

Henry Manufort (Vladimir Valenta) is a middle-aged man looking for something to do with his life who begins spending his evenings at the local zoo, endlessly watching the wolves. He meets Indian Smith (Lawrence Brown), a Northern Indian who shares his fascination with the animals. Together, they concoct a plan to free the wolf pack, but ultimately are defeated by the animals themselves, which don't care to leave the security of their cage. The film delivers its message with grace and subtlety, and the story is told with genuine feeling for its characters (including the wolf pack) while adding a nice comic touch. Another fine example of what an imaginative low-budget filmmaker can do.

p, Werner Aellen; d&w, Jack Darcus; ph, Hans Klardie; m, Don Druick.

Comedy/Drama   **(MPAA:NR)**

WONDER MAN *on tape*

(1945) 98m Goldwyn/RKO c

Danny Kaye *(Buzzy Bellew/Edwin Dingle)*, Virginia Mayo *(Ellen Shanley)*, Vera-Ellen *(Midge Mallon)*, Donald Woods *(Monte Rossen)*, S.Z. Sakall *(Schmidt)*, Allen Jenkins *(Chimp)*, Edward S. Brophy *(Torso)*, Steve Cochran *(Ten-Grand Jackson)*, Otto Kruger *(District Attorney R.J. O'Brien)*, Richard Land *(Assistant District Attorney Grosset)*, Natalie Schafer *(Mrs. Leland Hume)*, Huntz Hall *(Mike)*, Virginia Gilmore *(Girl Friend)*, Edward Gargan *(Cop in Park)*, Grant Mitchell *(Mr. Wagonseller)*, Gisela Werbiseck *(Mrs. Schmidt)*, Alice Mock *(Prima Donna)*, Mary Field *(Stenographer)*, Aldo Franchetti *(Opera Conductor)*, Maurice Cass *(Stage Manager)*, Luis Alberni *(Prompter)*, James Flavin *(Bus Driver)*, Jack Norton *(Drunk in Club)*, Frank Orth *(Bartender)*, Charles Irwin *(Drunk at Bar)*, Cecil Cunningham *(Barker)*, Eddie Dunn *(Cop)*, Byron Foulger *(Customer)*, Margie Stewart *(Page Girl)*, Frank Melton *(Waiter)*, Barbara La Rene *(Acrobatic Dancer)*, Al Ruiz, Willard Van Simons *(Specialty Dancers)*, Chester Clute *(Man on Bus)*, Eddie Kane *(Headwaiter)*, Ray Teal *(Ticket Taker)*, Leon Belasco *(Pianist)*, Carol Haney *(Dancer)*.

Danny Kaye takes on a dual role, playing two brothers—one an entertainer about to marry who is killed when he witnesses a mob hit, and the other an intellectual in love with a librarian. The dead brother approaches the living one and asks that he help bring the murderous mobsters to justice. Since the egghead is afraid to get involved, the spirit of the dead brother enters the body of the living one. Not surprisingly, this causes a great deal of confusion, especially for the two women who are now in love with him, the librarian and the dead brother's fiancee.

Filled with lots of laughs, WONDER MAN features a splendid performance by Kaye that is spiced with verve and zeal. There are a number of fine, funny musical numbers and the special effects are well deserving of the Oscar they earned.

p, Samuel Goldwyn; d, Bruce Humberstone; w, Don Hartman, Melville Shavelson, Philip Rapp, Jack Jevne, Eddie Moran (based on a story by Arthur Sheekman); ph, Victor Milner, William Snyder (Technicolor); m, Ray Heindorf.

Comedy/Musical   **Cas.**   **(MPAA:NR)**

WONDERFUL WORLD OF THE BROTHERS GRIMM, THE

(1962) 135m MGM-Cinerama/MGM c

Laurence Harvey *(Wilhelm Grimm)*, Karl Boehm *(Jacob Grimm)*, Claire Bloom *(Dorothea Grimm)*, Walter Slezak *(Stossel)*, Barbara Eden *(Greta Heinrich)*, Oscar Homolka *(The Duke)*, Arnold Stang *(Rumpelstiltskin)*, Martita Hunt *(Story Teller)*, Betty Garde *(Miss Bettenhausen)*, Bryan Russell *(Friedrich Grimm)*, Ian Wolfe *(Gruber)*, Tammy Marihugh *(Pauline Grimm)*, Cheerio Meredith *(Mrs. von Dittersdorf)*, Walter Rilla *(Priest)*, Regensburg Domspatzen Choir; "The Dancing Princess": Yvette Mimieux *(The Princess)*, Russ Tamblyn *(The Woodsman)*, Jim Backus *(The King)*, Beulah Bondi *(The Gypsy)*, Clinton Sundberg *(The Prime Minister)*; "The Cobbler and the Elves": Laurence Harvey *(The Cobbler)*, Walter Brooke *(The Mayor)*, Sandra Gale Bettin *(The Ballerina)*, Robert Foulk *(The Hunter)*, The Puppetoons; "The Singing Bone": Terry-Thomas *(Ludwig)*, Buddy Hackett *(Hans)*, Otto Kruger *(The King)*, Robert Crawford, Jr. *(The Shepherd)*, Sydney Smith *(The Spokesman)*.

Three stories from the Grimms are presented here, intertwined with a highly fictionalized look at the lives of the brothers, Wilhelm (Laurence Harvey) and Jacob (Karl Boehm). Early in the 1800s, the brothers are asked by Bavarian authorities to write a tale for the local squire's family. The first story is "The Dancing Princess," the story of a princess (Yvette Mimieux) who confounds her father, the king (Jim Backus), by wearing out one pair of slippers a day. The king hires a woodsman (Russ Tamblyn) to trail the princess, who dances with the gypsies, and eventually the two fall in love. The second story, "The Cobbler and the Elves," stars Harvey as aged cobbler who neglects his customers to carve elves for orphans who have no presents for Christmas. Exhausted, he falls asleep, and his creations come to life and finish the neglected work. The final story, "The Singing Bone," tells of Hans (Buddy Hackett), a humble servant who kills a fire-breathing dragon and, in turn, is killed by his boss, Ludwig (Terry-Thomas), who takes all the credit for the dragon's slaying. One of Hans' bones becomes a musical instrument and exposes the boss' lies. When Ludwig admits the truth, Hans returns to life and becomes Ludwig's boss. Produced by the masterful Puppetoon creator George Pal, the film boasts a number of technically impressive scenes, especially those of the elves in the cobbler shop.

WORLD OF HANS CHRISTIAN ANDERSEN—

p, George Pal; d, Henry Levin, George Pal; w, David P. Harmon, Charles Beaumont, William Roberts (based on *The Brothers Grimm* by Herman Gerstner); ph, Paul C. Vogel (Cinerama, Metrocolor); m, Leigh Harline.

Biography/Fantasy/Musical   Cas.   (MPAA:NR)

WORLD OF HANS CHRISTIAN ANDERSEN

(1971, Jap.) 75m Toei-Sean/UA c (HANSU KURISHITAN ANDERUSAN NO SEKAI)

Voices of: Chuck McCann *(Uncle Oley)*, Hetty Galen *(Hans Christian Andersen)*, Corinne Orr *(Elisa/Kitty Kat/ Little Boy/Match Girl/Mouse)*, Sidney Filson *(Karen)*, Jim MacGeorge *(Kaspar Kat/Governor/Hans' Father)*, Lionel Wilson *(Hannibal Mouse/Mayor/Watchdog)*, Ruth Ballew *(Elisa's Grandmother)*, Frances Russell, Jim Yoham *(Mice)*, Earl Hammond *(Ducks/Theater Manager)*.

This beautifully animated tale combines Hans Christian Andersen's stories "The Red Shoes" and "The Poor Little Match Girl." Little Hans is depressed because he cannot go to the opera. He is visited by the sympathetic Uncle Oley the Sandman, who provides Hans' father with some magic red leather with which to make a pair of shoes for a contest. The shoes take first prize, but the shifty mayor cheats the shoemaker out of his winnings. Refusing to give up, Hans takes a number of odd jobs and earns enough money to buy an opera ticket. Before he pays for it, however, Hans sees his friend Elisa, who has been forced by poverty to sell matches outside the theater. Instead of seeing the performance, Hans spends all his money on her matches and passes the evening spinning yarns for the crowd outside the theater. When the governor overhears the stories, he is so impressed he makes Hans his ward in this great heartwarmer for the kids.

p, Hiroshi Okawa; d&w, Al Kilgore, Chuck McCann; ph, (CinemaScope, Deluxe Color); m, Ron Frangiapane, Seiichiro Uno.

Animation   (MPAA:G)

WORLD OF HENRY ORIENT, THE

(1964) 115m UA c

Peter Sellers *(Henry Orient)*, Paula Prentiss *(Stella)*, Tippy Walker *(Valerie Boyd)*, Merrie Spaeth *(Marian "Gil" Gilbert)*, Angela Lansbury *(Isabel Boyd)*, Tom Bosley *(Frank Boyd)*, Phyllis Thaxter *(Mrs. Gilbert)*, Bibi Osterwald *(Boothy)*, Peter Duchin *(Joe Byrd)*, John Fiedler *(Sidney)*, Al Lewis *(Store Owner)*, Fred Stewart *(Doctor)*, Philippa Bevans *(Emma)*, Jane Buchanan *(Kafritz)*.

THE WORLD OF HENRY ORIENT is a charming comedy about the agony of adolescent infatuation. Valerie Boyd (Tippy Walker) and Gil Gilbert (Merrie Spaeth) are boarding school chums who keep busy pursuing egotistical concert pianist Henry Orient (Peter Sellers). The girls,

just 14 or so, believe that they are in love with Orient, a Casanova whose latest conquest is the married Stella (Paula Prentiss). Stella is convinced that the girls have been hired by her husband to trail her, and after that the girls' idolatry leads to a number of ridiculous situations. This is one of the rare films in which someone steals scenes from Sellers. Walker and Spaeth are a joy, with none of the professional, cloying sweetness so often seen in younger performers, and the best part of the movie is the depiction of the girls, which never strays from truth, even when the teens are on wild flights of fancy. Director George Roy Hill made another, equally charming, tale of young love 15 years later with A LITTLE ROMANCE.

p, Jerome Hellman; d, George Roy Hill; w, Nora Johnson, Nunnally Johnson (based on the novel by Nora Johnson); ph, Boris Kaufman, Arthur J. Ornitz (Panavision, Deluxe Color); m, Elmer Bernstein, Ken Lauber.

Comedy   Cas.   (MPAA:NR)

WORLD'S GREATEST ATHLETE, THE

(1973) 93m Disney/BV c

Tim Conway *(Milo Jackson)*, Jan-Michael Vincent *(Nanu)*, John Amos *(Coach Sam Archer)*, Roscoe Lee Browne *(Gazenga)*, Dayle Haddon *(Jane Douglas)*, Billy DeWolfe *(Maxwell)*, Nancy Walker *(Mrs. Petersen)*, Danny Goldman *(Leopold Maxwell)*, Vito Scotti *(Sports Fan)*, Don Pedro Colley *(Morumba)*, Clarence Muse *(Gazenga's Assistant)*, Liam Dunn *(Dr. Winslow)*, Leon Askin *(Dr. Gottlieb)*, Ivor Francis *(Dean Bellamy)*, Bill Toomey *(TV Spotter)*, Joe Kapp *(Buzzer Kozak)*, Howard Cosell, Frank Gifford, Jim McKay, Bud Palmer *(Announcers)*, Virginia Capers, John Lupton, Russ Conway, Dick Wilson, Jack Griffin, Leigh Christian, Philip Ahn, Sarah Selby, Al Checco, Dorothy Shay, David Manzy.

Coaches Sam Archer (John Amos) and Milo Jackson (Tim Conway) discover jungle boy Nanu (Jan-Michael Vincent) showing off his amazing super-physical abilities in the wilds of Africa. They bring him back to their college and transform him into a track star, thus saving their team from once again becoming the laughing stock of the league. Among the complications is a witch doctor's spell that shrinks Milo down to a roving miniature for a while. Howard Cosell appears as himself, doing a better parody of his own sportscasting than any comedian could. This snappy family entry from Disney is blessed with some inventive direction and a very funny performance from Conway.

p, Bill Walsh; d, Richard Scheerer; w, Gerald Gardner, Dee Caruso; ph, Frank Phillips (Technicolor); m, Marvin Hamlisch.

Comedy/Sports   Cas.   (MPAA:G)

XYZ

YANK AT OXFORD, A

(1938) 100m MGM bw

Robert Taylor *(Lee Sheridan)*, Lionel Barrymore *(Dan Sheridan)*, Maureen O'Sullivan *(Molly Beaumont)*, Vivien Leigh *(Elsa Craddock)*, Edmund Gwenn *(Dean of Cardinal College)*, Griffith Jones *(Paul Beaumont)*, C.V. France *(Dean Snodgrass)*, Edward Rigby *(Scatters)*, Morton Selten *(Cecil Davidson*, Claude Gillingwater *(Ben Dalton)*, Tully Marshall *(Cephas)*, Walter Kingsford *(Dean Williams)*, Robert Coote *(Wavertree)*, Peter Croft *(Ramsey)*, Noel Howlett *(Tom Craddock)*, Edmund Breon *(Capt. Wavertree)*, John Warwick, Ronald Shiner, Syd Saylor, Doodles Weaver, Richard Wattis, Anthony Hulme, Peter Murray-Hill, Jon Pertwee, Kenneth Villiers, Philip Ridgeway, Jr., John Varley.

This first British production for MGM was also the film that revived Robert Taylor's career. Lee Sheridan (Taylor), the brash son of a small-town newspaper publisher (Lionel Barrymore) and a college track star, is sent to Oxford after a dean gets him into the prestigious university. He arrives at Oxford convinced he'll show these Brits a thing or two, but he's soon taken down several pegs. Lee becomes enamored of Molly Beaumont (Maureen O'Sullivan), who unfortunately turns out to be the sister of one of his biggest rivals. Gradually, Lee becomes more accepting of Oxford traditions, and his popularity grows as he and his British friends learn mutual tolerance. A YANK AT OXFORD is an enjoyable feature, played with good spirit by Taylor and the rest of the cast. Appearing as a young English vamp is Vivien Leigh, just a year before her big success in GONE WITH THE WIND. The screenplay passed among several writers, finally ending with F. Scott Fitzgerald, who was then working as an MGM screenwriter. Fitzgerald was assigned to polish the screenplay, taking about three weeks to complete the job, but despite his work received no screen credit. A sequel of sorts, A YANK AT ETON, was made in 1942 with Mickey Rooney, and a dismal 1984 remake, OXFORD BLUES, featured Rob Lowe in Taylor's part.

p, Michael Balcon; d, Jack Conway; w, Malcolm Stuart Boylan, Walter Ferris, George Oppenheimer, Roland Pertwee, (uncredited) John Paddy Carstairs, F. Scott Fitzgerald, Frank Wead, Angus Macphail (based on a story by Leon Gordon, Sidney Gilliat and Michael Hogan, from an idea by John Monk Saunders); ph, Harold Rosson; m, Hubert Bath, Edmund Ward.

Comedy   **(MPAA:NR)**

YANK IN THE R.A.F., A

(1941) 98m FOX bw

Tyrone Power *(Tim Baker)*, Betty Grable *(Carol Brown)*, John Sutton *(Wing Comdr. Morley)*, Reginald Gardiner *(Roger Pillby)*, Donald Stuart *(Cpl. Harry Baker)*, John Wilde *(Graves)*, Richard Fraser *(Thorndyke)*, Morton Lowry *(Squadron Leader)*, Ralph Byrd *(Al Bennett)*, Denis Green *(Redmond)*, Bruce Lester *(Richardson)*, Gilchrist Stuart *(Wales)*, Lester Matthews *(Group Captain)*, Stuart Robertson *(Intelligence Officer)*, Frederick Worlock *(Canadian Major)*, Ethel Griffies *(Mrs. Fitzhugh)*, Claud Allister, Guy Kingsford *(Officers)*, John Rogers *(Chauffeur)*, John Hartley *(Copilot)*, Eric Lonsdale *(Radio Man)*, Alphonse Martell *(Headwaiter)*, Lynne Roberts *(Nurse at Boat)*, Fortunio Bonanova *(Headwaiter at Regency)*, Gladys Cooper *(Mrs. Pillby)*, Denis Hoey *(2nd Intelligence Officer)*, James Craven *(Instructor)*, Gavin Muir *(Wing Commander)*, Lillian Porter *(Chorus Girl)*, G.P. Huntley, Jr. *(Radio Operator)*, Forrester Harvey *(Cubby)*, Gil Perkins *(Sergeant)*, Charles Irwin *(Uniformed Man)*, John Meredith *(Cadet)*, Howard Davis *(Air Raid Warden)*, Patrick O'Hearn *(Navigator)*, Leslie Denison *(Group Commander)*, Otto Reichow, Kurt Kreuger *(German Pilots)*, Hans Von Morhart *(German Sergeant)*, Bobbie Hale *(Cab Driver)*, Hans Schumm *(German Soldier)*, Crauford Kent *(Group Captain)*, Maureen Roden-Ryan *(Barmaid)*.

Tyrone Power stars, in one of his most successful films, as Tim Baker, a brash American pilot (he easily could have been the model for TOP GUN's Tom Cruise) ferrying planes to Canada as part of the US government's WW II "Cash-and-Carry" policy to arm Britain while maintaining neutrality. In Canada, he accepts an offer to fly planes across the Atlantic. During a London air raid he meets an old girl friend, Carol Brown (Betty Grable). Now working at a London nightclub and volunteering daily for the war effort, Carol wants nothing to do with Tim, criticizing his ambivalence about the war. To impress her, he joins the RAF and is forced to go through flight school again, a routine that bores him silly, while finding competition for Carol in the person of his wing commander (John Sutton). The air battles, some taken from actual footage shot in combat over Europe, are seamlessly cut into the film, as is footage of the Dunkirk evacuation, with a huge reenactment of the battle staged on a beach in northern California. The film was a great success and helped prepare isolationist America for its upcoming role in the war.

p, Darryl F. Zanuck; d, Henry King; w, Darrel Ware, Karl Tunberg (based on a story by Melville Crossman [Darryl F. Zanuck]); ph, Leon Shamroy, Ronald Neame.

War   **Cas.**   **(MPAA:NR)**

YANKEE DOODLE DANDY

(1942) 126m WB bw

James Cagney *(George M. Cohan)*, Joan Leslie *(Mary)*, Walter Huston *(Jerry Cohan)*, Richard Whorf *(Sam Harris)*, George Tobias *(Dietz)*, Irene Manning *(Fay Templeton)*, Rosemary De Camp *(Nellie Cohan)*, Jeanne Cagney *(Josie Cohan)*, S.Z. Sakall *(Schwab)*, George Barbier *(Erlanger)*, Walter Catlett *(Manager)*, Frances Langford *(Nora Bayes)*, Minor Watson *(Ed Albee)*, Eddie Foy, Jr. *(Eddie Foy)*, Chester Clute *(Harold Goff)*, Douglas Croft

(George M. Cohan, Age 13), Patsy Lee Parsons (Josie, Age 12), Capt. Jack Young (Franklin D. Roosevelt), Audrey Long (Receptionist), Odette Myrtil (Mme. Bartholdi), Clinton Rosemond (White House Butler), Spencer Charters (Stage Manager in Providence), Dorothy Kelly, Marijo James (Sister Act), Henry Blair (George, Age 7), Jo Ann Marlow (Josie, Age 6), Thomas Jackson (Stage Manager), Phyllis Kennedy (Fanny), Pat Flaherty (White House Guard), Leon Belasco (Magician), Syd Saylor (Star Boarder), William B. Davidson (New York Stage Manager), Harry Hayden (Dr. Lewellyn), Francis Pierlot (Dr. Anderson), Charles Smith, Joyce Reynolds, Dick Chandlee, Joyce Horne (Teenagers), Frank Faylen (Sergeant), Wallis Clark (Theodore Roosevelt), Georgia Carroll (Betsy Ross), Joan Winfield (Sally), Dick Wessel, James Flavin (Union Army Veterans), Sailor Vincent (Schultz in "Peck's Bad Boy"), Fred Kelsey (Irish Cop in "Peck's Bad Boy"), Tom Dugan (Actor at Railway Station), Garry Owen (Army Clerk), Murray Alper (Wise Guy), Creighton Hale (Telegraph Operator).

The real George M. Cohan had just had a serious operation and was recuperating at his upstate New York home when he was shown, in a private screening, this film of his life starring the indefatigable James Cagney. The great showman watched the movie without a word. When it was finished he was asked how he liked it. Cohan grinned, shook his head, and paid the great Cagney his highest compliment: "My God, what an act to follow!" This beguiling film, which deservedly won Cagney a Best Actor Oscar, presents an irresistible portrait of song-and-dance man Cohan and of early 20th-century America. It's from-the-heart entertainment and anyone who ever whistled a tune, tapped a toe, or hummed a bar of music will love it. (For the musically deficient, it's still wonderful.) This was Cagney's favorite film and his favorite number was, in his own words, "when I did the 'wings' coming down the stairs at the White House. Didn't think of it until five minutes before I went on. I didn't consult with the director or anything, I just did it." YANKEE DOODLE DANDY made almost $5 million in its initial release and has been playing to packed houses ever since. The memorable collection of songs includes "Give My Regards to Broadway," "Yankee Doodle Dandy," "Harrigan," "Over There," and "Mary's a Grand Name." Remember to watch it in glorious black and white and avoid the fake-looking, candy-hued colorization that has recently surfaced.

p, Hal B. Wallis; d, Michael Curtiz; w, Robert Buckner, Edmund Joseph (based on a story by Robert Buckner); ph, James Wong Howe.

Biography/Musical   Cas.   (MPAA:NR)

YEARLING, THE

(1946) 134m MGM c

Gregory Peck (Pa Baxter), Jane Wyman (Ma Baxter), Claude Jarman, Jr. (Jody Baxter), Chill Wills (Buck Forrester), Clem Bevans (Pa Forrester), Margaret Wycherly (Ma Forrester), Henry Travers (Mr. Boyles), Forrest Tucker

(Lem Forrester), Donn Gift (Fodderwing), Daniel White (Millwheel), Matt Willis (Gabby), George Mann (Pack), Arthur Hohl (Arch), June Lockhart (Twink Weatherby), Joan Wells (Eulalie), Jeff York (Oliver), B.M. Chick York (Doc Wilson), Houseley Stevenson (Mr. Ranger), Jane Green (Mrs. Saunders), Victor Kilian (Captain), Robert Porterfield (Mate), Frank Eldredge (Deckhand).

THE YEARLING is a splendid family film set just after the Civil War in the wilds of southern Florida, where the Baxters—Ma, Pa, and their one surviving child, Jody (Gregory Peck, Jane Wyman, and Claude Jarman)—are having a tough time eking out a living on their small farm. Pa's ambition is to earn enough from his next crop to be able to sink a well nearer the house, so that Ma won't have to tote water. As an only child in the wilderness, Jody needs some company and asks his parents if he might have a pet. When Pa is bitten by a rattlesnake and in danger of dying, Ma and Jody must kill a deer and make an elixir out of its innards. The doe has a fawn, and when Jody begs his parents to allow him to raise the baby, they do. Time passes and the bond between boy and animal deepens, but as the deer grows it begins eating some of the crops so vital to the family's existence. Pa is left with no choice but to tell Jody that the youth must kill his beloved companion. Similar to OLD YELLER in its lessons, THE YEARLING was a huge success and one of MGM's top moneymakers, earning Oscar nominations for Best Film, Best Actor (Peck), and Best Actress (Wyman). Jarman, however, was the only cast member to take home a statuette—as Outstanding Child Actor of 1946. A remarkable film that is truly for the entire family.

p, Sidney Franklin; d, Clarence Brown; w, Paul Osborn (based on the novel by Marjorie Kinnan Rawlings); ph, Charles Rosher, Leonard Smith, Arthur Arling (Technicolor); m, Herbert Stothart.

Drama   Cas.   (MPAA:NR)

YOUNG PEOPLE

(1940) 78m FOX bw

Shirley Temple (Wendy), Jack Oakie (Joe Ballantine), Charlotte Greenwood (Kit Ballantine), Arleen Whelan (Judith), George Montgomery (Mike Shea), Kathleen Howard (Hester Appleby), Minor Watson (Dakin), Frank Swann (Fred Willard), Frank Sully (Jeb), Sarah Edwards (Mrs. Stinchfield), Mae Marsh (Marie Liggett), Irving Bacon (Otis), Charles Halton (Moderator), Arthur Aylesworth (Doorman), Olin Howland (Station Master), Billy Wayne (Stage Manager), Harry Tyler (Dave), Darryl Hickman (Tommy), Shirley Mills (Mary Ann), Diane Fisher (Susie), Bobby Anderson (Jerry Dakin), Robert Shaw (Usher), Syd Saylor (Vaudevillian), Del Henderson (Eddie's Father), Ted North (Eddie), Evelyn Beresford (English Woman), Billy Benedict (Boy).

At 12 years old, Shirley Temple's career as moviedom's cutest-ever child actress was just about over. In this last film on her 20th Century-Fox contract she's once more an orphan (didn't that poor girl ever have movie parents?), adopted by Joe and Kit Ballantine (Jack Oakie and Charlotte Greenwood). They're a couple retiring from the song-and-dance life to a more sedate existence in a small town. No one in town really likes the new family, but when a big storm hits, Joe becomes a hero and the family gives a fantastic show that ends all bitter feelings. Temple, as usual, carries the film. There is a fun use of clips from Temple's earlier films to show her character's past, making this a sort of full-circle picture for the young actress. Fans and anyone under the age of 10 will enjoy it thoroughly.

p, Harry Joe Brown; d, Allan Dwan; w, Edwin Blum, Don Ettlinger; ph, Edward Cronjager.

Musical (MPAA:NR)

YOUNG SHERLOCK HOLMES

(1985) 109m Amblin Entertainment/PAR c

Nicholas Rowe (Sherlock Holmes), Alan Cox (John H. Watson), Sophie Ward (Elizabeth), Anthony Higgins (Rathe), SusanFleetwood (Mrs. Dribb), Freddie Jones (Cragwitch), Nigel Stock (Waxflatter), Roger Ashton-Griffiths (Lestrade), Earl Rhodes (Dudley), Brian Oulton (Master Snelgrove), Patrick Newell (Bobster), Donald Eccles (Rev. Nesbitt), Matthew Ryan, Matthew Blaksted, Jonathan Lacey (Dudley's Friends), Walter Sparrow (Ethan Engle), Nadim Sawalha (Egyptian Tavern Owner), Roger Brierley (Mr. Holmes), Vivienne Chandler (Mrs. Holmes), Lockwood West (Curio Shop Owner), John Scott Martin (Cemetery Caretaker), George Malpas (School Porter), Willoughby Goddard (School Reverend), Michael Cule (Policeman with Lestrade), Ralph Tabakin (Policeman in Shop Window), Nancy Nevinson (Hotel Receptionist), Michael Hordern (Voice of Older Watson).

There was a time when every youngster was fascinated with Sherlock Holmes and his sidekick Watson, and movie screens were filled with their exploits. Today, however, the Baker Street sleuths have taken a back seat to the Indiana Joneses, Luke Skywalkers, and John Rambos of this world. Steven Spielberg, in an effort to rectify this generational oversight (which he himself helped to create), has brought to the screen a fresh look at the Holmes-Watson stories that proposes that their friendship dates back to their youth. The time is the late 1800s, the setting a private boys' school in London. Young Sherlock Holmes (Nicholas Rowe) is a tall, gangly, sharp-featured lad—just the way one would expect him to look as a teenager. John H. Watson (Alan Cox), the new boy at school, hails from the country and views his tall pal as a wiser mentor. No sooner does their friendship begin than they become involved in a mystery that even the local authorities ignore, showing early signs of the sleuthing expertise that would make them the subjects of scores of motion pictures. Good acting from all the lads and a beautiful re-creation of late 18th-century London with its foggy streets, hansom cabs, speeding carriages, and clip-clop of horses' hooves. Some of the scenes may be frightening for youngsters, hence the PG-13 rating and our cautionary warning.

p, Mark Johnson; d, Barry Levinson; w, Chris Columbus (based on the characters created by Sir Arthur Conan Doyle); ph, Stephen Goldblatt (Technicolor); m, Bruce Broughton.

Mystery **Cas.** (MPAA:PG-13)

YOUNG TOM EDISON

(1940) 85m MGM bw

Mickey Rooney (Tom Edison), Fay Bainter (Mrs. Samuel Edison), George Bancroft (Samuel Edison), Virginia Weidler (Tannie Edison), Eugene Pallette (Mr. Nelson), Victor Kilian (Mr. Dingle), Bobbie Jordan (Joe Dingle), J.M. Kerrigan (Mr. McCarney), Lloyd Corrigan (Dr. Pender), John Kellogg (Bill Edison), Clem Bevans (Mr. Waddell), Eily Malyon (Schoolteacher), Harry Shannon (Capt. Brackett).

This entertaining biography about two years in the boyhood of Menlo Park inventor Thomas A. Edison is made thoroughly enjoyable due to an energetic performance by Mickey Rooney. Rooney brings warmth and vitality to the title role as he goes about upsetting other people's lives with his experiments. He is branded crazy by his parents, teachers, and peers, but when his mother falls ill his inquisitive mind comes up with the very trick the doctor needs to perform a delicate operation. An enthusiastic film about an all-American boy who became a worldwide legend, this picture is perfect for children who are used to historical figures being portrayed as cardboard cutouts. Made in tandem with EDISON, THE MAN, both scripted by the same team.

p, John W. Considine, Jr.; d, Norman Taurog; w, Bradbury Foote, Dore Schary, Hugo Butler (based on material gathered by H. Alan Dunn); ph, Sidney Wagner; m, Edward Ward.

Biography (MPAA:NR)

YOUNGEST PROFESSION, THE

(1943) 81m MGM bw

Virginia Weidler (Joan Lyons), Edward Arnold (Mr. Lawrence Lyons), John Carroll (Hercules), Jean Porter (Patricia Drew), Marta Linden (Edith Lyons), Dick Simmons (Douglas Sutton), Ann Ayars (Susan Thayer), Agnes Moorehead (Miss Featherstone), Marcia Mae Jones (Vera Bailey), Raymond Roe (Schuyler), Scotty Beckett (Junior Lyons), Jessie Grayson (Lilybud), Greer Garson, William Powell, Lana Turner, Walter Pidgeon, Robert Taylor (Guest Stars), Beverly Tyler (Thyra Winters), Patricia Roe (Polly), Marjorie Gateson (Mrs. Drew), Thurston Hall (Mr. Drew), Aileen Pringle (Miss Farwood), Nora Lane (Hilda), Dorothy Christy (Sally), Mary Vallee (Mary), Gloria Tucker (Gladys), Jane Isbell (Jane), Hazel Dawn (Hazel), Beverly Boyd (Beverly), Randa Allen (Randa), Ann MacLean (Ann), Gloria Mackey (Gloria), Bobby Stebbins (Richard), Shirley Coates, Mary McCarty (Girls), Mark Daniels (Les Peterson), William Tannen (Hotel Clerk), Ann Codee (Sandra's Maid), Eddie Buzzell (Man in Theater), George Noisom (Delivery Boy), Leonard Carey (Va-

let), Harry Barris *(Man)*, Herberta Williams *(Hortense)*, Sara Haden *(Salvation Army Lass)*.

This juvenile comedy stars Virginia Weidler, a former child star struggling here to make it in adolescent territory. Joan Lyons (Weidler), the president of her high school's movie star fan club, has a passion for collecting autographs of major stars. Leading her pack of equally zealous girl friends on excursions resembling a big game safari, Joan stalks New York City train stations and hotels in search of the elusive signature. In the course of events Joan and friends waylay Lana Turner, Greer Garson, William Powell, Walter Pidgeon, and Robert Taylor. An innocent, silly-but-sweet episodic comedy, THE YOUNGEST PROFESSION is really an MGM tribute to the popularity of its stars, disguised as a vehicle for a newcomer. Weidler never caught on with the public after she "grew up" and made only one other film, BEST FOOT FORWARD (1943), before retiring from the movies.

p, B.F. Ziedman; d, Edward Buzzell; w, George Oppenheimer, Charles Lederer, Leonard Spigelgass (based on the book by Lillian Day); ph, Charles Lawton; m, David Snell.

Comedy (MPAA:NR)

YOU'RE TELLING ME

(1934) 67m PAR bw

W.C. Fields *(Sam Bisbee)*, Joan Marsh *(Pauline Bisbee)*, Larry "Buster" Crabbe *(Bob Murchison)*, Adrienne Ames *(H.R.H. Princess Lescaboura)*, Louise Carter *(Mrs. Bessie Bisbee)*, Kathleen Howard *(Mrs. Murchison)*, James B. "Pop" Kenton *(Doc Beebe)*, Robert McKenzie *(Charlie Bogle)*, George Irving *(President of the Tire Company)*, Jerry Stewart *(Frobisher)*, Del Henderson *(Mayor Brown)*, Nora Cecil *(Mrs. Price)*, George MacQuarrie *(Crabbe)*, John M. Sullivan *(Gray)*, Vernon Dent *(Fat Man in Train)*, Tammany Young *(Caddy)*, Lee Phelps *(1st Cop)*, Dorothy Vernon Bay *(Mrs. Kendall)*, Edward Le Saint *(Conductor)*, Elise Cavanna *(Mrs. Smith)*, Eddie Baker *(Motorcycle Police Escort)*, James C. Morton *(George Smith)*, Billy Engle *(1st Lounger)*, George Ovey *(2nd Lounger)*, Al Hart *(3rd Lounger)*, Alfred Del Cambre *(Phil Cummings)*, Frederic Sullivan *(Mr. Murchison)*, William Robyns *(Postman)*, Harold Berquist *(Doorman)*, Frank O'Connor *(2nd Cop)*, Florence Enright *(Mrs. Kelly)*, Isabelle La Mal *(Rosita)*, Hal Craig *(Motor Cop)*.

Sam Bisbee (W.C. Fields) is a struggling inventor having trouble scraping up enough money to support his family. He devises a puncture-proof tire, but a demonstration for auto company executives goes awry. Eventually, Bisbee's efforts are rewarded with a check for $1 million. While most of Fields' films were virtually plotless, YOU'RE TELLING ME has a complex, linear story line that gives him lots of room for comedy and a surprising number of opportunities to show off his talents as a serious actor. Fields demonstrates heretofore untapped sensitivity in several scenes—especially when he delivers an antisuicide speech. This is also a superior Fields vehicle in that the comedian is on screen throughout—

unlike many of his other films, in which his appearances are infrequent and sometimes almost incidental to other plot lines, romances, or musical numbers. Held to a taut 67 minutes, the film concentrates wholly on Fields and allows him to develop a full, emotionally complex, fascinating character. The stronger the characterization, the better the film, and YOU'RE TELLING ME is a great testament to Fields' skills as comedian and actor. One of its finest moments is Fields' famed golf routine, which is also seen in SO'S YOUR OLD MAN and in the sound short THE GOLF SPECIALIST in 1930.

p, William Le Baron; d, Erle C. Kenton; w, J.P. McEvoy, Walter De Leon, Paul M. Jones (based on the short story "Mr. Bisbee's Princess" by Julian Leonard Street); ph, Alfred Gilks; m, Arthur Johnston.

Comedy (MPAA:NR)

YOURS, MINE AND OURS

(1968) 111m Desilu-Walden/UA c

Lucille Ball *(Helen North)*, Henry Fonda *(Frank Beardsley)*, Van Johnson *(Darrell Harrison)*, Tom Bosley *(Doctor)*, Louise Troy *(Frank's Date)*, Ben Murphy *(Larry)*, Jennifer Leak *(Colleen North)*, Kevin Burchett *(Nicky North)*, Kimberly Beck *(Janette North)*, Mitch Vogel *(Tommy North)*, Margot Jane *(Jean North)*, Eric Shea *(Phillip North)*, Gregory Atkins *(Gerald North)*, Lynnell Atkins *(Teresa North)*, Tim Matthieson [Matheson] *(Mike Beardsley)*, Gil Rogers *(Rusty Beardsley)*, Nancy Roth *(Rosemary Beardsley)*, Gary Goetzman *(Greg Beardsley)*, Suzanne Cupito [Morgan Brittany]*(Louise Beardsley)*, Holly O'Brien *(Susan Beardsley)*, Michele Tobin *(Veronica Beardsley)*, Maralee Foster *(Mary Beardsley)*, Tracy Nelson *(Germaine Beardsley)*, Stephanie Oliver *(Joan Beardsley)*.

Frank Beardsley (Henry Fonda), a widowed Navy officer with 10 children, meets Helen North (Lucille Ball), a widowed nurse with eight children. They begin dating and finally marry, despite the unhappy prospect of raising 18 children under one roof. The expected problems with food, privacy, and bathroom rights abound, as do jealousies among the children. One of Helen's sons begins to see Frank's eldest son as a kind of hero, however, and barriers are broken even further when Helen announces that she's pregnant. With the new baby's birth the children decide they want a formal adoption so they can all be one family. In the end Frank's eldest goes to war and one of Helen's daughters falls in love, two events that knit the large family together for good. The potential for "Brady Bunch"-style saccharine is enormous here, but happily YOURS, MINE AND OURS never condescends to the true story it was based on, and the direction manages to place the enormous cast of children in believable situations. Ball, whose Desilu production company was behind the film, is surprisingly good, and Fonda, who was Ball's second choice after Fred ("My Three Sons") MacMurray proved unavailable, delivers a warm, fatherly performance.

p, Robert F. Blumofe; d, Melville Shavelson; w, Melville Shavelson, Mort Lachman (based on the story by Madelyn Davis, and Bob Carroll, Jr., from the book *Who Gets the Drumstick?* by Helen Beardsley); ph, Charles Wheeler (Deluxe Color); m, Fred Karlin.

Comedy/Drama **(MPAA:NR)**

INDEX

Individuals listed in the index are grouped by functions as follows:

Actors (major players only)
Cinematographers
Directors
Music Composers
Producers
Screenwriters
Source Authors (authors of the original material or creators of the characters upon which the film is based)

Individual names are followed by an alphabetical listing of the films in which they were involved.

ACTORS (major players)

Abbott, Bud
ABBOTT AND COSTELLO MEET FRANKENSTEIN (1948)
AFRICA SCREAMS (1949)
HERE COME THE CO-EDS (1945)
HOLD THAT GHOST (1941)
NOOSE HANGS HIGH, THE (1948)
ONE NIGHT IN THE TROPICS (1940)
RIDE 'EM COWBOY (1942)
TIME OF THEIR LIVES, THE (1946)

Abbott, Philip
INVISIBLE BOY, THE (1957)

Abel, Walter
KID FROM BOOKLYN, THE (1946)

Acosta, Rodolfo
LITTLEST OUTLAW, THE (1955)

Adams, Tom
FIGHTING PRINCE OF DONEGAL, THE (1966, Brit.)

Adler, Larry
SIDEWALKS OF LONDON (1940, Brit.)

Agar, John
SANDS OF IWO JIMA (1949)

Aherne, Brian
MY SISTER EILEEN (1942)

Albert, Eddie
ESCAPE TO WITCH MOUNTAIN (1975)
FULLER BRUSH GIRL, THE (1950)
OKLAHOMA! (1955)

Albertson, Jack
FOX AND THE HOUND, THE (1981)
WILLY WONKA AND THE CHOCOLATE FACTORY (1971)

Alderson, John
ALL THINGS BRIGHT AND BEAUTIFUL (1979, Brit.)

Alexander, Stan
BAMBI (1942)

Alford, Phillip
TO KILL A MOCKINGBIRD (1962)

Allan, Elizabeth
TALE OF TWO CITIES, A (1935)

Allen, Fred
O. HENRY'S FULL HOUSE (1952)

Allen, Barbara Jo [Vera Vague]
SLEEPING BEAUTY (1959)

Allen, Rex
CHARLOTTE'S WEB (1973)

Allyson, June
STRATTON STORY, THE (1949)
THREE MUSKETEERS, THE (1948)

Alphin, Patricia
MA AND PA KETTLE (1949)

Amarale, Nestor
THREE CABALLEROS, THE (1944)

Ambas, Genevieve
LITTLE ARK, THE (1972)

Ameche, Don
STORY OF ALEXANDER GRAHAM BELL, THE (1939)

Ames, Leon
ABSENT-MINDED PROFESSOR, THE (1961)

Amos, John
WORLD'S GREATEST ATHLETE, THE (1973)

Amsterdam, Morey
GAY PURR-EE (1962)

Anderson, Jean
JOHNNY ON THE RUN (1953, Brit.)
LITTLE KIDNAPPERS, THE (1954, Brit.)

Anderson, John
DOVE, THE (1974, Brit.)

Anderson, Jr., Michael
IN SEARCH OF THE CASTAWAYS (1962, Brit.)

Anderson, Mary
HENRY ALDRICH FOR PRESIDENT (1941)

Anderson, Richard
FEARLESS FAGAN (1952)

Andre, Marcel
BEAUTY AND THE BEAST (1947, Fr.)

Andrews, Dana
BATTLE OF THE BULGE (1965)

Andrews, Edward
FLUFFY (1965)

Andrews, Harry
BATTLE OF BRITAIN, THE (1969, Brit.)

MOBY DICK (1956, Brit.)

Andrews, Julie
MARY POPPINS (1964)
SOUND OF MUSIC, THE (1965)

Andrews Sisters, The
MAKE MINE MUSIC (1946)

Ankers, Evelyn
HOLD THAT GHOST (1941)

Ann-Margret
POCKETFUL OF MIRACLES (1961)

Annis, Francesca
FLIPPER'S NEW ADVENTURE (1964)

Arden, Eve
AT THE CIRCUS (1939)

Arlen, Richard
ALICE IN WONDERLAND (1933)

Armendariz, Pedro
LITTLEST OUTLAW, THE (1955)
THREE GODFATHERS, THE (1948)

Armstrong, Louis
HELLO, DOLLY! (1969)

Armstrong, Robert
KING KONG (1933)

Armstrong, Todd
JASON AND THE ARGONAUTS (1963, Brit.)

Arnaz, Desi
BATAAN (1943)

Arnold, Edward
DEAR WIFE (1949)
MR. SMITH GOES TO WASHINGTON (1939)
MY BROTHER TALKS TO HORSES (1946)
YOUNGEST PROFESSION, THE (1943)

Arthur, Jean
MR. SMITH GOES TO WASHINGTON (1939)
SHANE (1953)

Asherson, Renee
MAGIC BOX, THE (1952, Brit.)

Ashton, Frederick
PETER RABBIT AND TALES OF BEATRIX POTTER (1971, Brit.)

ACTORS

Asner, Edward
PINOCCHIO AND THE EMPEROR OF THE NIGHT (1987)

Astaire, Fred
EASTER PARADE (1948)

Astin, John
FREAKY FRIDAY (1976)

Astor, Mary
MEET ME IN ST. LOUIS (1944)

Attenborough, Richard
GREAT ESCAPE, THE (1963)
MAGIC BOX, THE (1952, Brit.)

Audley, Eleanor
CINDERELLA (1950)
SLEEPING BEAUTY (1959)

Aumont, Jean Pierre
LILI (1953)

Autry, Gene
LAST ROUND-UP, THE (1947)

Avalon, Frankie
ALAMO, THE (1960)

Avery, Tex
BUGS BUNNY, SUPERSTAR (1975)

Axton, Hoyt
BLACK STALLION, THE (1979)

Backus, Jim
FLUFFY (1965)
NOW YOU SEE HIM, NOW YOU DON'T (1972)
1001 ARABIAN NIGHTS (1959)
PETE'S DRAGON (1977)

Baddeley, Hermione
BELLES OF ST. TRINIAN'S, THE (1954, Brit.)
MARY POPPINS (1964)
SECRET OF NIMH, THE (1982)

Badham, Mary
TO KILL A MOCKINGBIRD (1962)

Baer, Buddy
AFRICA SCREAMS (1949)

Baer, Max
AFRICA SCREAMS (1949)

Bagdasarian [, Jr.], Ross
CHIPMUNK ADVENTURE, THE (1987)

Bailey, Pearl
FOX AND THE HOUND, THE (1981)

Bainter, Fay
JOURNEY FOR MARGARET (1942)
YOUNG TOM EDISON (1940)

Baio, Scott
BUGSY MALONE (1976, Brit.)

Baker, Carroll
HOW THE WEST WAS WON (1962)

Baker, Diane
JOURNEY TO THE CENTER OF THE EARTH (1959)

Baker, Kenny
AT THE CIRCUS (1939)

Baker, Tom
GOLDEN VOYAGE OF SINBAD, THE (1974, Brit.)

Balaban, Bob
CLOSE ENCOUNTERS OF THE THIRD KIND (1977)

Baldaro, Barrie
TIKI TIKI (1971, Can.)

Bale, Christian
EMPIRE OF THE SUN (1987)

Balfour, Michael
JOHNNY ON THE RUN (1953, Brit.)

Ball, Lucille
FULLER BRUSH GIRL, THE (1950)
YOURS, MINE AND OURS (1968)

Balsam, Martin
TRUMAN CAPOTE'S TRILOGY (1969)

Bancroft, Anne
MIRACLE WORKER, THE (1962)

Bancroft, George
YOUNG TOM EDISON (1940)

Barker, Patricia
NUTCRACKER: THE MOTION PICTURE (1986)

Barkworth, Peter
LITTLEST HORSE THIEVES, THE (1977)

Barnes, Binnie
THREE SMART GIRLS (1937)
TIME OF THEIR LIVES, THE (1946)

Barrie, Colin
MELODY (1971, Brit.)

Barrymore, Dolores Costello
LITTLE LORD FAUNTLEROY (1936)

Barrymore, Drew
E.T. THE EXTRA-TERRESTRIAL (1982)

Barrymore, Ethel
FARMER'S DAUGHTER, THE (1947)

Barrymore, Lionel
AH, WILDERNESS! (1935)
CAPTAINS COURAGEOUS (1937)
DAVID COPPERFIELD (1935)
IT'S A WONDERFUL LIFE (1946)
TREASURE ISLAND (1934)
YANK AT OXFORD, A (1938)

Bartholomew, Freddie
CAPTAINS COURAGEOUS (1937)
DAVID COPPERFIELD (1935)
KIDNAPPED (1938)
LITTLE LORD FAUNTLEROY (1936)

Bartlett, Bennie
JALOPY (1953)

Basehart, Richard
MOBY DICK (1956, Brit.)
ROSEANNA McCOY (1949)

Baskett, James
SONG OF THE SOUTH (1946)

Bates, Barbara
INSPECTOR GENERAL, THE (1949)

Baxter, Anne
CHARLEY'S AUNT (1941)
O. HENRY'S FULL HOUSE (1952)
TEN COMMANDMENTS, THE (1956)

Baxter, Warner
KIDNAPPED (1938)

Beal, John
LADDIE (1935)

Beatty, Ned
SUPERMAN (1978)
SUPERMAN II (1980)

Beatty, Robert
MAGIC BOX, THE (1952, Brit.)

Beaumont, Kathryn
ALICE IN WONDERLAND (1951)
PETER PAN (1953)

Bedelia, Bonnie
BOY WHO COULD FLY, THE (1986)

Beery, Jr., Noah
DAVY CROCKETT, INDIAN SCOUT (1950)
SERGEANT YORK (1941)
SEVEN FACES OF DR. LAO (1964)

Beery, Wallace
AH, WILDERNESS! (1935)
CHAMP, THE (1931)
DATE WITH JUDY, A (1948)
TREASURE ISLAND (1934)

Begley, Ed
IT HAPPENS EVERY SPRING (1949)

Behn, Peter
BAMBI (1942)

Bel Geddes, Barbara
I REMEMBER MAMA (1948)

Bell, Ann
MIDSUMMER NIGHT'S DREAM, A (1961, Czech.)

Benchley, Robert
SEE HERE, PRIVATE HARGROVE (1944)

Bendix, William
BABE RUTH STORY, THE (1948)
CONNECTICUT YANKEE IN KING ARTHUR'S COURT, A (1949)

Benedict, Billy
LET'S GO NAVY (1951)

Bennett, Constance
TOPPER (1937)

Bennett, Joan
FATHER'S LITTLE DIVIDEND (1951)
LITTLE WOMEN (1933)

Benny, Jack
CHARLEY'S AUNT (1941)
HORN BLOWS AT MIDNIGHT, THE (1945)

Benson, Martin
KING AND I, THE (1956)

Bergen, Edgar
FUN AND FANCY FREE (1947)

Bergman, Ingrid
BELLS OF ST. MARY'S, THE (1945)

INN OF THE SIXTH HAPPINESS, THE (1958)

Berle, Milton
IT'S A MAD, MAD, MAD, MAD WORLD (1963)
MUPPET MOVIE, THE (1979)

Berlin, Irving
THIS IS THE ARMY (1943)

Bernard, Thelonious
LITTLE ROMANCE, A (1979, US/Fr.)

Berry, Ken
CAT FROM OUTER SPACE, THE (1978)
HERBIE RIDES AGAIN (1974)

Best, Edna
GHOST AND MRS. MUIR, THE (1942)

Bey, Turhan
ALI BABA AND THE FORTY THIEVES (1944)

Beymer, Dick [Richard Beymer]
JOHNNY TREMAIN (1957)

Bickford, Charles
BABE RUTH STORY, THE (1948)
FARMER'S DAUGHTER, THE (1947)
LITTLE MISS MARKER (1934)
ROSEANNA McCOY (1949)
SONG OF BERNADETTE, THE (1943)

Bigney, Hugh
NUTCRACKER: THE MOTION PICTURE (1986)

Bikel, Theodore
DOG OF FLANDERS, A (1959)
LITTLE ARK, THE (1972)
LITTLE KIDNAPPERS, THE (1954, Brit.)
MY SIDE OF THE MOUNTAIN (1969)

Billingsley, Peter
CHRISTMAS STORY, A (1983)

Bing, Herman
DUMBO (1941)

Blackmer, Sidney
COUNT OF MONTE CRISTO, THE (1934)

Blair, Janet
FULLER BRUSH MAN (1948)
MY SISTER EILEEN (1942)

Blakely, Colin
ALL THINGS BRIGHT AND BEAUTIFUL (1979, Brit.)

Blanc, Mel
BUGS BUNNY, SUPERSTAR (1975)
GREAT AMERICAN BUGS BUNNY-ROAD RUNNER CHASE (1979)
MAN CALLED FLINTSTONE, THE (1966)
PHANTOM TOLLBOOTH, THE (1970)
WHO FRAMED ROGER RABBIT? (1988)

Bloom, Claire
WONDERFUL WORLD OF THE BROTHERS GRIMM, THE (1962)

Boddey, Martin
MAGIC BOX, THE (1952, Brit.)

Boehm, Karl
WONDERFUL WORLD OF THE BROTHERS GRIMM, THE (1962)

Bogart, Humphrey
AFRICAN QUEEN, THE (1951, US/Brit.)
ANGELS WITH DIRTY FACES (1938)

Boland, Mary
ONE NIGHT IN THE TROPICS (1940)

Boles, John
LITTLEST REBEL, THE (1935)

Bolger, Ray
DAYDREAMER, THE (1966)
HARVEY GIRLS, THE (1946)
WHERE'S CHARLEY? (1952, Brit.)
WIZARD OF OZ, THE (1939)

Bond, Ward
SERGEANT YORK (1941)
THREE GODFATHERS, THE (1948)

Bondi, Beulah
ONE FOOT IN HEAVEN (1941)
SO DEAR TO MY HEART (1949)

Boone, Pat
JOURNEY TO THE CENTER OF THE EARTH (1959)

Borgnine, Ernest
BEST THINGS IN LIFE ARE FREE, THE (1956)

Bosley, Tom
PINOCCHIO AND THE EMPEROR OF THE NIGHT (1987)
WORLD OF HENRY ORIENT, THE (1964)
YOURS, MINE AND OURS (1968)

Bottoms, Joseph
DOVE, THE (1974, Brit.)

Boudreaux, Joseph
LOUISIANA STORY (1948)

Bowie, David
LABYRINTH (1986)

Boyd, Stephen
FANTASTIC VOYAGE (1966)

Boyer, Charles
HAPPY TIME, THE (1952)
TALES OF MANHATTAN (1942)

Bracken, Eddie
CAUGHT IN THE DRAFT (1941)

Brand, Neville
ADVENTURES OF HUCKLEBERRY FINN, THE (1960)

Brando, Marlon
SUPERMAN (1978)

Bremer, Lucille
MEET ME IN ST. LOUIS (1944)

Brennan, Walter
ADVENTURES OF TOM SAWYER, THE (1938)
GNOME-MOBILE, THE (1967)
GOODBYE, MY LADY (1956)
HOME IN INDIANA (1944)
KENTUCKY (1938)
PRIDE OF THE YANKEES, THE (1942)

SERGEANT YORK (1941)
STANLEY AND LIVINGSTONE (1939)
THOSE CALLOWAYS (1964)

Brent, George
FIGHTING 69TH, THE (1940)

Brewster, Diane
INVISIBLE BOY, THE (1957)

Britton, Barbara
CHAMPAGNE FOR CAESAR (1950)

Bronson, Charles
GREAT ESCAPE, THE (1963)

Brooke, Hillary
FULLER BRUSH MAN (1948)
ROAD TO UTOPIA (1945)

Brooks, Geraldine
CHALLENGE TO LASSIE (1949)

Brooks, Mel
MUPPET MOVIE, THE (1979)

Brophy, Edward
DUMBO (1941)

Brown, Joe E.
SHUT MY BIG MOUTH (1942)

Brown, Vanessa
GHOST AND MRS. MUIR, THE (1942)

Browne, Roscoe Lee
WORLD'S GREATEST ATHLETE, THE (1973)

Bruce, Brenda
SWALLOWS AND AMAZONS (1977, Brit.)

Bruce, Nigel
ADVENTURES OF SHERLOCK HOLMES, THE (1939)
SON OF LASSIE (1945)

Brynner, Yul
KING AND I, THE (1956)
TEN COMMANDMENTS, THE (1956)

Buchanan, Edgar
BUFFALO BILL (1944)

Buchholz, Horst
TIGER BAY (1959, Brit.)

Buckton, Ben
GLITTERBALL, THE (1977, Brit.)

Bull, Peter
DOCTOR DOLITTLE (1967)

Burke, Billie
FATHER'S LITTLE DIVIDEND (1951)
TOPPER (1937)
WIZARD OF OZ, THE (1939)

Burke, Walter
JACK THE GIANT KILLER (1962)

Burlinson, Tom
PHAR LAP (1984, Aus.)

Burnett, Carol
ANNIE (1982)

Burnette, Smiley
KING OF THE COWBOYS (1943)

Burton, Richard
MIDSUMMER NIGHT'S DREAM, A (1961, Czech.)

ACTORS

Butler, Daws
PHANTOM TOLLBOOTH, THE (1970)

Buttons, Red
GAY PURR-EE (1962)
PETE'S DRAGON (1977)

Buttram, Pat
RESCUERS, THE (1977)

Bygraves, Max
CRY FROM THE STREET, A (1959, Brit.)

Byington, Spring
IN THE GOOD OLD SUMMERTIME
(1949)
STORY OF ALEXANDER GRAHAM
BELL, THE (1939)

Cabot, Bruce
KING KONG (1933)

Cabot, Sebastian
JOHNNY TREMAIN (1957)
JUNGLE BOOK, THE (1967)
TIME MACHINE, THE (1960, Brit./US)

Caesar, Sid
IT'S A MAD, MAD, MAD, MAD WORLD
(1963)

Cagney, James
ANGELS WITH DIRTY FACES (1938)
FIGHTING 69TH, THE (1940)
YANKEE DOODLE DANDY (1942)

Caine, Michael
BATTLE OF BRITAIN, THE (1969, Brit.)

Calhern, Louis
ANNIE GET YOUR GUN (1950)
COUNT OF MONTE CRISTO, THE
(1934)
DUCK SOUP (1933)
MAGNIFICENT YANKEE, THE (1950)

Callan, Michael
FRASIER, THE SENSUOUS LION (1973)
MYSTERIOUS ISLAND (1961, US/Brit.)

Calleia, Joseph
JUNGLE BOOK, THE (1942)
LITTLEST OUTLAW, THE (1955)
NOOSE HANGS HIGH, THE (1948)

Calthrop, Donald
SCROOGE (1935, Brit.)

Calvin, Henry
TOBY TYLER (1960)

Campbell, Glen
TRUE GRIT (1969)

Cantinflas
AROUND THE WORLD IN 80 DAYS
(1956)

Cantor, Eddie
KID FROM SPAIN, THE (1932)

Cardwell, Barry
SAND CASTLE, THE (1961)

Cardwell, Laurie
SAND CASTLE, THE (1961)

Carey, Harry
AIR FORCE (1943)
SO DEAR TO MY HEART (1949)

Carey, Jr., Harry
THREE GODFATHERS, THE (1948)

Carey, Macdonald
EXCUSE MY DUST (1951)

Cargol, Jean-Pierre
WILD CHILD, THE (1970, Fr.)

Carlisle, Kitty
NIGHT AT THE OPERA, A (1935)

Carlson, Richard
GHOST BREAKERS, THE (1940)
HOLD THAT GHOST (1941)
KING SOLOMON'S MINES (1950)

Carmichael, Ian
SCHOOL FOR SCOUNDRELS (1960,
Brit.)

Carney, Art
MUPPETS TAKE MANHATTAN, THE
(1984)

Caron, Leslie
FATHER GOOSE (1964)
LILI (1953)

Carpenter, Carleton
FEARLESS FAGAN (1952)

Carradine, John
KIDNAPPED (1938)
SECRET OF NIMH, THE (1982)

Carroll, John
YOUNGEST PROFESSION, THE (1943)

Carroll, Leo G.
PARENT TRAP, THE (1961)

Cartwright, Veronica
FLIGHT OF THE NAVIGATOR (1986)

Caselotti, Adriana
SNOW WHITE AND THE SEVEN
DWARFS (1937)

Cassell, Wally
SANDS OF IWO JIMA (1949)
STORY OF G.I. JOE, THE (1945)

Cassidy, Joanna
WHO FRAMED ROGER RABBIT? (1988)

Caulfield, Joan
DEAR WIFE (1949)

Cavanagh, Paul
FRANCIS IN THE HAUNTED HOUSE
(1956)

Chamberlain, Richard
SLIPPER AND THE ROSE, THE (1976,
Brit.)

Chaney, Jr., Lon
ABBOTT AND COSTELLO MEET
FRANKENSTEIN (1948)
HERE COME THE CO-EDS (1945)

Chapuis, Emeric
HERE COMES SANTA CLAUS (1984)

Charleson, Ian
CHARIOTS OF FIRE (1981, Brit.)

Cherry, Helen
FLIPPER'S NEW ADVENTURE (1964)

Cheryl, Karen
HERE COMES SANTA CLAUS (1984)

Chevalier, Maurice
ARISTOCATS, THE (1970)
IN SEARCH OF THE CASTAWAYS
(1962, Brit.)

Chillcot, Doris
WOLFPEN PRINCIPLE, THE (1974,
Can.)

Chylek, Eugeniusz
JOHNNY ON THE RUN (1953, Brit.)

Clampett, Bob
BUGS BUNNY, SUPERSTAR (1975)

Clarke, Angela
SEVEN LITTLE FOYS, THE (1955)

Cleese, John
TIME BANDITS (1981, Brit.)

Clooney, Rosemary
WHITE CHRISTMAS (1954)

Clyde, June
CUCKOOS, THE (1930)

Cobb, Lee J.
HOW THE WEST WAS WON (1962)

Coburn, Charles
EDISON, THE MAN (1940)
STANLEY AND LIVINGSTONE (1939)
STORY OF ALEXANDER GRAHAM
BELL, THE (1939)

Cochran, Robert
SCROOGE (1935, Brit.)

Coco, James
MUPPETS TAKE MANHATTAN, THE
(1984)

Colbourne, Maurice
LITTLEST HORSE THIEVES, THE
(1977)

Cole, George
BELLES OF ST. TRINIAN'S, THE (1954,
Brit.)

Coleman, Dabney
DOVE, THE (1974, Brit.)
MUPPETS TAKE MANHATTAN, THE
(1984)

Collet, Christopher
MANHATTAN PROJECT, THE (1986)

Collins, Ray
FRANCIS (1949)
MA AND PA KETTLE ON VACATION
(1953)

Colman, Ronald
CHAMPAGNE FOR CAESAR (1950)
TALE OF TWO CITIES, A (1935)

Colonna, Jerry
MAKE MINE MUSIC (1946)

Condon, David
JALOPY (1953)

Connelly, Jennifer
LABYRINTH (1986)

Connery, Sean
DARBY O'GILL AND THE LITTLE
PEOPLE (1959)
TIME BANDITS (1981, Brit.)

Connolly, Walter
HUCKLEBERRY FINN (1939)

Connors, Chuck
FLIPPER (1963)

Conried, Hans
DAVY CROCKETT, KING OF THE WILD FRONTIER (1955)
5,000 FINGERS OF DR. T., THE (1953)
1001 ARABIAN NIGHTS (1959)
PETER PAN (1953)
PHANTOM TOLLBOOTH, THE (1970)

Conroy, Frank
CALL OF THE WILD (1935)

Considine, Tim
SHAGGY DOG, THE (1959)

Conway, Tim
SHAGGY D.A., THE (1976)
WORLD'S GREATEST ATHLETE, THE (1973)

Coogan, Jackie
TOM SAWYER (1930)

Coogan, Robert
SKIPPY (1931)

Cooper, Gary
ALICE IN WONDERLAND (1933)
PRIDE OF THE YANKEES, THE (1942)
SERGEANT YORK (1941)

Cooper, Gladys
MY FAIR LADY (1964)
SECRET GARDEN, THE (1949)
SONG OF BERNADETTE, THE (1943)

Cooper, Jackie
CHAMP, THE (1931)
SKIPPY (1931)
SUPERMAN (1978)
SUPERMAN II (1980)
TREASURE ISLAND (1934)

Corcoran, Donna
ANGELS IN THE OUTFIELD (1951)

Corcoran, Kevin
OLD YELLER (1957)
TOBY TYLER (1960)

Corday, Claudia
DR. COPPELIUS (1968, US/Span.)

Corey, Jeff
MY FRIEND FLICKA (1943)

Corey, Wendell
LIGHT IN THE FOREST, THE (1958)

Corri, Adrienne
LITTLE KIDNAPPERS, THE (1954, Brit.)

Costello, Lou
ABBOTT AND COSTELLO MEET FRANKENSTEIN (1948)
AFRICA SCREAMS (1949)
HERE COME THE CO-EDS (1945)
HOLD THAT GHOST (1941)
NOOSE HANGS HIGH, THE (1948)
ONE NIGHT IN THE TROPICS (1940)
RIDE 'EM COWBOY (1942)
TIME OF THEIR LIVES, THE (1946)

Cotten, Joseph
FARMER'S DAUGHTER, THE (1947)

Coulouris, George
DOG AND THE DIAMONDS, THE (1962, Brit.)

Coutu, Jean
NIKKI, WILD DOG OF THE NORTH (1961, US/Can.)

Cowling, Bruce
PAINTED HILLS, THE (1951)

Cox, Alan
YOUNG SHERLOCK HOLMES (1985)

Cox, Ronny
HUGO THE HIPPO (1976, Hung./US)

Cox, Wally
BAREFOOT EXECUTIVE, THE (1971)

Coyote, Peter
E.T. THE EXTRA-TERRESTRIAL (1982)

Crabbe, Larry "Buster"
FLASH GORDON (1936)
YOU'RE TELLING ME (1934)

Craig, Michael
MYSTERIOUS ISLAND (1961, US/Brit.)

Crain, Jeanne
CHEAPER BY THE DOZEN (1950)
HOME IN INDIANA (1944)
O. HENRY'S FULL HOUSE (1952)

Cramer, Joey
FLIGHT OF THE NAVIGATOR (1986)

Craven, Gemma
SLIPPER AND THE ROSE, THE (1976, Brit.)

Crawford, Michael
HELLO, DOLLY! (1969)

Crenna, Richard
PRIDE OF ST. LOUIS, THE (1952)

Cribbins, Bernard
WATER BABIES, THE (1979, Brit.)

Criddle, Tom
MIDSUMMER NIGHT'S DREAM, A (1961, Czech.)

Crisp, Donald
ADVENTURES OF MARK TWAIN, THE (1944)
CHALLENGE TO LASSIE (1949)
DOG OF FLANDERS, A (1959)
GREYFRIARS BOBBY (1961, Brit.)
HILLS OF HOME (1948)
HOW GREEN WAS MY VALLEY (1941)
KNUTE ROCKNE--ALL AMERICAN (1940)
LADDIE (1935)
LASSIE, COME HOME (1943)
NATIONAL VELVET (1944)
POLLYANNA (1960)
SON OF LASSIE (1945)

Crosbie, Annette
SLIPPER AND THE ROSE, THE (1976, Brit.)

Crosby, Bing
ADVENTURES OF ICHABOD AND MR. TOAD (1949)
BELLS OF ST. MARY'S, THE (1945)

CONNECTICUT YANKEE IN KING ARTHUR'S COURT, A (1949)
EMPEROR WALTZ, THE (1948)
GOING MY WAY (1944)
ROAD TO MOROCCO (1942)
ROAD TO RIO (1947)
ROAD TO UTOPIA (1945)
ROAD TO ZANZIBAR (1941)
SING YOU SINNERS (1938)
WHITE CHRISTMAS (1954)

Cross, Ben
CHARIOTS OF FIRE (1981, Brit.)

Crothers, Scatman
ARISTOCATS, THE (1970)
JOURNEY OF NATTY GANN, THE (1985)

Crystal, Billy
PRINCESS BRIDE, THE (1987)

Cugat, Xavier
DATE WITH JUDY, A (1948)

Cullan, Peter
TIKI TIKI (1971, Can.)

Culver, Roland
EMPEROR WALTZ, THE (1948)

Cummings, Constance
BOY TEN FEET TALL, A (1965, Brit.)

Cummings, Robert
ONE NIGHT IN THE TROPICS (1940)

Cummins, Peter
STORM BOY (1976, Aus.)

Cusack, John
JOURNEY OF NATTY GANN, THE (1985)

Cushing, Peter
STAR WARS (1977)

Dahl, Arlene
JOURNEY TO THE CENTER OF THE EARTH (1959)
SOUTHERN YANKEE, A (1948)

Dailey, Dan
BEST THINGS IN LIFE ARE FREE, THE (1956)
PRIDE OF ST. LOUIS, THE (1952)

Damone, Vic
HIT THE DECK (1955)

Daniel, Ann
ISLAND OF THE BLUE DOLPHINS (1964)

Daniels, Anthony
EMPIRE STRIKES BACK, THE (1980)

Darby, Kim
TRUE GRIT (1969)

Darnell, Linda
BUFFALO BILL (1944)

Darren, James
GIDGET (1959)

Darwell, Jane
BRIGHT EYES (1934)

Davenport, Harry
COURAGE OF LASSIE (1946)

ACTORS

Davis, Bette
POCKETFUL OF MIRACLES (1961)

Davis, Joan
HOLD THAT GHOST (1941)

Davis, Lisa
ONE HUNDRED AND ONE
DALMATIANS (1961)

Davis, Nancy
NEXT VOICE YOU HEAR, THE (1950)

Davis, Sammi
HOPE AND GLORY (1987, Brit.)

Day, Josette
BEAUTY AND THE BEAST (1947, Fr.)

Day, Laraine
JOURNEY FOR MARGARET (1942)

De Camp, Rosemary
JUNGLE BOOK, THE (1942)

De Carlo, Yvonne
TEN COMMANDMENTS, THE (1956)

de Corsia, Ted
IT HAPPENS EVERY SPRING (1949)

de Havilland, Olivia
ADVENTURES OF ROBIN HOOD, THE
(1938)

de Kova, Frank
FRASIER, THE SENSUOUS LION (1973)

de Wilde, Brandon
GOODBYE, MY LADY (1956)
SHANE (1953)
THOSE CALLOWAYS (1964)

De Wolfe, Billy
DEAR WIFE (1949)

De Young, Cliff
FLIGHT OF THE NAVIGATOR (1986)

Deakins, Lucy
BOY WHO COULD FLY, THE (1986)

Decomble, Guy
FOUR HUNDRED BLOWS, THE (1959)

Dee, Frances
MR. SCOUTMASTER (1953)

Dee, Sandra
GIDGET (1959)

DeHaven, Gloria
SUMMER HOLIDAY (1948)

Del Rio, Evelyn
BANK DICK, THE (1940)

Dell, Dorothy
LITTLE MISS MARKER (1934)

Dell, Gabriel
NEWS HOUNDS (1947)

Deluca, Claudio
SMALL CHANGE (1976, Fr.)

DeLuise, Dom
AMERICAN TAIL, AN (1986)
SECRET OF NIMH, THE (1982)

Demarest, William
EXCUSE MY DUST (1951)

Dennehy, Brian
NEVER CRY WOLF (1983)

Dennek, Barbara
PLAYTIME (1973, Fr.)

Desmouceaux, Geory
SMALL CHANGE (1976, Fr.)

Devine, Andy
ALI BABA AND THE FORTY THIEVES
(1944)
ROBIN HOOD (1973)

Dewhurst, Colleen
BOY WHO COULD FLY, THE (1986)

Dillon, Melinda
CHRISTMAS STORY, A (1983)
CLOSE ENCOUNTERS OF THE THIRD
KIND (1977)

Dix, William
DOCTOR DOLITTLE (1967)

Domasin, Larry
ISLAND OF THE BLUE DOLPHINS
(1964)

Donald, James
GREAT ESCAPE, THE (1963)
PICKWICK PAPERS, THE (1952, Brit.)

Donat, Robert
COUNT OF MONTE CRISTO, THE
(1934)
GOODBYE MR. CHIPS (1939, Brit.)
INN OF THE SIXTH HAPPINESS, THE
(1958)

Donlevy, Brian
SOUTHERN YANKEE, A (1948)

Donnell, Jeff
FULLER BRUSH GIRL, THE (1950)

Donnelly, Ruth
BELLS OF ST. MARY'S, THE (1945)

Doohan, James
STAR TREK: THE MOTION PICTURE
(1979)
STAR TREK II: THE WRATH OF KHAN
(1982)
STAR TREK III: THE SEARCH FOR
SPOCK (1984)
STAR TREK IV: THE VOYAGE HOME
(1986)

Dorn, Philip
I REMEMBER MAMA (1948)

Dotrice, Karen
GNOME-MOBILE, THE (1967)

Douglas, Kirk
20,000 LEAGUES UNDER THE SEA
(1954)

Douglas, Melvyn
ANNIE OAKLEY (1935)
CAPTAINS COURAGEOUS (1937)

Douglas, Paul
ANGELS IN THE OUTFIELD (1951)
IT HAPPENS EVERY SPRING (1949)

Douglas, Robert
KIM (1950)

Dow, Peggy
HARVEY (1950)

Downs, Cathy
NOOSE HANGS HIGH, THE (1948)

Dragonette, Jessica
GULLIVER'S TRAVELS (1939)

Drainie, John
INCREDIBLE JOURNEY, THE (1963)

Drake, Betsy
CLARENCE, THE CROSS-EYED LION
(1965)
ROOM FOR ONE MORE (1952)

Drake, Charles
HARVEY (1950)

Drake, Tom
COURAGE OF LASSIE (1946)
GREAT RUPERT, THE (1950)
HILLS OF HOME (1948)

Drew, Ellen
DAVY CROCKETT, INDIAN SCOUT
(1950)

Dreyfuss, Richard
CLOSE ENCOUNTERS OF THE THIRD
KIND (1977)

Driscoll, Bobby
HAPPY TIME, THE (1952)
MELODY TIME (1948)
PETER PAN (1953)
SONG OF THE SOUTH (1946)
TREASURE ISLAND (1950, Brit.)

Dru, Joanne
LIGHT IN THE FOREST, THE (1958)
PRIDE OF ST. LOUIS, THE (1952)

Dudley, Lesley
JOHN AND JULIE (1957, Brit.)

Dugger, Florrie
BUGSY MALONE (1976, Brit.)

Duke, Patty
MIRACLE WORKER, THE (1962)

Dumbrille, Douglas
KENTUCKY (1938)

Dumont, Margaret
ANIMAL CRACKERS (1930)
AT THE CIRCUS (1939)
DAY AT THE RACES, A (1937)
NIGHT AT THE OPERA, A (1935)

Duncan, Sandy
CAT FROM OUTER SPACE, THE (1978)
FOX AND THE HOUND, THE (1981)

Dunn, James
BRIGHT EYES (1934)

Dunne, Irene
I REMEMBER MAMA (1948)
LIFE WITH FATHER (1947)

Duprez, June
THIEF OF BAGHDAD, THE (1940, Brit.)

Durante, Jimmy
GREAT RUPERT, THE (1950)
PALOOKA (1934)

Durbin, Deanna
AMAZING MRS. HOLLIDAY (1943)
THREE SMART GIRLS (1937)

Durkin, Junior
TOM SAWYER (1930)

Durning, Charles
MUPPET MOVIE, THE (1979)

Duryea, Dan
PRIDE OF THE YANKEES, THE (1942)

Duvall, Robert
TO KILL A MOCKINGBIRD (1962)
TRUE GRIT (1969)

Duvall, Shelley
TIME BANDITS (1981, Brit.)

Ebsen, Buddy
CAPTAIN JANUARY (1935)
DAVY CROCKETT, KING OF THE WILD
FRONTIER (1955)

Eccles, Teddy
MY SIDE OF THE MOUNTAIN (1969)

Eddy, Nelson
MAKE MINE MUSIC (1946)

Eden, Barbara
SEVEN FACES OF DR. LAO (1964)
VOYAGE TO THE BOTTOM OF THE
SEA (1961)
WONDERFUL WORLD OF THE
BROTHERS GRIMM, THE (1962)

Edwards, Cliff
DUMBO (1941)
PINOCCHIO (1940)

Egan, Richard
POLLYANNA (1960)

Eggar, Samantha
DOCTOR DOLITTLE (1967)

Eikenberry, Jill
MANHATTAN PROJECT, THE (1986)

Elliott, Eileen
DR. COPPELIUS (1968, US/Span.)

Ellison, James
CHARLEY'S AUNT (1941)

Elwes, Cary
PRINCESS BRIDE, THE (1987)

Emmet, Jesse
HUGO THE HIPPO (1976, Hung./US)

Erwin, Stuart
PALOOKA (1934)

Evans, Dale
BELLS OF ROSARITA (1945)
MY PAL TRIGGER (1946)

Evans, Edith
FITZWILLY (1967)
SCROOGE (1970, Brit.)
SLIPPER AND THE ROSE, THE (1976,
Brit.)

Evans, Joan
ROSEANNA McCOY (1949)

Evans, Linda
THOSE CALLOWAYS (1964)

Eyer, Richard
INVISIBLE BOY, THE (1957)
SEVENTH VOYAGE OF SINBAD, THE
(1958)

Fabian
MR. HOBBS TAKES A VACATION
(1962)

Fairbanks, Jr., Douglas
SINBAD THE SAILOR (1947)

Falk, Peter
POCKETFUL OF MIRACLES (1961)
PRINCESS BRIDE, THE (1987)

Farnsworth, Richard
SYLVESTER (1985)

Farnum, William
CONNECTICUT YANKEE, A (1931)

Farrell, Nicholas
CHARIOTS OF FIRE (1981, Brit.)

Faye, Alice
STOWAWAY (1936)

Feldon, Barbara
FITZWILLY (1967)

Felton, Verna
DUMBO (1941)
SLEEPING BEAUTY (1959)

Felton, Virginia
CINDERELLA (1950)

Fenton, Leslie
BOYS TOWN (1938)

Ferrer, Jose
DEEP IN MY HEART (1954)
FOREVER YOUNG, FOREVER FREE
(1976, South Africa)

Ferrer, Mel
LILI (1953)

Fields, W.C.
ALICE IN WONDERLAND (1933)
BANK DICK, THE (1940)
DAVID COPPERFIELD (1935)
IT'S A GIFT (1934)
YOU'RE TELLING ME (1934)

Finch, Peter
STORY OF ROBIN HOOD, THE (1952,
Brit.)

Finlayson, James
WAY OUT WEST (1937)

Finney, Albert
ANNIE (1982)
SCROOGE (1970, Brit.)

Finney, Bess
FOREVER YOUNG, FOREVER FREE
(1976, South Africa)

Fisher, Carrie
EMPIRE STRIKES BACK, THE (1980)
STAR WARS (1977)

Fiske, Richard
KONGA, THE WILD STALLION (1939)

Fitzgerald, Barry
AMAZING MRS. HOLLIDAY (1943)
GOING MY WAY (1944)

Flavin, James
FRANCIS IN THE HAUNTED HOUSE
(1956)

Fleming, Rhonda
CONNECTICUT YANKEE IN KING
ARTHUR'S COURT, A (1949)

Flynn, Errol
ADVENTURES OF ROBIN HOOD, THE
(1938)
KIM (1950)
PRINCE AND THE PAUPER, THE (1937)

Flynn, Joe
BAREFOOT EXECUTIVE, THE (1971)
COMPUTER WORE TENNIS SHOES,
THE (1970)
NOW YOU SEE HIM, NOW YOU DON'T
(1972)
RESCUERS, THE (1977)

Fonda, Henry
BATTLE OF THE BULGE (1965)
HOW THE WEST WAS WON (1962)
STORY OF ALEXANDER GRAHAM
BELL, THE (1939)
TALES OF MANHATTAN (1942)
YOURS, MINE AND OURS (1968)

Fontaine, Joan
EMPEROR WALTZ, THE (1948)
VOYAGE TO THE BOTTOM OF THE
SEA (1961)

Ford, Glenn
COURTSHIP OF EDDIE'S FATHER,
THE (1963)
POCKETFUL OF MIRACLES (1961)
SUPERMAN (1978)

Ford, Harrison
EMPIRE STRIKES BACK, THE (1980)
RETURN OF THE JEDI (1983)
STAR WARS (1977)

Ford, Paul
MUSIC MAN, THE (1962)

Forrest, Sally
EXCUSE MY DUST (1951)

Forrest, Steve
RASCAL (1969)

Fosse, Robert [Bob Fosse]
MY SISTER EILEEN (1955)

Foster, Jodie
BUGSY MALONE (1976, Brit.)
FREAKY FRIDAY (1976)
TOM SAWYER (1973)

Foster, Preston
ANNIE OAKLEY (1935)
HARVEY GIRLS, THE (1946)
MY FRIEND FLICKA (1943)
THUNDERHEAD-SON OF FLICKA
(1945)

Four Preps, The
GIDGET (1959)

Fox, James
THOSE MAGNIFICENT MEN IN THEIR
FLYING MACHINES OR HOW I FLEW
FROM LONDON TO PARIS IN 25
HOURS AND 11 MINUTES (1965, Brit.)

Frame, Philip
LITTLE ARK, THE (1972)

Francis, Anne
DREAMBOAT (1952)

Francis, Kay
CHARLEY'S AUNT (1941)

Franklin, Pamela
FLIPPER'S NEW ADVENTURE (1964)

Franz, Eduard
MAGNIFICENT YANKEE, THE (1950)

Fraser, Ronald
SWALLOWS AND AMAZONS (1977, Brit.)

Frawley, William
HUCKLEBERRY FINN (1939)

Freed, Stan
MR. BUG GOES TO TOWN (1941)

Freeman, Mona
DEAR WIFE (1949)

Freleng, Friz
BUGS BUNNY, SUPERSTAR (1975)

French, Norma
WHO SAYS I CAN'T RIDE A RAINBOW? (1971)

Frobe, Gert
CHITTY CHITTY BANG BANG (1968, Brit.)

Froud, Toby
LABYRINTH (1986)

Funicello, Annette
SHAGGY DOG, THE (1959)

Gable, Clark
CALL OF THE WILD (1935)

Gabor, Eva
ARISTOCATS, THE (1970)
RESCUERS, THE (1977)

Gabor, Zsa Zsa
LILI (1953)

Galen, Hetty
WORLD OF HANS CHRISTIAN ANDERSEN (1971, Jap.)

Gardiner, Reginald
CHRISTMAS IN CONNECTICUT (1945)
FLYING DEUCES, THE (1939)
HORN BLOWS AT MIDNIGHT, THE (1945)
YANK IN THE R.A.F., A (1941)

Gardner, Kenny
MR. BUG GOES TO TOWN (1941)

Garfield, John
AIR FORCE (1943)

Gargan, William
CANTERVILLE GHOST, THE (1944)

Garland, Judy
BABES IN ARMS (1939)
EASTER PARADE (1948)
GAY PURR-EE (1962)
GIRL CRAZY (1943)
HARVEY GIRLS, THE (1946)
IN THE GOOD OLD SUMMERTIME (1949)
LOVE FINDS ANDY HARDY (1938)
MEET ME IN ST. LOUIS (1944)

STRIKE UP THE BAND (1940)
WIZARD OF OZ, THE (1939)

Garner, James
GREAT ESCAPE, THE (1963)

Garner, Peggy Ann
BOMBA THE JUNGLE BOY (1949)

Garner, Shay
THUMBELINA (1970)

Garr, Teri
BLACK STALLION, THE (1979)
CLOSE ENCOUNTERS OF THE THIRD KIND (1977)

Garrett, Betty
MY SISTER EILEEN (1955)
TAKE ME OUT TO THE BALL GAME (1949)

Garrett, Patsy
BENJI (1974)
FOR THE LOVE OF BENJI (1977)

Garson, Greer
GOODBYE MR. CHIPS (1939, Brit.)
MADAME CURIE (1943)

Geeson, Judy
WINGS OF MYSTERY (1963, Brit.)

Genest, Emile
INCREDIBLE JOURNEY, THE (1963)

Genest, Emile
NIKKI, WILD DOG OF THE NORTH (1961, US/Can.)

Genn, Leo
MOBY DICK (1956, Brit.)

Gibson, Colin
JOHN AND JULIE (1957, Brit.)

Gibson, Henry
CHARLOTTE'S WEB (1973)

Gilbert, Billy
ARABIAN NIGHTS (1942)
BLOCKHEADS (1938)

Gilbert, Melissa
SYLVESTER (1985)

Gilford, Jack
DAYDREAMER, THE (1966)

Gillis, Ann
ADVENTURES OF TOM SAWYER, THE (1938)

Gingold, Hermione
GAY PURR-EE (1962)
MUSIC MAN, THE (1962)
PICKWICK PAPERS, THE (1952, Brit.)

Gish, Lillian
FOLLOW ME, BOYS! (1966)

Gleason, James
STORY OF WILL ROGERS, THE (1952)
TALES OF MANHATTAN (1942)

Goddard, Paulette
GHOST BREAKERS, THE (1940)

Goldman, Philippe
SMALL CHANGE (1976, Fr.)

Gombell, Minna
BLOCKHEADS (1938)

Gomez, Thomas
KIM (1950)

Good, Jack
FATHER GOOSE (1964)

Goodman, Dody
CHIPMUNK ADVENTURE, THE (1987)

Goodwin, Bill
SO THIS IS NEW YORK (1948)

Gorcey, David
LET'S GO NAVY (1951)

Gorcey, Leo
ANGELS WITH DIRTY FACES (1938)
JALOPY (1953)
LET'S GO NAVY (1951)
LIVE WIRES (1946)
NEWS HOUNDS (1947)
SO THIS IS NEW YORK (1948)

Gordon, Anita
FUN AND FANCY FREE (1947)

Gordon, Ruth
ABE LINCOLN IN ILLINOIS (1940)

Goulet, Robert
GAY PURR-EE (1962)

Grable, Betty
YANK IN THE R.A.F., A (1941)

Graham, John
HILDUR AND THE MAGICIAN (1969)

Grahame, Gloria
GREATEST SHOW ON EARTH, THE (1952)
OKLAHOMA! (1955)

Granger, Farley
HANS CHRISTIAN ANDERSEN (1952)
O. HENRY'S FULL HOUSE (1952)
ROSEANNA McCOY (1949)

Granger, Stewart
KING SOLOMON'S MINES (1950)

Grant, Alexander
PETER RABBIT AND TALES OF BEATRIX POTTER (1971, Brit.)

Grant, Cary
ALICE IN WONDERLAND (1933)
BACHELOR AND THE BOBBY-SOXER, THE (1947)
FATHER GOOSE (1964)
ROOM FOR ONE MORE (1952)
TOPPER (1937)

Grant, Kathryn
1001 ARABIAN NIGHTS (1959)
SEVENTH VOYAGE OF SINBAD, THE (1958)

Green, Nigel
AFRICA--TEXAS STYLE! (1967, US/Brit.)

Green, Mitzi
TOM SAWYER (1930)

Greene, Richard
KENTUCKY (1938)
LITTLE PRINCESS, THE (1939)
STANLEY AND LIVINGSTONE (1939)

Greenstreet, Sydney
CHRISTMAS IN CONNECTICUT (1945)

Greenwood, Charlotte
HOME IN INDIANA (1944)
YOUNG PEOPLE (1940)

Greenwood, Joan
MOON-SPINNERS, THE (1964)
MYSTERIOUS ISLAND (1961, US/Brit.)
WATER BABIES, THE (1979, Brit.)

Grenfell, Joyce
BELLES OF ST. TRINIAN'S, THE (1954, Brit.)

Grodin, Charles
GREAT MUPPET CAPER, THE (1981)

Guardino, Harry
ADVENTURES OF BULLWHIP GRIFFIN, THE (1967)

Guest, Christopher
PRINCESS BRIDE, THE (1987)

Guinness, Alec
OLIVER TWIST (1951, Brit.)
RETURN OF THE JEDI (1983)
SCROOGE (1970, Brit.)
STAR WARS (1977)

Gulpilil, David
STORM BOY (1976, Aus.)

Gwenn, Edmund
CHALLENGE TO LASSIE (1949)
CHARLEY'S AUNT (1941)
HILLS OF HOME (1948)
LASSIE, COME HOME (1943)
LIFE WITH FATHER (1947)
MIRACLE ON 34TH STREET, THE (1947)
MISTER 880 (1950)
MR. SCOUTMASTER (1953)
YANK AT OXFORD, A (1938)

Gwillim, David
ISLAND AT THE TOP OF THE WORLD, THE (1974)

Gwynne, Fred
BOY WHO COULD FLY, THE (1986)

Haas, Hugo
KING SOLOMON'S MINES (1950)

Hackett, Buddy
IT'S A MAD, MAD, MAD, MAD WORLD (1963)
LOVE BUG, THE (1968)
MUSIC MAN, THE (1962)

Hackman, Gene
SUPERMAN (1978)
SUPERMAN II (1980)

Hagen, Jean
SHAGGY DOG, THE (1959)

Hale, Alan
ADVENTURES OF MARK TWAIN, THE (1944)
FIGHTING 69TH, THE (1940)

Hale, Diana
THUNDERHEAD-SON OF FLICKA (1945)

Haley, Jack
WIZARD OF OZ, THE (1939)

Hall, Huntz
ANGELS WITH DIRTY FACES (1938)
GENTLE GIANT (1967)
JALOPY (1953)
LET'S GO NAVY (1951)
LIVE WIRES (1946)
NEWS HOUNDS (1947)

Hall, Jon
ALI BABA AND THE FORTY THIEVES (1944)
ARABIAN NIGHTS (1942)

Halpin, Luke
FLIPPER (1963)
FLIPPER'S NEW ADVENTURE (1964)

Hamill, Mark
EMPIRE STRIKES BACK, THE (1980)
RETURN OF THE JEDI (1983)
STAR WARS (1977)

Hamilton, Margaret
DAYDREAMER, THE (1966)
WIZARD OF OZ, THE (1939)

Hamilton, Murray
SPIRIT OF ST. LOUIS, THE (1957)

Hamilton, Neil
TARZAN THE APE MAN (1932)

Hampshire, Susan
FIGHTING PRINCE OF DONEGAL, THE (1966, Brit.)

Harding, Ann
MAGNIFICENT YANKEE, THE (1950)

Hardwicke, Sir Cedric
CONNECTICUT YANKEE IN KING ARTHUR'S COURT, A (1949)
I REMEMBER MAMA (1948)
STANLEY AND LIVINGSTONE (1939)

Hardy, Oliver
BABES IN TOYLAND (1934)
BLOCKHEADS (1938)
FLYING DEUCES, THE (1939)
WAY OUT WEST (1937)

Harris, Barbara
FREAKY FRIDAY (1976)

Harris, Phil
ARISTOCATS, THE (1970)
GOODBYE, MY LADY (1956)
JUNGLE BOOK, THE (1967)
ROBIN HOOD (1973)

Harrison, Kathleen
ALIVE AND KICKING (1962, Brit.)
DOG AND THE DIAMONDS, THE (1962, Brit.)

Harrison, Rex
DOCTOR DOLITTLE (1967)
GHOST AND MRS. MUIR, THE (1942)
MY FAIR LADY (1964)
SIDEWALKS OF LONDON (1940, Brit.)

Harrow, Lisa
ALL CREATURES GREAT AND SMALL (1975, Brit.)

Hartman, David
ISLAND AT THE TOP OF THE WORLD, THE (1974)

Hartman, Elizabeth
SECRET OF NIMH, THE (1982)

Harvey, Laurence
ALAMO, THE (1960)
WONDERFUL WORLD OF THE BROTHERS GRIMM, THE (1962)

Hasso, Signe
JOURNEY FOR MARGARET (1942)

Hatfield, Hurd
KING OF KINGS (1961)

Haver, June
HOME IN INDIANA (1944)

Havers, Nigel
CHARIOTS OF FIRE (1981, Brit.)
EMPIRE OF THE SUN (1987)

Hayakawa, Sessue
SWISS FAMILY ROBINSON (1960)

Haydn, Richard
ALICE IN WONDERLAND (1951)
CLARENCE, THE CROSS-EYED LION (1965)
EMPEROR WALTZ, THE (1948)
SITTING PRETTY (1948)
SOUND OF MUSIC, THE (1965)

Hayes, George "Gabby"
BELLS OF ROSARITA (1945)
MY PAL TRIGGER (1946)

Hayes, Helen
HERBIE RIDES AGAIN (1974)

Hayes, Peter Lind
5,000 FINGERS OF DR. T., THE (1953)

Hayman, David
HOPE AND GLORY (1987, Brit.)

Hayter, James
PICKWICK PAPERS, THE (1952, Brit.)
STORY OF ROBIN HOOD, THE (1952, Brit.)

Hayworth, Rita
TALES OF MANHATTAN (1942)

Healy, Mary
5,000 FINGERS OF DR. T., THE (1953)

Heather, Jean
LAST ROUND-UP, THE (1947)

Heayes, Neil
JOHN WESLEY (1954, Brit.)

Heflin, Van
SHANE (1953)
THREE MUSKETEERS, THE (1948)

Helmond, Katherine
TIME BANDITS (1981, Brit.)

Helmore, Tom
FLIPPER'S NEW ADVENTURE (1964)

Henreid, Paul
DEEP IN MY HEART (1954)
GOODBYE MR. CHIPS (1939, Brit.)

Henry, Charlotte
ALICE IN WONDERLAND (1933)

BABES IN TOYLAND (1934)
LADDIE (1935)

Henson, Jim
GREAT MUPPET CAPER, THE (1981)
MUPPET MOVIE, THE (1979)
MUPPETS TAKE MANHATTAN, THE (1984)

Hepburn, Audrey
MY FAIR LADY (1964)

Hepburn, Katharine
AFRICAN QUEEN, THE (1951, US/Brit.)
LITTLE WOMEN (1933)

Hersholt, Jean
HEIDI (1937)

Hesseman, Howard
FLIGHT OF THE NAVIGATOR (1986)

Heston, Charlton
GREATEST SHOW ON EARTH, THE (1952)
TEN COMMANDMENTS, THE (1956)

Heyes, Herbert
SEVEN LITTLE FOYS, THE (1955)

Hickman, Dwayne
1001 ARABIAN NIGHTS (1959)

Hicks, Sir Seymour
SCROOGE (1935, Brit.)

Higgins, Anthony
YOUNG SHERLOCK HOLMES (1985)

Hill, Arthur
LITTLE ROMANCE, A (1979, US/Fr.)

Hill, Benny
CHITTY CHITTY BANG BANG (1968, Brit.)
THOSE MAGNIFICENT MEN IN THEIR FLYING MACHINES OR HOW I FLEW FROM LONDON TO PARIS IN 25 HOURS AND 11 MINUTES (1965, Brit.)

Hinds, Samuel S.
RIDE 'EM COWBOY (1942)

Hobson, Valerie
GREAT EXPECTATIONS (1946, Brit.)

Hodges, Eddie
ADVENTURES OF HUCKLEBERRY FINN, THE (1960)
SUMMER MAGIC (1963)

Hodiak, John
HARVEY GIRLS, THE (1946)

Holden, Fay
JUDGE HARDY AND SON (1939)
JUDGE HARDY'S CHILDREN (1938)

Holden, William
DEAR WIFE (1949)

Holl, Milo
FABULOUS WORLD OF JULES VERNE, THE (1961, Czech.)

Holloway, Stanley
ALIVE AND KICKING (1962, Brit.)
FLIGHT OF THE DOVES (1971)
MY FAIR LADY (1964)

Holloway, Sterling
DUMBO (1941)

JUNGLE BOOK, THE (1967)

Holm, Celeste
CHAMPAGNE FOR CAESAR (1950)
COME TO THE STABLE (1949)
TOM SAWYER (1973)

Holm, Ian
CHARIOTS OF FIRE (1981, Brit.)

Holt, Jack
LITTLEST REBEL, THE (1935)
MY PAL TRIGGER (1946)

Homolka, Oscar
I REMEMBER MAMA (1948)

Hood, Noel
INN OF THE SIXTH HAPPINESS, THE (1958)

Hooks, Kevin
SOUNDER (1972)

Hope, Bob
CAUGHT IN THE DRAFT (1941)
GHOST BREAKERS, THE (1940)
ROAD TO MOROCCO (1942)
ROAD TO RIO (1947)
ROAD TO UTOPIA (1945)
ROAD TO ZANZIBAR (1941)
SEVEN LITTLE FOYS, THE (1955)

Hopkins, Anthony
ALL CREATURES GREAT AND SMALL (1975, Brit.)

Hopper, Dennis
TRUE GRIT (1969)

Hopper, William
GOODBYE, MY LADY (1956)

Hoskins, Bob
WHO FRAMED ROGER RABBIT? (1988)

Howard, Clint
GENTLE GIANT (1967)

Howard, Kathleen
IT'S A GIFT (1934)

Howard, Mary
ABE LINCOLN IN ILLINOIS (1940)

Howard, Robert
LASSIE'S GREAT ADVENTURE (1963)

Howard, Trevor
BATTLE OF BRITAIN, THE (1969, Brit.)
FATHER GOOSE (1964)

Howes, Sally Ann
CHITTY CHITTY BANG BANG (1968, Brit.)

Hudson, Rochelle
KONGA, THE WILD STALLION (1939)

Hull, Henry
BOYS TOWN (1938)

Hull, Josephine
HARVEY (1950)

Hunt, Marsha
HAPPY TIME, THE (1952)

Hunt, Martita
GREAT EXPECTATIONS (1946, Brit.)

Hunter, Ian
LITTLE PRINCESS, THE (1939)

Hunter, Jeffrey
DREAMBOAT (1952)

Hussey, Ruth
STARS AND STRIPES FOREVER (1952)

Huston, Walter
SUMMER HOLIDAY (1948)
YANKEE DOODLE DANDY (1942)

Hutchinson, Josephine
STORY OF LOUIS PASTEUR, THE (1936)

Hutton, Betty
ANNIE GET YOUR GUN (1950)
GREATEST SHOW ON EARTH, THE (1952)

Hyde, Tracy
MELODY (1971, Brit.)

Hyde-White, Wilfrid
IN SEARCH OF THE CASTAWAYS (1962, Brit.)
MY FAIR LADY (1964)

Ingram, Rex
HUCKLEBERRY FINN (1939)

Ireland, John
SOUTHERN YANKEE, A (1948)

Ishihara, Yuiro
ALONE ON THE PACIFIC (1964, Jap.)

Ittimangnaq, Zachary
NEVER CRY WOLF (1983)

Ives, Burl
SO DEAR TO MY HEART (1949)
SUMMER MAGIC (1963)

Izotov, Eduard
JACK FROST (1966, USSR)

Jackson, Gordon
FIGHTING PRINCE OF DONEGAL, THE (1966, Brit.)

Jacobi, Derek
SECRET OF NIMH, THE (1982)

Jaffe, Sam
BEDKNOBS AND BROOMSTICKS (1971)

Jagger, Dean
WHITE CHRISTMAS (1954)

Jamison-Olsen, Mikki
SEA GYPSIES, THE (1978)

Janssen, David
FRANCIS IN THE HAUNTED HOUSE (1956)

Jarman, Jr., Claude
SUN COMES UP, THE (1949)
YEARLING, THE (1946)

Jayne, Keith
GLITTERBALL, THE (1977, Brit.)

Jeanmaire [Renee]
HANS CHRISTIAN ANDERSEN (1952)

Jeans, Isabel
HEAVENS ABOVE! (1963, Brit.)

Jeffries, Lionel
CHITTY CHITTY BANG BANG (1968, Brit.)

Jenkins, Jackie "Butch"
MY BROTHER TALKS TO HORSES (1946)
SUMMER HOLIDAY (1948)

Johns, Glynis
COURT JESTER, THE (1956)
MARY POPPINS (1964)

Johnson, Gerry
MAN CALLED FLINTSTONE, THE (1966)

Johnson, Rita
EDISON, THE MAN (1940)
MY FRIEND FLICKA (1943)
THUNDERHEAD-SON OF FLICKA (1945)

Johnson, Van
IN THE GOOD OLD SUMMERTIME (1949)
YOURS, MINE AND OURS (1968)

Jones, Shirley
OKLAHOMA! (1955)

Jones, Allan
NIGHT AT THE OPERA, A (1935)
ONE NIGHT IN THE TROPICS (1940)

Jones, Carolyn
HOW THE WEST WAS WON (1962)

Jones, Dean
BLACKBEARD'S GHOST (1968)
LOVE BUG, THE (1968)
SHAGGY D.A., THE (1976)
THAT DARN CAT (1965)

Jones, Dickie
PINOCCHIO (1940)

Jones, James Earl
PINOCCHIO AND THE EMPEROR OF THE NIGHT (1987)
RETURN OF THE JEDI (1983)

Jones, Jennifer
SONG OF BERNADETTE, THE (1943)

Jones, Rickie Lee
PINOCCHIO AND THE EMPEROR OF THE NIGHT (1987)

Jones, Shirley
COURTSHIP OF EDDIE'S FATHER, THE (1963)
FLUFFY (1965)
MUSIC MAN, THE (1962)
OKLAHOMA! (1955)

Jordan, Bobby
LIVE WIRES (1946)
NEWS HOUNDS (1947)

Jordon, Patricia
HILDUR AND THE MAGICIAN (1969)

Jory, Victor
ADVENTURES OF TOM SAWYER, THE (1938)
FRASIER, THE SENSUOUS LION (1973)
MIRACLE WORKER, THE (1962)
SHUT MY BIG MOUTH (1942)

Joslyn, Allyn
HORN BLOWS AT MIDNIGHT, THE (1945)

Jourdan, Louis
HAPPY TIME, THE (1952)

Jurgens, Curt
BATTLE OF BRITAIN, THE (1969, Brit.)
INN OF THE SIXTH HAPPINESS, THE (1958)

Justice, James Robertson
STORY OF ROBIN HOOD, THE (1952, Brit.)

Justice, Katherine
FRASIER, THE SENSUOUS LION (1973)

Kahn, Madeline
AMERICAN TAIL, AN (1986)
WHAT'S UP, DOC? (1972)

Karloff, Boris
CHARLIE CHAN AT THE OPERA (1936)

Karman, Janice
CHIPMUNK ADVENTURE, THE (1987)

Kasznar, Kurt
LILI (1953)

Kaye, Celia
ISLAND OF THE BLUE DOLPHINS (1964)

Kaye, Danny
COURT JESTER, THE (1956)
HANS CHRISTIAN ANDERSEN (1952)
INSPECTOR GENERAL, THE (1949)
KID FROM BOOKLYN, THE (1946)
WHITE CHRISTMAS (1954)
WONDER MAN (1945)

Kaye, Stubby
LI'L ABNER (1959)
WHO FRAMED ROGER RABBIT? (1988)

Kazan, Lainie
JOURNEY OF NATTY GANN, THE (1985)

Keaton, Buster
ADVENTURES OF HUCKLEBERRY FINN, THE (1960)
IN THE GOOD OLD SUMMERTIME (1949)

Keel, Howard
ANNIE GET YOUR GUN (1950)
CALLAWAY WENT THATAWAY (1951)
SEVEN BRIDES FOR SEVEN BROTHERS (1954)

Keith, Brian
MOON PILOT (1962)
PARENT TRAP, THE (1961)
THOSE CALLOWAYS (1964)

Kellaway, Cecil
HARVEY (1950)

Kellerman, Sally
LITTLE ROMANCE, A (1979, US/Fr.)

Kelley, DeForest
STAR TREK: THE MOTION PICTURE (1979)
STAR TREK II: THE WRATH OF KHAN (1982)
STAR TREK III: THE SEARCH FOR SPOCK (1984)

STAR TREK IV: THE VOYAGE HOME (1986)

Kelly, Gene
TAKE ME OUT TO THE BALL GAME (1949)
THREE MUSKETEERS, THE (1948)

Kelly, Nancy
ONE NIGHT IN THE TROPICS (1940)
STANLEY AND LIVINGSTONE (1939)

Kelly, Patsy
FREAKY FRIDAY (1976)

Kelly, Paul
PAINTED HILLS, THE (1951)

Kelly, Tommy
ADVENTURES OF TOM SAWYER, THE (1938)

Kemp, Jeremy
BELSTONE FOX, THE (1976, Brit.)

Kennedy, Arthur
AIR FORCE (1943)

Kennedy, George
ISLAND OF THE BLUE DOLPHINS (1964)

Kerr, Deborah
KING AND I, THE (1956)
KING SOLOMON'S MINES (1950)

Khvylya, Aleksandr
JACK FROST (1966, USSR)

Kibbee, Guy
CAPTAIN JANUARY (1935)

Kidder, Margot
SUPERMAN (1978)
SUPERMAN II (1980)

Kiel, Richard
LASSIE'S GREAT ADVENTURE (1963)

Kilbride, Percy
MA AND PA KETTLE (1949)
MA AND PA KETTLE ON VACATION (1953)
SUN COMES UP, THE (1949)

Kilburn, Terry
CHRISTMAS CAROL, A (1938)
GOODBYE MR. CHIPS (1939, Brit.)

Kirk, Tommy
ABSENT-MINDED PROFESSOR, THE (1961)
OLD YELLER (1957)
SHAGGY DOG, THE (1959)
SON OF FLUBBER (1963)
SWISS FAMILY ROBINSON (1960)

Klugman, Jack
WHO SAYS I CAN'T RIDE A RAINBOW? (1971)

Knotts, Don
PINOCCHIO AND THE EMPEROR OF THE NIGHT (1987)

Kolb, Clarence
FIVE LITTLE PEPPERS AND HOW THEY GREW (1939)

Kossoff, David
MOUSE THAT ROARED, THE (1959, Brit.)

Kovack, Nancy
JASON AND THE ARGONAUTS (1963, Brit.)

Kove, Martin
KARATE KID, THE (1984)

Kruger, Otto
TREASURE ISLAND (1934)

Ladd, Alan
DOG OF FLANDERS, A (1959)
SHANE (1953)

Ladd, David
MISTY (1961)

Lahr, Bert
WIZARD OF OZ, THE (1939)

Lake, Arthur
BLONDIE (1938)

Lamour, Dorothy
CAUGHT IN THE DRAFT (1941)
GREATEST SHOW ON EARTH, THE (1952)
ROAD TO MOROCCO (1942)
ROAD TO RIO (1947)
ROAD TO UTOPIA (1945)
ROAD TO ZANZIBAR (1941)

Lancaster, Burt
MISTER 880 (1950)

Lanchester, Elsa
BLACKBEARD'S GHOST (1968)
COME TO THE STABLE (1949)
DREAMBOAT (1952)
INSPECTOR GENERAL, THE (1949)
RASCAL (1969)
SECRET GARDEN, THE (1949)
TALES OF MANHATTAN (1942)
THAT DARN CAT (1965)

Landi, Elissa
COUNT OF MONTE CRISTO, THE (1934)

Lane, Diane
LITTLE ROMANCE, A (1979, US/Fr.)

Lang, June
CAPTAIN JANUARY (1935)

Lange, Hope
POCKETFUL OF MIRACLES (1961)

Lansbury, Angela
BEDKNOBS AND BROOMSTICKS (1971)
COURT JESTER, THE (1956)
HARVEY GIRLS, THE (1946)
NATIONAL VELVET (1944)
THREE MUSKETEERS, THE (1948)
WORLD OF HENRY ORIENT, THE (1964)

Laughton, Charles
CANTERVILLE GHOST, THE (1944)
O. HENRY'S FULL HOUSE (1952)
SIDEWALKS OF LONDON (1940, Brit.)
TALES OF MANHATTAN (1942)

Laurel, Stan
BABES IN TOYLAND (1934)
BLOCKHEADS (1938)
FLYING DEUCES, THE (1939)
WAY OUT WEST (1937)

Law, John Phillip
GOLDEN VOYAGE OF SINBAD, THE (1974, Brit.)

Lawford, Peter
EASTER PARADE (1948)
MY BROTHER TALKS TO HORSES (1946)
SON OF LASSIE (1945)

Lawson, Priscilla
FLASH GORDON (1936)

Le Blanc, Lionel
LOUISIANA STORY (1948)

Leaud, Jean-Pierre
FOUR HUNDRED BLOWS, THE (1959)

Lederman, Caz
TAIL OF THE TIGER (1984, Aus.)

Lee, Anna
HOW GREEN WAS MY VALLEY (1941)

Lee, Michele
LOVE BUG, THE (1968)

Lee, Peggy
LADY AND THE TRAMP (1955)

Leibman, Ron
PHAR LAP (1984, Aus.)

Leigh, Janet
ANGELS IN THE OUTFIELD (1951)
FEARLESS FAGAN (1952)
HILLS OF HOME (1948)
MY SISTER EILEEN (1955)

Leigh, Vivien
SIDEWALKS OF LONDON (1940, Brit.)
YANK AT OXFORD, A (1938)

Lemmon, Jack
MY SISTER EILEEN (1955)

Leslie, Joan
SERGEANT YORK (1941)
THIS IS THE ARMY (1943)
YANKEE DOODLE DANDY (1942)

Lester, Mark
MELODY (1971, Brit.)
OLIVER! (1968, Brit.)

Levant, Oscar
O. HENRY'S FULL HOUSE (1952)

Levene, Sam
BABE RUTH STORY, THE (1948)

Linden, Eric
AH, WILDERNESS! (1935)

Lindfors, Viveca
KING OF KINGS (1961)

Linkletter, Art
CHAMPAGNE FOR CAESAR (1950)

Lipson, John
FLASH GORDON (1936)

Lister, Moira
JOHN AND JULIE (1957, Brit.)

Lithgow, John
MANHATTAN PROJECT, THE (1986)

Lloyd, Christopher
WHO FRAMED ROGER RABBIT? (1988)

Lloyd, Harold
MILKY WAY, THE (1936)

Lockhart, Gene
ABE LINCOLN IN ILLINOIS (1940)
BLONDIE (1938)
CHRISTMAS CAROL, A (1938)
EDISON, THE MAN (1940)
GOING MY WAY (1944)
INSPECTOR GENERAL, THE (1949)
MIRACLE ON 34TH STREET, THE (1947)

Lockhart, June
LASSIE'S GREAT ADVENTURE (1963)
MEET ME IN ST. LOUIS (1944)
SON OF LASSIE (1945)

Lockhart, Kathleen
CHRISTMAS CAROL, A (1938)

Logan, Robert F.
ADVENTURES OF THE WILDERNESS FAMILY, THE (1975)
SEA GYPSIES, THE (1978)

Loham, Gerald
JOHN WESLEY (1954, Brit.)

Lom, Herbert
MYSTERIOUS ISLAND (1961, US/Brit.)

Long, Richard
MA AND PA KETTLE (1949)

Lorre, Peter
20,000 LEAGUES UNDER THE SEA (1954)
VOYAGE TO THE BOTTOM OF THE SEA (1961)

Louis, Joe
THIS IS THE ARMY (1943)

Louise, Anita
LITTLE PRINCESS, THE (1939)
STORY OF LOUIS PASTEUR, THE (1936)

Loy, Myrna
BACHELOR AND THE BOBBY-SOXER, THE (1947)
CHEAPER BY THE DOZEN (1950)
CONNECTICUT YANKEE, A (1931)

Luddy, Barbara
LADY AND THE TRAMP (1955)

Lugosi, Bela
ABBOTT AND COSTELLO MEET FRANKENSTEIN (1948)

Lukas, Paul
GHOST BREAKERS, THE (1940)
KIM (1950)
LITTLE WOMEN (1933)
20,000 LEAGUES UNDER THE SEA (1954)

Luke, Keye
CHARLIE CHAN AT THE OPERA (1936)

Lupino, Ida
ADVENTURES OF SHERLOCK
HOLMES, THE (1939)

Luz, Dora
THREE CABALLEROS, THE (1944)

Lydon, Jimmy [James Lydon]
HENRY ALDRICH FOR PRESIDENT
(1941)

Lynde, Paul
CHARLOTTE'S WEB (1973)
HUGO THE HIPPO (1976, Hung./US)

Lynley, Carol
LIGHT IN THE FOREST, THE (1958)

Lynn, Jeffrey
FIGHTING 69TH, THE (1940)

MacArthur, James
LIGHT IN THE FOREST, THE (1958)
SWISS FAMILY ROBINSON (1960)

Macchio, Ralph
KARATE KID, THE (1984)

MacDonald, Jeanette
SUN COMES UP, THE (1949)

Mackay, Barry
CHRISTMAS CAROL, A (1938)

Mackenzie, Alexander
GREYFRIARS BOBBY (1961, Brit.)

MacLaine, Shirley
AROUND THE WORLD IN 80 DAYS
(1956)

MacLane, Barton
PRINCE AND THE PAUPER, THE (1937)

MacMurray, Fred
ABSENT-MINDED PROFESSOR, THE
(1961)
CALLAWAY WENT THATAWAY (1951)
FOLLOW ME, BOYS! (1966)
SHAGGY DOG, THE (1959)
SING YOU SINNERS (1938)
SON OF FLUBBER (1963)

MacNaughton, Robert
E.T. THE EXTRA-TERRESTRIAL (1982)

MacRae, Gordon
BEST THINGS IN LIFE ARE FREE, THE
(1956)
OKLAHOMA! (1955)

Macrae, Duncan
LITTLE KIDNAPPERS, THE (1954, Brit.)

Madison, Julian
IT'S A GIFT (1934)

Mahal, Taj
SOUNDER (1972)

Mahl, Hildur
HILDUR AND THE MAGICIAN (1969)

Mahoney, John
MANHATTAN PROJECT, THE (1986)

Main, Marjorie
MA AND PA KETTLE (1949)
MA AND PA KETTLE ON VACATION
(1953)

Mako
ISLAND AT THE TOP OF THE WORLD,
THE (1974)

Malcolm, Christopher
LABYRINTH (1986)

Malden, Karl
ADVENTURES OF BULLWHIP
GRIFFIN, THE (1967)
POLLYANNA (1960)

Malkovich, John
EMPIRE OF THE SUN (1987)

Mara, Adele
SHUT MY BIG MOUTH (1942)

Marais, Jean
BEAUTY AND THE BEAST (1947, Fr.)

March, Fredric
ADVENTURES OF MARK TWAIN, THE
(1944)
ONE FOOT IN HEAVEN (1941)

Marin, Jacques
ISLAND AT THE TOP OF THE WORLD,
THE (1974)

Marlowe, Hugh
COME TO THE STABLE (1949)

Mars, Kenneth
WHAT'S UP, DOC? (1972)

Marsh, Joan
YOU'RE TELLING ME (1934)

Marshall, Herbert
SECRET GARDEN, THE (1949)

Martin, Tony
HIT THE DECK (1955)

Martin, Vivienne
BELLES OF ST. TRINIAN'S, THE (1954,
Brit.)

Marx, Chico
ANIMAL CRACKERS (1930)
AT THE CIRCUS (1939)
DAY AT THE RACES, A (1937)
DUCK SOUP (1933)
NIGHT AT THE OPERA, A (1935)

Marx, Groucho
ANIMAL CRACKERS (1930)
AT THE CIRCUS (1939)
DAY AT THE RACES, A (1937)
DUCK SOUP (1933)
NIGHT AT THE OPERA, A (1935)

Marx, Harpo
ANIMAL CRACKERS (1930)
AT THE CIRCUS (1939)
DAY AT THE RACES, A (1937)
DUCK SOUP (1933)
NIGHT AT THE OPERA, A (1935)

Marx, Zeppo
ANIMAL CRACKERS (1930)
DUCK SOUP (1933)

Mason, James
JOURNEY TO THE CENTER OF THE
EARTH (1959)
20,000 LEAGUES UNDER THE SEA
(1954)
WATER BABIES, THE (1979, Brit.)

Massey, Raymond
ABE LINCOLN IN ILLINOIS (1940)
ROSEANNA McCOY (1949)

Mathews, Kerwin
JACK THE GIANT KILLER (1962)
SEVENTH VOYAGE OF SINBAD, THE
(1958)

Matthau, Walter
BAD NEWS BEARS, THE (1976)
HELLO, DOLLY! (1969)

Maurier, Claire
FOUR HUNDRED BLOWS, THE (1959)

Mayo, Virginia
KID FROM BOOKLYN, THE (1946)
WONDER MAN (1945)

McAndrew, Marianne
HELLO, DOLLY! (1969)

McCallister, Lon
HOME IN INDIANA (1944)

McCann, Chuck
WORLD OF HANS CHRISTIAN
ANDERSEN (1971, Jap.)

McClelland, Fergus
BOY TEN FEET TALL, A (1965, Brit.)

McCormack, Patty
ADVENTURES OF HUCKLEBERRY
FINN, THE (1960)

McCrea, Joel
BUFFALO BILL (1944)
CATTLE DRIVE (1951)

McDaniel, Hattie
SONG OF THE SOUTH (1946)

McDowall, Roddy
ADVENTURES OF BULLWHIP
GRIFFIN, THE (1967)
BEDKNOBS AND BROOMSTICKS
(1971)
CAT FROM OUTER SPACE, THE (1978)
HOW GREEN WAS MY VALLEY (1941)
LASSIE, COME HOME (1943)
MY FRIEND FLICKA (1943)
THAT DARN CAT (1965)
THUNDERHEAD-SON OF FLICKA
(1945)

McEnery, Peter
FIGHTING PRINCE OF DONEGAL,
THE (1966, Brit.)

McGavin, Darren
CHRISTMAS STORY, A (1983)

McGiver, John
FITZWILLY (1967)

McGuire, Don
FULLER BRUSH MAN (1948)

McGuire, Dorothy
CALLAWAY WENT THATAWAY (1951)
FLIGHT OF THE DOVES (1971)
MISTER 880 (1950)
OLD YELLER (1957)
SUMMER MAGIC (1963)
SWISS FAMILY ROBINSON (1960)

McHugh, Frank
GOING MY WAY (1944)

ACTORS

McIntire, John
FRANCIS (1949)
HERBIE RIDES AGAIN (1974)

McKenna, Virginia
BORN FREE (1966)
SWALLOWS AND AMAZONS (1977, Brit.)

McKern, Leo
MOUSE THAT ROARED, THE (1959, Brit.)

McLaglen, Victor
WEE WILLIE WINKIE (1937)

McLerie, Allyn
WHERE'S CHARLEY? (1952, Brit.)

McLiam, John
DOVE, THE (1974, Brit.)

McQueen, Steve
GREAT ESCAPE, THE (1963)

Meacham, Michael
MIDSUMMER NIGHT'S DREAM, A (1961, Czech.)

Medina, Patricia
FRANCIS (1949)

Meeker, Ralph
GENTLE GIANT (1967)

Meffre, Armand
HERE COMES SANTA CLAUS (1984)

Menjou, Adolphe
LITTLE MISS MARKER (1934)
MILKY WAY, THE (1936)

Mercer, Jack
MR. BUG GOES TO TOWN (1941)

Meredith, Burgess
STORY OF G.I. JOE, THE (1945)

Meredith, Judi
JACK THE GIANT KILLER (1962)

Merkel, Una
BANK DICK, THE (1940)
ROAD TO ZANZIBAR (1941)

Merman, Ethel
IT'S A MAD, MAD, MAD, MAD WORLD (1963)

Merrill, Dina
COURTSHIP OF EDDIE'S FATHER, THE (1963)

Merrill, Gary
MYSTERIOUS ISLAND (1961, US/Brit.)

Middleton, Charles
FLASH GORDON (1936)
FLYING DEUCES, THE (1939)

Middleton, Noelle
JOHN AND JULIE (1957, Brit.)

Miles, Bernard
GREAT EXPECTATIONS (1946, Brit.)

Miles, Sarah
HOPE AND GLORY (1987, Brit.)
THOSE MAGNIFICENT MEN IN THEIR FLYING MACHINES OR HOW I FLEW FROM LONDON TO PARIS IN 25 HOURS AND 11 MINUTES (1965, Brit.)

Miles, Vera
FOLLOW ME, BOYS! (1966)
GENTLE GIANT (1967)
THOSE CALLOWAYS (1964)

Milland, Ray
ESCAPE TO WITCH MOUNTAIN (1975)
IT HAPPENS EVERY SPRING (1949)
THREE SMART GIRLS (1937)

Miller, Ann
EASTER PARADE (1948)

Miller, Bodil
MA AND PA KETTLE ON VACATION (1953)

Miller, Cheryl
CLARENCE, THE CROSS-EYED LION (1965)

Miller, Eve
STORY OF WILL ROGERS, THE (1952)

Miller, Roger
ROBIN HOOD (1973)

Mills, Hayley
AFRICA--TEXAS STYLE! (1967, US/Brit.)
IN SEARCH OF THE CASTAWAYS (1962, Brit.)
MOON-SPINNERS, THE (1964)
PARENT TRAP, THE (1961)
POLLYANNA (1960)
SUMMER MAGIC (1963)
THAT DARN CAT (1965)
TIGER BAY (1959, Brit.)

Mills, John
AFRICA--TEXAS STYLE! (1967, US/Brit.)
GOODBYE MR. CHIPS (1939, Brit.)
GREAT EXPECTATIONS (1946, Brit.)
SWISS FAMILY ROBINSON (1960)
TIGER BAY (1959, Brit.)

Mimieux, Yvette
TIME MACHINE, THE (1960, Brit./US)

Miranda, Aurora
THREE CABALLEROS, THE (1944)

Miranda, Carmen
DATE WITH JUDY, A (1948)

Mitchell, Millard
MISTER 880 (1950)

Mitchell, Thomas
BATAAN (1943)
BUFFALO BILL (1944)
IT'S A WONDERFUL LIFE (1946)
MR. SMITH GOES TO WASHINGTON (1939)
TALES OF MANHATTAN (1942)

Mitchell, Yvonne
TIGER BAY (1959, Brit.)

Mitchum, Robert
STORY OF G.I. JOE, THE (1945)

Mobley, Roger
EMIL AND THE DETECTIVES (1964)

Molina, Carmen
THREE CABALLEROS, THE (1944)

Monroe, Marilyn
O. HENRY'S FULL HOUSE (1952)

Montalban, Ricardo
STAR TREK II: THE WRATH OF KHAN (1982)

Montez, Maria
ALI BABA AND THE FORTY THIEVES (1944)
ARABIAN NIGHTS (1942)

Montgomery, George
BATTLE OF THE BULGE (1965)
DAVY CROCKETT, INDIAN SCOUT (1950)
YOUNG PEOPLE (1940)

Moody, Ron
OLIVER! (1968, Brit.)
FLIGHT OF THE DOVES (1971)

Moore, Archie
ADVENTURES OF HUCKLEBERRY FINN, THE (1960)

Moore, Kieron
DARBY O'GILL AND THE LITTLE PEOPLE (1959)

Moore, Pauline
HEIDI (1937)

Moore, Robyn
DOT AND THE KOALA (1985, Aus.)

Moore, Terry
GREAT RUPERT, THE (1950)

Moorehead, Agnes
STRATTON STORY, THE (1949)
YOUNGEST PROFESSION, THE (1943)

Moran, Dolores
HORN BLOWS AT MIDNIGHT, THE (1945)

Moran, Jackie
ADVENTURES OF TOM SAWYER, THE (1938)

Moran, Peggy
KING OF THE COWBOYS (1943)

More, Kenneth
SCROOGE (1970, Brit.)

Morell, Pat
THUMBELINA (1970)

Moreno, Rita
KING AND I, THE (1956)

Morgan, Dennis
CHRISTMAS IN CONNECTICUT (1945)

Morgan, Frank
COURAGE OF LASSIE (1946)
STRATTON STORY, THE (1949)
SUMMER HOLIDAY (1948)
WIZARD OF OZ, THE (1939)

Morgan, Harry
BAREFOOT EXECUTIVE, THE (1971)
CAT FROM OUTER SPACE, THE (1978)
SO THIS IS NEW YORK (1948)

Morgan, Ralph
LAST ROUND-UP, THE (1947)

Morita, Noriyuki "Pat"
KARATE KID, THE (1984)

Morley, Karen
LITTLEST REBEL, THE (1935)

Morley, Robert
AFRICAN QUEEN, THE (1951, US/Brit.)
HUGO THE HIPPO (1976, Hung./US)

Morris, Howard
FLUFFY (1965)

Morrow, Vic
BAD NEWS BEARS, THE (1976)

Muir, Geraldine
HOPE AND GLORY (1987, Brit.)

Mumy, Bill
RASCAL (1969)

Muni, Paul
STORY OF LOUIS PASTEUR, THE
(1936)

Munro, Caroline
GOLDEN VOYAGE OF SINBAD, THE
(1974, Brit.)

Munro, Janet
DARBY O'GILL AND THE LITTLE
PEOPLE (1959)
SWISS FAMILY ROBINSON (1960)

Munshin, Jules
EASTER PARADE (1948)
TAKE ME OUT TO THE BALL GAME
(1949)

Murphy, George
BATAAN (1943)
THIS IS THE ARMY (1943)

Murray, Barbara
CRY FROM THE STREET, A (1959, Brit.)

Naish, J. Carrol
ANNIE GET YOUR GUN (1950)
KID FROM SPAIN, THE (1932)

Naismith, Laurence
GREYFRIARS BOBBY (1961, Brit.)
JASON AND THE ARGONAUTS (1963,
Brit.)

Natwick, Mildred
TRUMAN CAPOTE'S TRILOGY (1969)

Navara, Ernest
FABULOUS WORLD OF JULES
VERNE, THE (1961, Czech.)

Navin, Grant
TAIL OF THE TIGER (1984, Aus.)

Ndebele, Muntu
FOREVER YOUNG, FOREVER FREE
(1976, South Africa)

Negri, Pola
MOON-SPINNERS, THE (1964)

Newhart, Bob
RESCUERS, THE (1977)

Newley, Anthony
DOCTOR DOLITTLE (1967)
OLIVER TWIST (1951, Brit.)

Newmar, Julie
LI'L ABNER (1959)

Newton, Robert
AROUND THE WORLD IN 80 DAYS
(1956)
OLIVER TWIST (1951, Brit.)
TREASURE ISLAND (1950, Brit.)

Nimoy, Leonard
STAR TREK: THE MOTION PICTURE
(1979)
STAR TREK II: THE WRATH OF KHAN
(1982)
STAR TREK III: THE SEARCH FOR
SPOCK (1984)
STAR TREK IV: THE VOYAGE
HOME (1986)

Niven, David
AROUND THE WORLD IN 80 DAYS
(1956)

Nixon, Cynthia
MANHATTAN PROJECT, THE (1986)

Nolan, Jeanette
RESCUERS, THE (1977)

Nolan, Lloyd
BATAAN (1943)
SUN COMES UP, THE (1949)

North, Sheree
BEST THINGS IN LIFE ARE FREE, THE
(1956)

O'Brian, Hugh
AFRICA--TEXAS STYLE! (1967 US/Brit.)

O'Brien, Edmond
AMAZING MRS. HOLLIDAY (1943)
FANTASTIC VOYAGE (1966)
MOON PILOT (1962)

O'Brien, Margaret
CANTERVILLE GHOST, THE (1944)
JOURNEY FOR MARGARET (1942)
MEET ME IN ST. LOUIS (1944)
SECRET GARDEN, THE (1949)

O'Brien, Pat
ANGELS WITH DIRTY FACES (1938)
FIGHTING 69TH, THE (1940)
KNUTE ROCKNE--ALL AMERICAN
(1940)

O'Connell, Arthur
GIDGET (1959)
MISTY (1961)
POCKETFUL OF MIRACLES (1961)
SEVEN FACES OF DR. LAO (1964)

O'Connell, Bob
THUMBELINA (1970)

O'Connor, Donald
FRANCIS (1949)
SING YOU SINNERS (1938)

O'Dea, Jimmy
DARBY O'GILL AND THE LITTLE
PEOPLE (1959)

O'Driscoll, Martha
HENRY ALDRICH FOR PRESIDENT
(1941)
HERE COME THE CO-EDS (1945)

O'Hara, Maureen
BUFFALO BILL (1944)
HOW GREEN WAS MY VALLEY (1941)

MIRACLE ON 34TH STREET, THE
(1947)
MR. HOBBS TAKES A VACATION
(1962)
PARENT TRAP, THE (1961)
SINBAD THE SAILOR (1947)
SITTING PRETTY (1948)

O'Herlihy, Dan
ADVENTURES OF ROBINSON
CRUSOE, THE (1954)

O'Keefe, Paul
DAYDREAMER, THE (1966)

O'Neal, Ryan
WHAT'S UP, DOC? (1972)

O'Neal, Tatum
BAD NEWS BEARS, THE (1976)

O'Sullivan, Maureen
CONNECTICUT YANKEE, A (1931)
DAVID COPPERFIELD (1935)
DAY AT THE RACES, A (1937)
TARZAN THE APE MAN (1932)
YANK AT OXFORD, A (1938)

Oakie, Jack
CALL OF THE WILD (1935)
YOUNG PEOPLE (1940)

Oates, Warren
TOM SAWYER (1973)

Ober, Philip
MAGNIFICENT YANKEE, THE (1950)

Oberon, Merle
DEEP IN MY HEART (1954)

Oland, Warner
CHARLIE CHAN AT THE OPERA (1936)

Oliver, Edna May
DAVID COPPERFIELD (1935)
LITTLE WOMEN (1933)
TALE OF TWO CITIES, A (1935)

Olivier, Laurence
BATTLE OF BRITAIN, THE (1969, Brit.)
LITTLE ROMANCE, A (1979, US/Fr.)

Olson, Nancy
ABSENT-MINDED PROFESSOR, THE
(1961)
SON OF FLUBBER (1963)

Ostrum, Peter
WILLY WONKA AND THE
CHOCOLATE FACTORY (1971)

Oulton, Brian
DOG AND THE DIAMONDS, THE (1962,
Brit.)

Overman, Lynne
CAUGHT IN THE DRAFT (1941)
EDISON, THE MAN (1940)
LITTLE MISS MARKER (1934)

Owen, Reginald
CANTERVILLE GHOST, THE (1944)
CHRISTMAS CAROL, A (1938)
TALE OF TWO CITIES, A (1935)

Oz, Frank
GREAT MUPPET CAPER, THE (1981)
MUPPET MOVIE, THE (1979)

ACTORS

MUPPETS TAKE MANHATTAN, THE
(1984)

Page, Gale
KNUTE ROCKNE--ALL AMERICAN
(1940)

Page, Geraldine
RESCUERS, THE (1977)
TRUMAN CAPOTE'S TRILOGY (1969)

Paget, Debra
STARS AND STRIPES FOREVER (1952)

Palance, Jack
SHANE (1953)

Palin, Michael
TIME BANDITS (1981, Brit.)

Pallette, Eugene
STOWAWAY (1936)

Palmer, Peter
LI'L ABNER (1959)

Pangborn, Franklin
BANK DICK, THE (1940)

Pantoliano, Joe
EMPIRE OF THE SUN (1987)

Papas, Irene
MOON-SPINNERS, THE (1964)

Parker, Cecil
COURT JESTER, THE (1956)
HEAVENS ABOVE! (1963, Brit.)

Parker, Cecilia
JUDGE HARDY AND SON (1939)
JUDGE HARDY'S CHILDREN (1938)
LOVE FINDS ANDY HARDY (1938)

Parker, Eleanor
SOUND OF MUSIC, THE (1965)

Parker, Fess
DAVY CROCKETT, KING OF THE WILD
FRONTIER (1955)
LIGHT IN THE FOREST,
THE (1958)
OLD YELLER (1957)

Parker, Jean
FLYING DEUCES, THE (1939)
LITTLE WOMEN (1933)

Parker, Sarah Jessica
FLIGHT OF THE NAVIGATOR (1986)

Parrish, Leslie
LI'L ABNER (1959)

Patinkin, Mandy
PRINCESS BRIDE, THE (1987)

Patrick, Butch
PHANTOM TOLLBOOTH, THE (1970)

Patrick, Nigel
PICKWICK PAPERS, THE (1952, Brit.)

Patten, Luana
FUN AND FANCY FREE (1947)
JOHNNY TREMAIN (1957)
MELODY TIME (1948)

Payne, John
MIRACLE ON 34TH STREET, THE
(1947)

Peck, Gregory
MOBY DICK (1956, Brit.)
TO KILL A MOCKINGBIRD (1962)
YEARLING, THE (1946)

Perrine, Valerie
SUPERMAN (1978)
SUPERMAN II (1980)

Perry, Frank
MY SIDE OF THE MOUNTAIN (1969)

Persoff, Nehemiah
AMERICAN TAIL, AN (1986)

Peters, Jean
O. HENRY'S FULL HOUSE (1952)

Peters, Bernadette
ANNIE (1982)

Peters, Jean
IT HAPPENS EVERY SPRING (1949)
MAN CALLED PETER, A (1955)

Peters, Lauri
MR. HOBBS TAKES A VACATION
(1962)

Petersen, Colin
CRY FROM THE STREET, A (1959, Brit.)

Peterson, Dorothy
FIVE LITTLE PEPPERS AND HOW
THEY GREW (1939)

Petrella, Ian
CHRISTMAS STORY, A (1983)

Phipps, William
CINDERELLA (1950)

Pickens, Slim
STORY OF WILL ROGERS, THE (1952)

Pidgeon, Walter
DEEP IN MY HEART (1954)
HIT THE DECK (1955)
HOW GREEN WAS MY VALLEY (1941)
MADAME CURIE (1943)
RASCAL (1969)
VOYAGE TO THE BOTTOM OF THE
SEA (1961)

Pitts, ZaSu
FRANCIS (1949)
LIFE WITH FATHER (1947)

Pleasence, Donald
ESCAPE TO WITCH MOUNTAIN (1975)
FANTASTIC VOYAGE (1966)

Pleshette, Suzanne
ADVENTURES OF BULLWHIP
GRIFFIN, THE (1967)
BLACKBEARD'S GHOST (1968)
SHAGGY D.A., THE (1976)

Plummer, Christopher
AMERICAN TAIL, AN (1986)
SOUND OF MUSIC, THE (1965)

Poitier, Sidney
GOODBYE, MY LADY (1956)

Poole, Gordon
TAIL OF THE TIGER (1984, Aus.)

Porter, Eric
BELSTONE FOX, THE (1976, Brit.)

Powell, Jane
DATE WITH JUDY, A (1948)
HIT THE DECK (1955)
SEVEN BRIDES FOR SEVEN
BROTHERS (1954)

Powell, William
LIFE WITH FATHER (1947)

Power, Taryn
SINBAD AND THE EYE OF THE TIGER
(1977, US/Brit.)

Power, Tyrone
YANK IN THE R.A.F., A (1941)

Powers, Stefanie
HERBIE RIDES AGAIN (1974)

Preisser, June
HENRY ALDRICH FOR PRESIDENT
(1941)

Prentiss, Paula
WORLD OF HENRY ORIENT, THE
(1964)

Preston, Robert
MUSIC MAN, THE (1962)

Price, Vincent
CHAMPAGNE FOR CAESAR (1950)
SONG OF BERNADETTE, THE (1943)

Prima, Louis
JUNGLE BOOK, THE (1967)

Prine, Andrew
MIRACLE WORKER, THE (1962)

Provine, Dorothy
THAT DARN CAT (1965)

Provost, Jon
LASSIE'S GREAT ADVENTURE (1963)

Puglia, Frank
JUNGLE BOOK, THE (1942)

Pyott, Keith
JOHN WESLEY (1954, Brit.)

Qualen, John
JUNGLE BOOK, THE (1942)

Quinn, Aileen
ANNIE (1982)

Quinn, Anthony
BUFFALO BILL (1944)
ROAD TO MOROCCO (1942)
SINBAD THE SAILOR (1947)

Raffin, Deborah
DOVE, THE (1974, Brit.)

Ragland, Rags
GIRL CRAZY (1943)

Rains, Claude
ADVENTURES OF ROBIN HOOD, THE
(1938)
MR. SMITH GOES TO WASHINGTON
(1939)
PRINCE AND THE PAUPER, THE (1937)

Rambeau, Marjorie
MAN CALLED PETER, A (1955)

Randall, Meg
MA AND PA KETTLE (1949)

Randall, Tony
ADVENTURES OF HUCKLEBERRY
FINN, THE (1960)
FLUFFY (1965)
SEVEN FACES OF DR. LAO (1964)

Randell, Ron
KING OF KINGS (1961)

Rathbone, Basil
ADVENTURES OF ICHABOD AND MR.
TOAD (1949)
ADVENTURES OF ROBIN HOOD, THE
(1938)
ADVENTURES OF SHERLOCK
HOLMES, THE (1939)
COURT JESTER, THE (1956)
TALE OF TWO CITIES, A (1935)

Ratoff, Gregory
O. HENRY'S FULL HOUSE (1952)

Rattray, Heather
SEA GYPSIES, THE (1978)

Raye, Helen
FLIGHT OF THE DOVES (1971)

Raymond, Gary
JASON AND THE ARGONAUTS (1963,
Brit.)

Reagan, Ronald
KNUTE ROCKNE--ALL AMERICAN
(1940)
THIS IS THE ARMY (1943)

Reddy, Helen
PETE'S DRAGON (1977)

Reed, Oliver
OLIVER! (1968, Brit.)

Reed, Donna
IT'S A WONDERFUL LIFE (1946)
SEE HERE, PRIVATE HARGROVE
(1944)

Reed, Philip
DAVY CROCKETT, INDIAN SCOUT
(1950)

Reed, Sr., Alan
MAN CALLED FLINTSTONE, THE
(1966)

Reeve, Christopher
SUPERMAN (1978)
SUPERMAN II (1980)

Reicher, Frank
KING KONG (1933)

Reid, Carl Benton
FULLER BRUSH GIRL, THE (1950)

Reilly, Hugh
LASSIE'S GREAT ADVENTURE (1963)

Reinking, Ann
ANNIE (1982)

Remy, Albert
FOUR HUNDRED BLOWS, THE (1959)

Reno, Kelly
BLACK STALLION, THE (1979)

Rettig, Tommy
5,000 FINGERS OF DR. T., THE (1953)

Revere, Anne
NATIONAL VELVET (1944)

Reyna, Maurice
BOY WHO STOLE A MILLION, THE
(1960, Brit.)

Reynolds, Debbie
CHARLOTTE'S WEB (1973)
HIT THE DECK (1955)

Reynolds, Marjorie
TIME OF THEIR LIVES, THE (1946)

Rice, Joan
STORY OF ROBIN HOOD, THE (1952,
Brit.)

Rice-Edwards, Sebastian
HOPE AND GLORY (1987, Brit.)

Rich, Irene
CHAMP, THE (1931)

Richards, Jeff
SEVEN BRIDES FOR SEVEN
BROTHERS (1954)

Richards, Kim
ESCAPE TO WITCH MOUNTAIN (1975)

Richardson, Miranda
EMPIRE OF THE SUN (1987)

Richardson, Ralph
TIME BANDITS (1981, Brit.)

Ridgely, John
AIR FORCE (1943)

Robbins, Gale
FULLER BRUSH GIRL, THE (1950)

Roberti, Lyda
KID FROM SPAIN, THE (1932)

Roberts, Larry
LADY AND THE TRAMP (1955)

Roberts, Rachel
BELSTONE FOX, THE (1976, Brit.)

Robertson, Dale
O. HENRY'S FULL HOUSE (1952)

Robertson, Cliff
GIDGET (1959)

Robeson, Paul
TALES OF MANHATTAN (1942)

Robinson, Bartlett
SPIRIT OF ST. LOUIS, THE (1957)

Robinson, Bill
LITTLEST REBEL, THE (1935)

Robinson, Edward G.
BOY TEN FEET TALL, A (1965, Brit.)
TALES OF MANHATTAN (1942)
TEN COMMANDMENTS, THE (1956)

Robson, May
ADVENTURES OF TOM SAWYER, THE
(1938)

Rogers, Ginger
DREAMBOAT (1952)
TALES OF MANHATTAN (1942)

Rogers, Jean
FLASH GORDON (1936)

Rogers, Roy
BELLS OF ROSARITA (1945)
KING OF THE COWBOYS (1943)
MELODY TIME (1948)
MY PAL TRIGGER (1946)

Rogers, Will
CONNECTICUT YANKEE, A (1931)

Rogers, Jr., Will
STORY OF WILL ROGERS, THE (1952)

Romero, Cesar
COMPUTER WORE TENNIS SHOES,
THE (1970)
LITTLE PRINCESS, THE (1939)
NOW YOU SEE HIM, NOW YOU DON'T
(1972)
TALES OF MANHATTAN (1942)

Rooney, Mickey
AH, WILDERNESS! (1935)
BABES IN ARMS (1939)
BLACK STALLION, THE (1979)
BOYS TOWN (1938)
CAPTAINS COURAGEOUS (1937)
FOX AND THE HOUND, THE (1981)
FRANCIS IN THE HAUNTED HOUSE
(1956)
GIRL CRAZY (1943)
HUCKLEBERRY FINN (1939)
JUDGE HARDY AND SON (1939)
JUDGE HARDY'S CHILDREN (1938)
LITTLE LORD FAUNTLEROY (1936)
LOVE FINDS ANDY HARDY (1938)
NATIONAL VELVET (1944)
PETE'S DRAGON (1977)
STRIKE UP THE BAND (1940)
SUMMER HOLIDAY (1948)
YOUNG TOM EDISON (1940)

Rose, Jane
FLIPPER (1963)

Ross, Lanny
GULLIVER'S TRAVELS (1939)

Rouverol, Jean
IT'S A GIFT (1934)

Rowe, Greg
STORM BOY (1976, Aus.)

Rowe, Nicholas
YOUNG SHERLOCK HOLMES (1985)

Royle, Selena
COURAGE OF LASSIE (1946)

Rub, Christian
PINOCCHIO (1940)

Ruggles, Charlie
FOLLOW ME, BOYS! (1966)
MY BROTHER TALKS TO HORSES
(1946)
PARENT TRAP, THE (1961)

Russell, Bryan
ADVENTURES OF BULLWHIP
GRIFFIN, THE (1967)
EMIL AND THE DETECTIVES (1964)

Russell, Kurt
BAREFOOT EXECUTIVE, THE (1971)
COMPUTER WORE TENNIS SHOES,
THE (1970)

ACTORS

FOLLOW ME, BOYS! (1966)
FOX AND THE HOUND, THE (1981)
NOW YOU SEE HIM, NOW YOU DON'T (1972)

Russell, Rosalind
MY SISTER EILEEN (1942)

Ruth, Babe
PRIDE OF THE YANKEES, THE (1942)

Rutherford, Ann
JUDGE HARDY AND SON (1939)
JUDGE HARDY'S CHILDREN (1938)
LOVE FINDS ANDY HARDY (1938)

Rutherford, Margaret
WACKY WORLD OF MOTHER GOOSE, THE (1967)

Ruysdael, Basil
DAVY CROCKETT, KING OF THE WILD FRONTIER (1955)

Ryan, Peggy
HERE COME THE CO-EDS (1945)

Ryan, Robert
BATTLE OF THE BULGE (1965)

Sabu
ARABIAN NIGHTS (1942)
JUNGLE BOOK, THE (1942)
THIEF OF BAGHDAD, THE (1940, Brit.)

Sachs, Leonard
JOHN WESLEY (1954, Brit.)

Sakall, S.Z.
IN THE GOOD OLD SUMMERTIME (1949)
YANKEE DOODLE DANDY (1942)

Salenger, Meredith
JOURNEY OF NATTY GANN, THE (1985)

Sanders, George
GHOST AND MRS. MUIR, THE (1942)
IN SEARCH OF THE CASTAWAYS (1962, Brit.)
JUNGLE BOOK, THE (1967)
TALES OF MANHATTAN (1942)

Sarandon, Chris
PRINCESS BRIDE, THE (1987)

Saunders, Terry
KING AND I, THE (1956)

Savage, Fred
BOY WHO COULD FLY, THE (1986)

Saval, Dany
MOON PILOT (1962)

Saxon, John
MR. HOBBS TAKES A VACATION (1962)

Schallert, William
COMPUTER WORE TENNIS SHOES, THE (1970)

Schreck, Vicki
FREAKY FRIDAY (1976)

Schubert, Heinz
EMIL AND THE DETECTIVES (1964)

Scott, Connie
FLIPPER (1963)

Scott, Hennis
WINGS OF MYSTERY (1963, Brit.)

Scott, Janette
SCHOOL FOR SCOUNDRELS (1960, Brit.)

Scott, Keith
DOT AND THE KOALA (1985, Aus.)

Scott, Martha
CHARLOTTE'S WEB (1973)
ONE FOOT IN HEAVEN (1941)

Scott, Sandra
INCREDIBLE JOURNEY, THE (1963)

Searl, Jackie
SKIPPY (1931)

Seberg, Jean
MOUSE THAT ROARED, THE (1959, Brit.)

Sedykh, Natasha
JACK FROST (1966, USSR)

Sellers, Peter
HEAVENS ABOVE! (1963, Brit.)
MOUSE THAT ROARED, THE (1959, Brit.)
TOM THUMB (1958, Brit./US)
WORLD OF HENRY ORIENT, THE (1964)

Selling, Caj
DR. COPPELIUS (1968, US/Span.)

Servantie, Adrienne
MY UNCLE (1958, Fr.)

Seymour, Jane
SINBAD AND THE EYE OF THE TIGER (1977, US/Brit.)

Shackleton, Robert
WHERE'S CHARLEY? (1952, Brit.)

Sharp, Vanessa
NUTCRACKER: THE MOTION PICTURE (1986)

Sharpe, Albert
DARBY O'GILL AND THE LITTLE PEOPLE (1959)

Shatner, William
STAR TREK: THE MOTION PICTURE (1979)
STAR TREK II: THE WRATH OF KHAN (1982)
STAR TREK III: THE SEARCH FOR SPOCK (1984)
STAR TREK IV: THE VOYAGE HOME (1986)

Shaw, Robert
BATTLE OF THE BULGE (1965)

Shaw, Susan Damante
ADVENTURES OF THE WILDERNESS FAMILY, THE (1975)

Sheffield, Johnny
BOMBA THE JUNGLE BOY (1949)

Sheldon, Gene
TOBY TYLER (1960)

Sheridan, Ann
ANGELS WITH DIRTY FACES (1938)

Sherr, Francis
FABULOUS WORLD OF JULES VERNE, THE (1961, Czech.)

Shore, Dinah
FUN AND FANCY FREE (1947)
MAKE MINE MUSIC (1946)

Shue, Elisabeth
KARATE KID, THE (1984)

Sim, Alastair
BELLES OF ST. TRINIAN'S, THE (1954, Brit.)
LITTLEST HORSE THIEVES, THE (1977)
SCHOOL FOR SCOUNDRELS (1960, Brit.)
WEE GEORDIE (1956, Brit.)

Simms, Larry
BLONDIE (1938)

Sinatra, Frank
TAKE ME OUT TO THE BALL GAME (1949)

Sinclair, Ronald
FIVE LITTLE PEPPERS AND HOW THEY GREW (1939)

Sinden, Donald
ISLAND AT THE TOP OF THE WORLD, THE (1974)

Singleton, Penny
BLONDIE (1938)

Skelton, Red
EXCUSE MY DUST (1951)
FULLER BRUSH MAN (1948)
SOUTHERN YANKEE, A (1948)

Slezak, Walter
DR. COPPELIUS (1968, US/Span.)
EMIL AND THE DETECTIVES (1964)
INSPECTOR GENERAL, THE (1949)
SINBAD THE SAILOR (1947)
WONDERFUL WORLD OF THE BROTHERS GRIMM, THE (1962)

Smith, Alexis
ADVENTURES OF MARK TWAIN, THE (1944)
HORN BLOWS AT MIDNIGHT, THE (1945)

Smith, C. Aubrey
KIDNAPPED (1938)
LITTLE LORD FAUNTLEROY (1936)
WEE WILLIE WINKIE (1937)

Smith, Charles
HENRY ALDRICH FOR PRESIDENT (1941)

Smith, Charles Martin
NEVER CRY WOLF (1983)

Smith, Cynthia
FOR THE LOVE OF BENJI (1977)

Smith, Ethel
MELODY TIME (1948)

Smith, Pam
MISTY (1961)

Smith, Patricia
SPIRIT OF ST. LOUIS, THE (1957)

Sondergaard, Gale
ROAD TO RIO (1947)

Spaeth, Merrie
WORLD OF HENRY ORIENT, THE (1964)

Squire, Ronald
INN OF THE SIXTH HAPPINESS, THE (1958)

St. John, Howard
LI'L ABNER (1959)

Stalmaster, Hal
JOHNNY TREMAIN (1957)

Stamp, Terence
SUPERMAN II (1980)

Stander, Lionel
MILKY WAY, THE (1936)

Stanwyck, Barbara
ANNIE OAKLEY (1935)
CHRISTMAS IN CONNECTICUT (1945)

Stapleton, Maureen
TRUMAN CAPOTE'S TRILOGY (1969)

Steiger, Rod
OKLAHOMA! (1955)

Stephenson, Henry
LITTLE LORD FAUNTLEROY (1936)

Stevens, Onslow
BOMBA THE JUNGLE BOY (1949)

Stevens, Rise
GOING MY WAY (1944)

Stevens, Stella
COURTSHIP OF EDDIE'S FATHER, THE (1963)

Stevenson, McLean
CAT FROM OUTER SPACE, THE (1978)

Stewart, Bobby
BAMBI (1942)

Stewart, James
GREATEST SHOW ON EARTH, THE (1952)
HARVEY (1950)
IT'S A WONDERFUL LIFE (1946)
MR. HOBBS TAKES A VACATION (1962)
MR. SMITH GOES TO WASHINGTON (1939)
SPIRIT OF ST. LOUIS, THE (1957)
STRATTON STORY, THE (1949)

Stockwell, Dean
CATTLE DRIVE (1951)
KIM (1950)
SECRET GARDEN, THE (1949)

Stockwell, Harry
SNOW WHITE AND THE SEVEN DWARFS (1937)

Stone, Fred
KONGA, THE WILD STALLION (1939)

Stone, Harold J.
INVISIBLE BOY, THE (1957)

Stone, Lewis
JUDGE HARDY AND SON (1939)
JUDGE HARDY'S CHILDREN (1938)

LOVE FINDS ANDY HARDY (1938)

Strange, Glenn
ABBOTT AND COSTELLO MEET FRANKENSTEIN (1948)

Stratton, Gil
GIRL CRAZY (1943)

Streisand, Barbra
HELLO, DOLLY! (1969)
WHAT'S UP, DOC? (1972)

Strickland, Robert E.
GIRL CRAZY (1943)

Stuart, Gloria
LADDIE (1935)

Sullivan, Francis L.
GREAT EXPECTATIONS (1946, Brit.)

Summerville, Slim
CAPTAIN JANUARY (1935)

Sumner, Geoffrey
DOG AND THE DIAMONDS, THE (1962, Brit.)

Sweeney, Bob
TOBY TYLER (1960)

Swenson, Inga
MIRACLE WORKER, THE (1962)

Sydney, Basil
TREASURE ISLAND (1950, Brit.)

Sykes, Eric
HEAVENS ABOVE! (1963, Brit.)

Tafler, Sydney
JOHNNY ON THE RUN (1953, Brit.)

Takei, George
STAR TREK: THE MOTION PICTURE (1979)
STAR TREK II: THE WRATH OF KHAN (1982)
STAR TREK III: THE SEARCH FOR SPOCK (1984)
STAR TREK IV: THE VOYAGE HOME (1986)

Tamblyn, Russ
SEVEN BRIDES FOR SEVEN BROTHERS (1954)
TOM THUMB (1958, Brit./US)

Tamiroff, Akim
STORY OF LOUIS PASTEUR, THE (1936)

Tati, Jacques
MY UNCLE (1958, Fr.)
PLAYTIME (1973, Fr.)

Taylor, Deems
FANTASIA (1940)

Taylor, Don
FATHER'S LITTLE DIVIDEND (1951)

Taylor, Elizabeth
COURAGE OF LASSIE (1946)
DATE WITH JUDY, A (1948)
FATHER'S LITTLE DIVIDEND (1951)
LASSIE, COME HOME (1943)
LIFE WITH FATHER (1947)
NATIONAL VELVET (1944)

Taylor, Robert
BATAAN (1943)
YANK AT OXFORD, A (1938)

Taylor, Rod
ONE HUNDRED AND ONE DALMATIANS (1961)
TIME MACHINE, THE (1960, Brit./US)

Teasdale, Verree
MILKY WAY, THE (1936)

Temple, Shirley
BACHELOR AND THE BOBBY-SOXER, THE (1947)
BRIGHT EYES (1934)
CAPTAIN JANUARY (1935)
HEIDI (1937)
LITTLE MISS MARKER (1934)
LITTLE PRINCESS, THE (1939)
LITTLEST REBEL, THE (1935)
STOWAWAY (1936)
WEE WILLIE WINKIE (1937)
YOUNG PEOPLE (1940)

Terry-Thomas
ROBIN HOOD (1973)
SCHOOL FOR SCOUNDRELS (1960, Brit.)
THOSE MAGNIFICENT MEN IN THEIR FLYING MACHINES OR HOW I FLEW FROM LONDON TO PARIS IN 25 HOURS AND 11 MINUTES (1965, Brit.)
TOM THUMB (1958, Brit./US)

Texera, Virgilio
BOY WHO STOLE A MILLION, THE (1960, Brit.)
JACK THE GIANT KILLER (1962)

Thatcher, Torin
SEVENTH VOYAGE OF SINBAD, THE (1958)

Thomas, Henry
E.T. THE EXTRA-TERRESTRIAL (1982)

Thompson, Marshall
CLARENCE, THE CROSS-EYED LION (1965)

Thompson, Shelley
LABYRINTH (1986)

Thorndike, Sybil
ALIVE AND KICKING (1962, Brit.)

Tierney, Gene
GHOST AND MRS. MUIR, THE (1942)

Tobias, George
MY SISTER EILEEN (1942)
SEVEN LITTLE FOYS, THE (1955)
SINBAD THE SAILOR (1947)

Tock, Louis
FABULOUS WORLD OF JULES VERNE, THE (1961, Czech.)

Todd, Richard
MAN CALLED PETER, A (1955)
STORY OF ROBIN HOOD, THE (1952, Brit.)

Tomlinson, David
BEDKNOBS AND BROOMSTICKS (1971)
LOVE BUG, THE (1968)

ACTORS

MARY POPPINS (1964)

Townes, Harry
FITZWILLY (1967)

Tracy, Spencer
BOYS TOWN (1938)
CAPTAINS COURAGEOUS (1937)
EDISON, THE MAN (1940)
FATHER'S LITTLE DIVIDEND (1951)
HOW THE WEST WAS WON (1962)
IT'S A MAD, MAD, MAD, MAD WORLD (1963)
STANLEY AND LIVINGSTONE (1939)

Traubel, Helen
DEEP IN MY HEART (1954)

Travers, Bill
BORN FREE (1966)
WEE GEORDIE (1956, Brit.)

Travers, Henry
BELLS OF ST. MARY'S, THE (1945)
IT'S A WONDERFUL LIFE (1946)

Treacher, Arthur
HEIDI (1937)

Tree, Dorothy
ABE LINCOLN IN ILLINOIS (1940)

Treen, Mary Lou
ROOM FOR ONE MORE (1952)

Trevor, Claire
BABE RUTH STORY, THE (1948)

Trevor, Hugh
CUCKOOS, THE (1930)

Truffaut, Francois
CLOSE ENCOUNTERS OF THE THIRD KIND (1977)
WILD CHILD, THE (1970, Fr.)

Tryon, Tom
MOON PILOT (1962)

Tucker, Forrest
SANDS OF IWO JIMA (1949)

Turner, Lana
THREE MUSKETEERS, THE (1948)

Tuttle, Lurene
ROOM FOR ONE MORE (1952)

Tweed, Tommy
INCREDIBLE JOURNEY, THE (1963)

Tyler, Beverly
MY BROTHER TALKS TO HORSES (1946)

Tyrrell, Susan
CHIPMUNK ADVENTURE, THE (1987)

Tyson, Cicely
SOUNDER (1972)

Underwood, Jay
BOY WHO COULD FLY, THE (1986)

Urquhart, Molly
WEE GEORDIE (1956, Brit.)

Ustinov, Peter
BLACKBEARD'S GHOST (1968)
ROBIN HOOD (1973)

Valenta, Vladimir
WOLFPEN PRINCIPLE, THE (1974, Can.)

Valentine, Karen
FOREVER YOUNG, FOREVER FREE (1976, South Africa)

Vallee, Rudy
BACHELOR AND THE BOBBY-SOXER, THE (1947)
SO THIS IS NEW YORK (1948)

Van Dyke, Dick
CHITTY CHITTY BANG BANG (1968, Brit.)
FITZWILLY (1967)
MARY POPPINS (1964)

Van Patten, Joyce
BAD NEWS BEARS, THE (1976)

Vanderpyl, Jean
MAN CALLED FLINTSTONE, THE (1966)

Veidt, Conrad
THIEF OF BAGHDAD, THE (1940, Brit.)

Velasquez, Andres
LITTLEST OUTLAW, THE (1955)

Velez, Lupe
PALOOKA (1934)

Vera-Ellen
KID FROM BOOKLYN, THE (1946)
WONDER MAN (1945)

Vincent, Jan-Michael
WORLD'S GREATEST ATHLETE, THE (1973)

Wagner, Robert
STARS AND STRIPES FOREVER (1952)

Walker, Robert
MADAME CURIE (1943)
SEE HERE, PRIVATE HARGROVE (1944)

Walker, Tippy
WORLD OF HENRY ORIENT, THE (1964)

Wallace, Dee
E.T. THE EXTRA-TERRESTRIAL (1982)

Wallach, Eli
MOON-SPINNERS, THE (1964)

Walley, Deborah
SUMMER MAGIC (1963)

Wallis, Shani
OLIVER! (1968, Brit.)

Walsh, Kay
OLIVER TWIST (1951, Brit.)
GREYFRIARS BOBBY (1961, Brit.)

Ward, Simon
ALL CREATURES GREAT AND SMALL (1975, Brit.)

Ward, Sophie
YOUNG SHERLOCK HOLMES (1985)

Warner, David
TIME BANDITS (1981, Brit.)

Warner, John
MIDSUMMER NIGHT'S DREAM, A (1961, Czech.)

Warrick, Ruth
SONG OF THE SOUTH (1946)

Waters, Ethel
TALES OF MANHATTAN (1942)

Wayne, John
ALAMO, THE (1960)
SANDS OF IWO JIMA (1949)
THREE GODFATHERS, THE (1948)
TRUE GRIT (1969)

Wayne, Patrick
SINBAD AND THE EYE OF THE TIGER (1977, US/Brit.)

Weaver, Dennis
GENTLE GIANT (1967)

Webb, Clifton
CHEAPER BY THE DOZEN (1950)
DREAMBOAT (1952)
MR. SCOUTMASTER (1953)
SITTING PRETTY (1948)
STARS AND STRIPES FOREVER (1952)

Weidler, Virginia
LADDIE (1935)
YOUNGEST PROFESSION, THE (1943)

Weingaertner, Vit
WISHING MACHINE (1971, Czech.)

Weissmuller, Johnny
TARZAN THE APE MAN (1932)

Welch, Raquel
FANTASTIC VOYAGE (1966)

Welles, Orson
BUGS BUNNY, SUPERSTAR (1975)
MOBY DICK (1956, Brit.)

Welles, Virginia
FRANCIS IN THE HAUNTED HOUSE (1956)

Westley, Helen
HEIDI (1937)

Wheeler, Bert
CUCKOOS, THE (1930)

Whelan, Arleen
KIDNAPPED (1938)

Whitaker, Johnny
TOM SAWYER (1973)

White, Jesse
CALLAWAY WENT THATAWAY (1951)

Whitelaw, Billie
WATER BABIES, THE (1979, Brit.)

Whiting, Margaret
SINBAD AND THE EYE OF THE TIGER (1977, US/Brit.)

Whitman, Stuart
THOSE MAGNIFICENT MEN IN THEIR FLYING MACHINES OR HOW I FLEW FROM LONDON TO PARIS IN 25 HOURS AND 11 MINUTES (1965, Brit.)

Whitmore, James
NEXT VOICE YOU HEAR, THE (1950)
OKLAHOMA! (1955)

Whitty, Dame May
LASSIE, COME HOME (1943)
MADAME CURIE (1943)

Widmark, Richard
ALAMO, THE (1960)
O. HENRY'S FULL HOUSE (1952)

Wiggins, Tudi
MY SIDE OF THE MOUNTAIN (1969)

Wild, Jack
FLIGHT OF THE DOVES (1971)
MELODY (1971, Brit.)
OLIVER! (1968, Brit.)

Wilde, Cornel
GREATEST SHOW ON EARTH, THE
(1952)

Wilder, Gene
WILLY WONKA AND THE
CHOCOLATE FACTORY (1971)

Williams, Billy Dee
EMPIRE STRIKES BACK, THE (1980)

Williams, Esther
TAKE ME OUT TO THE BALL GAME
(1949)

Williams, Gwen
MR. BUG GOES TO TOWN (1941)

Williams, Rhys
FARMER'S DAUGHTER, THE (1947)
HILLS OF HOME (1948)

Wills, Chill
CATTLE DRIVE (1951)
YEARLING, THE (1946)

Wilmer, Douglas
GOLDEN VOYAGE OF SINBAD, THE
(1974, Brit.)

Wilson, Dana
CRY FROM THE STREET, A (1959, Brit.)

Winchell, Paul
ARISTOCATS, THE (1970)

Windom, William
NOW YOU SEE HIM, NOW YOU DON'T
(1972)

Winfield, Paul
SOUNDER (1972)
STAR TREK II: THE WRATH OF KHAN
(1982)

Winninger, Charles
BABES IN ARMS (1939)
THREE SMART GIRLS (1937)

Winslow, George "Foghorn"
MR. SCOUTMASTER (1953)
ROOM FOR ONE MORE (1952)

Winters, Jonathan
IT'S A MAD, MAD, MAD, MAD WORLD
(1963)

Winters, Shelley
PETE'S DRAGON (1977)

Winwood, Estelle
ALIVE AND KICKING (1962, Brit.)

Wise, Ray
JOURNEY OF NATTY GANN, THE
(1985)

Witherspoon, Cora
BANK DICK, THE (1940)

Wolfe, Ian
MAGNIFICENT YANKEE, THE (1950)

Wood, Natalie
MIRACLE ON 34TH STREET, THE
(1947)

Wood, Peggy
SOUND OF MUSIC, THE (1965)

Woods, Ilene
CINDERELLA (1950)

Woolsey, Robert
CUCKOOS, THE (1930)

Wray, Fay
KING KONG (1933)

Wright, Teresa
PRIDE OF THE YANKEES, THE (1942)

Wyman, Jane
POLLYANNA (1960)
STORY OF WILL ROGERS, THE (1952)
YEARLING, THE (1946)

Wynn, Ed
ALICE IN WONDERLAND (1951)
GNOME-MOBILE, THE (1967)
SON OF FLUBBER (1963)
THOSE CALLOWAYS (1964)

Wynn, Keenan
ABSENT-MINDED PROFESSOR, THE
(1961)
ANGELS IN THE OUTFIELD (1951)
FEARLESS FAGAN (1952)
HERBIE RIDES AGAIN (1974)
SEE HERE, PRIVATE HARGROVE
(1944)
SHAGGY D.A., THE (1976)
SON OF FLUBBER (1963)
THREE MUSKETEERS, THE (1948)

York, Richard [Dick York]
MY SISTER EILEEN (1955)

York, Jeff
JOHNNY TREMAIN (1957)

York, Susannah
SUPERMAN II (1980)

Young, Alan
TIME MACHINE, THE (1960, Brit./US)
TOM THUMB (1958, Brit./US)

Young, Gig
AIR FORCE (1943)

Young, Loretta
CALL OF THE WILD (1935)
COME TO THE STABLE (1949)
FARMER'S DAUGHTER, THE (1947)
KENTUCKY (1938)
STORY OF ALEXANDER GRAHAM
BELL, THE (1939)

Young, Robert
CANTERVILLE GHOST, THE (1944)
JOURNEY FOR MARGARET (1942)
KID FROM SPAIN, THE (1932)
SITTING PRETTY (1948)
STOWAWAY (1936)

Young, Roland
TOPPER (1937)

Zerman, Milan
WISHING MACHINE (1971, Czech.)

Zola, Jean-Pierre
MY UNCLE (1958, Fr.)

CINEMATOGRAPHERS

Ahern, Lloyd
MIRACLE ON 34TH STREET, THE
(1947)
O. HENRY'S FULL HOUSE (1952)
SAND CASTLE, THE (1961)

Alekan, Henri
BEAUTY AND THE BEAST (1947, Fr.)

Allen, James
BELSTONE FOX, THE (1976, Brit.)

Almendros, Nestor
WILD CHILD, THE (1970, Fr.)

Alonzo, John A.
BAD NEWS BEARS, THE (1976)
CLOSE ENCOUNTERS OF THE THIRD
KIND (1977)
SOUNDER (1972)

Alton, John
FATHER'S LITTLE DIVIDEND (1951)

Anders, Gunther
SWAN LAKE, THE (1967)

Andriot, Lucien
CHARLIE CHAN AT THE OPERA (1936)

Arling, Arthur
YEARLING, THE (1946)

Ash, Jerry
FLASH GORDON (1936)

Assuerus, Jacques
HERE COMES SANTA CLAUS (1984)

Avil, Gordon
CHAMP, THE (1931)

Bacon III, William V.
NIKKI, WILD DOG OF THE NORTH
(1961, US/Can.)

Badal, Jean
PLAYTIME (1973, Fr.)

Ballard, Lucien
O. HENRY'S FULL HOUSE (1952)
PARENT TRAP, THE (1961)
TRUE GRIT (1969)

Barnes, George
BELLS OF ST. MARY'S, THE (1945)
EMPEROR WALTZ, THE (1948)
GREATEST SHOW ON EARTH, THE
(1952)
SINBAD THE SAILOR (1947)
STANLEY AND LIVINGSTONE (1939)

Beebe, Lloyd
NIKKI, WILD DOG OF THE NORTH
(1961, US/Can.)

Beeson, Paul
AFRICA--TEXAS STYLE! (1967 US/Brit.)

CINEMATOGRAPHERS

GREYFRIARS BOBBY (1961, Brit.)
IN SEARCH OF THE CASTAWAYS (1962, Brit.)
LITTLEST HORSE THIEVES, THE (1977)
MOON-SPINNERS, THE (1964)
THREE LIVES OF THOMASINA, THE (1963, US/Brit.)

Berenguer, Manuel
KING OF KINGS (1961)

Biddle, Adrian
PRINCESS BRIDE, THE (1987)

Biroc, Joseph
FITZWILLY (1967)
IT'S A WONDERFUL LIFE (1946)

Biziou, Peter
BUGSY MALONE (1976, Brit.)
TIME BANDITS (1981, Brit.)

Blundell, Dick
CHARLOTTE'S WEB (1973)
MAN CALLED FLINTSTONE, THE (1966)

Blythe, Sydney
SCROOGE (1935, Brit.)

Boren, Lamar
CLARENCE, THE CROSS-EYED LION (1965)
FLIPPER (1963)
FLIPPER'S NEW ADVENTURE (1964)

Borghi, Gene
MAN CALLED FLINTSTONE, THE (1966)

Borrodaile, Osmond
THIEF OF BAGHDAD, THE (1940, Brit.)

Bourgoin, Jean
MY UNCLE (1958, Fr.)

Boyd, Russell
PHAR LAP (1984, Aus.)

Boyle, Charles
DAVY CROCKETT, KING OF THE WILD FRONTIER (1955)
FUN AND FANCY FREE (1947)
JOHNNY TREMAIN (1957)
OLD YELLER (1957)

Boyle, John W.
RIDE 'EM COWBOY (1942)

Bradford, William
LAST ROUND-UP, THE (1947)
MY PAL TRIGGER (1946)

Bredell, Elwood
AMAZING MRS. HOLLIDAY (1943)
HOLD THAT GHOST (1941)
INSPECTOR GENERAL, THE (1949)

Brodine, Norbert
SITTING PRETTY (1948)
TOPPER (1937)

Bronner, Robert
POCKETFUL OF MIRACLES (1961)
SEVEN FACES OF DR. LAO (1964)

Brower, Otto
STANLEY AND LIVINGSTONE (1939)

Brun, Joseph
FLIPPER (1963)
TRUMAN CAPOTE'S TRILOGY (1969)

Buehre, John
OF STARS AND MEN (1961)

Burks, Robert
MUSIC MAN, THE (1962)
ROOM FOR ONE MORE (1952)
SPIRIT OF ST. LOUIS, THE (1957)

Burton, Geoff
STORM BOY (1976, Aus.)

Burum, Stephen H.
NUTCRACKER: THE MOTION PICTURE (1986)

Bush, Dick
JOURNEY OF NATTY GANN, THE (1985)

Butler, David L.
FRASIER, THE SENSUOUS LION (1973)

Butler, Laurence
ADVENTURES OF MARK TWAIN, THE (1944)

Caparros, Ernesto
MIRACLE WORKER, THE (1962)

Carbajal, J. Carlos
LITTLEST OUTLAW, THE (1955)

Cardiff, Jack
AFRICAN QUEEN, THE (1951, US/Brit.)
MAGIC BOX, THE (1952, Brit.)

Cavelli, Daniel
DAYDREAMER, THE (1966)

Challis, Christopher
CHITTY CHITTY BANG BANG (1968, Brit.)
THOSE MAGNIFICENT MEN IN THEIR FLYING MACHINES OR HOW I FLEW FROM LONDON TO PARIS IN 25 HOURS AND 11 MINUTES (1965, Brit.)

Clarke, Charles
MIRACLE ON 34TH STREET, THE (1947)
STARS AND STRIPES FOREVER (1952)
THUNDERHEAD-SON OF FLICKA (1945)

Cline, Wilfrid
ADVENTURES OF TOM SAWYER, THE (1938)
STORY OF WILL ROGERS, THE (1952)

Clothier, William H.
ALAMO, THE (1960)
GOODBYE, MY LADY (1956)

Colman, Edward
ABSENT-MINDED PROFESSOR, THE (1961)
ADVENTURES OF BULLWHIP GRIFFIN, THE (1967)
BLACKBEARD'S GHOST (1968)
GNOME-MOBILE, THE (1967)
LOVE BUG, THE (1968)
MARY POPPINS (1964)
SHAGGY DOG, THE (1959)
SON OF FLUBBER (1963)
THAT DARN CAT (1965)

THOSE CALLOWAYS (1964)

Coop, Denys
LITTLE ARK, THE (1972)
MY SIDE OF THE MOUNTAIN (1969)

Cooper, Wilkie
JASON AND THE ARGONAUTS (1963, Brit.)
MYSTERIOUS ISLAND (1961, US/Brit.)
PICKWICK PAPERS, THE (1952, Brit.)
SEVENTH VOYAGE OF SINBAD, THE (1958)
WEE GEORDIE (1956, Brit.)

Corby, Francis
BABES IN TOYLAND (1934)

Correll, Charles
STAR TREK III: THE SEARCH FOR SPOCK (1984)

Couffer, Jack
NIKKI, WILD DOG OF THE NORTH (1961, US/Can.)

Crabe, James
KARATE KID, THE (1984)

Cronenweth, Jordon
TRUMAN CAPOTE'S TRILOGY (1969)

Cronjager, Edward
HOME IN INDIANA (1944)
YOUNG PEOPLE (1940)

Cross, Eric
LITTLE KIDNAPPERS, THE (1954, Brit.)
TIGER BAY (1959, Brit.)

Cundey, Dean
WHO FRAMED ROGER RABBIT? (1988)

Daniels, William
GIRL CRAZY (1943)
HARVEY (1950)
HOW THE WEST WAS WON (1962)

Daviau, Allen
E.T. THE EXTRA-TERRESTRIAL (1982)
EMPIRE OF THE SUN (1987)

de Grasse, Robert
BACHELOR AND THE BOBBY-SOXER, THE (1947)

De Vinna, Clyde
AH, WILDERNESS! (1935)

Decae, Henri
FOUR HUNDRED BLOWS, THE (1959)

Dempster, Austin
LITTLE ARK, THE (1972)
PETER RABBIT AND TALES OF BEATRIX POTTER (1971, Brit.)

Deschanel, Caleb
BLACK STALLION, THE (1979)

DeVinna, Clyde
TARZAN THE APE MAN (1932)
TREASURE ISLAND (1934)

Diskant, George
DAVY CROCKETT, INDIAN SCOUT (1950)

Dyer, Elmer
AIR FORCE (1943)

Eckes, Jack
1001 ARABIAN NIGHTS (1959)

Edeson, Arthur
PALOOKA (1934)
SERGEANT YORK (1941)

Epperson, George
CHARLOTTE'S WEB (1973)

Fapp, Daniel L.
GREAT ESCAPE, THE (1963)
LI'L ABNER (1959)

Fitzgerald, Ed
LASSIE'S GREAT ADVENTURE (1963)

Flekal, Charles
MAN CALLED FLINTSTONE, THE
(1966)

Folsey, George
ANIMAL CRACKERS (1930)
DEEP IN MY HEART (1954)
HARVEY GIRLS, THE (1946)
HIT THE DECK (1955)
MEET ME IN ST. LOUIS (1944)
SEVEN BRIDES FOR SEVEN
BROTHERS (1954)
TAKE ME OUT TO THE BALL GAME
(1949)

Fraker, William A.
CLOSE ENCOUNTERS OF THE THIRD
KIND (1977)

Fredericks, Ellsworth
LIGHT IN THE FOREST, THE (1958)

Freulich, Henry
BLONDIE (1938)
FIVE LITTLE PEPPERS AND HOW
THEY GREW (1939)
SHUT MY BIG MOUTH (1942)

Fryer, Richard
FLASH GORDON (1936)

Gabbani, Till
20,000 LEAGUES UNDER THE SEA
(1954)

Garmes, Lee
JUNGLE BOOK, THE (1942)
MISTY (1961)
ROSEANNA McCOY (1949)

Gaudio, Tony
ADVENTURES OF ROBIN HOOD, THE
(1938)
FIGHTING 69TH, THE (1940)
KNUTE ROCKNE--ALL AMERICAN
(1940)
STORY OF LOUIS PASTEUR, THE
(1936)

Gerrard, Henry
LITTLE WOMEN (1933)

Gerstad, Merritt B.
NIGHT AT THE OPERA, A (1935)

Gertsman, Maury
CATTLE DRIVE (1951)
MA AND PA KETTLE (1949)

Gibbs, Gerald
JOHNNY ON THE RUN (1953, Brit.)

Gilks, Alfred
EXCUSE MY DUST (1951)
LITTLE MISS MARKER (1934)
MILKY WAY, THE (1936)
PAINTED HILLS, THE (1951)
YOU'RE TELLING ME (1934)

Gilliam, Harry
CRY FROM THE STREET, A (1959, Brit.)

Glassberg, Irving
FRANCIS (1949)

Glendinning, Hone
JOHN WESLEY (1954, Brit.)

Glenn, Pierre William
LITTLE ROMANCE, A (1979, US/Fr.)
SMALL CHANGE (1976, Fr.)

Glennon, Bert
ALICE IN WONDERLAND (1933)
DRUMS ALONG THE MOHAWK (1939)
THIS IS THE ARMY (1943)

Glennon, James
FLIGHT OF THE NAVIGATOR (1986)
RETURN OF THE JEDI (1983)

Goldblatt, Stephen
YOUNG SHERLOCK HOLMES (1985)

Grant, Arthur
JOHN AND JULIE (1957, Brit.)

Grant, Stanley
JOHN WESLEY (1954, Brit.)

Green, Guy
GREAT EXPECTATIONS (1946, Brit.)
OLIVER TWIST (1951, Brit.)
STORY OF ROBIN HOOD, THE (1952,
Brit.)

Green, W. Howard
ALI BABA AND THE FORTY THIEVES
(1944)

Greene, Max
HEAVENS ABOVE! (1963, Brit.)

Griggs, Loyal
SHANE (1953)
TEN COMMANDMENTS, THE (1956)
WHITE CHRISTMAS (1954)

Guffey, Burnett
GIDGET (1959)

Guthrie, Carl
CHRISTMAS IN CONNECTICUT (1945)

Hall, Alan
GLITTERBALL, THE (1977, Brit.)

Hall, Conrad
TRUMAN CAPOTE'S TRILOGY (1969)

Hall, Robert
CLOSE ENCOUNTERS OF THE THIRD
KIND (1977)

Hammeras, Ralph
20,000 LEAGUES UNDER THE SEA
(1954)

Harlan, Russell
POLLYANNA (1960)
TO KILL A MOCKINGBIRD (1962)

Harris, John
HOPE AND GLORY (1987, Brit.)

Heller, Otto
DOG OF FLANDERS, A (1959)

Hickox, Sid
HORN BLOWS AT MIDNIGHT, THE
(1945)

Hildyard, Jack
BATTLE OF THE BULGE (1965)

Hillier, Erwin
BOY TEN FEET TALL, A (1965, Brit.)
SCHOOL FOR SCOUNDRELS (1960,
Brit.)
WHERE'S CHARLEY? (1952, Brit.)

Hoch, Winton C.
DARBY O'GILL AND THE LITTLE
PEOPLE (1959)
SO DEAR TO MY HEART (1949)
THREE GODFATHERS, THE (1948)
VOYAGE TO THE BOTTOM OF THE
SEA (1961)

Holender, Adam
BOY WHO COULD FLY, THE (1986)

Hora, Anthony
FABULOUS WORLD OF JULES
VERNE, THE (1961, Czech.)

Horsley, David S.
JACK THE GIANT KILLER (1962)

Howe, James Wong
ABE LINCOLN IN ILLINOIS (1940)
ADVENTURES OF TOM SAWYER, THE
(1938)
AIR FORCE (1943)
YANKEE DOODLE DANDY (1942)

Huke, Bob
BATTLE OF BRITAIN, THE (1969, Brit.)

Hume, Alan
RETURN OF THE JEDI (1983)

Hunt, J. Roy
ANNIE OAKLEY (1935)

Hutchcroft, Roy
GAY PURR-EE (1962)

Ibbetson, Arthur
ALL THINGS BRIGHT AND
BEAUTIFUL (1979, Brit.)
FIGHTING PRINCE OF DONEGAL,
THE (1966, Brit.)
WILLY WONKA AND THE
CHOCOLATE FACTORY (1971)

Imi, Tony
SLIPPER AND THE ROSE, THE (1976,
Brit.)

Ivano, Paul
CHAMPAGNE FOR CAESAR (1950)

Jarel, Don
CLOSE ENCOUNTERS OF THE THIRD
KIND (1977)

Jewell, Ray
NIKKI, WILD DOG OF THE NORTH
(1961, US/Can.)

Jiuliano, Joe
SECRET OF NIMH, THE (1982)

CINEMATOGRAPHERS

Jordan, Larry
HILDUR AND THE MAGICIAN (1969)

June, Ray
BABES IN ARMS (1939)
CALLAWAY WENT THATAWAY (1951)
COURT JESTER, THE (1956)
JOURNEY FOR MARGARET (1942)
SECRET GARDEN, THE (1949)
SOUTHERN YANKEE, A (1948)
STRIKE UP THE BAND (1940)
SUN COMES UP, THE (1949)
TREASURE ISLAND (1934)

Kaplan, Ervin L.
PINOCCHIO AND THE EMPEROR OF THE NIGHT (1987)

Kaufman, Boris
WORLD OF HENRY ORIENT, THE (1964)

Keegan, Duane
GAY PURR-EE (1962)

Kelley, Wallace
GREATEST SHOW ON EARTH, THE (1952)
TEN COMMANDMENTS, THE (1956)

Klardie, Hans
WOLFPEN PRINCIPLE, THE (1974, Can.)

Kline, Benjamin
KONGA, THE WILD STALLION (1939)

Kline, Richard H.
STAR TREK: THE MOTION PICTURE (1979)

Kolin, Jiri
WISHING MACHINE (1971, Czech.)

Kotler, Bill
MAN CALLED FLINTSTONE, THE (1966)

Kovacs, Laszlo
CLOSE ENCOUNTERS OF THE THIRD KIND (1977)
WHAT'S UP, DOC? (1972)

Krasner, Milton
ARABIAN NIGHTS (1942)
BANK DICK, THE (1940)
COURTSHIP OF EDDIE'S FATHER, THE (1963)
DREAMBOAT (1952)
FARMER'S DAUGHTER, THE (1947)
HOW THE WEST WAS WON (1962)
KING OF KINGS (1961)
O. HENRY'S FULL HOUSE (1952)

Kruger, Jules
SIDEWALKS OF LONDON (1940, Brit.)

La Shelle, Joseph
COME TO THE STABLE (1949)
MR. SCOUTMASTER (1953)

Lang, Charles
FATHER GOOSE (1964)
GHOST AND MRS. MUIR, THE (1942)
GHOST BREAKERS, THE (1940)
HOW THE WEST WAS WON (1962)
TOM SAWYER (1930)

Lanning, Reggie
KING OF THE COWBOYS (1943)
SANDS OF IWO JIMA (1949)

Lapierre, Claude
TIKI TIKI (1971, Can.)

LaShelle, Joseph
HOW THE WEST WAS WON (1962)
MISTER 880 (1950)

Laszlo, Ernest
FANTASTIC VOYAGE (1966)
IT'S A MAD, MAD, MAD, MAD WORLD (1963)
ROAD TO RIO (1947)

Lawton, Charles
FULLER BRUSH GIRL, THE (1950)
HAPPY TIME, THE (1952)
MY SISTER EILEEN (1955)
SEE HERE, PRIVATE HARGROVE (1944)
YOUNGEST PROFESSION, THE (1943)

Le Picard, Marcel
LET'S GO NAVY (1951)
NEWS HOUNDS (1947)

Leacock, Richard
LOUISIANA STORY (1948)

Leicester, James
ADVENTURES OF MARK TWAIN, THE (1944)

Lewiston, Denis
SWALLOWS AND AMAZONS (1977, Brit.)

Linden, Edward
ADVENTURES OF MARK TWAIN, THE (1944)
KING KONG (1933)

Lindon, Lionel
AROUND THE WORLD IN 80 DAYS (1956)
GOING MY WAY (1944)
GREAT RUPERT, THE (1950)
ROAD TO UTOPIA (1945)

Lipstein, Harold
FEARLESS FAGAN (1952)
MAN CALLED PETER, A (1955)
PAINTED HILLS, THE (1951)

Lloyd, Art
BABES IN TOYLAND (1934)
BLOCKHEADS (1938)
FLYING DEUCES, THE (1939)
WAY OUT WEST (1937)

Lowin, Jack
RETURN OF THE JEDI (1983)

Luff, William
SCROOGE (1935, Brit.)

Lundin, Walter
WAY OUT WEST (1937)

MacDonald, Joe
IT HAPPENS EVERY SPRING (1949)
O. HENRY'S FULL HOUSE (1952)

Mankofsky, Isidore
MUPPET MOVIE, THE (1979)

Marley, J. Peverell
GREATEST SHOW ON EARTH, THE (1952)
CHARLEY'S AUNT (1941)
COUNT OF MONTE CRISTO, THE (1934)
LIFE WITH FATHER (1947)
SPIRIT OF ST. LOUIS, THE (1957)
TEN COMMANDMENTS, THE (1956)

Marsh, Oliver T.
DAVID COPPERFIELD (1935)
TALE OF TWO CITIES, A (1935)

Mate, Rudolph
PRIDE OF THE YANKEES, THE (1942)

McAdoo, Tom
COURT JESTER, THE (1956)

McCord, Ted
ADVENTURES OF HUCKLEBERRY FINN, THE (1960)
SOUND OF MUSIC, THE (1965)

McHugh, Thomas
SEA GYPSIES, THE (1978)

Mellor, William C.
MR. HOBBS TAKES A VACATION (1962)
NEXT VOICE YOU HEAR, THE (1950)
ROAD TO MOROCCO (1942)

Mellquist, Jeff
SECRET OF NIMH, THE (1982)

Mescall, John
DAVY CROCKETT, INDIAN SCOUT (1950)
HENRY ALDRICH FOR PRESIDENT (1941)

Metty, Russell
STORY OF G.I. JOE, THE (1945)

Michalak, Richard
TAIL OF THE TIGER (1984, Aus.)

Migliori, Ralph
CHARLOTTE'S WEB (1973)

Miller, Arthur
BRIGHT EYES (1934)
HEIDI (1937)
HOW GREEN WAS MY VALLEY (1941)
LITTLE PRINCESS, THE (1939)
SONG OF BERNADETTE, THE (1943)
STOWAWAY (1936)
WEE WILLIE WINKIE (1937)

Miller, Dan
GAY PURR-EE (1962)

Miller, Ernest
BELLS OF ROSARITA (1945)

Milner, Victor
WONDER MAN (1945)

Mochinag, Tad
DAYDREAMER, THE (1966)

Moore, Richard
ANNIE (1982)

Moore, Ted
GOLDEN VOYAGE OF SINBAD, THE (1974, Brit.)

SINBAD AND THE EYE OF THE TIGER (1977, US/Brit.)

Morris, Oswald
GREAT MUPPET CAPER, THE (1981)
MOBY DICK (1956, Brit.)
OLIVER! (1968, Brit.)
SCROOGE (1970, Brit.)

Morris, Reginald H.
CHRISTMAS STORY, A (1983)

Muren, Dennis
CLOSE ENCOUNTERS OF THE THIRD KIND (1977)

Musuraca, Nicholas
BACHELOR AND THE BOBBY-SOXER, THE (1947)
I REMEMBER MAMA (1948)

Narita, Hiro
NEVER CRY WOLF (1983)
SYLVESTER (1985)

Neame, Ronald
YANK IN THE R.A.F., A (1941)

Neumann, Harry
JALOPY (1953)

Nykvist, Sven
DOVE, THE (1974, Brit.)

Ornitz, Arthur J.
FOREVER YOUNG, FOREVER FREE (1976, South Africa)
WORLD OF HENRY ORIENT, THE (1964)

Palmer, Ernest
CONNECTICUT YANKEE, A (1931)
KENTUCKY (1938)

Paniagua, Cecilio
DR. COPPELIUS (1968, US/Span.)

Parrish, Frank
MAN CALLED FLINTSTONE, THE (1966)

Pavey, Stanley
BELLES OF ST. TRINIAN'S, THE (1954, Brit.)

Paynter, Robert
MUPPETS TAKE MANHATTAN, THE (1984)
SUPERMAN II (1980)

Peach, Kenneth
INCREDIBLE JOURNEY, THE (1963)

Perinal, Georges
THIEF OF BAGHDAD, THE (1940, Brit.)
TOM THUMB (1958, Brit./US)

Peterman, Don
STAR TREK IV: THE VOYAGE HOME (1986)

Philips, Alex
ADVENTURES OF ROBINSON CRUSOE, THE (1954)
LITTLEST OUTLAW, THE (1955)

Phillips, Frank
BEDKNOBS AND BROOMSTICKS (1971)

COMPUTER WORE TENNIS SHOES, THE (1970)
ESCAPE TO WITCH MOUNTAIN (1975)
HERBIE RIDES AGAIN (1974)
ISLAND AT THE TOP OF THE WORLD, THE (1974)
NOW YOU SEE HIM, NOW YOU DON'T (1972)
PETE'S DRAGON (1977)
SHAGGY D.A., THE (1976)
WORLD'S GREATEST ATHLETE, THE (1973)

Piccard, B.S.
FABULOUS WORLD OF JULES VERNE, THE (1961, Czech.)

Planck, Robert
CANTERVILLE GHOST, THE (1944)
GIRL CRAZY (1943)
LILI (1953)
THREE MUSKETEERS, THE (1948)

Planer, Franz F.
5,000 FINGERS OF DR. T., THE (1953)
KING OF KINGS (1961)
20,000 LEAGUES UNDER THE SEA (1954)

Polito, Sol
ADVENTURES OF MARK TWAIN, THE (1944)
ADVENTURES OF ROBIN HOOD, THE (1938)
ANGELS WITH DIRTY FACES (1938)
PRINCE AND THE PAUPER, THE (1937)
SERGEANT YORK (1941)
THIS IS THE ARMY (1943)

Pope, R.W.
MIGHTY MOUSE IN THE GREAT SPACE CHASE (1983)

Poster, Steven
BOY WHO COULD FLY, THE (1986)

Pratt, John
MAN CALLED FLINTSTONE, THE (1966)

Reddy, Don
BENJI (1974)
FOR THE LOVE OF BENJI (1977)

Reed, Michael
MOON-SPINNERS, THE (1964)

Rennahan, Ray
CONNECTICUT YANKEE IN KING ARTHUR'S COURT, A (1949)
DRUMS ALONG THE MOHAWK (1939)
KENTUCKY (1938)
THREE CABALLEROS, THE (1944)

Rescher, Gayne
STAR TREK II: THE WRATH OF KHAN (1982)

Robinson, George
ALI BABA AND THE FORTY THIEVES (1944)
FRANCIS IN THE HAUNTED HOUSE (1956)
HERE COME THE CO-EDS (1945)
MA AND PA KETTLE ON VACATION (1953)

Rosher, Charles
ANNIE GET YOUR GUN (1950)
CALL OF THE WILD (1935)
LITTLE LORD FAUNTLEROY (1936)
ONE FOOT IN HEAVEN (1941)
YEARLING, THE (1946)

Rosson, Harold
CAPTAINS COURAGEOUS (1937)
EDISON, THE MAN (1940)
MY BROTHER TALKS TO HORSES (1946)
STRATTON STORY, THE (1949)
TARZAN THE APE MAN (1932)
TREASURE ISLAND (1934)
WIZARD OF OZ, THE (1939)
YANK AT OXFORD, A (1938)

Rousselot, Philippe
HOPE AND GLORY (1987, Brit.)

Russell, Jack
SO THIS IS NEW YORK (1948)

Ruttenberg, Joseph
DAY AT THE RACES, A (1937)
MADAME CURIE (1943)
MAGNIFICENT YANKEE, THE (1950)

Scaife, Ted
WATER BABIES, THE (1979, Brit.)

Schettler, Charles
GULLIVER'S TRAVELS (1939)

Schnettler, Charles
MR. BUG GOES TO TOWN (1941)

Schoenbaum, Charles
CHALLENGE TO LASSIE (1949)
HILLS OF HOME (1948)
SON OF LASSIE (1945)
SUMMER HOLIDAY (1948)

Seitz, John
CAPTAIN JANUARY (1935)
HUCKLEBERRY FINN (1939)
LITTLEST REBEL, THE (1935)

Senftleben, Gunther
EMIL AND THE DETECTIVES (1964)

Seresin, Michael
BUGSY MALONE (1976, Brit.)

Shamroy, Leon
ADVENTURES OF SHERLOCK HOLMES, THE (1939)
BEST THINGS IN LIFE ARE FREE, THE (1956)
BUFFALO BILL (1944)
CHEAPER BY THE DOZEN (1950)
KING AND I, THE (1956)
STORY OF ALEXANDER GRAHAM BELL, THE (1939)
YANK IN THE R.A.F., A (1941)

Sharp, Henry
ALICE IN WONDERLAND (1933)
DUCK SOUP (1933)
IT'S A GIFT (1934)

Sharpe, Graham
DOT AND THE KOALA (1985, Aus.)

Shiffman, Hal
MAN CALLED FLINTSTONE, THE (1966)

CINEMATOGRAPHERS

Shorr, Lester
PHANTOM TOLLBOOTH, THE (1970)

Sickner, William
BOMBA THE JUNGLE BOY (1949)
LIVE WIRES (1946)

Siegel, Don
ADVENTURES OF MARK TWAIN, THE
(1944)

Skall, William V.
KIM (1950)
LIFE WITH FATHER (1947)
LITTLE PRINCESS, THE (1939)

Skinner, Frank
ABBOTT AND COSTELLO MEET
FRANKENSTEIN (1948)

Slocombe, Douglas
BOY WHO STOLE A MILLION, THE
(1960, Brit.)
CLOSE ENCOUNTERS OF THE THIRD
KIND (1977)

Smith, Leonard M.
AT THE CIRCUS (1939)
COURAGE OF LASSIE (1946)
LASSIE, COME HOME (1943)
NATIONAL VELVET (1944)
YEARLING, THE (1946)

Snyder, William
MOON PILOT (1962)
RASCAL (1969)
SUMMER MAGIC (1963)
TOBY TYLER (1960)
WONDER MAN (1945)

Stainback, Norman
MAN CALLED FLINTSTONE, THE
(1966)

Stanley, Frank
TOM SAWYER (1973)

Stevens, Jack
GAY PURR-EE (1962)

Stewart, Dave
CLOSE ENCOUNTERS OF THE THIRD
KIND (1977)

Stine, Clifford
FLUFFY (1965)
FOLLOW ME, BOYS! (1966)

Strading, Harry
EASTER PARADE (1948)
HANS CHRISTIAN ANDERSEN (1952)
HELLO, DOLLY! (1969)
IN THE GOOD OLD SUMMERTIME
(1949)
MY FAIR LADY (1964)

Struss, Karl
CAUGHT IN THE DRAFT (1941)
SING YOU SINNERS (1938)
SKIPPY (1931)

Sundby, Harry
TRUMAN CAPOTE'S TRILOGY (1969)

Surenskiy, Dmitriy
JACK FROST (1966, USSR)

Surtees, Robert
DATE WITH JUDY, A (1948)

DOCTOR DOLITTLE (1967)
KING SOLOMON'S MINES (1950)
OKLAHOMA! (1955)

Suschitzky, Peter
ALL CREATURES GREAT AND SMALL
(1975, Brit.)
MELODY (1971, Brit.)
EMPIRE STRIKES BACK, THE (1980)

Talbot, Kenneth
BORN FREE (1966)

Tannura, Phillip
BABE RUTH STORY, THE (1948)

Taran, George
FABULOUS WORLD OF JULES
VERNE, THE (1961, Czech.)

Taylor, Gilbert
ALIVE AND KICKING (1962, Brit.)
STAR WARS (1977)

Taylor, J.O.
KING KONG (1933)

Tetzlaff, Ted
ROAD TO ZANZIBAR (1941)

Thompson, Stuart
DEAR WIFE (1949)

Thomson, Alex
LABYRINTH (1986)

Tobin, Bill
THUMBELINA (1970)

Toland, Gregg
KID FROM BOOKLYN, THE (1946)
KID FROM SPAIN, THE (1932)
KIDNAPPED (1938)
SONG OF THE SOUTH (1946)

Tover, Leo
ISLAND OF THE BLUE DOLPHINS
(1964)
JOURNEY TO THE CENTER OF THE
EARTH (1959)
MISTY (1961)
PRIDE OF ST. LOUIS, THE (1952)

Unsworth, Geoffrey
SUPERMAN (1978)
SUPERMAN II (1980)

Valentine, Joseph
HOLD THAT GHOST (1941)
ONE NIGHT IN THE TROPICS (1940)
THREE SMART GIRLS (1937)

Van Enger, Charles
ABBOTT AND COSTELLO MEET
FRANKENSTEIN (1948)
AFRICA SCREAMS (1949)
NOOSE HANGS HIGH, THE (1948)
TIME OF THEIR LIVES, THE (1946)

Vasu, Nick
BON VOYAGE, CHARLIE BROWN
(AND DON'T COME BACK) (1980)
SNOOPY, COME HOME (1972)

Vogel, Paul C.
ANGELS IN THE OUTFIELD (1951)
TIME MACHINE, THE (1960, Brit./US)
WONDERFUL WORLD OF THE
BROTHERS GRIMM, THE (1962)

Vojta, Jiri
MIDSUMMER NIGHT'S DREAM, A
(1961, Czech.)

Wade, Roy
CHARLOTTE'S WEB (1973)
MAN CALLED FLINTSTONE, THE
(1966)

Wagner, Sidney
BATAAN (1943)
BOYS TOWN (1938)
CHRISTMAS CAROL, A (1938)
YOUNG TOM EDISON (1940)

Walker, Joseph
IT'S A WONDERFUL LIFE (1946)
MR. SMITH GOES TO WASHINGTON
(1939)
MY SISTER EILEEN (1942)
TALES OF MANHATTAN (1942)

Walker, Vernon L.
KING KONG (1933)

Warren, Charles
SECRET OF NIMH, THE (1982)

Warren, John F.
SEVEN LITTLE FOYS, THE (1955)
TEN COMMANDMENTS, THE (1956)

Watkin, David
CHARIOTS OF FIRE (1981, Brit.)

Waxman, Harry
FLIGHT OF THE DOVES (1971)
SWISS FAMILY ROBINSON (1960)

Weaver, Dennis
CHARLOTTE'S WEB (1973)

Wellman, Harold
HOW THE WEST WAS WON (1962)
INVISIBLE BOY, THE (1957)

Wenstrom, Harold
LADDIE (1935)

Wheeler, Charles F.
BAREFOOT EXECUTIVE, THE (1971)
CAT FROM OUTER SPACE, THE (1978)
FREAKY FRIDAY (1976)
YOURS, MINE AND OURS (1968)

White, Lester
FULLER BRUSH MAN (1948)
JUDGE HARDY AND SON (1939)
JUDGE HARDY'S CHILDREN (1938)
LOVE FINDS ANDY HARDY (1938)

Wilcox, John
BELSTONE FOX, THE (1976, Brit.)
MOON-SPINNERS, THE (1964)
MOUSE THAT ROARED, THE (1959,
Brit.)

Wilder, Donald
NIKKI, WILD DOG OF THE NORTH
(1961, US/Can.)

Williams, Billy
MANHATTAN PROJECT, THE (1986)

Winding, Andreas
PLAYTIME (1973, Fr.)

Winner, Howard
GENTLE GIANT (1967)

Woxholt, Egil
MYSTERIOUS ISLAND (1961, US/Brit.)

Wrigley, Dewey
MY FRIEND FLICKA (1943)

Yamazaki, Yoshihiro
ALONE ON THE PACIFIC (1964, Jap.)

Young, Freddie
BATTLE OF BRITAIN, THE (1969, Brit.)
GOODBYE MR. CHIPS (1939, Brit.)
INN OF THE SIXTH HAPPINESS, THE (1958)
TREASURE ISLAND (1950, Brit.)
Yuricich, Richard
CLOSE ENCOUNTERS OF THE THIRD KIND (1977)

Zsigmond, Vilmos
CLOSE ENCOUNTERS OF THE THIRD KIND (1977)

DIRECTORS

Algar, James
ADVENTURES OF ICHABOD AND MR. TOAD (1949)
FANTASIA (1940)

Allen, Irwin
VOYAGE TO THE BOTTOM OF THE SEA (1961)

Anderson, Michael
AROUND THE WORLD IN 80 DAYS (1956)

Annakin, Ken
BATTLE OF THE BULGE (1965)
STORY OF ROBIN HOOD, THE (1952, Brit.)
SWISS FAMILY ROBINSON (1960)
THOSE MAGNIFICENT MEN IN THEIR FLYING MACHINES OR HOW I FLEW FROM LONDON TO PARIS IN 25 HOURS AND 11 MINUTES (1965, Brit.)

Armstrong, Samuel
FANTASIA (1940)

Arnold, Jack
MOUSE THAT ROARED, THE (1959, Brit.)

Avildsen, John G.
KARATE KID, THE (1984)

Bacon, Lloyd
FULLER BRUSH GIRL, THE (1950)
IT HAPPENS EVERY SPRING (1949)
KNUTE ROCKNE--ALL AMERICAN (1940)

Ballard, Carroll
BLACK STALLION, THE (1979)
NEVER CRY WOLF (1983)
NUTCRACKER: THE MOTION PICTURE (1986)

Barbera, Joseph
MAN CALLED FLINTSTONE, THE (1966)

Barton, Charles
ABBOTT AND COSTELLO MEET FRANKENSTEIN (1948)
AFRICA SCREAMS (1949)
FIVE LITTLE PEPPERS AND HOW THEY GREW (1939)
NOOSE HANGS HIGH, THE (1948)
SHAGGY DOG, THE (1959)
SHUT MY BIG MOUTH (1942)
TIME OF THEIR LIVES, THE (1946)
TOBY TYLER (1960)

Bass, Jules
DAYDREAMER, THE (1966)
WACKY WORLD OF MOTHER GOOSE, THE (1967)

Beaudine, William
JALOPY (1953)
LASSIE'S GREAT ADVENTURE (1963)
LET'S GO NAVY (1951)
NEWS HOUNDS (1947)

Beebe, Ford
BOMBA THE JUNGLE BOY (1949)
FANTASIA (1940)

Bellamy, Earl
FLUFFY (1965)

Bennett, Compton
KING SOLOMON'S MINES (1950)

Bennett, Hugh
HENRY ALDRICH FOR PRESIDENT (1941)

Benson, Leon
FLIPPER'S NEW ADVENTURE (1964)

Berger, Ludwig
THIEF OF BAGHDAD, THE (1940, Brit.)

Berkeley, Busby
BABES IN ARMS (1939)
STRIKE UP THE BAND (1940)
TAKE ME OUT TO THE BALL GAME (1949)

Berman, Ted
FOX AND THE HOUND, THE (1981)

Binyon, Claude
DREAMBOAT (1952)

Bluth, Don
AMERICAN TAIL, AN (1986)
SECRET OF NIMH, THE (1982)

Blystone, John G.
BLOCKHEADS (1938)

Bogdanovich, Peter
WHAT'S UP, DOC? (1972)

Boorman, John
HOPE AND GLORY (1987, Brit.)

Boulting, John
HEAVENS ABOVE! (1963, Brit.)
MAGIC BOX, THE (1952, Brit.)

Branss, Truck
SWAN LAKE, THE (1967)

Brickman, Marshall
MANHATTAN PROJECT, THE (1986)

Brown, Clarence
AH, WILDERNESS! (1935)

ANGELS IN THE OUTFIELD (1951)
EDISON, THE MAN (1940)
NATIONAL VELVET (1944)
YEARLING, THE (1946)

Bunuel, Luis
ADVENTURES OF ROBINSON CRUSOE, THE (1954)

Butler, David
BRIGHT EYES (1934)
CAPTAIN JANUARY (1935)
CAUGHT IN THE DRAFT (1941)
CONNECTICUT YANKEE, A (1931)
KENTUCKY (1938)
LITTLEST REBEL, THE (1935)
ROAD TO MOROCCO (1942)
WHERE'S CHARLEY? (1952, Brit.)

Butler, Robert
BAREFOOT EXECUTIVE, THE (1971)
COMPUTER WORE TENNIS SHOES, THE (1970)
NOW YOU SEE HIM, NOW YOU DON'T (1972)

Buzzell, Edward
AT THE CIRCUS (1939)
YOUNGEST PROFESSION, THE (1943)

Camp, Joe
BENJI (1974)
FOR THE LOVE OF BENJI (1977)

Capra, Frank
IT'S A WONDERFUL LIFE (1946)
MR. SMITH GOES TO WASHINGTON (1939)
POCKETFUL OF MIRACLES (1961)

Castle, Nick
BOY WHO COULD FLY, THE (1986)

Chaffey, Don
GREYFRIARS BOBBY (1961, Brit.)

Chaffey, Don
JASON AND THE ARGONAUTS (1963, Brit.)
PETE'S DRAGON (1977)
THREE LIVES OF THOMASINA, THE (1963, US/Brit.)

Clark, Bob
CHRISTMAS STORY, A (1983)

Clark, James B.
DOG OF FLANDERS, A (1959)
FLIPPER (1963)
ISLAND OF THE BLUE DOLPHINS (1964)
LITTLE ARK, THE (1972)
MISTY (1961)
MY SIDE OF THE MOUNTAIN (1969)

Clark, Les
SLEEPING BEAUTY (1959)

Cline, Edward
BANK DICK, THE (1940)

Cockliss, Harley
GLITTERBALL, THE (1977, Brit.)

Cocteau, Jean
BEAUTY AND THE BEAST (1947, Fr.)

Conway, Jack
TALE OF TWO CITIES, A (1935)

DIRECTORS

YANK AT OXFORD, A (1938)

Cooper, Merian C.
KING KONG (1933)

Cormack, Robert
MAKE MINE MUSIC (1946)

Cottrell, William
SNOW WHITE AND THE SEVEN
DWARFS (1937)

Couffer, Jack
NIKKI, WILD DOG OF THE NORTH
(1961, US/Can.)

Crichton, Charles
BOY WHO STOLE A MILLION, THE
(1960, Brit.)

Cromwell, John
ABE LINCOLN IN ILLINOIS (1940)
LITTLE LORD FAUNTLEROY (1936)
TOM SAWYER (1930)

Cukor, George
DAVID COPPERFIELD (1935)
LITTLE WOMEN (1933)
MY FAIR LADY (1964)

Cummings, Irving
STORY OF ALEXANDER GRAHAM
BELL, THE (1939)

Curtiz, Michael
ADVENTURES OF ROBIN HOOD, THE
(1938)
ADVENTURES OF HUCKLEBERRY
FINN, THE (1960)
ANGELS WITH DIRTY FACES (1938)
BEST THINGS IN LIFE ARE FREE, THE
(1956)
LIFE WITH FATHER (1947)
STORY OF WILL ROGERS, THE (1952)
THIS IS THE ARMY (1943)
WHITE CHRISTMAS (1954)
YANKEE DOODLE DANDY (1942)

DaCosta, Morton
MUSIC MAN, THE (1962)

Darcus, Jack
WOLFPEN PRINCIPLE, THE (1974,
Can.)

Dassin, Jules
CANTERVILLE GHOST, THE (1944)

Daugherty, Herschel
LIGHT IN THE FOREST, THE (1958)

de Heer, Rolf
TAIL OF THE TIGER (1984, Aus.)

Del Ruth, Roy
BABE RUTH STORY, THE (1948)

DeMille, Cecil B.
GREATEST SHOW ON EARTH, THE
(1952)
TEN COMMANDMENTS, THE (1956)

Dieterle, William
STORY OF LOUIS PASTEUR, THE
(1936)

Donen, Stanley
DEEP IN MY HEART (1954)
FEARLESS FAGAN (1952)

SEVEN BRIDES FOR SEVEN
BROTHERS (1954)

Donner, Richard
SUPERMAN (1978)

Dukas, Paul
FANTASIA (1940)

Duvivier, Julien
TALES OF MANHATTAN (1942)

Dwan, Allan
HEIDI (1937)
SANDS OF IWO JIMA (1949)
YOUNG PEOPLE (1940)

Edwards, Henry
SCROOGE (1935, Brit.)

Endfield, Cy
MYSTERIOUS ISLAND (1961, US/Brit.)

English, John
LAST ROUND-UP, THE (1947)

Fairchild, William
JOHN AND JULIE (1957, Brit.)

Feigenbaum, Bill
HUGO THE HIPPO (1976, Hung./US)

Ferguson, Norman
FANTASIA (1940)
THREE CABALLEROS, THE (1944)

Flaherty, Robert J.
LOUISIANA STORY (1948)

Fleischer, Dave
GULLIVER'S TRAVELS (1939)
MR. BUG GOES TO TOWN (1941)

Fleischer, Richard
DOCTOR DOLITTLE (1967)
FANTASTIC VOYAGE (1966)
HAPPY TIME, THE (1952)
SO THIS IS NEW YORK (1948)
20,000 LEAGUES UNDER THE SEA
(1954)

Fleming, Victor
CAPTAINS COURAGEOUS (1937)
TREASURE ISLAND (1934)
WIZARD OF OZ, THE (1939)

Forbes, Bryan
SLIPPER AND THE ROSE, THE (1976,
Brit.)

Ford, John
DRUMS ALONG THE MOHAWK (1939)
HOW GREEN WAS MY VALLEY (1941)
HOW THE WEST WAS WON (1962)
THREE GODFATHERS, THE (1948)
WEE WILLIE WINKIE (1937)

Foster, Harve
SONG OF THE SOUTH (1946)

Foster, Norman
DAVY CROCKETT, KING OF THE WILD
FRONTIER (1955)

Frank, Melvin
CALLAWAY WENT THATAWAY (1951)
COURT JESTER, THE (1956)
LI'L ABNER (1959)

Frankel, Cyril
ALIVE AND KICKING (1962, Brit.)

Frawley, James
MUPPET MOVIE, THE (1979)

Friedman, Ed
MIGHTY MOUSE IN THE GREAT
SPACE CHASE (1983)

Garnett, Tay
BATAAN (1943)
CONNECTICUT YANKEE IN KING
ARTHUR'S COURT, A (1949)
SEE HERE, PRIVATE HARGROVE
(1944)

Gavaldon, Roberto
LITTLEST OUTLAW, THE (1955)

Geronimi, Clyde
ADVENTURES OF ICHABOD AND MR.
TOAD (1949)
ALICE IN WONDERLAND (1951)
CINDERELLA (1950)
LADY AND THE TRAMP (1955)
MAKE MINE MUSIC (1946)
MELODY TIME (1948)
ONE HUNDRED AND ONE
DALMATIANS (1961)
PETER PAN (1953)
SLEEPING BEAUTY (1959)
THREE CABALLEROS, THE (1944)

Gilbert, Lewis
CRY FROM THE STREET, A (1959, Brit.)
JOHNNY ON THE RUN (1953, Brit.)

Gilliam, Terry
TIME BANDITS (1981, Brit.)

Gion, Christian
HERE COMES SANTA CLAUS (1984)

Godfrey, Peter
CHRISTMAS IN CONNECTICUT (1945)

Goulding, Edmund
MISTER 880 (1950)

Gross, Yoram
DOT AND THE KOALA (1985, Aus.)

Gunn, Gilbert
WINGS OF MYSTERY (1963, Brit.)

Haldane, Donald
NIKKI, WILD DOG OF THE NORTH
(1961, US/Can.)

Hall, Alexander
LITTLE MISS MARKER (1934)
MY SISTER EILEEN (1942)

Hamer, Robert
SCHOOL FOR SCOUNDRELS (1960,
Brit.)

Hamilton, Guy
BATTLE OF BRITAIN, THE (1969, Brit.)

Hand, David
SNOW WHITE AND THE SEVEN
DWARFS (1937)

Handley, Jim
FANTASIA (1940)

Hanna, William
MAN CALLED FLINTSTONE, THE
(1966)

Harris, Vernon
JOHNNY ON THE RUN (1953, Brit.)

Haskin, Byron
TREASURE ISLAND (1950, Brit.)

Hathaway, Henry
HOME IN INDIANA (1944)
HOW THE WEST WAS WON (1962)
O. HENRY'S FULL HOUSE (1952)
TRUE GRIT (1969)

Hawks, Howard
AIR FORCE (1943)
O. HENRY'S FULL HOUSE (1952)
SERGEANT YORK (1941)

Haydn, Richard
DEAR WIFE (1949)

Hee, T. [Walt Disney]
FANTASIA (1940)

Heerman, Victor
ANIMAL CRACKERS (1930)

Henson, Jim
GREAT MUPPET CAPER, THE (1981)
LABYRINTH (1986)

Hessler, Gordon
GOLDEN VOYAGE OF SINBAD, THE
(1974, Brit.)

Hill, George Roy
LITTLE ROMANCE, A (1979, US/Fr.)
WORLD OF HENRY ORIENT, THE
(1964)

Hill, James
BELSTONE FOX, THE (1976, Brit.)
BORN FREE (1966)

Hill, Jerome
SAND CASTLE, THE (1961)

Hoffman, Herman
INVISIBLE BOY, THE (1957)

Horne, James W.
WAY OUT WEST (1937)

Hough, John
ESCAPE TO WITCH MOUNTAIN (1975)

Hubley, John
OF STARS AND MEN (1961)

Hudson, Hugh
CHARIOTS OF FIRE (1981, Brit.)

Hughes, Ken
CHITTY CHITTY BANG BANG (1968,
Brit.)

Humberstone, Bruce
CHARLIE CHAN AT THE OPERA (1936)
WONDER MAN (1945)

Hunter, Tim
SYLVESTER (1985)

Hussein, Waris
MELODY (1971, Brit.)

Huston, John
AFRICAN QUEEN, THE (1951, US/Brit.)
ANNIE (1982)
MOBY DICK (1956, Brit.)

Ichikawa, Kon
ALONE ON THE PACIFIC (1964, Jap.)

Jackson, Larry
BUGS BUNNY, SUPERSTAR (1975)

Jackson, Wilfred
CINDERELLA (1950)
FANTASIA (1940)
LADY AND THE TRAMP (1955)
MELODY TIME (1948)
PETER PAN (1953)
SNOW WHITE AND THE SEVEN
DWARFS (1937)
SONG OF THE SOUTH (1946)

Jarrott, Charles
DOVE, THE (1974, Brit.)
LITTLEST HORSE THIEVES, THE
(1977)

Jaxon, Wilfred
ALICE IN WONDERLAND (1951)

Jeffries, Lionel
WATER BABIES, THE (1979, Brit.)

Jones, Chuck
GREAT AMERICAN BUGS BUNNY-
ROAD RUNNER CHASE (1979)
PHANTOM TOLLBOOTH, THE (1970)

Jones, Harmon
PRIDE OF ST. LOUIS, THE (1952)

Jordan, Larry
HILDUR AND THE MAGICIAN (1969)

Juran, Nathan
JACK THE GIANT KILLER (1962)
SEVENTH VOYAGE OF SINBAD, THE
(1958)

Kachivas, Lou
MIGHTY MOUSE IN THE GREAT
SPACE CHASE (1983)

Kagan, Jeremy
JOURNEY OF NATTY GANN, THE
(1985)

Kane, Joseph
KING OF THE COWBOYS (1943)

Karlson, Phil
LIVE WIRES (1946)

Karman, Janice
CHIPMUNK ADVENTURE, THE (1987)

Keighley, William
ADVENTURES OF ROBIN HOOD, THE
(1938)
FIGHTING 69TH, THE (1940)
PRINCE AND THE PAUPER, THE (1937)

Kelly, Gene
HELLO, DOLLY! (1969)

Kenton, Erle C.
YOU'RE TELLING ME (1934)

Kershner, Irvin
EMPIRE STRIKES BACK, THE (1980)

Kilgore, Al
WORLD OF HANS CHRISTIAN
ANDERSEN (1971, Jap.)

King, Henry
O. HENRY'S FULL HOUSE (1952)
SONG OF BERNADETTE, THE (1943)
STANLEY AND LIVINGSTONE (1939)

YANK IN THE R.A.F., A (1941)

King, Louis
THUNDERHEAD-SON OF FLICKA
(1945)

Kinney, Jack
ADVENTURES OF ICHABOD AND MR.
TOAD (1949)
FUN AND FANCY FREE (1947)
MAKE MINE MUSIC (1946)
MELODY TIME (1948)
1001 ARABIAN NIGHTS (1959)
THREE CABALLEROS, THE (1944)

Kleiser, Randal
FLIGHT OF THE NAVIGATOR (1986)

Kneeland, Ted
DR. COPPELIUS (1968, US/Span.)

Korda, Alexander
THIEF OF BAGHDAD, THE (1940, Brit.)

Korda, Zoltan
JUNGLE BOOK, THE (1942)
THIEF OF BAGHDAD, THE (1940, Brit.)

Koster, Henry
COME TO THE STABLE (1949)
HARVEY (1950)
INSPECTOR GENERAL, THE (1949)
MAN CALLED PETER, A (1955)
MR. HOBBS TAKES A VACATION
(1962)
O. HENRY'S FULL HOUSE (1952)
STARS AND STRIPES FOREVER (1952)
THREE SMART GIRLS (1937)

Kramer, Stanley
IT'S A MAD, MAD, MAD, MAD WORLD
(1963)

Kress, Harold F.
PAINTED HILLS, THE (1951)

Lamont, Charles
FRANCIS IN THE HAUNTED HOUSE
(1956)
MA AND PA KETTLE ON VACATION
(1953)
MA AND PA KETTLE (1949)

Lamore, Marsh
MIGHTY MOUSE IN THE GREAT
SPACE CHASE (1983)

Landers, Lew
DAVY CROCKETT, INDIAN SCOUT
(1950)

Lang, Walter
CHEAPER BY THE DOZEN (1950)
KING AND I, THE (1956)
LITTLE PRINCESS, THE (1939)
SITTING PRETTY (1948)

Langley, Noel
PICKWICK PAPERS, THE (1952, Brit.)

Larson, Eric
SLEEPING BEAUTY (1959)

Launder, Frank
BELLES OF ST. TRINIAN'S, THE (1954,
Brit.)
WEE GEORDIE (1956, Brit.)

DIRECTORS

Lazarus, Ashley
FOREVER YOUNG, FOREVER FREE (1976, South Africa)

Leacock, Philip
LITTLE KIDNAPPERS, THE (1954, Brit.)

Lean, David
GREAT EXPECTATIONS (1946, Brit.)
OLIVER TWIST (1951, Brit.)

Lee, Rowland V.
COUNT OF MONTE CRISTO, THE (1934)

Leonard, Robert Z.
IN THE GOOD OLD SUMMERTIME (1949)

LeRoy, Mervyn
MADAME CURIE (1943)

Lester, Richard
SUPERMAN II (1980)

Levin, Henry
JOURNEY TO THE CENTER OF THE EARTH (1959)
MR. SCOUTMASTER (1953)
WONDERFUL WORLD OF THE BROTHERS GRIMM, THE (1962)

Levinson, Barry
YOUNG SHERLOCK HOLMES (1985)

Levitow, Abe
GAY PURR-EE (1962)
PHANTOM TOLLBOOTH, THE (1970)

Lounsbery, John
RESCUERS, THE (1977)

Lubin, Arthur
ALI BABA AND THE FORTY THIEVES (1944)
FRANCIS (1949)
HOLD THAT GHOST (1941)
RIDE 'EM COWBOY (1942)

Lucas, George
STAR WARS (1977)

Luske, Hamilton
ALICE IN WONDERLAND (1951)
CINDERELLA (1950)
FANTASIA (1940)
FUN AND FANCY FREE (1947)
LADY AND THE TRAMP (1955)
MAKE MINE MUSIC (1946)
MELODY TIME (1948)
ONE HUNDRED AND ONE DALMATIANS (1961)
PETER PAN (1953)
PINOCCHIO (1940)

Mackendrick, Alexander
BOY TEN FEET TALL, A (1965, Brit.)

Mahon, Barry
THUMBELINA (1970)

Mamoulian, Rouben
SUMMER HOLIDAY (1948)

Mankiewicz, Joseph L.
GHOST AND MRS. MUIR, THE (1942)

Mann, Delbert
FITZWILLY (1967)

Mann, Edward
WHO SAYS I CAN'T RIDE A RAINBOW? (1971)

Manning, Bruce
AMAZING MRS. HOLLIDAY (1943)

Marin, Edwin L.
CHRISTMAS CAROL, A (1938)

Markle, Fletcher
INCREDIBLE JOURNEY, THE (1963)

Marquand, Richard
RETURN OF THE JEDI (1983)

Marshall, George
GHOST BREAKERS, THE (1940)
HOW THE WEST WAS WON (1962)

Marton, Andrew
AFRICA--TEXAS STYLE! (1967 US/Brit.)
CLARENCE, THE CROSS-EYED LION (1965)
KING SOLOMON'S MINES (1950)

Mayo, Archie
CHARLEY'S AUNT (1941)

McCarey, Leo
BELLS OF ST. MARY'S, THE (1945)
DUCK SOUP (1933)
GOING MY WAY (1944)
KID FROM SPAIN, THE (1932)
MILKY WAY, THE (1936)

McDonald, Frank
BELLS OF ROSARITA (1945)
MY PAL TRIGGER (1946)

McLeod, Norman Z.
ALICE IN WONDERLAND (1933)
IT'S A GIFT (1934)
KID FROM BOOKLYN, THE (1946)
ROAD TO RIO (1947)
TOPPER (1937)

Meador, Joshua
MAKE MINE MUSIC (1946)

Meins, Gus
BABES IN TOYLAND (1934)

Melendez, Bill
BON VOYAGE, CHARLIE BROWN (AND DON'T COME BACK) (1980)
SNOOPY, COME HOME (1972)

Menzies, William Cameron
THIEF OF BAGHDAD, THE (1940, Brit.)

Meyer, Nicholas
STAR TREK II: THE WRATH OF KHAN (1982)

Mills, Reginald
PETER RABBIT AND TALES OF BEATRIX POTTER (1971, Brit.)

Minnelli, Vincente
COURTSHIP OF EDDIE'S FATHER, THE (1963)
FATHER'S LITTLE DIVIDEND (1951)
MEET ME IN ST. LOUIS (1944)

Monahan, David
PHANTOM TOLLBOOTH, THE (1970)

Morey, Larry
SNOW WHITE AND THE SEVEN DWARFS (1937)

Morgan, William
FUN AND FANCY FREE (1947)

Mulligan, Robert
TO KILL A MOCKINGBIRD (1962)

Neame, Ronald
SCROOGE (1970, Brit.)

Negulesco, Jean
O. HENRY'S FULL HOUSE (1952)

Neilson, James
ADVENTURES OF BULLWHIP GRIFFIN, THE (1967)
GENTLE GIANT (1967)
MOON PILOT (1962)
MOON-SPINNERS, THE (1964)
SUMMER MAGIC (1963)

Nelson, Gary
FREAKY FRIDAY (1976)

Nelson, Ralph
FATHER GOOSE (1964)
FLIGHT OF THE DOVES (1971)

Nelson, Sam
KONGA, THE WILD STALLION (1939)

Neumann, Kurt
CATTLE DRIVE (1951)

Nichols, Charles A.
CHARLOTTE'S WEB (1973)

Nimoy, Leonard
STAR TREK IV: THE VOYAGE HOME (1986)
STAR TREK III: THE SEARCH FOR SPOCK (1984)

O'Herlihy, Michael
FIGHTING PRINCE OF DONEGAL, THE (1966, Brit.)

Carol Reed
OLIVER! (1968, Brit.)

Oz, Frank
MUPPETS TAKE MANHATTAN, THE (1984)

Pal, George
SEVEN FACES OF DR. LAO (1964)
TIME MACHINE, THE (1960, Brit./US)
TOM THUMB (1958, Brit./US)
WONDERFUL WORLD OF THE BROTHERS GRIMM, THE (1962)

Panama, Norman
CALLAWAY WENT THATAWAY (1951)
COURT JESTER, THE (1956)

Parker, Alan
BUGSY MALONE (1976, Brit.)

Pearce, Perce
SNOW WHITE AND THE SEVEN DWARFS (1937)

Penn, Arthur
MIRACLE WORKER, THE (1962)

Perry, Frank
TRUMAN CAPOTE'S TRILOGY (1969)

Pichel, Irving
GREAT RUPERT, THE (1950)

Pinkava, Josef
WISHING MACHINE (1971, Czech.)

Potter, H.C.
FARMER'S DAUGHTER, THE (1947)

Potterton, Gerald
TIKI TIKI (1971, Can.)

Powell, Michael
THIEF OF BAGHDAD, THE (1940, Brit.)

Quine, Richard
MY SISTER EILEEN (1955)

Raffil, Stewart
ADVENTURES OF THE WILDERNESS
FAMILY, THE (1975)
SEA GYPSIES, THE (1978)

Rankin, Jr., Arthur
WILLIE MCBEAN AND HIS MAGIC
MACHINE (1965, US/Jap.)

Rapper, Irving
ADVENTURES OF MARK TWAIN, THE
(1944)
ONE FOOT IN HEAVEN (1941)

Rawlins, John
ARABIAN NIGHTS (1942)

Ray, Nicholas
KING OF KINGS (1961)

Reiner, Rob
PRINCESS BRIDE, THE (1987)

Reis, Irving
BACHELOR AND THE BOBBY-SOXER,
THE (1947)
ROSEANNA McCOY (1949)

Reitherman, Wolfgang
ARISTOCATS, THE (1970)
JUNGLE BOOK, THE (1967)
ONE HUNDRED AND ONE
DALMATIANS (1961)
RESCUERS, THE (1977)
ROBIN HOOD (1973)
SLEEPING BEAUTY (1959)

Rich, Richard
FOX AND THE HOUND, THE (1981)

Ritchie, Michael
BAD NEWS BEARS, THE (1976)

Ritt, Martin
SOUNDER (1972)

Roberts, Bill
FANTASIA (1940)
THREE CABALLEROS, THE (1944)

Roberts, W.O.
FUN AND FANCY FREE (1947)

Robson, Mark
INN OF THE SIXTH HAPPINESS, THE
(1958)

Rogers, Charles
BABES IN TOYLAND (1934)

Rowland, Roy
EXCUSE MY DUST (1951)
HIT THE DECK (1955)
5,000 FINGERS OF DR. T., THE (1953)

Ruggles, Wesley
SEE HERE, PRIVATE HARGROVE
(1944)
SING YOU SINNERS (1938)

Sackler, Howard
MIDSUMMER NIGHT'S DREAM, A
(1961, Czech.)

Safran, Henri
STORM BOY (1976, Aus.)

Sarecky, Louis
CUCKOOS, THE (1930)

Satterfield, Paul
FANTASIA (1940)

Saville, Victor
KIM (1950)

Scheerer, Richard
WORLD'S GREATEST ATHLETE, THE
(1973)

Schertzinger, Victor
ROAD TO ZANZIBAR (1941)

Schoedsack, Ernest B.
KING KONG (1933)

Schuster, Harold
MY FRIEND FLICKA (1943)
SO DEAR TO MY HEART (1949)

Seaton, George
MIRACLE ON 34TH STREET, THE
(1947)

Sedgwick, Edward
SOUTHERN YANKEE, A (1948)

Seiter, William A.
STOWAWAY (1936)

Seitz, George B.
JUDGE HARDY AND SON (1939)
JUDGE HARDY'S CHILDREN (1938)
LOVE FINDS ANDY HARDY (1938)

Sharpsteen, Ben
DUMBO (1941)
PINOCCHIO (1940)
SNOW WHITE AND THE SEVEN
DWARFS (1937)

Shavelson, Melville
SEVEN LITTLE FOYS, THE (1955)
YOURS, MINE AND OURS (1968)

Shields, Pat
FRASIER, THE SENSUOUS LION (1973)

Sidney, George
ANNIE GET YOUR GUN (1950)
HARVEY GIRLS, THE (1946)
THREE MUSKETEERS, THE (1948)

Simon, S. Sylvan
FULLER BRUSH MAN (1948)
SON OF LASSIE (1945)

Sloane, Paul
CUCKOOS, THE (1930)

Spielberg, Steven
CLOSE ENCOUNTERS OF THE THIRD
KIND (1977)
E.T. THE EXTRA-TERRESTRIAL (1982)
EMPIRE OF THE SUN (1987)

Stephani, Frederick
FLASH GORDON (1936)

Stevens, Art
FOX AND THE HOUND, THE (1981)
RESCUERS, THE (1977)

Stevens, George
ANNIE OAKLEY (1935)
I REMEMBER MAMA (1948)
LADDIE (1935)
SHANE (1953)

Stevenson, Robert
ABSENT-MINDED PROFESSOR, THE
(1961)
BEDKNOBS AND BROOMSTICKS
(1971)
BLACKBEARD'S GHOST (1968)
DARBY O'GILL AND THE LITTLE
PEOPLE (1959)
GNOME-MOBILE, THE (1967)
HERBIE RIDES AGAIN (1974)
IN SEARCH OF THE CASTAWAYS
(1962, Brit.)
ISLAND AT THE TOP OF THE WORLD,
THE (1974)
JOHNNY TREMAIN (1957)
LOVE BUG, THE (1968)
MARY POPPINS (1964)
OLD YELLER (1957)
SHAGGY D.A., THE (1976)
SON OF FLUBBER (1963)
THAT DARN CAT (1965)

Stoloff, Benjamin
PALOOKA (1934)

Strayer, Frank R.
BLONDIE (1938)

Stuart, Mel
WILLY WONKA AND THE
CHOCOLATE FACTORY (1971)

Sturges, John
GREAT ESCAPE, THE (1963)
MAGNIFICENT YANKEE, THE (1950)

Sutherland, A. Edward
FLYING DEUCES, THE (1939)
ONE NIGHT IN THE TROPICS (1940)

Sutherland, Hal
PINOCCHIO AND THE EMPEROR OF
THE NIGHT (1987)

Swift, David
PARENT TRAP, THE (1961)
POLLYANNA (1960)

Takamoto, Iwao
CHARLOTTE'S WEB (1973)

Tati, Jacques
MY UNCLE (1958, Fr.)
PLAYTIME (1973, Fr.)

Taurog, Norman
ADVENTURES OF TOM SAWYER, THE
(1938)
BOYS TOWN (1938)
GIRL CRAZY (1943)
ROOM FOR ONE MORE (1952)
SKIPPY (1931)
YOUNG TOM EDISON (1940)

MUSIC COMPOSERS

Taylor, Don
TOM SAWYER (1973)

Tewksbury, Peter
EMIL AND THE DETECTIVES (1964)

Thomas, Ralph
DOG AND THE DIAMONDS, THE (1962, Brit.)

Thompson, J. Lee
TIGER BAY (1959, Brit.)

Thorpe, Richard
CHALLENGE TO LASSIE (1949)
DATE WITH JUDY, A (1948)
HOW THE WEST WAS WON (1962)
HUCKLEBERRY FINN (1939)
SUN COMES UP, THE (1949)

Till, Eric
ALL THINGS BRIGHT AND BEAUTIFUL (1979, Brit.)

Tokar, Norman
CAT FROM OUTER SPACE, THE (1978)
FOLLOW ME, BOYS! (1966)
RASCAL (1969)
THOSE CALLOWAYS (1964)

Trnka, Jiri
MIDSUMMER NIGHT'S DREAM, A (1961, Czech.)

Truffaut, Francois
FOUR HUNDRED BLOWS, THE (1959)
SMALL CHANGE (1976, Fr.)
WILD CHILD, THE (1970, Fr.)

Van Dyke II, W.S.
JOURNEY FOR MARGARET (1942)

Van Dyke, W.S.
TARZAN THE APE MAN (1932)

Vidor, Charles
HANS CHRISTIAN ANDERSEN (1952)

Vidor, King
CHAMP, THE (1931)
WIZARD OF OZ, THE (1939)

Walker, Hal
ROAD TO UTOPIA (1945)

Walker, Norman
JOHN WESLEY (1954, Brit.)

Wallace, Richard
SINBAD THE SAILOR (1947)

Walsh, Raoul
HORN BLOWS AT MIDNIGHT, THE (1945)

Walters, Charles
EASTER PARADE (1948)
LILI (1953)

Wanamaker, Sam
SINBAD AND THE EYE OF THE TIGER (1977, US/Brit.)

Wayne, John
ALAMO, THE (1960)

Wellman, William A.
BUFFALO BILL (1944)
CALL OF THE WILD (1935)
GOODBYE, MY LADY (1956)
NEXT VOICE YOU HEAR, THE (1950)

STORY OF G.I. JOE, THE (1945)

Wendkos, Paul
GIDGET (1959)

Werker, Alfred
ADVENTURES OF SHERLOCK HOLMES, THE (1939)
KIDNAPPED (1938)

Wetzler, Gwen
MIGHTY MOUSE IN THE GREAT SPACE CHASE (1983)

Whatham, Claude
ALL CREATURES GREAT AND SMALL (1975, Brit.)
SWALLOWS AND AMAZONS (1977, Brit.)

Whelan, Tim
SIDEWALKS OF LONDON (1940, Brit.)
THIEF OF BAGHDAD, THE (1940, Brit.)

Whorf, Richard
CHAMPAGNE FOR CAESAR (1950)

Wilcox, Fred M.
COURAGE OF LASSIE (1946)
HILLS OF HOME (1948)
LASSIE, COME HOME (1943)
SECRET GARDEN, THE (1949)

Wilder, Billy
EMPEROR WALTZ, THE (1948)
SPIRIT OF ST. LOUIS, THE (1957)

Wincer, Simon
PHAR LAP (1984, Aus.)

Wise, Robert
SOUND OF MUSIC, THE (1965)
STAR TREK: THE MOTION PICTURE (1979)

Wood, Sam
DAY AT THE RACES, A (1937)
GOODBYE MR. CHIPS (1939, Brit.)
NIGHT AT THE OPERA, A (1935)
PRIDE OF THE YANKEES, THE (1942)
STRATTON STORY, THE (1949)

Wright, Kay
MIGHTY MOUSE IN THE GREAT SPACE CHASE (1983)

Yarbrough, Jean
HERE COME THE CO-EDS (1945)

Young, Harold
THREE CABALLEROS, THE (1944)

Zeman, Karel
FABULOUS WORLD OF JULES VERNE, THE (1961, Czech.)

Zemeckis, Robert
WHO FRAMED ROGER RABBIT? (1988)

Zinnemann, Fred
MY BROTHER TALKS TO HORSES (1946)
OKLAHOMA! (1955)

Zukor, Lou
MIGHTY MOUSE IN THE GREAT SPACE CHASE (1983)

MUSIC COMPOSERS

Addinsell, Richard
GOODBYE MR. CHIPS (1939, Brit.)

Addison, John
SCHOOL FOR SCOUNDRELS (1960, Brit.)

Adler, Larry
CRY FROM THE STREET, A (1959, Brit.)

Akatagawa, Yasushi
ALONE ON THE PACIFIC (1964, Jap.)

Almeida, Laurindo
GOODBYE, MY LADY (1956)

Alwyn, William
IN SEARCH OF THE CASTAWAYS (1962, Brit.)
MAGIC BOX, THE (1952, Brit.)
SWISS FAMILY ROBINSON (1960)
WEE GEORDIE (1956, Brit.)

Amfitheatrof, Daniele
ANGELS IN THE OUTFIELD (1951)
LASSIE, COME HOME (1943)
PAINTED HILLS, THE (1951)
SONG OF THE SOUTH (1946)

Andrews, Joel
HILDUR AND THE MAGICIAN (1969)

Applebaum, Louise
STORY OF G.I. JOE, THE (1945)

Arnold, Malcolm
AFRICA--TEXAS STYLE! (1967 US/Brit.)
BELLES OF ST. TRINIAN'S, THE (1954, Brit.)
INN OF THE SIXTH HAPPINESS, THE (1958)

Arnold, Steve
TAIL OF THE TIGER (1984, Aus.)

Astley, Edwin
MOUSE THAT ROARED, THE (1959, Brit.)

Auric, Georges
BEAUTY AND THE BEAST (1947, Fr.)

Bach, Johann Sebastian
FANTASIA (1940)
20,000 LEAGUES UNDER THE SEA (1954)

Baker, Buddy
FOX AND THE HOUND, THE (1981)
GNOME-MOBILE, THE (1967)
RASCAL (1969)
SHAGGY D.A., THE (1976)
SUMMER MAGIC (1963)
TOBY TYLER (1960)

Banks, Brian
PINOCCHIO AND THE EMPEROR OF THE NIGHT (1987)

Barcellini, Franck
MY UNCLE (1958, Fr.)

Barry, John
BORN FREE (1966)
DOVE, THE (1974, Brit.)

Bart, Lionel
OLIVER! (1968, Brit.)

Bassett, R.H.
STANLEY AND LIVINGSTONE (1939)

Bassman, George
CANTERVILLE GHOST, THE (1944)

Bath, Hubert
YANK AT OXFORD, A (1938)

Bax, Sir Arnold
OLIVER TWIST (1951, Brit.)

Baxter, Les
INVISIBLE BOY, THE (1957)

Bee-Gees, The
MELODY (1971, Brit.)

Beethoven, Ludwig van
FANTASIA (1940)

Bennett, Richard Rodney
HEAVENS ABOVE! (1963, Brit.)

Bennett, Robert R.
STANLEY AND LIVINGSTONE (1939)

Berlin, Irving
WAY OUT WEST (1937)

Bernstein, Elmer
GREAT ESCAPE, THE (1963)
TEN COMMANDMENTS, THE (1956)
TO KILL A MOCKINGBIRD (1962)
TRUE GRIT (1969)
WORLD OF HENRY ORIENT, THE
(1964)

Blais, Yvette
MIGHTY MOUSE IN THE GREAT
SPACE CHASE (1983)

Blatt, Jerry
TIKI TIKI (1971, Can.)

Bogas, Ed
BON VOYAGE, CHARLIE BROWN
(AND DON'T COME BACK) (1980)

Box, Euel
BENJI (1974)
FOR THE LOVE OF BENJI (1977)

Bradley, Scott
COURAGE OF LASSIE (1946)

Bricusse, Leslie
SCROOGE (1970, Brit.)

Broughton, Bruce
BOY WHO COULD FLY, THE (1986)
YOUNG SHERLOCK HOLMES (1985)

Brunner, Robert F.
BAREFOOT EXECUTIVE, THE (1971)
BLACKBEARD'S GHOST (1968)
COMPUTER WORE TENNIS SHOES,
THE (1970)
NOW YOU SEE HIM, NOW YOU DON'T
(1972)
THAT DARN CAT (1965)

Bruns, George
ABSENT-MINDED PROFESSOR, THE
(1961)
ADVENTURES OF BULLWHIP
GRIFFIN, THE (1967)
ARISTOCATS, THE (1970)
DAVY CROCKETT, KING OF THE WILD
FRONTIER (1955)

FIGHTING PRINCE OF DONEGAL,
THE (1966, Brit.)
FOLLOW ME, BOYS! (1966)
HERBIE RIDES AGAIN (1974)
JOHNNY TREMAIN (1957)
JUNGLE BOOK, THE (1967)
LOVE BUG, THE (1968)
ONE HUNDRED AND ONE
DALMATIANS (1961)
ROBIN HOOD (1973)
SLEEPING BEAUTY (1959)
SON OF FLUBBER (1963)

Budashkin, Nikolay
JACK FROST (1966, USSR)

Budd, Roy
FLIGHT OF THE DOVES (1971)
SINBAD AND THE EYE OF THE TIGER
(1977, US/Brit.)

Bukovy, William
WISHING MACHINE (1971, Czech.)

Bullock, Walter
LITTLE PRINCESS, THE (1939)

Burns, Ralph
MUPPETS TAKE MANHATTAN, THE
(1984)

Burnstein, L.
TIKI TIKI (1971, Can.)

Butler, Artie
RESCUERS, THE (1977)
WHAT'S UP, DOC? (1972)

Buttolph, David
BUFFALO BILL (1944)
ROSEANNA McCOY (1949)
STANLEY AND LIVINGSTONE (1939)

Campbell, James
PLAYTIME (1973, Fr.)

Carlos, Michael
STORM BOY (1976, Aus.)

Cary, Tristram
BOY TEN FEET TALL, A (1965, Brit.)
BOY WHO STOLE A MILLION, THE
(1960, Brit.)

Chagrin, Francis
GREYFRIARS BOBBY (1961, Brit.)

Churchill, Frank
BAMBI (1942)
SNOW WHITE AND THE SEVEN
DWARFS (1937)

Coleman, Cy
FATHER GOOSE (1964)

Collins, Anthony
ADVENTURES OF ROBINSON
CRUSOE, THE (1954)

Constantin, Jean
FOUR HUNDRED BLOWS, THE (1959)

Conti, Bill
KARATE KID, THE (1984)

Coppola, Carmine
BLACK STALLION, THE (1979)

Daniel, Eliot
FUN AND FANCY FREE (1947)

Darby, Ken
HOW THE WEST WAS WON (1962)

Delerue, Georges
LITTLE ROMANCE, A (1979, US/Fr.)

Delibes, Clement
DR. COPPELIUS (1968, US/Span.)

Deutsch, Adolph
FIGHTING 69TH, THE (1940)

Dolan, Robert Emmett
BELLS OF ST. MARY'S, THE (1945)

Dragon, Carmen
KID FROM BOOKLYN, THE (1946)

Druick, Don
WOLFPEN PRINCIPLE, THE (1974,
Can.)

Duning, George
1001 ARABIAN NIGHTS (1959)
MY SISTER EILEEN (1955)

Edelman, Randy
CHIPMUNK ADVENTURE, THE (1987)

Edens, Robert
TAKE ME OUT TO THE BALL GAME
(1949)

Elliott, Dean
GREAT AMERICAN BUGS BUNNY-
ROAD RUNNER CHASE (1979)
PHANTOM TOLLBOOTH, THE (1970)

Emenegger, Robert
FRASIER, THE SENSUOUS LION (1973)

Field, George
GOODBYE, MY LADY (1956)

Fielding, Jerry
BAD NEWS BEARS, THE (1976)

Fox, Sydney
FABULOUS WORLD OF JULES
VERNE, THE (1961, Czech.)

Frangiapane, Ron
WORLD OF HANS CHRISTIAN
ANDERSEN (1971, Jap.)

Frankel, Benjamin
BATTLE OF THE BULGE (1965)

Franklyn, Milt
GREAT AMERICAN BUGS BUNNY-
ROAD RUNNER CHASE (1979)

Franklyn, Robert
HILLS OF HOME (1948)

Freidhofer, Hugo
HOME IN INDIANA (1944)
TOPPER (1937)

Gamley, Douglas
TOM THUMB (1958, Brit./US)

Garcia, Russell
TIME MACHINE, THE (1960, Brit./US)

Gertz, Irving
FLUFFY (1965)

Goehr, Walter
GREAT EXPECTATIONS (1946, Brit.)

Gold, Ernest
IT'S A MAD, MAD, MAD, MAD WORLD
(1963)

MUSIC COMPOSERS

Goldsmith, Jerry
SECRET OF NIMH, THE (1982)
STAR TREK: THE MOTION PICTURE (1979)

Goodwin, Ron
BATTLE OF BRITAIN, THE (1969, Brit.)
LITTLEST HORSE THIEVES, THE (1977)
THOSE MAGNIFICENT MEN IN THEIR FLYING MACHINES OR HOW I FLEW FROM LONDON TO PARIS IN 25 HOURS AND 11 MINUTES (1965, Brit.)

Grainer, Ron
MOON-SPINNERS, THE (1964)

Gray, Alan
AFRICAN QUEEN, THE (1951, US/Brit.)

Green, Johnny
INSPECTOR GENERAL, THE (1949)

Green, Philip
ALIVE AND KICKING (1962, Brit.)
JOHN AND JULIE (1957, Brit.)

Hageman, Richard
THREE GODFATHERS, THE (1948)

Hamlisch, Marvin
WORLD'S GREATEST ATHLETE, THE (1973)

Harline, Leigh
BACHELOR AND THE BOBBY-SOXER, THE (1947)
FARMER'S DAUGHTER, THE (1947)
IT HAPPENS EVERY SPRING (1949)
PRIDE OF THE YANKEES, THE (1942)
ROAD TO UTOPIA (1945)
SEVEN FACES OF DR. LAO (1964)
SNOW WHITE AND THE SEVEN DWARFS (1937)
WONDERFUL WORLD OF THE BROTHERS GRIMM, THE (1962)

Hatley, Marvin
WAY OUT WEST (1937)

Hayton, Lenny
HELLO, DOLLY! (1969)

Heindorf, Ray
KNUTE ROCKNE--ALL AMERICAN (1940)
WONDER MAN (1945)

Herrmann, Bernard
GHOST AND MRS. MUIR, THE (1942)
JASON AND THE ARGONAUTS (1963, Brit.)
JOURNEY TO THE CENTER OF THE EARTH (1959)
MYSTERIOUS ISLAND (1961, US/Brit.)
SEVENTH VOYAGE OF SINBAD, THE (1958)

Hewson, Richard
MELODY (1971, Brit.)

Hill, J.L.
WAY OUT WEST (1937)

Holdridge, Lee
FOREVER YOUNG, FOREVER FREE (1976, South Africa)
SYLVESTER (1985)

Hollander, Frederick
CHRISTMAS IN CONNECTICUT (1945)
5,000 FINGERS OF DR. T., THE (1953)

Hopkins, Antony
PICKWICK PAPERS, THE (1952, Brit.)

Horner, James
AMERICAN TAIL, AN (1986)
JOURNEY OF NATTY GANN, THE (1985)
STAR TREK III: THE SEARCH FOR SPOCK (1984)
STAR TREK II: THE WRATH OF KHAN (1982)

Iger, Julie
HILDUR AND THE MAGICIAN (1969)

Isham, Mark
NEVER CRY WOLF (1983)

Jarre, Maurice
ISLAND AT THE TOP OF THE WORLD, THE (1974)

Jaubert, Maurice
SMALL CHANGE (1976, Fr.)

Johnson, Arthur
SIDEWALKS OF LONDON (1940, Brit.)

Johnson, Laurie
ALL THINGS BRIGHT AND BEAUTIFUL (1979, Brit.)
BELSTONE FOX, THE (1976, Brit.)
TIGER BAY (1959, Brit.)

Johnston, Arthur
YOU'RE TELLING ME (1934)

Jones, Ken
TOM THUMB (1958, Brit./US)

Jones, Trevor
LABYRINTH (1986)

Josephs, Wilfred
ALL CREATURES GREAT AND SMALL (1975, Brit.)
MY SIDE OF THE MOUNTAIN (1969)
SWALLOWS AND AMAZONS (1977, Brit.)

Jurmann, Walter
DAY AT THE RACES, A (1937)

Kahn, Gus
DAY AT THE RACES, A (1937)

Kaper, Bronislau
BATAAN (1943)
DAY AT THE RACES, A (1937)
LILI (1953)
SECRET GARDEN, THE (1949)

Kaplan, Sol
MISTER 880 (1950)
TALES OF MANHATTAN (1942)

Karlin, Fred
LITTLE ARK, THE (1972)
YOURS, MINE AND OURS (1968)

Kauer, Gene
ADVENTURES OF THE WILDERNESS FAMILY, THE (1975)

Kaye, Buddy
GREAT RUPERT, THE (1950)

Keyes, Burt
HUGO THE HIPPO (1976, Hung./US)

Knopfler, Mark
PRINCESS BRIDE, THE (1987)

Kopp, Rudolph G.
MY BROTHER TALKS TO HORSES (1946)

Korngold, Eric Wolfgang
ADVENTURES OF ROBIN HOOD, THE (1938)
PRINCE AND THE PAUPER, THE (1937)

Kostal, Irwin
MARY POPPINS (1964)
PETE'S DRAGON (1977)

Kupferman, Meyer
TRUMAN CAPOTE'S TRILOGY (1969)

Lackey, Douglas
ADVENTURES OF THE WILDERNESS FAMILY, THE (1975)

Lai, Francis
HERE COMES SANTA CLAUS (1984)

Lange, Arthur
KIDNAPPED (1938)
PRIDE OF ST. LOUIS, THE (1952)

Lauber, Ken
WORLD OF HENRY ORIENT, THE (1964)

Lava, William
LITTLEST OUTLAW, THE (1955)

Laws, Maury
DAYDREAMER, THE (1966)

Lemarque, Francis
PLAYTIME (1973, Fr.)

Leopold, John
FLYING DEUCES, THE (1939)

Loesser, Frank
HANS CHRISTIAN ANDERSEN (1952)

Loewe, Frederick
MY FAIR LADY (1964)

Mack, Al
CLARENCE, THE CROSS-EYED LION (1965)

Mahal, Taj
SOUNDER (1972)

Mancini, Henry
MR. HOBBS TAKES A VACATION (1962)

Mandel, Johnny
ESCAPE TO WITCH MOUNTAIN (1975)
FREAKY FRIDAY (1976)

Marinelli, Anthony
PINOCCHIO AND THE EMPEROR OF THE NIGHT (1987)

Martin, Peter
HOPE AND GLORY (1987, Brit.)

Matlovsky, Samuel
GENTLE GIANT (1967)

Michael, Jeff
MIGHTY MOUSE IN THE GREAT SPACE CHASE (1983)

Mockridge, Cyril
CHEAPER BY THE DOZEN (1950)
COME TO THE STABLE (1949)
DREAMBOAT (1952)
MIRACLE ON 34TH STREET, THE (1947)
MR. SCOUTMASTER (1953)
STANLEY AND LIVINGSTONE (1939)
THUNDERHEAD-SON OF FLICKA (1945)

Montgomery, Bruce
LITTLE KIDNAPPERS, THE (1954, Brit.)

Moran, Mike
TIME BANDITS (1981, Brit.)

Moross, Jerome
ADVENTURES OF HUCKLEBERRY FINN, THE (1960)

Munsen, Judy
BON VOYAGE, CHARLIE BROWN (AND DON'T COME BACK) (1980)

Mussorgsky, Modest
FANTASIA (1940)

Newman, Alfred
CALL OF THE WILD (1935)
CHARLEY'S AUNT (1941)
COUNT OF MONTE CRISTO, THE (1934)
DRUMS ALONG THE MOHAWK (1939)
HOW GREEN WAS MY VALLEY (1941)
HOW THE WEST WAS WON (1962)
MAN CALLED PETER, A (1955)
MY FRIEND FLICKA (1943)
O. HENRY'S FULL HOUSE (1952)
SITTING PRETTY (1948)
SONG OF BERNADETTE, THE (1943)

Newman, Lionel
BEST THINGS IN LIFE ARE FREE (1956)
HELLO, DOLLY! (1969)

Nichols, Ted
MAN CALLED FLINTSTONE, THE (1966)

Paich, Marty
MAN CALLED FLINTSTONE, THE (1966)

Papathanassiou, Vangelis
CHARIOTS OF FIRE (1981, Brit.)

Parker, Clifton
STORY OF ROBIN HOOD, THE (1952, Brit.)

Parker, Clifton
TREASURE ISLAND (1950, Brit.)

Plumb, Edward
BAMBI (1942)
PETER PAN (1953)

Pokrass, Samuel
LITTLE PRINCESS, THE (1939)

Ponchielli, Amilcare
FANTASIA (1940)

Powell, Edward
TOPPER (1937)

Previn, Andre
CHALLENGE TO LASSIE (1949)
KIM (1950)
SUN COMES UP, THE (1949)

Rainger, Ralph
LITTLE MISS MARKER (1934)

Raksin, David
MAGNIFICENT YANKEE, THE (1950)
NEXT VOICE YOU HEAR, THE (1950)

Ralke, Donald
SNOOPY, COME HOME (1972)

Reed, Henry
JOHN WESLEY (1954, Brit.)

Riddle, Nelson
LI'L ABNER (1959)

Rodgers, Richard
KING AND I, THE (1956)
OKLAHOMA! (1955)
SOUND OF MUSIC, THE (1965)

Roemheld, Heinz
FULLER BRUSH MAN (1948)
FULLER BRUSH GIRL, THE (1950)

Romans, Alains
MY UNCLE (1958, Fr.)

Romberg, Sigmund
DEEP IN MY HEART (1954)

Ronell, Ann
STORY OF G.I. JOE, THE (1945)

Rosen, Milton
TIME OF THEIR LIVES, THE (1946)

Rosenman, Leonard
FANTASTIC VOYAGE (1966)
STAR TREK IV: THE VOYAGE HOME (1986)

Rosenthal, Laurence
MIRACLE WORKER, THE (1962)

Rowland, Bruce
PHAR LAP (1984, Aus.)

Rozsa, Miklos
GOLDEN VOYAGE OF SINBAD, THE (1974, Brit.)
JUNGLE BOOK, THE (1942)
KING OF KINGS (1961)
THIEF OF BAGHDAD, THE (1940, Brit.)

Salter, H.J.
AMAZING MRS. HOLLIDAY (1943)

Sangster, John
DOT AND THE KOALA (1985, Aus.)

Sarde, Philippe
MANHATTAN PROJECT, THE (1986)

Sawtell, Paul
DAVY CROCKETT, INDIAN SCOUT (1950)
DOG OF FLANDERS, A (1959)
ISLAND OF THE BLUE DOLPHINS (1964)
JACK THE GIANT KILLER (1962)
MISTY (1961)
VOYAGE TO THE BOTTOM OF THE SEA (1961)

Scharf, Walter
POCKETFUL OF MIRACLES (1961)
WILLY WONKA AND THE CHOCOLATE FACTORY (1971)

Schifrin, Lalo
CAT FROM OUTER SPACE, THE (1978)

Schoen, Victor
COURT JESTER, THE (1956)

Schrager, Rudy
STANLEY AND LIVINGSTONE (1939)

Schreiter, Heinz
EMIL AND THE DETECTIVES (1964)

Schubert, Franz
FANTASIA (1940)

Schumann, Walter
NOOSE HANGS HIGH, THE (1948)

Schwarzwald, Milton
MA AND PA KETTLE (1949)

Scott, Bobby
WHO SAYS I CAN'T RIDE A RAINBOW? (1971)

Sendrey, Albert
FATHER'S LITTLE DIVIDEND (1951)
HILLS OF HOME (1948)

Shefter, Bert
DOG OF FLANDERS, A (1959)
JACK THE GIANT KILLER (1962)
MISTY (1961)
VOYAGE TO THE BOTTOM OF THE SEA (1961)

Sherman, Richard M.
CHARLOTTE'S WEB (1973)
SLIPPER AND THE ROSE, THE (1976, Brit.)
TOM SAWYER (1973)

Sherman, Robert B.
CHARLOTTE'S WEB (1973)
SLIPPER AND THE ROSE, THE (1976, Brit.)
TOM SAWYER (1973)

Shield, LeRoy
WAY OUT WEST (1937)

Shilkret, Nathaniel
WAY OUT WEST (1937)

Shuken, Leo
FLYING DEUCES, THE (1939)

Silvers, Louis
STANLEY AND LIVINGSTONE (1939)
WEE WILLIE WINKIE (1937)

Silvestri, Alan
FLIGHT OF THE NAVIGATOR (1986)
WHO FRAMED ROGER RABBIT? (1988)

Skiles, Marlin
CALLAWAY WENT THATAWAY (1951)
JALOPY (1953)

Skinner, Frank
AMAZING MRS. HOLLIDAY (1943)
ARABIAN NIGHTS (1942)
FRANCIS (1949)
HARVEY (1950)

MUSIC COMPOSERS

Smith, Paul J.
CINDERELLA (1950)
FUN AND FANCY FREE (1947)
LIGHT IN THE FOREST, THE (1958)
MOON PILOT (1962)
PARENT TRAP, THE (1961)
PINOCCHIO (1940)
POLLYANNA (1960)
SHAGGY DOG, THE (1959)
SNOW WHITE AND THE SEVEN
DWARFS (1937)
SO DEAR TO MY HEART (1949)
SONG OF THE SOUTH (1946)
THREE LIVES OF THOMASINA, THE
(1963, US/Brit.)
20,000 LEAGUES UNDER THE SEA
(1954)

Snell, David
JUDGE HARDY AND SON (1939)
JUDGE HARDY'S CHILDREN (1938)
LOVE FINDS ANDY HARDY (1938)
SEE HERE, PRIVATE HARGROVE
(1944)
SOUTHERN YANKEE, A (1948)
YOUNGEST PROFESSION, THE (1943)

Spielman, Fred
GREAT RUPERT, THE (1950)

Stainton, Philip
MOBY DICK (1956, Brit.)

Stalling, Carl
GREAT AMERICAN BUGS BUNNY-
ROAD RUNNER CHASE (1979)

Steiner, Fred
SEA GYPSIES, THE (1978)

Steiner, Max
ADVENTURES OF MARK TWAIN, THE
(1944)
ANGELS WITH DIRTY FACES (1938)
KING KONG (1933)
LIFE WITH FATHER (1947)
LITTLE LORD FAUNTLEROY (1936)
LITTLE WOMEN (1933)
ONE FOOT IN HEAVEN (1941)
ROOM FOR ONE MORE (1952)
SERGEANT YORK (1941)
THOSE CALLOWAYS (1964)

Stoll, George
COURTSHIP OF EDDIE'S FATHER,
THE (1963)
IN THE GOOD OLD SUMMERTIME
(1949)

Stoloff, Morris
GIDGET (1959)

Stothart, Herbert
AH, WILDERNESS! (1935)
DAVID COPPERFIELD (1935)
EDISON, THE MAN (1940)
HILLS OF HOME (1948)
MADAME CURIE (1943)
NATIONAL VELVET (1944)
NIGHT AT THE OPERA, A (1935)
SON OF LASSIE (1945)
TALE OF TWO CITIES, A (1935)
THREE MUSKETEERS, THE (1948)
TREASURE ISLAND (1934)

WIZARD OF OZ, THE (1939)
YEARLING, THE (1946)

Stravinsky, Igor
FANTASIA (1940)

Takemitsu, Tohru
ALONE ON THE PACIFIC (1964, Jap.)

Tardif, Graham
TAIL OF THE TIGER (1984, Aus.)

Tchaikovsky, Peter Ilyich
FANTASIA (1940)
NUTCRACKER: THE MOTION
PICTURE (1986)
POCKETFUL OF MIRACLES (1961)
SWAN LAKE, THE (1967)
SLEEPING BEAUTY (1959)

Thomson, Virgil
LOUISIANA STORY (1948)

Thorne, Ken
SUPERMAN II (1980)

Tiomkin, Dimitri
ALAMO, THE (1960)
ALICE IN WONDERLAND (1933)
CHAMPAGNE FOR CAESAR (1950)
HAPPY TIME, THE (1952)
IT'S A WONDERFUL LIFE (1946)
MR. SMITH GOES TO WASHINGTON
(1939)
SO THIS IS NEW YORK (1948)

Toch, Ernst
GHOST BREAKERS, THE (1940)

Trojan, Vaclav
MIDSUMMER NIGHT'S DREAM, A
(1961, Czech.)

Uno, Seiichiro
WORLD OF HANS CHRISTIAN
ANDERSEN (1971, Jap.)

Van Alstyne, Egbert
WAY OUT WEST (1937)

Vars, Henry
FLIPPER (1963)
FLIPPER'S NEW ADVENTURE (1964)

Vivaldi, Antonio
WILD CHILD, THE (1970, Fr.)

von Suppe, Franz
WAY OUT WEST (1937)

Wallace, Oliver
ALICE IN WONDERLAND (1951)
CINDERELLA (1950)
DARBY O'GILL AND THE LITTLE
PEOPLE (1959)
FUN AND FANCY FREE (1947)
INCREDIBLE JOURNEY, THE (1963)
LADY AND THE TRAMP (1955)
NIKKI, WILD DOG OF THE NORTH
(1961, US/Can.)
OLD YELLER (1957)
PETER PAN (1953)

Walton, Sir William
BATTLE OF BRITAIN, THE (1969, Brit.)

Ward, Edmund
YANK AT OXFORD, A (1938)

Ward, Edward
ALI BABA AND THE FORTY THIEVES
(1944)
BABE RUTH STORY, THE (1948)
BOYS TOWN (1938)
YOUNG TOM EDISON (1940)

Warren, Harry
SUMMER HOLIDAY (1948)

Waxman, Franz
AIR FORCE (1943)
AT THE CIRCUS (1939)
CAPTAINS COURAGEOUS (1937)
CHRISTMAS CAROL, A (1938)
FLASH GORDON (1936)
HORN BLOWS AT MIDNIGHT, THE
(1945)
HUCKLEBERRY FINN (1939)
JOURNEY FOR MARGARET (1942)
SPIRIT OF ST. LOUIS, THE (1957)

Webb, Roy
ABE LINCOLN IN ILLINOIS (1940)
I REMEMBER MAMA (1948)
SINBAD THE SAILOR (1947)

Wilder, Alec
SAND CASTLE, THE (1961)

Williams, John
CLOSE ENCOUNTERS OF THE THIRD
KIND (1977)
E.T. THE EXTRA-TERRESTRIAL (1982)
EMPIRE OF THE SUN (1987)
EMPIRE STRIKES BACK, THE (1980)
RETURN OF THE JEDI (1983)
STAR WARS (1977)
SUPERMAN (1978)

Williams, Johnny
FITZWILLY (1967)

Williams, Paul
BUGSY MALONE (1976, Brit.)
MUPPET MOVIE, THE (1979)

Willson, Meredith
MUSIC MAN, THE (1962)

Wilson, Raymond Guy
DR. COPPELIUS (1968, US/Span.)

Young, Bob
DOT AND THE KOALA (1985, Aus.)

Young, Victor
AROUND THE WORLD IN 80 DAYS
(1956)
CAUGHT IN THE DRAFT (1941)
CONNECTICUT YANKEE IN KING
ARTHUR'S COURT, A (1949)
EMPEROR WALTZ, THE (1948)
GREATEST SHOW ON EARTH, THE
(1952)
GULLIVER'S TRAVELS (1939)
ROAD TO ZANZIBAR (1941)
SANDS OF IWO JIMA (1949)
SHANE (1953)
STORY OF WILL ROGERS, THE (1952)

Zaza, Paul
CHRISTMAS STORY, A (1983)

Ziffrer, Carl
CHRISTMAS STORY, A (1983)

PRODUCERS

Adelson, Gary
BOY WHO COULD FLY, THE (1986)

Adler, Buddy
INN OF THE SIXTH HAPPINESS, THE (1958)

Aellen, Werner
WOLFPEN PRINCIPLE, THE (1974, Can.)

Algar, James
GNOME-MOBILE, THE (1967)
INCREDIBLE JOURNEY, THE (1963)
RASCAL (1969)

Allen, Irwin
VOYAGE TO THE BOTTOM OF THE SEA (1961)

Allen, Lewis
NEVER CRY WOLF (1983)

Ames, Stephen
SINBAD THE SAILOR (1947)

Anderson, Bill
ADVENTURES OF BULLWHIP GRIFFIN, THE (1967)
BAREFOOT EXECUTIVE, THE (1971)
COMPUTER WORE TENNIS SHOES, THE (1970)
FIGHTING PRINCE OF DONEGAL, THE (1966, Brit.)
MOON PILOT (1962)
MOON-SPINNERS, THE (1964)
SHAGGY D.A., THE (1976)
SWISS FAMILY ROBINSON (1960)

Arthur, Robert
ABBOTT AND COSTELLO MEET FRANKENSTEIN (1948)
FATHER GOOSE (1964)
FRANCIS (1949)
FRANCIS IN THE HAUNTED HOUSE (1956)
STORY OF WILL ROGERS, THE (1952)

Attwooll, Hugh
MOON-SPINNERS, THE (1964)
THREE LIVES OF THOMASINA, THE (1963, US/Brit.)

Bagdasarian [, Jr.], Ross
CHIPMUNK ADVENTURE, THE (1987)

Balcon, Michael
YANK AT OXFORD, A (1938)

Barbera, Joe
CHARLOTTE'S WEB (1973)
MAN CALLED FLINTSTONE, THE (1966)

Barton, Charles
NOOSE HANGS HIGH, THE (1948)

Bassler, Robert
THUNDERHEAD-SON OF FLICKA (1945)

Beck, John
HARVEY (1950)

Bennett, Harve
STAR TREK III: THE SEARCH FOR SPOCK (1984)
STAR TREK IV: THE VOYAGE HOME (1986)

Berbeet, Marcel
WILD CHILD, THE (1970, Fr.)

Berman, Pandro S.
FATHER'S LITTLE DIVIDEND (1951)
LADDIE (1935)
NATIONAL VELVET (1944)
THREE MUSKETEERS, THE (1948)

Bischoff, Sam
ANGELS WITH DIRTY FACES (1938)

Blanke, Henry
ADVENTURES OF ROBIN HOOD, THE (1938)
ROOM FOR ONE MORE (1952)
STORY OF LOUIS PASTEUR, THE (1936)

Blaustein, Julian
MISTER 880 (1950)

Bloom, Jim
RETURN OF THE JEDI (1983)

Blumofe, Robert F.
YOURS, MINE AND OURS (1968)

Bluth, Don
AMERICAN TAIL, AN (1986)
SECRET OF NIMH, THE (1982)

Bogdanovich, Peter
WHAT'S UP, DOC? (1972)

Bogle, Duane
ALL CREATURES GREAT AND SMALL (1975, Brit.)

Boorman, John
HOPE AND GLORY (1987, Brit.)

Bosustow, Stephen
1001 ARABIAN NIGHTS (1959)

Boulting, Roy
HEAVENS ABOVE! (1963, Brit.)

Brackett, Charles
EMPEROR WALTZ, THE (1948)
JOURNEY TO THE CENTER OF THE EARTH (1959)
KING AND I, THE (1956)

Brahm, Hans [John]
SCROOGE (1935, Brit.)

Brickman, Marshall
MANHATTAN PROJECT, THE (1986)

Broccoli, Albert R.
CHITTY CHITTY BANG BANG (1968, Brit.)

Bronston, Samuel
KING OF KINGS (1961)

Brown, Clarence
ANGELS IN THE OUTFIELD (1951)
SECRET GARDEN, THE (1949)

Brown, George H.
BOY WHO STOLE A MILLION, THE (1960, Brit.)

Brown, Harry Joe
YOUNG PEOPLE (1940)

Buckner, Robert
LIFE WITH FATHER (1947)

Burton, Val
TIME OF THEIR LIVES, THE (1946)

Camp, Joe
BENJI (1974)

Capra, Frank
IT'S A WONDERFUL LIFE (1946)
MR. SMITH GOES TO WASHINGTON (1939)
POCKETFUL OF MIRACLES (1961)

Carroll, Matt
STORM BOY (1976, Aus.)

Carroll, Willard
NUTCRACKER: THE MOTION PICTURE (1986)

Chester, Hal E.
SCHOOL FOR SCOUNDRELS (1960, Brit.)

Christensen, Don
MIGHTY MOUSE IN THE GREAT SPACE CHASE (1983)

Clark, Bob
CHRISTMAS STORY, A (1983)

Coe, Fred
MIRACLE WORKER, THE (1962)

Considine, Jr., John W.
BOYS TOWN (1938)
EDISON, THE MAN (1940)
YOUNG TOM EDISON (1940)

Cooper, Merian C.
KING KONG (1933)
THREE GODFATHERS, THE (1948)

Couffer, Jack
NEVER CRY WOLF (1983)

Courtland, Jerome
ESCAPE TO WITCH MOUNTAIN (1975)
PETE'S DRAGON (1977)

Cowan, Lester
STORY OF G.I. JOE, THE (1945)

Crawford, Robert L.
LITTLE ROMANCE, A (1979, US/Fr.)

Cummings, Jack
EXCUSE MY DUST (1951)
SEVEN BRIDES FOR SEVEN BROTHERS (1954)
STRATTON STORY, THE (1949)

DaCosta, Morton
MUSIC MAN, THE (1962)

Dalrymple, Ian
CRY FROM THE STREET, A (1959, Brit.)

Dancigers, Oscar
ADVENTURES OF ROBINSON CRUSOE, THE (1954)

Dare, Daniel
ROAD TO RIO (1947)

Daven, Andre
HOME IN INDIANA (1944)

PRODUCERS

David, Saul
FANTASTIC VOYAGE (1966)

Dean, Vaughan N.
MOBY DICK (1956, Brit.)

DeMille, Cecil B.
GREATEST SHOW ON EARTH, THE (1952)
TEN COMMANDMENTS, THE (1956)

DeSylva, B.G.
CAUGHT IN THE DRAFT (1941)
LITTLEST REBEL, THE (1935)
STOWAWAY (1936)

Deutsch, Armand
MAGNIFICENT YANKEE, THE (1950)

Dietrich, Ralph
MY FRIEND FLICKA (1943)

Disney, Walt
ABSENT-MINDED PROFESSOR, THE (1961)
ADVENTURES OF ICHABOD AND MR. TOAD (1949)
ADVENTURES OF BULLWHIP GRIFFIN, THE (1967)
ALICE IN WONDERLAND (1951)
BAMBI (1942)
CINDERELLA (1950)
DARBY O'GILL AND THE LITTLE PEOPLE (1959)
DUMBO (1941)
EMIL AND THE DETECTIVES (1964)
FANTASIA (1940)
FIGHTING PRINCE OF DONEGAL, THE (1966, Brit.)
FOLLOW ME, BOYS! (1966)
FUN AND FANCY FREE (1947)
GNOME-MOBILE, THE (1967)
GREYFRIARS BOBBY (1961, Brit.)
IN SEARCH OF THE CASTAWAYS (1962, Brit.)
INCREDIBLE JOURNEY, THE (1963)
JOHNNY TREMAIN (1957)
JUNGLE BOOK, THE (1967)
LADY AND THE TRAMP (1955)
LIGHT IN THE FOREST, THE (1958)
MARY POPPINS (1964)
MELODY TIME (1948)
NIKKI, WILD DOG OF THE NORTH (1961, US/Can.)
OLD YELLER (1957)
ONE HUNDRED AND ONE DALMATIANS (1961)
PETER PAN (1953)
PINOCCHIO (1940)
POLLYANNA (1960)
SHAGGY DOG, THE (1959)
SLEEPING BEAUTY (1959)
SNOW WHITE AND THE SEVEN DWARFS (1937)
SO DEAR TO MY HEART (1949)
SONG OF THE SOUTH (1946)
SUMMER MAGIC (1963)
THOSE CALLOWAYS (1964)
20,000 LEAGUES UNDER THE SEA (1954)

Dolan, Robert Emmett
WHITE CHRISTMAS (1954)

Dryhurst, Michael
HOPE AND GLORY (1987, Brit.)

Dubbs, Arthur R.
ADVENTURES OF THE WILDERNESS FAMILY, THE (1975)

Dull, Orville O.
EDISON, THE MAN (1940)

Dupont, Rene
CHRISTMAS STORY, A (1983)

Eagle [Sam Spiegel], S.P.
AFRICAN QUEEN, THE (1951, US/Brit.)
TALES OF MANHATTAN (1942)

Edens, Roger
DEEP IN MY HEART (1954)

Ehrlich, Henry
ADVENTURES OF ROBINSON CRUSOE, THE (1954)

Engel, Samuel G.
COME TO THE STABLE (1949)
MAN CALLED PETER, A (1955)
SITTING PRETTY (1948)

Ephron, Henry
BEST THINGS IN LIFE ARE FREE, THE (1956)

Fellows, Robert
CONNECTICUT YANKEE IN KING ARTHUR'S COURT, A (1949)

Ferguson, Norman
THREE CABALLEROS, THE (1944)

Feuer, Cy
WHERE'S CHARLEY? (1952, Brit.)

Field, Arthur L.
CANTERVILLE GHOST, THE (1944)

Fier, Jack
FIVE LITTLE PEPPERS AND HOW THEY GREW (1939)

Fineman, B.P.
JOURNEY FOR MARGARET (1942)

Fisz, S. Benjamin
BATTLE OF BRITAIN, THE (1969, Brit.)

Flaherty, Robert J.
LOUISIANA STORY (1948)

Fleischer, Max
GULLIVER'S TRAVELS (1939)
MR. BUG GOES TO TOWN (1941)

Ford, John
THREE GODFATHERS, THE (1948)

Forstater, Mark
GLITTERBALL, THE (1977, Brit.)

Frank, Melvin
CALLAWAY WENT THATAWAY (1951)
COURT JESTER, THE (1956)

Franklin, Chester M.
PAINTED HILLS, THE (1951)

Franklin, Sidney
MADAME CURIE (1943)
YEARLING, THE (1946)

Freed, Arthur
ANNIE GET YOUR GUN (1950)
BABES IN ARMS (1939)

EASTER PARADE (1948)
GIRL CRAZY (1943)
HARVEY GIRLS, THE (1946)
MEET ME IN ST. LOUIS (1944)
STRIKE UP THE BAND (1940)
SUMMER HOLIDAY (1948)
TAKE ME OUT TO THE BALL GAME (1949)

Gilkison, Anthony
WINGS OF MYSTERY (1963, Brit.)

Gilliam, Terry
TIME BANDITS (1981, Brit.)

Gilliat, Sidney
BELLES OF ST. TRINIAN'S, THE (1954, Brit.)
WEE GEORDIE (1956, Brit.)

Gion, Christian
HERE COMES SANTA CLAUS (1984)

Golden, Robert
LASSIE'S GREAT ADVENTURE (1963)

Goldman, Gary
AMERICAN TAIL, AN (1986)
SECRET OF NIMH, THE (1982)

Goldman, Les
PHANTOM TOLLBOOTH, THE (1970)

Goldstein, Leonard
MA AND PA KETTLE ON VACATION (1953)
MA AND PA KETTLE (1949)
MR. SCOUTMASTER (1953)

Goldwyn, Jr., Samuel
ADVENTURES OF HUCKLEBERRY FINN, THE (1960)

Goldwyn, Samuel
HANS CHRISTIAN ANDERSEN (1952)
KID FROM BOOKLYN, THE (1946)
KID FROM SPAIN, THE (1932)
PRIDE OF THE YANKEES, THE (1942)
ROSEANNA McCOY (1949)
WONDER MAN (1945)

Golitzen, George
PARENT TRAP, THE (1961)

Goodwin, Richard
PETER RABBIT AND TALES OF BEATRIX POTTER (1971, Brit.)

Gordon, Leon
KIM (1950)

Gordon, Max
ABE LINCOLN IN ILLINOIS (1940)
MY SISTER EILEEN (1942)

Gottleib, Alex
RIDE 'EM COWBOY (1942)
HOLD THAT GHOST (1941)

Grainger, Edmund
SANDS OF IWO JIMA (1949)

Grant, Joe
MAKE MINE MUSIC (1946)

Grant, John
HERE COME THE CO-EDS (1945)

Grey, Harry
KING OF THE COWBOYS (1943)

Griffith, Raymond
DRUMS ALONG THE MOHAWK (1939)
HEIDI (1937)
Grippo, Jan
LET'S GO NAVY (1951)
LIVE WIRES (1946)
NEWS HOUNDS (1947)
Gross, Sandra
DOT AND THE KOALA (1985, Aus.)
Gross, Yoram
DOT AND THE KOALA (1985, Aus.)
Hagen, Julius
SCROOGE (1935, Brit.)
Haight, George
SEE HERE, PRIVATE HARGROVE
(1944)
Hakim, Andre
O. HENRY'S FULL HOUSE (1952)
Hale, Frank J.
DR. COPPELIUS (1968, US/Span.)
Halmi, Robert
HUGO THE HIPPO (1976, Hung./US)
Hammer, Jerry
WHO SAYS I CAN'T RIDE A
RAINBOW? (1971)
Hand, David D.
BAMBI (1942)
Hanna, William
MAN CALLED FLINTSTONE, THE
(1966)
CHARLOTTE'S WEB (1973)
Harryhausen, Ray
GOLDEN VOYAGE OF SINBAD, THE
(1974, Brit.)
SINBAD AND THE EYE OF THE TIGER
(1977, US/Brit.)
Havelock-Allan, Anthony
OLIVER TWIST (1951, Brit.)
Hawkesworth, John
TIGER BAY (1959, Brit.)
Hayward, Leland
SPIRIT OF ST. LOUIS, THE (1957)
Hellinger, Mark
HORN BLOWS AT MIDNIGHT, THE
(1945)
Hellman, Jerome
WORLD OF HENRY ORIENT, THE
(1964)
Henson, Jim
MUPPET MOVIE, THE (1979)
Hibler, Winston
ARISTOCATS, THE (1970)
ISLAND AT THE TOP OF THE WORLD,
THE (1974)
NIKKI, WILD DOG OF THE NORTH
(1961, US/Can.)
THOSE CALLOWAYS (1964)
Hill, Jerome
SAND CASTLE, THE (1961)
Hornblow, Jr., Arthur
GHOST BREAKERS, THE (1940)

OKLAHOMA! (1955)
Hubley, Faith
OF STARS AND MEN (1961)
Hubley, John
OF STARS AND MEN (1961)
Huston, John
MOBY DICK (1956, Brit.)
Jacobs, Arthur P.
DOCTOR DOLITTLE (1967)
TOM SAWYER (1973)
Jacobs, William
CHRISTMAS IN CONNECTICUT (1945)
Jaffe, Sam
BORN FREE (1966)
Jaffe, Stanley R.
BAD NEWS BEARS, THE (1976)
Johnson, Mark
YOUNG SHERLOCK HOLMES (1985)
Jones, Chuck
GREAT AMERICAN BUGS BUNNY-
ROAD RUNNER CHASE (1979)
PHANTOM TOLLBOOTH, THE (1970)
Jones, Paul
ROAD TO UTOPIA (1945)
ROAD TO ZANZIBAR (1941)
ROAD TO MOROCCO (1942)
SOUTHERN YANKEE, A (1948)
Jordan, Larry
HILDUR AND THE MAGICIAN (1969)
Jurow, Martin
SYLVESTER (1985)
Kaufman, Joe
BABE RUTH STORY, THE (1948)
Kaufman, Leonard B.
CLARENCE, THE CROSS-EYED LION
(1965)
Kay, Gordon
FLUFFY (1965)
Kazanjian, Howard
RETURN OF THE JEDI (1983)
Kennedy, Kathleen
E.T. THE EXTRA-TERRESTRIAL (1982)
EMPIRE OF THE SUN (1987)
Knopf, Edwin H.
FEARLESS FAGAN (1952)
LILI (1953)
Kohlmar, Fred
GHOST AND MRS. MUIR, THE (1942)
MY SISTER EILEEN (1955)
Korda, Alexander
JUNGLE BOOK, THE (1942)
THIEF OF BAGHDAD, THE (1940, Brit.)
Kramer, Stanley
5,000 FINGERS OF DR. T., THE (1953)
HAPPY TIME, THE (1952)
IT'S A MAD, MAD, MAD, MAD WORLD
(1963)
SO THIS IS NEW YORK (1948)
Kurtz, Gary
EMPIRE STRIKES BACK, THE (1980)

STAR WARS (1977)
Kushner, Donald
NUTCRACKER: THE MOTION
PICTURE (1986)
Langley, Noel
PICKWICK PAPERS, THE (1952, Brit.)
Lansburgh, Larry
LITTLEST OUTLAW, THE (1955)
Lasky, Jesse L.
ADVENTURES OF MARK TWAIN, THE
(1944)
SERGEANT YORK (1941)
Launder, Frank
BELLES OF ST. TRINIAN'S, THE (1954,
Brit.)
WEE GEORDIE (1956, Brit.)
Laurel, Stan
WAY OUT WEST (1937)
Lazer, David
GREAT MUPPET CAPER, THE (1981)
MUPPETS TAKE MANHATTAN, THE
(1984)
Le Baron, William
IT'S A GIFT (1934)
YOU'RE TELLING ME (1934)
Lehman, Ernest
HELLO, DOLLY! (1969)
Leroy, Mervyn
AT THE CIRCUS (1939)
WIZARD OF OZ, THE (1939)
Levine, Joseph E.
FABULOUS WORLD OF JULES
VERNE, THE (1961, Czech.)
Levitow, Abe
PHANTOM TOLLBOOTH, THE (1970)
Lighton, Louis D.
ALICE IN WONDERLAND (1933)
CAPTAINS COURAGEOUS (1937)
SKIPPY (1931)
TOM SAWYER (1930)
Lobell, Mike
JOURNEY OF NATTY GANN, THE
(1985)
Locke, Peter
NUTCRACKER: THE MOTION
PICTURE (1986)
Lyndon, Victor
JOHNNY ON THE RUN (1953, Brit.)
Lyons, Stuart
SLIPPER AND THE ROSE, THE (1976,
Brit.)
MacDonald, Wallace
KONGA, THE WILD STALLION (1939)
MacGowan, Kenneth
KIDNAPPED (1938)
LITTLE WOMEN (1933)
STORY OF ALEXANDER GRAHAM
BELL, THE (1939)
MacRae, Henry
FLASH GORDON (1936)

PRODUCERS

Mahon, Barry
THUMBELINA (1970)

Maibaum, Richard
DEAR WIFE (1949)

Malvern, Paul
ALI BABA AND THE FORTY THIEVES (1944)

Mankiewicz, Herman
DUCK SOUP (1933)

Mankiewicz, Joseph L.
CHRISTMAS CAROL, A (1938)
HUCKLEBERRY FINN (1939)

Manning, Bruce
AMAZING MRS. HOLLIDAY (1943)

Margulies, Stan
THOSE MAGNIFICENT MEN IN THEIR FLYING MACHINES OR HOW I FLEW FROM LONDON TO PARIS IN 25 HOURS AND 11 MINUTES (1965, Brit.)
WILLY WONKA AND THE CHOCOLATE FACTORY (1971)

Markey, Gene
ADVENTURES OF SHERLOCK HOLMES, THE (1939)
KENTUCKY (1938)
WEE WILLIE WINKIE (1937)

Marshall, Alan
BUGSY MALONE (1976, Brit.)

Marshall, Frank
EMPIRE OF THE SUN (1987)
WHO FRAMED ROGER RABBIT? (1988)

Martin, Ernest
WHERE'S CHARLEY? (1952, Brit.)

Marton, Andrew
KING SOLOMON'S MINES (1950)

Marx, Samuel
LASSIE, COME HOME (1943)
MY BROTHER TALKS TO HORSES (1946)
SON OF LASSIE (1945)

Mason, Hal
BOY TEN FEET TALL, A (1965, Brit.)

Mason, Herbert
JOHN AND JULIE (1957, Brit.)

Matheson, Margaret
ALL THINGS BRIGHT AND BEAUTIFUL (1979, Brit.)

McCarey, Leo
BELLS OF ST. MARY'S, THE (1945)
GOING MY WAY (1944)

Melendez, Bill
BON VOYAGE, CHARLIE BROWN (AND DON'T COME BACK) (1980)
SNOOPY, COME HOME (1972)

Mendelson, Lee
BON VOYAGE, CHARLIE BROWN (AND DON'T COME BACK) (1980)
SNOOPY, COME HOME (1972)

Miller, Ron
CAT FROM OUTER SPACE, THE (1978)
FREAKY FRIDAY (1976)

LITTLEST HORSE THIEVES, THE (1977)
NOW YOU SEE HIM, NOW YOU DON'T (1972)
PETE'S DRAGON (1977)
SON OF FLUBBER (1963)
SUMMER MAGIC (1963)
THAT DARN CAT (1965)

Minter, George
PICKWICK PAPERS, THE (1952, Brit.)

Mirisch, Walter
BOMBA THE JUNGLE BOY (1949)
FITZWILLY (1967)

Morros, Boris
FLYING DEUCES, THE (1939)
TALES OF MANHATTAN (1942)

Moskov, George
CHAMPAGNE FOR CAESAR (1950)

Mull, Edward
ISLAND OF THE BLUE DOLPHINS (1964)

Nakai, Akira
ALONE ON THE PACIFIC (1964, Jap.)

Nassour, Edward
AFRICA SCREAMS (1949)

Nayfack, Nicholas
INVISIBLE BOY, THE (1957)

Neame, Ronald
GREAT EXPECTATIONS (1946, Brit.)
MAGIC BOX, THE (1952, Brit.)
OLIVER TWIST (1951, Brit.)

Nelson, Ralph
FLIGHT OF THE DOVES (1971)

Nolbandov, Sergei
LITTLE KIDNAPPERS, THE (1954, Brit.)

Ogden, Jennifer
MANHATTAN PROJECT, THE (1986)

Okawa, Hiroshi
WORLD OF HANS CHRISTIAN ANDERSEN (1971, Jap.)

Ostrow, Lou
JUDGE HARDY AND SON (1939)

Oz, Frank
GREAT MUPPET CAPER, THE (1981)

Pakula, Alan J.
TO KILL A MOCKINGBIRD (1962)

Pal, George
GREAT RUPERT, THE (1950)
SEVEN FACES OF DR. LAO (1964)
TIME MACHINE, THE (1960, Brit./US)
TOM THUMB (1958, Brit./US)
WONDERFUL WORLD OF THE BROTHERS GRIMM, THE (1962)

Panama, Norman
CALLAWAY WENT THATAWAY (1951)
COURT JESTER, THE (1956)
LI'L ABNER (1959)

Parkyn, Leslie
LITTLE KIDNAPPERS, THE (1954, Brit.)

Parsons, Harriet
I REMEMBER MAMA (1948)

Parsons, Lindsley
LIVE WIRES (1946)

Pasternak, Joe
COURTSHIP OF EDDIE'S FATHER, THE (1963)
DATE WITH JUDY, A (1948)
HIT THE DECK (1955)
IN THE GOOD OLD SUMMERTIME (1949)
THREE SMART GIRLS (1937)

Paulve, Andre
BEAUTY AND THE BEAST (1947, Fr.)

Pearce, Perce
SO DEAR TO MY HEART (1949)
STORY OF ROBIN HOOD, THE (1952, Brit.)
TREASURE ISLAND (1950, Brit.)

Peck, Gregory
DOVE, THE (1974, Brit.)

Pennington, Jon
MOUSE THAT ROARED, THE (1959, Brit.)

Perlberg, William
CHARLEY'S AUNT (1941)
IT HAPPENS EVERY SPRING (1949)
SONG OF BERNADETTE, THE (1943)

Perry, Frank
TRUMAN CAPOTE'S TRILOGY (1969)

Phillips, Julia
CLOSE ENCOUNTERS OF THE THIRD KIND (1977)

Phillips, Michael
CLOSE ENCOUNTERS OF THE THIRD KIND (1977)

Pieterse, Andre
FOREVER YOUNG, FOREVER FREE (1976, South Africa)

Pilbrow, Richard
SWALLOWS AND AMAZONS (1977, Brit.)

Pomeroy, John
AMERICAN TAIL, AN (1986)
SECRET OF NIMH, THE (1982)

Pommer, Eric
SIDEWALKS OF LONDON (1940, Brit.)

Popkin, Harry
CHAMPAGNE FOR CAESAR (1950)

Prescott, Norm
MIGHTY MOUSE IN THE GREAT SPACE CHASE (1983)

Puttnam, David
CHARIOTS OF FIRE (1981, Brit.)
MELODY (1971, Brit.)

Rachmil, Lewis J.
GIDGET (1959)

Radin, Paul
BORN FREE (1966)

Radnitz, Robert B.
LITTLE ARK, THE (1972)
MISTY (1961)
MY SIDE OF THE MOUNTAIN (1969)

SOUNDER (1972)

Radnitz, Robert D.
DOG OF FLANDERS, A (1959)
ISLAND OF THE BLUE DOLPHINS (1964)

Rafill, Joseph C.
SEA GYPSIES, THE (1978)

Rankin, Douglas
SCHOOL FOR SCOUNDRELS (1960, Brit.)

Rankin, Jr., Arthur
DAYDREAMER, THE (1966)
WACKY WORLD OF MOTHER GOOSE, THE (1967)
WILLIE MCBEAN AND HIS MAGIC MACHINE (1965, US/Jap.)

Rapf, Harry
CHAMP, THE (1931)

Rattray, Eric
LABYRINTH (1986)

Reid, Cliff
ANNIE OAKLEY (1935)

Reiner, Rob
PRINCESS BRIDE, THE (1987)

Reitherman, Wolfgang
ARISTOCATS, THE (1970)
FOX AND THE HOUND, THE (1981)
RESCUERS, THE (1977)
ROBIN HOOD (1973)

Roach, Hal
BABES IN TOYLAND (1934)
BLOCKHEADS (1938)
TOPPER (1937)

Roddenberry, Gene
STAR TREK: THE MOTION PICTURE (1979)

Rogers, Peter
DOG AND THE DIAMONDS, THE (1962, Brit.)

Roos, Fred
BLACK STALLION, THE (1979)

Rose, Jack
SEVEN LITTLE FOYS, THE (1955)

Rosenberg, Aaron
CATTLE DRIVE (1951)

Rousset-Rouard, Yves
LITTLE ROMANCE, A (1979, US/Fr.)

Rowland, Roy
EXCUSE MY DUST (1951)

Ruggles, Wesley
SING YOU SINNERS (1938)

Sallin, Robert
STAR TREK II: THE WRATH OF KHAN (1982)

Saltzman, Harry
BATTLE OF BRITAIN, THE (1969, Brit.)

Sandler, Allan
FRASIER, THE SENSUOUS LION (1973)

Saperstein, Henry G.
GAY PURR-EE (1962)

Saville, Victor
GOODBYE MR. CHIPS (1939, Brit.)

Schaefer, Armand
LAST ROUND-UP, THE (1947)
MY PAL TRIGGER (1946)

Schary, Dore
BACHELOR AND THE BOBBY-SOXER, THE (1947)
FARMER'S DAUGHTER, THE (1947)
NEXT VOICE YOU HEAR, THE (1950)

Scheimer, Lou
MIGHTY MOUSE IN THE GREAT SPACE CHASE (1983)
PINOCCHIO AND THE EMPEROR OF THE NIGHT (1987)

Scheinman, Arnold
PRINCESS BRIDE, THE (1987)

Schermer, Jules
PRIDE OF ST. LOUIS, THE (1952)

Schneer, Charles H.
GOLDEN VOYAGE OF SINBAD, THE (1974, Brit.)
JASON AND THE ARGONAUTS (1963, Brit.)
MYSTERIOUS ISLAND (1961, US/Brit.)
SEVENTH VOYAGE OF SINBAD, THE (1958)
SINBAD AND THE EYE OF THE TIGER (1977, US/Brit.)

Schoedsack, Ernest B.
KING KONG (1933)

Schulberg, B.P.
LITTLE MISS MARKER (1934)

Schwalb, Ben
JALOPY (1953)

Selznick, David O.
ADVENTURES OF TOM SAWYER, THE (1938)
DAVID COPPERFIELD (1935)
LITTLE LORD FAUNTLEROY (1936)
TALE OF TWO CITIES, A (1935)

Sexton, John
PHAR LAP (1984, Aus.)

Shaw, Peter
WATER BABIES, THE (1979, Brit.)

Sheldon, E. Lloyd
MILKY WAY, THE (1936)

Shenson, Walter
MOUSE THAT ROARED, THE (1959, Brit.)

Sherman, Harry A.
BUFFALO BILL (1944)

Siegel, Sol C.
DREAMBOAT (1952)
HENRY ALDRICH FOR PRESIDENT (1941)

Silvera, Rene
PLAYTIME (1973, Fr.)

Sisk, Robert
CHALLENGE TO LASSIE (1949)
COURAGE OF LASSIE (1946)
HILLS OF HOME (1948)

SUN COMES UP, THE (1949)

Skutezky, Victor
ALIVE AND KICKING (1962, Brit.)

Small, Edward
COUNT OF MONTE CRISTO, THE (1934)
DAVY CROCKETT, INDIAN SCOUT (1950)
FULLER BRUSH MAN (1948)
JACK THE GIANT KILLER (1962)

Smith, Bernard
HOW THE WEST WAS WON (1962)

Solo, Robert H.
SCROOGE (1970, Brit.)

Sparks, Robert
BLONDIE (1938)
SHUT MY BIG MOUTH (1942)

Spengler, Pierre
SUPERMAN II (1980)
SUPERMAN (1978)

Sperling, Milton
BATTLE OF THE BULGE (1965)

Spielberg, Steven
E.T. THE EXTRA-TERRESTRIAL (1982)
EMPIRE OF THE SUN (1987)

Spigelgass, Leonard
ONE NIGHT IN THE TROPICS (1940)

Stark, Ray
ANNIE (1982)

Starr, Irving
BATAAN (1943)

Sternberg, Tom
BLACK STALLION, THE (1979)

Stevens, Art
FOX AND THE HOUND, THE (1981)

Stevens, George
I REMEMBER MAMA (1948)
SHANE (1953)

Stone, John
CHARLIE CHAN AT THE OPERA (1936)

Strick, Joseph
NEVER CRY WOLF (1983)

Stromberg, Hunt
AH, WILDERNESS! (1935)
TREASURE ISLAND (1934)

Sturges, John
GREAT ESCAPE, THE (1963)

Susskind, David
ALL CREATURES GREAT AND SMALL (1975, Brit.)

Tati, Jacques
MY UNCLE (1958, Fr.)

Teasdale, Verree
MILKY WAY, THE (1936)

Thalberg, Irving
NIGHT AT THE OPERA, A (1935)
TARZAN THE APE MAN (1932)

Todd, Michael
AROUND THE WORLD IN 80 DAYS (1956)

SCREENWRITERS

Tokar, Norman
CAT FROM OUTER SPACE, THE (1978)

Tors, Ivan
AFRICA--TEXAS STYLE! (1967)
FLIPPER (1963)
FLIPPER'S NEW ADVENTURE (1964)
GENTLE GIANT (1967)

Trnka, Jiri
MIDSUMMER NIGHT'S DREAM, A
(1961, Czech.)

Trotti, Lamar
CHEAPER BY THE DOZEN (1950)
STARS AND STRIPES FOREVER (1952)

Truffaut, Francois
FOUR HUNDRED BLOWS, THE (1959)

Vaughn, Ven
FOR THE LOVE OF BENJI (1977)

Vernon, James M.
TAIL OF THE TIGER (1984, Aus.)

Villard, Dimitri
FLIGHT OF THE NAVIGATOR (1986)

Wald, Jerry
INSPECTOR GENERAL, THE (1949)
MR. HOBBS TAKES A VACATION
(1962)

Wald, Robby
FLIGHT OF THE NAVIGATOR (1986)

Wallis, Hal B.
ADVENTURES OF ROBIN HOOD, THE
(1938)
AIR FORCE (1943)
KNUTE ROCKNE--ALL AMERICAN
(1940)
ONE FOOT IN HEAVEN (1941)
PRINCE AND THE PAUPER, THE (1937)
SERGEANT YORK (1941)
THIS IS THE ARMY (1943)
TRUE GRIT (1969)
YANKEE DOODLE DANDY (1942)

Walsh, Bill
BEDKNOBS AND BROOMSTICKS
(1971)
BLACKBEARD'S GHOST (1968)
DAVY CROCKETT, KING OF THE WILD
FRONTIER (1955)
HERBIE RIDES AGAIN (1974)
LOVE BUG, THE (1968)
MARY POPPINS (1964)
SHAGGY DOG, THE (1959)
SON OF FLUBBER (1963)
THAT DARN CAT (1965)
TOBY TYLER (1960)
WORLD'S GREATEST ATHLETE, THE
(1973)

Wanger, Walter
ARABIAN NIGHTS (1942)

Warner, Jack L.
FIGHTING 69TH, THE (1940)
KNUTE ROCKNE--ALL AMERICAN
(1940)
MY FAIR LADY (1964)
ONE FOOT IN HEAVEN (1941)
THIS IS THE ARMY (1943)

Watts, Robert
RETURN OF THE JEDI (1983)
WHO FRAMED ROGER RABBIT? (1988)

Wayne, John
ALAMO, THE (1960)

Weingarten, Lawrence
DAY AT THE RACES, A (1937)

Weintraub, Jerry
KARATE KID, THE (1984)

White, Edward J.
BELLS OF ROSARITA (1945)

Wilhite, Thomas L.
NUTCRACKER: THE MOTION
PICTURE (1986)

Wilson, Carey
LOVE FINDS ANDY HARDY (1938)

Wintle, Julian
BELSTONE FOX, THE (1976, Brit.)

Wise, Robert
SOUND OF MUSIC, THE (1965)

Wolper, David L.
WILLY WONKA AND THE
CHOCOLATE FACTORY (1971)

Woolf, John
OLIVER! (1968, Brit.)

Wright, William H.
ADVENTURES OF TOM SAWYER, THE
(1938)

Wurtzel, Sol
BRIGHT EYES (1934)

Yordan, Philip
BATTLE OF THE BULGE (1965)

Zanuck, Darryl F.
ADVENTURES OF SHERLOCK
HOLMES, THE (1939)
CALL OF THE WILD (1935)
CAPTAIN JANUARY (1935)
HOW GREEN WAS MY VALLEY (1941)
KENTUCKY (1938)
LITTLE PRINCESS, THE (1939)
LITTLEST REBEL, THE (1935)
STANLEY AND LIVINGSTONE (1939)
STORY OF ALEXANDER GRAHAM
BELL, THE (1939)
YANK IN THE R.A.F., A (1941)

Ziedman, B.F.
YOUNGEST PROFESSION, THE (1943)

Zimbalist, Sam
KING SOLOMON'S MINES (1950)

SCREENWRITERS

Adams, Max
LET'S GO NAVY (1951)

Adler, Felix
BLOCKHEADS (1938)
WAY OUT WEST (1937)

Agee, James
AFRICAN QUEEN, THE (1951, US/Brit.)

Algar, James
INCREDIBLE JOURNEY, THE (1963)

Allen, Irwin
VOYAGE TO THE BOTTOM OF THE
SEA (1961)

Allen, R.S.
MAN CALLED FLINTSTONE, THE
(1966)

Ambler, Eric
MAGIC BOX, THE (1952, Brit.)

Anderson, Ken
ARISTOCATS, THE (1970)
JUNGLE BOOK, THE (1967)
MELODY TIME (1948)
RESCUERS, THE (1977)
CINDERELLA (1950)

Andrews, Robert D.
BATAAN (1943)

Annakin, Ken
THOSE MAGNIFICENT MEN IN THEIR
FLYING MACHINES OR HOW I FLEW
FROM LONDON TO PARIS IN 25
HOURS AND 11 MINUTES (1965, Brit.)

Ardrey, Robert
SECRET GARDEN, THE (1949)
THREE MUSKETEERS, THE (1948)

Arthur, Art
FLIPPER'S NEW ADVENTURE (1964)

Atlas, Leopold
STORY OF G.I. JOE, THE (1945)

Bagdasarian [, Jr.], Ross
CHIPMUNK ADVENTURE, THE (1987)

Baker, Herbert
SO THIS IS NEW YORK (1948)

Baldwin, Earl
AFRICA SCREAMS (1949)

Banta, Milt
PETER PAN (1953)

Barrett, Lawrence
JOHN WESLEY (1954, Brit.)

Bartlett, Jeanne
SON OF LASSIE (1945)

Battaglia, Aurelius
PINOCCHIO (1940)

Battle, John Tucker
SO DEAR TO MY HEART (1949)

Baum, Thomas
MANHATTAN PROJECT, THE (1986)
HUGO THE HIPPO (1976, Hung./US)

Beagle, Peter
DOVE, THE (1974, Brit.)

Beaumont, Charles
SEVEN FACES OF DR. LAO (1964)
WONDERFUL WORLD OF THE
BROTHERS GRIMM, THE (1962)

Behrman, S.N.
TALE OF TWO CITIES, A (1935)

Belden, Charles S.
CHARLIE CHAN AT THE OPERA (1936)

Belgard, Arnold
BLOCKHEADS (1938)

Beloin, Edmund
TALES OF MANHATTAN (1942)
CONNECTICUT YANKEE IN KING
ARTHUR'S COURT, A (1949)
HARVEY GIRLS, THE (1946)
ROAD TO RIO (1947)

Bennett, Charles
VOYAGE TO THE BOTTOM OF THE
SEA (1961)

Bennett, Harve
STAR TREK IV: THE VOYAGE HOME
(1986)
STAR TREK III: THE SEARCH FOR
SPOCK (1984)

Benson, Sally
COME TO THE STABLE (1949)
SUMMER MAGIC (1963)

Benton, Robert
SUPERMAN (1978)
WHAT'S UP, DOC? (1972)

Berg, Sonia
STORM BOY (1976, Aus.)

Berman, Ted
FOX AND THE HOUND, THE (1981)
RESCUERS, THE (1977)

Binyon, Claude
DREAMBOAT (1952)
SING YOU SINNERS (1938)
THIS IS THE ARMY (1943)

Biro, Lajos
THIEF OF BAGHDAD, THE (1940, Brit.)

Blackburn, Tom
DAVY CROCKETT, KING OF THE WILD
FRONTIER (1955)
JOHNNY TREMAIN (1957)

Blank, Dorothy Ann
SNOW WHITE AND THE SEVEN
DWARFS (1937)

Blankford, Henry
TALES OF MANHATTAN (1942)

Blazek, Jiri
WISHING MACHINE (1971, Czech.)

Blum, Edwin
ADVENTURES OF SHERLOCK
HOLMES, THE (1939)
CANTERVILLE GHOST, THE (1944)
KIDNAPPED (1938)
YOUNG PEOPLE (1940)

Bluth, Don
SECRET OF NIMH, THE (1982)

Boardman, True
ARABIAN NIGHTS (1942)
PAINTED HILLS, THE (1951)
RIDE 'EM COWBOY (1942)

Boasberg, Al
NIGHT AT THE OPERA, A (1935)

Bodeen, DeWitt
I REMEMBER MAMA (1948)

Bodrero, James
MAKE MINE MUSIC (1946)
THREE CABALLEROS, THE (1944)

Bolton, Guy
EASTER PARADE (1948)

Boorman, John
HOPE AND GLORY (1987, Brit.)

Boulting, John
HEAVENS ABOVE! (1963, Brit.)

Bowers, William
BEST THINGS IN LIFE ARE FREE, THE
(1956)

Boylan, Malcolm Stuart
YANK AT OXFORD, A (1938)

Brackett, Charles
EMPEROR WALTZ, THE (1948)
JOURNEY TO THE CENTER OF THE
EARTH (1959)

Brackett, Leigh
EMPIRE STRIKES BACK, THE (1980)

Bradbury, Ray
MOBY DICK (1956, Brit.)

Brady, Fred
CHAMPAGNE FOR CAESAR (1950)

Brdecka, Jiri
MIDSUMMERS NIGHT'S DREAM, A
(1961, Czech.)

Brecher, Irving
AT THE CIRCUS (1939)
MEET ME IN ST. LOUIS (1944)
SUMMER HOLIDAY (1948)

Breen, Richard
O. HENRY'S FULL HOUSE (1952)

Brennan, Frederick Hazlitt
FEARLESS FAGAN (1952)

Brickman, Marshall
MANHATTAN PROJECT, THE (1986)

Bricusse, Leslie
DOCTOR DOLITTLE (1967)
SCROOGE (1970, Brit.)

Brightman, Homer
ADVENTURES OF ICHABOD AND MR.
TOAD (1949)
CINDERELLA (1950)
FUN AND FANCY FREE (1947)
MAKE MINE MUSIC (1946)
MELODY TIME (1948)
THREE CABALLEROS, THE (1944)

Brodney, Oscar
HARVEY (1950)

Brown, Harry
SANDS OF IWO JIMA (1949)

Brown, Leigh
CHRISTMAS STORY, A (1983)

Buchman, Sidney
MR. SMITH GOES TO WASHINGTON
(1939)

Buchwald, Art
PLAYTIME (1973, Fr.)

Bucknall, Nathalie
FIVE LITTLE PEPPERS AND HOW
THEY GREW (1939)

Buckner, Robert
KNUTE ROCKNE--ALL AMERICAN
(1940)
YANKEE DOODLE DANDY (1942)

Bullock, Harvey
MAN CALLED FLINTSTONE, THE
(1966)

Bullock, Walter
O. HENRY'S FULL HOUSE (1952)

Bunuel, Luis
ADVENTURES OF ROBINSON
CRUSOE, THE (1954)

Burke, Edwin
BRIGHT EYES (1934)
LITTLEST REBEL, THE (1935)

Burnett, W.R.
GREAT ESCAPE, THE (1963)

Burns, Allan
LITTLE ROMANCE, A (1979, US/Fr.)

Burns, Jack
MUPPET MOVIE, THE (1979)

Burton, Michael
FLIGHT OF THE NAVIGATOR (1986)

Burton, Val
HENRY ALDRICH FOR PRESIDENT
(1941)
TIME OF THEIR LIVES, THE (1946)

Butler, David
BRIGHT EYES (1934)

Butler, Frank
BABES IN TOYLAND (1934)
GOING MY WAY (1944)
MILKY WAY, THE (1936)
ROAD TO ZANZIBAR (1941)
ROAD TO MOROCCO (1942)

Butler, Hugo
CHRISTMAS CAROL, A (1938)
HUCKLEBERRY FINN (1939)
LASSIE, COME HOME (1943)
YOUNG TOM EDISON (1940)

Butler, John K.
MY PAL TRIGGER (1946)

Caillou, Alan
CLARENCE, THE CROSS-EYED LION
(1965)

Callahan, George
BABE RUTH STORY, THE (1948)

Camp, Joe
BENJI (1974)
FOR THE LOVE OF BENJI (1977)

Campbell, Alan
TALES OF MANHATTAN (1942)

Cannan, Denis
ALIVE AND KICKING (1962, Brit.)
BOY TEN FEET TALL, A (1965, Brit.)

Cannon, Jimmy
POCKETFUL OF MIRACLES (1961)

SCREENWRITERS

Capote, Truman
TRUMAN CAPOTE'S TRILOGY (1969)

Capra, Frank
IT'S A WONDERFUL LIFE (1946)

Carothers, A.J.
EMIL AND THE DETECTIVES (1964)

Carstairs, John Paddy
YANK AT OXFORD, A (1938)

Caruso, Dee
WORLD'S GREATEST ATHLETE, THE (1973)

Castle, Nick
BOY WHO COULD FLY, THE (1986)

Cavett, Frank
GOING MY WAY (1944)

Chandlee, Harry
ADVENTURES OF MARK TWAIN, THE (1944)
SERGEANT YORK (1941)

Chase, Mary
HARVEY (1950)

Cheney, J. Benton
KING OF THE COWBOYS (1943)

Chester, Hal E.
SCHOOL FOR SCOUNDRELS (1960, Brit.)

Chodorov, Jerome
MY SISTER EILEEN (1942)
TIKI TIKI (1971, Can.)

Clark, Bob
CHRISTMAS STORY, A (1983)

Clavell, James
GREAT ESCAPE, THE (1963)

Clemens, Brian
GOLDEN VOYAGE OF SINBAD, THE (1974, Brit.)

Clemmons, Larry
ARISTOCATS, THE (1970)
JUNGLE BOOK, THE (1967)
RESCUERS, THE (1977)
ROBIN HOOD (1973)
FOX AND THE HOUND, THE (1981)

Cleworth, Eric
ARISTOCATS, THE (1970)

Cocteau, Jean
BEAUTY AND THE BEAST (1947, Fr.)

Collier, John
ROSEANNA McCOY (1949)

Collins, Pierre
STORY OF LOUIS PASTEUR, THE (1936)

Columbus, Chris
YOUNG SHERLOCK HOLMES (1985)

Comandini, Adele
THREE SMART GIRLS (1937)
CHRISTMAS IN CONNECTICUT (1945)

Connell, Del
THREE CABALLEROS, THE (1944)

Connell, Richard
MILKY WAY, THE (1936)

Connelly, Marc
CAPTAINS COURAGEOUS (1937)

Conselman, William
BRIGHT EYES (1934)
CONNECTICUT YANKEE, A (1931)
STOWAWAY (1936)

Considine, Bob
BABE RUTH STORY, THE (1948)

Cooper, Dorothy
DATE WITH JUDY, A (1948)

Cooper, Olive
KING OF THE COWBOYS (1943)

Copley, Gerald L.C.
BORN FREE (1966)

Corr, Eugene
NEVER CRY WOLF (1983)

Cottrell, William
MELODY TIME (1948)
PINOCCHIO (1940)
THREE CABALLEROS, THE (1944)

Crane, Harry
HARVEY GIRLS, THE (1946)
TAKE ME OUT TO THE BALL GAME (1949)

Crawford, Joanna
LITTLE ARK, THE (1972)
MY SIDE OF THE MOUNTAIN (1969)

Creedon, Richard
SNOW WHITE AND THE SEVEN DWARFS (1937)

Creelman, James
KING KONG (1933)

Crichton, Charles
BOY WHO STOLE A MILLION, THE (1960, Brit.)

Crosby, Percy
SKIPPY (1931)

Cross, Beverley
JASON AND THE ARGONAUTS (1963, Brit.)
SINBAD AND THE EYE OF THE TIGER (1977, US/Brit.)

Crutcher, Jack
JALOPY (1953)

Cummins, Dwight
THUNDERHEAD-SON OF FLICKA (1945)

Cunningham, Jack
IT'S A GIFT (1934)

Curtis, Nathaniel
HARVEY GIRLS, THE (1946)

DaGradi, Don
BEDKNOBS AND BROOMSTICKS (1971)
BLACKBEARD'S GHOST (1968)
LOVE BUG, THE (1968)
MARY POPPINS (1964)
SON OF FLUBBER (1963)
LADY AND THE TRAMP (1955)

Dahl, Roald
CHITTY CHITTY BANG BANG (1968, Brit.)
WILLY WONKA AND THE CHOCOLATE FACTORY (1971)

Dane, Clemence
SIDEWALKS OF LONDON (1940, Brit.)

Darcus, Jack
WOLFPEN PRINCIPLE, THE (1974, Can.)

Darling, Scott
CHARLIE CHAN AT THE OPERA (1936)

Davies, Jack
THOSE MAGNIFICENT MEN IN THEIR FLYING MACHINES OR HOW I FLEW FROM LONDON TO PARIS IN 25 HOURS AND 11 MINUTES (1965, Brit.)

Davies, Valentine
IT HAPPENS EVERY SPRING (1949)

Davis, Frank
STORY OF WILL ROGERS, THE (1952)

Davis, Owen
CONNECTICUT YANKEE, A (1931)

de Heer, Rolf
TAIL OF THE TIGER (1984, Aus.)

De Leon, Walter
GHOST BREAKERS, THE (1940)
TIME OF THEIR LIVES, THE (1946)
YOU'RE TELLING ME (1934)

De Maris, Merrill
SNOW WHITE AND THE SEVEN DWARFS (1937)

De Wolf, Karen
SHUT MY BIG MOUTH (1942)

Dedini, Eldon
FUN AND FANCY FREE (1947)

Deutsch, Helen
KIM (1950)
KING SOLOMON'S MINES (1950)
LILI (1953)
NATIONAL VELVET (1944)

DeWitt, Jack
BOMBA THE JUNGLE BOY (1949)

Dickey, Basil
FLASH GORDON (1936)

Doyle, Laird
PRINCE AND THE PAUPER, THE (1937)

Drake, Oliver
SHUT MY BIG MOUTH (1942)

Drake, William
ADVENTURES OF SHERLOCK HOLMES, THE (1939)

Duff, Warren
ANGELS WITH DIRTY FACES (1938)

Duncan, David
FANTASTIC VOYAGE (1966)
TIME MACHINE, THE (1960, Brit./US)

Dunne, Philip
COUNT OF MONTE CRISTO, THE (1934)
GHOST AND MRS. MUIR, THE (1942)

HOW GREEN WAS MY VALLEY (1941)
STANLEY AND LIVINGSTONE (1939)

Dyne, Michael
MOON-SPINNERS, THE (1964)

Edwards, Blake
MY SISTER EILEEN (1955)

Edzard, Christine
PETER RABBIT AND TALES OF
BEATRIX POTTER (1971, Brit.)

Elder III, Lonne
SOUNDER (1972)

Eldridge, John
BOY WHO STOLE A MILLION, THE
(1960, Brit.)

Endore, Guy
STORY OF G.I. JOE, THE (1945)

Englander, Otto
PINOCCHIO (1940)
SNOW WHITE AND THE SEVEN
DWARFS (1937)

Ephron, Phoebe
BEST THINGS IN LIFE ARE FREE, THE
(1956)

Erdman, Nikolay
JACK FROST (1966, USSR)

Estabrook, Howard
DAVID COPPERFIELD (1935)

Ettlinger, Don
YOUNG PEOPLE (1940)

Fairchild, William
JOHN AND JULIE (1957, Brit.)

Faragoh, Frances Edwards
MY FRIEND FLICKA (1943)

Felton, Earl
HAPPY TIME, THE (1952)
20,000 LEAGUES UNDER THE SEA
(1954)

Ferris, Walter
HEIDI (1937)
LITTLE PRINCESS, THE (1939)
YANK AT OXFORD, A (1938)

Fields, Herbert
STRIKE UP THE BAND (1940)

Fields, Joseph
MY SISTER EILEEN (1942)

Fields, W.C.
IT'S A GIFT (1934)

Finkel, Abem
SERGEANT YORK (1941)

Finklehoffe, Fred
GIRL CRAZY (1943)
MEET ME IN ST. LOUIS (1944)
STRIKE UP THE BAND (1940)

Finn, Will
SECRET OF NIMH, THE (1982)

Fisz, Benjamin
BATTLE OF BRITAIN, THE (1969, Brit.)

Fitts, Margaret
SUN COMES UP, THE (1949)

Fitzgerald, F. Scott
YANK AT OXFORD, A (1938)

Flaherty, Frances
LOUISIANA STORY (1948)

Flaherty, Robert J.
LOUISIANA STORY (1948)

Fleischman, Sid
GOODBYE, MY LADY (1956)

Fleisher, Dave
MR. BUG GOES TO TOWN (1941)

Flournoy, Richard
BLONDIE (1938)

Flynn, Greg
DOT AND THE KOALA (1985, Aus.)

Fodor, Ladislas
TALES OF MANHATTAN (1942)
TOM THUMB (1958, Brit./US)

Foote, Bradbury
EDISON, THE MAN (1940)
YOUNG TOM EDISON (1940)

Foote, Horton
TO KILL A MOCKINGBIRD (1962)

Foote, John Taintor
KENTUCKY (1938)

Forbes, Bryan
SLIPPER AND THE ROSE, THE (1976,
Brit.)

Foreman, Carl
SO THIS IS NEW YORK (1948)

Fowler, Gene
CALL OF THE WILD (1935)

Frank, Fredric M.
GREATEST SHOW ON EARTH, THE
(1952)
TEN COMMANDMENTS, THE (1956)

Frank, Melvin
CALLAWAY WENT THATAWAY (1951)
COURT JESTER, THE (1956)
LI'L ABNER (1959)
ROAD TO UTOPIA (1945)
WHITE CHRISTMAS (1954)

Franklin, Dean
FIGHTING 69TH, THE (1940)

Franklin, Sidney
GOODBYE MR. CHIPS (1939, Brit.)

Freeman, Devery
FULLER BRUSH MAN (1948)

Freudberg, Judy
AMERICAN TAIL, AN (1986)

Gabrielson, Frank
FLIGHT OF THE DOVES (1971)

Gardner, Gerald
WORLD'S GREATEST ATHLETE, THE
(1973)

Gariss, Jack
TEN COMMANDMENTS, THE (1956)

Gay, John
COURTSHIP OF EDDIE'S FATHER,
THE (1963)

Geisel, Ted [Dr. Seuss]
5,000 FINGERS OF DR. T., THE (1953)

Geiss, Tony
AMERICAN TAIL, AN (1986)

Gerry, Vance
ARISTOCATS, THE (1970)
FOX AND THE HOUND, THE (1981)
JUNGLE BOOK, THE (1967)
RESCUERS, THE (1977)

Gibney, Sheridan
STORY OF LOUIS PASTEUR, THE
(1936)

Gibson, William
MIRACLE WORKER, THE (1962)

Gilliam, Terry
TIME BANDITS (1981, Brit.)

Gilliat, Sidney
BELLES OF ST. TRINIAN'S, THE (1954,
Brit.)
WEE GEORDIE (1956, Brit.)

Gion, Christian
HERE COMES SANTA CLAUS (1984)

Gipson, Fred
OLD YELLER (1957)

Goff, Ivan
O. HENRY'S FULL HOUSE (1952)

Goldman, Gary
SECRET OF NIMH, THE (1982)

Goldman, William
PRINCESS BRIDE, THE (1987)

Goodrich, Frances
AH, WILDERNESS! (1935)
EASTER PARADE (1948)
FATHER'S LITTLE DIVIDEND (1951)
IN THE GOOD OLD SUMMERTIME
(1949)
IT'S A WONDERFUL LIFE (1946)
SEVEN BRIDES FOR SEVEN
BROTHERS (1954)
SUMMER HOLIDAY (1948)

Goodwin, Richard
PETER RABBIT AND TALES OF
BEATRIX POTTER (1971, Brit.)

Gordon, Dan
GULLIVER'S TRAVELS (1939)
MR. BUG GOES TO TOWN (1941)

Gordon, Gordon
THAT DARN CAT (1965)

Gordon, Leon
KIM (1950)

Gordon, Mildred
THAT DARN CAT (1965)

Gorog, Laslo
TALES OF MANHATTAN (1942)

Graham, Erwin
MAKE MINE MUSIC (1946)

Gramatky, Hardie
MELODY TIME (1948)

Grant, James Edward
ALAMO, THE (1960)
SANDS OF IWO JIMA (1949)

SCREENWRITERS

Grant, Joe
DUMBO (1941)

Grant, John
ABBOTT AND COSTELLO MEET
FRANKENSTEIN (1948)
HERE COME THE CO-EDS (1945)
HOLD THAT GHOST (1941)
NOOSE HANGS HIGH, THE (1948)
RIDE 'EM COWBOY (1942)
TIME OF THEIR LIVES, THE (1946)

Grant, Morton
SONG OF THE SOUTH (1946)

Grayson, Charles
ONE NIGHT IN THE TROPICS (1940)

Greatorex, Wilfred
BATTLE OF BRITAIN, THE (1969, Brit.)

Griffin, Eleanore
MAN CALLED PETER, A (1955)

Grinde, Nick
BABES IN TOYLAND (1934)

Gross, Francis
FABULOUS WORLD OF JULES
VERNE, THE (1961, Czech.)

Gross, Yoram
DOT AND THE KOALA (1985, Aus.)

Gruault, Jean
WILD CHILD, THE (1970, Fr.)

Gunn, Gilbert
WINGS OF MYSTERY (1963, Brit.)

Gurney, Eric
MAKE MINE MUSIC (1946)

Guthrie, Jr., A.B.
SHANE (1953)

Hackett, Albert
AH, WILDERNESS! (1935)
EASTER PARADE (1948)
FATHER'S LITTLE DIVIDEND (1951)
IN THE GOOD OLD SUMMERTIME
(1949)
IT'S A WONDERFUL LIFE (1946)
SEVEN BRIDES FOR SEVEN
BROTHERS (1954)
SUMMER HOLIDAY (1948)

Hamm, Sam
NEVER CRY WOLF (1983)

Hamner, Jr., Earl
CHARLOTTE'S WEB (1973)

Hampton, Orville H.
JACK THE GIANT KILLER (1962)

Hanson, Curtis
NEVER CRY WOLF (1983)

Hargrove, Marion
MUSIC MAN, THE (1962)

Harmon, David P.
WONDERFUL WORLD OF THE
BROTHERS GRIMM, THE (1962)

Harris, Eleanor
KIDNAPPED (1938)

Harris, Howard
NOOSE HANGS HIGH, THE (1948)

Harris, Joel Chandler
SONG OF THE SOUTH (1946)

Harris, Ray
LADDIE (1935)

Harris, Vernon
CRY FROM THE STREET, A (1959, Brit.)
OLIVER! (1968, Brit.)

Hart, Moss
HANS CHRISTIAN ANDERSEN (1952)

Hartman, Don
KID FROM BOOKLYN, THE (1946)
ROAD TO ZANZIBAR (1941)
ROAD TO MOROCCO (1942)
WONDER MAN (1945)

Hartmann, Edmund L.
ALI BABA AND THE FORTY THIEVES
(1944)

Harvey, Frank
HEAVENS ABOVE! (1963, Brit.)

Hatch, Eric
TOPPER (1937)

Hauer, Daniel
WHO SAYS I CAN'T RIDE A
RAINBOW? (1971)

Hauser, Dwight
NIKKI, WILD DOG OF THE NORTH
(1961, US/Can.)

Havelock-Allan, Anthony
GREAT EXPECTATIONS (1946, Brit.)

Hawkesworth, John
TIGER BAY (1959, Brit.)

Hawley, Lowell S.
ADVENTURES OF BULLWHIP
GRIFFIN, THE (1967)
IN SEARCH OF THE CASTAWAYS
(1962, Brit.)
SWISS FAMILY ROBINSON (1960)

Haynes, Stanley
OLIVER TWIST (1951, Brit.)

Hayward, Lillie
CATTLE DRIVE (1951)
MY FRIEND FLICKA (1943)
SHAGGY DOG, THE (1959)
TOBY TYLER (1960)

Hecht, Ben
TALES OF MANHATTAN (1942)

Hee, T. [Walt Disney]
MAKE MINE MUSIC (1946)

Heerman, Victor
LITTLE WOMEN (1933)

Hellman, Sam
CAPTAIN JANUARY (1935)
HORN BLOWS AT MIDNIGHT, THE
(1945)
LITTLE MISS MARKER (1934)

Henley, Jack
MA AND PA KETTLE ON VACATION
(1953)

Henry, Buck
WHAT'S UP, DOC? (1972)

Herbert, F. Hugh
SITTING PRETTY (1948)

Hertz, David
JOURNEY FOR MARGARET (1942)

Hibler, Winston
ADVENTURES OF ICHABOD AND MR.
TOAD (1949)
CINDERELLA (1950)
MELODY TIME (1948)
NIKKI, WILD DOG OF THE NORTH
(1961, US/Can.)
PETER PAN (1953)

Hicks, Seymour
SCROOGE (1935, Brit.)

Hill, Ethel
LITTLE PRINCESS, THE (1939)

Hill, Jerome
SAND CASTLE, THE (1961)

Hoffenstein, Samuel
TALES OF MANHATTAN (1942)

Hogan, Michael
ARABIAN NIGHTS (1942)

Holland, Sylvia
MAKE MINE MUSIC (1946)

Holloway, Jean
SUMMER HOLIDAY (1948)

Horman, Arthur T.
HERE COME THE CO-EDS (1945)

Hornstein, Martin
TIKI TIKI (1971, Can.)

Houser, Lionel
CHRISTMAS IN CONNECTICUT (1945)
COURAGE OF LASSIE (1946)

Howard, Cal
MR. BUG GOES TO TOWN (1941)

Hubley, Faith
OF STARS AND MEN (1961)

Hubley, John
OF STARS AND MEN (1961)

Huemer, Dick
DUMBO (1941)
MAKE MINE MUSIC (1946)

Hughes, Ken
CHITTY CHITTY BANG BANG (1968,
Brit.)

Hulett, Steve
FOX AND THE HOUND, THE (1981)

Hume, Cyril
INVISIBLE BOY, THE (1957)
TARZAN THE APE MAN (1932)

Hurd, Earl
SNOW WHITE AND THE SEVEN
DWARFS (1937)

Huston, John
AFRICAN QUEEN, THE (1951, US/Brit.)
MOBY DICK (1956, Brit.)
SERGEANT YORK (1941)

Jacoby, Hans
CHAMPAGNE FOR CAESAR (1950)

Jacoby, John
AMAZING MRS. HOLLIDAY (1943)

Jeeves, Mahatma Kane [W.C. Fields]
BANK DICK, THE (1940)

Jennings, Talbot
EDISON, THE MAN (1940)

Jevne, Jack
PALOOKA (1934)
TOPPER (1937)
WONDER MAN (1945)

Johnson, Nora
WORLD OF HENRY ORIENT, THE
(1964)

Johnson, Nunnally
MR. HOBBS TAKES A VACATION
(1962)
O. HENRY'S FULL HOUSE (1952)
WORLD OF HENRY ORIENT, THE
(1964)

Jones, Chuck
GAY PURR-EE (1962)
GREAT AMERICAN BUGS BUNNY-
ROAD RUNNER CHASE (1979)
PHANTOM TOLLBOOTH, THE (1970)

Jones, Dorothy
GAY PURR-EE (1962)

Jones, Grover
MILKY WAY, THE (1936)
TOM SAWYER (1930)

Jones, Paul M.
YOU'RE TELLING ME (1934)

Jones, Terry
LABYRINTH (1986)

Jordan, Larry
HILDUR AND THE MAGICIAN (1969)

Joseph, Edmund
YANKEE DOODLE DANDY (1942)

Josephson, Julien
HEIDI (1937)
STANLEY AND LIVINGSTONE (1939)
WEE WILLIE WINKIE (1937)

Juhl, Jerry
GREAT MUPPET CAPER, THE (1981)
MUPPET MOVIE, THE (1979)

Juran, Nathan
JACK THE GIANT KILLER (1962)

Kadison, Ellis
GNOME-MOBILE, THE (1967)

Kalmar, Bert
DUCK SOUP (1933)
KID FROM SPAIN, THE (1932)
NIGHT AT THE OPERA, A (1935)

Kamen, Robert Mark
KARATE KID, THE (1984)

Kaminka, Didier
HERE COMES SANTA CLAUS (1984)

Kanter, Hal
POCKETFUL OF MIRACLES (1961)

Karman, Janice
CHIPMUNK ADVENTURE, THE (1987)

Kasdan, Lawrence
EMPIRE STRIKES BACK, THE (1980)

Kaufman, George S.
NIGHT AT THE OPERA, A (1935)

Keaton, Buster
TALES OF MANHATTAN (1942)

Kelsey, Dick
MAKE MINE MUSIC (1946)

Kennaway, James
BATTLE OF BRITAIN, THE (1969, Brit.)

Kennedy, Adam
DOVE, THE (1974, Brit.)

Kern, James V.
HORN BLOWS AT MIDNIGHT, THE
(1945)

Kerr, Laura
FARMER'S DAUGHTER, THE (1947)

Key, Ted
CAT FROM OUTER SPACE, THE (1978)

Kilgore, Al
WORLD OF HANS CHRISTIAN
ANDERSEN (1971, Jap.)

Kingsley, Dorothy
ANGELS IN THE OUTFIELD (1951)
DATE WITH JUDY, A (1948)
GIRL CRAZY (1943)
SEVEN BRIDES FOR SEVEN
BROTHERS (1954)

Kinney, Dick
MAKE MINE MUSIC (1946)

Kleiner, Harry
FANTASTIC VOYAGE (1966)

Kletter, Richard
NEVER CRY WOLF (1983)

Klove, Jane
ISLAND OF THE BLUE DOLPHINS
(1964)
MY SIDE OF THE MOUNTAIN (1969)

Kneeland, Ted
DR. COPPELIUS (1968, US/Span.)

Kober, Arthur
PALOOKA (1934)

Kobrin, Jerry
FRASIER, THE SENSUOUS LION (1973)

Koch, Howard
SERGEANT YORK (1941)

Kolb, Kenneth
SEVENTH VOYAGE OF SINBAD, THE
(1958)

Kramer, Cecile
BUFFALO BILL (1944)

Krasna, Norman
WHITE CHRISTMAS (1954)

Kress, Earl
FOX AND THE HOUND, THE (1981)

Krikes, Peter
STAR TREK IV: THE VOYAGE HOME
(1986)

Kurnitz, Harry
INSPECTOR GENERAL, THE (1949)

SEE HERE, PRIVATE HARGROVE
(1944)

L'Hote, Jean
MY UNCLE (1958, Fr.)

Lachman, Mort
YOURS, MINE AND OURS (1968)

Lagrange, Jacques
MY UNCLE (1958, Fr.)
PLAYTIME (1973, Fr.)

Lakso, Edward J.
GENTLE GIANT (1967)

Lancaster, Bill
BAD NEWS BEARS, THE (1976)

Langdon, Harry
BLOCKHEADS (1938)
FLYING DEUCES, THE (1939)

Langley, Noel
PICKWICK PAPERS, THE (1952, Brit.)
WIZARD OF OZ, THE (1939)

Lasky, Jr., Jesse L.
TEN COMMANDMENTS, THE (1956)

Latham, Patricia
DOG AND THE DIAMONDS, THE (1962,
Brit.)
JOHNNY ON THE RUN (1953, Brit.)

Launder, Frank
BELLES OF ST. TRINIAN'S, THE (1954,
Brit.)
WEE GEORDIE (1956, Brit.)

Lavery, Emmet
MAGNIFICENT YANKEE, THE (1950)

Lawrence, Bert
JALOPY (1953)
LET'S GO NAVY (1951)

Lawson, John Howard
TREASURE ISLAND (1934)

Lazarus, Ashley
FOREVER YOUNG, FOREVER FREE
(1976, South Africa)

Lean, David
GREAT EXPECTATIONS (1946, Brit.)
OLIVER TWIST (1951, Brit.)

Lederer, Charles
FEARLESS FAGAN (1952)
SPIRIT OF ST. LOUIS, THE (1957)
YOUNGEST PROFESSION, THE (1943)

Lee, James
ADVENTURES OF HUCKLEBERRY
FINN, THE (1960)

Lee, Rowland V.
COUNT OF MONTE CRISTO, THE
(1934)

Lees, Robert
ABBOTT AND COSTELLO MEET
FRANKENSTEIN (1948)
HOLD THAT GHOST (1941)

Lehman, Gladys
CAPTAIN JANUARY (1935)
LITTLE MISS MARKER (1934)

Lehman, Ernest
HELLO, DOLLY! (1969)

SCREENWRITERS

KING AND I, THE (1956)
SOUND OF MUSIC, THE (1965)

LeMay, Alan
ADVENTURES OF MARK TWAIN, THE (1944)

Lennart, Isobel
FITZWILLY (1967)
INN OF THE SIXTH HAPPINESS, THE (1958)

Lerner, Alan Jay
MY FAIR LADY (1964)

Levien, Sonya
DRUMS ALONG THE MOHAWK (1939)
HIT THE DECK (1955)
KIDNAPPED (1938)
OKLAHOMA! (1955)

Lewis, Al
MA AND PA KETTLE (1949)

Lipman, William R.
LITTLE MISS MARKER (1934)

Lipscomb, W.P.
TALE OF TWO CITIES, A (1935)

Livingston, Harold
STAR TREK: THE MOTION PICTURE (1979)

London, Robby
PINOCCHIO AND THE EMPEROR OF THE NIGHT (1987)

Lucas, George
RETURN OF THE JEDI (1983)
STAR WARS (1977)

Lucky, Fred
RESCUERS, THE (1977)

Ludwig, William
CHALLENGE TO LASSIE (1949)
GIRL CRAZY (1943)
HILLS OF HOME (1948)
HIT THE DECK (1955)
JOURNEY FOR MARGARET (1942)
LOVE FINDS ANDY HARDY (1938)
OKLAHOMA! (1955)
SUN COMES UP, THE (1949)

Luescher, Christina
NEVER CRY WOLF (1983)

Lyndon, Barre
GREATEST SHOW ON EARTH, THE (1952)

MacDougall, Roger
MOUSE THAT ROARED, THE (1959, Brit.)

MacKenzie, Aeneas
BUFFALO BILL (1944)
TEN COMMANDMENTS, THE (1956)

MacManus, Matt
FLIGHT OF THE NAVIGATOR (1986)

Macphail, Angus
YANK AT OXFORD, A (1938)

Mahin, John Lee
CAPTAINS COURAGEOUS (1937)
TREASURE ISLAND (1934)

Maibaum, Richard
CHITTY CHITTY BANG BANG (1968, Brit.)

Malleson, Miles
THIEF OF BAGHDAD, THE (1940, Brit.)

Maltese, Mike
GREAT AMERICAN BUGS BUNNY-ROAD RUNNER CHASE (1979)

Mankiewicz, Herman J.
PRIDE OF THE YANKEES, THE (1942)
PRIDE OF ST. LOUIS, THE (1952)

Mankiewicz, Joseph L.
ALICE IN WONDERLAND (1933)
SKIPPY (1931)

Mann, Edward
WHO SAYS I CAN'T RIDE A RAINBOW? (1971)

Mann, Stanley
MOUSE THAT ROARED, THE (1959, Brit.)

Manning, Monroe
LASSIE'S GREAT ADVENTURE (1963)

Margolis, Herbert
FRANCIS IN THE HAUNTED HOUSE (1956)
MA AND PA KETTLE (1949)

Marmorstein, Malcolm
PETE'S DRAGON (1977)

Marquis, Don
SKIPPY (1931)

Marsh, Jesse
MAKE MINE MUSIC (1946)
MELODY TIME (1948)

Martin, Francis
ONE NIGHT IN THE TROPICS (1940)
SHUT MY BIG MOUTH (1942)

Maschwitz, Eric
GOODBYE MR. CHIPS (1939, Brit.)

Mason, Sarah Y.
LITTLE WOMEN (1933)

Mathison, Melissa
BLACK STALLION, THE (1979)
E.T. THE EXTRA-TERRESTRIAL (1982)

Mattinson, Burny
FOX AND THE HOUND, THE (1981)
RESCUERS, THE (1977)

Mayes, Wendell
SPIRIT OF ST. LOUIS, THE (1957)

McEveety, Joseph L.
BAREFOOT EXECUTIVE, THE (1971)
COMPUTER WORE TENNIS SHOES, THE (1970)
NOW YOU SEE HIM, NOW YOU DON'T (1972)

McEvoy, J.P.
YOU'RE TELLING ME (1934)

McGivern, Cecil
GREAT EXPECTATIONS (1946, Brit.)

McGowan, Jack
BABES IN ARMS (1939)

McGowan, Tom
ARISTOCATS, THE (1970)

McGuire, William Anthony
KID FROM SPAIN, THE (1932)

McLeod, Norman
SKIPPY (1931)

McNutt, William Slavens
TOM SAWYER (1930)

Mear, H. Fowler
SCROOGE (1935, Brit.)

Meehan, John
BOYS TOWN (1938)

Meerson, Steve
STAR TREK IV: THE VOYAGE HOME (1986)

Melson, John
BATTLE OF THE BULGE (1965)

Menzies, William Cameron
ALICE IN WONDERLAND (1933)

Meyer, Mike
MR. BUG GOES TO TOWN (1941)

Meyer, Nicholas
STAR TREK IV: THE VOYAGE HOME (1986)

Meyjes, Menno
EMPIRE OF THE SUN (1987)

Michener, David
FOX AND THE HOUND, THE (1981)
RESCUERS, THE (1977)

Millard, Oscar
COME TO THE STABLE (1949)

Miller, Seton I.
ADVENTURES OF ROBIN HOOD, THE (1938)

Miller, Winston
HOME IN INDIANA (1944)

Mintz, Sam
SKIPPY (1931)
TOM SAWYER (1930)

Mischel, Josef
LIVE WIRES (1946)

Moffitt, John C.
STORY OF WILL ROGERS, THE (1952)

Molnar, Ferenc
TALES OF MANHATTAN (1942)

Monks, Jr., John
STRIKE UP THE BAND (1940)
WHERE'S CHARLEY? (1952, Brit.)

Moore, Bob
MELODY TIME (1948)

Moran, Eddie
TOPPER (1937)
WONDER MAN (1945)

Morey, Larry
BAMBI (1942)

Morheim, Louis
MA AND PA KETTLE (1949)

Morrow, Bill
TALES OF MANHATTAN (1942)

Morrow, Douglas
STRATTON STORY, THE (1949)

Moussy, Marcel
FOUR HUNDRED BLOWS, THE (1959)

Moyes, Patricia
SCHOOL FOR SCOUNDRELS (1960, Brit.)

Muller, Romeo
WACKY WORLD OF MOTHER GOOSE, THE (1967)

Nash, N. Richard
DEAR WIFE (1949)

Natteford, Jack
CATTLE DRIVE (1951)

Neame, Ronald
GREAT EXPECTATIONS (1946, Brit.)

Nelson, Ralph
FLIGHT OF THE DOVES (1971)

Newman, David
SUPERMAN (1978)
SUPERMAN II (1980)
WHAT'S UP, DOC? (1972)

Newman, Leslie
SUPERMAN (1978)
SUPERMAN II (1980)

Niblo, Jr., Fred
FIGHTING 69TH, THE (1940)

Nichols, Dudley
AIR FORCE (1943)
BELLS OF ST. MARY'S, THE (1945)

Nolley, Lance
FUN AND FANCY FREE (1947)

Novello, Ivor
TARZAN THE APE MAN (1932)

Nugent, Frank S.
THREE GODFATHERS, THE (1948)

O'Brien, Barry
PINOCCHIO AND THE EMPEROR OF THE NIGHT (1987)

O'Flaherty, Dennis
PINOCCHIO AND THE EMPEROR OF THE NIGHT (1987)

O'Hanlon, James
HARVEY GIRLS, THE (1946)

O'Neal, Charles
LASSIE'S GREAT ADVENTURE (1963)

O'Neill, Ella
FLASH GORDON (1936)

Oppenheimer, George
DAY AT THE RACES, A (1937)
YANK AT OXFORD, A (1938)
YOUNGEST PROFESSION, THE (1943)

Oreb, Tom
FUN AND FANCY FREE (1947)
MAKE MINE MUSIC (1946)

Ormonde, Czeni
1001 ARABIAN NIGHTS (1959)

Osborn, Paul
MADAME CURIE (1943)
YEARLING, THE (1946)

Oz, Frank
MUPPETS TAKE MANHATTAN, THE (1984)

Palin, Michael
TIME BANDITS (1981, Brit.)

Palmer, Cap
MAKE MINE MUSIC (1946)

Panama, Norman
CALLAWAY WENT THATAWAY (1951)
COURT JESTER, THE (1956)
LI'L ABNER (1959)
ROAD TO UTOPIA (1945)
WHITE CHRISTMAS (1954)

Parker, Alan
BUGSY MALONE (1976, Brit.)
MELODY (1971, Brit.)

Parker, Austin
THREE SMART GIRLS (1937)

Parker, Jefferson
FIVE LITTLE PEPPERS AND HOW THEY GREW (1939)

Parrott, James
BLOCKHEADS (1938)
WAY OUT WEST (1937)

Pascal, Ernest
KIDNAPPED (1938)
WEE WILLIE WINKIE (1937)

Patchett, Tom
GREAT MUPPET CAPER, THE (1981)
MUPPETS TAKE MANHATTAN, THE (1984)

Paterson, Neil
LITTLE KIDNAPPERS, THE (1954, Brit.)

Pearce, Perce
BAMBI (1942)

Peet, Bill
CINDERELLA (1950)
ONE HUNDRED AND ONE DALMATIANS (1961)
PETER PAN (1953)
SONG OF THE SOUTH (1946)
THREE CABALLEROS, THE (1944)

Pelletier, Louis
FOLLOW ME, BOYS! (1966)
THOSE CALLOWAYS (1964)

Penner, Ed
MAKE MINE MUSIC (1946)

Penner, Erdman
ADVENTURES OF ICHABOD AND MR. TOAD (1949)
CINDERELLA (1950)
LADY AND THE TRAMP (1955)
MELODY TIME (1948)
PETER PAN (1953)
PINOCCHIO (1940)

Perelman, S.J.
AROUND THE WORLD IN 80 DAYS (1956)

Perrin, Nat
DUCK SOUP (1933)
STOWAWAY (1936)

Perry, Eleanor
TRUMAN CAPOTE'S TRILOGY (1969)

Pertwee, Roland
YANK AT OXFORD, A (1938)

Pierce, Ted
GULLIVER'S TRAVELS (1939)
MR. BUG GOES TO TOWN (1941)

Pinkava, Josef
WISHING MACHINE (1971, Czech.)

Pirosh, Robert
DAY AT THE RACES, A (1937)

Place, Graham
MR. BUG GOES TO TOWN (1941)

Plater, Alan
ALL THINGS BRIGHT AND BEAUTIFUL (1979, Brit.)

Plymmer, Elmer
THREE CABALLEROS, THE (1944)

Plympton, George
FLASH GORDON (1936)

Pomeroy, John
SECRET OF NIMH, THE (1982)

Potterton, Gerald
TIKI TIKI (1971, Can.)

Praskins, Leonard
CALL OF THE WILD (1935)
CHAMP, THE (1931)
MR. SCOUTMASTER (1953)
TREASURE ISLAND (1934)

Prebble, John
MYSTERIOUS ISLAND (1961, US/Brit.)

Price, Jeffrey
WHO FRAMED ROGER RABBIT? (1988)

Purcell, Gertrude
ONE NIGHT IN THE TROPICS (1940)
PALOOKA (1934)

Puzo, Mario
SUPERMAN (1978)
SUPERMAN II (1980)

Quine, Richard
MY SISTER EILEEN (1955)

Radnitz, Robert B.
ISLAND OF THE BLUE DOLPHINS (1964)

Raffil, Stewart
ADVENTURES OF THE WILDERNESS FAMILY, THE (1975)
SEA GYPSIES, THE (1978)

Raine, Norman Reilly
ADVENTURES OF ROBIN HOOD, THE (1938)
FIGHTING 69TH, THE (1940)

Rameau, Paul H.
MADAME CURIE (1943)

Rankin, Jr., Arthur
DAYDREAMER, THE (1966)
WILLIE MCBEAN AND HIS MAGIC MACHINE (1965, US/Jap.)

Rapf, Maurice
SO DEAR TO MY HEART (1949)

SCREENWRITERS

SONG OF THE SOUTH (1946)

Raphaelson, Samson
HARVEY GIRLS, THE (1946)
IN THE GOOD OLD SUMMERTIME
(1949)

Rapp, Philip
INSPECTOR GENERAL, THE (1949)
WONDER MAN (1945)

Raymond, Dalton
SONG OF THE SOUTH (1946)

Raynor, William
FRANCIS IN THE HAUNTED HOUSE
(1956)

Reed, Jan
JASON AND THE ARGONAUTS (1963,
Brit.)

Reeves, Harry
ADVENTURES OF ICHABOD AND MR.
TOAD (1949)
CINDERELLA (1950)
FUN AND FANCY FREE (1947)
MELODY TIME (1948)

Reeves, Theodore
NATIONAL VELVET (1944)

Reisch, Walter
JOURNEY TO THE CENTER OF THE
EARTH (1959)

Richard, Dick
SNOW WHITE AND THE SEVEN
DWARFS (1937)

Rinaldi, Joe
ADVENTURES OF ICHABOD AND MR.
TOAD (1949)
CINDERELLA (1950)
LADY AND THE TRAMP (1955)
MELODY TIME (1948)
PETER PAN (1953)

Rinaldo, Frederic I.
ABBOTT AND COSTELLO MEET
FRANKENSTEIN (1948)
HOLD THAT GHOST (1941)

Ripley, Clements
BUFFALO BILL (1944)

Riskin, Robert
MISTER 880 (1950)

Rivkin, Allen
FARMER'S DAUGHTER, THE (1947)

Roberts, Ben
O. HENRY'S FULL HOUSE (1952)

Roberts, Marguerite
TRUE GRIT (1969)

Roberts, Stanley
STORY OF WILL ROGERS, THE (1952)

Roberts, William
WONDERFUL WORLD OF THE
BROTHERS GRIMM, THE (1962)

Robinson, Casey
ONE FOOT IN HEAVEN (1941)
THIS IS THE ARMY (1943)

Robson, Michael
WATER BABIES, THE (1979, Brit.)

Roddenberry, Gene
STAR TREK: THE MOTION PICTURE
(1979)

Rodgers, Mary
FREAKY FRIDAY (1976)

Roeca, Samuel
FLUFFY (1965)

Rogers, Charles
BLOCKHEADS (1938)
FLYING DEUCES, THE (1939)
WAY OUT WEST (1937)

Roll, Philip
ADVENTURES OF ROBINSON
CRUSOE, THE (1954)

Ropes, Bradford
TIME OF THEIR LIVES, THE (1946)

Rose, Jack
GREAT MUPPET CAPER, THE (1981)
ROAD TO RIO (1947)
ROOM FOR ONE MORE (1952)
SEVEN LITTLE FOYS, THE (1955)

Rose, Ruth
KING KONG (1933)

Rose, Tania
IT'S A MAD, MAD, MAD, MAD WORLD
(1963)

Rose, William
IT'S A MAD, MAD, MAD, MAD WORLD
(1963)

Rosen, Sam
PHANTOM TOLLBOOTH, THE (1970)

Rosenberg, Jeanne
BLACK STALLION, THE (1979)
JOURNEY OF NATTY GANN, THE
(1985)

Roth, Murray
PALOOKA (1934)

Rowe, Tom
ARISTOCATS, THE (1970)

Ruby, Harry
DUCK SOUP (1933)
KID FROM SPAIN, THE (1932)
NIGHT AT THE OPERA, A (1935)

Ryan, Ben
PALOOKA (1934)

Ryan, Frank
AMAZING MRS. HOLLIDAY (1943)

Ryan, Tim
JALOPY (1953)
LIVE WIRES (1946)
NEWS HOUNDS (1947)

Ryerson, Florence
WIZARD OF OZ, THE (1939)

Ryskind, Morrie
ANIMAL CRACKERS (1930)
NIGHT AT THE OPERA, A (1935)

Sabo, Joseph
PINOCCHIO (1940)

Sackler, Howard
MIDSUMMER NIGHT'S DREAM, A
(1961, Czech.)

Sayre, Joel
ANNIE OAKLEY (1935)

Schary, Dore
BOYS TOWN (1938)
YOUNG TOM EDISON (1940)

Schayer, Richard
DAVY CROCKETT, INDIAN SCOUT
(1950)
KIM (1950)

Schiffmann, Suzanne
SMALL CHANGE (1976, Fr.)

Schiller, Alfred
FLYING DEUCES, THE (1939)

Schnee, Charles
NEXT VOICE YOU HEAR, THE (1950)

Schulz, Charles M.
BON VOYAGE, CHARLIE BROWN
(AND DON'T COME BACK) (1980)
SNOOPY, COME HOME (1972)

Scola, Kathryn
ONE NIGHT IN THE TROPICS (1940)

Scott, Allan
5,000 FINGERS OF DR. T., THE (1953)

Scott, Art
MELODY TIME (1948)

Seamon, Peter S.
WHO FRAMED ROGER RABBIT? (1988)

Sears, Ted
ADVENTURES OF ICHABOD AND MR.
TOAD (1949)
CINDERELLA (1950)
FUN AND FANCY FREE (1947)
MELODY TIME (1948)
PETER PAN (1953)
PINOCCHIO (1940)
SNOW WHITE AND THE SEVEN
DWARFS (1937)
SO DEAR TO MY HEART (1949)
THREE CABALLEROS, THE (1944)

Seaton, George
CHARLEY'S AUNT (1941)
DAY AT THE RACES, A (1937)
MIRACLE ON 34TH STREET, THE
(1947)
SONG OF BERNADETTE, THE (1943)

Sebast, Dick
RESCUERS, THE (1977)

Sendak, Maurice
NUTCRACKER: THE MOTION
PICTURE (1986)

Seward, Edmond
GULLIVER'S TRAVELS (1939)

Seward, Edmond
JALOPY (1953)
NEWS HOUNDS (1947)

Shapley, Harlow
OF STARS AND MEN (1961)

Shavelson, Melville
KID FROM BROOKLYN, THE (1946)
ROOM FOR ONE MORE (1952)
SEVEN LITTLE FOYS, THE (1955)
WONDER MAN (1945)

YOURS, MINE AND OURS (1968)

Shaw, Dick
MAKE MINE MUSIC (1946)

Sheekman, Arthur
DEAR WIFE (1949)
DUCK SOUP (1933)
STOWAWAY (1936)

Sheldon, Sidney
ANNIE GET YOUR GUN (1950)
BACHELOR AND THE BOBBY-SOXER, THE (1947)
EASTER PARADE (1948)

Shepherd, Jean
CHRISTMAS STORY, A (1983)

Sher, Jack
SHANE (1953)

Sherdeman, Ted
DOG OF FLANDERS, A (1959)
ISLAND OF THE BLUE DOLPHINS (1964)
MISTY (1961)
MY SIDE OF THE MOUNTAIN (1969)

Sherman, Richard M.
TOM SAWYER (1973)
SLIPPER AND THE ROSE, THE (1976, Brit.)

Sherman, Robert B.
SLIPPER AND THE ROSE, THE (1976, Brit.)
TOM SAWYER (1973)

Sherriff, R.C.
GOODBYE MR. CHIPS (1939, Brit.)

Sherwood, Robert E.
ABE LINCOLN IN ILLINOIS (1940)

Shumate, Harold
KONGA, THE WILD STALLION (1939)
RIDE 'EM COWBOY (1942)

Silvers, Sid
GIRL CRAZY (1943)

Sisson, Rosemary Anne
LITTLEST HORSE THIEVES, THE (1977)

Slater, Barney
MR. SCOUTMASTER (1953)

Smith, C.M.
NEVER CRY WOLF (1983)

Smith, Shelley
TIGER BAY (1959, Brit.)

Smith, Webb
PINOCCHIO (1940)
SNOW WHITE AND THE SEVEN DWARFS (1937)

Snell, Earle
LAST ROUND-UP, THE (1947)

Sobieski, Carol
ANNIE (1982)
SYLVESTER (1985)

Sowards, Jack B.
STAR TREK II: THE WRATH OF KHAN (1982)

Sparber, Isidore
GULLIVER'S TRAVELS (1939)
MR. BUG GOES TO TOWN (1941)

Spence, Ralph
FLYING DEUCES, THE (1939)

Sperling, Milton
BATTLE OF THE BULGE (1965)

Spielberg, Steven
CLOSE ENCOUNTERS OF THE THIRD KIND (1977)

Spigelgass, Leonard
DEEP IN MY HEART (1954)
YOUNGEST PROFESSION, THE (1943)

St. John, Theodore
GREATEST SHOW ON EARTH, THE (1952)

Stallings, George
SONG OF THE SOUTH (1946)

Stallings, Laurence
JUNGLE BOOK, THE (1942)
THREE GODFATHERS, THE (1948)

Stephani, Frederick
FLASH GORDON (1936)

Stern, David
FRANCIS (1949)

Stevenson, Philip
STORY OF G.I. JOE, THE (1945)

Stewart, Donald Ogden
LIFE WITH FATHER (1947)
TALES OF MANHATTAN (1942)

Stone, Peter
FATHER GOOSE (1964)

Stoppard, Tom
EMPIRE OF THE SUN (1987)

Stowell, Kent
NUTCRACKER: THE MOTION PICTURE (1986)

Svendsen, Julius
ARISTOCATS, THE (1970)

Swanton, Harold
RASCAL (1969)

Swerling, Jo
IT'S A WONDERFUL LIFE (1946)
PRIDE OF THE YANKEES, THE (1942)

Swift, David
PARENT TRAP, THE (1961)
POLLYANNA (1960)

Tait, Don
SHAGGY D.A., THE (1976)

Tarloff, Frank
FATHER GOOSE (1964)

Tarses, Jay
GREAT MUPPET CAPER, THE (1981)
MUPPETS TAKE MANHATTAN, THE (1984)

Tashlin, Frank
FULLER BRUSH MAN (1948)
FULLER BRUSH GIRL, THE (1950)

Tati, Jacques
MY UNCLE (1958, Fr.)

PLAYTIME (1973, Fr.)

Tchaikovsky, Peter Ilyich
SWAN LAKE, THE (1967)

Terrazzas, Ernest
THREE CABALLEROS, THE (1944)

Thomas, Frank
ARISTOCATS, THE (1970)
RESCUERS, THE (1977)

Thompson, Howard
GLITTERBALL, THE (1977, Brit.)

Thompson, Morton
MY BROTHER TALKS TO HORSES (1946)

Tombragel, Maurice
MOON PILOT (1962)

Tors, Ivan
IN THE GOOD OLD SUMMERTIME (1949)

Totheroh, Dan
COUNT OF MONTE CRISTO, THE (1934)

Townley, Jack
BELLS OF ROSARITA (1945)
LAST ROUND-UP, THE (1947)
MY PAL TRIGGER (1946)

Trnka, Jiri
MIDSUMMER NIGHT'S DREAM, A (1961, Czech.)

Trosper, Guy
STRATTON STORY, THE (1949)

Trotti, Lamar
CHEAPER BY THE DOZEN (1950)
DRUMS ALONG THE MOHAWK (1939)
KENTUCKY (1938)
O. HENRY'S FULL HOUSE (1952)
STARS AND STRIPES FOREVER (1952)
STORY OF ALEXANDER GRAHAM BELL, THE (1939)
TALES OF MANHATTAN (1942)

Truffaut, Francois
FOUR HUNDRED BLOWS, THE (1959)
SMALL CHANGE (1976, Fr.)
WILD CHILD, THE (1970, Fr.)

Tugend, Harry
CAPTAIN JANUARY (1935)
CAUGHT IN THE DRAFT (1941)
LITTLEST REBEL, THE (1935)
POCKETFUL OF MIRACLES (1961)
SOUTHERN YANKEE, A (1948)
TAKE ME OUT TO THE BALL GAME (1949)

Tunberg, Karl
YANK IN THE R.A.F., A (1941)

Tunberg, William
OLD YELLER (1957)

Turner, William
MR. BUG GOES TO TOWN (1941)

Twist, John
ANNIE OAKLEY (1935)
SINBAD THE SAILOR (1947)

SOURCE AUTHORS

Ullman, Daniel
MYSTERIOUS ISLAND (1961, US/Brit.)

Upton, Gabrielle
GIDGET (1959)

Ustinov, Peter
SCHOOL FOR SCOUNDRELS (1960, Brit.)

Vacca, Milan
FABULOUS WORLD OF JULES VERNE, THE (1961, Czech.)

Vadnai, Laszlo
TALES OF MANHATTAN (1942)
GREAT RUPERT, THE (1950)

Vajda, Ernest
STARS AND STRIPES FOREVER (1952)

Valentine, Val
BELLES OF ST. TRINIAN'S, THE (1954, Brit.)

Van Every, Dale
CAPTAINS COURAGEOUS (1937)

Van Riper, Kay
BABES IN ARMS (1939)
JUDGE HARDY'S CHILDREN (1938)
STRIKE UP THE BAND (1940)

Volpin, Mikhail
JACK FROST (1966, USSR)

Wada, Natto
ALONE ON THE PACIFIC (1964, Jap.)

Walbridge, John
MAKE MINE MUSIC (1946)
MELODY TIME (1948)

Walpole, Hugh
DAVID COPPERFIELD (1935)
LITTLE LORD FAUNTLEROY (1936)

Walsh, Bill
ABSENT-MINDED PROFESSOR, THE (1961)
BEDKNOBS AND BROOMSTICKS (1971)
BLACKBEARD'S GHOST (1968)
HERBIE RIDES AGAIN (1974)
LITTLEST OUTLAW, THE (1955)
LOVE BUG, THE (1968)
MARY POPPINS (1964)
SHAGGY DOG, THE (1959)
SON OF FLUBBER (1963)
THAT DARN CAT (1965)
TOBY TYLER (1960)

Walsh, Kay
GREAT EXPECTATIONS (1946, Brit.)

Ware, Darrel
YANK IN THE R.A.F., A (1941)

Watkin, Lawrence E.
DARBY O'GILL AND THE LITTLE PEOPLE (1959)
LIGHT IN THE FOREST, THE (1958)
STORY OF ROBIN HOOD, THE (1952, Brit.)
TREASURE ISLAND (1950, Brit.)

Wead, Frank
YANK AT OXFORD, A (1938)

Weaver, John V.A.
ADVENTURES OF TOM SAWYER, THE (1938)

Webb, James R.
HOW THE WEST WAS WON (1962)

Weiss, Arthur
FLIPPER (1963)

Welland, Colin
CHARIOTS OF FIRE (1981, Brit.)

Wells, George
ANGELS IN THE OUTFIELD (1951)
EXCUSE MY DUST (1951)
TAKE ME OUT TO THE BALL GAME (1949)

West, Claudine
GOODBYE MR. CHIPS (1939, Brit.)

Westerby, Robert
FIGHTING PRINCE OF DONEGAL, THE (1966, Brit.)
GREYFRIARS BOBBY (1961, Brit.)
THREE LIVES OF THOMASINA, THE (1963, US/Brit.)

Wexley, John
ANGELS WITH DIRTY FACES (1938)

Whedon, John
ISLAND AT THE TOP OF THE WORLD, THE (1974)

White, Andy
AFRICA--TEXAS STYLE! (1967 US/Brit.)
GENTLE GIANT (1967)

Whitemore, Hugh
ALL CREATURES GREAT AND SMALL (1975, Brit.)

Wickersham, Bob
MR. BUG GOES TO TOWN (1941)

Wilbur, Crane
MYSTERIOUS ISLAND (1961, US/Brit.)

Wilder, Billy
EMPEROR WALTZ, THE (1948)
SPIRIT OF ST. LOUIS, THE (1957)

Williams, Roy
MAKE MINE MUSIC (1946)
THREE CABALLEROS, THE (1944)

Williamson, David
PHAR LAP (1984, Aus.)

Wilson, Carey
JUDGE HARDY AND SON (1939)

Witliff, William
BLACK STALLION, THE (1979)

Wood, David
SWALLOWS AND AMAZONS (1977, Brit.)

Woods, Cy
CUCKOOS, THE (1930)

Woolf, Edgar Allen
WIZARD OF OZ, THE (1939)

Wright, Ralph
ARISTOCATS, THE (1970)
GAY PURR-EE (1962)
JUNGLE BOOK, THE (1967)
LADY AND THE TRAMP (1955)

NIKKI, WILD DOG OF THE NORTH (1961, US/Can.)
PETER PAN (1953)
SONG OF THE SOUTH (1946)
THREE CABALLEROS, THE (1944)

Yordan, Philip
BATTLE OF THE BULGE (1965)
KING OF KINGS (1961)

Yost, Dorothy
LADDIE (1935)
THUNDERHEAD-SON OF FLICKA (1945)

Young, Peter
FOX AND THE HOUND, THE (1981)

Young, Robert Malcolm
ESCAPE TO WITCH MOUNTAIN (1975)

Zeman, Karel
FABULOUS WORLD OF JULES VERNE, THE (1961, Czech.)

SOURCE AUTHORS

Abbott, George
WHERE'S CHARLEY? (1952, Brit.)

Aberson, Helen
DUMBO (1941)

Abrashkin, Raymond
SON OF FLUBBER (1963)

Adams, Samuel Hopkins
HARVEY GIRLS, THE (1946)

Adamson, Ewart
ANNIE OAKLEY (1935)

Adamson, Joy
BORN FREE (1966)

Albee, George Sumner
NEXT VOICE YOU HEAR, THE (1950)

Alcott, Louisa May
LITTLE WOMEN (1933)

Allan, Ted
1001 ARABIAN NIGHTS (1959)

Allen, Irwin
VOYAGE TO THE BOTTOM OF THE SEA (1961)

Allen, R.S.
MAN CALLED FLINTSTONE, THE (1966)

Allen, Ted
GREAT RUPERT, THE (1950)

Allister, Ray
MAGIC BOX, THE (1952, Brit.)

Andersen, Hans Christian
DAYDREAMER, THE (1966)
THUMBELINA (1970)

Anderson, Ken
ROBIN HOOD (1973)

Annixter, Paul
THOSE CALLOWAYS (1964)

Armstrong, William H.
SOUNDER (1972)

Arnold, Elliott
DEEP IN MY HEART (1954)

Arthur, Art
CLARENCE, THE CROSS-EYED LION (1965)

Atkinson, Eleanor
CHALLENGE TO LASSIE (1949)
GREYFRIARS BOBBY (1961, Brit.)

Bagnold, Enid
NATIONAL VELVET (1944)

Baker, Mark H.
FLIGHT OF THE NAVIGATOR (1986)

Ballard, J.G.
EMPIRE OF THE SUN (1987)

Barbera, Joseph
MAN CALLED FLINTSTONE, THE (1966)

Barnett, S.H.
FATHER GOOSE (1964)

Barrie, Sir James M.
PETER PAN (1953)

Bart, Lionel
OLIVER! (1968, Brit.)

Bartlett, Sy
ROAD TO ZANZIBAR (1941)

Baum, L. Frank
WIZARD OF OZ, THE (1939)

Beardsley, Helen
YOURS, MINE AND OURS (1968)

Beebe, Ford
DAVY CROCKETT, INDIAN SCOUT (1950)

Benet, Stephen Vincent
SEVEN BRIDES FOR SEVEN BROTHERS (1954)

Bennett, Harve
STAR TREK II: THE WRATH OF KHAN (1982)
STAR TREK IV: THE VOYAGE HOME (1986)

Benson, Sally
MEET ME IN ST. LOUIS (1944)

Berlin, Irving
THIS IS THE ARMY (1943)

Biddle, Francis
MAGNIFICENT YANKEE, THE (1950)

Biggers, Earl Derr
CHARLIE CHAN AT THE OPERA (1936)
ONE NIGHT IN THE TROPICS (1940)

Billett, Stewart C.
BAREFOOT EXECUTIVE, THE (1971)

Bixby, Jay Lewis
FANTASTIC VOYAGE (1966)

Blaustein, Julian
NOOSE HANGS HIGH, THE (1948)

Bogdanovich, Peter
WHAT'S UP, DOC? (1972)

Bogle, Charles [W.C. Fields]
IT'S A GIFT (1934)

Bolton, Guy
CUCKOOS, THE (1930)
GIRL CRAZY (1943)

Bretherton, Vivian B.
LOVE FINDS ANDY HARDY (1938)

Brickhill, Paul
GREAT ESCAPE, THE (1963)

Brown, Harry
SANDS OF IWO JIMA (1949)

Brown, Rowland
ANGELS WITH DIRTY FACES (1938)

Browning, Ricou
FLIPPER (1963)
FLIPPER'S NEW ADVENTURE (1964)

Buckner, Robert
MOON PILOT (1962)
YANKEE DOODLE DANDY (1942)

Buford, Gordon
HERBIE RIDES AGAIN (1974)
LOVE BUG, THE (1968)

Bullock, Harvey
MAN CALLED FLINTSTONE, THE (1966)

Burgess, Alan
INN OF THE SIXTH HAPPINESS, THE (1958)

Burness, Pete
1001 ARABIAN NIGHTS (1959)

Burnett, Frances Hodgson
LITTLE LORD FAUNTLEROY (1936)
LITTLE PRINCESS, THE (1939)
SECRET GARDEN, THE (1949)

Burnford, Sheila
INCREDIBLE JOURNEY, THE (1963)

Burroughs, Edgar Rice
TARZAN THE APE MAN (1932)

Butler, Frank
KID FROM BOOKLYN, THE (1946)

Butler, Hugo
EDISON, THE MAN (1940)

Calef, Noel
TIGER BAY (1959, Brit.)

Cameron, Ian
ISLAND AT THE TOP OF THE WORLD, THE (1974)

Camp, Joe
FOR THE LOVE OF BENJI (1977)

Canaway, W.H.
BOY TEN FEET TALL, A (1965, Brit.)

Capote, Truman
TRUMAN CAPOTE'S TRILOGY (1969)

Capp, Al
LI'L ABNER (1959)

Cappy, George
NEWS HOUNDS (1947)

Carey, Ernestine Gilbreth
CHEAPER BY THE DOZEN (1950)

Carroll, Jr., Bob
YOURS, MINE AND OURS (1968)

Carroll, Lewis
ALICE IN WONDERLAND (1933)
ALICE IN WONDERLAND (1951)

Cauvin, Patrick
LITTLE ROMANCE, A (1979, US/Fr.)

Cavett, Frank
GREATEST SHOW ON EARTH, THE (1952)

Chamberlain, George Agnew
HOME IN INDIANA (1944)

Charnin, Martin
ANNIE (1982)

Chase, Mary
HARVEY (1950)

Chodorov, Jerome
MY SISTER EILEEN (1942)
MY SISTER EILEEN (1955)

Clork, Harry
KID FROM BOOKLYN, THE (1946)
MILKY WAY, THE (1936)

Cochran, Rice E.
MR. SCOUTMASTER (1953)

Collins, Pierre
STORY OF LOUIS PASTEUR, THE (1936)

Collodi [Carlo Lorenzini]
PINOCCHIO (1940)
PINOCCHIO AND THE EMPEROR OF THE NIGHT (1987)

Comandini, Adele
THREE SMART GIRLS (1937)

Conan Doyle, Sir Arthur
ADVENTURES OF SHERLOCK HOLMES, THE (1939)
YOUNG SHERLOCK HOLMES (1985)

Conlin, Richard
ANGELS IN THE OUTFIELD (1951)

Connell, Richard
KID FROM BOOKLYN, THE (1946)

Connolly, Myles
HANS CHRISTIAN ANDERSEN (1952)

Considine, Bob
BABE RUTH STORY, THE (1948)

Cooper, Edmund
INVISIBLE BOY, THE (1957)

Cooper, Merian C.
KING KONG (1933)

Cowan, Sam K.
SERGEANT YORK (1941)

Cowden, Jack
FLIPPER (1963)
FLIPPER'S NEW ADVENTURE (1964)

Coxhead, Elizabeth
CRY FROM THE STREET, A (1959, Brit.)

Crosby, Percy
SKIPPY (1931)

Cross, Beverley
SINBAD AND THE EYE OF THE TIGER (1977, US/Brit.)

SOURCE AUTHORS

Crossman, Melville [Darryl F. Zanuck]
YANK IN THE R.A.F., A (1941)

Crouse, Russel
LIFE WITH FATHER (1947)
SOUND OF MUSIC, THE (1965)

Crutcher, Jack
JALOPY (1953)

Curie, Eve
MADAME CURIE (1943)

Curwood, James Oliver
NIKKI, WILD DOG OF THE NORTH
(1961, US/Can.)

Cushing, Catherine Chishold
PRINCE AND THE PAUPER, THE (1937)

Dahl, Roald
WILLY WONKA AND THE
CHOCOLATE FACTORY (1971)

Dane, Clemence
SIDEWALKS OF LONDON (1940, Brit.)

Davenport, Gwen
SITTING PRETTY (1948)

Davies, Valentine
IT HAPPENS EVERY SPRING (1949)

Davies, Valentine
MIRACLE ON 34TH STREET, THE
(1947)

Davis, Madelyn
YOURS, MINE AND OURS (1968)

Day, Jr., Clarence
LIFE WITH FATHER (1947)

Day, Lillian
YOUNGEST PROFESSION, THE (1943)

de Beaumont, Mme. Leprince
BEAUTY AND THE BEAST (1947, Fr.)

De Hartog, Jan
LITTLE ARK, THE (1972)

de Leon, Antonio
BOY WHO STOLE A MILLION, THE
(1960, Brit.)

Defoe, Daniel
ADVENTURES OF ROBINSON
CRUSOE, THE (1954)

Delibes, Clement
DR. COPPELIUS (1968, US/Span.)

Dick, R.A.
GHOST AND MRS. MUIR, THE (1942)

Dickens, Charles
CHRISTMAS CAROL, A (1938)
DAVID COPPERFIELD (1935)
GREAT EXPECTATIONS (1946, Brit.)
OLIVER TWIST (1951, Brit.)
OLIVER! (1968, Brit.)
PICKWICK PAPERS, THE (1952, Brit.)
SCROOGE (1935, Brit.)
SCROOGE (1970, Brit.)
TALE OF TWO CITIES, A (1935)

Dickey, Paul
GHOST BREAKERS, THE (1940)

Dore, Sandy
FRASIER, THE SENSUOUS LION (1973)

Drake, Oliver
SHUT MY BIG MOUTH (1942)

Dumas pere, Alexandre
COUNT OF MONTE CRISTO, THE
(1934)
THREE MUSKETEERS, THE (1948)

Dunn, H. Alan
YOUNG TOM EDISON (1940)

Edmonds, Walter D.
DRUMS ALONG THE MOHAWK (1939)

Engel, Samuel G.
STOWAWAY (1936)

Farley, Walter
BLACK STALLION, THE (1979)

Field, Joseph
MY SISTER EILEEN (1955)

Field, S.S.
PETE'S DRAGON (1977)

Fields, Dorothy
ANNIE GET YOUR GUN (1950)

Fields, Herbert
ANNIE GET YOUR GUN (1950)
HIT THE DECK (1955)

Fields, Joseph
ANNIE OAKLEY (1935)
MY SISTER EILEEN (1942)

Finney, Charles G.
SEVEN FACES OF DR. LAO (1964)

Fins, Bernard
NOOSE HANGS HIGH, THE (1948)

Fisher, Ham
PALOOKA (1934)

Fleischman, Sid
ADVENTURES OF BULLWHIP
GRIFFIN, THE (1967)

Fleming, Ian
CHITTY CHITTY BANG BANG (1968,
Brit.)

Fontaine, Robert
HAPPY TIME, THE (1952)

Foote, John Taintor
KENTUCKY (1938)

Forbes, Esther
JOHNNY TREMAIN (1957)

Forbes, Kathryn
I REMEMBER MAMA (1948)

Forester, C.S.
AFRICAN QUEEN, THE (1951, US/Brit.)

Foster, Alan Dean
STAR TREK: THE MOTION PICTURE
(1979)

Foster, Lewis R.
MR. SMITH GOES TO WASHINGTON
(1939)

Foster, Warren
MAN CALLED FLINTSTONE, THE
(1966)

Frank, Fredric M.
GREATEST SHOW ON EARTH, THE
(1952)

Frank, Melvin
SOUTHERN YANKEE, A (1948)

Franklin, Jr., Sidney
FEARLESS FAGAN (1952)

Freudberg, Judy
AMERICAN TAIL, AN (1986)

Gallico, Paul
LILI (1953)
PRIDE OF THE YANKEES, THE (1942)
THREE LIVES OF THOMASINA, THE
(1963, US/Brit.)

Gangelin, Paul
MY PAL TRIGGER (1946)

Garrett, Lila
BAREFOOT EXECUTIVE, THE (1971)

Gaspard Itard, Jean-Marc
WILD CHILD, THE (1970, Fr.)

Geiss, Tony
AMERICAN TAIL, AN (1986)

George, Jean Craighead
MY SIDE OF THE MOUNTAIN (1969)

Gershwin, George
GIRL CRAZY (1943)

Gershwin, Ira
GIRL CRAZY (1943)

Gerstner, Herman
WONDERFUL WORLD OF THE
BROTHERS GRIMM, THE (1962)

Gibney, Sheridan
STORY OF LOUIS PASTEUR, THE
(1936)

Gilbreth, Jr., Frank B.
CHEAPER BY THE DOZEN (1950)

Gill, Derek
DOVE, THE (1974, Brit.)

Gillette, William
ADVENTURES OF SHERLOCK
HOLMES, THE (1939)

Gilliat, Sidney
YANK AT OXFORD, A (1938)

Gipson, Fred
OLD YELLER (1957)

Goddard, Charles
GHOST BREAKERS, THE (1940)

Gogol, Nikolai
INSPECTOR GENERAL, THE (1949)

Goldman, William
PRINCESS BRIDE, THE (1987)

Goldsmith, Clifford
HENRY ALDRICH FOR PRESIDENT
(1941)

Goodrich, Frances
EASTER PARADE (1948)

Gordon, Gordon
THAT DARN CAT (1965)

Gordon, Leon
YANK AT OXFORD, A (1938)

Gordon, Mildred
THAT DARN CAT (1965)

Graham, John
HILDUR AND THE MAGICIAN (1969)

Graham, Robin Lee
DOVE, THE (1974, Brit.)

Grahame, Kenneth
ADVENTURES OF ICHABOD AND MR.
TOAD (1949)

Greene, Ward
LADY AND THE TRAMP (1955)

Griffin, Eleanore
BOYS TOWN (1938)
HARVEY GIRLS, THE (1946)

Griffiths, Eldon W.
FEARLESS FAGAN (1952)

Grimm, Jacob
SNOW WHITE AND THE SEVEN
DWARFS (1937)
TOM THUMB (1958, Brit./US)

Grimm, Wilhelm
SNOW WHITE AND THE SEVEN
DWARFS (1937)
TOM THUMB (1958, Brit./US)

Hackett, Albert
EASTER PARADE (1948)

Haggard, Sir Henry Rider
KING SOLOMON'S MINES (1950)

Hamilton, Aileen
CHRISTMAS IN CONNECTICUT (1945)

Hammerstein II, Oscar
KING AND I, THE (1956)
OKLAHOMA! (1955)
SOUND OF MUSIC, THE (1965)

Hampton, Orville H.
JACK THE GIANT KILLER (1962)

Hanna, William
MAN CALLED FLINTSTONE, THE
(1966)

Hannum, Alberta
ROSEANNA McCOY (1949)

Hargrove, Marion
SEE HERE, PRIVATE HARGROVE
(1944)

Harris, Joel Chandler
SONG OF THE SOUTH (1946)

Harris, Ray
STORY OF ALEXANDER GRAHAM
BELL, THE (1939)

Harryhausen, Ray
SINBAD AND THE EYE OF THE TIGER
(1977, US/Brit.)

Hart, Lorenz
BABES IN ARMS (1939)

Hartman, Don
ROAD TO ZANZIBAR (1941)

Hartmann, Edmund L.
HERE COME THE CO-EDS (1945)
RIDE 'EM COWBOY (1942)

Hellman, Sam
STANLEY AND LIVINGSTONE (1939)

Henry, Marguerite
MISTY (1961)

Henson, Jim
LABYRINTH (1986)

Herbert, Victor
BABES IN TOYLAND (1934)

Herriot, James
ALL CREATURES GREAT AND SMALL
(1975, Brit.)
ALL THINGS BRIGHT AND
BEAUTIFUL (1979, Brit.)

Hilton, James
GOODBYE MR. CHIPS (1939, Brit.)

Hoffman, E.T.A.
NUTCRACKER: THE MOTION
PICTURE (1986)

Hogan, Michael
YANK AT OXFORD, A (1938)

Horie, Kenichi
ALONE ON THE PACIFIC (1964, Jap.)

Huggins, Roy
FULLER BRUSH MAN (1948)

Hull, Alexander
PAINTED HILLS, THE (1951)

Ingraham, Rev. J.H.
TEN COMMANDMENTS, THE (1956)

Ingster, Boris
AMAZING MRS. HOLLIDAY (1943)

Irving, Washington
ADVENTURES OF ICHABOD AND MR.
TOAD (1949)

Jevne, Jack
WAY OUT WEST (1937)

Johnson, Nora
WORLD OF HENRY ORIENT, THE
(1964)

Jones, Grover
KID FROM BOOKLYN, THE (1946)

Jordan, Patricia
HILDUR AND THE MAGICIAN (1969)

Juster, Norton
PHANTOM TOLLBOOTH, THE (1970)

Kahn, Bernie
BAREFOOT EXECUTIVE, THE (1971)

Kaler, James Otis
TOBY TYLER (1960)

Kalmar, Bert
CUCKOOS, THE (1930)

Kantor, MacKinlay
FOLLOW ME, BOYS! (1966)

Kastner, Erich
EMIL AND THE DETECTIVES (1964)
PARENT TRAP, THE (1961)

Kaufman, George S.
ANIMAL CRACKERS (1930)

Kavanagh, H.T.
DARBY O'GILL AND THE LITTLE
PEOPLE (1959)

Keller, Helen
MIRACLE WORKER, THE (1962)

Keller, Lew
1001 ARABIAN NIGHTS (1959)

Kennedy, Burt
LITTLEST HORSE THIEVES, THE
(1977)

Key, Alexander
ESCAPE TO WITCH MOUNTAIN (1975)

King, Robert L.
NOW YOU SEE HIM, NOW YOU DON'T
(1972)

Kingsley, Charles
WATER BABIES, THE (1979, Brit.)

Kinney, Dick
1001 ARABIAN NIGHTS (1959)

Kipling, Rudyard
CAPTAINS COURAGEOUS (1937)
JUNGLE BOOK, THE (1942)
JUNGLE BOOK, THE (1967)
KIM (1950)
WEE WILLIE WINKIE (1937)

Kirschner, David
AMERICAN TAIL, AN (1986)

Klement, Otto
FANTASTIC VOYAGE (1966)

Knight, Eric
LASSIE, COME HOME (1943)
SON OF LASSIE (1945)

Kohner, Frederick
GIDGET (1959)

Krasna, Norman
DEAR WIFE (1949)

Kyne, Peter B.
THREE GODFATHERS, THE (1948)

Lacey, Franklin
MUSIC MAN, THE (1962)

Landon, Margaret
KING AND I, THE (1956)

Lansburgh, Larry
LITTLEST OUTLAW, THE (1955)

Lardner, Ring
SO THIS IS NEW YORK (1948)

Larsen, Neils West
BOY WHO STOLE A MILLION, THE
(1960, Brit.)

Laszlo, Miklos
IN THE GOOD OLD SUMMERTIME
(1949)

Lavery, Emmet
MAGNIFICENT YANKEE, THE (1950)

Lee, Harper
TO KILL A MOCKINGBIRD (1962)

Lees, Robert
HOLD THAT GHOST (1941)

LeMay, Alan
ADVENTURES OF MARK TWAIN, THE
(1944)

Lerner, Alan Jay
MY FAIR LADY (1964)

SOURCE AUTHORS

Leslie, Aleen
DATE WITH JUDY, A (1948)

Less, Dennis
LABYRINTH (1986)

Lewenhak, H.K.
WINGS OF MYSTERY (1963, Brit.)

Lewis, Sinclair
FUN AND FANCY FREE (1947)

Lindbergh, Charles A.
SPIRIT OF ST. LOUIS, THE (1957)

Lindsay, Howard
LIFE WITH FATHER (1947)
SOUND OF MUSIC, THE (1965)

Llewellyn, Richard
HOW GREEN WAS MY VALLEY (1941)

Loesser, Frank
WHERE'S CHARLEY? (1952, Brit.)

Loewe, Frederick
MY FAIR LADY (1964)

Lofting, Hugh
DOCTOR DOLITTLE (1967)

London, Jack
CALL OF THE WILD (1935)

Long, Hal
KING OF THE COWBOYS (1943)
STANLEY AND LIVINGSTONE (1939)

Long, Sumner Arthur
LASSIE'S GREAT ADVENTURE (1963)

Lovy, Alex
MAN CALLED FLINTSTONE, THE (1966)

Lucas, George
EMPIRE STRIKES BACK, THE (1980)
RETURN OF THE JEDI (1983)

Luce, Clare Boothe
COME TO THE STABLE (1949)

MacDonald, Betty
MA AND PA KETTLE (1949)

Macken, Walter
FLIGHT OF THE DOVES (1971)

MacLaren, Ian
HILLS OF HOME (1948)

Mannix, Daniel P.
FOX AND THE HOUND, THE (1981)

Marion, Frances
CHAMP, THE (1931)

Marshall, Catherine
MAN CALLED PETER, A (1955)

McCarey, Leo
BELLS OF ST. MARY'S, THE (1945)
GOING MY WAY (1944)

McEvoy, J.P.
IT'S A GIFT (1934)

McGowan, Jack
GIRL CRAZY (1943)

McGuinness, James Kevin
NIGHT AT THE OPERA, A (1935)

McKelway, St. Clair
MISTER 880 (1950)

McKenney, Ruth
MY SISTER EILEEN (1942)

McKenney, Ruth
MY SISTER EILEEN (1955)

Meehan, Thomas
ANNIE (1982)

Melville, Herman
MOBY DICK (1956, Brit.)

Meredyth, Bess
CHARLIE CHAN AT THE OPERA (1936)

Miller, Seton I.
PETE'S DRAGON (1977)

Morey, Walt
GENTLE GIANT (1967)

Morrow, Douglas
STRATTON STORY, THE (1949)

Mowat, Farley
NEVER CRY WOLF (1983)

Muggeridge, Malcolm
HEAVENS ABOVE! (1963, Brit.)

Nimoy, Leonard
STAR TREK IV: THE VOYAGE HOME (1986)

Nofziger, Ed
1001 ARABIAN NIGHTS (1959)

North, Sterling
RASCAL (1969)
SO DEAR TO MY HEART (1949)

Norton, Mary
BEDKNOBS AND BROOMSTICKS (1971)

Nuitter, Charles
DR. COPPELIUS (1968, US/Span.)

O. Henry
O. HENRY'S FULL HOUSE (1952)

O'Brien, Robert C.
SECRET OF NIMH, THE (1982)

O'Dell, Scott
ISLAND OF THE BLUE DOLPHINS (1964)

O'Flaherty, Dennis
PINOCCHIO AND THE EMPEROR OF THE NIGHT (1987)

O'Hara, John
BEST THINGS IN LIFE ARE FREE, THE (1956)

O'Hara, Mary
MY FRIEND FLICKA (1943)
THUNDERHEAD-SON OF FLICKA (1945)

O'Neill, Eugene
AH, WILDERNESS! (1935)
SUMMER HOLIDAY (1948)

Osborne, Hubert
HIT THE DECK (1955)

Ouida
DOG OF FLANDERS, A (1959)

Panama, Norman
SOUTHERN YANKEE, A (1948)

Patchett, Tom
MUPPETS TAKE MANHATTAN, THE (1984)

Pearl, Harold
DUMBO (1941)

Peet, William
SONG OF THE SOUTH (1946)

Peple, Edward
LITTLEST REBEL, THE (1935)

Perrault, Charles
CINDERELLA (1950)
WACKY WORLD OF MOTHER GOOSE, THE (1967)

Pieterse, Andre
FOREVER YOUNG, FOREVER FREE (1976, South Africa)

Pirosh, Robert
DAY AT THE RACES, A (1937)

Porter, Eleanor H.
POLLYANNA (1960)

Portis, Charles
TRUE GRIT (1969)

Potter, Beatrix
PETER RABBIT AND TALES OF BEATRIX POTTER (1971, Brit.)

Potter, Stephen
SCHOOL FOR SCOUNDRELS (1960, Brit.)

Puzo, Mario
SUPERMAN (1978)
SUPERMAN II (1980)

Pyle, Ernie
STORY OF G.I. JOE, THE (1945)

Rankin, William
HARVEY GIRLS, THE (1946)

Ransome, Arthur
SWALLOWS AND AMAZONS (1977, Brit.)

Rawlings, Marjorie Kinnan
SUN COMES UP, THE (1949)
YEARLING, THE (1946)

Raymond, Alex
FLASH GORDON (1936)

Raymond, Dalton
SONG OF THE SOUTH (1946)

Reilly, Robert T.
FIGHTING PRINCE OF DONEGAL, THE (1966, Brit.)

Richards, Laura E.
CAPTAIN JANUARY (1935)

Richter, Conrad
LIGHT IN THE FOREST, THE (1958)

Riggs, Lynn
OKLAHOMA! (1955)

Rinaldo, Frederic I.
HOLD THAT GHOST (1941)

Riskin, Robert
POCKETFUL OF MIRACLES (1961)

Rockwood, Roy
BOMBA THE JUNGLE BOY (1949)

Roddenberry, Gene
STAR TREK: THE MOTION PICTURE (1979)
STAR TREK II: THE WRATH OF KHAN (1982)
STAR TREK III: THE SEARCH FOR SPOCK (1984)
STAR TREK IV: THE VOYAGE HOME (1986)

Rodgers, Mary
FREAKY FRIDAY (1976)

Rodgers, Richard
BABES IN ARMS (1939)
KING AND I, THE (1956)
OKLAHOMA! (1955)
SOUND OF MUSIC, THE (1965)

Rogers, Betty Blake
STORY OF WILL ROGERS, THE (1952)

Rogers, Charles
WAY OUT WEST (1937)

Root, Lynn
KID FROM BOOKLYN, THE (1946)
MILKY WAY, THE (1936)

Rose, Anna Perrott
ROOM FOR ONE MORE (1952)

Rouverol, Aurania
JUDGE HARDY AND SON (1939)
JUDGE HARDY'S CHILDREN (1938)
LOVE FINDS ANDY HARDY (1938)

Ruby, Harry
CUCKOOS, THE (1930)

Runyon, Damon
LITTLE MISS MARKER (1934)
POCKETFUL OF MIRACLES (1961)

Ryan, Tim
JALOPY (1953)
NEWS HOUNDS (1947)

Ryskind, Morris
ANIMAL CRACKERS (1930)

Salkin, Leo
1001 ARABIAN NIGHTS (1959)

Salten, Felix
BAMBI (1942)
SHAGGY D.A., THE (1976)
SHAGGY DOG, THE (1959)

Saunders, John Monk
YANK AT OXFORD, A (1938)

Schaefer, Jack
SHANE (1953)

Schary, Jeb [Dore Schary]
LIVE WIRES (1946)

Schary, Dore
BOYS TOWN (1938)
EDISON, THE MAN (1940)

Schneider, Margaret
1001 ARABIAN NIGHTS (1959)

Schneider, Paul
1001 ARABIAN NIGHTS (1959)

Schultz, Charles M.
BON VOYAGE, CHARLIE BROWN (AND DON'T COME BACK) (1980)

SNOOPY, COME HOME (1972)

Seaton, George
DAY AT THE RACES, A (1937)

Seward, Edmond
GULLIVER'S TRAVELS (1939)
NEWS HOUNDS (1947)

Shakespeare, William
MIDSUMMER NIGHT'S DREAM, A (1961, Czech.)

Shapley, Harlow
OF STARS AND MEN (1961)

Sharp, Margery
RESCUERS, THE (1977)

Shaw, Dick
1001 ARABIAN NIGHTS (1959)

Shaw, George Bernard
MY FAIR LADY (1964)

Sheekman, Arthur
WONDER MAN (1945)

Shelley, Mary
ABBOTT AND COSTELLO MEET FRANKENSTEIN (1948)

Shepherd, Jean
CHRISTMAS STORY, A (1983)

Sherman, Harold M.
ADVENTURES OF MARK TWAIN, THE (1944)

Sherwood, Robert E.
ABE LINCOLN IN ILLINOIS (1940)

Shuster, Joe
SUPERMAN II (1980)
SUPERMAN (1978)

Sidney, Margaret
FIVE LITTLE PEPPERS AND HOW THEY GREW (1939)

Siegel, Jerry
SUPERMAN (1978)
SUPERMAN II (1980)

Sinclair, Upton
GNOME-MOBILE, THE (1967)

Sisson, Rosemary Anne
LITTLEST HORSE THIEVES, THE (1977)

Skeyhill, Tom
SERGEANT YORK (1941)

Smith, Dodie
ONE HUNDRED AND ONE DALMATIANS (1961)

Smith, Shirley W.
IT HAPPENS EVERY SPRING (1949)

Smith, Thorne
TOPPER (1937)

Sousa, John Philip
STARS AND STRIPES FOREVER (1952)

Southon, Rev. G.E.
TEN COMMANDMENTS, THE (1956)

Sowards, Jack B.
STAR TREK II: THE WRATH OF KHAN (1982)

Spence, Hartzell
ONE FOOT IN HEAVEN (1941)

Spence, William
ONE FOOT IN HEAVEN (1941)

Spyri, Johanna
HEIDI (1937)

St. John, Theodore
GREATEST SHOW ON EARTH, THE (1952)

Stahl, Ben
BLACKBEARD'S GHOST (1968)

Stallings, George
SONG OF THE SOUTH (1946)

Stern, David
FRANCIS (1949)
FRANCIS IN THE HAUNTED HOUSE (1956)

Stern, Philip Van Doren
IT'S A WONDERFUL LIFE (1946)

Stevenson, Robert Louis
KIDNAPPED (1938)
TREASURE ISLAND (1934)
TREASURE ISLAND (1950, Brit.)

Stewart, Mary
MOON-SPINNERS, THE (1964)

Stratton-Porter, Gene
LADDIE (1935)

Street, James
GOODBYE, MY LADY (1956)

Street, Julian Leonard
YOU'RE TELLING ME (1934)

Streeter, Edward
FATHER'S LITTLE DIVIDEND (1951)
MR. HOBBS TAKES A VACATION (1962)

Strouse, Charles
ANNIE (1982)

Swift, Jonathan
GULLIVER'S TRAVELS (1939)

Taradash, Daniel
NOOSE HANGS HIGH, THE (1948)

Tarses, Jay
MUPPETS TAKE MANHATTAN, THE (1984)

Taylor, Samuel A.
HAPPY TIME, THE (1952)

Taylor, Samuel W.
ABSENT-MINDED PROFESSOR, THE (1961)
SON OF FLUBBER (1963)

Tervataa, Juhni
FARMER'S DAUGHTER, THE (1947)

Thiele, Colin
STORM BOY (1976, Aus.)

Thomas, Brandon
CHARLEY'S AUNT (1941)
WHERE'S CHARLEY? (1952, Brit.)

Thompson, Marshall
CLARENCE, THE CROSS-EYED LION (1965)

SOURCE AUTHORS

Toby, Mark
COURTSHIP OF EDDIE'S FATHER, THE (1963)

Tors, Ivan
FLIPPER'S NEW ADVENTURE (1964)

Townsend, Leo
AMAZING MRS. HOLLIDAY (1943)

Travers, P.L.
MARY POPPINS (1964)

Trosper, Guy
PRIDE OF ST. LOUIS, THE (1952)

Truffaut, Francois
FOUR HUNDRED BLOWS, THE (1959)

Tugend, Harry
CAUGHT IN THE DRAFT (1941)

Twain, Mark
ADVENTURES OF HUCKLEBERRY FINN, THE (1960)
ADVENTURES OF TOM SAWYER, THE (1938)
CONNECTICUT YANKEE, A (1931)
CONNECTICUT YANKEE IN KING ARTHUR'S COURT, A (1949)
HUCKLEBERRY FINN (1939)
PRINCE AND THE PAUPER, THE (1937)
TOM SAWYER (1930)
TOM SAWYER (1973)

Twist, John
SINBAD THE SAILOR (1947)

Tyler, Poyntz
FITZWILLY (1967)

Van Druten, John
I REMEMBER MAMA (1948)

Vaughn, Ven
FOR THE LOVE OF BENJI (1977)

Verne, Jules
AROUND THE WORLD IN 80 DAYS (1956)
FABULOUS WORLD OF JULES VERNE, THE (1961, Czech.)
IN SEARCH OF THE CASTAWAYS (1962, Brit.)
JOURNEY TO THE CENTER OF THE EARTH (1959)
MYSTERIOUS ISLAND (1961, US/Brit.)
20,000 LEAGUES UNDER THE SEA (1954)

Walker, David
WEE GEORDIE (1956, Brit.)

Wallace, Edgar
KING KONG (1933)

Weaver, John D.
DREAMBOAT (1952)

Wells, H.G.
TIME MACHINE, THE (1960, Brit./US)

Werfel, Franz
SONG OF BERNADETTE, THE (1943)

White, E.B.
CHARLOTTE'S WEB (1973)

White, William L.
JOURNEY FOR MARGARET (1942)

Wibberley, Leonard
MOUSE THAT ROARED, THE (1959, Brit.)

Wiggin, Kate Douglas
SUMMER MAGIC (1963)

Wilde, Oscar
CANTERVILLE GHOST, THE (1944)

Wilder, Thornton
HELLO, DOLLY! (1969)

Wilkinson, Michael
PHAR LAP (1984, Aus.)

Williams, Jay
SON OF FLUBBER (1963)

Willson, Meredith
MUSIC MAN, THE (1962)

Wilson, Dorothy Clarke
TEN COMMANDMENTS, THE (1956)

Winch, Frank
BUFFALO BILL (1944)

Wisberg, Aubrey
HORN BLOWS AT MIDNIGHT, THE (1945)

Wolf, Gary K.
WHO FRAMED ROGER RABBIT? (1988)

Wright, Ralph
SONG OF THE SOUTH (1946)

Wyss, Johann
SWISS FAMILY ROBINSON (1960)

Yates, George Worthing
SINBAD THE SAILOR (1947)

Young, Chic
BLONDIE (1938)

CineBooks

THE CINEBOOKS HOME LIBRARY SERIES

The CineBooks Home Library Series features volumes devoted to comprehensive and entertaining reviews of movies in specific categories.

Subjects covered in the series are:

Horror Movies	Sports Movies
Westerns	Musicals
Science Fiction Movies	Comedies
International Films	Crime Films
	War Films

In addition, CineBooks publishes:

THE MOTION PICTURE GUIDE ™ a 12-volume encyclopedia covering 53,000 films from Silents to 1984, with index volumes offering filmographies of more than 180,000 actors and technical personnel. The set is kept up to date with illustrated annual supplements, currently available for 1985, 1986 and 1987.

THE MOTION PICTURE ANNUAL, a complete review of the film year in the US, with photos, awards, obituaries, and profiles of rising stars. The 1988 MOTION PICTURE ANNUAL (covering the films of 1987) is now available; THE 1989 MOTION PICTURE ANNUAL (covering the films of 1988) will be available in May of 1989.

For more information about the CineBooks Home Library Series, complete and return the coupon below.

- -

Please send me more information about CineBooks publications on:

☐ Musicals	☐ Sports	☐ Horror
☐ Science Fiction	☐ Westerns	☐ Comedies
☐ Motion Picture Guide	☐ Crime	☐ International Films
		☐ Motion Picture Annual

Name_____

Address_____

City/State/Zip_____.

Return to: CineBooks, Inc.
  990 Grove St.
  PO Box 1407, Dept. FC
  Evanston, IL 60204